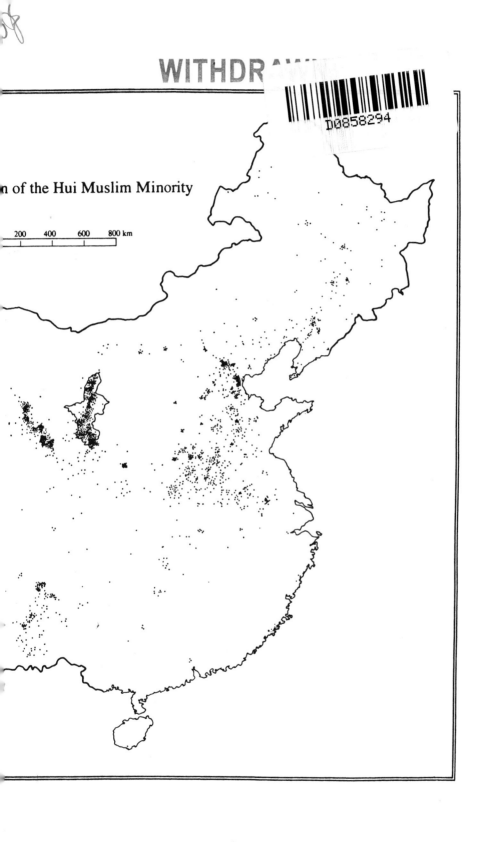

n of the Hui Muslim Minority

200   400   600   800 km

Muslim Chinese

HARVARD EAST ASIAN MONOGRAPHS
149

Publication of this book was substantially assisted by the An Wang Fund for Research on China at the John K. Fairbank Center for East Asian Research at Harvard University.

MUSLIM CHINESE
Ethnic Nationalism in the People's Republic

Dru C. Gladney

Published by COUNCIL ON EAST ASIAN STUDIES, HARVARD UNIVERSITY, and distributed by HARVARD UNIVERSITY PRESS, Cambridge (Massachussetts) and London   *1991*

The Council on East Asian Studies at Harvard University publishes a monograph series and, through the Fairbank Center for East Asian Research and the Reischauer Institute of Japanese Studies, administers research projects designed to further scholarly understanding of China, Japan, Korea, Vietnam, Inner Asia, and adjacent areas.

Library of Congress Cataloging-in-Publication Data

Gladney, Dru C.
    Muslim Chinese : ethnic nationalism in the People's Republic / Dru
C. Gladney.
        p. cm. – (Harvard East Asian monographs ; 149)
    Includes bibliographical references and index.
    ISBN 0-674-59495-9. – ISBN 0-674-59496-7 (pbk.)
    1. Muslims–China.   2. China–Ethnic relations.   I. Title.
II. Series.
DS731.M87G53   1991
305.6′971051–dc20   90-26582
                                                            CIP

To my true parents,
my "dry" parents,
and Mary

Preface

The melting pot has erupted into a "cauldron" of ethnicities.[1] In China, the Soviet Union, and around the globe, ethnic and national movements have risen to the forefront of social and political action. Though both modernization and Marxist theories of nationalism have predicted the demise of national identities, the recent assertion of these identities in the political arena has cast doubt on, if not repudiated, these assimilationist assumptions. Russification, though accepted by many as an inexorable inevitability, has not occurred among the many strident nationalities of the Soviet Union. Sinicization, predicted as well for the minorities of China, is called into question in the face of rising nationalism and the persistence of ethnic identities.

While much has been written about the resurgence of national, often Muslim, ethnic movements in the Soviet Union, there has been little discussion of similar processes in China. This book will examine some of the reasons why. The minorities, and Muslims, of China have generally been marginalized on the geographic and social horizons of discourse and power in China, often confined to remote, officially closed communities difficult to research and often reluctant to admit outsiders. This study, based on field research in concentrated Muslim communities in China, represents an attempt to understand the identity of one of the Muslim minorities of China, as well as to reintroduce the problem of ethnic nationalism to the study and understanding of Chinese society and national identity.

Nearly 20 million of the peoples in the People's Republic are Muslim. Though they are a small percentage of China's entire population, the reassertion of their identity on a national and transnational level calls into question many assumptions about the nature of Chinese society, ethnicity, and national identity. Relegated to the borders of territory and power in China, and to the periphery of scholarly interest, they are beginning to challenge this marginalization, forcing a reconsideration of the traditional categorization by which Chinese society is divided and analyzed. This is why, in the words of Peter Stallybrass and Allon White, the "Others" who were *socially* peripheral have become so *symbolically* central."[2] The internal Others of China are now beginning to challenge the conceptualization of the Chinese "Self."

The "Salman Rushdie in China" protest, a nationwide demonstration of Muslims that took place at the peak of the 1989 "Democracy Movement" in Beijing (pictured on the cover of this book and discussed in Chapter 1), illustrates many of the issues with which this study is concerned: the nationalization and transnationalization of Muslim identity in China, the challenge posed to the state by minority voices, and the rise in ethnic nationalism. Both of these last terms are key: *ethnicity*, in that the Muslims who took part in the protest see themselves as vibrant ethnic groups with a self-assurance and an identity that is very much their own; and *nationalism*, in that they are expressing their identities as nationalities, recognized by the state as belonging to the 55 official minority nationalities who have been given a voice and a right, guaranteed by the constitution, to speak out on their own affairs—a voice they are now using with considerable effect.

This book concerns itself primarily with one of the 10 Muslim nationalities in China, the Hui minority, who make up over half of all Muslims in China and live in every province and city across the nation. A vital part of the Chinese social landscape, they have rarely been studied by Westerners. The last book in English to be written about these Muslims that was based on field research in China was published in 1910, by the Protestant missionary Marshall Broomhall, entitled, *Islam in China: A Neglected Problem*. Despite Broomhall's monumental effort to highlight the importance of Muslims to Chinese society, they have remained a neglected and problematic minority.

The reasons behind this continued neglect are explored in the first two chapters, and the problem of Hui Muslim identity is a central concern throughout the work. My thesis is that Hui Muslim identity in China has been inadequately understood in the past due to Western ethnicity theories that failed to take into account both cultural and political aspects of that identity, their dynamic dialectical interaction at local levels, and, most important, the role of the state in defining and, to some extent, objectifying that identity. Official Chinese portrayals of the Hui are also limited in understanding this dynamic identity by their overemphasis upon nationality identification programs, relying on, in Partha Chatterjee's terms, the "derivative discourses" of Marxist-Stalinist nationality theory,[3] Lewis Henry Morgan-style stage evolutionism, and traditional Chinese ideas of identity and nationhood, which are very much tied to the idea of country—China as "Zhong Guo," the central state.

This unique combination of nationality discourse and political rhetoric has resulted in a considerable blurring of genres, to use Clifford Geertz's phrase, unfortunately obfuscating much of Hui identity.[4] This confusion has led scholars in the past to take two diametrically opposed views of the Hui Muslims in China, either predicting that, since they are Muslims and similar to their brethren elsewhere, they would inevitably rise in an attempt to violently secede from the Chinese nation-state, or, by contrast, assuming that, if they have not risen up against the state, it is only because they have already, or soon will, become entirely assimilated to the dominant Han Chinese tradition—what in China scholarship is known as "Sinicization." Since the Hui are thought to be culturally "closer" to the Han majority than other minorities in China—they generally speak Chinese, wear Chinese dress, and lack many of the "colorful" cultural markers of identity that other minorities display—many have completely doubted their distinct ethnicity, seeing them as merely Han who may share a vestigial belief in Islam.

These positions are seriously challenged by resurgent Hui Muslim ethnic nationalism (as demonstrated by the "Salman Rushdie in China" case, in which protesters appealed to the Communist Party for protection and assistance), as well as the dramatic rise in those who (for whatever reason) identify themselves, and want to be recognized by the state, as minorities. Some Han now prefer to marry these minorities, giving themselves, or their children, access to the rights and privileges accorded to minority nationalities in China, even as other Han are becoming increasingly disgruntled by the favoritism shown toward these minorities. These shifts in ethnic sentiments are matched by a growing seriousness with which the state has begun to address the national question in China.

These "social facts" of the modern Chinese world require a radical reassessment of former thinking about the assimilation and marginalization of minorities in China. Based on the case of the Hui, I propose a theory of ethnic national identity in the Chinese nation-state that takes into consideration the dynamic, even dialectical, interaction of culture, socioeconomics, and the state in fashioning the expression and identification of the Hui, and other minorities, in China today. In Benedict Anderson's terms, this study challenges the way Chinese national identity is "imagined" by both Chinese and Western China scholars, as well as exploring how the identity of one people has been shaped at local levels by these social imaginings, the derivative discourses of ethnicity and nationalism in China.[5]

This study of Muslim ethnic nationalism and identity in China is based on a total of 3 years' field research in the People's Republic, primarily among Hui Muslims, from 1982 to 1990. The bulk of the research was carried out during my dissertation fieldwork, from 1983 to 1985, when I spent 22 months in China. In addition, several follow-up trips were taken to Muslim areas every year following the completion of the dissertation research, with the most recent in January 1990. On every trip I was able to meet again with many of my Hui colleagues, informants, and villagers in China and to discuss with them my earlier conclusions. For those who have gone to the trouble to read the original dissertation, this study represents a significant revision, based on follow-up interviews, and provides new information and resolutions. The four case communities remain the same, however, with additional material added. Though many of my original ideas and questions have changed, my basic conclusion has remained the same: The wide diversity of local Hui ethnic identity, and their national unity under the state's minority policy, has led to the emergence of a new ethnoreligious identity in China, an identity that challenges many of the assumptions about ethnicity and national identity in Chinese society.

The 4 ethnographic chapters discuss how Hui ethnic identity is expressed with reference to cultural symbols and national policies at the local level. In the northwestern Sufi village of Na Homestead, located in the Ningxia Hui autonomous region, Islamic belief and ritual embody the most salient expressions of Hui identity. In the capital of Beijing city, the urban Hui of the Niujie "Oxen Street" community express their ethnicity in terms of occupational specializations and dietary restrictions. In the rural village of Changying, a Hui autonomous village on the Hebei North China plain outside of Beijing, Hui identity is often expressed in terms of ethnic marriage endogamy, that has led to the establishment of national networks. Finally, in the Chendai Ding lineage on the southeast coast of Fujian province, genealogical ideas of descent that reflect traditional Chinese constructions of ethnicity become the key marker of identity for these Hui who no longer practice Islam.

These divergent identities reflect a wide variety of Hui Muslims in China: from Sufi fundamentalists to urban workers, from northern wheat farmers to southeastern fishermen, from noodle-makers to Party leaders, from smartly dressed "Western" urbanites to veiled northwestern melon-sellers, from imam to cadre, *hajji* to athiest, these people all call themselves Hui, are identified by the state as such, and strongly resent all attempts to regard them otherwise as an insult to their heritage. That all of these different peoples could see themselves as one ethnic group wreaks havoc on modern ethnicity theory; that they have united together as one nationality with a growing population, connections to the Middle East, and political clout, makes Chinese Communist cadres give serious consideration to many of their demands and requestion Marxist dogma about the fading of national differences in socialist societies. It is in the particularities of their differences, and the shared imaginings of their similarities, that their identity is to be located—not in any reified notion of what a "Hui Muslim" is, or an assumed construction of "Chinese-ness."

As China finds itself once again at the center of a growing Asian sphere of economic and international dominance, situated between the Central Asian plain (commanded by the nation-states of the Muslim Middle East, South Asia, and the Soviet Union), and the vibrant political economies of East Asia (led by Japan, Taiwan, and Korea), the Muslims of China may be very well positioned to resume their traditional role as the "middle men" of the Silk Road, somewhere in between East and West, and no longer marginal to our understanding of the complex nature of Chinese society.

Acknowledgments

In the course of this study, I have incurred enormous debts of assistance which no simple acknowledgment of my gratitude could begin to repay; nevertheless I will attempt to do so, as simply as possible. I am particularly indebted to my dissertation committee, whose chair, Stevan Harrell, guided me through the fieldwork and writing-up stages, with insight, humor, and acumen. Charles F. Keyes challenged me to not become mired in the ethnographic intricacies of Chinese and Hui Muslim society, but to ask the larger questions of ethnicity, nationality, and identity in the modern nation-state that sustained the theoretical commitment of this study. "Sino-Muslim" experts advised me at several stages of this venture, most notably Jonathan N. Lipman and Barbara L. K. Pillsbury. China scholars, from many different fields, who nevertheless took an interest in a very different side of Chinese society, included: Frederick Brandauer, K. C. Chang, David and Isobel Crook, Jack Dull, Arthur Glasser, Hue-Tam Ho Tai, William Lavely, Roderick MacFarquhar, Elizabeth Perry, Morris Rossabi, Collin Tong, Ezra Vogel, and James L. Watson. Scholars outside the "China field" who provided considerable advice and support included: Sayid Z. Abedin, Thomas Barfield, Robert Hefner, Paul Hiebert, Chris Kruegler, Beatrice Manz, Henry Rosovsky, Nur Yalman, and Farhat Ziadeh.

In China, I was hosted and advised by many individuals and organizations, to whom I am most grateful. My main *danwei* and host institutions included the Central Institute for Nationalities and the Ningxia Academy of Social Sciences. I was also assisted tremendously by the State Commission for Nationalities Affairs and the China Islamic Association (as well as the provincial and regional level branches of these organizations in Ningxia, Gansu, Xinjiang, Sichuan, Yunnan, Guangzhou, and Fujian), the Gansu Provincial Nationalities Research Institute, the Xinjiang Academy of Social Sciences, Xinjiang University, the Tibetan Academy of Social Sciences, the Yunnan Institute for Nationalities, the Anthropology Department of Xiamen University, the Quanzhou Maritime Museum, and the Ningxia Educational College. Among the many scholars and leaders from these institutions (both inside and outside China) who assisted my research, sometimes facilitating requests, arranging interviews, and challenging ideas, included, in alphabetical order: Kahar Barat, Chen Yongling, Ding Guoyong, Fu Yunqi, Gao Zhanfu, Guo Zhichao, He Yan, Huang Tianzhu, Huang Ying, Hui Jingfang, Jiger Jenabel, Li Beshu, Li Yangqing, Lin Yaohua, Liu Xianzhao, Lü Lin, Ma Jun, Ma Qicheng, Ma Shouqian, Ma Tengai, Ma Tong, Ma Weiliang, Ren Shiqi, Song Shuhua, Su Wei, Tian Guang Uerliq, Wang Jianguo, Wang Lianmao, Yang Huaizhong, Yu Zhengui, and Zhang Tianlu. These individuals do not necessarily agree with (and some are strongly opposed to) the conclusions in this book, but they all expended much time and personal effort to allow me to "seek truth from facts," and decide for myself how the two were aligned in China.

Numerous funding and academic institutions provided the "iron noodle bowl" that made this study possible. My field research was funded by the Committee on Scholarly Communication with the People's Republic of China, the Fulbright-Hays Doctoral Disseration Research Abroad program, and the Wenner-Gren Foundation for Anthropological Research. Write-up support, both pre- and postdoctoral, was provided by the Charlotte W. Newcombe Doctoral Dissertation Fellowship of the Woodrow Wilson National Fellowship Foundation, the Hsiao Kung-ch'uan Dissertation Fellowship program of the Henry S. Jackson School of International Studies at the University of Washington, and the Harvard Academy for International and Area Studies. While at Harvard, the John King Fairbank Center provided considerable support for the project, agreeing to host (with Andrew W. Mellon Foundation funding) a conference, "The Legacy of Islam in China: An International Symposium in Memory of Joseph F. Fletcher" in 1989, that brought many Chinese, Soviet, Japanese, and Western scholars together for the first time, providing tremendous further insights to this study on the Hui. Considerable assistance was provided by librarians at the East Asia Library of the University of Washington, the Harvard-Yenching Library, the Fairbank Center East Asia Library, and the Social Science Library of the Institute for Advanced Study, including Karl Lo, Eugene W. Wu, Raymond D. Lum, Nancy Hearst, and Elliot Shore. John King Fairbank took a personal interest in the study and addressed the international conference on Islam in China, evidencing his long-term commitment to the multi-national aspects of Chinese society. I also want especially to thank Mary Ellen Alonso and Jacqueline Armijo-Hussein for their many suggestions and assistance with the photographic archives of Owen Lattimore, Claude Pickens, and Frederick Wulsin at Harvard, and to Mary Beth Bresolin and Pat MacDowell for their help with maps. Through the long process of revising, editing, and re-editing, the anonymous reviewers and editors of the East Asian Monograph Series, and especially Florence Trefethen, went beyond the call of duty to help bring this manuscript to fruition. Final touches were made while serving as a Catherine D. and John T. MacArthur Foundation scholar at the Institute for Advanced Study, where I received considerable input from my colleagues and fellow members, particularly Thomas Abercrombie, Arjun Appadurai, Carol Breckenridge, Nicholas Dirks, Sherry Ortner, and Robert Thornton. I am particularly grateful to Clifford Geertz for inviting me to the Institute and engaging in many of the issues of this study.

I would like also to express appreciation to the *Journal of Asian Studies* and the *Fletcher Forum* for allowing me to make use of previously published material. I am also grateful to the Harvard-Yenching Library and the Pickens family for the reproduction of Claude Pickens's photographs, to the Lattimore family and the Peabody Museum for the use of Owen Lattimore's photographs, and to Agence France-Presse and Associated-Press for the use of their photographs.

I wish it were possible to thank the scores of villagers, workers, and religious and political leaders in the communities where I carried out my research. They were so hospitable and open to me as a foreigner not well versed in the ways of Islam that I am not surprised that Ibn Battuta, and perhaps Marco Polo, felt quite at home among them several centuries earlier. I especially wish to express my appreciation to the members of the communities in Na Homestead, Ningxia; Chendai and Baiqi, Fujian; and Niujie and Changying, Beijing.

Finally, special thanks go to Mary Hammond, who enthusiastically supported my research, providing a constant inspiration to me while pursuing her own career and research in China. She is most responsible for making the study possible and enormously enjoyable. I alone, unfortunately, must accept responsibility for any shortcomings in the study, and its final conclusions.

A Note on Romanization

Chinese terms are transliterated using the *pinyin* system that is now standard in the People's Republic. Frequently used Chinese ideographs, as well as Hui Islamic terms and phrases, are given in the glossary (Appendix B), using the *jiantize* script, which is also standard in China. Names and places traditionally glossed according to popularly accepted systems are given in their most widely known forms (Sun Yat-sen, Canton, Hakka, Manchu, etc.). Arabic and Persian terms are romanized according to the *Encyclopedia of Islam*. For Turkic terms and place names I usually follow the romanized forms given by D. M. Farquhar, G. Jarring, and E. Norin, *Sven Hedin Central Asian Atlas: Index of Geographic Names* (Sven Hedin Foundation: Stockholm, 1967). Thus *Kashgar* is used instead of the Chinese *Kashi*, and *Tibet*, instead of *Xizang*. Let the reader beware: In a work portraying such a truly transnational group, whose linguistic codes, socioreligious traditions and ethnic roots extend from the Far to the Middle East, and beyond, there are bound to be gross inconsistencies (*Ahong*, instead of the *pinyin*, *Ah hong*, since it better reflects its Persian origins, *Ahund*) and a few personal idiosyncracies (such as the use of plurals for languages that use them, e.g., Imams, Uigurs, and Tibetans; and singular for Chinese terms, which do not, e.g., the many Hui, Han, and Dongxiang who inhabit this text). For these variances I depend upon the reader's indulgence.

Contents

Tables

Photographs

Figures

Maps

Muslim protesters in Beijing, holding government documents permitting them to march, 12 May 1989. Note that, in the front row, Hui, Uigur, and Kirghiz Muslim nationalities are represented. Courtesy of Associated Press.

ONE

Muslim Nationalism in China: A Fourth Tide

During my stay in China, whenever I saw any Muslims I always felt as though I were meeting my own family and close kinsmen.
— *Ibn Battuta, Fourteenth Century*

Just prior to the bloody suppression of the 1989 democracy movement in China, in the midst of the flood of protesting students and workers who, for a remarkably lengthy moment in history, marched relatively unimpeded across Tiananmen Square and the screens of the world's television sets, another comparatively unnoticed, but nevertheless significant, procession took place. Starting at the Central Institute for Nationalities, the state-sponsored college that attempts to "educate" some of the most elite representatives of China's 91 million minority nationalities, the protest began with mainly Hui Muslim students who were joined by representatives of all 10 Muslim nationalities in China, including some sympathetic members of the Han Chinese majority. The rather unwieldy procession made its way down China's "high-tech corridor" in the northwest corner of the city, where Beijing University, People's University, Qinghua University, and a host of other colleges had gorged forth innumerable student protesters in the heady days before June 4th. Like these zealous student marchers, this procession was on its way to Tiananmen Square, the so-called "Gate of Heavenly Peace," which soon opened on to a hellish nightmare of indiscriminate warfare in the streets of the terrorized city. This procession to the Square also made its way along Changan Jie, "the Avenue of Eternal Peace," that shortly thereafter was to be renamed "Blood Alley" by Beijing's citizens, but, instead of proceeding directly to the Square, it veered south, for its second point of destination: the central "Oxen Street" (Niujie) Mosque patronized by many of Beijing's 200,000 Muslims and the nearby Chinese Islamic Association.

Instead of calls for "Democracy!" and "Freedom!," this protest raised banners that proclaimed: "Death to China's Salman Rushdie!" "Respect China's Freedom of Religion!" "Uphold the Constitution!" "Uphold the Party's Nationality and Religion Policies!" "Preserve Nationality Unity!" "Love our Country, Love our Religion!" "Oppose Blasphemy against Islam!" "Allahu Akbar! (God is Great)" and "Ban the Book *Sexual Customs*, the *Satanic Verses* of China!"[1] Unlike the students and workers dressed in their street clothes, these protesters wore the emblems of Islam in China: Men donned the white hat by which Muslims are frequently distinguished, while women Muslims, many for first time, adopted the *hijab*, or head-covering (Chinese: *gai tou*), worn publicly only in very conservative Muslim areas in China, but found adorning Muslim women throughout the Islamic world.

Numbering almost 3,000 by the time they reached their final destination, Tiananmen Square, these Muslims, primarily students from the Nationalities Institute, were protesting the publication of a book in Chinese entitled *Sexual Customs* (*Xing fengsu*), that they claimed denigrated Islam, just, they said, "like the 'Satanic Verses.'" Marching at the front of the long procession as it wound its way through the streets of the capital were Hui, Uigur, Kirghiz, and Kazak Muslim students who held above their heads both their official certificate permitting them to protest, issued by the Public Security Bureau, and their letter of protest over the publication of *Sexual Customs*. The book was an innocuous description of the history of sexuality around the world, which guaranteed it a strong market in China where few official books address the subject.[2] Muslims in China would normally pay little attention to such popular literature. They were violently incensed, however, by sections of the book dealing with Islam which compared minarets to phalli, Muslim tombs and domes to the "mound of Venus," and the Meccan pilgrimage to orgies, which were an excuse, the book claimed, for homosexual relations and sodomy, *with camels*, no less.[3]

The denigration of Islam and religious practices not thought to be Chinese has had a long history in China, and this was by no means the most degrading. The response this time, however, was the most violent in recent years. In addition to the protest of 3,000 Muslims in Beijing on 12 May, the Chinese press reported that over 20,000 Muslims marched in Lanzhou, the capital of Gansu, at the end of April, and up to 100,000 Muslims filled the streets of Xining, the capital of Qinghai, in mid-May, including smaller protests in Urumqi, Shanghai, Inner Mongolia, Wuhan, and Yunnan.

Remarkably, and in another dramatic contrast to the crackdown on the student Pro-Democracy Movement, the state took the following actions in response to this Muslim protest over an insignificant Chinese book: The government granted full permission for all the Muslim protests,[4] often despatching police to close streets, stop traffic, and direct the marchers, many of whom were organized by the China Islamic Association, a state-sponsored organization established in the 1950s. In the Beijing instance, the police even provided a car for a Hui Muslim professor from the Central Institute for Nationalities to escort the protesting students. At the end of their long day of protesting, the state provided buses to bring the students back across town to their home universities. Perhaps as a factor influencing the state's rapid response, China's Muslims received a large boost from the visit of Iran's President Ali Khameini, who on 11 May, just one day before the Beijing protest that ignited protests across China, stated that he was in full solidarity with the Muslims' demands and that the Ayatollah Khomeini continued to maintain the Rushdie death threat, despite international outrage.

Most notably, the state immediately met all the demands of the protestors: The book was banned, and supposedly 13 million copies were confiscated, with 95,240 copies publicly burned in the main square of Lanzhou; the Shanghai editors were fired and the authors required to make a public apology; and the publication houses in Shanghai and Shanxi were closed for "reorganization."

Perhaps even more significantly, the government decided to be lenient against Muslims who had gotten carried away in the largely peaceful demonstrations, breaking laws and damaging state property. In a Lanzhou Muslim protest on 12 May, over 200 Muslims rampaged through the downtown offices of the provincial government, breaking windows and office equipment, and severely injuring the driver of a car suspected of transporting copies of the book. The Public Security Bureau, after a prolonged struggle, arrested 35 Muslims, who were detained overnight. However, instead of prosecuting the Muslims, the government released them, after an emergency meeting with representatives of the local Chinese Islamic Association who arbitrated on their behalf.[5] In an interesting development, after the authors of *Sexual Customs* were released, and their formerly pseudonymous identities revealed, they were then re-arrested for their own safety: Muslims in Qinghai had taken up a reward of 600,000 yuan ($200,000 US) for their execution. They are now in hiding under police protection, Salman Rushdie-style.

The protests were not well covered in the Western media.[6] Given that they occurred in the midst of the student demonstrations, hunger strikes, and Gorbachev visit, it is not surprising. What is noteworthy is that the Chinese media covered every detail of the Muslim protests, and the procession in Beijing on 12 May shared the front-page headlines of the *People's Daily* with both the student strikes and the Gorbachev visit.

This case serves as a useful introduction to this book on Hui Muslim identity in that it bears important parallels to past protests as well as initiating a new stage in ethnic nationalism in China, what I have termed, following Joseph Fletcher, a fourth tide in Muslim identity in China.[7] In terms of past Muslim movements, similar anti-Islamic publication protests have taken place since the rise of the popular press in China. Rudolf Löwenthal, one of the many scholars who paid serious attention to Islam in China in the 1930s and 1940s, recorded another Beijing incident in 1939 when Muslim protesters wrecked the publication offices of the *Shijie wanbao*, the *Gongmin bao*, and forced China's largest publishing house, the Commercial Press, to publish a formal retraction of an article the Muslims found "insulted Muslim womanhood."[8] Between 1926–1936, Barbara Pillsbury noted more than 24 articles published by "Han" Chinese magazines and newspapers denigrating "peculiar customs" of Muslims in China, including such statements as: "The pig is the most beloved son of the Muslim gods," and describing how Muslims are descended from a pig which they worship (which is why they do not eat pork, out of veneration for their ancestors!).[9] Just such an article appeared in Shanghai in 1932, entitled "Why Muslims Do Not Eat Pork," which led to an attack on the magazine's editor and closure of the publication house.[10] These incidents were not limited to pre-revolutionary China, however. The 12 May letter held aloft by the protesting students and read at each stop along the protest route, contained references to a 1984 *Youth News* article in Shanghai and a 1988 *History of Religion* volume published in Shaanxi that was "barbarian and impertinent to Muslims."[11] The rise of the Muslim nationalist protests over published insults to Islam and their heritage supports Benedict Anderson's argument that the proliferation of print media in Europe gave currency to national and transnational identities, reaching out to isolated groups and individuals.[12] What is unique about this protest is the use of the Salman Rushdie incident as a rallying point for the Beijing protesters, now elevated to an international metaphor for local Muslim complaints anywhere, even in China, underscoring the new transnationalism of Chinese Islam.[13] In addition, and perhaps because of the international attention given to the matter (note Khameini's support for the Beijing protestors), the Chinese government's response and acquiescence to Muslim demands has never been as thoroughgoing, nor the protest as national, or even transnational.[14]

In this book I seek to argue that the Rushdie incident in China reveals the ways in which modern religious and ethnic identities are shaped, the ways in which local Muslims move within the specific "contours of power" in Chinese society.[15] These contours are shaped by what Partha Chatterjee notes as the "derivative discourse" of nationalism and religion—the definition of what it means to be a member of an identified nationality or officially approved religious group in China.[16] By appealing to these state-imposed rationalizations of religion and ethnicity, Muslims were able to turn these discursive restraints to their own advantage. By stressing the legality of the Muslim protests, what Barbara Pillsbury noted as their *"protest to* the government," rather than *against* it—the fact that the Muslims had permission and were often escorted by police—the state-controlled press sought to juxtapose the legal Muslim protest with the *illegality* of the student protests. The students, as an unrecognized voluntary association, were considered unlawful, riotous, and a threat to the state's order. For that they were met by a military crackdown. The actions of the Muslims, as members of state-assigned minority nationalities and believing in a world religion approved by the state, were considered permissible. For that they were inundated with state-sponsored media and assisted in their demands. The difference, from the Chinese state's standpoint, was one of order and disorder, rationality and confusion, law and criminality, reward and punishment.

The Muslims demonstrating in the streets of China's major cities protested not only as Muslims but also as members of the state-assigned Islamic nationalities, in a demonstration of what Geertz has called "primordial politics."[17] This is illustrated in the means by which Muslims justified their participation in the Salman Rushdie protest in China. In several accounts, it was reported that many Muslims felt compelled to take part in the protests because the book was an affront to their identity as members of state-assigned Muslim national groups. In Qinghai, the following statement was made to the Xining news service:

> Han Fucai, a Hui leading cadre, said: "*As a Hui cadre*, in common with all Muslims, I am extremely angry. The masses have called for punishment according to the law for those concerned with publishing, distributing, and editing this book. This is quite fair and reasonable."[18]

As a member of the Hui minority, one of 10 Muslim nationalities in China, this man felt insulted by the portrayal of Islam in the book *Sexual Customs*, though he himself was a cadre, probably a Communist Party member, and undoubtedly not very religious. The state-assigned label of Hui identity became the means by which this man's claims were placed before the state, an immensely useful circularity, revealing what I shall argue to be an important dialectical interaction in China between ethnicity and nationality.

Confusion in the literature on minority nationality identity in China has arisen over the interchangeability of the terms *ethnicity* and *nationality*.[19] *Nationality* is what the state in China has conferred upon the 56 nationalities who were identified mainly in the 1950s, and expressed in the Chinese term for nationality, *minzu*. *Ethnicity*, for which there is no separate term in Chinese (see below), is something entirely different, but not unrelated, in that it is tied into one's own self-perceived identity, which is often influenced by state policy. It is the interaction of self-perceived identity and its relation to state definition and nationality policy that is at the heart of the new rise in ethnic nationalism and the fourth tide of Islam in China. The confusion over ethnic and national identity has led to a misunderstanding of Hui Muslim identity in China, which is couched in terms of notions of purity, Islamic heritage, and descent from Muslim ancestors, as well as state policy.

QING ZHEN: *EXPRESSIONS OF HUI IDENTITY*

The Chinese book *Sexual Customs*, like many publications before it, offended Muslim notions of purity and identity in China. Central to Muslim identity is the Chinese translation and interpretation of Islam, as revealed in a nineteenth-century Muslim tract appended at the end of the Marshal Broomhall's *Islam in China* written in 1910, the first and only book on Muslims in China based upon extensive field and survey work. If we are to understand Hui Muslim identity in China, we must begin here. The Muslim tract stated:

> But our Pure and True Faith [*Qing Zhen Jiao*], the Correct Religion, arose and gradually reached this land from the Sui and T'ang dynasties onward. The statement of the recognition of the Lord (derived) from Adam was not yet lost. Moreover they obtained the most Holy Mohammed's very detailed account of the plain commands of the True Lord. Therefore our Religion is very Pure and very True, and only holds what is correct, not vainly taking the name, while lacking the ability to prove its truth. . . . Why (have we written) like this? Only in the hope that those who look at (the words) will clarify their heart and breast, and enlarge their horizon beyond the common and the visible, and sweeping away heresy will consider the traces of origin and exit, (and) will investigate the essential matter of reversion to the Source. Thus you will almost get hold of the correct Doctrine of Purity and Truth.[20]

The "Pure and True" mentioned in this Muslim tract refer to the two Chinese characters *qing zhen* (清真) that one encounters wherever the people known as Hui are found. The importance of this concept initially caught my attention in 1982 while in China as a language student at Beijing University. One of the first Hui with whom I became acquainted came to my room but refused a cup of tea I offered. The cup,

Muslim graves outside the "Bell Tomb" of Wahb Abu Kabcha in Guangzhou, whom many Hui believe to be the cousin of Muhammad sent to China in the mid-seventh century. Note that the two upright tombstones have different Chinese ideographs for "ahong," the Hui term for teacher (see glossary), revealing earlier variants of the transliterated Persian term. The horizontal inscription (lower left) reads, "The Pure and True (religion, *Qing Zhen*) is without ceasing." Photo: Gladney

Qing zhen pickling buckets produced by villagers in a Hui autonomous village south of Kunming, Yunnan. Note the Chinese ideographs for Hui nationality (*Hui zu*). Photo: Gladney

Christian Missionary Alliance missionary Carter Holton's photograph of a Hui restauranteer holding traditional *Qing Zhen* sign indicating the restaurant is pure according to Islamic regulations. Note pictured symbols of teapot, incense vase, tree of life, and two GMD Nationalist emblems (c. 1935). Photo: Holton. Courtesy of Harvard-Yenching Library.

he said, was not "pure and true enough" (*bu gou qing zhen*). He explained that he did not want to drink from the same cup or eat with the same utensils that may have been used formerly by someone who had eaten pork; the residue might still be on the cup, no matter how often or how well I had washed it. I later found out that this person was a member of the Communist Party, a well-educated urbanite, and, although he attended the local Haidian district mosque on Islamic "National Minority" holidays twice a year, a self-avowed atheist.

During the rest of the summer in Beijing, I began to notice the characters *qing zhen* on restaurants, food shops, bakeries, ice-cream stands, candy wrappers, mosques, Islamic literary works, and even on packages of incense produced in the Dachang Hui autonomous county just east of Beijing. It became clear to me that the concept expressed by these Chinese ideographs meant more to the Hui than the absence of lard or pork. It had become, in the Geertzian sense,[21] a "sacred symbol" marking Hui identity and thus provides a good starting point for this study of Hui ethnicity.

Wherever the Hui have traveled, both in and outside China proper,

Weizhou Great Mosque, southern Ningxia, which Claude Pickens described as the most beautiful mosque in China (c. 1930). It was destroyed during the Cultural Revolution. Photo: Pickens. Courtesy of Harvard-Yenching Library.

Interior of Hui mosque in Dali, Yunnan, with *mihrab* at center bordered by Quranic citations. The stylized Chinese characters for "longevity" (*wan shou*) are displayed on either side of the *mihrab* (lower left and lower right). Photo: Gladney this concept of *qing zhen* has followed. Barbara Pillsbury reports that, until recently, a Hui Chinese restaurant could be found in Los Angeles bearing the large characters for *qing zhen* on a sign in front, and serving traditional ceremonially purified Hui Chinese dishes cooked by a Hui immigrant from Taiwan. Most Chinese restaurants in the Muslim Middle East are run by Muslims from China and are *qing zhen* restaurants. In Kirghizia and Kazakistan, Soviet Central Asia, where Hui fled after the failure of their mid-nineteenth-century rebellions and established themselves in close-knit communities, the title of *qing zhen* is found on all their restaurants and food stands, written in the Dungan Cyrillic script they have adapted over the years. In Bangkok, I found a small Chinese restaurant run by Hui from Yunnan, named *Chien Jan*, a Thai transliteration of *qing zhen*, reflecting Southern Chinese and Thai pronunciation. "The China Islamic Restaurant" in Rosemead, California, is run by Hui Muslims and entitled in Chinese Qing Zhen Ma Jia Guan (Pure and True Ma Family Restaurant). The importance of this label on all "Pure and True" Hui restaurants and caravansary was apparent to the Protestant missionaries Cable and French, when they stopped in Dunhuang on their long trek across the Gobi Desert in the early part of this century:

> At Tunhwang we temporarily exchanged tent life for inn life. From half a dozen possible hostelries we chose a *serai* where a wooden sign, in the shape of a teapot, swung at the main entrance. This sign bore the inscription "Pure and True Religion," which indicated to passers-by that it was a Moslem inn and offered lodging more particularly to followers of the prophet.
>
> Chinese travellers avoid any such inn because of the rudeness to which they may be subjected when using it. Even though they abstain from eating pork during their stay, every pot and pan which they possess is considered unclean, and will not be allowed inside the kitchen. This is not conducive to good feeling between host and guest, and may at any time lead to high words and even to blows.[22]

Donald Leslie suggests that *qing zhen* might have originated with the Chinese Jews and referred to Judaism in many of their ancient inscriptions.[23] Beijing's East Mosque (Dong Si) is the earliest structure referred to as a *Qing Zhen Si* in 1447, the 20th year of the Ming Emperor Zheng

Tong.[24] The early-eleventh-century Arab-style mosque in Quanzhou was known as the Qing Jing Si (Pure and Clean Mosque), and the Islamicist Yang Yongchang gives several examples of mosques with Purity and Truth in their early titles.[25] In his etymological study of the term, the prominent Hui historian Ma Shouqian concludes that, before the Yuan dynasty, *qing zhen* referred loosely to both Islam and Judaism, but, by the Ming dynasty, its meaning was generally restricted to the religion of the Hui people.[26] The French Commandant d'Ollone,[27] in his study of the Hui in Yunnan, reported that *Qing Zhenjiao* (The Pure and True Religion) was the name officially given to Islam in a fourteenth-century edict.[28]

The Chinese etymological dictionary *Ci Yuan* traces *qing zhen* to a Tang-dynasty expression: "Pure and True lacks desire, it is everything that cannot change" (*qing zhen guayu, wanwu bu neng yi ye*).[29] In the seventeenth-century work *Qing Zhen jiao shuo* (Speaking of the pure and true religion), Liu Sanxiu, father of the famous Ming-dynasty Islamic scholar Liu Zhi, wrote that Islam comprises 3 elements: "The purity and truth of Allah, religion, and humankind" (*zhu de qing zhen, jiao de qing zhen he ren de qing zhen*). Ma Fuchu (1794–1874), the Yunnan Hui scholar, defined *qing zhen* in terms of Confucian ideals when he wrote: "To deny oneself is pure, to restore propriety is true" (*Keji zhiwei qing, fuli zhiwei zhen*).[30] Here we see the two complementary but distinct usages of the term. Ma Fuchu explicitly tied the Islamic concept of *qing zhen* to traditional Confucian principles expressed in the phrase "denying oneself and restoring propriety" (*keji fuli*).[31]

Hui scholars in China today generally suggest that *qing zhen* means "clean and authentic" (*qingjie zhenshi*), emphasizing both the sanitary and authoritarian aspects of the term. Matthews translates *qing* as clear, pure, and lucid.[32] A Beijing "sanitation worker" or "street cleaner" is known as a *qingjie gongren*. *Qing jiaotu* is the Chinese gloss for the Christian "Puritan." *Zhen*, Matthews informs us, refers to what is true, real, unfeigned, and genuine.[33] "Authenticity" or "truthfulness" is generally rendered as *zhen shi xing*. Vernon Fowler, in an interesting recent etymological study of the term *zhen*, concludes that the graph appears in early sacrificial texts related to "ritual cooking."[34] It is noteworthy that early Muslim attempts to represent the foreign term *Islam* in Chinese writing should turn to ideographs that connote ritual purity and sacrificial authenticity.

The concept of *qing zhen*, I argue, reveals two aspects of Islam in China central to Hui community interests and self-understanding: purity (*qing*), in the sense of ritual cleanliness and moral conduct; and truth (*zhen*), in the sense of authenticity and legitimacy. This wider meaning of *qing zhen* goes beyond the Arabic term *halal*, as *qing zhen* is sometimes translated, for it involves much more than food ritually prepared according to Islamic dietary prescriptions. The concept of *qing zhen* governs all one's life. The Arabic term *tahára* (ritual or moral purity) is perhaps a better translation for this all-encompassing concept.[35] However, for the Hui, the two aspects of *qing zhen*, purity and truth, define important tensions in their identity: Islamic moral purity and the authenticity of ethnic ancestry, lifestyle, and heritage.

Anthropologists have explored in many different contexts the notion of purity and social tabu in terms of symbolic import and influence on social relations. Louis Dumont has argued that, in South Asia, an emphasis on moral and ritual purity contains within it the basis for ideas of hierarchy:

> The opposition of pure and impure appears to us the very principle of hierarchy, to such a degree that it merges with the opposition of superior and inferior; moreover, it also governs separation. We have seen it leads at many levels to seclusion, isolation. The preoccupation with purity leads to the getting rid of the recurrent personal impurities of organic life, to organizing contact with purificatory agents and abolishing it with external agents of impurity, whether social or other.[36]

Clearly, for the Hui, social and ideological priorities have superseded ecological and economic concerns. (In China, pork has been the basic meat protein for centuries and regarded by Chairman Mao as "a national treasure.")[37]

As Mary Douglas has so eloquently described, social pollution is structured in the context of marginality and boundedness: People make moral distinctions between what they regard as pure and impure in the context of social exclusivity and inclusivity.[38] Arnold van Gennep's work on tabu and totemism in Madagascar emphasized, in a way similar to Douglas, that these practices were more than just religious concerns with ideological purity; they marked the boundaries of one's identity, separating Self from Other.[39] For the Hui to have perceived, even re-ordered, their moral universe in terms of the dictates of a *qing zhen* life-style indicates its centrality to their identity in China. Foreign Muslim visitors to Hui areas have commented on the scrupulous attention paid by Hui to Islamic dietary restrictions, even surpassing other Muslims in the Middle East.[40] In Victor Turner's terms, the polysemic symbolic expression of ritual purity is intricately tied to the structure and power of social relations.[41] Confucian notions of propriety and hierarchy may have also contributed to the ways in which the Hui conceived of them-selves in relations to others.

In China, the Hui have always been ritually and perhaps morally sus-pect, not merely because of their foreign origins—there have been many foreigners easily assimilated into Chinese society without developing ethnic, enduring social collectivities—but perhaps, more fundamen-tally, because of their avoidance of those objects, such as pork, that have been a fundamental part of the elementary structure of Chinese ritual and food prestations.[42] Yet, as Julia Kristeva has so acutely described, there is a basic powerfulness, even horror, related to defilement and impurity that goes beyond social structure.[43] It strikes at the very core of one's self and ontology. There may be something more fundamental than food proscription at stake here: The Hui's defining and ordering of their world into one that is pure and true turns the tables on Chinese society. It reverses the Durkheimian polarities of what is sacred and pro-fane in China, making the Hui *the pure* community that rejects Chinese ritual values, and *the true* believers who follow the one God above all others.[44] This notion and its wide variety of expression and reinterpre-tation among various Hui communities is basic to their identity.

This book explores the expression of Hui identity according to their different interpretations of *qing zhen*. It also highlights the basis for fun-damental questions with which the Hui themselves are concerned. How does one maintain moral purity and ritual cleanliness in a society that is non-Muslim and uses pork as its basic source of meat protein and cooking oil? More fundamentally, how does one legitimate one's ethno-religious identity as true, authentic, and valid, in the context of a Communist state influenced by the "three great teachings" (*san da jiao*) of Confucianism, Buddhism, and Daoism? As we have seen with the Salman Rushdie protest, Hui notions of purity and identity define the context and content of their ethnic nationalism.

The concept of *qing zhen* is so central to Hui ethnoreligious concern that it has become the very confession of their faith.[45] The monotheistic formula—that there is no God but Allah and Muhammad is his Prophet—is known in Arabic as the *Shahadah*; to the Hui, it is known in Chinese as the *Qing Zhen Yan*, the very words of *qing zhen*. It is not surprising that Muslims since the Yuan settled upon the concept of *qing zhen* to translate the meaningfulness of Islam for them living in Chinese society. Significantly, they could have settled on Chinese translations of "submission," "obedience," or "faithfulness," arguably closer to the original meaning of Islam. They also did not simply transliterate the term *Islam* as *Yisilam* until very recently. Instead, the combination of *qing* and *zhen* seemed to capture and express their deepest concerns as Muslims living in the Chinese world. *Pure* reflected their concern to morally legitimate themselves in a Confucian society preoccupied with moral propriety and order. *Truth* and belief in the "True Lord" (Zhen Zhu) distinguished them as monotheists in a land where polytheistic belief and practice predominated. There is clearly a subtle irony here, as in China the Han have typically looked down on the Hui as dirty, larcenous, and immoral, while the Hui, by their very choice of translation, portray their ethnoreligious identity as more "pure and true" than the Han. The different ways Hui have sought to adapt their ethnoreligious identity, their ideas of a pure and true lifestyle, to the various Chinese sociopolitical contexts and to the tides of Islamic influence arriving from the Middle East and Central Asia have led to a wide diversity of Hui identities and Islamic orders in China, as well as influencing the nature of their conflict and interaction with the Chinese state.

STATE POWER AND THE EVOLUTION OF AN ETHNONYM

The Hui have exercised originality and flexibility in interpreting their understanding of Islam to a Chinese audience, and thus have sought interpretive control over their internal understanding of Islam. Externally, however, the state has traditionally labeled their faith simply as the "religion of the Hui" (*Hui jiao*). While archaeological evidence has revealed that Muslim peoples traded and settled in China since the very advent of Islam, there was no consistent term in Chinese to refer to these peoples and their religion until the thirteenth century. The emergence of this term and its institutionalization as the accepted ethnonym for one people is intimately bound to the increasing power of the state in China and its authority over the naming of social entities. According to Bernard Cohn, the power of the British colonial authorities to conduct a census and institutionalize labels and castes in India contributed to the "objectification" of their cultures and identities:

> Through the asking of questions and the compiling of information in categories which the British rulers could utilize for governing, [the census] provided an arena for Indians to ask questions about themselves, and Indians utilized the fact that the British census commissioners tried to order tables on caste in terms of social precedence.[46]

It is not that these social labels did not exist in some form prior to their institutionalization by the state in China. People referred to themselves as Huihui, believed in the Hui religion, and lived ethnically distinct lives. However, naming by the state, legislating who was and was not a nationality, then quantifying the numbers of certain groups, solidified those groups and gave them a social life unknown before. While Judith Banister has related that there has been little written about the reason the PRC chose to initiate a census along Western models and categorize its population according to nationalities,[47] H. Yuan Tien's analysis of the development of the early Chinese policy toward population planning indicates that the census was very much tied into the Nationalists' concerns about building and documenting a strong Chinese nation. Just before his death, Sun Yat-sen gave a series of lectures in which he declared:

> We Chinese are constantly boasting of our large population [of 400 million] which cannot easily be destroyed by another nation. . . . Gentlemen, do you know when China's four hundred million census was taken?—In the reign of Ch'ien Lung [A.D. 1734–1795] in the Manchu dynasty. Since Ch'ien Lung, there has been no census. In this period of nearly two hundred years our pop-

ulation has remained the same—four hundred millions. A hundred years ago it was four hundred millions; then a hundred years hence it will still be four hundred millions.... Our new policy calls for increase of population and *preservation of the race*, so that the Chinese people may perpetuate their existence along with the ... races of the world.[48]

Sun Yat-sen's speech illustrates that the census played an important role in the formulation of Chinese national identity. The early Nationalists (and later Communist Party leaders) argued that only by counting and categorizing their population, as the Western nations did, could they begin to compete in the age of nation-states and engender a national movement. The first census of the People's Republic, conducted in 1953, registered only 41 nationalities. After the minority nationality identification campaigns in the late 1950s (see below), the 1964 census registered 53 nationalities, with the 1982 census reporting a total of 56 nationalities in China. The transformation and ethnogenesis of these peoples into recognized nationalities is crucial to our understanding of ethnic nationalism in China. With regard to the Hui, where once there were Muslims interacting as co-religionists, the state identified, institutionalized, and in short, invented a nationality. As we shall see below, the modern term for the Hui nationality in China is directly related to the creation of the census and the rise of the nation-state in China.

As early as the seventh century, Tang-dynasty historians documented the presence of large groups of foreign merchants dwelling in the southeast coastal communities of Canton (Guangzhou), Xiamen, and Quanzhou.[49] Among these foreigners there were increasingly large numbers of mainly Persian and Arab Muslims who were grouped with the other foreigners as *fan ke* (barbarian guests). As they settled and took on local spouses, their offspring became known as *tusheng fan ke* (autochthonous or native-born barbarian guests). Ma Shouqian reports that, during this early period, the foreign Muslims rarely interacted with non-Muslim Chinese outside the marketplace, and Islam was of little interest to local officials.[50] Islamic religious activities were described in Tang and Song texts simply as the worship of other spirits (*shen*), ghosts (*gui*), and even heaven (*tian*). Professor Ma reports early terms for Islam such as the "Law of the Arabs" (*Da Shi Fa*), the Religion of the Celestial Square (*Tian Fang Jiao*), and Muhammadanism.[51]

The Chinese term *Hui* (回) or *Hui jiao* (回教) for the Hui people or Islam in China did not gain widespread usage until the Yuan dynasty, when large populations of Central Asian Muslims began to migrate to China under Yuan-dynasty administration.[52] The Mongols, under Khubilai Khan's leadership, were the first to make an official, legal hierarchical distinction between four kinds of peoples in China: The Mongols were at the highest level of society; next were the Semu, or other foreigners, that included other Central Asians, Europeans, and Muslims, known as the Hui hui; then came the Han people, which included not only Northern Chinese, but also Koreans, Khitans, and Jurchen; and at the lowest end were the Nan, or "Southern" people, the Chinese populations in the south, including the Cantonese, Fujianese, and others, who were the "least desirable and least trustworthy group."[53]

The term that was later adopted as the modern Hui ethnonym derives from a medieval Chinese transliteration for the Uigur people (*Huihu* or *Huihe*).[54] William Samolin, a Central Asian historian, notes that it was a confused attempt by early Chinese officials to generalize about the Muslim peoples with whom they came into contact:

> Later the Chinese used Hui-hu, originally Uygur, for Muslim. This served to add to the confusion. Strictly speaking, the tribal confederation which succeeded the Turkish dynasty of the [Orkhon] Inscriptions in 742 and possessed itself of the Ötükän refugium became generally known as Uygur after the seizure of power.[55]

The term *Hui hui*, or *Hui jiao*, was used generally until the modern era to refer to all Muslims and Islam in China, no matter what their ethnolinguistic background. It received its first official institutionalization under the Nationalist Government. More specific terms were often employed by locals to distinguish between various Muslims; thus, in Xinjiang, *Chantou Hui* (turban Hui) literally referred to those Muslims who wore wound cloths on their heads, particularly the Uigur. Other more specific ethnonyms included *Wei Hui, Dongxiang Hui, Sala Hui,* and even *Han Hui,* which referred to those Hui who were more culturally close to the Han.[56]

Djamal al-Din Bai Shouyi, the famous Hui Marxist historian, was the first to argue persuasively that *Islam* should be glossed in Chinese as

Yisilan jiao (Islam), not the Hui religion (*Hui jiao*).[57] In a chapter entitled "The Hui hui People and the Hui hui Religion," Bai argued that, even though Hui are descendants of Muslims and have inherited certain Muslim cultural traditions such as pork abstention, they do not all necessarily believe in Islam. "Muslim" is different from "Hui person" (*Hui min*), and one should not use the term *Hui jiao* (Hui religion) but *Islam* (*Yisilan jiao*). He argued that the Hui believed not in their own religion, but in the world religion of Islam, and therefore are Muslims in faith. In ethnicity they are the Hui people, not Hui religion disciples. In Marxist terms, he identified a process of the indigenization of a world religion, in this case Islam, to a local context, which for the communities now known as the Hui had been going on for 1,200 years. Muslim groups identified by Chinese linguists with supposedly their own language derived their ethnonym from their language family; in this way the Uigur, Kazak, Tadjik, Uzbek, Kirghiz, and Tatar were identified. In this, the Chinese were heavily influenced by the 1920s Soviet identification of these peoples in Soviet Central Asia.[58] Bai Shouyi went on to identify the Muslim peoples not distinguished by language or locality as a catch-all residual group known as *Hui min*, not *Hui jiao*. Thus, the official category of the Hui was legitimated, one might even say invented so far as the legal definition of who is considered Hui is concerned.

In Taiwan today, the term *Hui* still continues to refer to all Muslim peoples, and Islam is often referred to as *Hui jiao*, though this usage is opposed by some Hui.[59] The refusal to recognize the Hui as a separate nationality in Taiwan but instead as a religious group—the believers in the Hui religion (*Hui jiao tu*) rather than members of the Hui ethnic group (*Hui minzu*) is intimately tied to different policies in both states, as we shall see below. These contrasting policies and ethnonyms play an important role in the construction of Hui identity on both sides of the Taiwan Strait.

After the founding of the People's Republic, many of these Muslim peoples were identified as specific nationalities, leading to the creation or recognition of 10 so-called Muslim nationalities in China: the Hui, Uigur, Kazak, Dongxiang, Kirghiz, Salar, Tadjik, Uzbek, Baoan, Tatar (see Table 1). Other Muslims in Tibet, Mongolia, Yunnan, and Sichuan

TABLE 1 Ethnonyms and Populations of Muslim Minorities in China

Minority	Location	Language	1990 Census
Hui	All China, esp.* Ningxia, Gansu, Henan, Xinjiang, Qinghai, Yunnan Hebei, Shandong	Sino-Tibetan	8,602,978
Uigur	Xinjiang	Altaic (Turkic)	7,214,431
Kazak	Xinjiang, Gansu Qinghai	Altaic (Turkic)	1,111,718
Dongxiang	Gansu, Xinjiang	Altaic (Turkic)	373,872
Kirghiz	Xinjiang, Heilongjiang	Altaic (Turkic)	141,549
Salar	Qinghai, Gansu	Altaic (Turkic)	87,697
Tadjik	Xinjiang	Indo-European	33,538
Uzbek	Xinjiang	Altaic (Turkic)	14,502
Baoan	Gansu	Altaic (Mongolian)	12,212
Tatar	Xinjiang	Altaic (Turkic)	4,873

Source: *Renmin ribao*, "Guanyu 1990 nian ren kou pucha zhu yao shuju de gongbao," 14 November 1990, p. 3.

Note: *Listed in order of size; total Muslim population, 17,597,370.

who were smaller in number and did not have a language of their own, however, were merely grouped with the Hui as one nationality.

In general, the Communist Government has used the ethnonym *Hui nationality* (*Hui minzu*) to refer to those Muslims who do not have a language of their own but speak the dialects of the peoples among whom they live, as opposed to the other 9 Turkic-Altaic and Indo-European Muslim language groups. In China I rarely heard Hui refer to themselves as *Hui jiao tu* (Hui religion disciples) and only occasionally heard *Hui jiao*. Instead, Hui generally preferred *Huimin* or *Huizu* (Hui nationality) and sometimes *Huihui* in rural areas. Urban Hui and intellectuals often use the Chinese renderings for "Islam" (*Yisilan jiao*) and "Muslim" (*Musilin*), and even Muslim people (*Mumin*). Urban Hui often found the term *Huihui* to be offensive, and slightly demeaning, connoting rural origins. Other terms used to refer to the Hui in the literature include: *Dungan* in Soviet Central Asia and Xinjiang,[60] *Panthay* in Southeast Asia and Yunnan,[61] as well as *Hanhui, Huihui, Khojem, Khalkhas*, and, most frequently, *Chinese Muslims*.[62] Though the Hui are often referred to as the *Chinese Muslims* because they generally speak Chinese and are more culturally similar to the Han than, say, the Turkish-speaking Muslims, this term is inappropriate and misleading since, by law, all Muslims in China are citizens of the Chinese state, and thus Chinese. The Hui, in this respect, are no more Chinese than the Uigur or Kazak.[63] However, through over 1,200 years of intimate contact with the so-called Han majority and other peoples they have lived among, the nature of the Hui as a people is, at the very least, exceedingly complex and, at most, questionable.

The appropriateness of many of these ethnonyms and categories is heavily contested in China. The question of whether the Hui are indeed a nationality (*minzu*) was the basis of several Communist Party documents dating from the 1940s, published for the first time publicly in 1980 as *Huihui minzu wenti* (The question of the Hui hui nationality). One may debate the appropriateness of the application of such ethnic labels *Hui* and *Uigur*.[64] What is not disputed, however, is the right of the Chinese state to legalize these labels and employ them in collecting national census materials. The continued use of these labels, their creation, institutionalization, and quantification have spurred a process of "objectification" that has engendered a resurgence of nationalism in China along certain contours of power relations—often defined by the state.[65] Problematizing what it means to be a member of an official ethnic group, the so-called Hui *minzu*, in the Chinese state is one of the main purposes of this book.

THE PROBLEM: WHO ARE THE HUI?

The wide diversity within Hui communities and the various ways different Hui have sought to resolve the tension of maintaining a "pure and true" lifestyle in Chinese society have often obfuscated their identity. At one extreme are those who portray the Hui as "Muslims in China"—communities defined solely in terms of their religion. This position has led one scholar to assert that "Islam in China is, by definition, potentially rebellious and secessionist, and Chinese Islam is, perhaps, a contradiction in terms."[66] The Hui are often portrayed as members of a homogeneous Muslim community in a hostile Chinese world, like Muslims everywhere who reside outside the Muslim world (*Dar-al-Islam*) in non-Muslim states (*Dar-al-Harb*, literally, "territory of war").[67] In this case the Hui are depicted as Muslims in China totally distinct from the Han majority, and likely to either rebel against the non-Muslim state or, failing in that endeavor, to totally assimilate. Assimilation or secession are the only options available to Muslims in China, according to this view.

The idea that the Muslims in China were an isolated religious enclave, stigmatized by the broader Chinese population to the extent that they were pushed to either rebellion or assimilation, led Protestant missionaries in China to regard them as a potential pool of willing converts to Christianity. Missionary organizations, such as the China Inland Mission, were already heavily engaged in medical, educational, and evangelical mission projects in the northwest where Muslims were prominent. Several missionaries working in these areas argued that, given the Muslims' marginalized existence in Chinese society, their monotheism, their poverty, and their respect for the shared-Semitic traditions of Christianity and Judaism, even recognizing Jesus (Yisa) as one of their own prophets, these Muslims would be more open to the Protestant evangelical message. Converts among Muslims in China would also help improve the record in China and the Muslim Middle East, where, after years of preaching, Protestant missions had met with little evangelical success. As a result, Marshall Broomhall was specifically commissioned at the World Missionary Congress in Edinburgh to carry out missions and research among the Muslims in China, resulting in his impressive volume, *Islam in China: A Neglected Problem*, published in 1910. In 1917, after the first of two trips to China, Samuel M. Zwemer, the Islamic scholar and Protestant missionary who had spent a lifetime of mission work among Muslims in the Middle East, declared: "The Chinese Moslems are more accessible to Christian work and workers than their co-religionists in any other land." This encouraged a host of missionary scholars, including G. Findlay Andrew, Mark Botham, Marshall Broomhall, M. G. Griebenow, Carter Holton, Isaac Mason, Claude L. Pickens, Jr. (who was Zwemer's son-in-law), F. W. Martin

Taylor, W. A. Saunders, and Leonard A. Street, to dedicate their lives to work among Muslims in China. Though the missionaries overestimated the willingness of Muslims in China to convert to Christianity, and underestimated the strength of their commitment to Islam, their research and photographic collections provide a vast treasure-trove of material on late-nineteenth-century and early-twentieth-century Islam in China.

The notion that the Hui are "Muslims in China," living isolated existences on the far periphery of the Muslim world, may have also contributed to the general lack of interest in studying them by historians and Islamic specialists in the past. The only exceptions were the missionaries, mentioned above, and the occasional intrepid explorer and traveler, like Owen Lattimore, Sven Hedin, or Frederick Wulsin, who passed through the northwest and took an interest in these unique Muslim peoples. Assumed to be small and insignificant, or perhaps already assimilated, the Muslims in China held little interest for those Islamic historians who saw Muslims as defined by the standards of the Middle East. This Arab-centered view of the Muslim world has led to what Lila Abu-Lughod termed "zones of theory" in the study of Islam that have directed inquiry away from the so-called "periphery" to what has been accepted as the "center" or "core" of Islam.[68] In their recent discussion of pilgrimage and travel in Islam, Eickelman and Piscatori challenge this notion, arguing that studies of the Muslim world should begin to consider "multiple centers" of Islam, instead of the essentializing core-periphery dichotomy.[69] Just as this study may help broaden our understanding of Chinese society through the examination of one of its integral peoples, deconstructing assumptions about a monolithic Chinese culture, so it may contribute to a fuller understanding of what it means to be a Muslim in a context radically different from the "Islamic world."

Those who portray the Hui as entirely distinct from the Han and other peoples among whom they live frequently point to unique, often foreign, physical features that characterize many of them. In the northwest, where Hui are more concentrated and perhaps continue to preserve more of their Central Asian heritage, physical differences distinguishing them from the Han often strike the casual observer. Hazel-green eyes, long beards, high-bridged noses, and light, even red, hair are not unusual among the Hui. Frederick R. Wulsin, who traveled throughout Chinese Inner Asia on the celebrated 1923 National Geographic expedition, observed:

> The individual Moslems that one meets show much physical diversity. Some cannot be distinguished from ordinary Chinese except by the way they cut their moustaches. Others are quite distinct from the Chinese in appearance. Near Ningsia and Lanchou one sees many tall Moslems, standing from 5 ft. 7 in. to 5 ft. 11 in. They are spare, long limbed and active. The forehead is high, the face long, and the nose well developed and aquiline, the eye horizontal and large. I cannot say whether the Mongol eye fold is always present. The beard is abundant, though never as great as in the European. Men like this are spoken of as the Arab Hui Hui.[70]

Even in eastern urban areas like Beijing and Shanghai, one is often surprised to meet Hui who look decidedly unlike the majority of the Han they live among. Hui in Beijing have complained to me that, as children, they were often taunted by their playmates, called "little Hui hui," "big nose," "foreigner," and other such derogatory epithets. There are, however, many Hui who take great pride in their different looks. Upon one's first arrival in a Hui village or home, the locals frequently bring out the individual with the largest nose, longest beard, fullest eyebrows, most extended earlobes, and say: "Look at this guy, he's a real Hui!" Hui often cultivate their beards, regarding it as a duty of Islam to let them grow as long as possible and keep them meticulously clean. In North China, where heavier bearded men are common, I was pulled aside once by a Hui friend who pointed out a Han merchant who also sported a black cap and long beard, like many Hui in the marketplace. When I asked how he knew he was a Han, he answered: "Of course he's a Han, you can tell by his dirty cap, his long messy beard (*luan huzi*), and, besides, he's smoking a cigarette in public!"

At the other extreme are those who regard the Hui as virtually indistinguishable from the larger population, referring to them as "Chinese Muslims." In this case, the Hui are said to have essentially assimilated to the Han, the majority ethnic group in China, differing from them only in certain religious beliefs and archaic customs, as a Buddhist might differ from a Daoist.[71] This position is appealing at first glance because Hui often appear culturally and linguistically similar to the Han among whom they live. To many observers, the Hui do not stand out from the broader Han majority, and this physical and linguistic invisibility has led to a questioning of the existence of a Hui ethnic identity. Isaac Mason wrote in 1929 that he "found little in the facial or physical appearance of Moslems [he had] known to distinguish them from their neighbors of other faiths."[72] Owen Lattimore, who traveled for many years in Northwest China and became very interested in Muslim life, found that this ethnic ambiguity of the Hui often made them suspect:

> In times of political crisis, Moslem Chinese in Sinkiang are invariably caught on one or the other horn of a dilemma. If they stand with their fellow Moslems, sooner or later an attempt is made to reduce them to a secondary position and to treat them as "untrustworthy" because, in spite of their Moslem religion, they are after all, Chinese. If they stand with their fellow Chinese, there is a similar tendency to suspect them of subversion and disloyalty, because, it is feared, their religion may prove politically more compelling than their patriotism.[73]

Many writers continue to suggest that the Hui differ from the Han only in religion. As recently as March 1987, a reporter could find little difference between Han and Hui: "Frequently indistinguishable in features and dress from Han Chinese. . . . It is often only their rejection of pork, the common surname Ma (Mohammed), and Arabic inscriptions in mosques built like Buddhist temples, that serve to distinguish them from their Han Chinese neighbors."[74] Judith Banister writes that the Hui are "distinct from the Han only in their religion."[75] The following description of the Hui was found in *Aramco World Magazine*'s impressive pictorial on Muslims in China:

> The largest of China's Muslim minorities, the Hui, is racially Chinese rather than Turkic; and though classified by the government as a "national minority," is not really a "nationality." Generally indistinguishable from the Han Chinese in physical appearance, similar in social and familiar form and speaking only Chinese, the Hui are classified as a "nationality" largely on religious grounds.[76]

In areas where Hui are less openly religious, the pork tabu becomes the most distinguishing marker of identity. "Hui are just Han who do not eat pork," I was told by a cadre in Tianjin. This was echoed by sim-

ilar comments from Han throughout China. Barbara Pillsbury claims
that, for the Hui, pork abstention has become the "essential distinguishing characteristic, the *sine qua non,* of a Muslim [in China]."[77] Interestingly, despite the difficulty of adherence to Islamic dietary restrictions
in a country where Chairman Mao once regarded pork as a "national
treasure" and sought to induce Hui to raise and consume pigs (see Chapter 3), Hui have never invoked the accepted Islamic practice of *taqiya,*
or "dissimulation,"[78] where the requirements of Islam may be ignored
in life-threatening situations, as is often practiced by Shi'ite Muslims.[79]
Most Hui agree that one of the central notions of their understanding
of *qing zhen* and Islamic purity is the abstention from pork. I was surprised when several informants even included the pork tabu as one of
the 5 central tenets of Islam. Yet, as we shall discover in the following
chapters, while the pork issue is highly salient for many Hui, there are
large populations of Hui recognized by the state who no longer practice
Islam nor maintain Islamic dietary restrictions. In addition, pork abstention is becoming less critical to younger-generation Hui workers and
intellectuals who live in Han-dominated urban centers. Nevertheless, all
these people continue to regard themselves as Hui, and, most important, the state labels them as such.

If the Hui are so similar to the Han, is it merely religion that separ-
ates them, or do they really constitute a separate ethnic group? Traditional ethnicity models have not been very helpful in providing an
answer to this question. The wide ethnographic and religious variety
found among the Hui who, despite this diversity, continue to regard
themselves as one group, and are recognized by the state as a minority
nationality, wreaks havoc on most of these theories. I shall first introduce the sociocultural and religious diversity found among the Hui and
then discuss various attempts at explaining Hui identity before proposing a new approach that I think provides a more comprehensive interpretation of the diversity and unity of Hui ethnoreligious identity.

SOCIOCULTURAL DIVERSITY AMONG THE HUI

According to the official nationality census and literature in China, the
Hui people are the third most populous of China's 55 recognized minor-

ity nationalities, who altogether constitute 8.04 percent of the total population. The sociocultural uniqueness of the Hui can be readily seen by briefly examining their wide distribution, dispersed population, manifold administrative units, occupational diversity, linguistic variety, and cultural complexity.

WIDE DISTRIBUTION. The Hui are the most widespread minority, inhabiting every region, province, city, and over 97 percent of the nation's counties. Incredibly, the 1982 census revealed that there are Hui living in 2,308 of 2,372 counties and cities across China.[80] This substantiates the popular Hui conception that they are "spread widely and concentrated narrowly" (*da fen can, xiao ji zhong*). It is noteworthy that, while the Hui may represent a small fragment of the population in most areas (with the exception of Ningxia), they often make up the vast majority of the minority population in Han-dominated areas (see Table 2). In Anhui, only 0.5 percent of the provincial population are Hui, but they represent over 97 percent of all the minorities. This is also true for most of China's cities where the Hui are the main urban ethnic group (see Beijing, Shanghai, and Tianjin).

In border areas, where most of China's minorities are concentrated, the Hui are also numerous, but they represent only a small proportion of the minorities. For example, in Yunnan, the southwest province bordering Burma and Vietnam, the Hui are the 8th largest minority group (behind the Yi, Bai, Hani, Zhuang, Dai, Miao, and Lisu); they represent only 4.2 percent of the minority population, and 1.3 percent of the entire provincial population. It is conventionally thought that China's Muslim minorities are concentrated in the northwest corner, near Soviet Central Asia. The Hui minority, however, are mainly spread throughout China's Inner Asia.[81] This region is at the juncture of four distinct cultures—the Central Asian, Tibetan, Mongolian, and Chinese (Han)—and encompasses a vast area including Xinjiang, Ningxia, Gansu, and Qinghai, which has been justifiably referred to as China's "Quran belt."[82]

DISPERSED POPULATION. With a population of at least 8.6 million according to the 1990 census, the Hui are the most numerous of the 10 nation-

TABLE 2 Distribution of the Hui Minority
         (%)

Municipality Region or Province	Population	% of Total Population	% of Hui in China	% of Minorities in Area
Ningxia	1,235,207	31.6	17.1	99.3
Gansu	950,974	4.8	13.2	61.4
Henan	727,146	0.9	10.0	91.3
Xinjiang	570,788	4.3	7.9	7.3
Qinghai	533,750	13.7	7.4	34.7
Yunnan	438,883	1.3	6.1	4.2
Hebei	418,853	0.8	5.8	49.2
Shandong	389,506	0.5	5.4	95.5
Anhui	254,602	0.5	3.5	97.3
Liaoning	239,200	0.7	3.3	8.2
Beijing	184,693	2.0	2.5	57.3
In. Mongolia	169,096	0.9	2.3	5.6
Tianjin	142,847	1.8	1.9	87.2
Heilongjiang	126,427	0.3	1.7	7.8
Shaanxi	118,389	0.4	1.6	89.0
Jilin	110,673	0.4	1.5	6.0
Jiangsu	103,822	0.1	1.4	94.1
Guizhou	100,058	0.3	1.3	1.3
Hubei	70,516	0.1	0.9	3.9
Hunan	67,205	0.1	0.9	3.0
Shanxi	51,585	0.2	0.7	81.1
Shanghai	44,123	0.3	0.6	89.0
Fujian	31,060	0.1	0.4	12.4
Guangxi	19,279	0.1	0.3	0.1
Guangdong	10,849	0.0	0.2	1.0
Sichuan	10,000	0.0	0.1	0.3
Zhejiang	9,435	0.0	0.1	5.9
Jiangxi	7,926	0.0	0.1	35.9
Tibet	1,788	0.1	0.0	0.1
Total:	7,138,680	1.4.	98.3	10.7

Source: 1982 Census (*Minzu tuanjie* 1984).

alities recognized by the state as adhering to Islam as their nationality religion. According to the *1990 Census*, the total population of the 10 Muslim nationalities in China is 17.5 million (see Table 1). This represents about 1.98 percent of the total population.[83] However, the census registered people by ethnic group, not by religion, so the actual number of Muslims is still unknown, and local figures I have collected range widely from the census reports.

The figure for the Hui was increased to 8.6 million in 1990 from 7.2 million in 1982, an increase of 19 percent. *The Population Atlas of China*[84] gives 13 excellent maps and diagrams documenting the distribution and economic diversity of China's minority nationalities. County-level population figures are not published, and we shall not be able to arrive at an accurate assessment of the full extent of Hui distribution until these are fully analyzed.[85] While totals for Muslim population have been obstructed by the lack of a category in the 1982 census for religion, a minimum of 15 million and a maximum of 20 million seem the most reasonable estimates. More wide-ranging population figures of as many as 40 million Muslims among the Hui alone in China[86] appear to be influenced by political concerns similar to those that, in the earlier part of this century, led people purposively to inflate Muslim population in China.[87]

MANIFOLD ADMINISTRATION. As the most widespread and third most numerous of China's minority nationalities, the Hui have more autonomous administrative units assigned to them than any other minority, including 1 autonomous region, 2 autonomous prefectures, and 9 autonomous counties, as well as numerous autonomous townships that have only recently been established (see Table 3 and Map 1).

While the Hui have their own Ningxia autonomous region, they constitute only one-third of its population, the Han being in the vast majority. Only one-sixth of the total Hui population is concentrated in their only autonomous region. By contrast, 99.8 percent of the Uigur population live in Xinjiang Uigur autonomous region, and the vast majority of Tibetan, Zhuang, and Mongolian populations are concentrated in their autonomous regions. Surprisingly, after Ningxia and Gansu, the 3rd largest population of Hui is found in Henan province

TABLE 3 Hui Autonomous Administrative Units

Province or Region	Autonomous Administrative Unit	Founded
Ningxia	Ningxia Hui autonomous region	1958
Gansu	Linxia autonomous prefecture	1956
	Zhangjiachuan autonomous county	1953
Xinjiang	Changji autonomous prefecture	1954
	Yanqi autonomous county	1954
Hebei	Dachang autonomous county	1955
	Mengcun autonomous county	1955
Qinghai	Hualong autonomous county	1954
	Menyuan autonomous county	1953
Guizhou	Weining Yi, Hui and Miao autonomous counties	1954
Yunnan	Weishan Yi and Hui autonomous county	1956
	Xundian Hui and Yi autonomous county	1979

Source: *Zhongguo shaoshu minzu*, pp. 587–593.

in Central China. Their 6th largest concentration is in Yunnan (see Table 2).

OCCUPATIONAL SPECIALIZATION. In addition to the wide distribution of the Hui across China, there is also extensive economic and occupational diversity among them, from cadres to clergy, rice farmers to factory workers, schoolteachers to camel drivers, and poets to generals. Hui have occupied a large variety of economic niches throughout the history of China. Most of these were related to their Islamic restrictions in diet and hygiene, leading them to take up such occupations as restauranteur, innkeeper, shepherd, cavalryman, caravaneer, butcher, tanner, tea trader, jeweler, interpreter, and clergyman. In the north, the majority of Hui are wheat and dry-rice agriculturalists, while, in the south, they are primarily engaged in wet-rice cultivation and aquaculture. In urban centers, the majority are employed in common labor and industry. Since the collectivization campaigns of the 1950s, most Hui have been prevented from engaging in the small private businesses that were their traditional specializations. Nevertheless, Table 4 reveals that the Hui con-

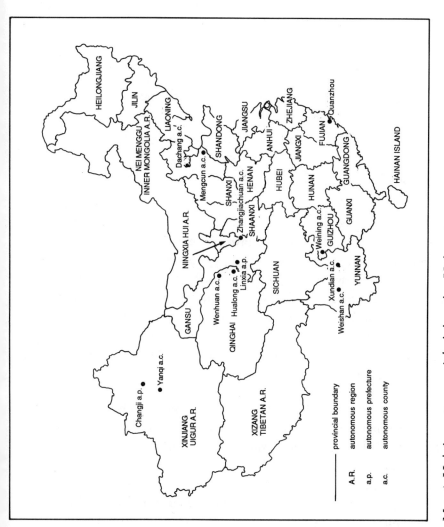

MAP 1 Hui Autonomous Administrative Units

provincial boundary

A.R.   autonomous region
a.p.   autonomous prefecture
a.c.   autonomous county

HEILONGJIANG

JILIN

LIAONING

NEI MENGGU
INNER MONGOLIA A.R.

Dachang a.c.

SHANDONG

JIANGSU

ZHEJIANG

Mengcun a.c.

SHANXI

NINGXIA HUI A.R.

Zhangjiachuan a.c.

HENAN

ANHUI

FUJIAN

Quanzhou

SHAANXI

HUBEI

JIANGXI

GUANGDONG

GANSU

Wenhuan a.c.

Hualong a.c.

Linxia a.p.

QINGHAI

SICHUAN

HUNAN

Weining a.c.

GUIZHOU

GUANXI

HAINAN ISLAND

Xundian a.c.

Weishan a.c.

YUNNAN

Yanqi a.c.

Changji a.p.

XINJIANG
UIGUR A.R.

XIZANG
TIBETAN A.R.

TABLE 4 Occupational Structure of Muslim Minorities in China, 1982 (%)

Occupation	Hui	Uigur	Kazak	Dong-xiang	Kirghiz	Salar	Tajik	Uzbek	Bao-an	Tatar	All Ethnic Groups
Skilled technical staff	5.7	4.2	11.2	1.0	7.0	3.2	5.7	17.2	1.5	23.5	4.0
Administration	1.7	0.7	2.0	0.2	1.5	0.7	2.7	3.7	2.2	4.5	1.0
Office & related workers	1.7	1.0	2.0	0.2	1.7	0.7	2.0	3.2	0.7	4.2	1.0
Commercial workers	3.5	1.5	1.2	0.2	0.7	0.7	0.5	10.7	0.5	5.2	1.2
Service workers	4.0	1.5	1.5	0.2	1.0	0.7	0.7	6.5	0.5	4.5	1.2
Farming, forestry, fishing & animal husbandry	60.7	84.0	74.5	96.7	84.0	90.5	85.7	31.5	92.2	38.5	84.0
Factory, production & transport workers	22.2	7.0	7.5	1.2	4.0	3.2	2.5	27.0	2.2	19.2	7.5
Others	0.2	–	–	–	–	–	–	–	–	.2	–

Source: Adapted from the Population Census Office 1987, pp. xx, 28.

tinue to be occupied in trade and commerce. In contrast to the Uigur, 84 percent of whom are primarily involved in agriculture and husbandry, only 60.7 percent of the total Hui population are engaged in such occupations. It is significant that the census reveals that 29 percent of the Hui are in occupations of service, commerce, production, and transport, more than any other ethnic group in China, including the Han. However, these figures do not begin to take into account the many private and part-time small businesses now dominating the local village business economies in which the Hui play an active part.

LINGUISTIC VARIETY. The Hui are distinguished from the other 9 Muslim nationalities in China by not having a language of their own; they speak the dialects of the other ethnic groups with whom they live, mainly the Han. Thus, in the past, they have been somewhat inaccurately labeled as the "Chinese-speaking Muslims."[88] Among those recognized by the state as Hui, however, there is extremely wide linguistic variety. These include Hui in non-Han majority areas who have adopted the language, dress, and customs of their minority neighbors, such as the "Tibetan Hui" (Zang Hui) in Lhasa; the "Mongolian Hui" (Meng Hui) of Alashan district, Inner Mongolia; the "Dai Hui" in Xishuangbana and the "Bai Hui" in Eryuan county, both in Yunnan.[89] When I spoke in Alma Ata with the Dungan of Soviet Central Asia, who call themselves Hui Min,[90] we spoke in a hybrid Gansu dialect that combined Turkish and Russian lexical items, which had been written in Cyrillic for over 30 years.[91] These Muslims are culturally indistinguishable from the minority group with whom they live, but they identify themselves as Hui and are recognized by the state as members of the Hui nationality.

In one Bai (Minjia) nationality village north of Erhu Lake in Dali prefecture, I interviewed 5 Hui women who were training to become imams. They wore traditional Bai dress and spoke only the Tibeto-Burman Bai language, yet they were studying Arabic and Islamic doctrine under a female imam from their village. Bilingual in Bai and Mandarin, this woman had studied for 5 years in a Hui mosque in southern Yunnan.[92] It is significant that, in order to receive further Islamic training beyond her village, she had to go to a predominantly Hui area where there were no Bai people. Most of these Hui say that they fled to the Bai concentrated area north of Dali city after the failed Panthay Muslim uprising (1855–1873) led by the Hui hero, Du Wenxiu.[93] They say that they gradually assimilated to Bai culture in the last 100 years. One village elder, however, described an origin myth where the Hui in that village descended from the "Black Cloth" early Turkish-speaking Muslims who settled there under the Tang or perhaps Yuan dynasties.[94]

The so-called "Tibetan Hui" are a community of about 6,000 Muslims living in Lhasa, who speak Tibetan, wear Tibetan clothes, and worship in a mosque decorated with Tibetan floral designs and carpets. Theirs is one of two mosques left in the city since the Chinese occupation and suppression of the Tibetan uprising in 1959. At that time, another community of "Kashmiri" Muslims, who came from the northern Pakistani/India border region of Kashmir, fled en masse with the Dalai Lama. I was told that there was only one household of "Kashmiri Hui" left in Lhasa. Xue Wenbo, the late Hui intellectual, who conducted 2 years' research among the Hui in Tibet after he was sent there with the People's Liberation Army in 1951, argued that "the majority of them are Sichuanese, a minority are Western Shaanxi Hui, and a few are from Gansu, Qinghai, and Yunnan."[95] He suggests that most fled to Tibet after the failed nineteenth-century rebellions. During several interviews in February 1985, I was impressed at how distinct they regarded themselves to be from the other Hui traders in Lhasa. At any one time, there are from 20,000 to 30,000 Hui merchants from Ningxia, Gansu, and Qinghai working primarily in Lhasa as well as the other major trade centers throughout Tibet.[96] The local "Tibetan Hui" did not interact with these traders, whom they regarded with suspicion, and preferred to marry their children to other Tibetans instead of to their co-religionists from outside Tibet.

In Yunnan, I attended the ordination service at the well-known Wukeng Mosque in the Weishan Yi and Hui autonomous county of an acolyte who called himself a Hui from Hainan Island. He had traveled almost a 1,000 kilometers from Hainan to study under a famous Hui *hajji* in southwestern Yunnan on the Burmese border. At the time, his brother was studying at the national *madrassah* in Beijing, sponsored by the China Islamic Association. When I visited one of two Muslim villages along the southern coast of Hainan Island in January 1984, the local imam said in Mandarin that his people were Hui. However, in their own Malayo-Austronesian language, Pang Keng-fong has found that they call themselves *Utsat*, which simply means Muslim.[97] It is significant that, while speaking Mandarin, the national language, these people call themselves Hui, and they send their sons to far-away Hui religious centers in Yunnan and Beijing to obtain the necessary training in order to become imams.

Three other identified Muslim groups, the Dongxiang, Baoan, and Salar, located primarily on the Gansu-Qinghai Tibetan plateau, did not derive their ethnonyms from the Soviet Central Asian model but were decided upon by the Chinese state. Each of these groups speaks a combination of Turkic, Mongolian, and Han Chinese dialects; thus, they are defined mainly by locality; for example, the Dongxiang (East Township) derive their name from the eastern prefecture of old Hezhou (Linxia) where they were concentrated. The question remains, however, why these groups received their separate identifications, when other groups such as the Mongolian, Tibetan, Bai, and Hainan Muslims

Young Hui acolytes studying the Quran in Arabic with Persian commentary in a Hui village outside of Xining, Qinghai. Photo: Gladney

Young Muslims with Arabic text inscribed on camel bones that Pickens termed "horn books." These were still used in the 1930s before Qurans were more readily available. Photo: Pickens.
Courtesy of Harvard-Yenching Library.

described above, are all identified as Hui and did not receive separate identities, despite their divergent localities and languages. Their populations are not insignificant enough to warrant refusal as a distinct nationality. The Baoan numbered 9,027 in 1982 and the Tatar 4,127; Chinese minority publications proudly proclaim the recognition of such insignificant groups as the Hezhe, despite their possessing a population of only 300 at the time of the Revolution, and 450 at the time of their identification in 1953, and a 1982 population of 1,476.[98]

All these seemingly multi-ethnic peoples—the Bai, Tibetan, and Hainanese Muslims—are registered as Hui by the State Commission for Nationality Affairs and are considered members of the Hui nationality. Just as the Muslim Cantonese, Shanghainese, Fujianese and other non-Mandarin speakers are registered as Hui, so these groups do not have their own ethnonym, or legal separate ethnic status. Unlike the Dongxiang and Baonan peoples in Gansu, these Hui peoples are counted by the state simply as Hui. Interestingly enough, after living for 30 years under this policy, despite their linguistic diversity and multi-cultural background, they themselves claim membership in the same Hui ethnic group as other Hui in China and often quoted to me the popular phrase: "All Hui under Heaven are one family" (*Tianxia Hui hui shi yi jia*).

THREE TIDES OF ISLAM IN CHINA

In addition to geographic, economic, cultural, and linguistic differences, the Hui also subscribe to a wide spectrum of Islamic beliefs. The variety of religious orders represents a long history of reforms and Islamic movements, resulting from interaction with the Islamic world. The late Joseph Fletcher, who dedicated the last years of his life to the study of the connections of Islam in China to Central Asia and the Middle East, was the first to suggest that the nature of China's present-day Islamic communities and orders can be traced to successive "tides" of influence and individuals who entered China during critical periods of exchange with the outside world.[99] Like a swelling and ebbing tide, the influence of these movements grew or diminished with the interaction of China's Muslims and the Islamic world. This influence was not based on population movements as much as on a gradual and profound exchange between the two regions. While this study does not begin to address Islam's complex history in China, an introduction to the various Islamic movements in China will help illustrate the wide Islamic diversity within China's Hui Muslims.

THE FIRST TIDE: GEDIMU TRADITIONAL CHINESE ISLAM. The earliest Muslim communities were descended from the Arab, Persian, Central Asian, and Mongolian Muslim merchants, militia, and officials who settled along China's southeast coast and in the northwest in large and small numbers from the seventh to the fourteenth centuries. Generally residing in independent small communities clustered around a central mosque (*danyi jiaofangzhi*), they became known as the Gedimu (from the Arabic *qadîm* for "old"). They followed the traditional Sunni, Hanafi Islam.[100] With the exception of the 33,000 Tadjik nomads of the Pamir Mountains in southwestern Xinjiang, the vast majority of Muslims in China are Sunni. Few Hui I spoke with in the northwest knew the difference between Shi'i and Sunni, even though the Iran/Iraq War was at its height during my fieldwork and in the daily news.[101]

These "old" Islamic communities established an early Hui pattern of zealously preserving and protecting their identity as enclaves ensconced in the dominant Han society. Each village was centered upon a single mosque headed by an ahong (from the Persian, *akhun[d]*) who was invited to teach on a more or less temporary basis. These ahong generally moved on an average of every three years from one mosque to another. A council of senior local elders and ahong were responsible for the affairs of each village and the inviting of the itinerant imam. Late nineteenth-century and early twentieth-century travelers noted the maintenance of these isolated communities. "I know of no strictly farming village where there is an equal mixture of the two groups [Han and Hui]"; Ekvall observed, "in every case the village is predominantly one or the other. In some instances, the population is composed almost entirely of one group, with only a few hangers-on of the other."[102] He went on to suggest that, due to different cultural, ritual, and dietary preferences that sometimes led to open conflict, the communities preferred physical separation. Another frequent northwest traveler noted:

> In some districts throughout the province [Gansu] the Moslems are found in
> such numbers as to outnumber the Chinese in the proportion of seven to one.
> Again, in other districts it is possible to travel for days without coming across
> one Moslem family, and in such districts it would be next to impossible for
> a Moslem family to settle. . . . To find Chinese and Moslems living harmon-
> iously intermingled is but on the rarest occasion.[103]

This isolation was mitigated somewhat during the collectivization campaigns in the 1950s, when Han and Hui villages were often administered
as clusters by a single commune. They have also been brought closer
together through national telecommunications and transportation networks established by the state, including such umbrella organizations as
the China Islamic Organization, established in 1955, which seeks to
coordinate religious affairs among all Muslim groups. With the recent
dismantling of the commune in many areas, however, these homogeneous Hui communities are once again becoming more segregated (see
Chapter 3).

Urban mosque-centered communities prior to 1949 tended to be relegated to ghetto-like concentrations of Hui inside or outside the city
walls. During the Socialist Transformation of Industry Campaign in the
1950s, however, this spatial concentration was largely disrupted.[104]
Some cities, like Beijing, Xi'an, Lanzhou, and Jiaxing, continue to preserve more discrete Hui neighborhoods, while in others, such as Shanghai and Guangzhou, previously concentrated Hui areas have been
dispersed through a policy of assigning housing according to work unit
(see Chapter 4). This decentralization has led, I argue, to a displacement
of the mosque by other more secular institutions as the principal locus
of Hui social organization and leadership.

The isolation of these individual Gedimu communities and their
thin dispersion throughout China reveals the importance of trade and
migration history among the Hui. Although the early origins of the
Hui can be traced to the descendants of migrants from the southeast
along the Spice Route, and from the northwest along the Silk Road, it
is interesting that the major concentrations of the Hui are no longer in
those border areas. After Gansu and Ningxia, Henan province contains
the third largest concentration of Hui. Hui villages can be found
throughout China, especially evident along the main transport nodes of

the Yellow River in the north, and the Burma Road in the south, revealing the traditional Hui proclivity for exploiting trade opportunities.
Iwamura Shinobu's perceptive analysis of the Inner Mongolian Hui
communities in Huhehot and Baotou revealed that the vast majority of
them were populated with Hui native to central and northern China,
not Mongolia, who left poorer areas to engage in business and seek
opportunities in the new frontier.[105] James Millward has persuasively
documented that almost all interior wool collection and transshipment
agencies in the northwest were increasingly taken over by Hui after the
problems of taxation, banditry, and warlord politics led the previously
foreign-owned companies to return to the safer enclaves of Tianjin.[106] It
is not surprising, therefore, that the major wool-trade towns and cities
during the heyday of wool trade in the early Republican period continued to be populated with many Hui communities. The recent paving of
the Qing-Zang highway linking Golmud, Qinghai, with Lhasa, Tibet,
has facilitated travel for numerous Hui businessmen from Gansu, Qinghai, and Ningxia interested in potential trade with local Tibetans who
have access to foreign products from India through Nepal. There is at
least one Hui restaurant and family in every major bus stop along the
1,155-km. Qing-Zang road.[107] While traveling from Moscow to Beijing
through the Ili Valley in 1988, I met several Hui businessmen in Alma
Ata who were taking advantage of the Sino-Soviet rapprochement to
reestablish contact with their Dungan Hui relatives and resume long-
broken small-trade relations.

In addition to seeking trade opportunities, many Hui migrations
resulted from the displacement caused by calamity and impoverish-
ment. Most of the Hui I interviewed in Shanghai migrated there from
Henan and Anhui during the Republican period to escape floods and
famine and to engage in business. Jingyuan county in southern Ningxia
is 97 percent Hui, with the vast majority of the population having fled
or been forcibly relocated there after the Shaanxi Hui Rebellion
(1862–1877). In this mountainous area near the Liu Pan range, one can
still find the remains of Qing forts built on the tops of hills, established
to keep watch on the Hui refugees below. While these disparate communities among the Gedimu were generally linked only by trade and a
sense of a common religious heritage, it was the Sufi brotherhoods that

Hui merchant on road to Tibetan Kumbum Lamasery, Qinghai. Note Buddhas, prayer beads, and Muslim handmade knives for sale, in addition to Nang, the Hui flatbread. Photo: Gladney

Hui Muslim poster on wall of home in Na Homestead, Ningxia. The Arabic *Shahada* and *Bismallah* are pictured vertically, with the Ka'ba of Mecca featured in the center. Photo: Gladney

eventually tied many of them together through extensive socioreligious networks.

THE SECOND TIDE: SUFI COMMUNITIES AND NATIONAL NETWORKS. Sufism did not begin to make a substantial impact in China until the late seventeenth century, during the "second tide" of Islam's entrance into China.[108] Like Sufi centers that proliferated after the thirteenth century in other countries,[109] many of these Sufi movements in China developed socioeconomic and religiopolitical institutions built around the schools established by descendants of early Sufi saintly leaders. The institutions became known in Chinese as the *menhuan*, the "leading" or "saintly" descent groups.[110]

The important contribution that Sufism made to religious organization in China was that the leaders of mosques throughout their order owed their allegiance to their *shaykh*, the founder of the order who appointed them. These designated followers were loyal to the leader of their order and remained in the community for long periods of time, unlike the Gedimu ahong who were generally itinerant, not well connected to the community, and less imbued with appointed authority. Gedimu mosque elders were loyal to their village first, and connected only by trade to other communities. While it is beyond this paper to delineate the history and distribution of these Sufi *menhuan*, the late Joseph Fletcher's cogent introductory discussion of their development is worth citing:

> Over the course of the eighteenth, nineteenth, and early twentieth centuries a considerable number of these "saintly lineages" came into being in northwest China, most of them within the Naqšbandi "path." Typically, each saint's tomb had a shrine, or *qubba* (Chinese *gongbai* or *gongbei*), and the main shrines became centers of devotional activity. The "saintly lineages" obtained contributions from their followers and amassed substantial amounts of property. The growth in the number and importance of the *menhuan* represented an important change, because they gradually replaced the "old" (*gedimu*) pattern by linking together the *menhuan* adherents all over the northwest. The widening compass of social integration that resulted made it easier for the "saintly lineages" and other leaders to harness the Muslims' political and economic potential, facilitating the rise of Muslim warlordism in that region in the twentieth century.[111]

Hui Sufis of the Naqshbandia Jahriyya order chant their traditional Mathanawi text in a small *dao tang* (ritual center) in Tongxin, Ningxia. Note picture of Medina with traditional Hui Chinese-Arabic art work on wall. Chinese vertical texts read: "Believe in Allah (Zhu) and transform your self" and "Believe in the Prophet (Shengren), awaken the people of the world." At center is the Arabic *Bismallah.* Photo: Gladney.

Many Sufi reforms spread throughout Northwest China during the early decades of the Qing dynasty (mid-seventeenth to the early eighteenth centuries). Increased travel and communication between Muslims, both east and west, during what Fletcher terms the "general orthodox revival" of the eighteenth century, had great influence on Muslims from West Africa to Indonesia and, not least of all, on China's Hui Muslims.[112] Exposure to these new ideas led to a reformulation of traditional Islamic concepts that rendered them more meaningful and practical for the Hui Muslims of that time. Sufi orders were gradually institutionalized into such forms as the *menhuan.*[113] Only 4 orders maintain significant influence among the Hui today, what Claude Pickens as a Protestant missionary in northwest China first discovered as the 4 *menhuan* of China:[114] the Qadiriyya, Khufiyya, Jahriyya, and Kubrawiyya.[115] While these are the 4 main *menhuan,* they are subdivided into a myriad smaller *menhuan* and branches along ideological, political, geographical, and historical lines (see Appendix A). If a detailed history of these divisions and alliances could ever be written, it would reveal the tensions and new meanings created by Hui communities attempting to reconcile perceived disparities between Islamic ideals and changing social realities.[116]

It is unfortunate but perhaps quite natural that Western scholarship has prolonged the confusion of early Chinese writers over the rise of Sufism and later Islamic orders in China. As each Islamic reformer established a new following in China, often in conflict with other older Islamic orders, these "new" arrivals replaced or converted the "old" traditional Islamic communities. Chinese officials during the Ming and the Qing naturally referred to these communities with their new teachings as *xin jiao* (literally, "new religion" or "new teaching," not "new sect" as it has been erroneously translated). As each new arrival replaced the older, they became known as the "new," or even "new new" teachings (*xin xin jiao*), as in the case of the arrival of the Ikhwan in China. Traditional Islam among the Hui generally was referred to as *lao jiao*, the old teaching(s), and even some orders that were new at one time, when others arrived were gradually classed as old, *lao jiao*, which is the case with the Khufiyya, an early Naqshbandiyya Sufi order (see below). These designations became important in that, during the mid-nineteenth northwest rebellions, some led by Sufi leaders, the Chinese state proscribed all of these "new teachings" in order to root out the more rebellious Hui communities.[117] This is precisely the rationale whereby all Buddhist sectarian movements were proscribed under the general rubric of the "White Lotus" Rebellion in China.[118] Unfortunately, Chinese and Western scholars perpetuated these designations and, until recently, there were no accurate descriptions of Hui Islamic orders in China.[119] The post-1979 opening of China to the West has allowed, for the first time, the appearance of Chinese publications on these groups as well as Western fieldwork, giving us a better glimpse into their origins and socioreligious complexity.

The Qadiriyya. While there is some dispute among the Sufis themselves as to which order was the earliest to enter China proper, (there had been regular contacts on an individual basis with the Sufi orders of Central Asia that had already begun to proliferate in Xinjiang in the early part of the fifteenth century), it is generally agreed that one of the earliest to be established firmly on Chinese soil was the Qadiri *ṭarîqa*

(Arabic for "path," or Islamic "order"). The founder of the Qadariyya *menhuan* in China was Qi Jingyi, Hilal al-Din (1656–1719). Known among the Hui as Qi Daozu (Grand Master Qi), he was buried in Linxia's "great tomb" (*da gongbei*) shrine complex, which became the center of Qadiriyya Sufism in China.[120] One of the reasons Grand Master Qi continues to be greatly revered among all Sufis in China is that the tradition suggests he received his early training under two of the most famous Central Asian Sufi teachers, Khoja Afaq and Khoja Abd Alla. Qi Jingyi supposedly met with the revered Naqshbandi leader Khoja Afaq (see below) in Xining in 1672, where, according to Qadariyya records, the master sent the 16-year-old acolyte home, saying: "I am not your teacher (*yu er fei shi*); my ancient teaching is not to be passed on to you; your teacher has already crossed the Eastern Sea and arrived in the Eastern land. You must therefore return home quickly, and you will become a famous teacher in the land."[121] Qadiriyya followers today feel that their saint received the blessing of the great Naqshbandi Khoja Afaq, while their order was formally founded by his second teacher, Khoja Abd Alla, a 29th-generation descendant of Muhammad.[122] Chinese Sufi records state that he entered China in 1674 and preached in Guangdong, Guangxi, Yunnan, Guizhou, and Linxia, Gansu, before his eventual death in Guizhou in 1689.[123] While Abd al-Kadir al-Jilani is the reputed founder of the Qadiri *ṭarîqa*, it is not surprising to find that Abd Alla perhaps studied in Medina under the reknowned Kurdish mystic Ibrahim b. Hasan al-Kurani (1616–1690), who was initiated into both the Naqshbandi and Qadiri *ṭarîqas*, as well as several other Sufi orders.

The appeal of Qadiriyya Sufism as a renewal movement among the Hui is related to its combining ascetic mysticism with a non-institutionalized form of worship, which centers around the tomb complex of deceased saints rather than the mosque.[124] The early Qadiriyya advocated long-term isolated meditation, poverty, and vows of celibacy. The head of the order did not marry and eschewed family life, a radical departure from other Islamic traditions in China. Qadiri Sufi continue to attend the Gedimu mosques in the local communities in which they live, gathering at the tombs for holidays and individual worship. Qi Jingyi was known for his emphasis upon ascetic withdrawal from society, poverty, and self-cultivation. Formalized Islamic ritual as represented by the "5 pillars" (fasting, pilgrimage, prayer, almsgiving, and recitation of the *Shahadah*) was deemphasized by Qi Jingyi in favor of private meditation. Qadiri maintain: "Those who know themselves clearly will know Allah" and "The Saints help us to know ourselves first before knowing Allah." Union with the divine is accomplished through meditation and self-cultivation, rather than formalized public ritual. "The moment of thinking about Allah," they maintain, "is superior to worshiping him for a thousand years."[125]

The terminology of Sufi mysticism in China is similar to that of Daoism. Islam, among Sufis, began to be known as the *Dao men* (the "order" or "school" of the Dao), whereas traditional Islam was known as the *Jiao men* (the "teaching order"). Three stages of initiation among Sufis began to be taught, and while debate often centers on which stage is most important, or in what order they should be followed, they are generally given as the first stage of *Jiaocheng* or *Changdao*, known in Arabic as the *Sharia*; the middle stage of *Daocheng* or *Zhongdao*, the *Tarīqah*; the final stage of *Zhencheng* or *Zhidao*, the *Haqiqah*. Individual Sufis would be initiated into each of these stages under the guidance of their *Daozu* ("master of the Dao"), which often took place in the *Dao tang* (ritual center of the Sufi *shaykh*, Arabic, "elder"). The system of succession became known as the *Dao tong* ("tradition of the Dao," Arabic, *silsila*). At one point there were even Sufis who became known as the *qingzhen Daoshi* ("pure and true master") and the *qingzhen heshang* ("pure and true monk") because they wore the robes of the Daoist and Buddhist monks. Ma Hualong, the Jahriyya saint, said in one of his poems, "It is in the human stomach that the elixir of life is made," and "It is on the phoenix land that white cranes come to rest."[126] These Daoist metaphors and terms were familiar to Sufis throughout China and infused their ascetic discourse and practice.

A Chinese inscription above the entrance to a Qadiriyya branch tomb complex in Beishan Hui cemetery, Linxia, reads: "The True Dao is Unceasing" (*Ti Dao wu she*). Through religious terminology familiar to the Hui in China, Confucian moral tenets, Daoist mystical concepts, and Buddhist folk rituals infused with new Islamic content pervade Qadiriyya Sufism.[127] Athough the Qadiriyya *menhuan* has always been less

influential than other Sufi orders in China due to its rejection of
"worldly" political involvement, it set the stage for many Sufi orders to
follow.

The Naqshbandiyya. The Naqshbandi *ṭarîqa* became most rooted in
Chinese soil through the establishment of 2 *menhuan*, the Khufiyya and
Jahriyya, which were to exercise tremendous influence on the history of
Islam in China and the northwest. As Joseph Fletcher argued, "the history of the Naqshbandiyya is the history of Islam" from eighteenth- to
nineteenth- century China. Fletcher went on to explain that the reform
movement emphasized the following:

> . . . a shar'ist orthopraxy, political activism, propagation of the religion, and
> a strong Sunni orientation [which] came to mark the Naqshbandiyya in a
> way that proved definitive in the mystical path's subsequent history. . . . Two
> other general characteristics of popular mysticism, namely the veneration of
> saints (misleadingly called "saint worship" by non-Muslim writers) and the
> seeking of inspiration by visiting and meditating at the saints' tombs (mislead-
> ingly referred to as "tomb worship"), were also prominent features of the Alti-
> shahr Naqshbandiyya."[128]

Founded by Baha' ad-Din Naqshband (d. 1389), who lived in Mawa-
rannahr (a Central Asian region west of the Pamirs), the Naqshbandiyya order gradually spread east across the trade routes and, by the
middle of the fifteenth century, gained ascendance over other Central
Asian Sufi orders in the oasis cities of Altishahr, surrounding the Tarim
River Basin in what is now southern Xinjiang. The Naqshbandi order
that gained the most prominence in the Tarim Basin and played an
important role in later eighteenth- and nineteenth-century politics in
Xinjiang was the Makhdumzada, established by Makhdum-i A'zam
(also known as Ahmad Kasani, 1461–1542). It was his great grandson,
Khoja Afaq (d. 1694), known in the Chinese sources as Hidayat Allah,
who was the saint most responsible for establishing the Naqshbandiyya
among the Hui in Northwest China.[129] Khoja Afaq (Khwaja-yi Afaq,
"the Master of the Horizons") founded the Afaqiyya in Xinjiang, and,
from 1671–1672, visited Gansu, where his father, Muhammad Yusuf,
had previously visited and preached, reportedly converting a few Hui
and a substantial number of the Salars to Naqshbandi Sufism. During
this influential tour, Khoja Afaq visited the northwest cities of Xining,

Lintao, and Hezhou (now Linxia, China's "little Mecca"), preaching to Hui, Salar, and northeastern Tibetan Muslims. Two of these early Hui Gansu Muslims became his disciples and went to Central Asia and the pilgrimage cities to become further trained in the order. When they returned to China, they established the two most important Naqshbandi brotherhoods among the Hui in the northwest, the Khufiyya and the Jahriyya.

Throughout its history, the Naqshbandiyya has stressed an active participation in worldly affairs.[130] Their *shaykhs* worked wonders, chanted the powerful Mathanawi texts of the Turkish mystic Rumi al-Balkhi, Maulana Jalluddin (d. 1273), and advocated scriptural reforms. They emphasized both self-cultivation and formal ritual, withdrawal from and involvement in society. Unlike the Qadiriyya, their leaders enjoyed families and the material wealth accrued from the donations of their followers. They also became committed to political involvement and social change based on the principles of Islam. Some of the Naqshbandiyya orders in China advocated, I argue, more of a "transformationist" perspective, in which they sought to change the social order in accord with their own visions of propriety and morality. This inevitably led to conflicts with Chinese rule and local governments, causing some orders of the Naqshbandiyya, especially the Jahriyya, to be singled out for suppression and persecution. "Due to the arduous way it has traversed," Yang Huaizhong writes, "the branch [Jahriyya] has always advocated the militant spirit of the Muslims, organizing uprisings to resist the oppression of the Qing and GMD Governments against the ethnic Hui minority and their religious belief."[131] By contrast, the Khufiyya tended to seek more conformist solutions to local conflicts, stressing personal internal reform over political change. The different stance that the Naqshbandiyya orders took in China with regard to the state and Chinese culture reflects their dialectical interaction with local interpretations of identity and changing sociopolitical realities in the northwest.

The Naqshbandi Khufiyya. During his 1672 visit to Hezhou, Khoja Afaq played an important role in the life of a certain Ma Laichi (d. 1766), a Hezhou Hui of incredible talent who went on to found one of the earliest and most influential Naqshbandiyya orders in China, the Khufiyya *menhuan*. According to Sufi tradition, Ma Laichi was born to a childless couple after receiving Khoja Afaq's blessing, and was later raised and trained by one of his disciples, Ma Tai Baba ("Great Father"), who later gave him his daughter in marriage and passed on to him the leadership of the mystical path that he had received from Khoja Afaq.[132] From 1728–1733, Ma Laichi went on pilgrimage to Mecca, Yemen, and Bukhara, where he studied several Sufi orders and became particularly influenced by Mawlana Makhdum, a man of uncertain origin, who Fletcher hypothesizes may have been Indian.[133] When he returned from his pilgrimage, Ma Laichi established the most powerful of the Khufiyya schools, the Huasi ("flowery mosque") branch, propagating the order for 32 years among the Hui and Salar in Gansu and Qinghai, before his death in 1766 at the age of 86.[134] The *menhuan* is still quite active and centered in Linxia Hui autonomous region, Gansu, at the tomb of Ma Laichi, which was restored in 1986.

Originating in an earlier Central Asian and Yemeni Naqshbandi Sufism, the Khufiyya order was permeated with an emphasis on a more active participation in society, the veneration of saints, the seeking of inspiration at tombs and the silent *dhikr* ("remembrance," properly "Khufiyya," the "silent" ones).[135] There are now over 20 sub-branch *menhuan* throughout China, with mosques in Yunnan, Xinjiang, and Beijing. Most Khufiyya orders are concentrated in Gansu, Qinghai, Ningxia, and Xinjiang, with several of the original Khufiyya practices in some outlying areas such as northern Ningxia beginning to lose their distinctiveness over time (see Chapter 3).

The Naqshbandi Jahriyya. The second Naqshbandi *ṭarîqa*, the Jahriyya order, was founded in China under the dynamic leadership of Ma Mingxin (1719–1781).[136] One of the most fascinating detective stories in historical discovery is the tracing by Joseph Fletcher of Ma Mingxin's spiritual lineage to Mizjaja, a village on the outskirts of Zabid in northern Yemen. While Chinese Sufis have known for generations that their saint Ma Mingxin studied in the Middle East and Yemen, it was never clear whom he received his "New Teaching" from or where he studied. Middle Eastern Sufi accounts recorded the presence of Chinese Muslims studying in certain Sufi areas, but only Joseph Fletcher was able to put the two together. This was an important discovery, as Ma Mingxin's Sufi practice was thought to be novel, even heterodox, and the subject of many conflicts in Northwest China. This is primarily the *jahr* in remembrance ("vocal *dhikr*," whence comes the name *Jahriyya*, the "vocal" ones), which Ma Mingxin openly advocated in opposition to the Khufiyya's silent remembrance, the more standard Naqshbandi practice.[137] After an extensive search through arcane Sufi documents in Arabic, Persian, Turkish, and Chinese, and a final personal trip to Yemen, Fletcher discovered that the name of the Sufi saint under whom Ma Mingxin studied was 'Abd al-Khāliq (c. 1705–1740), a Naqshbandi Sufi, who had derived his teaching from his father, az-Zayn b. Muhammad 'Abd al-Baqī al-Mizjaji (1643/4–1725), whose family home was in Mizjaja, the Zabid, Yemen. Chinese Sufi records indicate only that Ma Mingxin studied in Yemen in a Sufi order known as the Shazilinye, whose *shaykh* was Muhammad Bulu Seni, but did not know the full ancestry and origins of the order. Most Jahriyya say only: "The root of our order is Arabia, the branches and leaves are in China."

Fletcher discovered the actual name of the Yemeni saint in Sufi *silsila* genealogical lists contained in two separate letters from the China Inland Missionary, F. W. Martin Taylor, who was based in Jinji, Ningxia, the headquarters of the Banqiao branch of the Jahriyya. Taylor obtained the generations of the Jahriyya through interviews with the local Jahriyya elders, most probably Ma Jinxi, the grandson of Ma Hualong, the son of Ma Mingxin. Taylor recorded that there were 9 generations of Sufi saints in the Middle East, beginning first with al-Kurani and then Rumi, and ending with the 9th generation saint "Abu Duha Halik." (Jahriyya Sufis predicted that, since there were only 9 generations of Sufi saints in the Middle East before their teaching was transmitted to China, after the 9th generation of Sufi saints in China the world would end—the failure of that prediction has led to considerable debate and reinterpretation among Sufis in China today.) Fletcher identified "Abu Duha Halik," whom Ma Mingxin studied under, as 'Abd al-Khaliq, thus firmly establishing the link between the direct line of Sufis extending from the early seventeenth century in the Middle East to its inception in China in the mid-eighteenth century, down to today.[138]

This discovery is extremely significant in the history of ideas, as it is known that az-Zayn had studied in Medina under the famous Kurdish mystic Ibrahim b. Hasan al-Kurani (1616–1690), who also advocated the use of vocal formulae in the remembrance of Allah (*al-jahr bi-'dh-*

dhikr). Al-Kurani's students were at the forefront of Islamic reform and fundamentalist movements throughout the Islamic world:

> Through his students and his students' students and those of his son Abu 't-Tahir Muhammad al-Kurdi (d. 1733), al-Kurani's influence spread far and wide. One of his pupils was 'Abd ar-Ra'uf as-Sinkili (d. post 1693), who studied with him for many years in Medina and then returned home to Sumatra, where he laid the groundwork for a future surge of Islam in Indonesia. Abu 't-Tahir was the principle influence on the life of the great Indian orthodox reformer Shah Wali Allah of Delhi (d. 1762), a figure to be reckoned with in much of the subsequent Islamic history of the Indo-Pakistani subcontinent. Al-Kurdi also taught Muhammad Hayat as-Sindi (d. 1750 or 1752), who was the teacher of Muhammad b. 'Abd al-Wahhab (d. 1891), founder of the anti-Sufi "Wahhabi" movement. As-Sindi taught Muhammad as-Samman (d. 1775), who disseminated his fundamentalist Sufism through his own students to both west and east Africa, to Afghanistan, India, and Indonesia.[139]

Under al-Kurani's student's direction, it is not surprising that Ma Mingxin returned after 16 years of study in Yemen and the Arabian Peninsula in 1744 with more activist, fundamentalist reforms on his mind. While advocating the use of the vocal *dhikr*, he generally opposed the heavy emphasis upon the veneration of Islamic saints, which had become popular in China. As the disputes grew worse and conflicts erupted, Qing troops, tired from the conquest of Xinjiang in 1759, did not wish to have any more trouble among Muslims in Gansu. They arrested Ma Mingxin in 1781 and executed him as his followers attempted to free him. Three years later, they crushed another uprising led by a Jahriyya Sufi, Tian Wu. From this point on, the Qing sought to limit the spread and outlawed many of the so-called "New Teachings," primarily the Jahriyya. The great Northwest Hui Rebellion (1862–1876) was led by Ma Hualong, another Jahriyya Sufi *murshid* and 5th generation descendant of Ma Mingxin. His rebellion was responsible for cutting the Qing state off from the northwest, making way for the great 1864–1877 Uigur-led rebellion in Xinjiang under Yakub Beg.[140] In 1871, Ma Hualong was captured and purportedly executed with his entire family. His body is entombed in Dongta township, Jinji, just east of the Yellow River in Ningxia, while his head is supposedly buried in Xuanhuagang, a Jahriyya center, north of Zhangjiachuan in south Gansu. There is also evidence that suggests Du Wenxiu, of the Panthay

Hui Muslim Rebellion in Yunnan (1855–1873), who called himself the Sultan Suleiman, was also influenced by Jahriyya ideas.[141] Following the failure of these uprisings, the Jahriyya became much more secretive and dispersed, leading to the establishment of 5 main Jahriyya branch orders, all named after their ritual and historical centers: Shagou, Beishan, Xindianzi, Banqiao, and Nanchuan.[142]

Of these, there are 2 main sub-branches of the Jahriyya that continue to exercise significant influence among Naqshbandi Sufi Hui throughout China today. The Shagou *menhuan* claims spiritual descent from Ma Yuanzhang, the son-in-law of Ma Hualong, who is said to have received the "oral transmission" (*kouhuan*) from one or two other chosen ahong initiated by Ma Hualong himself, just before his death. Shagou members maintain that all Ma Hualong's blood descendants were lost in the Qing pogrom mentioned above that executed 130 of his family members. Hence, only the spiritual mantle of leadership could be conferred on Ma Yuanzhang. Upon Ma Yuanzhang's death, during the 1920 earthquake in Shagou, Xiji county, southern Ningxia, his fourth son, Ma Zhenwu, took up the leadership of the order, later followed by his son, the current *murshid*. The Shagou branch is said to have 145 mosque communities (*jiaofang*) in southern Ningxia, 40 in Xinjiang, 20 in Guizhou, more than 10 in Yunnan, and at least 1 in Beijing, Tianjin, Jinan, and Jilin province, with over 100,000 followers.[143] In the 1958 document criticizing Ma Zhenwu and justifying his arrest, they mentioned his receiving support in 1954 from as far away as Chuanchang, Jilin province.[144]

The Banqiao order, the second main Jahriyya *menhuan*, traces direct blood descent from Ma Jinxi, the grandson of Ma Hualong, who they claim escaped the massacre of Ma Hualong's descendants. The Banqiao Jahriyya say that two of Ma Hualong's grandsons escaped the Qing pogrom. The eldest of the two surviving grandsons, Ma Jinchang, was castrated by Zuo Zongtang's forces and exiled to Kaifeng, where he died as a bondservant. The younger grandson, Ma Jinxi, was secreted to Yunnan and raised among Jahriyya until he was old enough to take on the mantle of the *jiaozhu* of the Banqiao order. Thus, the Shagou and Banqiao orders derive their legitimacy from either spiritual or blood descent, and therein lies the basis to their claims of authority. Concentrated in Zhangjiachuan, Gansu, and Banqiao, Ningxia, the Banqiao

Sufis have more than 25,000 followers, with 120 mosques in Ningxia, 20 in Xinjiang, and others in Gansu, Qinghai, Jiangsu, Sichuan, and Yunnan.[145] The present *murshid* of the Banqiao *menhuan* is also vice-chairman of the Ningxia Regional People's Government.

The Kubrawiyya. Of minor influence in China is the fourth main Sufi order, the Kubrawiyya.[146] An Arab, Mohidin, is said to have first introduced the order to China in the 1600s (or perhaps as early as 1370).[147] He taught in Henan, Qinghai, Gansu, and died in Dawantou, Dongxiang prefecture, Gansu province. Presently, many of the Dongxiang Muslim minority concentrated in that area are members of the Kubrawiyya *menhuan*.

Sufi Networks and Islamic Resurgence. The importance and extensiveness of these Sufi orders for uniting disparate Hui communities across China cannot be underestimated. Gellner's suggestion that "Sufism provides a theory, terminology, and technique of leadership"[148] seems applicable to understanding the rapid proliferation of various orders during the turmoil of the late eighteenth and nineteenth centuries, when China was faced with widespread domestic social unrest and the advancing encroachment of Western imperialist powers. Unlike the isolated "patchwork" Gedimu communities that had been the norm until that time, Sufi orders provided the leadership and organization that could help Hui survive politically and economically.[149] During the fragmented Republican period (1911–1949), extensive Sufi networks proved helpful to some Hui warlords in the northwest and disruptive to others. In the 1930s, Pickens and a few other missionary scholars were becoming aware of Sufi networks that extended across the country:

> Although in East China we do not think much of the Derwish Orders yet when we get to know something of what goes on we find that even in Shanghai branches of the Djahariah [Jahriyya] can be found. From Yunnan right north to Kansu and Ningsia, even Peiping and probably Manchuria, the influence of this order is felt.[150]

At the 1985 commemoration ceremony (*ermaili*) of the death of the Jahriyya order's founder, Ma Mingxin, over 20,000 adherents gathered for 3 days at the site of his original tomb outside Lanzhou. The local municipality had intended originally to refrain from participation in the ceremony, but, owing to the unexpected number of participants, the city eventually supplied sanitation facilities and food. The Provincial Islamic Society subsequently agreed to allow Ma Mingxin's tomb to be rebuilt. Two months earlier, a similar *ermaili* was held in remembrance of Ma Hualong, the Jahriyya Rebellion leader. A crowd of over 10,000 followers from as far away as Urumqi, Kunming, and Harbin arrived at his grave in Lingwu county, Dongta township, demonstrating the extensive influence of this order and the important focus the Sufi leader's tomb provides for galvanizing collective action.[151]

Membership in various Islamic orders often significantly influences social interaction, especially among the Sufi orders who sometimes distinguish themselves by dress. Unlike the rounded white cap worn by most Hui men, Sufi followers often wear a 6-cornered hat, sometimes black.[152] Many Jahriyya Hui shave the sides of their beards to commemorate their founder, Ma Mingxin, whose beard is said to have been shorn by Qing soldiers before his execution in 1781. While these markers are almost universally unnoticed by the Han majority—for whom a Hui is a Hui—northwest Hui can easily identify in the marketplace members of the various orders that divide them internally. The exclusivity of Sufi orders in China illustrates the cruciality of identity and authority for Sufi Hui. Hui can enter these orders through ritual vow or by birth, but seldom maintain allegiance to two *menhuan* at once. This is unlike Sufi orders in other parts of the world that tend to be less exclusive and allow simultaneous membership in several orders.[153]

THE THIRD TIDE: SCRIPTURALIST CONCERNS AND MODERNIST REFORMS. The third tide in Chinese Islam began at the end of the Qing dynasty, a period of accelerated exchange between China and the outside world, when many Muslims began traveling to and returning from the Middle East. In the early decades of the twentieth century, China was exposed to many new foreign ideas and, in the face of Japanese and Western imperialist encroachment, sought a Chinese approach to governance. Intellectual and organizational activity by Chinese Muslims during this period was also intense. Increased contact with the Middle East led Chinese Muslims to reevaluate their traditional notions of Islam. Pickens records that, from 1923 to 1934, there were 834 known Hui Muslims who made the Hajj, or pilgrimage, to Mecca.[154] In 1937, according to one observer, over 170 Hui pilgrims boarded a steamer in Shanghai bound for Mecca.[155] By 1939, at least 33 Hui Muslims had studied at Cairo's prestigious Al-Azhar University. While these numbers are not significant when compared with pilgrims on the Hajj from other Southeast Asian Muslim areas, the influence and prestige attached to these returning Hui *hajji* was profound, particularly in isolated communities. "In this respect," Fletcher observed, "the more secluded and remote a Muslim community was from the main centers of Islamic cultural life in the Middle East, the more susceptible it was to those centers' most recent trends."[156]

As a result of political events and the influence of foreign Muslim ideas, numerous new Hui organizations emerged. In 1912, one year after Sun Yat-sen was inaugurated as provisional president of the Chinese Republic in Nanjing, the Chinese Muslim Federation was also formed in that city. This was followed by the establishment of other Hui Muslim associations: the Chinese Muslim Mutual Progress Association (Beijing, 1912), the Chinese Muslim Educational Association (Shanghai, 1925), the Chinese Muslim Association (1925), the Chinese Muslim Young Students Association (Nanjing, 1931), the Society for the Promotion of Education Among Muslims (Nanjing, 1931), and the Chinese Muslim General Association (Jinan, 1934).

The Muslim periodical press flourished as never before. Although Löwenthal reported that circulation was low, there were over 100 known Muslim periodicals produced before the outbreak of the Sino-Japanese War in 1937.[157] Thirty journals were published between 1911 and 1937 in Beijing alone, prompting one author to suggest that, while Chinese Islam's traditional religious center was still Linxia (Hezhou), its cultural center had shifted to Beijing.[158] This took place when many Hui intellectuals traveled to Japan, the Middle East, and the West. Caught up in the nationalist fervor of the first half of this century, they published magazines and founded organizations, questioning their identity as never before in a process that one Hui historian, Ma Shouqian, has recently termed "The New Awakening of the Hui at the end of 19th and beginning of the 20th centuries."[159] As many of these Hui *hajji* returned from their pilgrimages to the Middle East, they initiated several reforms, engaging themselves once again in the contested space between Islamic ideals and Chinese culture.

Wahhabi Muslim Brotherhood. Influenced by fundamentalist Wahhabi ideals in the Arabian Peninsula, returning Hui reformers introduced the Ikwan Muslim Brotherhood to China—a religious movement in tune, in some cases, with China's nationalist concerns and, in others, with warlord politics.[160] While the Muslim Brotherhood elsewhere in the Islamic world has been depicted as anti-modernist and fundamentalist, this is not true of the movement in China. "There a fundamentalist, revivalist impulse among returned pilgrims influenced by Wahhabi notions," Lipman suggests, "was transformed into a nationalist, modernist, anti-Sufi solidarity group which advocated not only Muslim unity but Chinese national strength and conciousness."[161]

The beginnings of the Ikhwan movement in China can be traced to Ma Wanfu (1849–1934), who returned from the Hajj in 1892 to teach in the Linxia, Dongxiang area. Eventually known as the Yihewani (Chinese for the Ikhwan al-Muslimin), the initial reformers were primarily concerned with religious scripturalist orthodoxy—so much so that they are still known as the "venerate-the-scriptures faction" (*zunjing pai*).[162] Seeking perhaps to replace "Islamic theater" with scripture,[163] they proscribed the veneration of saints, their tombs and shrines, and sought to stem the growing influence of well-known individual ahong and Sufi *menhuan* leaders. Advocating a purified, "non-Chinese" Islam, they criticized such cultural accretions as the wearing of white mourning dress (*dai xiao*) and the decoration of mosques with Chinese or Arabic texts. At one point, Ma Wanfu even proposed the exclusive use of Arabic and Persian instead of Chinese in all education.[164] Following strict Wahhabi practice, Yihewani mosques are distinguished by their almost complete lack of adornment on the inside, with white walls and no inscriptions, as well as a preference for Arabian-style mosque architecture. This contrasts sharply with other more Chinese-style mosques in China, typical of the "old" Gedimu, whose architecture resembles Confucian temples with sweeping roofs and symmetrical courtyards (the Xi'an Huajue Great Mosque being the best example).[165] The Yihewani also proscribed the adornment of their mosques with Arabic, especially Chinese,

Quranic texts and banners; these are the most striking markers of Sufi mosques and worship centers in the northwest, whose walls are often layered with calligraphy and unique Hui-style art.[166]

Within the Yihewani, another reform movement emerged in the 1930s, the Salafiyya, that stressed a non-politicized fundamentalist return to Wahhabi scripturalist ideals.[167] In turn, in the last few years, a controversy has arisen within the Salafiyya in Gansu over the immanence or transcendence of Allah. Those who believe in transcendence — that Allah dwells in a high place above the affairs of humankind (*gao weizhishang*) — demonstrate their position by cutting their hair short. Immanentalists, by contrast, let their hair grow down to their collars, symbolizing God's presence in the world.

The Yihewani continue to be a powerful Islamic group throughout China. Like the Gedimu, the Yihewani emphasize leadership through training and Islamic education rather than inheritance and succession. The Yihewani differ from the Gedimu primarily in ritual matters and their stress upon reform through Chinese education and modernism. Because of their emphasis on nationalist concerns, education, modernization, and decentralized leadership, the order has attracted more urban intellectual Muslims. The Yihewani are also especially numerous in areas like Qinghai and Gansu where they proliferated during the Republican period under the patronage of Hui warlords. Many of the large mosques and Islamic schools rebuilt with government funds throughout China in the late 1970s and early 1980s tend to be staffed by Yihewani Imam.

The Xi Dao Tang. A small Islamic movement that did not gain much popularity in China is important because of its historical and cultural significance. The Xi Dao Tang was the only completely "native" Islamic movement in China, which arose at the beginning of this century through a fascinating combination of Chinese and Islamic learning. Known publically as the "Study the Han Faction" (Han xue pai), they called themselves the Xi Dao Tang ("Western School" or "Mosque"). Xi Dao Tang originated in Lin Tan (Tao Zhou old city), a market town that served as an important economic center and crossroads for Sichuan, Shaanxi, Yunnan, Gansu, Tibet, and Qinghai. The site of incredible turmoil in the aftermath of the 1862 Hui Rebellion, Tao Zhou was the center of fierce Han, Hui, and Tibetan ethnic violence, as well as sectarian divisions among the competing Islamic orders in the area. The movement took its inspiration from Ma Qixi (1857–1914, note that his name means, "one who reveals the West"), a Qing *xiucai* scholar, who wrote several works along the same lines as the Qing-dynasty Islamic-Confucian texts of Liu Zhi, which sought to legitimize Islam in terms of Confucian moral tenets and discourse. Originally a member of the Khufiyya Beizhuang branch *menhuan*, in 1901 he established his own movement, which emphasized study of the Quran as the only scripture as opposed to other Sufi texts. Significantly, he promoted the study of the Chinese Confucian-Islamic classics, communal living, and cordial relations between Han, Hui, and Tibetan. Ma Qixi strongly stressed both classical Chinese and Arabic learning, even the study of the Quran in Chinese, and his following grew quickly. He was able, in a relatively short time, to establish a modernist, accomodationist movement that was supported by the pillars of Tao Zhou Hui commercial society. There is much mixed opinion as to the source of Ma Qixi's popularity and wealth. George Andrew, the Protestant missionary who worked in the area, gives the following account of the rise of this "New Sect":

> By this time he had quiet a large following, and to them he commenced to expound his new teaching, which proved a strange mixture of Mohammedanism, Confucianism, and Spiritualism. He held regular seances, and mystified his followers by exhibitions of black art. Strange to say, this retirement had resulted in the restoration of his health. Numbers joined him, till one morning the members of the Old Sect awoke to the fact that a large, powerful, and dangerous organization had sprung up in their midst. This was no sooner realized than they took steps to suppress it, but the root had already struck deeper than they thought.[168]

With its approximately 10,000 followers, one of the early unique contributions of the association was an emphasis upon communal living and holding all economic assets in common. About 400 lived this way in Tao Zhou, with other adherents spread throughout Gansu, Qinghai, and Xinjiang. The Xi Dao Tang also emphasized the passing of succession through merit, not blood, and criticized the accumulation of wealth by the leaders of the association. The 400 in Tao Zhou lived in community, seeking equal distribution of their goods. As a trading center, Tao Zhou proved to be an excellent environment for this kind of community corporation. They must have derived great wealth from dominating the trade in leather, tea, and, perhaps, opium along the southern mule-caravan routes to Sichuan, and thence to Burma. The movement had grown so strong militarily that it repulsed a savage attack by the "Bai Lang" ("White Wolf") bandits who were terrorizing the northwest and, according to eye-witness accounts, completely devastated the city in 1914.[169] Their increasing strength and wealth apparently roused the envy and fear of other Hui associations, and Ma Anliang, a Khufi Hez-hou official, had Ma Qixi and his family assassinated later that year. After Ma Qixi's death, however, the movement revived briefly but grad-ually declined, and, by 1957, it supposedly dispersed. This may have been related to the collectivization and land reforms initiated by the state, but I as yet have no information on the effects of these policies on the Xi Dao Tang.[170]

While the total population of the various Islamic associations in China has not been published, Yang Huaizhong writes that, of the 2,132 mosques in Ningxia Hui autonomous region, 560 belong to the Yihewani, 560 to the Khufiyya, 464 to the Jahriyya, 415 to the tradi-tional Gedimu, and 133 belong to Qadiriyya religious worship sites (some of which include mosques).[171] The most comprehensive estimate given so far for Hui membership in Islamic orders throughout China is by Ma Tong. Out of his total of 6,781,500 Hui Muslims, he records that there are 58.2 percent Gedimu, 21 percent Yihewani, 10.9 percent Jah-riyya, 7.2 percent Khufiyya, 1.4 percent Qadiriyya, 0.5 percent Xidao-tang, and 0.7 percent Kubrawiyya (see Appendix A).[172]

Internal Conversion. While these Islamic associations are as confus-ing to the non-initiate as the numerous schools of Buddhist thought in China, membership is not hotly disputed as in China. Unlike Central Asian Islamic orders, where one might belong to two or even three brotherhoods at once, the Hui belong only to one. Among the Hui, one is generally born into one's Islamic order or converts dramatically to another. In fact, this is the only instance of conversion I encountered among my sojourn among the Hui. I never met a Han who had con-verted to Islam in China without having been married to a Hui or adopted into a Hui family, though I heard of a few isolated instances. Fletcher recorded the conversion of 28 Tibetan tribes as well as their

"Living Buddha" by Ma Laichi in Xunhua, Qinghai, in the mid-eighteenth century.[173] After the 1784 Ma Mingxin uprising, the Qing government forbade non-Muslims from converting to Islam, and this may account for the few Han conversions recorded in history. This goes against the common assumption that Islam in China was spread through proselytization and conversion. Islamic preachers in China, including Ma Laichi, Ma Mingxin, Qi Jingyi, and Ma Qixi, spent most of their time trying to convert other Muslims. Islam in China for the most part, had expanded through migration, intermarriage, and adoption. Hui frequently adopted Han children in the past, raising them as Muslims, and eventually accepting them as Hui. They were also concerned enough about preserving the identities of Muslim children while away from home that they frequently practiced the tradition of "dry adoption," where young Hui would be accepted into a home and treated as an adopted child so that they might more easily preserve a *qing zhen* Muslim lifestyle.

HUI ISLAMIC ORDERS AND CHINESE CULTURE. The tensions and conflicts that led to the rise and divisions of the Sufi *menhuan* in Northwest China, and subsequent non-Sufi reforms, are impossible to enumerate in their complexity. They give evidence, however, of the ongoing struggles that continue to make Islam meaningful to Hui Muslims. These tensions between Islamic ideals and social realities are often left unresolved.[174] Their very dynamism derives from the questions they raise and the doubts they engender among people struggling with traditional meanings in the midst of changing social contexts. The questions of purity and legitimacy (*qing zhen*) become paramount when the Hui are faced with radical internal socioeconomic and political change, and exposed to different interpretations of Islam from the outside Muslim world. These conflicts and reforms reflect an ongoing debate in China over Islamic orthodoxy, revealing an important disjunction between "scripturalist" or "mystical" interpretations.[175]

In a similar fashion, the study of Southeast Asian Islam has often centered on the contradiction and compromise between the native culture of the indigenous Muslims and the *shariʿa* of orthodox Islam, the mystical and the scriptural, the real and the ideal.[176] The supposed accommodation of orthodox Islamic tenets to local cultural practices has led scholars to dismiss or explain such compromise as syncretism, assimilation, and "Sinicization," as has been described among the Hui.[177] An alternative approach, and one perhaps more in tune with the interests of Hui themselves, sees this incongruence as the basis for ongoing dialectical tensions that have often led to reform movements and conflicts within Muslim communities.[178] Following Weber,[179] one can see the wide variety of Islamic expression as reflecting processes of local world construction and programs for social conduct whereby a major religious tradition becomes meaningful to an indigenous society.[180]

In the competition for scarce resources, these conflicts are also prompted by and expressed in economic concerns, such as we saw in the defeat of the Xi Dao Tang above by the Khufiyya leader Ma Anliang—clearly a case of coveting his Muslim brother's wealth. Fletcher, in "The Naqshbandiyyas in Northwest China," noted that one of the criticisms of the Khufiyya was that their recitation of the *Ming sha le* took less time than the normal Quranic *suras* by non-Sufi clergy, and therefore their imams were cheaper to hire at ritual ceremonies. He suggested that this assisted their rise in popularity and criticism by the Gedimu religious leaders. The Yihewani criticized both the Gedimus and Sufis for performing rituals in believers' homes only for profit, and advocated the practice, "If you recite, do not eat; if you eat, do not recite" (*Nian jing bu chi, chi by nian jing*). The Chinese state has generally found economic reasons for criticizing certain Islamic orders among the Hui. During the Land Reform Campaigns of the 1950s, which appropriated mosque and *wagf* (Islamic endowment) holdings, they met with great resistance from the Sufi *menhuan*, which had accumulated a great deal due to their hierarchical centralized leadership. In the 1958 document criticizing Ma Zhenwu, the Jahri Sufi *shaykh*, the following accusations are quite revealing:

> According to these representatives, Ma Chen-wu instituted many "A-mai-lis," or festival days to commemorate the dead ancestors to which the A-hungs must be invited to chant the scriptures and be treated with big feasts, thereby squeezing money out of the living for the dead. For example, he has kept a record of the days of birth and death of all the family members of this followers and has seen to it that religious services be held on such days. These include "Grandmother's Day," "Wife's Day," "Aunt's Day," and others, sixty-five of such "A-mai-lis" in a year. On the average, one of such "A-mai-lis" is held every six or seven days, among which are seven occasions of big festival.

... All the A-hungs of the Islamic mosques have been appointed by Ma Chen-wu. Through the appointment of A-hungs he has squeezed a big sum of money. ... Ma has regularly, in the name of repairing the "kung-peis" [i.e., tombs], squeezed the Hui people for money.[181]

The tensions arising from the conflict of Chinese cultural practices and Islamic ideals have led to the rise and powerful appeal of Islamic movements among Hui Muslims (see Figure 1).[182] At one extreme there are those who reject any integration of Islam with Chinese culture, such as Ma Wanfu's fundamentalist return to an Arabicized "pure" Islam. Conversely, at the other extreme, there are those leaders of the Gedimu, such as Hu Dengzhou, who accepted more of an integration with traditional Chinese society. Likewise, Ma Qixi's Xi Dao Tang stressed the complete compatibility of Chinese and Islamic culture, the importance of Chinese Islamic Confucian texts, the harmony of the two systems, and the reading of the Quran in Chinese.

FIGURE 1 Hui Islam and Chinese Culture: A Range of Alternatives

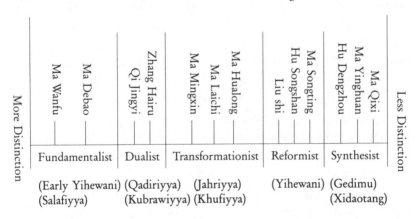

In between, one finds various attempts at changing Chinese society to "fit" a Muslim world, through transformationist or militant Islam, as illustrated by the largely Naqshbandiyya-led nineteenth-century Hui uprisings. The Jahriyya sought to implement an alternative vision of the world in their society, and this posed a threat to the Qing, as well as other Hui Muslims, earning them the label of "heterodox" (*xie jiao*) and persecution by the Chinese state. By contrast, other Hui reformers have attempted throughout history to make Islam "fit" Chinese society, such as Liu Zhi's monumental effort to demonstrate the Confucian morality of Islam. The Qadiriyya alternative represents resolution of this tension through ascetic withdrawal from the world. Qi Jingyi advocated an inner mystical journey where the dualism of Islam and the Chinese world is absolved through grasping the oneness of Allah found inside every believer. These various approaches in China's Islam represent sociohistorical attempts to deal with the problem of relating the world religion of Islam to the local Chinese realm.

THE FOURTH TIDE: ETHNIC NATIONALISM IN AN AGE OF NATION-STATES

The Salman Rushdie incident with which this chapter began illustrates a significant new way in which Muslims in China are now expressing themselves. Accepting the labels of Hui, Uigur, and Kazak, by which the state has designated them, and making use of the organizations of the China Islamic Association, the Nationalities Institute, and the State Nationalities Commission, by which the state has sought to administer them, the Muslims *as nationalities*, not merely as Muslims, are now calling for a greater voice in their own affairs. And by the response to their protest, it is clear that the state is listening. Much of this new tide in ethnic nationalism and "primordial politics" sweeping China, and much of the world, is due to the internationalism arising from the organization of the world into nation-states. No longer content to sit on the sidelines, the nations within these states are playing a greater role in the public sphere, which Jürgen Habermas suggests is the defining characteristic of civil society in the modern nation-state.[183]

The three previous "tides" of Islam in China, according to Joseph Fletcher, were precipitated by China's opening to the outside world. A new tide may now be washing across China's terrain. The Salman Rushdie event has demonstrated that China, no matter what conservative leaders in the government might wish, has reached a new stage of openness. If China wants to continue to participate in the international political sphere of the nation-states, this is unavoidable. The President of Iran's visit in May 1989 to China, during the midst of the democracy protests, and just prior to the *Sexual Customs* uprising, indicates that China can no longer isolate its Muslims from the currents of the Islamic world, nor its people from nationalistic ferment. China is part of the Muslim Asian sphere where James Piscatori argues international Islamic politics are taking on new significance in domestic relations.[184] The new technologies of communication and travel have assisted this change, and led to a fourth tide in Chinese Islam.

With the opening to the West in recent years, travel to and from the Islamic heartlands has dramatically increased in China. In 1984, over 1,400 Muslims left China to go on the Hajj.[185] This number increased to over 2,000 in 1987, representing a return to pre-1949 levels. Several Hui students are presently enrolled in Islamic and Arabic studies at the Al-Azhar University in Egypt.

In September 1987, I visited the home of a Hui elder in Xi'an who had just returned from the Hajj. He was escorted home from the airport in a procession of over 100 taxis, all owned and operated privately by Hui. His trip was financed by local Hui, who turned over 10,000 yuan ($3,300 US) to the China Islamic Society in Beijing. The Islamic Society arranged his travel to Pakistan, where his visa was procured at the Saudi Embassy (at that time China had no formal diplomatic relations with Saudi Arabia), and supplied him with $80 US for use on the trip, since local currency is nonconvertible. Upon his return, he traveled throughout the northwest, preaching and lecturing about his pilgrimage experiences and the need to reform Islam along Middle Eastern lines.

Encouraged by the Chinese state, relations between Muslims in China and the Middle East are becoming stronger and more frequent, partly from a desire to establish trading partners for arms, commodities, and currency exchanges,[186] and partly because of China's traditional view of itself as a leader of the Third World. Delegations of foreign Muslims regularly travel to prominent Islamic sites in China, in a kind of state-sponsored religious tourism, and donations are encouraged. While the state hopes that private Islamic investment will assist economic development, the vast majority of grants by visiting foreign Muslims have been donated to the rebuilding of Islamic mosques, schools, and hospitals. As Hui in China are further exposed to Islamic internationalism, and they return from studies and pilgrimages abroad, traditional Hui identities will once again be reshaped and called into question, giving rise to a fourth tide of Islam in China.

Hui saleswoman peddling Nang (*da bing*), the traditional flatbread, in the doorway to her home in a Hui neighborhood of Lanzhou, Gansu. Note the sign for *Qing Zhen* (*Halal*) suspended from the doorway. Photo: Gladney

TWO

Ethnographic Research and the Chinese State

A "nation" has been cynically but not inaptly defined as a society united by a common error as to its origin and a common aversion to its neighbors.
—*Julian S. Huxley and A. C. Haddon,*
We Europeans: A Survey of "Racial" Problems

The complex and diffuse identity of the Hui as outlined in the preceding chapter challenges traditional approaches to ethnicity theory. Anthropology in the past was ill-equipped to address this kind of expansive ethnic identity. Given their widespread distribution and lack of cohesion, one may very rightly question the validity of Hui ethnic identity. The Hui regard themselves as an ethnic group, however, and the Chinese state registers them as an official nationality. The Hui are also beginning to play an increasingly important role in the Chinese state's domestic affairs and in international ethnopolitics. The Hui thus pose an interesting problem for modern ethnicity theory and studies of nationalism.

The Hui raise another issue for contemporary anthropological studies: Given their diffuse and diverse nature, how does one study them according to traditional fieldwork? In addition, since the restrictions placed on foreigners doing research in the Chinese nation-state are still substantial, the question remains whether this kind of research is worthwhile or even possible. I argue that the challenge of understanding Hui identity will not only push us toward more comprehensive ethnicity theory, but assist us in problematizing the issue of developing alternative research methodologies appropriate to modern complex nation-states.

THEORETICAL PERSPECTIVES ON HUI IDENTITY

Despite the wide cultural and religious diversity of Hui communities discussed above, several theories have been advanced to explain how the Hui regard themselves as an ethnic group and why the state chose to recognize them as a nationality. These theories may be grouped under 3 main approaches: the Chinese Stalinist, the cultural-primordial, and the circumstantialist-instrumentalist. After briefly discussing these theories and their limitations when applied to the Hui, I shall propose a fourth approach that I suggest more adequately interprets the unity and diversity of Hui identity.

IDENTIFYING THE HUI: THE CHINESE STALINIST APPROACH. After the People's Republic of China was founded in 1949, the state embarked upon a monumental endeavor to identify and recognize as nationalities those who qualified among the hundreds of groups applying for national minority status. In his review of this process, Fei Xiaotong records that, by 1955, over 400 minority groups had registered names for themselves and applied for recognition.[1] In the late 1950s, teams of researchers were sent out to identify these people in the border areas and, as a result, 55 were labeled as nationalities (*minzu*, from the Japanese term *minzoku*, introduced by Sun Yat-sen, see below). The Han *minzu* were recognized as the majority nationality, with 91 percent of the 1990 population. This process has continued, with the Jinno recognized as an official nationality as late as 1979. Currently, there are 15 other groups applying for recognition to the State Commission for Nationality Affairs (SCNA). Significantly, the 1990 census[2] revealed that there are still 749,341 individuals of "unidentified ethnicity" waiting to be recognized.

Since its founding in the mid-1950s, the SCNA has relied on Stalin's 4 criteria for defining a nationality (*minzu*): "a common language, a common territory, a common economic life, and a common psychological make-up manifested in common specific features of national culture."[3] "Psychological make-up" was synonymous with "culture," in Stalin's

view: "Of course the elements of nationhood–language, territory, common culture, etc.–did not fall from the skies."[4] These 4 criteria are still
viewed as normative for defining nationalities in a socialist society such
as China.[5] In a summary of its policy, the State Commission for Nationality Affairs concluded:

> Stalin's nationality criteria are a universal truth (*pubian zhenli*), they have
> been proved through a long period of actual investigation. . . . After Libera-
> tion, our country, in the work of nationality research and nationality
> identification, accurately utilized Stalin's theory, causing the nationality iden-
> tification work to meet with success.[6]

Fei Xiaotong's description of the process of identifying several questionable nationality groups assumes these 4 criteria and generally begins
with the study of their linguistic history. In one case, Fei describes how
Chinese sociologists applied the Stalinist criteria in determining the
identity of the Chuanqing "Blacks" in Guizhou. He suggests that,
although the Blacks have a close relationship with the Han, "the Blacks
seemed to have certain features in their language, areas of settlement,
economic life, and psychological makeup which might qualify them as
a national minority."[7] Following a linguistic and historical analysis of
the Blacks, Fei concludes that they are not a minority, but descendants
of Han garrison troops sent to conquer remnant Yuan forces in Yunnan
at the beginning of the Ming dynasty. While linguistic data often appear
most decisive in assessing a group's identity, they are not the only factor,
and must be tested historically, according to Fei.[8]

By the same criteria, we must assume that the more than 350 other
applicant groups were refused recognition. While many of them were
collapsed into other groups, creating larger umbrella-like nationalities
such as the Yi[9] and the Qiang,[10] many others continue to seek recognition. The Ku Cong in the southwest and the so-called Danmin (Boat
People) along the southeast coast have been continually denied recognition, despite their strong self-ascribed identity and common culture. As
long as China continues to subscribe to the Stalinist nationality policies, it is doubtful that these and other peoples will be able to convince
the state of their claim to nationality status.

Despite their failure to meet the Stalinist criteria for recognition, the Hui were among the first minorities to be recognized. Most Chinese publications that discuss Hui ethnic identification tend to see them in a situation similar to the Manchu (Man) and She minorities, who have lived for such a long time among the Han majority that they have lost their own language and many cultural distinctions.[11] Historical records document that each of these minorities once spoke a common language different from the Han, and, since they maintain some cultural distinctions, they are recognized as minorities in a historical application of the Stalinist criteria. While this may be true of the Manchu and the She minorities, it does not adequately account for the identity of the Hui. The Hui are descendants of foreign Muslim merchants, militia, and officials who came to China in large numbers from the seventh through fourteenth centuries and later intermarried with the local Han populace. These foreign residents did not speak a single language—they spoke Persian, Arabic, Turkish, or Mongolian—and there is no record that the foreign languages of these early Muslim ancestors were adopted by their Hui descendants beyond the Ming dynasty.[12]

While Quranic Arabic is used in Hui Islamic ritual, it has never served as a common language for communication. Hui do use certain Persian and Arabic loan words (known as *Huihui hua*) that are unintelligible to Han, but these in no way constitute a separate language (see Appendix B). Of course, to the Hui themselves, these distinctive non-Han expressions of speech, though not a separate language in any sense, continue to serve as important markers of ethnic identity.[13] I have been in many public market situations in the northwest where Hui easily identified other Hui in a group of people bargaining, just by listening to their speech. In setting the price among themselves, Hui will often use Arabic or Persian numbers that the Han do not understand, before announcing to Han buyers in Chinese what the price is. For this and other entrepreneurial practices, Hui have been traditionally denigrated as the *zei Huihui*, "larcenous Hui people." This linguistic switching has assisted their mediating role in trade throughout history in the northwest, as the missionaries Cable and French related:

Wang was a trusted friend and confidant of Yolbas and was consulted by all the important men of Central Asia as representing Tungan [Hui] interests. He had excellent manner, and conducted his household, as his business, with capacity and conspicuous success. His mother-tongue was Chinese, and this was the language of his home, his children and his womenfolk, but though he spoke Chinese and Turki with equal fluency, in Chinese his intonation was foreign, his vocabulary restricted and his speech mixed with a *patois* interspersed with Arabic words. The construction of his phrases had none of the sprightly idiomatic short-cuts which spring to the lips of the man from China proper and make his speech so terse and unforgettable. Likewise, his Turki talk lacked the racy crispness which constitutes the unique charm of that tongue. His clumsy speech was typical of the Tungan.[14]

DEFINING THE HUI: THE CULTURAL APPROACH. It is evident that national identification in China relies on an analysis of a group's cultural traits and history. This approach is similar to what Naroll and other Western scholars have carried out, and later termed the "cultunit" or "historical-idealist" model.[15] Naroll has defined a "cultunit" as a "people who are domestic speakers of a common distinct language and who belong either to the same state or the same contact group."[16] These studies of ethnic phenomena have treated ethnic groups as units of population distinguished by characteristic cultural features or traits, such as language, religion, economy, locality origin, and biogenetic physical features.

Fredrik Barth and others have sharply criticized this approach in recent years for its inability to define any core cultural features that consistently provide a means for distinguishing between ethnic groups.[17] This is a critical problem, since the model seeks to use these core cultural traits as a means for identifying a cultunit or ethnic group, primarily for the purpose of cross-cultural comparison with other cultunits. Ethnic change is seen as the attrition or alteration of these core cultural traits. It is not surprising that "religion" is listed as simply one more of the traits on the cultural grocery list—the *Oxford English Dictionary* reveals that the early connotation of *ethnic* meant "heathen" to Western English speakers, while the Greek origin of the term simply refers to "people" or "nation." Discussion in this approach is generally limited to cross-cultural comparison of these discrete "culture units" or their traits, and often overlooks such important issues as ethnogenesis (how new ethnic groups form), inter-ethnic relations, and the social organization of ethnic groups.

In his classic study, E. R. Leach demonstrated that the Kachin people in highland Burma, although often identified as a single people or distinctive ethnic group, could not be said to be a discrete unit living within the same society, speaking the same language, or having the same culture.[18] The ethnic identity of the Kachin could be understood only by reference to their political and social opposition to the Shan, another group with whom they interacted. The manipulation of their ethnic identities by individuals in different social situations was also problematic for this approach to ethnic identification, which focused mainly on the distinct cultural features of a group.

> Differences between groups become differences in trait inventories; the attention is drawn to the analysis of cultures, not of ethnic organization. The dynamic relationship between groups will then be depicted in acculturation studies of the kind that have been attracting decreasing interest in anthropology, though their theoretical inadequacies have never been seriously discussed.[19]

The identity of the Hui is problematic under a model that emphasizes cultural criteria. If we examine the Hui with reference to the 4 Stalinist criteria, we find the following discrepancies: The Hui do not share a common language, but speak the dialect of the area where they live; they do not live in a common locality, but are distributed throughout China in rural and urban areas, in large and small concentrations; they do not share a common economic life, as their employment ranges from peasant farmers, to small business people, to government cadres; and, finally, they do not share a common psychological makeup or culture, as there are Hui who maintain traditional Islamic customs, Hui who are atheist Communist Party members, and many young urban Hui who have ceased to follow any Islamic customs traditionally associated with being Hui.

It is evident that more factors are involved in the state's recognition of the Hui people than language, economy, locality, or culture. Cultural factors alone are inadequate consistently to distinguish the Hui as a minority people. In addition to linguistic distinctives, Fei emphasizes the historical background of a group for determining nationality status.[20] If the historical descent of modern Hui from foreign Muslim ancestors is considered a crucial determinant in their identification, then it becomes important to ask why the southeastern Hui lineages were so late in being recognized (see Chapter 6). No other Hui group in China can lay claim to as much historical evidence for descent from foreign Muslims as the Ding, Guo, and Jin lineages of Fujian province. If historical tradition is the basis for national identification, then these Hui have more claim to nationality status than other more conservative and religious Hui in the northwest, who have little written record of their foreign Muslim ancestry.

Finally, the inclusion as Hui of the aforementioned Muslims who culturally belong to the Tibetan, Dai, Bai, Yi, and Mongolian peoples certainly indicates that the Hui category could not be based on Stalin's 4 criteria. In this, and I would argue, every national identification decision, political factors came into play. It was expedient to enlist the Hui's and other groups' support at the very founding of the People's Republic. Clearly, a cultural theory of ethnic identification, whether the Stalinist or cultunit approach, is inadequate to account for the Hui as a distinctive ethnic group, or their historical continuity and wide diversity. The leaders of the Chinese Communist Party had other reasons for accepting some groups such as the Hui, and rejecting others, such as the Chuanqing Blacks or the Sherpas.

It is clear, however, that the Chinese state is not interested in multiplying its minority nationalities. If it had been fully committed to a cultural approach as portrayed in the Soviet Stalinist model, it would not have hesitated to increase its number of recognized minority nationalities to more than 100, as in the case of the USSR. Instead, in China, we find a much greater commitment to the evolutionary hypothesis within Marxist theory, a stronger linking between class and ethnicity. Walker Connor has documented that, in Leninist-Marxist theory, national difference should fade with the loss of class distinction.[21] The Bolsheviks, however, were willing to allow this process to take its time, and to encourage national sentiment strategically for the sake of the revolution. The evolution into a socialist society would take much longer. Chinese social thinkers were heavily influenced by stage evolutionary theory, particularly as represented in the writings of the American anthropologist Lewis Henry Morgan, who in his famous 1878 treatise, *Ancient Society,* described in his first chapter, entitled the "Ethnical Period," the development of society from savagery, to barbarism, and then to civilization.[22] Tong Enzheng, the Sichuanese anthropologist and museologist, criticized Chinese anthropology's heavy reliance, almost reverence, for this theory of societal evolution:

> Because of the esteem in which both Marx and Engels held [Morgan's] works, and especially because Engels, in *The Origin of the Family, Private Property, and the State,* affirmed many of his views, there has been a tendency among scholars to mistakenly equate his positions with specific positions taken by Marx and Engels, positions which themselves were mistakenly equated with the fundamental principle of Marxism. As a result, Morgan's most representative work, *Ancient Society,* has been canonized, and for the past 30 years has been regarded as something not to be tampered with. . . . therefore, to cast any doubt on it would be to cast doubt on Marxism itself.[23]

The anthropological enterprise in China became one of proving Morgan to be right, over and over again, through the examination of minorities as representatives of earlier forms of society, "living fossils" of savagery and barbarism.[24] The Han, as representative of "higher" forms of civilization, were thought to be clearly more evolved, and were to lead the way for minorities to follow. As if to underline the continued dominance of this theory, Fei Xiaotong presented a 1988 Tanner lecture in Hong Kong, entitled "Plurality and Unity in the Configuration of the Chinese Nationality," which was later published in the *Beijing University Journal.* In the article, Fei traces the rise of the Han people from multi-ethnic origins prior to the Qin dynasty, and their almost unilineal descent down to the present day, despite absorbing and being conquered by various foreign tribes and nations. In the following statements, Fei reveals his commitment to this stage developmentalist view, with the Han as the most evolved:

> The first step of this gigantic process was the coming into being of the Hua Xia group; the second the formation of the nation of the Han, which meant that the nucleus evolved and became enlarged. The unification of Central China by the Qin Empire was the last step which completed the development of the Han community into a nationality entity (*minzu*). . . . As soon as it

came into being, the Han nationality became a nucleus of concentration. Its people radiated in all directions into the areas around it and, centripetally, absorbed them into their own groups and made them a part of themselves. . . . As the non-Han rulers' regimes were mostly shortlived, one minority conqueror was soon replaced by another, and eventually all were assimilated into the Han.[25]

Under the section entitled "The Han Received New Blood from the Northern Nationalities," Fei describes the ethnogenesis of the Han 2,000 years ago:

The Han magnified themselves by taking from other groups, while the Qiang [a Tibeto-Tangut nomadic people] factually gave out so that other groups could grow. . . . Such densely intermingled habitation makes it possible for some Han to be melted into the local ethnic groups; but it is mainly for Han groups, who have infiltrated into non-Han communities, to work as the centripetal force around which to build a unified entity participated in by various groups.[26]

The vast technical superiority of the Han, Fei argues, led to the almost automatic assimilation of the various non-Han peoples, and supports the continued policy of national unification (*minzu tuanjie*, or *ronghe*) promoted by the Chinese state today:

What, then, has made the Han a nucleus with such centripetal force? The main factor, in my view, has been their agricultural economy. Once a nomad tribe made its entrance into the plain and found itself in the midst of the careful, orderly society of the farmers, it would eventually throw itself all too voluntarily into the embrace of the Han. . . . But as the national minorities generally are inferior to the Han in the level of culture and technology indispensable for the development of modern industry, they would find it difficult to undertake industrial projects in their own regions, their advantage of natural resources notwithstanding. . . . Therefore, our principle is for the better developed groups to help the underdeveloped ones by furnishing economic and cultural aids.[27]

Fei Xiaotong's understanding of ethnic change and national identity is informed by a strong commitment to Stalinist-Leninist nationality policy, based on Morgan's theory of stage-development evolutionism, and Engel's prediction of the withering away of class and national identity with the removal of private property. While there are many nationalities in China, the Han are so defined as to be in the cultural and technical vangaurd, the manifest destiny of all the minorities. While many younger scholars, like Tong Enzheng, are beginning to challenge the dominance of the Marxist-Stalinist-Morganian paradigm, it still heavily influences the discourse of nationalism in China, state policy, and social practice.

SHIFTING HUI BOUNDARIES: THE CIRCUMSTANTIALIST APPROACH. In response to a cultunit approach that portrays ethnic identity as posited in a distinct corpus of cultural traits that may be shaped or assimilated, an alternative theory focuses on the socioeconomic and political circumstances influencing a group's identity. This "circumstantialist"[28] or "functional-ecological"[29] model sees ethnicity as a dependent variable, created and controlled by a combination of external instrumental interests and strategies, and investing it with potential for action and mobilization. Ethnicity, portrayed as "reactive,"[30] is regarded as dependent on such single-value explanatory factors as the environment,[31] economics,[32] politics,[33] and class.[34] Culture, central to the earlier cultunit paradigm, is now treated as tertiary to ethnicity. Cultural symbols are seen as justifying interest groups and often easily manipulated to rationalize identity.[35]

Pillsbury finds this situational approach to ethnicity most useful in her detailed study of Hui in Taiwan who migrated from divergent ecological and socioeconomic circumstances throughout China.[36] In her analysis, Pillsbury concentrates on the "emergence, maintenance and disintegration of boundaries between Hui and Han and on the ultimate question of acculturation and assimilation."[37] She finds continued identity but acculturation to Han customs among the "Hui-Hui."[38] This continued identity is a result of their maintaining the "Hui way of life," emphasizing descent from Arab ancestors, and thus possessing "Arab blood."[39] One group of Hui, however, known as the "Taiwanese Muslims" (seventeenth-century Hui migrants, see Chapter 6), have almost completely lost any Hui, or Islamic, ethnic identity; "For most, assimilation has been almost complete."[40] In this case, the boundaries separating Han and Hui, Muslim and non-Muslim, have almost totally disintegrated.

While a circumstantialist approach has helped isolate the phenomenological and practical usage of ethnicity in real-life situations, when taken alone it has serious limitations. This is particularly the case when applied to the Hui. Ethnic identity is not always instrumental; it often possesses a power of its own that the actors may or may not be able to use to their own advantage. A circumstantialist view fails to account for the central place these powerful, enduring ideas of identity—what Shils terms "primordial" loyalties[41]—have for the Hui in China, as well as for other ethnic groups. Michael Fischer describes the "id-like" power of ethnicity,

> the paradoxical sense that ethnicity is something reinvented and reinterpreted in each generation by each individual, something over which he or she lacks control. Ethnicity is not something that is simply passed on from generation to generation, taught and learned; it is something dynamic, often unsuccessfully repressed or avoided. It can be potent even when not consciously taught; it is something that institutionalized teaching easily makes chauvinist, sterile, and superficial, something that emerges in full—often liberating—flower only through struggle.[42]

This fundamental aspect of identity is particularly important for groups that have maintained an identity for centuries despite intense periods of persecution. A situationalist theory, taken alone, cannot account for why groups like the Hui in late Qing China, or Jews in Spain prior to World War II, refused to renounce their ethnoreligious identity when it was in their best interest to do so. Despite prolonged ethnic persecution and ethnocide, these people remained ethnic, often by choice. While there is evidence of factional strife between different Hui communities during these periods of social upheaval, there is little to suggest that the Hui denied or rejected their identity.

A further limitation of this functional approach is the assumption that ethnic identity is a matter of rational choice that actors are free to assume, discard, or manipulate. Worsley argues that a situational approach removes the ethnic groups from the field of power and social relations.[43] An approach that assumes ethnic identity is always utilitarian fails to account for the fact that ethnic groups often have little control over their identification by others. Government policy in many cases determines who is defined in ethnic terms, and the state often dictates who may register as such.

Moreover, O'Brien,[44] following Wolf,[45] suggests that Barth's "functional-ecological" approach still takes the bounded unit as the basis for analysis, undervaluing the connections between groups and social relations. The theory takes us no farther in determining the expanding and contracting nature of ethnicity—how people can have articulated hierarchies of identity adopted in different social situations, or maintain multiple selves. The ability of the Hui to be radically different in the expression of their identity across China, and yet continue to identify themselves by the same ethnic designation is difficult to explain with an approach that takes a bounded unit as the basis for analysis.

Finally, the theories discussed above fail to make a distinction between a group's subjective self-perception of itself as an ethnic group, and the state's role in objectifying that identity, through conferring nationality status, or contesting the group's ethnicity, by refusing recognition. There are many cases of groups in China who perceive themselves as ethnic, and seek nationality status, such as the Chinese Jews, Sherpas, Khmer, Ku Cong, and Boat People, yet whom the state has continued to deny. Heberer reports that, in the early 1980s when many groups reapplied for nationality recognition, in Guizhou province alone, over 900,000 persons petitioned to be identified as nationalities, including the Chuanqing Blacks discussed above who Fei Xiaotong argued in the 1950s had been ineligible.[46] It is this dynamic interplay between self- and state-definition and contested identities that is crucial to our understanding of ethnic nationalism in China.

TOWARD A DIALOGICAL INTERPRETATION. Barth's "circumstantialist" approach has helped us understand how ethnicity is manipulated and altered under varying socioeconomic and political situations. It has been less useful in clarifying the persistence of ethnicity, the attachment a group has to a certain idea of common identity and loyalty. Charles Keyes has argued persuasively that this primordial loyalty stems from a group's basic agreement upon and attachment to an idea of shared descent, which constitutes the basis of an ethnic group's identity.[47] Yet these loyalties only become explicit, salient, and empowered in the context of social relations—in dialogical interaction with sociopolitical context. Just as the Self is often defined in terms of the Other,[48] so ethnic groups coalesce in the context of relation and opposition. Similarly, Marcus and Fischer have argued that cultural identity is established through a process of social and political "negotiation," continuously changing, depending on relations of power and hierarchy.[49] In a dialogical approach to ethnicity, social relations of power become the focus of attention, while both the symbolic and instrumental aspects of ethnicity, its enduring and mutable nature, are taken seriously.

In dialectical theory, the cultural traits of an ethnic group, such as language, religion, dress, and location, may take on a primordial quality if they become fundamental "markers" or "charters" of one's shared descent.[50] These cultural markers become defined and significant to a group's ethnicity in the process of social interaction with other groups, acting like "operational sorting devices."[51] "While ethnic groups are based fundamentally on the ideas of shared descent," Keyes proposes, "they take their particular form as a consequence of the structure of intergroup relations."[52] In this approach, ethnic change is not an alteration or manipulation of cultural traits but an ongoing dialectical process that results from tensions arising between social contexts and cultural meanings. Change is often precipitated by radical shifts in the political-economic contexts in which people live.[53] Realignments in the structural oppositions distinguishing two ethnic groups may not necessarily mean assimilation of one group by another. Assimilation is viewed as the "reduction of cultural distance" between competing groups, rather than the loss of one's ethnic identity.[54]

While Keyes has emphasized the dialectical process of ethnic adaptation involved in making shared ideas of ethnic identity salient for changing social contexts, I argue that, for the Hui in China, the dialogue with government policy plays a privileged role in the socioeconomic arena, exerting a large influence on ethnic change and identity.[55] In expansive nation-states faced with the task of administering macro-regions inhabited by competing minority nationalities, the importance of power relations and shifting government policy in influencing ethnic identity must be further explored.[56] Recent attempts to resolve the primordial/ circumstantial antinomy have sought to focus on practice[57] and interplay, without specific attention to the role of the nation-state in often creating and institutionalizing ethnic identities. As John Comaroff suggests, in the high-stakes game of contestation over national identity in modern nation-states, ethnicity can be compared to totemic relations, which often serve as categories of relation. "In as much as collective social identity always entails some form of communal self-definition," Comaroff argues, "it is invariably founded on a marked opposition between 'we' and 'other/s'; identity, that is, is a *relation* inscribed in culture."[58]

In China, nationality status marks one group from another, and is stamped on one's identity card. Like class, nationality in China objectifies social relations and modes of production, in that some minorities are given certain privileges and encouraged to maintain cultural and economic niches.[59] In China one may regard oneself as a member of an ethnic group, such as the Chinese Jews, but unless that group is recognized as a minority nationality by the state, one is denied the privileges accorded to certain minorities, such as the allowance to have more than one child and subsidized food purchases. Conversely, even if one does not regard oneself as ethnic, but is a member of a nationality designated by the state, such as the Manchu, one may be stigmatized by an identity stamped on one's work card one might not want. This may have been especially onerous during radical periods when Manchus were singled out as being feudal remnants of the oppressive Qing Empire. This dialogical interaction between ethnic and national identity has led to the invention of some identities, the resurgence of others, and the loss of many. Though it was once thought that ethnicity would quickly fade in authoritarian Marxist-Leninist states like China or Russia through Sinicization or Russification campaigns that sought to wipe out ethnic difference as another manifestation of fuedal class distinctions, the recent resurgence of ethnic identities along national lines, some of which were once thought artificial or imposed by the state, calls for more dynamic interpretations of identity in these nation-states.[60] The Hui case makes an important contribution to our understanding of the dialogic and dialectical nature of ethnic identity and state policy.

Ethnic identities in the modern world became particularly salient with the decline of the empires and the rise of the nation-state. E. K. Francis, in his extensive and profound analysis, *Interethnic Relations*, was one of the first to argue that the rise of ethnic identities and interethnic conflict was a phenomenon of the modern nation-state—as nation-states were built on the ashes of former empires, decidedly ethnic identities became more meaningful for social interaction and discourse.[61] David Maybury-Lewis, in his discussion of ethnicity in plural societies, has argued that it was the French Revolution's ideal of equality and participation in governance that formed the basis for the idea of the modern nation-state.[62] It was precisely these notions of identity and participation that the French elite later drew upon in World War I in order to mobilize the peasantry, who had previously never really thought of themselves as "French."[63] Even though Rousseau himself would have opposed the recognition of ethnic groups for fear that they would interfere with individual representation, "the social pact," which Rousseau argued "established equality among all citizens," allowed for its possibility.[64] Hobbes's famous dictum, "Nature hath made men so equal,"[65] was couched in the awareness of the differences separating them, which he encouraged the state to resolve without the necessity for war as a final means of adjudicating inequity and exploitation. The recognition of equality rests on the admission of difference.

Lloyd Fallers, one of the few anthropologists to attempt the "anthropology of the nation-state," notes: "The logic of populistic nationalism . . . encourages scrutiny to discover and eradicate diversity and thus exacerbates diversity."[66] "Since sovereignty in the modern nation-state is vested in the people, rather than in a monarch legitimated by descent or religious charisma," Charles Keyes perceptively argues, "the subjects of the modern nation-state must be integrated into the people."[67] Ernest Gellner proposes that "nationalism engenders nations, not the other way around."[68] It is culture or, I propose, cultural expression, that is manipulated and invented for the sake of nationalist interests, either the state's or those of the community in question, as Gellner argues:

Dead languages can be revived, traditions invented, quite fictitious pristine pur-
ities restored. But this culturally creative, fanciful, positively inventive aspect
of nationalist ardour ought not to allow anyone to conclude, erroneously,
that nationalism is a contingent, artificial, ideological invention, which might
not have happened, if only those damned busy-body interfering European
thinkers, not content to leave well alone, had not concocted it and fatefully
injected it into the bloodstream of otherwise viable political communities.
The cultural shreds and patches used by nationalism are often arbitrary historical inventions. Any old shred and patch would have served as well. But in no
way does it follow that the principle of nationalism itself, as opposed to the
avatars it happens to pick up for its incarnations, is itself in the least contingent and accidental.[69]

This may be going to the extreme. If culture did not exist, Gellner
seems to suggest, nationalist movements would have had to invent it. As
I shall argue below, these "inventions of tradition"[70] are better understood as negotiations over, and reinterpretations of, symbolic representations of identity—an unceasing process that becomes particularly
salient when the nation-state takes upon itself the task of legislating
national identity.

One's identity becomes particularly critical during modern state
incorporation, where citizenship may be imposed rather than sought.
In this case, it is not so much actual participation in the government process that is crucial as it is the *idea* that it should take place in the modern nation-state. The precise nature of the group itself becomes a matter
for negotiation and genesis.

The vast majority of these instances of ethnogenesis occur in the context of incorporation into and identity within a larger nation-state,
often dominated by another ethnic group. These ethnic identities form
and reform according to articulated asymmetries of interaction with the
particular oppositional power in question. Sir Edmund Leach was the
first anthropologist to argue that ethnic identity is formed as the result
of power oppositions: The Kachin in Highland Burma only acted ethnically when in opposition to the Shans.[71] Evans-Pritchard's classic
study of the Nuer determined the unique expansive-contractive nature
of hierarchical segmentary lineages among acephelous nomadic societies. When the Nuer were confronted with an outside power, they
unified and organized to a high degree of political complexity in order to

respond to the challenge. When the threat subsided, they diversified and atomized.[72]

Ethnic identities are often seen to coalesce and crystallize in the face of higher-order oppositions. In *From Empire to Nation*, Rupert Emerson provides a perceptive definition of the nation as "the largest community which, when the chips are down, effectively commands men's loyalty."[73] In the modern era, it is often the nation-state apparatus itself to which ethnic groups find themselves in opposition. By agreeing to articulate their identities along the contours shaped by national identification policies and censuses, ethnic groups demonstrate their desire to form coalitions at the highest possible level of nationality in order to interact as as powerful a collectivity as possible within the state apparatus.

HAN NATIONALISM AND THE CREATION OF NATIONALITIES IN CHINA

For he might have been a Roosian,
A French, or Turk, or Proosian,
Or perhaps Italian!
But in spite of all temptations
To belong to other nations,
He remains an Englishman!
— *W. S. Gilbert*, H. M. S. Pinafore

While research on the rise of Russian nationalism has been popular in Soviet studies since the 1970s, both by foreign and Russian scholars,[74] as yet no larger studies of the creation of Han nationalism have emerged— mainly because it is assumed, by Sinologists trained in the dominant tradition, that "Han" is generally equal to "Chinese"—a tradition created and promoted by the current regime in power. It is the lack of fit of "Russian" with "Soviet" that has led to so much discussion regarding Russian nationalism in Soviet studies.[75] This has not been considered in studies of Chinese nationalism, which generally ignore the creation of the Han majority in favor of the larger question of Chinese identity. Few have questioned how the Han became the 94-percent majority of China. Perhaps, the traditional Confucian preoccupation with order and harmony in a society held tenuously together by proper relationships may be one reason why these categories have never been challenged. The very Confucian practice of the "rectification of names" (*zheng ming*) is of primary concern to the Chinese ethnographers: Once the Han and all the minority nationalities have been identified or named, order is restored, and all is well in the world. As François Thierry has noted:

> The importance given in China to the harmony between the thing and its name is well known: every name must agree perfectly with the profound nature of what is named. Thus the graphic classification of the name of each type of Barbarian under a radical marking his animal nature is an ontological necessity. So one finds in the ideograms designating some Barbarians the root "reptile" (the Mo, the Wei, the Lao, etc.), the root "worm" (the Ruan, the Bie, the Dan, the Man, etc.), and above all the root "dog" (the Di, the Yan, the Qiang, the Tong, etc.); some may be written equally with the root "dog" or the root "reptile" (the Wei, the Lao).[76]

Though these root graphs were removed from the names of the minority nationalities after the founding of the People's Republic, the corrected labels themselves crystallized as official designations. Some were inappropriate, as the Hani call themselves Akha, the Miao call themselves Hmong, and some Naxi also go by Moso,[77] and others, such as the Hui, had a wider meaning, indicating more than one nationality. These designations assist the Chinese state in its traditional role of bringing order out of chaos, and the Confucian practice of rectifying names. It is not surprising that Engels's *Origin of the Family, Private Property, and the State* is so popular in China, since it is clear in this work that the state's primary role is to invoke order out of conflict.

The notion of *Han ren* (Han person) has existed for many centuries to designate those descendants of the Han dynasty which had its beginnings in the Wei River Valley. As noted above, the term narrowed under the Mongols to refer to inhabitants of North China. However, I submit that the notion of *Han zu* or *Han min* (Han nationality) is an entirely modern phenomenon—it arises with the shift from empire to nation, as argued above. While the concept of a Han person certainly existed, the notion of a unified Han nationality that occupies 94 percent of China's population gained its greatest popularity under Dr. Sun Yat-sen. The leader of the Nationalist movement that toppled the last empire of China, Dr. Sun was most certainly influenced by strong currents of Japanese nationalism during his long-term stay there. Sun argued that the ruler-subject relationship which had persisted throughout China's dynastic history would need to be fundamentally transformed if a true nationalist movement were to sweep China and engender support among all its peoples. More practically, Dr. Sun needed a way to mobilize all Chinese against the imperial rule of the Qing, a dynasty founded by a northeastern collection of tribes who became known as the Manchu.[78] By invoking the argument that the majority of the people in China were Han, Sun effectively found a symbolic metaphorical opposition to the Manchu to which the vast majority of peoples in China would easily rally. He was one of the earliest and perhaps best practitioners of "primordial politics."

FROM NATIONALITIES TO NATIONALISM. Dr. Sun Yat-sen advocated the idea that there were "5 Peoples of China" (*wuzu gonghe*): the Han, Man (Manchu), Meng (Mongolian), Zang (Tibetan), and Hui (a term that included all Muslims in China, now divided into the Uigur, Kazak, Hui, and so forth). This recognition of the 5 Peoples of China served as the main platform for his Nationalist Revolution, which overthrew the Qing Empire and established the first "People's Republic." One must have peoples if there is to be a peoples' revolution. The critical link between Sun Yat-sen's 5-peoples policy and his desire to unify all of China is made crystal clear in his discussion of nationalism, the first of his *Three Principles of the People* (*Sanmin zhuyi*). While Sun recognized 5 peoples of China, his ultimate goal was still assimilationist, to unify and fuse all the peoples into one Chinese race:

> The Chinese people have shown the greatest loyalty to family and clan with the result that in China there have been family-ism and clan-ism but no real nationalism. Foreign observers say that the Chinese are like a sheet of loose sand. . . . The unity of the Chinese people has stopped short at the clan and has not extended to the nation. . . . China, since the Ch'in and Han dynasties, has been developing a single state out of a single race, while foreign countries have developed many states from one race and have included many nationalities within one state. . . . The Chinese race totals four hundred million people; for the most part, the Chinese people are of the Han or Chinese race with common blood, common language, common religion, and common customs—a single, pure race.[79]

Stalin's 4 nationality criteria are already seen to have had a substantial parallel with and influence on this creation of Han nationalism. The overriding purpose of the rhetoric is clear: a call for the unity of the Chinese nation based on a common charter of descent in opposition to foreign powers. While the idea of the unity of the Chinese state and/or country certainly existed before, it was the stress upon cultural and national unity, with the rising importance of the Han *nation*, that was a crucial component of Chinese nationalism in the early twentieth century.

The assimilationist aspect of this early Nationalist policy was further promoted in 1939 by Chiang Kai-shek when he presided over the 1st National Congress of the Chinese Hui People's National Salvation Association in Chongqing. At that time, he declared that all non-Han groups within China are sub-varieties of an ancient Chinese race.[80] This policy was more fully stated in Chiang's treatise *China's Destiny*:

> As to the so-called Mohammedans [Huijiaotu] in present-day China, they are for the most part actually members of the Han clan [*minzu*] who embraced Islam. Therefore, the difference between the Hans and Mohammedans is only in religion and different habits of life. In short, our various clans actually belong to the same nation, as well as to the same racial stock. Therefore, there is an inner factor closely linking the historical destiny of common existence and common sorrow and joy of the whole Chinese nation. That there are five peoples designated in China [i.e., Chinese, Manchus, Mongols, Tibetans, Mohammedans] is not due to differences in race or blood, but to religion and geographical environment. In short, the differentiation among China's five peoples is due to regional and religious factors, and not to race or blood. This fact must be thoroughly understood by all our fellow countrymen.[81]

Under this policy, the Hui were not considered a separate *minzu* (people, nationality) but a religious group with special characteristics and were to be referred to as *Hui jiaoren* or *Hui jiaotu*. The name of the Hui People's (*Huimin*) National Salvation Association was changed to China Muslim (*Huijiao*) National Salvation Association in 1939, and the Hui (and other Muslims grouped with them) have been subsequently dealt with as a religious group by the Nationalist Government in Taiwan.[82] Interestingly, both the rationale and end purpose of Sun Yat-sen's and Chiang Kai-shek's nationality discourses were the same: national unity.

From Sun Yat-sen's earlier policy of 5 peoples we see the basis of the later Communist minority-nationality platform.

The origins of Sun's 5-peoples policy are unclear. It is not surprising that he made use of the term *minzu* (民族 nation, nationality, people, ethnic group—all legitimate English glosses of the multi-vocal Chinese term). *Minzu* is not a native Chinese term—it derives from the Japanese term for people or nation, *minzoku* (民族). According to the nationality volume of the *Chinese Complete Encyclopaedia*, the term was introduced to China in 1903 by the "capitalist Swiss-German political theorist and legal scholar, Johannes Kaspar Bluntschli."[83] Whether the term had gained earlier currency in China is not important. What is critical is that it proved particularly useful to Sun Yat-sen in his efforts to engender support for a nationalist movement.

It is also not at all surprising that Dr. Sun should turn to the use of the all-embracing idea of the Han as the national group, which included all the regional peoples and Sino-linguistic speech communities. Sun Yat-sen was Cantonese, raised as an overseas Chinese in Hawaii. As one who spoke little Mandarin, and with few connections in North China, he would have easily aroused traditional northern suspicions of southern radical movements extending back to the Song dynasty (tenth century), which were, of course, well known to him. This recurring historical pattern and the traditional antipathy between the Cantonese and northern peoples would have posed an enormous barrier to his promotion of a nationalist movement. Dr. Sun found an ingenious way to rise above deeply embedded north-south ethnocentrisms. The use and perhaps invention of the term *Han minzu* was a brilliant attempt to mobilize other non-Cantonese, especially northern Mandarin speakers, and the powerful Zhejiang and Shanghainese merchants, into one overarching national group against the Manchu and other foreigners threatening China during the unstable period following the Unequal Treaties. The Han were seen to stand in opposition to the Others on their borders, the Manchu, Tibetan, Mongol, and Hui, as well as the Western imperialists. By distinguishing these "Others" in their midst, the Nationalists cultivated the imagined identity of the "We" Han, as opposed to the "They" minorities and foreigners. Hobsbawm notes that this is a typical practice in the legitimization of new nations through the authentication of them-

Samuel Zwemer and fellow China Inland Mission Protestant missionaries read Arabic Christian pamphlets to Hui in Gansu (1933). Pickens's note reads: "A Zwemer tract in Arabic, its author and ready listeners." Photo: Pickens. Courtesy of Harvard-Yenching Library.

Owen Lattimore, intrepid explorer and student of Inner Asia, 1930s. Original caption reads: "Mr. Lattimore and the T'ung-kan or Chinese Mohammedan [Hui] commanding the Chinese patrol which arrested him at the frontier of Chinese Turkistan. Mr. Lattimore is wearing the half-Chinese costume and Chinese shoes in which he travelled a great part of the time. The officer, for the sake of the photograph, borrowed a pair of boots belonging to Mr. Lattimore, as well as his revolver and cartridge belt."
Courtesy of the Peabody Museum, Harvard University, and reproduced with the permission of David Lattimore.

selves.[84] In Benedict Anderson's poignant terms, Dr. Sun was engaged in "stretching the short tight skin of the nation over the gigantic body of the empire."[85] The "imagined" Han nationality that was created, like Victor Mudimbe's "invention of Africa," through the objectivizing of the "Other" led to the invention and legitimization of the Self.[86] By drawing together under the collective imagination of one Han people, the Nationalists thought they could prevent the total dismemberment of the Chinese state. Neither the Nationalists in Taiwan nor the Communists on the mainland have since challenged this generic ethnonym; it proved too fundamentally useful. It is surprising, however, that this concept of the Han as one ethnic group occupying 94 percent of China's population has never been seriously challenged by non-Chinese scholars.[87]

PEOPLES FOR THE PEOPLE'S REPUBLIC. The nationality policy of the People's Republic of China was formulated during the 1930s for the strategic purpose of enlisting the support of the peoples disgruntled by Qing rule and Chiang Kai-shek's nationality policy, which deemphasized ethnic difference in favor of the unity of all peoples as members of the Chinese race. This policy was formed most fully on the Long March.

During the Long March, the Chinese Communist leaders became acutely aware of the vibrant ethnic identity of the Muslims and other peoples they encountered on their arduous 371-day trek from the southeast to the northwest which led them for 124 days through the most concentrated minority areas. Edgar Snow, and the recent chronicler Harrison Salisbury, graphically describe the desperate plight of the Long Marchers, harried on one side by the Japanese and the Nationalists and on the other by the "fierce barbarian tribesmen."[88] The fathers of the yet-to-be-born Chinese nation were faced with extermination or making promises of special treatment to the minorities, specifically including the Miao, Yi (Lolo), Tibetan, and Hui. The first Hui autonomous county was set up in the 1930s in Tongxin, southern Ningxia, as a demonstration of the early Communists' goodwill toward the Hui.

In a chapter entitled "Moslem and Marxist," Snow recorded several encounters with militant conservative Hui Muslims and subsequent strong lectures to 8th Route Army troops to respect Hui customs lest

they offend them and provoke conflicts. Mao[89] issued an appeal to the
northwest Hui to support the Communists' cause, even mentioning the
renaissance of Turkey under Ataturk as an example for China's Muslims.[90] One slogan that Snow observed posted by Hui soldiers training
under the Communist 15th Army Corps was: "Build our own anti-
Japanese Mohammedan Red Army."[91] Perhaps Chairman Mao was
more sensitive to the Muslim issue since his brother had been killed in
Xinjiang in 1942 due to interethnic and intra-Muslim factionalism.[92]
Later Party documents (*Dangshi wenshi ziliao*) that have come to light
from the Long March reveal that Chairman Mao explicitly promised
self-determination to the minorities until the year 1937, offering them
not only privileges but also the right to secede, as is still the case in the
Soviet constitution. However, that right was withdrawn by 1940 and
instead limited regional "autonomy" was offered.[93] The transition in Chinese terminology from "self-determination" (*zi jue* 自决, or "self-rule,"
zi zhu 自主) to "autonomy" (*zi zhi* 自治) is slight, but for the minorities
it represented a major shift in policy. Unlike the Soviet Union, where
requests for Baltic and Central Asian secession must now be taken seriously because that right was written into the constitution, any such
request in China is regarded as criminal. As Walker Connor noted, "a
request that prerevolutionary promises be honored became counterrev-
olutionary and reactionary."[94]

Though the CCP promised autonomy, it quashed any illusions of
separatism, in hopes of preserving "national unity." The contradiction
between a policy that promotes both autonomy and assimilation is an
irony that continues to plague China's nationality policy. As June
Dreyer has observed:

> The Communist government of China may be said to have inherited a policy
> of trying to facilitate the demise of nationality identities through granting self-
> government to minorities. It has in fact been struggling with the conse-
> quences to this day.[95]

Although the Yan'an leaders gradually withdrew the promise of possible secession, the institution of national identities was carried out
shortly after the founding of the People's Republic. For the Hui, this
resolved a debate that had been going on since the 1920s over whether

they were a nationality or merely a religious community. While the debate over Hui identity within the Communist Party has never been published, several nationality scholars have confirmed that it raged throughout the years in Yan'an, with Hui cadres such as Ma Yin and Yang Jingren arguing that the Hui were a nationality and should be recognized as such, and Han scholars, such as Ya Hanzhang, disagreeing. Hui scholars have related to me the perhaps apocryphal story that Joseph Stalin, on first meeting Chairman Mao in Moscow, argued that the Hui should not be recognized as a nationality but only as Muslims. Mao, however, supposedly replied that the political necessity of enlisting Hui support for the establishment of the early People's Republic required their recognition as a nationality. Though the right to secede was never granted them, as it was to the nationalities in the Soviet Union, they did receive hard-earned recognition as a nationality by a Han-dominated government which was in need of their support. This, apparently, was enough.

After the founding of the PRC, the minority areas were brought under military control, awarded limited autonomy, and subjected to integrationist policies. Walker Connor has shown that the fundamental characteristic of Marxist-Leninist nationality policy and theory is its primary concern with nation building. The strategic importance attached to obtaining the support of the minorities lessened with the establishment of central authority—it was no longer necessary to promise or grant full autonomy. This dramatic policy shift due to changing power relations is strikingly revealed in a cable from the Central Party Propaganda Office of the New China News Agency to the Northwestern Branch Office, which has only recently come to light:

> On 20 October 1949, in document number 62, you reported the statement by Ma Gecai, 19th Army Corps Party Director, regarding the Communist Party's proposition: "Resolutely Oppose Great Han Chauvinism," and the slogan, "Nationality Self-Determination". ... Today the question of each minority's "self-determination" should not be stressed any further. In the past, during the period of civil war, for the sake of strengthening the minorities opposition to the Guomindang's [KMT] reactionary rule, we emphasized this slogan. This was correct at the time. But today the situation has fundamentally changed. The KMT's reactionary rule has been basically destroyed and the party leaders of the New China have already arisen. For the sake of completing our state's great purpose of unification, for the sake of opposing the

conspiracy of imperialists and other running dogs to divide China's nationality unity, we should not stress this slogan in the domestic nationality question and should not allow its usage by imperialists and reactionary elements
among various domestic nationalities. . . . . The Han occupy the majority population of the country; moreover, the Han today are the major force in
China's revolution. Under the leadership of the Chinese Communist Party,
the victory of China's peoples' democratic revolution mainly relied on the
industry of the Han people.[96]

In this one cable we see both the hegemonic role of the Han nationality and the declining importance of minority identity under the context of new power relations. While the idea of the nations was critical
to the founding of the People's Republic, the real autonomy of the
minority peoples was no longer necessary for garnering support. Once
it had gained complete control, the Party was free to coopt the leading
role over all the peoples, with the Han majority in the vanguard. This
method exactly follows Lenin's 3 "commandments" described by
Walker Connor for harnessing nationalism in a socialist state:

1. Prior to the assumption of power, promise to all national groups the right
   of self-determination (expressly including the right of secession), while
   proffering national equality to those who wish to remain within the state.
2. Following the assumption of power, terminate the fact—though not necessarily the fiction—of a right to secession, and begin the lengthy process of
   assimilation via the dialectical route of territorial autonomy for all compact
   national groups.
3. Keep the party centralized and free of all nationalist proclivities.[97]

The Chinese Communists were very effective in carrying out these
"commandments" as a means of solidifying power and control over
every aspect of national life in the early days of the PRC. As Vivienne
Shue has argued, in China the "Reach of the State" still pervades much
of life, and it is able to use nationality policy as one of its main avenues
of power.[98] Mayfair Yang has recently argued that, in China, the "contours" of power exercised by the state socialist economy infuse everyday
life and identity, perhaps much more than that of the state in a capitalist
welfare economy.[99] Nationality policy plays an important role in the
exercise of power in China and other authoritarian regimes. When
power is concentrated in the hands of a few, as Deleuze and Guattari per-

haps facetiously suggest, it becomes egg-like, a body without organs, and the nationalities are subsumed in the nationalism of one nation.[100] Claude Lefort has argued that the fundamental nature of totalitarianism in the modern era is the concentration of nationalism in the hands of one nationality:

> But if the image of the people is actualized, if a party claims to identify with it and to appropriate power under the cover of this identification, then it is the very principle of the distinction between the state and society, the principle of the difference between the norms that govern the various between types of relations between individuals, ways of life, beliefs and opinions, which is denied; and, at a deeper level, it is the very principle of a distinction between what belongs to the order to power, to the order of law, and to the order of knowledge which is negated. The economic, legal and cultural dimensions are, as it were, interwoven into the political. This phenomenon is characteristic of totalitarianism.[101]

Since the founding of the PRC, the fluctuation of Chinese policy depending on political shifts between right and left has been documented elsewhere.[102] China has moved radically between poles of pluralism and ethnocentric hegemonic repression, depending on the political winds. These shifts, of course, have had dramatic effects on the identities of the nationalities in question, and the expression of their ethnic identities. In the following chapters, I shall attempt to document the effects of these policies in the communities I studied, particularly since the 1978 policies of liberalization were initiated.

The fluctuations in former nationality policies and repudiation of former mistakes by the 1978 3rd Party Plenum, such as confusing class struggle with national conflict, was summarized trenchantly by a Yunnan Hui political scientist, Ma Weiliang, and worth quoting at length:

> Early in 1953, when our Party's Central Committee laid down the general line of the transitional period, it also laid down the following task in the work among minority nationalities during the transitional period: For the common cause of the reconstruction of our mother land, we must promote gradually political, economic, and cultural affairs among all minority nationalities; eliminate gradually actual inequalities left over by history among these nationalities; and help the backward nationalities stride into the ranks of advanced nationalities and gradually go through the transition to socialism. ... Chairman Mao placed the economic construction of minority national-

ity regions in the forefront in solving the nationality problem. However, due to the interference of the "left," the nationality problem was aggravated in the aspect of class struggle, and was ignored in the aspect of economic and cultural construction. . . . For instance, in our struggle against local nationalism in 1957, we magnified class struggle, accused some minority national cadres of attacking the party because they explained the true conditions in their regions and expressed the complaints and wishes of their people, and labeled them as local nationalists. We criticized proper national feelings, national desires, and demands as bourgeois nationalism. In 1962, the national conference on the work among the minority nationalities correctly summed up our experience and lessons drawn, and pointed out profoundly that . . . [we must] understand fully many inherent features of minority nationalities in the socialist period and the protracted nature of the existing national differences. . . . But later in 1964, under the domination of "left" deviation, we again vigorously criticized the so-called "right capitulationism" and "revisionism" in the national united front work, and refuted many of our good experiences. In particular, some comrades arbitrarily emphasized the viewpoint that national struggle was class struggle in essence. . . . During the Great Cultural Revolution, Lin Biao and the Gang of Four even confused national struggles in foreign countries with our domestic problem of minority nationalities, equated the nationality problem with the class problem, exaggerated the aspect of class struggle, artificially created large numbers of horrible, unjust, false, and wrong cases, and used the big stick of class struggle to attack and persecute many minority national cadres and the masses. They slandered minority national customs and habits and spoken and written languages as "four old things," replaced our work among the minority nationalities with class struggle, undermined very seriously the party's policy towards the minority nationalities and the economic cultural reconstruction in their regions, and caused serious calamities. This is an extremely bitter experience from which we learned a lesson.[103]

The recent return to pluralistic policies is excellent news for the 55 minorities who were recognized. But what about the over 350 other peoples who never were awarded nationality status? Now that more positive policies have been reestablished, nationality status is even more desired by these peoples. In this sense, the state *invented* nationality and institutionalized it for the 55 peoples that were recognized, while the remaining groups are legally prevented from organizing along ethnic lines, though informally many of them continue to attempt to do so (see Chapter 7).

That the state originally employed and still maintains a Stalinist cultural definition of nationality is very important for our understanding of how local ethnic communities responded to policies of incorporation. Whereas the original creation of national groups was a strategic temporary recognition of ethnic difference in order to solicit support in the revolutionary process,[104] it later led to the hardening of ethnic boundaries—the creation of identities, which were supposed to be only provisional. After reviewing the resurgence and reinterpretation of so-called traditions, Eric Hobsbawm emphasized their relevance

> to that comparatively recent historical innovation, the "nation," with its associated phenomena: nationalism, the nation-state, national symbols, histories and the rest. All these rest on exercises in social engineering which are often deliberate and always innovative. . . . the national phenomenon cannot be adequately investigated without careful attention to the "invention of tradition."[105]

Attention to the creation of culture has become a preoccupation since Hobsbawm and Ranger's important volume. What I am proposing is the examination of the unique process involved in the creation not only of culture, but of "cultures" by authoritarian regimes, as the case of the Hui so clearly reveals. While the ethnogenesis of new ethnic groups has been well documented by anthropologists, the role of the state in creating or legislating these groups for its purposes has been downplayed in favor of internal or socioeconomic factors. The invention and legitimation of Hui ethnicity provides an excellent example of modern ethnic identity in China and other authoritarian regimes.

DERIVATIVE DISCOURSES AND CHINESE TRADITIONAL NATIONALISM

I have discussed above the derived sources of modern Chinese nationalism, which included Western, Japanese, and Soviet influences in the middle of the nineteenth century when China had its doors forced open by the West. These modern theories of nationalist discourse interacted with traditional Chinese ideas of identity and ethnicity. While the Nationalists employed the borrowed term of *minzu* for people, or nationality, in traditional Chinese society the term for "people" was merely *ren* (human, or person). "Humanism," in Chinese, is simply defined as "the school of thought that is basic, or at the root of *ren*" (*ren ben zhuyi*). Peoples who are not a formal *minzu* in Chinese society, but subsumed under the state's formal designations, are still referred to as *ren*, for example, the Chinese Jews (Youtai *ren*), Cantonese (Guangdong *ren*), Hakka (Kejia *ren*), Ku Cong *ren*, and so on.

The most elemental notion of Chinese nationality, then, is "a person of China" (Zhongguo *ren*). Those who live in the land known as Zhongguo, the "Central Kingdom," are Chinese. What is at issue for Chinese nationality is the land, and those who dwell under the central authority of the Kingdom or State (*Guo*) of that land. Similarly, Thomas Heberer, in his recent book on minorities in China, finds the concept of "territory" to be central to traditional ideas of nationality. Citing an article from the Central Nationalities Institute Journal, which concluded that "all peoples who have at any time lived on the territory of what is today China" are Chinese, Heberer argues, "The European concept of nation defines 'nation' as the sum of the government plus its people, whereas the Chinese define nation as the historically legitimated territory plus the whole population."[106]

In a forthcoming volume, Clifford Geertz has proposed the term *country* as a more simple and basic concept by which many people understand their nationality.[107] Most people think of themselves as living in a certain locality within natural boundaries rather than as members of "nation-states," "nationalities," or other political entities. Nations rise and fall, but countries usually stay much the same, though the people in them may be under one administration or another. While this may not hold true for nomadic peoples who move between countries, or displaced persons who have adopted new identities, it is helpful for understanding Chinese notions of territorial identity.

It also helps to explain China's relations with her subject peoples and foreign countries. Tibet, in Chinese historiography, is always thought to have been part of China, and is therefore, still, a part of China. The same goes for Chinese ideas about Xinjiang, Yunnan, and Mongolia. Debate centers over when control over the land was established, and bears little relation to the identities, or the opinions, of the peoples therein. As Thomas Barfield has discussed with regard to the Han dynasty and the Hsiung-nu, peoples on China's frontier were considered equals until control was established over the *territory* in which these peoples moved.[108] It was only under the foriegn conquest dynasties of Liao, Mongol, and Manchu that domination over these border areas moved to the center of concern. Earlier Chinese ideas of the nation had less to do with territory than with civilization and hierarchy.

Central to earlier Chinese notions of identity and authority was the Confucian concept of hierarchy. The country was defined in terms of spatial hierarchy, with China at the center of the civilized world. The center defined the core of the nation, and the emperor's responsiblity for maintaining order and harmony at that center took precedence over conquest. While the country was important, it was viable only so long as the central moral authority maintained the Mandate of Heaven. The periphery, in a classic sociological paradigm outlined by Shils,[109] is defined by the center of Chinese society, and only bears importance in relation to that center. Border skirmishes, raids by nomads, and lack of control over China's periphery were of little concern to those in the capital, unless they threatened the security of the emperor and, by extension, the nation. Membership in that nation belonged to those who owed their allegiance to him, and could trace descent to the legendary Yellow Emperor, whose realm was in the heart of China, in the Wei River Valley, a tributary of the Yellow River.

François Thierry, in a fascinating recent article, outlines this progression of Chinese thought on national authority and identity:

> Traditional Chinese thought is based on two ideas, Order and Totality. Everything is one, and it is placed in a hierarchy, in a cosmic order, where its position is proportionate to its nature. ... Three conceptions of empire, and hence of minority, have guided the practice of the states that have followed one another in China: a traditional conception, based on a hierarchy of spaces, a military conception, deriving from the conquest dynasties, which were of nomadic origin, and a Jacobian conception, ending in its "socialist" avatar.[110]

Pamela Crossley, in a forthcoming article on ethnicity in early modern China, suggests that an important shift took place at the end of the Qing when racial theories of identity began to replace cultural and hierarchical ideas of space and civilization, perhaps precipitated by the Taiping Rebellion, which in turn had an influence on the ethnogenesis of peoples at the end of dynasty, particularly the Manchu and Mongol.[111] As people at the end of the Qing era began to construct their past in terms of genealogy, exposure to foreign nations and nationalism introduced a whole new discourse by which to conceptualize and imagine these emergent identities. The emphasis upon genealogy and history as criteria for ethnicity that Fei Xiaotong describes in his article "Ethnic Identification in China" indicates that this is still a valid means for legitimating one's ethnicity. As we shall see in Chapter 4, one community was recently admitted to membership in the Hui nationality by virtue of their genealogy alone: They possessed none of the Stalinist cultural traits listed above as requirements for nationality. The state recognized their claim to nationality because of race alone: physical proof of blood descent from foreign Muslim ancestors.

Sun Yat-sen wrote: "China since the Ch'in (Qin) and Han dynasties has been developing a single state out of a single race"; and Fei Xiaotong revealed his continued commitment to this belief when he wrote: "The Qin empire was the last step which completed the development of the Han community into a nationality. . . . As soon as it came into being the Han nationality became a nucleus of concentration." In these statements we see an uninterrupted vision of imagined national identity and myth of origin that is at once territorial, hierarchical, and racial. It is not surprising, then, that certain aspects of Morganian, Leninist, and Stalinist views of evolution and nationality were taken up with such vigor, and employed so rigorously in the identification of its peoples, at the founding of the People's Republic.

THE ETHNOGENESIS OF THE HUI: FROM MUSLIM TO MINORITY NATIONALITY

Official histories and minority nationality maps to the contrary, before their identification by the state in the 1950s, the Hui were not a *minzu*, a nationality, in the modern sense of the term. Like many other groups, the Hui emerged only in the transition from empire to nation-state. The people now known as the Hui are descended from Persian, Arab, Mongolian, and Turkish Muslim merchants, soldiers, and officials who settled in China from the seventh to fourteenth centuries and intermarried with local non-Muslim women. Largely living in isolated communities, the only thing that some but not all had in common was a belief in Islam. Until the 1950s in China, Islam was known simply as the "Hui religion" (*Hui jiao*)—believers in Islam were *Huijiao* believers. Until then, any person who was a believer in Islam was a "Hui religion disciple" (*Huijiao tu*). One was accepted into Hui communities and mosques simply on the basis of being a Muslim. If one stopped believing in Islam, one lost one's membership in that community of faith. Han could become Hui through conversion, and Hui could revert to being Han through apostasy. After the fall of the last empire and rise of nationalism in the first half of this century, the Hui emerged as one of several nationalities pressing for recognition. Through a dialogical process of self-examination and state-recognition, the Hui emerged fully as a nationality, a *minzu*, only after their institutionalization by the state. This recognition as a nationality has helped to objectify their ethnicity. Not that the Hui previously had no ethnic consciousness. Rather, prior to state recognition, Hui ethnic identity was localized and less fully articulated. Hui related to each other as fellow Muslims, not as *minzu*. Now that Hui national identity has been legitimated and legalized by the state, the Hui are beginning to objectify their identity, to think of themselves and relate to each other in inter-referential, ethnic terms.

Hui in China, no matter where one travels, now refer to themselves as the Hui people (Hui *minzu*). Hui are generally offended in China when asked if they believe in *Hui jiao*, the Hui religion, as they take great pride in being members of a world religion, the international Islamic *Umma*. Sometimes, however, less informed members of the community slip into old habits. I was amused when one of my Hui colleagues who was present at an interview corrected a wheat farmer and sideline rope maker in Wuzhong, central Ningxia: "No you are not a 'Hui religion disciple' (*Huijiao tu*)," he reprimanded, "you are a 'Hui person' (*Huimin*). Hui believe in Islam (*Yisilan jiao*), not their own Hui religion." I was even at times asked if I was a *Meiguo Hui hui* (an "American Hui") when locals mistook me for a Muslim, since, they reasoned, only a Muslim would be interested in Hui history. Nevertheless, the label *Hui nationality* is beginning to stick, particularly as participation in the ethnic group carries with it important practical benefits (see below).

These labels are becoming more and more accepted by the people as inclusive ethnonyms, stimulating further communication, exchange, and inter-referentiality between the so-called Hui communities.

Despite the continued diversity among these communities, a process of ethnogenesis has also brought them closer together, through dialogue with state policy and local traditions. Nationalization, as noted by Benedict Anderson, is assisted by the acceptance of the label *Hui*, increased "pan-Hui" interaction, and mandatory education in special state-sponsored Hui schools.[112] The Hui, of course, desire more political power through larger numbers, and they are beginning to argue for and experience the national unity of their people.

THE RESEARCH: IN SEARCH OF THE HUI

My reflections on the question of ethnic identity in China were guided by a feeling of ambiguity similar to what Michael Moerman experienced when confronted with the question: "Whom did you study in the field?"[113] After almost 3 years of fieldwork in China, I experienced great difficulty in attempting adequately to answer this question. I went to China in the fall of 1983 to begin study of the Hui, one of the 55 officially identified minority nationalities portrayed clearly in government nationality publications as one nationality with a long and uninterrupted history in China. Unlike many of the other minority nationalities of China, the Hui are distinguished negatively: They generally do not have their own language, peculiar dress, literature, music, or the other cultural inventories by which more "colorful" minorities are portrayed. As one Hui ethnologist put it to me, "We Hui don't sing, we don't dance, but we're still ethnic!" How was I to find, let alone describe in classical ethnographic fashion, this people who supposedly lacked any special cultural characteristics?

When I arrived in Beijing, I set out to carry out my rather narrowly defined original proposal: an in-depth social study of an urban Muslim community concentrated mainly in one neighborhood, with a citywide population of over 200,000 Hui. Through the auspices of the Central Institute for Nationalities, as a visiting graduate student I was assigned a supervisoral committee with two Hui professors to oversee my research in Beijing and study at the Institute. It was not long, however, before my advisors and other Hui classmates at the Institute said that, if I wanted to *really* understand the Hui, I would have to travel to where they are "typical," such as, I was told, the northwest. During my year of fieldwork on the Hui workers in Beijing city, I went on two trips through the northwest and the southeast. On a 1-month research trip to northwest China, I followed the historic 1936 northwestern route of the Chinese journalist Fan Changjiang, recorded in his book *China's Northwest Corner (Zhongguode xibeijiao)*, and visited Hui communities in Inner Mongolia (Huhehot), Ningxia (Yinchuan, Wuzhong), Gansu (Lanzhou), and Shaanxi (Xi'an). In the spring, I made a 6-week escorted trip to dispersed Hui communities in southern and southeastern China, including Shanghai, Hangzhou, Suzhou, Nanjing, Zhenjiang, Yangzhou, Jiaxing, Fuzhou, Quanzhou, Xiamen, and Guangzhou. The problem was that, in all these trips, the farther I traveled, the less I found that tied all of these diverse peoples together into one ethnic group. With Moerman, the more I learned about them, the less sure I became of who they *really* were.

I was permitted to renew for another year, and, through delicate and protracted bureaucratic negotiations, managed to move to Ningxia, the Hui autonomous region in the rural northwest. After 10 months in Ningxia, I returned to the United States to begin the process affectionately known as "writing up." Because this endeavor raised more questions than it answered, in the summer of 1986, I went back to China to do some follow-up and carry out further research on the southeast coast. Since then, I have made 3 more shorter trips to China where I had the opportunity to meet with Hui colleagues and interview again several key informants.

On escorted research trips, I was generally accompanied by a Hui scholar (never a Han), who assisted me in obtaining permission from the local authorities to carry out research and gain entré to the local Hui communities. I also established the research pattern of visiting as many mosques as possible in the various communities, conducting interviews with religious leaders and students, visiting Islamic *madrassahs* or government Hui schools, touring Hui factories and cooperatives, eating only in Hui restaurants, attending local rituals and celebrations, especially holiday celebrations, weddings, and funerals, as well as interviewing local government leaders active in minority affairs and well-known Hui scholars. In each community visited, I conducted household interviews with an informal interview schedule focusing on 3 major areas: migration and family ethnohistories; basic household economic and occupational data; and ethnoreligious knowledge of the Islamic world, Hui history, minority polity, and Hui cultural and religious differentiation. Whenever possible, I attempted to be sensitive to longitudinal and gender distinctions. When there were two or more generations present in one household, I often asked the same ethnoreligious-knowledge questions to different age groups and obtained widely divergent responses. Talking with Hui rural women in the northwest was much more difficult, since they tend to be even more conservative than Han women. Much that I learned of their identity was obtained informally in Hui homes, among those Hui families who knew me well. I also benefited enormously from the insights of Mary Hammond, my companion and spouse, who was naturally and widely accepted among both younger and older Hui women.

On formal research forays, local authorities were generally helpful in allowing me to interview well-known "model" households as well as worker and farming households of average income. In addition to the Hui scholar accompanying me on arranged visits to mosques and households, I was occasionally accompanied by 1, and once as many as 5, cadres from the local Commission for Nationality Affairs (CNA) (Minzu Shiwu Weiyuanhui), the United Front Bureau (Tongzhanbu), or the Chinese Islamic Society (Zhongguo Yisilanjiao Xiehui). While these cadres were sometimes a hindrance to more casual unrestricted conversation, they often proved to be extremely knowledgeable and forthcoming about local conditions and policies, as well as helpful in providing the official stamp of approval on my research. I often revisited households alone on later occasions, sometimes several times.

Since I did not have much control over whom I was able to interview during the more structured arranged meetings, I do not regard my survey as statistically significant or reliable. However, the interview schedule informed many of the issues that I address below with regard to the diversity and unity of ethnoreligious identity among the Hui. It provided a useful framework on which to hang many of my questions regarding overriding issues with which Hui themselves are concerned: personal ethnohistory, changing socioeconomic conditions, religious knowledge and differentiation, and government policy. Use of a tape recorder proved cumbersome and obtrusive to more casual conversation, although I was able to make recordings of some sermons and rituals. Most Hui expressed appreciation for the slides I made of their mosques, rituals, and historical artifacts.[114]

Finally, and most important, in addition to these more formal, arranged interviews and research trips, I engaged wherever possible in informal "participant observation" in which I talked with local Hui regarding their ethnic background on an individual basis without being accompanied by any local officials or scholars. Since I lived continuously in China for 2 years as a "foreign student," it was not difficult to spend almost all of my time with Hui. This, of course, was much easier when living in Beijing and Yinchuan than on the more intensive escorted survey trips. I was able, however, to make several individual trips without escort to various Hui centers, including Tibet, Yunnan, and Hainan Island.

Travel in China is generally tedious, troublesome, and time-consuming. The innumerable hours I spent on trains and buses—or waiting to buy tickets for them—provided ample opportunity to discuss questions of Hui identity and ethnic nationalism with fellow Han and Hui travelers. For this reason and personal preference, I always traveled in hard berth or seat (3rd and 4th class) and ate exclusively in Hui *qing zhen* restaurants. This last requirement became most difficult when traveling in southern China where Hui restaurants are less numerous, but it gave me an "insider's" view of the hardships imposed on a *qing zhen* lifestyle.

In Ningxia, I negotiated a research contract that guaranteed unrestricted and unescorted individual informal access to Hui households in Yinchuan city and two nearby Hui villages (Luojiazhuang and Najiahu). This was cleared with city and village officials—at one point while riding through the countryside on my bicycle I even heard an official open-air radio broadcast on the local loudspeaker system explaining my research project and purpose to workers busy with the fall harvest. Our presence as the only and first Americans to live long term in Ningxia since 1949 was a source of interest and concern to residents and officials throughout the region. Due to restrictions on foreign researchers in China, I never lived independently in a peasant home, though I stayed at length in the village retirement unit in Na Homestead (Chapter 3). In Ningxia, residence in the Chinese faculty building of Ningxia Educational College (Ningxia Jiaoyu Xueyuan), where my spouse taught, provided normal social living conditions and frequent unrestricted access to Chinese society. My wife's Hui students, drawn from throughout Ningxia, were a constant source of companionship and instruction. Fortunately, the college itself was located on the land of the Luo Family village (Luojiazhuang). I only had to walk out the front gate to be in the village and look out my back window to see Hui villagers in their fields.

Language was a problem. In the north, I was able to rely on the so-called "standard language" (*putong hua*) of Northern Mandarin based on the Beijing dialect. In the northwest, I had to cope with Ningxia, Gansu, and Shaanxi dialects, and, by the end of my stay, was able to understand general conversation without too much repetition. Familiarity with these dialects became useful when visiting with Soviet Central Asian Dungans in Alma Ata, who maintained their Gansu dialect. In that case, my limited Turkish was helpful, but in Xinjiang I relied primarily on Mandarin. Only in Quanzhou did it become necessary to work through a research assistant, who was a Hui from the village and spoke Southern Min (Hokkien). In Tibet, Yunnan, Guangdong, Hainan, and Sichuan, most of the younger Hui spoke Mandarin or interpreted their elders' speech into something more or less understandable to me.

"BEING THERE" IN THE CHINESE NATION-STATE. Given the well-known restrictions placed on foreign social-science researchers in China, by now you, the reader, must be wondering how I was seemingly able to so easily "waddle in."[115] More important, once there, why did I keep moving? This is a fundamental issue for my research on the Hui in the Chinese nation-state. It certainly departs from the traditional Malinowski-style ethnography where an anthropologist attempts to "squat" in one community for an extended period of time. Not only was I urged to visit as

many Hui communities as possible by my Hui colleagues, but it also became immediately apparent that a book on the Hui based solely on one community would mislead rather than inform readers about their identity. Unlike Raymond Firth's classic ethnography, *We, the Tikopia*, there was no single voice that spoke for the Hui. For the Hui, there is no "We." There is no community or individual who even begins to represent all the Hui of China.

Certainly the voice of the state in its numerous nationality publications could not be taken as definitive, nor the view of the imam, the worker, the villager, or the entrepreneur. Instead, we find heteroglossia, to quote Bakhtin,[116] a polyphony of voices, from urban to rural, religious to secular, elite to commoner, modernist to "traditionalist"—each contradicting the other, sharing different visions of Hui-ness, and subscribing to separate imagined communities.[117] Of course, I could have remained in Beijing and spent all my 27 months among the Oxen Street Hui community. An urban ethnography of the Hui in Beijing would reveal much about Hui identity in the city—and this very much needs to be undertaken—but it would reveal very little about the vast majority of agriculturalist Hui. Moreover, how would one begin to understand the devoutly religious northwestern Hui communities from the reference point of the secularized workers who predominate in the city?

At an even more fundamental level, the basic nature of nationality identity in the nation-state is diffused—it depends on the local juxtapositions of power, constantly in flux, interacting dialogically with the significant others in socially specific contexts as well as the local state apparati. Central nationality policy, as this study will show, often bears little relation to what happens at the local level. Particularized, long-term ethnographies are indeed needed to gain a greater understanding of unique Hui identities, and it is hoped that these may become available. The problem this study seeks to address, however, is one of national identity: what it means to be Hui in the Chinese nation-state. To pursue this question, I realized that I needed an over-all perspective. My research trips exposed me to widely divergent communities of Hui living in varying ecological and socioeconomic contexts and expressing their identity in radically different ways. This diversity convinced me that I should not concentrate on one isolated community, but should use the time and opportunities provided to travel and observe as much of Hui life as possible in order to build a more comprehensive under-standing of Hui identity and nationalism in the Chinese state. These travels allowed me to observe the wide variety of Hui communities, an aspect of Hui identity not expressed in earlier accounts of the Hui in China.[118]

There were, of course, practical considerations. Field research when I was in China was still formally limited to a 2-week stay in any one vil-lage. I was able to circumvent some limitations by returning often to cer-tain villages and by living long term as a foreign graduate student in Chinese institutional housing, with other Chinese, including Hui. Bus and bicycle carried me to most outlying households and communities, such as Na Homestead, Changying, and Niujie. However, there were frustrating times when I was restricted and denied access to Hui com-munities for various reasons. Once, after traveling in southern Ningxia for 4 days by Beijing jeep on dirt roads across a good chunk of the Gobi Desert and over the Liu Pan Mountains, I finally arrived late one evening in Xiji, a major Hui Sufi Naqshbandiyya center (for the Shagou order) and one of the poorest towns in China, only to be told by the local County Chairman that it would be inconvenient (*bu fangbian*) for me to stay beyond the next morning. Out of respect for China's national sovereignty and laws, I never transgressed these boundaries by entering off-limit areas (*fei kaifang diqu*) without permission or passing as a local—which would have been easy to do in the northwest where I was often mistaken for another minority.[119] I doubt, too, that I would have been given the same kind of access had I been a visiting foreign scholar, generally watched much more closely than graduate students in China.

I spent a total of almost 3 years in China conducting research primar-ily on the Hui. While I was not in any one village during my entire stay, I did manage to invest substantial time and energy in at least 4 commu-nities, while visiting several others. Under the constraints of fieldwork in China, I was fortunate to have picked the Hui, since they are found everywhere, in every city, small town, and village. On occasions when

I could not be among Hui, it was often just as enlightening to discuss ethnic problems with Han colleagues and informants.

The state could keep me from going to the Hui, but it could not always keep them from coming to me. On my first trip to Quanzhou on the southeast coast, I was particularly interested in visiting the Ding lineage who had only recently been recognized in 1979 as members of the Hui nationality. The Chinese Islamic Society in Beijing told me about this interesting community and I made a specific request of the Fujian Provincial Commission for Nationality Affairs and the Fujian Chinese Islamic Society for permission to visit them. I also had special approval and travel documents issued by the State Commission for Nationality Affairs in Beijing to conduct research on Hui communities during this trip, and was accompanied by a professor from the Central Institute for Nationalism. Once again, it turned out that it was "inconvenient" for me to go to the village, only 20 minutes from the city center and part of the city district administration. When the Hui in the village heard of my interest, however, 10 of them rented a bus and met with me the entire day in the local mosque—a case of the followers of Muhammad coming to the interviewer. I was able eventually to travel to the village in 1986 and carry out further study (see Chapter 6).

In many ways, this kind of research seeks to avoid the reification of a certain community or individual as exemplary of the whole. It is also does not lend itself to Marcus's "salvage" or "redemptive" modes of ethnography, where the community is thought to be either on the verge of modernization, or still struggling to preserve remnants of its tradition, "after the deluge" of modernity has set in.[120] Each community, and individual, must speak for it-, him-, or herself. By not assuming a certain identity for each community or individual, or reifying it as representative of some abstract whole, this approach seeks more particularized understanding, attempting to avoid the "Orientalism" upon which so many of our travelogues, and even some ethnographies, are based.[121] The attempt to convey a false sense of objectivity through the well-defined and throughly described Other does not necessarily bring us any closer to understanding. As James Clifford has found problematic in some ethnographic portrayals:

This Orient, occulted and fragile, is brought lovingly to light, salvaged in the work of the outside scholar. The effect of domination in such spatial/temporal deployments (not limited, of course to Orientalism proper) is that they confer on the other a discrete identity, while also providing the knowing observer with a standpoint from which to see without being seen, to read without interruption.[122]

There are, of course, important costs. My research suffered from the lack of long-term daily observation that only comes with classic-style ethnography in one locality. The study was thesis- and problem-oriented, rather than village- or locale-oriented. Thus, it represents a substantial departure from traditional fieldwork. I do not attempt to describe the complete community, but examine certain problems of identity across several communities. The project was extensive, rather than intensive, not in the Margaret Mead style of studying one culture for 6 months and then moving to a totally new one—I did spend almost 3 years in China studying primarily one nationality, all of whom could communicate in the national language—but in the sense that I did not devote my entire study to one specific community in time and place.

I have no single central paradigmatic community or individual around whom my ideas of Hui-ness revolve. I can point to no standard ideal type by which to judge all other varieties (though, I would argue, this is not necessarily a flaw). I missed the opportunity to see the year-round daily agricultural cycle in one community, though was able to observe many of the major ecological transitions in Luo village across from my home. I might have formed deeper relationships with the locals if I had stayed in one village the whole time. I also discovered, however, that some people were often more willing to tell me things about themselves (and their neighbors) if they thought I was not too tightly woven into the web of their immediate social relations. In a politically permeated society such as China, a foreigner staying in one place for a very long time tends to focus and intensify attention on that place and those individuals, whereas my approach may have diffused some of that exposure.

I am also not able to point to any one community as "my village," as Philip Salzman notes other "lone stranger" anthropologists have traditionally claimed with exclusivity and pride.[123] I not only have difficulty in briefly answering the question "Whom did you study?" but also "Where did you study them?" The claim of exclusivity may become more difficult to make as fieldwork continues to become more public and publicized in complex societies, occurring, as Mary Louis Pratt has noted, in less exotic "common places."[124] This is particularly true when the actions of the fieldworker become interesting, or even perhaps threatening, to the regimes where s/he works. As Marcus argues, no longer can the world of larger systems be "seen as externally impinging on and bounding little worlds, but not as integral to them."[125] Smaller ethnic communities are tied into the larger nationality to which they belong and may be assigned by the state, and these are influenced by international events and relations. I, of course, plan to go back and "camp out" in one place for a longer term myself and, more important, hope that my carefulness has made it easier for others to follow. It is my desire that they start with the communities I have most come to know and enjoy, which certainly are not "mine."

FIELDWORK AND ANTHROPOLOGICAL CAREERS IN A POST-COLONIAL WORLD. There is another issue at stake here: Classical long-term fieldwork has traditionally been modeled on those situations where the ethnographer is able to exercise at least some control over lifestyle and environment. Geertz reminds us that "being there" for the anthropologist in the past involved

> at the minimum hardly more than a travel booking and permission to land; a willingness to endure a certain amount of loneliness, invasions of privacy, and physical discomfort; a relaxed way with odd growths and unexplained fevers; a capacity to stand still for artistic insults, and the sort of patience that can support an endless search for invisible needles in infinite haystacks.[126]

Having endured these "minimal" difficulties, the anthropologist was generally left to do what he or she wanted. The thought of government employees looking over one's shoulder, residence in state-owned institutions or hotels, restricted access to one's informants, and the need for multiple bureaucratic applications and approvals is distasteful, if not completely unacceptable, to most anthropologists. As a result, modern ethnographers have tended to avoid those places where such restrictions apply, favoring fieldwork where they can, for the most part, pitch their tents with impunity. It is no surprise that this "fetishism of the field," in James Boon's terms, is generally practiced in countries closely tied to Western economic and political interests.[127]

Western field research in China basically ground to a halt at the end of World War II with the decline of the notion of Western "extra-territoriality"–a right to immunity from Chinese prosecution that foreigners generally possessed to one degree or another since the Un-equal Treaties were signed in the mid-nineteenth century. It became ille-gal to conduct field research in China without specific permission from the People's Republic, and, for the most part, few Westerners were granted it.[128] Those who were allowed to conduct fieldwork were so cir-cumscribed and sympathetic to state policy that their works generally lacked the dispassionate stance thought necessary for ethnographic cred-ibility.

Since 1949, field research on Chinese communities has been carried out primarily in Taiwan, Hong Kong, and Southeast Asia. There, due to international economic and power alliances, fieldwork could be con-ducted with the degree of autonomy deemed necessary by many West-ern anthropologists. When I first proposed to conduct fieldwork in the PRC in 1981, I often received the advice generally given at the time by American Sino-anthropologists: Since it was assumed I would never be able to do "real" fieldwork in China, it would be better to go to Taiwan or Hong Kong where I "could do what I wanted." In China I might waste my time and then never be able to get a job. After writing a "solid" dissertation in Taiwan and obtaining an academic position, I was advised, I could afford to risk some short stints in China. When I then came up with the idea of working on minorities, several warned that I would be putting my career in jeopardy. I was constantly reminded that, since there were so few minorities in China ("less than 7 percent of the population"), research on them would not be of any long-term value to our understanding of "Chinese society." The head of a major Chinese studies center on the west coast once said to me, "Why study the minorities? We still don't know enough about the Han." One prominent China political historian (who asked that his name be withheld), once publicly stated: "I don't mind saying in public that I am a Han chauvinist. I don't care anything about those border barbarians, Tibetans, and the like. They do not matter at all to China." One of my students at Harvard mentioned that he was warned by a senior American Sino-anthropologist at another university in the spring of 1989 that he would never find a job in a reputable university if he did his dissertation research on minorities in China.

The issue of anthropological careers and the limitations placed on anthropological research by the academic industry is of paramount concern when we consider contemporary research in complex nations.[129] I discovered in China, however, what few Sinologists could have predicted: It was precisely the work on the Han that was often most restricted, and minority research was not only possible but encouraged. Traditionally, it was Chinese anthropologists who, influenced by the British social anthropological tradition, worked mainly on minorities. In a classic division of labor, sociologists devoted themselves to the Han. When Western anthropologists attempt to study the Han in China, it is not only bureaucratically difficult; I have also noticed a tangible resentment and conviction that anthropologists should study only "backward peoples." The Han, as the "vanguard of the proletariat," certainly do not wish to be regarded or studied as backward. Anthropology (*ren lei xue*) in China, until very recently, has been almost exclusively limited to physical anthropology. Ethnography (*minzu xue*) was devoted to the study of minorities and was generally carried out in the nationalities institutes (*shaoshu minzu*) and nationalities research centers, rather than in the universities. As David Arkush has so clearly documented in the life of China's senior social anthropologist, Fei Xiaotong, it was sociology that in the late 1950s received the full brunt of the Maoist critique:

> It was said that bourgeois sociology had been progressive at first, when subverting feudalism, but had lost its revolutionary nature when the bourgeoisie became the ruling class. It had consistently supported the bourgeois capitalist order by justifying its social division, extolling social harmony, and generally depicting capitalist society as just and the highest stage of social development.[130]

Anthropology, on the other hand, was generally given approval due to its practical usefulness in understanding and incorporating the minorities:

> As for anthropology, it had served imperialism by providing information on primitive colonial peoples that was used in controlling them. Firth's *Human Types*, which Fei had translated, was quoted to show that anthropologists provide this service knowingly: "Modern anthropology is practical. . . . Colonial governments have known it is important to use anthropology in dealing with aborigines." Functionalism, it was said, had not been concerned with explaining origins or the history of systems but with pointing out functions, in order that colonial administrators could handle peoples more effectively.[131]

Ethnography and anthropology, though later criticized, were in general more protected than sociology as a tool of the state in dominating the minorities. In China, anthropology became the "people's anthropology,"[132] because it concerned itself exclusively with the cultural study of the minority peoples, generally ignoring such issues as political economy, social structure, religious authority, and socioeconomic change.

When I introduced myself in China as an ethnographer studying minorities, I generally was better received than when I said I was an anthropologist. (Now that Western sociologists have been allowed back into China, they are expected to work among the Han.) My application to study minorities appeared to follow the contours of power within the Chinese social-science tradition, and though still difficult, it met with less resistance. It is hoped that it will not be used by "colonial administrators" in "handling" their people more effectively in the future.

But one is never detached from the power structures of Chinese, or any, society. "Waddling in" always involves leaving a wake behind. To some degree I was, of course, perceived by locals as a representative of the Chinese state (since I had their approval to be there), as well as American interests. Most cadres simply assumed I was a spy and treated me as such. A Han official challenged me in Yinchuan one day asking "Why else would you be in the middle of nowhere studying such an uninteresting, insignificant people?" I am sure he never believed my lengthy explanation of why I found the Hui so fascinating. More practically, the institutes and individuals who hosted me were very aware of the political risks, costs, and benefits involved. My presence as a foreign researcher, in addition to being a threat, added prestige and some compensation to their institutions. There was an exchange of symbolic benefits, but not one that can be measured in quantifiable terms.

The past 5 years have demonstrated that, for whatever reasons, anthropological research has indeed made progress among the minorities. While my situation was admittedly quite unique, due to the subject of study, others (generally graduate students) have been granted longterm admittance to villages and communities in diverse minority areas from Yunnan to Xinjiang. In the 1987–1988 grant year, the Committee on Scholarly Communication with the People's Republic of China funded 5 anthropologists to carry out research in China; all proposed to study minorities. I suggest that not only will this research among minorities continue to offer more opportunity in China, but, most significantly, it will reveal much about the power relations and social identities within China. Ethnicity studies have the potential to reveal a great deal about the Chinese state and society in general, including the Han. After all, the Han are also a *minzu*.[133]

THE UNITY AND DIVERSITY OF HUI IDENTITY: FOUR COMMUNITIES IN FLUX

For the purposes of this study's argument regarding the dialectical nature of ethnic identity in the Chinese nation-state, I settled on 4 Hui communities that provide revealing examples of the widely divergent expression of Hui identity and its recent adaptation to the contemporary Chinese social context and power relations. These communities should be viewed as case communities, not complete ethnographies of certain villages or places.

I focused my research on a mosque-centered Naqshbandiyya Sufi village in the northwest; an urban-worker ethnic enclave in Beijing city; a northern suburban village, and a lineage community on the southeast coast. Thus, I conducted fieldwork in urban and rural, northern and southern, Islamic and traditional Chinese folk religious communities in an attempt to examine the broad spectrum of ethnic identity across the breadth of the modern nation-state. I noted a similar range of ethnoreligious diversity as Clifford Geertz observed in his comparison of Moroccan scripturalist fundamentalism and Indonesian "syncretistic" Islam, which he argued existed by necessity in "two countries, two cultures"[134]—yet I found even more varied identity among Muslims defined by the Chinese state as a *single* national minority. In each Hui community, I sought to address what Michel Foucault noted as a dynamic interaction between power and ideology, expressed through state hegemonic structures and local ethnoreligious symbols of identity.[135] This interaction is fundamental to ethnic identity in Inner Asia: The dialectic both empowers identity and draws divergent communities together under a dominant hegemony.

In Chapter 3, I describe northwest Hui identity with reference to Na Homestead (Najiahu), one village with which I am most familiar in Ningxia Hui autonomous region and, in many ways, typical of Mosque-centered Hui communities in Northwest China. The dispersion of Hui across China is due partly to their traditional proclivity for engaging in long-distance trade and small business operations that are linked to urban and market centers. Like the Jews of Eastern Europe prior to World War II, the Hui are the main urban ethnic minority in almost every major city and town in China. In Chapter 4, I address the question of the identity of urban Hui with reference to the Niujie (Oxen Street) community in Beijing. The issue of marriage within isolated Hui communities in rural Han-dominant areas throughout Central China is a paramount problem for Hui concerned with the perpetuation of their identity. Marriage endogamy among Hui, some from very distant communities, is an important strategy these Hui use to preserve and express the purity of their descent from foreign ancestors. This issue is discussed in Chapter 5 with reference to Changying, a suburban Hui village east of Beijing. In Chapter 6, I deal with the identity of one Hui community in Southeastern China, the Ding lineage, recognized only recently by the government as belonging to the Hui nationality owing to their unique and controversial non-Islamic identity.

In each of these studies, I discuss how Hui identity is rooted in local shared ideas of descent based on accepted texts and rituals. The relevance of Hui identity for each case is then discussed with respect to its expression in the local social context. I attempt to show how Hui identity makes a difference in the lives of the Hui in each community—how it affects their lifestyle, work, marriage, and social relations. Finally, I analyze the dialectical emergence of new Hui identities and government policies through the interaction of local identities with the state in each social context.

While much of this study attempts to understand ethnographically who the Hui are and the role they play in modern Chinese society, as well as the government's dealings with them, I analyze the above proposed approach to ethnicity with regard to its power adequately to interpret Hui ethnoreligious expression in each case. Unlike most ethnographic reports, which tend to describe an isolated village community frozen in time apart from changing sociopolitical realities, I examine these 4 Hui communities in the political-economic context of their recent history and the PRC today. I propose that these communities represent processes or "types" of Hui ethnoreligious identity that illuminate varieties of Hui identity and community interests throughout China.[136] While no particular community or individual will be representative of the whole, this spectrum of expression illustrates the issues that often confront each community and individual in different contexts.

A SPECTRUM OF ETHNORELIGIOUS EXPRESSION. First, at one end of the spectrum there are highly concentrated communities of Hui, especially in Northwest China, where religious identity is the most salient aspect of Hui identity. In these communities, to be Hui is to be Muslim, and purity (*qing*) derives from one's moral and religious integrity. At the other extreme, one finds southeastern Hui lineages for whom Islam is almost totally irrelevant, and Hui identity is based entirely on genealogical descent from foreign Arab ancestors: To be Hui is to be different in ancestry from the Han, and authenticity (*zhen*) is based on the truth of one's ancestry. In between these two extreme expressions of identity one finds urban Hui communities for whom identity is a mixture of ethnic ancestry and religious commitment, in varying degrees. While Islam continues to be meaningful to most of these Hui, and to some more than others, the mosque generally has ceased to be a locus of religious authority and cultural activity, replaced by more secular organizations, such as the restaurant, school, or voluntary association. A fourth type are those traditional communities of isolated Hui villages in Han-majority areas where the mosque continues to maintain its central role in the affairs of the community, but for whom issues of religious author-ity and orthodoxy are less important than more practical concerns such as marriage and social cohesiveness.

While these communities are portrayed as types across a wide spec-trum of expression, I do not intend to suggest that this scheme has any predictive value for ethnic change. I discuss how the Hui express their identity in different contexts because of widely divergent historical, eco-logical, socioeconomic, and political forces. I do not presuppose or intend to suggest any stage or developmental scheme.

In my interviews in over 400 Hui households throughout China, I always asked: "What, if any, is the difference between Han and Hui?" In Na Homestead, and other similar Hui communities throughout Ning-xia, Gansu, and Qinghai, I almost always received the response: "Hui believe in Islam. Han believe in Buddhism or Marxism." In those areas, both Han and Hui tended to couch their differences in religious dis-course. When I interviewed a Han who lived in the almost all-Muslim village of Na Homestead, he said: "Hui and Han have different reli-gions. We eat pork, they don't." Among Hui lineages near Quanzhou, the response was generally: "We are Hui because we are descended from foreign Muslims." Differences were perceived genealogically. In urban areas and Hui communities in central and southern China, I often heard: "Hui are different because we have different customs than the Han; we don't eat pork." Here, cultural practice epitomized ethnic differ-ence. In rural northern villages, they told me: "We are Hui because our parents are, and we maintain the *qing zhen* life." For those isolated com-munities, not only was practice important; its perpetuation through association and intermarriage was a central issue.

These responses indicate the wide variety of Hui self-understanding and ethnic ascription. I argue that expressions of ethnic identity and interpretations of *qing zhen* will also differ among these communities. Though there is much variety of ethnic expression, the shared idea of descent from common ancestors is the root that grounds Hui identity in a shared ethnoreligious tradition. While it might be plausible to argue that these communities and individuals are so different that they are not ethnic, they nevertheless think they are, and believe they maintain discursive relations with other Hui, no matter how different. This feeling becomes institutionalized and defined by the state, which, in dialogical fashion, leads to further expression, even invention, of ethnicity. Genealogical or historical evidence to the contrary, this common self-perception of descent from common ancestors forms the basis of a meaningful ethnoreligious identity that continues to maintain "All Hui under Heaven are one family."

Na Homestead graveyard attached to mosque within the confines of the village. Main tombstone belongs to Na Yongxiang (1906–1982). Note Hui Muslim at prayer with Ming dynasty mosque (c. 1522–1567) in background. Photo: Gladney

THREE

Ethnoreligious Resurgence in
a Northwestern Sufi Community

The loathsome mask has fallen,
  the man remains
Sceptreless, free, uncircumscribed,
  but man
Equal, unclassed, tribeless, and nationless.
Exempt from awe, worship, degree, the king
Over himself, just, gentle, wise,
  but man.

— *Percy B. Shelley,* Prometheus Unbound

Na Homestead (Najiahu), in Ningxia Hui autonomous region, is, in many respects, typical of other Hui Muslim communities throughout the northwest. A collection of adobe houses clustered around a central mosque, Na Homestead has been the site of an Islamic resurgence in recent years. As several visitors to other northwestern Muslim communities have noted, Islamic conservatism has become more pronounced among the Hui since 1979.[1] This rising radical, even fundamentialist, emphasis upon Islamic purity (*qing*) in Hui communities has caused concern among local government cadres.

In Ningxia Hui autonomous region, where over 1.2 million of China's Hui minority reside, local cadres and government researchers are alarmed about the possibility of an Islamic "revival" among Hui youth.[2] They are also questioning whether the private-responsibility system has engendered too much personal and religious freedom in rural areas. Cadres are surprised to find that some Hui peasants hold the mistaken idea that the Party not only allows religious belief, but encourages it.[3] In order to quell these rising concerns, studies by local academies of social sciences in Muslim areas are used to show that, while ethnic customs are maintained, religious belief is not necessarily strong.[4] Reflecting traditional Chinese policy toward nationality religions, this approach clearly distinguishes between the minority itself and its religion. The policy often encourages the expression of traditional nationality customs and culture, while depicting religion as extraneous to ethnicity.[5]

In this chapter, I argue that Hui ethnic identity in the northwest is inseparably identified with an Islamic tradition handed down to them by their Muslim ancestors. It is more than an ethnic identity; it is ethnoreligious, in that Islam is intimately tied to the northwest Hui's self-understanding. Recent reemergence of the meaning of Islam and stress upon the requirements of a decidedly Islamic *qing zhen* lifestyle represent a return to northwestern Hui ethnoreligious roots. In this regard, an examination of Na Homestead discloses some of the expressions of this northwestern Hui ethnoreligious identity as well as its recent transformation in the midst of rapid socioeconomic change. A close analysis of salient Hui institutions, rituals, and texts reveals that a policy that seeks to make a clear distinction between religion and ethnicity is based on an inadequate understanding of Hui identity. The resurgence of Islamic practice and conservativism in Na Homestead, under recent liberalized policies, illustrates the importance of Islam in this context. The interaction of Na ethnic identity with recently liberalized government policies has also led to important changes in the expression of that identity and in the reformulation of local nationality policies.

A FUNDAMENTALIST REVIVAL IN NA HOMESTEAD?

Na Homestead is part of Yongning county, Yang He township, 15 km. south of Yinchuan city in central Ningxia.[6] Traveling south on the main north-south highway linking Yinchuan with Wuzhong city and southern Ningxia, one finds a dirt road leading off to Na Homestead at the main intersection of the Yongning county seat. Separated from the intersection by 3 km. of fields, Na Homestead is a somewhat isolated, formerly walled community of mud houses clustered around a central mosque (*qing zhen si*). The sloping eaves of the mosque rising up above the flat-roofed houses are visible from the road, providing a striking visual contrast with other surrounding communities.

This compact collection of households comprises 9 teams that are almost 100 percent Hui, a rarity in central and northern Ningxia, where Hui are thinly distributed among the majority Han population (see Table 5). Yongning county is only 12.9 percent Hui, a relatively small minority in contrast to neighboring Lingwu county in the southeast, which is 47 percent Hui, and southern Jingyuan county, which is 97 percent Hui (the highest concentration of Hui in one county in China, see Map 2).

Just north of the all-Hui community in Na Homestead, separated by about 2 km. of fields, is another collection of households belonging to the village administratively and containing 2 teams (numbers 1 and 11) of mixed Han and Hui. All 22 households (264 people) of the Han families belonging to Na Homestead are located in this smaller community, separate from the 9 all-Hui teams. Based on 1984 statistics, Na Homestead comprises 767 households, with a total population of 3,871. Hui households number 745, amounting to more than 95 percent of the population. Over 60 percent of the Hui in the village are surnamed Na.

RELIGIOUS REVITALIZATION IN NA HOMESTEAD. I first became aware of changing Hui-Han social dynamics in the village from a discussion with one of the Han villagers in Team 1. She explained:

> Since 1979, we have had less and less social contact with the Hui in the other teams. There are no problems between us, but the Hui are more devout (*qiancheng*) now and less willing to come to our homes and visit or borrow tools. We raise pigs in our yards and eat pork, so they are afraid it will influence their religion (*yingxiang tamende jiaomen*).

Like many conservative northwest Hui, most Na villagers have become more conscientious about Islamic purity (*qing*) through attention to dietary restrictions. In order to preserve one's *qing zhen* lifestyle, conservative Hui who do visit Han homes accept, at the most, sunflower seeds or

TABLE 5 Population of the Hui Nationality in Ningxia Hui
Autonomous Region by City and County, 1983

County or City	Total Population	Hui Population	Percent of Hui in County Population	Percent of Regional Hui Population in County
Jingyuan	82,464	79,823	96.8	6.3
Tongxin	218,967	172,906	79.0	13.5
Haiyuan	249,672	170,732	68.4	13.4
Xiji	316,298	156,477	49.5	12.3
Lingwu	184,289	86,424	47.0	6.8
Guyuan	377,634	154,875	41.0	12.0
Pingluo	234,375	71,511	30.5	5.6
Pengyang	186,334	52,636	28.3	4.1
Helan	159,953	37,337	23.3	2.9
Yinchuan	371,250	69,636	18.8	5.5
Qingtongxia	188,362	26,510	14.1	2.1
Yongning	156,504	20,282	13.0	1.6
Shizuishan	301,957	32,422	10.8	2.5
Taole	19,017	1,842	9.7	0.1
Longde	162,572	13,233	8.1	1.0
Wuzhong	217,704	12,081	5.6	9.4
Yanchi	121,741	3,274	2.7	0.3
Zhongning	180,778	4,463	2.5	0.3
Zhongwei	251,329	1,924	.8	0.3
Total:	3,981,200	1,168,388	29.3	100.0

Source: 1983 Regional Census

fruit when offered by their host. When Han come to their homes, Hui
offer them tea from a separate set of cups that the family itself does not
use, lest the family *qing zhen* utensils become contaminated. Hui are
also free to offer Han prepared dishes of lamb and beef, but the Han cannot reciprocate. Gradually this imbalance of obligation leads to less and
less contact. Increased scrupulous attention to the culturally defined
notions of Islamic purity—especially in a culture that traditionally

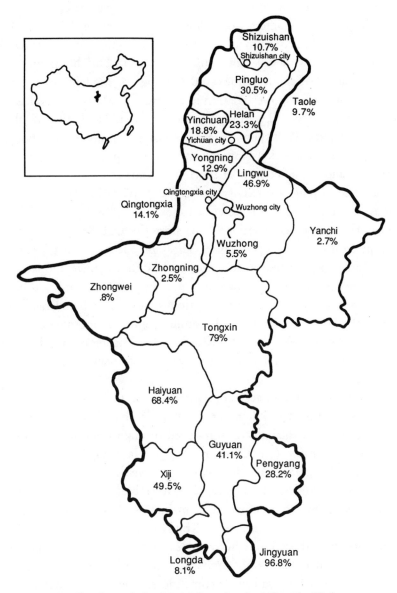

MAP 2 Distribution of the Hui Minority in Ningxia Hui
Autonomous Region by Percentage of County

places high priority on extending social courtesies—has increasingly limited Hui-Han social interaction. This is not surprising. Careful Hui attention to this tradition maintains the purity/impurity power reversal in which Han, who can never fully reciprocate Hui hospitality by offering them social prestations and offerings of food in return, are placed in an inferior power relation to the Hui. As Marcel Mauss has so eloquently described, "The thing given is not inert,"[7] and Hui refusal to receive Han gifts places them in a position of moral superiority, though they may occupy a socially inferior and marginal position in the socio-economic and ethnic context of Northwest China.

This rise in religious activity and conservativism in Na Homestead stands in stark contrast to the closed mosques and restricted religious behavior common elsewhere in China since the 1958 Religious System Reform Campaigns (*Zongjiao Zhidu Gaige*). Frequent Na-villager participation in mosque ritual is also noticeably different from the lack of popular participation in urban mosques in northern and southern China. In those areas—with the exception of holidays, where large turn-outs of the Hui community are becoming common—mosques are generally frequented only by a few bearded old men sitting on benches and sunning themselves while awaiting the next call to prayer. Not so in Na Homestead.

The Hui of Na Homestead are associated with the Khufiyya brotherhood, a very popular Sufi order in Ningxia that developed from a branch of the Naqshbandiyya introduced through Central Asia in the seventeenth century (see Chapter 1). Yet Na villagers, like many Khufiyya in Ningxia, do not subscribe to the *menhuan* that venerate the descendants of Sufi saints. Hence, they resemble an isolated mosque-centered Gedimu community that maintains Sufi forms of ritual. Although they regard themselves as Khufiyya, Na villagers are not connected to the other Sufi Khufiyya networks extending throughout Northwest China. This is not unusual in northern Ningxia and other areas where the Khufiyya have become more decentralized. While they are thus not closely connected to other Khufiyya orders, their Sufi background continues to influence daily life and ritual.

On any weekday morning, at least 150 people kneel at prayer on the hard floor of the mosque an hour before dawn. One wintry morning,

I arose from my warm *kang* to the call for prayer (heard throughout the village) at 6:00 a.m. and walked over to the mosque. In this season, the ground is frozen and the temperature hovers around 13 to 14 degrees below zero centigrade. I was surprised to find the large prayer hall full of men when I arrived, illustrating that, though China was on one time zone, these villagers lived life according to a different clock. Many villagers prayed 5 times a day and followed the Islamic calendar, suggesting that the rhythm of their lives was much different than for the rest of China. As the service began, 2 or 3 stragglers came running up, hastily donning fleece-lined coats over their bare backs and removing their boots as they entered the prayer hall. They prayed in unison on the bare concrete floor for the duration of the 30–45 minute service, some of them kneeling upon lamb pelts or on small carpets purchased from a Zhejiang factory that makes the colorful rayon Islamic-style prayer mats sold throughout the northwest. Because of the sermon, the main prayer on Fridays (*zhuma ri*) generally lasts over an hour. This differed markedly from mosques in other parts of China where latecomers straggled in at the last minute, knowing they could always "make up prayers" (*bu li*) later.

One official count of attendance on a Thursday morning in January 1985 recorded 141 worshipers, including 31 between 14 and 50 years of age.[8] On Fridays, an attendance of up to 500 worshipers is not unusual (13 percent of the village), with an average of 100–200 praying at least once in the mosque during the week. On holidays, the whole village, including women and children, turns out. While some say that participation has not yet reached 1950 levels, this is perceived as a new peak (*gaofeng*) since 1949 of religious activity among the Hui.[9] During the month of Ramadan in 1984, the mosque reported that one third of all households had at least one member who took part in the fast. I have also visited concentrated Hui areas such as Linxia Hui autonomous prefecture, Gansu province, and southern Ningxia where 100 percent of the villagers above the age of 12 (boys) or 9 (girls) fast. The level of participation in the fast among Na villagers is still considered rather high in a predominantly Han area.

Mosque income (*sifei*) derived from offerings (*nietie*) has also risen dramatically. According to the mosque's own careful accounting records, in the last 2 years it averaged over 20,000 yuan ($6,700 US) annual income from offerings. Based on an outside study, over a 4-month period during 1984 and 1985, offerings of grain produce, goods, or money totaled 8,997.23 yuan (about $3,000 US). An economic survey of expenditures of 113 Hui households in Na Homestead revealed that average giving to the mosque was 47 yuan per household, or 8.40 yuan per person in 1984.[10] If this average is applied to the entire Hui community of the village, then the mosque's total income last year was well over 32,500 yuan ($10,833 US). The money supports the staff of 7 ahong including 1 "teaching" or head ahong (*kaixue ahong* or *jiaozhang*), and 4 student ahong (*halifat* from *khalîfa*, "successor," or *manla*, from *mullah*), and the daily upkeep of the mosque.[11] Offerings are given during the 3 main religious holidays and to individual ahong when they read the Quran at weddings, funerals, and naming ceremonies. Giving at funerals by the family to guests and to the mosque ranges from 100 to 1,000 yuan. As much as 2,500 yuan has been reported when the status of the deceased was extremely high.

On one holiday celebrated in Na Homestead, the "Prophet's Day" or "Muhammad's Birthday" (*Shengji*) on 7 December 1984, I witnessed offerings brought by children and adults—bags of flour or rice and fistfulls of money. A group of mosque officials dutifully registered each offering according to amount, name, and team number. Gifts totaled 3,000 kilograms of wheat, 2,500 kilograms of rice, and 300 yuan ($100 US), equal to approximately 3,313 yuan ($1,100 US). None of the donated money is required for the restoration of the mosque building (*qianliang*). The mosque has received over 90,000 yuan ($30,000 US) from the State Nationalities Affairs Commission since it was identified as a national monument in 1981. Dating from the Ming dynasty's Jia Jing period (1522–1567), it is the oldest remaining mosque in Ningxia.[12]

Donations to the mosque come from a village considered fairly poor by neighboring village standards, with an average annual income of 300 yuan (about $100 US) per household.[13] Average per capita annual income in Yongning county for 1982 was substantially higher, 539 yuan according to the Population Census Office.[14] Poor households (*pinkun hu*) occupy 2 percent of the village.[15] Mosque income, however, does not necessarily reflect total giving per household. The mosque also received income from outside the village, such as from the state or from other Muslim communities. A study of 17 households from 3 different villages belonging to different Islamic orders found that, out of an annual average income of 96.67 yuan, 8.96 yuan (9.26 percent) was given to religious concerns in 1980.[16]

THE ASCENDANCE OF QURANIC EDUCATION. A decrease in public-school enrollment, and an increase in children studying the Quran in private *madrassah* attached to local mosques is another phenomenon that concerns local cadres. This growing interest in pursuing religious education has not yet reached large proportions among the Hui in Na Homestead, since only 10 school-age children were not attending public school in 1985. Instead, they are studying the Quran at home privately. There are 4 officially permitted *manla* in the village. In more heavily populated Hui areas, however, this is becoming a more noticeable practice. In Guyuan county, Jiefangxiang (Liberation township), only 12 out of 104 school-age children in the village are attending school, and 27 of those not in school are studying the Quran in the mosque.

This trend has become even more pronounced in conservative Muslim areas such as Linxia Hui autonomous prefecture, in Gansu province, where Muslim minorities are 52.7 percent of the population.[17] School enrollment has regularly decreased since 1978, from 77.2 percent to 66.6 percent in 1979, to 60 percent in 1980, to 57.3 percent in 1981, and to a low of 50 percent in 1982. In Hanfeng commune, a completely Han area, enrollment of children has reached as high as 93.9 percent; among girls it is 79 percent. In the neighboring mountainous Badan commune, an all-Muslim area, enrollment was 23.9 percent in 1982, with only 9.05 percent of girls enrolled. By the end of the school year, only 2.9 percent of the girls remained in school. This reflects the common practice of children attending school for the first few weeks of registration, but returning full time to the farm before completing the term.[18]

In a *China Daily* front-page article entitled "Keep rural girls in school," Liu Su,[19] Vice-Governor of Gansu province, reported that, out of 157,300 school-aged children not in school in Gansu, 85 percent were girls. Children leave school for a variety of reasons, including the farm's need for income-producing labor under the newly introduced responsibility system. Yet many Hui point to traditional Islamic views that have made them reluctant to send their children, especially daughters, to public schools.

When asked about such reluctance, Na Homestead parents expressed doubts about "the value of learning Chinese and mathematics." "It would be much more useful," I was told by one mother, "for our children to learn the Quran, Arabic, and Persian." If a child excelled, he or she might become a *manla*, and eventually perhaps an ahong. Their status in the village would be much higher than the average middle-school or even high-school graduate, as would their income (estimated at 100 to 500 yuan a month for a well-known teaching ahong). Children who are in poor health are often kept at home to study the Quran. In large families with more than one son, generally one child is encouraged to study to become an ahong. Although the government officially allows each mosque to support from 2 to 4 full-time *manla*—who should be at least 18 years old and junior-middle-school graduates— many younger children study at home without official approval.

Ningxia, as the only autonomous region for China's Hui Muslims, tends to monitor ahong training and religious practice more closely than other areas where Hui are concentrated. In Yunnan's Weishan Yi and Hui autonomous county, several mosques had over 20 resident *manla* studying under well-known ahong. In Gansu's Linxia Hui autonomous prefecture, at the South Great Mosque there were over 130 full-time students. In Linxia city's Bafang district, where most of the Hui are concentrated, there were at least 60 full-time *manla* in each mosque. Mirroring the spiritual importance of Mecca and the centrality of theological learning of the Iranian city of Qum for China's Hui Muslims, Linxia's famous mosques and scholars attract students from all over China.[20]

Renowned mosques in Yunnan's Shadian and Weishan counties tend to attract students from throughout the southwest, including Hainan Island. At an ordination (*chuanyi*) service I attended at the Xiao Weigeng Mosque in Weishan county in February 1985, the 10 graduates included 1 Hainan Island student and 6 students from outside the county who had studied there for 5 years. The Hainan student had a brother studying the Quran in Beijing. The next class admitted 30 students, 10 from the local village, 10 from other villages, 10 from outside the county, including 1 from outside Yunnan. The fact that these *manla* travel long distances to study under celebrated ahong demonstrates that national ties continue to link disparate Hui communities. It also reveals the growing importance of religious education in the countryside.

THE RISE IN ISLAMIC CONSERVATISM. The increasing conservatism of the Hui in Na Homestead, noted by the Han villager above, is apparent to any visitor. Smoking and drinking are now prohibited in the village for the simple reason that "the elders are against it" (*laoren fandui*). When pressed for their reasons, the elders invariably refer to the dictates of maintaining a pure (*qing zhen*) lifestyle according to Islamic prescriptions. According to the local store clerk, very few people buy cigarettes anymore. Smoking and drinking were commonplace in the village during the Cultural Revolution. The clerk now keeps only a few bottles of low-alcohol-content "champagne" (*xiangbin jiu*) under a back shelf for rare occasions when outside cadres need to be entertained. When young men want to drink or smoke, they go outside the village to the Yongning county seat or to Yinchuan city. It came as quite a shock to the elders of this village when visited by foreign Muslim "friendship delegations" who openly drank or smoked.

While only the older women wear the head covering (*gaitou*) associated with the Muslim custom of *purdah*,[21] younger Hui admit that male-female interaction is much more restricted than in neighboring Han villages.[22] Men and women rarely work together in the fields, and the majority of marriages are arranged through introductions. In a survey of 50 newly married young couples, only 8 (16 percent) met their partners on their own, without an intermediary. The average courtship period was less than 5 months for 76 percent of the couples surveyed.[23] While some younger Hui complain about this conservativism, change in the near future appears unlikely. In fact, "modern" marriage practice has continued to decline since the high point of male-female "free love" (*lianai ziyou*) encouraged during the Cultural Revolution. The only "love match" I knew of took place between a local Na villager who had met his bride while studying for 2 years at a vocational training college.

One of a handful to receive higher education above the middle-school level, the case of this young intellectual was anything but typical.

When I asked several Hui villagers if there was anyone in their team who did not believe in Islam (*buxinjiao de huizu*), I was always told that they did not know of anyone. By contrast, in urban areas such as Yinchuan, the capital of Ningxia region, Hui youth often openly discuss their belief in Marxism or secularism and the lack of relevance of Islam for their lives.[24] Several have told me that they believe in neither Marxism nor Islam, but in "individualism," or only in "making money." This attitude is even more prevalent in cities like Beijing and Shanghai where urbanized Hui youth are becoming attracted to Western ideas (see Chapter 4). One Shanghai Hui youth married to a Han woman told me: "Buddhism is for peasants, Islam is for old Huihui, and Christianity is for those interested in the West."

In Na Homestead, however, even the local cadres who say they do not believe in Islam and belong to the Communist Party always invite the ahong to read the Quran at their family weddings, funerals, and parents' deathdays. The chairman of one team in Na Homestead, a prominent Party member, openly invited the ahong and participated in the reciting of the Quran at his son's wedding.[25]

Perhaps of greatest concern to local Party officials in Ningxia is the lack of participation in the local Party apparatus and the "problem of Party members who believe in religion" (*dangyuan xinjiaode wenti*). There are 63 Party members in Na Homestead, representing only 1.7 percent of the total population. Of those 63, 22 publicly worship at the mosque and say they believe in Islam. Three of these believers go to mosque 5 times daily, and one has officially quit his Party membership in order to become an ahong.[26] Many of these Muslim Party members have at one time been team-level chairmen, and 4 have been brigade (*da dui*) Party vice-secretaries in the past. The United Front Department estimated that 70–80 percent of Party members in Hui villages take part in religious activities, and about 10 percent openly admit they are believers in Islam.[27] When I asked one Hui state cadre who openly prayed at the mosque in another city about this contradiction, he rationalized, "I believe in Marxism in my head, but I believe in Islam in my heart."

Mason remarkably reported a similar explanation offered by Confucian Hui officials in the Qing dynasty:

> It may be added that military officials in the Manchu times were not altogether exempt from certain ceremonies of worship at temples; but Moslems seem to have made a compromise with conscience and went with the rest; one said to me long ago in Szechwan that though his bodily presence was there, and he shared in the prostrations, his heart was not there, so it didn't matter![28]

Local cadres give many reasons for religious behavior among Hui Party officials. In Na Homestead, it is explained that 80 percent entered the Party in the 1950s and are too old and uninvolved with Party affairs.[29] As they grow older, these veteran Party members are becoming more interested in religion. Yet it should be noted that no one has been admitted to the Party in Na Homestead since October 1976.

Involvement of Party members in religious activities, state support of mosque reconstruction, and recent visits by foreign Muslims and guests to the historic mosque have been interpreted by some Hui as the Party's encouragement of religion. Na villagers have been quoted as saying: "Whoever does not believe in religion does not do good works (*xingshan*) and does not carry out the policy of the Communist Party."[30] Acceptance of the Party's position on atheism has been declining in religious minority nationality areas, to the extent that some youths accept Islamic doctrines such as the creation of the world in place of scientific materialism. These trends have led many local cadres to argue that there has indeed been a revival of Islam among the Hui to the point of fundamentalist "fanaticism" (*kuanre* or *zongjiao re*, "religious heat.")[31]

ISLAMIC CONSERVATIVISM AND GOVERNMENT POLICY. What is the official response to these accelerating trends in religious conservatism? Based on several interviews with local and state officials, I find 3 approaches. (1) More conservative cadres say these religious activities and excesses should be stopped (*shoule*) immediately. (2) Others propose that political thought-reform campaigns should be taught again in the countryside to correct these misunderstandings of Party policy. (3) More moderate cadres would suggest reforms in the local Party itself rather than changes in policy; they point to recent research by Chinese sociologists that suggests Islam's influence is only superficial and is not important to youths and others in the village who are pressured to conform by mosque leaders[32] and claim that Islamic activities merely represent maintenance of minority customs, not real religious belief.

To support this last position, a Ningxia Academy of Social Sciences (NASS) survey on religious belief was conducted among 60 Hui secondary-school graduates under 30 years old; 14 said they did not believe in Islam, while 46 professed either complete or partial belief. Of those who did not believe, 5 expressed belief in Marxism, 4 in "individualism" (*geren zhuyi*), and 5 in both Marxism and Islam.[33] Of those 46 who said they believed in Islam, 26 expressed complete adherence, while the others professed only partial belief and unbelief. When the 26 believers were asked if this meant that they believed in an afterlife, heaven or hell, only one said he did. At one point, the young believers were asked: "When you say you believe in Islam, can it be that what you believe is that you shouldn't smoke, shouldn't drink, shouldn't eat pork, and should go to mosque on holidays and give offerings?" The natural response was "That's exactly what we mean."[34]

The NASS researchers cite this response to support their claim that few young people have "objective" reasons for believing in religion. Objective reasons, they maintain, would include beliefs in an afterlife, in the involvement of God in personal prosperity, and in Islam as the right religion. The researchers argue that most believe in Islam for "subjective" reasons, in which they include social pressure and ethnic background. The most common "subjective" answer given was: "We believe in Islam because we are Hui."[35] This response, and the fact that over 70 percent of those who attend daily prayer service are over 50 years old, demonstrates that religion is unpopular among the young, according to the researchers. When the Hui villagers say they believe in religion, according to these observers, they have confused the influence of ethnic customs with Islamic belief.[36]

Moderate cadres point out that many social benefits have derived from the relaxed religious policy. One of the most important advantages is the opportunity to use the mosque for disseminating Party and government policy. Imams have begun to preach both government policy and religious practice at the Friday prayer in a new style of preaching called *chuan jiang* ("combined talks"). Since 1979, the crime rate and social-disturbance problems that I was told were "fairly messy" (*bijiao luan*) in Na Homestead have declined dramatically. Wang Xiren of the Ningxia Academy of Social Sciences reported that only 0.06 percent of the whole Hui population had been charged with committing crimes, while the Han crime rate was 0.1 percent.[37] The government's family-planning policy and other reforms have been carried out quite effectively compared with other areas, a fact attributed to the willingness of the ahong to permit use of the mosque for promoting public policies. On 17 November 1984, the government invited 63 ahong from throughout the region to gather at the Yinchuan Hotel where they were praised and encouraged in their efforts to raise the educational level of Hui in their areas, at a "Meeting Praising the Services of Islam in Building the Four Modernizations," a ceremony reported in the national press.[38] Most important, the religious policy has instilled in the villagers a new openness to dialogue with the Communist Party[39] — a trust strongly shaken during the Cultural Revolution's "10 years of internal confusion" (*shinian neiluan*).

Moderate cadres argue that the solution to the misinterpretation of the Party's free-religion policy does not lie in restricting religious activity or returning to the reform campaigns of the Gang of Four period. Rather, they advocate resolving the problems and contradictions in the local Party apparatus whose inactivity and "paralysis" (*tanhuan*) is responsible for these false conceptions of Party policy.[40] Errant Party members who openly believe should be educated or asked to resign. While the Party policy is one of "freedom of religion," it should be clearly explained that the Party itself does not promote religion and still regards it as an "opiate" that deters the masses from better production.[41] As one cadre in Yinchuan explained to me:

> The Hui are allowed to maintain their ethnic customs that are influenced by Islamic traditions, but religion and ethnicity are two separate matters and should not be confused.

THE REROOTING OF IDENTITY IN NA HOMESTEAD

The policy of clearly distinguishing between religion and ethnicity is becoming the most important formula applied to the minority-religion question.[42] This distinction is useful to cadres working in urban or Han-majority areas among minorities who no longer practice their traditional religion but who maintain certain ethnic customs. Many Beijing and Shanghai Hui who do not practice Islam continue to maintain Islamic dietary restrictions and celebrate traditional Islamic holidays (Chapter 4). The distinction between ethnicity and religion is particularly evident among Hui along the southeastern coast; these recently recognized Hui eat pork and practice Chinese folk religion (see Chapter 6). What might be applicable to ethnic policy in these areas, however, does not make sense for the majority of Hui in the northwest. Nevertheless, this policy is promoted in these areas, as the cadre's comment above demonstrates.

The distinction between Hui ethnicity and Islam was an important corrective to the traditional Chinese idea that Islam was the "Hui religion" (*Hui jiao*), rather than a world religion in which most Hui believe.[43] Controversy has arisen recently, however, over the idea that the Hui can be entirely separated from the Islamic religious tradition.[44] This debate came to a head during the 1983 Northwest Five Province Islamic Studies discussion meetings held in Yinchuan. Conferees concluded that, while the Hui nationality must be distinguished from Islam analytically, nevertheless Hui cultural heritage has been intimately influenced by Islam. Without Islam, there would be no Hui minority.

The policy of distinguishing between religion and ethnicity arises from a Chinese Marxist approach to ethnicity that tends to view ethnic consciousness, customs, and religion as circumstantial, epiphenomenal traits. These cultural traits are often class-based, and assume importance only in the competition for scarce resources. Like Barth's "situational" approach outlined above,[45] ethnic identity will lose its relevance when socioeconomic conditions change, and eventually should disappear with erosion of class or interest-based differences. Yet, for Na villagers, the religiosity is not instrumental;[46] it is part of their very sense of self and identity.

Islam is integral to their self-perception as Hui—it is part of how they see and construct their world.[47] What some might regard as a revival of Islamic fundamentalism in Hui communities is, I argue, but one aspect of a general return to and reinterpretation of their ethnoreligious roots. The resurgence in the countryside has come about in the midst of rapid socioeconomic change in the last few years since the liberalization of religious and economic policies. Current developments in Na Homestead illustrate that accepted cultural meanings of Hui identity are becoming more relevant in the social context under liberalized government policies that allow freer expression of Hui identity.

ETHNORELIGIOUS ROOTS

When I made my first visit to Na Homestead during a short 1983 trip through central Ningxia, I was immediately presented with the story that the Na villagers like to tell about their ancestry. This origin myth was often repeated to me throughout 1984 and 1985:

> We are all Muslims in this village. Most of us are surnamed Na. The Chinese character for "Na" is not in the classical book of Chinese surnames, and this proves that we are descended not from Han Chinese but from a foreign Muslim from the west. Our ancestor was none other than Nasredin, the son of Sai Dianchi (Sayyid 'Ajall), the Muslim Governor of Yunnan under the Yuan dynasty. Nasredin had four sons, and those sons changed their names to Chinese under the Ming government's ethnic-oppression policy. The four sons adopted the surnames "Na, Su, La, Ding" corresponding to the four Chinese characters that made up his name. This is why so many northwest Huihui in the Ming dynasty had these surnames. The son surnamed Na moved to this place and had five sons, of which we still have five Na leading lineages (*men*) in the village. There is also a Na village in Yunnan province, Tonghua county, where some of our relatives live.[48]

Based partly on historical records and partly on oral traditions that may or may not be accurate, this story is nevertheless critical for illuminating Na self-understanding. The ability to trace ancestral origins to the 5 leading Na lineages is an important aspect of personal status in Na Homestead. Those surnamed Na are buried together in one part of the large cemetery connected to the mosque and village. The cultural reckoning of their descent from an ancestor not only foreign but Muslim is critical for Na self-identity.

The Na have maintained this cohesive identity over centuries of inter-action with Han neighbors and in the face of prolonged oppressive local-government policies and socioeconomic instability. Na villagers are proud that their ancestors participated in Ma Hualong's Northwest Hui Rebellion (1862–1877). They say they surrendered to the Qing army general, Zuo Zongtang, only after 3 months of siege by 2 of his commanders with over 12,000 troops. They often mentioned to me that Ma Hualong's birthplace, Jinji, and gravesite, Dong Ta, are within 40 km. of Na Homestead.[49] While Zuo Zongtang's commanders spared most of the men because they surrendered, the Hui say his soldiers carried off many of their women to Henan. According to some elders, the Sichuan general Wang Tuan and his army fought the Hui for over 3 years but were never able to enter the walled village. During a conflict in the 1920s with the local Han warlord, Sun Dianying, Na villagers resisted his efforts to incorporate them into his domain. When many of the Na men were inducted into the large standing army of the Ningxia Hui war-lord, Ma Hongkui, Hui women in Na Homestead refused to marry men outside the village. Unmarried girls wore their hair up, so that Han men would think they were married and not approach them (*mei bianzi, mei hanzi,* "no ponytails, no men"). One ahong, they say, even agreed to marry a young girl to a chicken, so she would not have to leave home. Ethnic independence and a proud tradition of Muslim self-reliance during periods of adversity are reflected in these stories.

After 1949, Hui ethnoreligious identity was profoundly influenced by political campaigns that discouraged "local nationality chauvinism" (*difang minzu zhuyi*) in favor of "nationality unity" (*minzu tuanjie*). Liu Keping, the first Hui Chairman of the Ningxia Hui autonomous region, in a *Beijing Daily* speech criticized minority groups with "separatist ideas" who desire "the right of self-determination" or "independence." There was concern that the Hui in Ningxia might be influenced by Tibetan separatist movements and seek to turn the newly established Ningxia autonomous region into their own "Israel."[50] During the 1958 Religious System Reform Campaign (*Zongjiao Zhidu Gaige*) most of Ningxia's smaller mosques were closed in order to concentrate worship in larger mosques. As the largest and oldest in the area, the Na Homestead mosque was not closed and remained the main mosque in the area until the advent of the Cultural Revolution in 1966. In the mid-1950s, Na village had been recognized as an autonomous Hui village (*Najiahu Huizu zizhixiang*). However, with the 1958 drive to establish communes in the countryside, Na Homestead was incorporated as Chaoyang brigade of the Yongning county Yanghe commune. It was not renamed Na Homestead and recognized as an official village (*xinzheng cun*) of Yang He township until 1983. Since many of the religious restrictions imposed upon Muslims in China began with these campaigns in the late 1950s, and were not lifted until the 1979 reforms, many Hui referred to this period as the "20 lost years" instead of the "10 lost years" (*shinian haojie*) generally restricted to the Cultural Revolution.

A cadre from another area told me that, at a 1960 Northwest Region United Front meeting, several cadres outside Ningxia advocated a policy of requiring Hui to raise pigs. This was in response to Chairman Mao's call during the Great Leap Forward for every household to raise pigs, the perfect "fertilizer factory," reflected in the saying: "The more pigs, the more manure; the more manure, the more grain; the more grain, the greater contribution to our country." Hui who were reluctant to raise pigs risked criticism for feudalist ideas and refusal to answer Mao's call.

Despite resistance by some local cadres who were later accused of "local ethnic chauvinism" (*difang minzu zhuyi*), by 1966 at least 10 Hui households in Na Homestead were raising pigs. Most of these were cadre activists who volunteered. Some ahong in other villages also volunteered in order to show their support for the Party. These were later disparagingly called "policy ahong" (*zhengce ahong*) and recently have been rejected by many Hui as unqualified to be religious leaders.[51]

Na villagers say that many people got sick and died in the village during the time when they were forced to raise pigs. Hui regard pigs as dirty and unhealthful animals, the very antithesis of *qing zhen*.[52] A neighboring Han villager told me that many of the Hui who raised pigs did not take care of them well, and, consequently, many of the animals died prematurely. One Hui villager recounted a familiar story of the dilemma of having to feed the pig or face criticism. He would look at the animal and say: "Oh you black bug (*hei chongzi*, a Hui euphemism), if you get fat, you will die. If you get thin, I'll die!"

By 1966, during the Cultural Revolution's Smash 4 Olds (*posijiu*) Campaign, the mosque was closed and the ahong worked in the fields with the production teams. Other local ahong often returned to their original homes. Na Youxi, head ahong of the neighboring Xinzhaizi (New Stockade) Mosque, left to join his relatives in northern Ningxia, where he worked in a store.[53] I was told that no local youth took part in the Red Guard activity of that time. The mosque was converted to a county ball-bearing factory, and, although it was reopened for prayer in 1979, the factory was not relocated until 1981. By 1982, open participation in mosque affairs had resumed. Throughout this stormy period, the Hui in Na Homestead maintained their ethnic identity, and there were no cases that I could find of people attempting to deny or conceal their Hui heritage.

Reactions to oppressive policies in Na Homestead were apparently milder than in other parts of China and Ningxia. There were reported Hui uprisings in Ningxia shortly after 1949 and during the Great Leap Forward. In 1952, the "2 April" and "4 April" uprisings took place in Guyuan (now southern Ningxia) and Zhangjiachuan, Gansu, led by Ma Zhenwu's Jahriyya order. Other local uprisings by Hui followed, disenchanted by the failed promises for religious freedom and autonomy. In 1953, an "independent Islamic kingdom" was declared during an uprising by a Hui group in Henan. In Ningxia, Ma Zhenwu supposedly issued *pierhan* ("letters of introduction to the afterworld") for those who might fall in battle defending the mosques, Daotang, and tomb *waqf* lands that were being confiscated under land reform. Labeled the "protecting the Gongbei" movement, it gained wide support, before it was finally crushed on 1 June during another attempt at local control.[54] Ma Zhenwu was arrested in 1958 and publicly criticized in the news media throughout the country as a "counter-revolutionary" and exploitative "religious landlord," due to his control over the Sufi order's large *waqf* holdings. Ma Zhenwu died in prison, but was posthumously rehabilitated in August 1983 as a victim of "leftist radicalism."

THE SHADIAN INCIDENT. During the Cultural Revolution there were several minor protests led by Hui in Beijing, Ningxia, Henan, and Hebei, and at least one major uprising. This became known throughout the country as the "Shadian Incident," and is the only large-scale ethnic rebellion that I know of during the Cultural Revolution. Though the details concerning the event are unclear, based on refugee accounts and unpublished reports,[55] one new private publication was issued by the Shadian Hui History Committee in 1989, in which one essay is entitled, "A General Account of the 'Shadian Incident.'" Many of the details of the article were confirmed by several interviews I conducted in 1985 with nationality officials and eyewitnesses to the event in Yunnan.

The Shadian Incident took place in a small Hui village that is located in the southwestern corner of Yunnan, near the border of Vietnam, in Ahmi prefecture, Mengzi county, Jijie township.[56] Muslims frequently passed through the area as a result of its location on a major trading link near the Burma Road between Vietnam, Burma, and Southeast Asia, and thus one of the main overland routes for Muslim merchants traveling to the Malaysian Penninsula and the Bay of Bengal with its famous port of Chittagong near the Ganges River Delta, and from there to the Middle Eastern pilgrimage cities. With the widespread use of Muslim muleteers for transport along the Burma Road, Muslim villages still dot the old trade route from Sichuan to Burma. As a result, a flourishing Muslim community was established in Shadian as early as the Ming dynasty. It became a center for Islamic learning throughout Southeast Asia and Southwest China, producing the first Chinese translation of the Quran and several famous Muslim Chinese scholars. It was also a silver-mining and weapons-manufacturing center that played an important role in the Panthay Muslim Rebellion of 1855–1873.[57]

Though the actual uprising and massacre did not take place until 1975, the incident had its roots in an earlier conflict that took place during the height of the Cultural Revolution's "Smash-4-Olds" attack on "feudalist" practice. One of these "olds," of course, was religion, and a well-known center of Islam such as Shadian was an obvious target. The initial conflict began in July 1968 and was confined within the Hui community itself, and not along Hui-Han ethnic lines. After "Leftist" and "Revisionist" factions emerged in the village, the Leftist faction, located near an army base in the mountains, obtained weapons from the base and the conflict escalated, with several on both sides killed in related incidents of violence. In November, a People's Liberation Army propoganda team of mainly Han soldiers was welcomed by leaders of the village in order to help restore order, but they accomplished this in the full spirit of the Cultural Revolution by criticizing the "feudal" ahong and religious leaders of the village. According to the reports, over 200 Hui were struggled against, with the criticisms taking particular aims at such "backward" customs as pork avoidance and Islamic practice (shades of the Salman Rushdie scandal two decades later). Under the slogan "Purifying Class Ranks," those being criticized were not only required to denounce themselves, but also eat pork, and even imitate pigs, by being forced to "cry out," "crawl," and "roll" like the animals. One pregnant woman who was forced to undergo this humiliation suffered a miscarriage, according to the reports. Pork bones and carcasses were thrown into the water wells located in the mosque courtyard, polluting the main source of *qing zhen* water for the villagers.

By 1973, as in most of China, the situation had stabilized with life gradually returning to a semblance of normality. Several villages near Shadian had begun to reopen their mosques and openly practice their faith. When the elders at Shadian made the request to reopen their mosque, prefectural and county level cadres refused, stating: "National struggle is actually a form of class struggle," equating interest in reviving Islam with "local nationalism." About the same time, Jiang Qing, Chairman Mao's wife and member of the Gang of Four, made her famous statement: "Why do we need national minorities anyway? National identity should be done away with!" In Shadian, this meant further repression and refusal to reopen the mosque. When they attempted to celebrate Ramadan, it was labeled a "counter-revolutionary meeting" (*fan geming jihui*).

In October 1974, leaders from Shadian went to Kunming, the capital, to request that the state honor the freedom of religion and nationality laws of the Constitution. They were accused of "making a disturbance" (*nao shi*) and "opposing the leadership of the Party" (similar to the charges brought against the students of Tiananmen in 1989). When a Han "people's militia" was formed in the Jijie township to oversee the affairs in Shadian, they in turn organized their own "Huihui militia." In late December, the two well-armed militias clashed, leaving several dead. This incident came to Beijing's attention, and Hui leaders from Shadian were brought to the national Capitol to explain their position. Under Premier Zhou Enlai's guidance, they agreed to lay down their arms and were allowed to reopen their mosque.

In mid-February, another clash occurred between the two rival militias, leaving 9 Hui dead. After yet another delegation to Kunming, and further incidents, they were required to turn over any remaining arms and allow People's Liberation Army troops to enter the village and help restore order. However, the government sent many more troops than the villagers expected, and they surrounded the village. The villagers had originally welcomed the troops, but they balked at the large occupation force. In mid-July the villagers complained:

> We don't have any new weapons, and therefore, of course, have no more real arms to hand over to the soldiers. As to homemade weapons (*tu wuqi*), everyone agreed that we would hand them over if they accepted the masses' one condition: We welcome a select few of the troops to enter our village and implement the state's policy (*luo shi zhengce*). Shadian is such a small village, how can it hold several regiments of troops? At the time of Shadian's liberation [in 1949], only one small company of People's Liberation Army was needed to throw out the Nationalist regiment; why do you need so many regiments now to carry out the policy in Shadian? What are you planning on doing? The lesson we learned from letting in the army in 1968 is still fresh in everyone's mind.[58]

When this response was received by the central authorities, the Shadian Hui were accused of opposing the Party and "attempting to establish an Islamic state" like the Panthays before them. A crackdown was ordered in the middle of the night on 29 July. At 3:00 a.m. several regiments of PLA soldiers entered the village and began firing indiscriminately. Fighting in the streets, homes, and mosque lasted until noon. On 30 July the entire village was razed, and the conflagration spread to surrounding villages. "It was a nightmare," one villager told me; "every family had someone killed, and some entire households were wiped out." After 7 days and 8 nights of fighting, there were more than 1,600 Hui massacred, with 866 coming from the village of Shadian alone (whose individual names and production teams are listed in the village history).[59] One eyewitness told me that in the "clean-up" (*qing jiao*) campaign, the village itself was leveled, destroying 4,400 houses, which were completely reduced to rubble no higher than one meter. Another eyewitness reported that, in addition to using heavy cannon and artillery, the army called in Chinese MIG jets to fire rockets into the village.

It was not until February 1979, following the fall of the Gang of Four, that those responsible for the crackdown on the village were criticized, apologies were made, and reparations paid to the surviving relatives. The village was entirely rebuilt, and 7 new mosques have been constructed by the government in the area. Though the city is now open to foreign tourists as a "model community," and the government has recognized its grievous error, few are still willing to speak openly about the incident, since some of the provincial-level leaders involved in the crackdown are still in positions of influence. No one knows when the policy might reverse itself again.

With such shifting policies, the rehabilitation of the "evil landlord" Ma Zhenwu, the reparations made to Shadian, and the admissions of past "Leftist" mistakes by former leaders of the Party, it is no wonder that Hui villagers in Na Homestead, who were well aware of these events in Yunnan and elsewhere, remain skeptical about the current reforms. Most of them, when they look at all, turn instead to traditional sources of authority. As one Na villager told me, "No matter which political winds blow, I am going to stick to Islam—the Quran doesn't change its mind."

THE RECURRING TEXTS OF NA ETHNORELIGIOUS IDENTITY. Recurrent rituals play an important role in reaffirming and maintaining a group's ethnic identity. DeVos proposes:

> A major source of ethnic identity is found in the cultural traditions related to crises in the life cycle, such as coming of age, marriage, divorce, illness, or death. It is particularly in rites of passage that one finds highly emotional symbolic reinforcement of ethnic patterns.[60]

Keyes,[61] following Ricoeur,[62] has also stressed the importance of ritualized behavior, or "texts," in expressing and informing ethnic identity. In the life of Hui villagers in Na Homestead, these texts are frequently and regularly reinforced. They have become a part of the daily practice of communal life.[63] On the 3rd day after the birth of each child, every Na villager invites the local ahong to come to the home, read the scriptures, and give the child a Quranic name (*jingming*). Usually based on Arabic or Persian, such Muslim names as Muhammad, Yusuf, Usiar, Dawud, Salima, and Fatima are often heard around the Hui household.[64] Chinese names, or *Hanming* (Han nationality names) are used for official purposes and in school (sometimes referred to as *xiaoming*, literally, "school name"). After the naming ceremony, a large feast and *nietie* are provided for the ahong and guests.

At weddings, every Hui family invites the ahong to come to the bride's home, read the scriptures, and then accompany her to the new home. At one of the weddings I attended, the ahong arrived with the bride at about 8:00 in the morning. The father and mother of the groom came out of the house into the yard and everyone gathered for the reading of the special Quranic text reserved for weddings (*nikaha*). The ahong first addressed a series of questions (*yizabu*) to the father of the groom, interestingly enough, and not to the groom himself. "Are you the father of this boy?" "Do you agree to the marriage with this girl?" "Do you guarantee that their children will be raised as Muslims?" Following the father's affirmative replies, the ahong turned to the groom and asked him to quote the *Shahadah*. The groom then proclaimed the monotheistic formula (*qing zhen yan*) in fluid Arabic, "There is no God but Allah, and Muhammad is his prophet." The ahong then recited the scripture and signed their marriage certificate, at which time the guests repaired to the groom's home for a large feast. The symbolic import of reinforcing group corporate identity through rites of passage is illuminated by Bourdieu:

> Rite must resolve by means of an operation socially approved and collectively assumed—that is, in accordance with the logic of the taxonomy that gives rise to it—the specific contradiction which the primal dichotomy makes inevitable in constituting as separate and antagonistic principles that must be reunited in order to ensure the reproduction of the group. . . . Marriage rites and ploughing rites owe their numerous similarities to the fact that their *objective intention* is to sanction the union of contraries which is the condition of the resurrection of the grain and the reproduction of the group.[65]

The Hui not only regularly reaffirm their group solidarity to themselves through rites of passage, but it behooves them to demonstrate their unique ethnic separation from the outside Han world. Thus, the Islamic content of the rituals becomes particularly powerful. Perhaps underscoring the responsibility of the parents and elders for maintaining ethnoreligious tradition, male guests were seated in the main room of the house, with the ahong and several elders on the *kang* in the front, while the groom and his friends waited on the tables. It is the responsibility of the elders and the whole community to make sure ethnoreligious identity is impressed upon each new generation. Thus, marriage and parenthood, the increasing of the community, are indivisible actions that must receive sanction through Islamic ritual that stresses the purity of their identity.

Funerals are a significant part of Na community life, ensuring that ethnoreligious identity is crucial in death as well as life. Membership in the community does not end with the last breath. Death ceremonies do not terminate after the funeral, which must take place within 3 days after death (Hui use the Buddhist term *wuchang*, "impermanence," not the normal Chinese term, *chushi*). Important commemoration rituals take place on days 7, 14, 21, 40, 100, and years 1 and 3 after the death date. At one 21-day commemoration ritual (*jinqi* or *sanqi*) for a 92-year-old man, there were separate prayers and banquets at the older and younger sons' homes. The prayer began when the ahong sat down on the *kang* in the front of the younger son's house. A semicircle of other ahong and village elders was formed around him facing the gathered men. The women packed into the back room of the house or stood outside and participated in the prayer. Several people who could not fit into the small room, crowded with over 100 men, knelt on the ground in the freezing weather outside. The prayer began with a loud chanting of the *Shahadah* in unison, then a recitation by the assistant head ahong (whose voice was stronger than the 77-year-old head ahong's) of several passages of scripture with others joining, and a final chanting of the *Shahadah* by all present, including the women.

Although the Na villagers are members of a Khufiyya Sufi order, they do not practice the silent *dhikr* traditionally associated with the Khufiyya. As described above, when the Khufiyya order was first introduced to China it was known for promoting the silent *dhikr*, as opposed to the later Jahriyya order, known for the vocal use of the *jahr* in remembrance. However, like many Khufiyya members in north and central Ningxia, the Na villagers now practice an oral *dhikr*. Local historians suggest that the interesting combination of Jahriyya and Khufiyya ritual practices among the Na may result from their participation in Ma Hualong's Jahriyya-led uprising (1862–1876), after they had already been Khufiyya for many generations.[66] As a result, when they pray in unison at certain rituals, the *dhikr* is expressed aloud.[67]

At this ritual, they chant the *Shahadah* in a rhythmic cadence unique to their Khufiyya order. The last syllable of the *Shahadah* receives special stress; participants raise their voices and sway their bodies rhythmically from side to side. It is from this movement among Sufi Hui that their religion became known in earlier accounts as the "shaking-head religion" (*yaotou jiao*).[68] As I sat in the rear, wedged between several older men, I had no choice but to be swayed back and forth with them. I tried to accustom my ears to the loud chanting that went on for 15 to 30 minutes. It was always under the control of the lead ahong, and occasionally "primed" by worshipers when the reciting began to die down in intensity. After some duration, the lead ahong intoned a sort of "mm" sound and the service ended. As the men departed, each received a small donation (*dajiawangren*) of about 2 to 4 *mao* (7 to 13 cents), while several stayed for a 9-course banquet.

Following the meal, the entire ceremony was repeated in a more elaborate and lengthy fashion at the older brother's home. Mourners also chant the *dhikr* at funeral ceremonies (*zhenazi*). There, men remove their shoes and kneel in orderly rows behind the deceased, whose body is placed upon a mat on the ground and wrapped in a white shroud. After the recitation of remembrance, the body is carried by hand from the mosque environs where the ceremony is performed to the grave site. At one funeral I attended in Xining, the men carried the body for over 50 km. from the mosque to the "Public Hui Graveyard" (Hui Gong Mu) in the mountains behind the city. The rest of us went by truck. At the grave site, to the accompaniment of several readings or recitations of Quranic *suras*, the body was lowered into the earth in the shroud without a coffin, whereupon most of those present assisted in replacing the soil.

As an outside observer who has attended other Muslim funerals and Sufi rituals in Central Asia, I was struck by the attention paid to order in these ceremonies. Chanting and remembrance of the *dhikr* in most Sufi rituals often leads to trance states and loud singing, shaking, and even dancing. Funerals are often accompanied by loud mourners and community tumult. While the more silent Khufiyya tradition may have had some influence, I was told by Na villagers that they did not want to arouse the suspicions of their Han neighbors or the state, so they took care not to let things get out of control. One Han joked with me that, in the old days, after the loud chanting in the mosque, the Hui would run out excitedly shouting, "Kill the Han!" The slightest hint of this kind of activity is quashed by the Hui. Allowing me, a foreigner, to attend to the ritual, generally closed to Han and non-Muslims, is certainly an indication of their desire not to appear secret in their practices. In Islamic ritual in China, the far-reaching hand of the state is heavily felt.

I subsequently learned that the prayer and funeral ceremony for this 92-year-old man were more elaborate due to his venerable age and standing in the community. Well over 1,000 yuan in *nietie* were distributed to those attending.[69] By contrast, while I was there, another man was given a very simple funeral. One older man complained: "Only 250 yuan was distributed to guests." He explained that this particular individual was not well cared for by his family, nor very religious. He was often left alone in a room and died at the comparatively young age of 60. "No wonder he died young," one villager told me; "its like repairing old pants. If you just keep patching them rather than caring for them or getting new ones, when winter comes they won't last." Consequently, fewer than 100 villagers attended his funeral, the others displaying their disapproval by their absence.

Hui often say that longevity is the result of Allah's blessing (*Zhenzhu baoyou*) for a devout *qing zhen* life. They attribute their good health to their maintaining Islamic dietary restrictions and attention to personal hygiene. Hui say they are cleaner than Han because they must engage in the "small wash" (*xiao jin*) 5 times a day before prayer, and the "complete wash" (*da jin*) every Friday. Hui are proud to note that, though the Hui are only one third of Ningxia's population, the 1982 census revealed 21 of the 23 centenarians in Ningxia region were Hui[70] — veritable proof of the benefits of living a pure *qing zhen* life.

Wang Zixiao is held up by the Na villagers as an example of God's blessing. At 101 years old, even though his legs are too weak for him to go to the mosque, Wang Lao still regularly prays at home. The walls surrounding his warm *kang* are covered with Arabic texts and flowery Islamic paintings containing Quranic verses arranged in traditional Chinese *duilian* style. His wife lived to 113 years old, and his eldest son is 86. His mother was a Han woman who converted to Islam at marriage, and her children were raised in a strict Muslim household. When I asked Lao Wang what his secret was for longevity, he responded; "good religion" (*jiaomende hao*). The Hui in Na Homestead feel that Allah rewards a *qing zhen* lifestyle with health and longevity. Religious devotion is critical to this understanding of *qing zhen*, where purity (*qing*) exemplifies the authenticity (*zhen*) of one's religion.

Along with rituals that take place at important stages of the Hui life cycle, Islamic holidays interrupt the normal course of the agricultural year. In addition to the Ramadan and Corban festivals, Na-village Hui celebrate the Prophet's Day, or Muhammad's Birthday, as well as Fatima's Birthday. When I attended the Prophet's Day Festival, I was surprised by the turnout of the entire village for the event. The men attending the festival entered the mosque and knelt for prayer in the front with their shoes off, while the women and children assembled in the back of the mosque. The presence of women and men together in a mosque anywhere in the Muslim world is rare, and China is no exception. This allowance was perhaps due to the fact that the mosque was under construction, and the place where the women stood was not yet repaired and well behind the men. There are no women's mosques in Ningxia, and only one women's prayer room that I know of, located in the Yihewani "South Great Mosque" in Wuzhong city. The women wore shoes and many of their heads were uncovered, but they continued to recite the scriptures in unison.

The ahong, elders, and several young *manla* were the last in a procession to enter the mosque. They were seated in a circle at the front around low tables on which they had placed the Quran, divided into 30 separate chapters. After a short sermon (*hutubai*) on the significance of the Prophet's birth, the men divided up the chapters and simultaneously read the entire Quran (*yuanjing* or *da nian*). The ahong later explained that this was so the entire village would receive the benefit of being present when the whole Quran was read, since most of them could only recite memorized Quranic texts and could not read them. Young *manla* who learn to read the Quran are often employed by villagers to read portions at the graves of their ancestors. They are accorded high status in the village. Hence, several of the young *manla* were seated at the head of the mosque in front of the entire village to read the Quran along with the other elders and ahong. As the worshipers left the mosque they were given traditional Hui pastries, "fragrant oil cakes" (*youxiang*), with a slice of boiled mutton on top.

THE CULTURAL ORGANIZATION OF NA IDENTITY. The cultural organization of space in Hui villages and homes also distinguishes them from their Han neighbors. Hui homes are often decorated with brightly painted mirrors depicting Mecca or Medina as well as ornate Quranic calligraphic drawings and paintings in Chinese and Arabic. These mirrors and texts are generally placed where Han traditionally would have their ancestral altars. Hui homes, like those of the Han, usually open to the south, but for the Hui there is generally no communication or doorways linking the side homes of the sons with the central hall of the parents. Hui claim that this reflects a more conservative perspective because the women are more secluded from their in-laws. The gates of Hui homes are less ornate than Han and not fixed according to *fengshui* (geomantic) principles. Hui also say their houses are cleaner than Han houses. Unlike most Han, the Hui usually do not allow domestic animals like dogs or chickens into the home. Hui often set aside places for ritual washing, and some even build separate small prayer rooms for the women to use. Hui pay scrupulous attention to order and cleanliness in their homes. I turn again to Cable and French for a pithy desciption of northwestern Hui homes where they spent much time, which they contrasted with Han and Central Asian Muslim homes:

> In the home of the Tungan [Hui] there is neither shrine nor ancestral tablet, but its pattern is as defined as the ancestor-controlled home of the Confucian,

only here the scheme of life is ordered by the rules and regulations of the Islamic faith. Five times a day, beginning with the hour of sunrise, the man must prostrate himself with face toward Mecca and recite the liturgy of the hour. He never dares to neglect the endless ceremonial purifications which his religion demands, and for one full month of each year he observes the exacting and rigid fast of the *Ramazan*. . . . A visit to a Turki home is quiet unlike a stay in a Tungan house. In the latter all is order, thrift and propriety, for existence has progressed on definite and established lines until it has mastered the technique of orderly conduct. Among the Turkis all is noise and turmoil. Gay clothing, swinging draperies and light muslin veiling combine with the rapid talk of girls and the gutturals of men's voices to fill the air with noise and movement.[71]

The central location of the mosque in virtually every Hui village marks its importance as the focal point of the village in ritual and social organization. A Han temple, by contrast, is traditionally located wherever the *fengshui* determines best, which may place it either within or well outside the village. Those who maintain Han temples are not necessarily regarded by the locals as leaders or integral to the affairs of the village. The ahong in a Hui village, however, are regarded as the primary actors. They must approve every marriage and are intimately acquainted with the villagers' lives. Most ahong are regularly invited to Hui homes for meals on a revolving basis (*chuanfan*). The ahong also often assist in resolving local conflicts. For example, I witnessed the intervention by a Na-village ahong in one dispute over the construction of a water pipe that one villager thought was being installed too close to his yard. If the pipe broke, the spillage would ruin his grain storage. As the argument escalated to the point of violence, several villagers ran to get the ahong to help settle the matter. When he arrived, the dispute calmed down considerably.

Unlike their Han neighbors, Hui often build their graveyards either adjacent to or within the confines of their village. This land is held in common by the community and often frequented by the villagers for regular prayer and meditation. Ekvall also noticed this unique aspect of the Hui social landscape:

> The Moslems take great pains to make their graveyards like parks or semi-public groves, which become places for informal religious meditation and acquire a peculiar odor of sanctity. Among the Chinese the graveyards are

open, and there is no prejudice against allowing sheep or cattle to graze over them—in fact, they are in a way community pastures.[72]

Lattimore described two Hui graveyards outside Huhehot, Inner Mongolia, where "good Moslems" are buried in grave sites separate from the "backsliders."[73] In Na Homestead, an average of 4 to 8 individuals went to the graveyard (*shangfen*) every day to pray, with 30 or more visitors on Fridays. Someone from the extended household made at least one trip a week to the graveyard. Hui do not believe in ghosts and gods like their Han neighbors, and are not afraid of the graveyards at night. A popular Hui folk saying is:

> When on the road the safest place for Hui to sleep is the Han graveyard; the ghosts won't bother us because we don't believe in them, and local Han bandits won't bother us because they are too afraid of the ghosts.

In his book, *Under the Ancestors' Shadow*, Francis L. K. Hsu[74] relates that, in the religious cosmology of Han villagers (actually, they were Bai),[75] the Hui's ancestral spirits were neither feared nor welcomed: "They do not influence the West Towners' relations with the other world at all." Hence, Han, and, in this case, Bai villagers, did not object to the close proximity of a neighboring Hui village's graveyard. Red Guard desecration of graveyards and tombs in Hui areas during the Cultural Revolution led to major and minor confrontations throughout China.

The role of the graveyard among the Hui and the influence of the ancestors buried there resembles the place of traditional temples dotting the Taiwan countryside.[76] Women often take their daughters to these temples, seeking otherworldly help for them to have sons, or resolving financial problems. Miracles also are known to occur in the vicinity of these folk Chinese shrines, and they influence the natural powers of the earth, bringing good weather and fruitful harvests.[77] Local communities may adopt non-lineage ghosts and historic heroes as patron deities over time.[78] Similarly, among the Hui, especially well-known deceased religious leaders or *hajji* are often honored with local tombs (*tu gongbei*) that are patronized like these traditional Han temples. Deceased Sufi saints are built more elaborate tombs and shrines.[79] The value attached to these local symbols has often been viewed as a threat to the state.

While criticizing the Jahriyya *shaykh* Ma Zhenwu in 1958, prosecutors representing the state recorded the following ways in which he supposedly extorted money from his followers:

> Before the Liberation, Ma Chen-wu even sold his hair, beard, the dirt from the "kung-pei," his household firewood ashes, dry bread, small pieces of his ragged clothes, and even his own manure to the Hui masses as "miracle drugs" to cure their diseases. By so doing, he not only has swindled big sums of money but also has caused many deaths.[80]

While Hui do not have any known institutionalized practice of geomancy (*fengshui*) with professionals skilled in selecting sites for buildings and graves, it is interesting that many of these graves are placed in similar locations. Many Hui graveyards and tombs are on the sides of hills with a stream or plain below. The most notable example is the graveyard and *gongbei* complex at North Mountain, in Linxia, Gansu. Following their own Islamic customs, Hui arrange their graves on a north-south axis, with the entrance to tombs almost always to the south. The body lies with the head to the north, the feet to the south and the face turned west, toward Mecca.

Near the famous Bell Tomb of a Muslim saint buried outside Canton (see Chapter 6), there is a tombstone for the "Pure and True Religious Leader Ma Ahong by the Name of Yunting" (*qing zhen jiaozhang Ma lao ahheng zi Yunting*) dated 1939. It is engraved with the following epitaph: "Another Home for Purity and Truth (Islam)" (*qing zhen bieshe*). This marks the graveyard, and the ancestors buried there, as a powerful focal place in the *qing zhen* Hui village.

THE SOCIOECONOMIC CONTEXT

Shared ideas and rituals illustrate the solidarity of the Hui community and the important role the texts of their faith play in defining ethnic identity. The texts become particularly meaningful during periods of intense socioeconomic change. The years since 1979, not to mention the "10 catastrophic years" (*shinian haojie*) of the Cultural Revolution, have called into question the relevance of Islam, and the nature of Hui identity in Na Homestead. Hui identity has also been expressed and altered by interaction with recent government policies and renewed participation in the marketplace under the private-responsibility system.

Na Homestead has 5,036 *mu* (805.7 acres) of land under cultivation, planting mainly rice, winter wheat, sorghum, and some fruit in a few orchards. Average land per person is 1.37 *mu* (0.21 acres), and 6.95 *mu* (1.1 acres) per household, somewhat less than in neighboring Han villages. Average grain yield per *mu* in Na Homestead is about 200 kgms., less than the regional average of 238 kgms. Important shifts in the involvement of the local labor force since the private-responsibility system was introduced in 1979 include a significant decline in collective activity and power since the dismantling of the commune, as documented elsewhere in China.[81] In 1978, 27.8 percent of the village population was involved in the labor force. However, by 1984, that figure had grown to 49.6 percent of the village, reflecting pre-1950 levels (see Table 6). Agriculture and husbandry, industry and construction, and small sideline enterprises (such as cottage industries, private shops and food stands, transportation and service industries) are the 3 main sectors. A significant change in sideline industries has absorbed much of the increased labor. While only 1.6 percent of the labor force was involved in these small enterprises in 1978, involvement increased to 16 percent by 1984, slightly less than the 1950 level of 17.6 percent.

In the 113 households studied, 60 people are engaged in sideline businesses, representing 19 percent of the labor force. In 1978, only 1 person was involved in food-related small business, and no one from the village was involved in service or transportation. By 1984, however, 85 people were in the food trade, 26 in service industry, and 24 in transport.[82] In the food industry, 8 households opened small restaurants in Yanghe township with several others selling *yang zasui*—a traditional Hui spicy stew made from the internal organs of sheep. This surpassed the reported 4 households who operated small restaurants before 1950.[83]

Participation in the free market and the private-responsibility system has also encouraged Hui in Na Homestead to increase their planting of vegetables and cash crops, significantly higher than 1978 levels (see Table 7). While agricultural income derived from cash crops in 1984 was only half as much as in 1957, it was more than 3 times that of 1978 before the responsibility system was instituted in Na Homestead.

TABLE 6 Change in Labor Force in Na Village since 1949

Year	Popu- lation	Labor Force		Agriculture & Husbandry		Industry & Construction		Private Enterprise		Other	
		N	%	N	%	N	%	N	%	N	%
1950	2,004	985	49.0	607	61.6	55	5.6	175	17.8	148	15.0
1978	3,378	937	27.8	760	81.1	162	17.3	15	1.6	0	0
1984	3,871	1,921	49.6	1,439	74.9	175	9.1	307	16.0	0	0

Source: Adapted from Zhu Yuntao, p. 3.

TABLE 7 Grain, Vegetables, and Cash Crops in Na Homestead since 1957

Year	% Land Planted with Grains	% Agricultural Income from Grain	% Land Planted with Cash Crops	% Agricultural Income From Cash Crops
1957	61.7	33.5	38.3	66.5
1978	91.0	89.6	9.0	10.4
1984	82.2	66.8	17.8	33.2

Source: Zhu Yuntao, p. 5.

Before 1949, Hui proclivity for growing cash crops in this area was noted by Fan Changjiang. He observed that the opium produced by Han and Hui peasants in the Yanghe area was of a very high quality, but the Han could not make much of a profit from it. The Han smoked too much of it themselves and thus were too weak-willed to gain financially. The Hui, on the other hand, did not smoke opium. Furthermore, their fields produced 120 *liang* per *mu,* whereas Han fields yielded only 70 *liang* per *mu.*[84] The Hui in this area were prosperous and healthy:

> Because the Hui do not smoke opium, their health is good, they are able to endure hardship and share each other's burdens. . . . The Han situation is quite the opposite in comparison, therefore they naturally are not able to compete with the Hui.[85]

ECONOMIC VALUES AND NA ENTREPRENEURSHIP. Some Hui complain that they have no alternative but to engage in small business, because the land they have been allotted is too little or too unproductive. Since the

Na Homestead villager, "The longest beard in the village." Northwestern Hui are proud of their Central Asian physical features, which, they believe, mark their Muslim ancestry. Photo: Gladney

Third-generation Hui camel herdsmen selling camels in Wuzhong, Ningxia. These are no longer used for transport but are now raised for their pelts and meat. Photo: Gladney

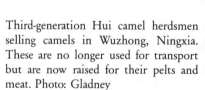

nineteenth-century Hui rebellions, the Hui in Shaanxi, Gansu, and Ningxia were often forced to live in areas with steep mountains and saline flatlands, which Han avoided. While attempts to redress many of these inequities were made during the Land-Reform Campaigns of the early 1950s, some Hui feel that they still have poorer land than Han and are thus compelled to be more interested in business. On his 1980 tour of southern Ningxia's Guyuan district (6 counties) where the Hui are most concentrated (constituting 45.7 percent of the total population in Guyuan and 49.1 percent of Ningxia region's total Hui population), Hu Yaobang remarked that this area was China's most impoverished region. In 1983, the State Council set up a special committee to encourage economic development in Guyuan district, Ningxia, Longxi, and Dingxi counties, Gansu.[86]

Until its large hydraulic works were recently developed, Tongxin county (78.96 percent Hui) was unable to receive any of the water from the nearby Yellow River and remained a barren wasteland. Many of the peasants continue to live in caves built into the sides of loess hills. Though cheaper and cooler than adobe houses, one man explained to me that he would like to move out of his cave house because it was not "modern." Most villagers seek to build houses in their yards and keep the caves for livestock and storage. During a large market-day gathering in Tongxin, a peasant from a nearby all-Hui village said that, instead of doing business at the market, he had come to get his monthly allotment of grain. Because of the previous year's drought, his entire village had no harvest whatsoever. He had come to buy or borrow grain from the government at a reduced price (0.14 yuan a kgm. instead of 0.20+ yuan a kgm. on the open market). He would eventually repay the government with either money or grain, a common practice in Tongxin during drought-stricken seasons. Since he had a family of 12, and received 20 kgms. a month for each person, he picked up 240 kgm. a month. He said over 90 percent of Tongxin's peasants depended on trade and government subsidies for a living. Only 10 percent depended on farming, because the land was just not productive enough. A local doggerel poem depicts the harshness of this area where Hui are concentrated in southern Ningxia:

The wind blows, the stones roll	*Fengchui shitou pao*
Everywhere is camel grass	*Biandi luotou cao*
The housetops are so flat you can run races	*Fangding neng saipao*
There is no water, no one bathes	*Meishui bu xizao*

Several visits to local Tongxin households disclosed a large amount of sundry and decorative goods produced in Guangzhou and rarely seen in Yinchuan. The main intersection of town lies along the Yinchuan-Guyuan arterial road and is always crowded with young people selling digital watches purchased from southern China and Guangzhou. These items were still a rare commodity in Yinchuan where they were far more expensive. On one occasion, a Hui companion from Yinchuan bought 10 watches for 3 yuan ($1.00 US) each. Similar watches might cost 30 yuan each in Yinchuan.

The Hui from Na Homestead are also playing an important role in the local free-market economy. Hui operate 70 percent of the new restaurants, food stands, and private sales stalls in the nearby Yongning county seat market area, even though they constitute only 12.6 percent of the population. The Hui from Na Homestead own most of the stands. They also participate in the central free market in Wuzhong city, 30 km. south. There, Hui merchants make up over 90 percent of those doing business in a city that is 95 percent Han. Most of the Hui come into the city to do business from outlying Hui villages, like Dongfeng township, 95 percent Hui. This active entrepreneurial participation is an important aspect of Hui ethnoreligious identity. As one Han peasant from Na Homestead remarked, "The Hui are good at doing business; the Han are too honest and can't turn a profit. Han are good at planting, Hui at trade."

Only 2 percent of households in Na Homestead are *wanyuan hu*, that is, reporting an annual income of over 10,000 yuan. While not a large percentage compared to some areas in China, it is unusual in a fairly poor Hui area. The prestige and influence of these *wanyuan hu* is significant. Na Jingling, the most successful of Na Homestead's new entrepreneurs, made his fortune through setting up a popsicle (*binggun*) factory in 1982. A former mechanic for the commune, he and his brother have now moved into the transportation and construction business. They have recently entered into a contract with two other investors to build an "Islamic" hotel in Yinchuan city at a cost of 1.4 million yuan. The hotel will feature a restaurant and shopping facilities with "Arabic" architecture. "We want a real Hui hotel," his brother said, "not like other Hui restaurants in town where you aren't sure if its *qing zhen*."

The government's encouragement of economic development and market-oriented enterprise among Hui is having an important impact on Han-Hui relations and ethnoreligious identity. In several Hui villages in Northwest China, active Hui participation in trade and food businesses has led to faster economic development than their Han neighbors. In Tang Ma village, a Hui and Han village that I visited outside Xining on the road to the Kumbum Tibetan monastery (Taersi) in 1983, there are 2 all-Hui teams and 1 Han team that separated along ethnic lines in 1979. There are 3 private (*geti*) restaurants in the village, all run by Hui and patronized by local residents and tourists who stop on their way to Kumbum. Since 1979, dramatic changes have taken place in Han and Hui economic levels. In addition to running restaurants, Hui began raising cattle in the late 1970s, selling their beef in Xining. Before 1949, the Hui there raised cattle, but in 1956 they were confiscated by the commune as trappings of bourgeois capitalism. As a result of their new-found income, the Hui now have 18 tractors, while the Han only have 3. The village chairman estimates Hui household income to be twice that of the Han.

Recent economic prosperity among rural Hui as a result of favorable government policy and Hui entrepreneurial abilities has led to increased support for religious affairs. Na Jingling, for example, wants to use his profits to help the Hui in Ningxia support the mosque, and build a "really *qing zhen*" Islamic hotel. Other Hui *wanyuan hu* have told me that, because Allah is responsible for their new-found wealth under the new government policies, they should devote some of their profits to promoting Islam and mosque construction. Red posters on the walls in every mosque clearly list by name and amount who has given to the construction projects, with names of these *wanyuan hu* and their donations writ large. More wealthy Hui sometimes complained to me of the pressures brought to bear on them to contribute to the mosque.

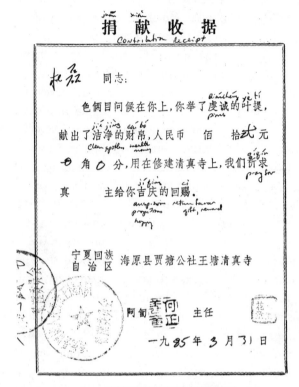

CONTRIBUTION RECEIPT

_____ Comrade (*Tongzhi*):

When this is presented in your presence, carry out your pious work (*qiancheng de yeti*) and contribute spotless money (*jiejing de caibo*), renminbi _____ hundred _____ ten _____ yuan _____ mao _____ fen, when used in building the mosque, we will pray for Allah (*Zhenzhu*) to return to you auspicious favor (*jijing de huici*).

Ningxia Hui

       Haiyuan County Jiatan Commune Wangtan Mosque

Autonomous Region

          Ahong _____ Director

             19 __ year _____ month _____ day

FIGURE 2 A Mosque Contribution Receipt

While I was in Tongxin on one Friday prayer day, a venerable Hui with a long white beard grabbed my arm. He strongly encouraged me to give my weekly *nietie* (alms) to the mosque. He desisted only when he was satisfied that I was a non-Muslim and a foreigner. Lacking adequate funds to restore their own mosques, Hui frequently send out itinerant travelers to request donations. These travelers give receipts with official seals and the admonition: "We will pray for Allah (Zhenzhu) to return auspicious favor to you" (see Figure 2). The pressure brought to bear on Hui to use their new-found wealth for higher purposes is clearly set forth in the following text painted next to the doorway of the *dadian* (main prayer hall) at a mosque just 20 km. south of Na Homestead:

"SUGGESTIONS FOR MUSLIMS"

We suggest that Muslims practice the 5 tenets regularly; do not put off today until tomorrow, tomorrow to the next day.

When natural and national disasters come, it is too late to regret. Days and months pass, and the truth is lost.

In a glance, children become adults, and adults become elderly; very many people do not consider death (*wuchang*).

Everyday you clean and order your house to establish its future but abandon prayer, neglect to give alms, and are very stingy.

You have 100, but want 1,000, you get it and desire 10,000. Your desire is uncontrollable; do not know satisfaction; the more you have the more you desire.

Today you go east, tomorrow west; mind and body are never at peace. Anxiety becomes happiness, happiness becomes anxiety, anxiety is great, happiness is limited.

You don't practice the prayers on time; they are postponed until tomorrow. Because of laziness, you waste forever (10,000 years), what a pity!

You are a created person; why not consider the results more carefully? Maintaining the prayers will not interfere with your daily life.

Because of contentedness you disregard the lessons, committing myriad errors. If you were very wealthy, but you died suddenly, your wealth would be gone forever.

Money hoarded amounts to nothing; in the end even a little bit can't be taken with you; you build many houses, but in daily life you have need of only one.

Stocking up on food, you can only eat to the full one *jin* and a half *liang;* your trunks stuffed with clothes, they amount to nothing; you can only wear one outfit.

Abounding in grace, extreme wealth looks good for a little while: You enjoy it for this life, but, in the afterlife, you certainly will owe a great deal.

MARRIAGE EXCHANGE AND ETHNORELIGIOUS IDENTITY. Marital practices are an important indicator of changing social relations and ethnic solidarity. Growing prosperity in Na Homestead has led to an increase in the bride wealth given at marriage and a decrease in intermarriage with the Han. In Na Homestead, there were many Hui-Han intermarriages during the Cultural Revolution when young Hui were strongly encouraged to marry Han as an indication that they rejected "local ethnic chauvinism" (*difang minzu zhuyi*). With the increasing conservativism in Na Homestead in recent years, however, intermarriages have been rare. The most recent intermarriage occurred in 1984; a Han women living outside the village on the market street in the Yongning county seat married into a Hui family. This is typical of Hui-Han intermarriage in the northwest. Hui families take in Han women, but rarely permit Hui women to marry out (Chapter 5). The village chairman could remember only one marriage between a Han man and Hui woman, which took place 10 years earlier. A Han villager told me of a 37-year-old Han man who married a 35-year-old Hui woman in 1972. The man converted at marriage and is now regarded as a Hui. He maintains little contact with his Han relatives.

Marriage among the Hui within Na Homestead or with other rural Hui in the vicinity is the norm. Surname endogamous marriage between Na villagers still takes place—almost unheard of among the Han. Government regulations strictly prohibit endogamous marriage with someone who has a common ancestor within 5 generations. As more accurate government records restrict close intermarriage, the *lunzi paibie* system of marking generations by the first character of one's personal name has begun to break down only in the last 2 generations among the Na. The characters Wan, Yu, Zhang, Dian, and Hong mark the last 5 generations in Na Homestead. Surname endogamy is justified by some Hui to Han who reject this practice as unfilial because, the Hui reason, their surnames are translations of foreign surnames (for example, Ma for Muhammad) and not indicative of familial relations. It is a different matter for Na villagers, however, who trace descent to a single ancestor.

Cross-cousin marriage, as well as marriage between matrilateral parallel cousins (*yibiao xiongmei*), is frequently practiced. The custom of "swapping relatives" (*huandui qin*), where a daughter is exchanged for a brother's son, is common in Na Homestead, as was the case in the venerable Wang Zixiao's family. He gave his daughter in marriage to his brother's son. A survey of 50 young people already married in Na Homestead showed that 4 percent were cross-cousin or matrilateral parallel cousin (*gubiao, yibiao*) marriages, with 8 percent in some kind of familial relationship with their spouses. Since dowry value was increasing throughout the rural areas in China, due to a general increase in rural income, I cannot tell if it correlated with rising surname endogamy. In general, however, Hui dowries tended to be 20-30 percent higher than Han.

Some Hui leaders believe that the preference for endogamous marriages among the Hui has led to mental illness among their offspring (*jinqin hunbing*). The Na Homestead chairman said that, in 1982, there were 4 cases of mentally handicapped children attributed to too close intermarriage. In one case, 2 malformed children were born to a household where a maternal uncle's (*jiujiu*) daughter was married to a paternal aunt's (*gumu*) son. In another household all 3 children were malformed, with one son dying at childbirth. I often encountered these mentally handicapped children (simply called *xiazi*, "idiots") in Hui villages throughout the northwest.[87]

Hui say mental retardation is a particularly serious problem in areas where certain conservative Islamic orders restrict intermarriage with Hui in other Islamic orders. Membership in various Islamic orders often significantly influences social interaction. While intermarriage between different orders of Hui is common elsewhere in China, in stronger Islamic areas of Northwest China Hui prefer to marry within their own order. This is particularly true of the Jahriyya order, and, in

Ningxia, Shagou, and Banqiao, *menhuan* branch members rarely inter-marry.

In Chengdu, Sichuan, I met 3 Hui travelers from the northwest, who were easily marked by their strong Gansu accents, long beards, and distinctive dress. They were on their way to Kunming where they planned to purchase tea; as Rossabi documented, this was an important trade niche of the Hui in this area over 400 years ago.[88] Bringing the tea back to the northwest, they could sell it at as a profit of 1 yuan per half kilo, averaging 300 yuan profit each trip, with 3 trips scheduled per year. Chengdu is a frequent stopping place for travelers from the northwest on their way to the southwest, since it is the most central rail and transportation hub. This accounts for the high proportion of Hui restaurants and the large mosque in the city, despite a relatively small indigenous Hui population. The 3 businessmen complained that the religious fervor (*jiaomen*) at the local mosque was inadequate; they were the only ones at prayer that day. They then discussed their Islamic differences. One was a Gedimu, another a Yihewani, and the last a member of a Jahriyya Sufi order. When I asked if they would allow their children to intermarry, they themselves were somewhat surprised to learn that the Gedimu was willing to marry his child to the Yihewani, but not to the Jahriyya. Neither the Yihewani nor the Jahriyya were willing to let his children marry someone from another order.

LOCAL GOVERNMENT POLICIES AND NA NATIONAL IDENTITY

The Ningxia Hui autonomous region was established in 1958 with its present boundaries redrawn in 1976. Since its founding, Hui throughout China have taken an active involvement in its leadership and civic affairs. While the first Party secretary of the region has always been Han, the chairman of the People's Government (Renmin Zhengfu) has always been Hui. Four of the 5 current vice-chairmen are Hui. Concerned to involve different Hui Islamic leaders, the government is represented by influential members of several religious orders. One regional vice-chairman is the acknowledged *murshid* of the Banqiao branch of the Sufi Jahriyya order (see Appendix A). The current leader of the

Shagou Jahriyya branch is a vice-chairman of the Regional Chinese People's Political Consultative Conference (CPPCC).[89]

Hui cadre representation in the People's Government and CPPCC exceeds their one-third proportion of the population. Party membership, however, is comparatively much lower than among the Han. While published figures on total Hui participation in the Party are unavailable, Hui membership in the Yanchi county Party was published as 79 out of 4,286 (1.8 percent). Party enrollment among Hui, especially in rural areas, has been a high government priority. A *Ningxia rebao* 8 November 1984 article stressing the importance of encouraging Hui to join the Party in Tongxin county stated that, since 1979, 799 new Party members had enrolled, including 536 new Hui members (67.1 percent). The current low percentage of Hui in the Party is attributed to continuing "leftist influences" that have begun to be corrected only since the 3rd Party Plenum. In order to increase Party enrollment in Tongxin, entrance exams will be held twice a year. In Na Homestead, as noted above, no one has been introduced into the Party since 1976, and membership stands at 1.7 percent of the village.

AUTONOMOUS ADMINISTRATION AND LOCAL CONCERNS. As an autonomous region, Ningxia has more jurisdiction over regional affairs than centrally controlled provinces.[90] A higher percentage of tax revenues are allowed to be used locally rather than turned over to the central government. Production quotas may be set according to local plans. Those minority-affairs policies having the most effect on the Hui relate to the following: religious expression, education, marriage and birth planning, expanded relations with Middle Eastern Muslim nations, and more liberalized economic policies.[91]

Greater religious freedom is evident throughout the region in the rapid rebuilding of mosques that were either closed or destroyed during the "Smash-4-Olds" Campaign of the Cultural Revolution and the 1958 Religious System Reform Campaign. The government has spent large sums of money to rebuild and restore famous mosques in Na Homestead (90,000 yuan), Tongxin (800,000 yuan), and Yinchuan's Southgate Great Mosque (over 1 million yuan). Hui are allowed to rebuild mosques in almost every village where they existed before 1949, as well as in newer areas where Hui have become concentrated. As a result, there are now more mosques in Ningxia than before 1949—almost one in every Hui village.

The shifting religious landscape in the northwest is a direct result of recent nationality reforms that have had an important impact, not only on the Hui, but on the Han majority as well. Many of Ningxia's recently rebuilt 2,132 mosques are visible from the window of the bus as one travels the main arterial from Yinchuan to Jingyuan. On one trip in 1985, I counted well over 100 on either side of the road. While many of these mosques were being built on my first trip through central Ningxia in 1983, there were then few Han temples noticeable. As a response to the rapid rebuilding of Hui mosques, Han have since become actively engaged in rebuilding their temples; many were visible along the highway in 1985. The Han were able effectively to argue the validity of rebuilding their *mazu* and *tudigong* folk religious temples since the Hui had already rebuilt their mosques. It is arguable whether the Han would have been granted the privilege had the Hui not first been able to exploit the opportunity. One Han villager in Qingtongxia said: "The Hui get to rebuild their temples, why can't we? Their temples rise up and block our wind/water alignments (*darao fengshui*, geomantic principles of ecological-ontological order), and the gods are angry that only the Hui spirits have temples built to them."

In newly developed areas where there are mixed Islamic orders among the Hui, conflicts have arisen over obtaining permission to build separate mosques for different orders, instead of the united service in a single mosque that the government encourages. In Shizuishan, Ningxia's northernmost city, there was only one mainly Yihewani mosque before 1949, later destroyed in 1966. When the government donated 90,000 yuan to help rebuild the mosque in 1981, Gedimu, who had migrated to the area in large numbers to engage in the expanding coal industry, claimed they wanted their own mosque. The Yihewani objected and one night pulled down a prayer room the Gedimu had used and planned to convert to a mosque. After much strife and debate, the local government agreed to build a separate Gedimu mosque in October 1982. Increasing numbers of Qadariyya Sufi in the area have now requested their own mosque. Qadariyya generally worship at the shrines and tombs of their saints, but, because there are no such places in northern Ningxia and Qadariyya numbers are growing, they want to worship in their own mosque. The city government is reluctant to approve the request because the absolute number of Qadariyya in the area is still too small.

Occasionally, participants in these disputes attempt to resolve their differences in the streets. To help settle the conflicts, the regional government often brings in respected religious leaders from the city as mediators. While local cadres say these conflicts give them many headaches in their nationality work (*minzu gongzuo*), they have as yet not led to any widescale violence. The conflicts seem to have remained at the local, intra-factional level, and I have not heard of any of them being directed toward the local government or Han neighbors.[92] Instead, I have witnessed the concern by local government cadres and Chinese Islamic Society leaders to attempt to work out the differences without enforcing any rigid policies. To avoid sectarian struggles, they encourage the policy of "Each to his own matter, mutual unity, and mutual non-interference" (*Ge gan ge de, huxiang tuanjie, hu bu gan she*).[93] The existence of these conflicts and the flexibility on the part of the government to help resolve them illustrates that the state policy of freedom of religion, though not without its problems, is having a significant effect in the countryside.

EDUCATION. In addition to allowing from 2 to 4 students (*halifat*) to train privately in each mosque, the government has approved and funded 2 Islamic schools (*yixueyuan*) in Yinchuan and Tongxin. Plans were being drawn up in early 1985 to establish a large Islamic seminary and mosque complex outside the West Gate of Yinchuan near Luo village. The Number 2 Northwest Nationalities Institute was established in 1984 to raise the educational level of Hui in Ningxia. A special 1-year preparatory course for Hui students (*minzu yubei ban*) at Ningxia University was established to raise Hui students to college level. There are Hui high schools in Yinchuan, Lingwu, Tongxin, and Guyuan, as well as numerous Hui primary schools. The curriculum of these schools is the same as in Han public schools, using materials published by the Education Bureau. The main difference is that entrance requirements for middle schools and colleges are lower for Hui, and no pork is served in the student cafeterias.

BIRTH PLANNING. The Hui minority in Ningxia follow a "1-2-3" policy: allowing 1 child in the city, 2 children in the countryside, and 3 children in mountainous or desert areas. In 1985, a law was promoted that minorities above 1 million population in urban areas would have to follow the birth-planning policies of 1 child only. In general, however, the Hui are often allowed to have at least 1 child more than their Han neighbors. This leads to not a little resentment among Han, who often feel the Hui are just the same as they and should not be given any advantages.

In rural areas where population is sparse, Hui have been known to have even more than their allotted children. One man from a village outside Guyuan told me his wife was pregnant with her 9th child. However, with the support of the ahong and use of the mosque for disseminating policy, birth planning has been judged relatively successful among most Hui. Infractions by the Hui tend to be judged more lightly than among the Han. I knew of one Hui village chairman with 3 sons and another child on the way in early 1985. A Hui villager north of Yinchuan had 3 daughters and was officially allowed to have 1 more child in order to see if he might have a son. He began spending every morning in the mosque praying for a son.

Perhaps because of this flexibility among the Hui, I heard of no female infanticide in Na Homestead or elsewhere in Ningxia. Hui villagers claimed that their Han neighbors practiced it, and said they occasionally found Han female infants in the fields. Hui youth are permitted to get married 2 years earlier than Han, Hui girls at age 18 and boys at 20. I encountered several Hui weddings, however, where the bride was from 14 to 16 years old.

INTERNATIONAL ISLAMIC EXCHANGE. The Ningxia government is interested in promoting closer ties with foreign Muslim countries to foster economic development. In a 14 November 1984 *China Daily* interview Hei Boli, the Hui Chairman of the Ningxia People's Government, stated:

The delegations of the World Islamic Association that came to our region are quite impressed by the sincerity of the Party's policy of guaranteeing freedom of religious belief. Our Muslims are true believers and pay meticulous attention to Muslim customs.[94]

In another article, Ye Zhikun, director of the region's economic commission, stated: "Ningxia, the home of Chinese Muslims, expects loans from Arab countries to help develop foodstuffs and light industrial goods for the Muslim world."[95] The government has sponsored several economic and "Muslim Friendship" delegations to the Middle East to correspond with the Hajj, with the delegations including important religious leaders and well-known ahong fluent in Arabic. Delegations of foreign Muslim government and religious leaders have been hosted by Ningxia and escorted to visit historic mosques in Yinchuan, Na Homestead, and Tongxin. Hui "Muslim Construction Teams" formed by collectives and encouraged by the government have been sent to Third World Muslim nations on state development projects.[96] While many of the workers are Han, several leaders are Hui and some translators are Hui trained in the Islamic schools. The son of the current leader of the Jahriyya Shagou branch, trained in Arabic at Beijing's Foreign Language Institute, spent 2 years (1984–1986) in Yemen as the translator for a Chinese development project. He sought the roots of China's Naqshbandiyya Sufism in Yemen, where it is thought Ma Mingxin studied in the seventeenth century.[97]

This exchange with the outside Muslim world and visits by foreign Muslims to Hui villages are having a profound impact on Hui ethnoreligious self-understanding. Na villagers told me that they were deeply impressed by the religious power and prestige of Islam after the first visit of foreign Muslims to their village in May 1984. Previously, they had no idea that foreign Muslims enjoyed such high levels of prestige and education. The excitement with which these foreign Muslims are greeted was evident to the Protestant missionary George Andrew (perhaps because they did not welcome him in the same way):

Itinerant mullahs from Persia, Arabia, India, Turkey, and Egypt are found, from time to time, visiting the Hwei-hwei [Hui]. . . . These visiting mullahs are greeted with great respect by the Hwei-hwei, who purchase from them copies of the Koran, prayer-caps and turbans. They not only provide them with the necessaries of life, but also bring them free-will offerings of money. They are escorted form one Hwei-hwei community to the next with great pomp and ceremony.[98]

Religious knowledge of the Islamic world outside China is very limited among Na villagers and Hui throughout the northwest. I often asked if they knew of the religious differences in the Iraq-Iran conflict or the identity of Khomeini. Few people outside the city knew. Two young *halifat* in a mosque near Na Homestead who had studied in the *madrassah* for 4 years could not tell me why they faced west to pray. Few knew the country where Muhammad's birthplace is located. Mecca was generally only known to be in Arabia, the *Ahlabo* country west of China.

Now that Hui are becoming increasingly exposed to the Islamic world through visiting delegations and returned work teams or *hajji*, their awareness of the Islamic world is changing significantly. The Tongxin Mosque Halifat wear colorful silk turbans sent them by friends and relatives working in the Middle East, or given to them by visiting Muslim delegations. While the government hopes for development assistance and increased trade through improved relations with the Middle East, many delegations are interested only in supporting religious development, mosque and *madrassah* reconstruction. In the spring of 1986, an Arab visitor to the Central Mosque in Yinchuan wrote out a check for $10,000 US to assist its restoration and expansion.

ETHNORELIGIOUS TOURISM. The government is conscious of these unexpected results of its program, but, for the sake of improved international relations and the earning of foreign-exchange currency, it continues to promote travel to Islamic holy sites in China. Prestige associated with historic Islamic sites has led to a growing interest on the part of local cadres in developing "Muslim tourist attractions" in places like Na Homestead. While the mosque leaders are still not supportive of the idea, economic interests are beginning to prevail. Construction was begun in 1986 on an "Islamic Hotel" (*Yisilanjiao bingguan*), featuring Arab and Islamic architectural motifs. Na villagers do not want their mosque to become a tourist site like the South District Mosque in Yinchuan, which sells tickets at the gate to visitors interested in seeing the new Arab-style complex built in 1982 with government funds. The government's encouragement of tourism to foster better relations with Middle Eastern Muslim nations is an important factor influencing the ethnic identity of Na villagers, who are beginning to conceive of themselves in more international religious terms.[99] This promotion on the part of the state is clearly evident in the introductory paragraph of the glossy pictorial *The Religious Life of Chinese Muslims*, published in English, Chinese, and Arabic, by the state-sponsored Chinese Islamic Association:

> It is our wish that this pictorial will contribute to strengthening the unity among the Muslim community of China and encouraging leading Islamic personages and the rest of the Muslim community to do their bit in the socialist modernization of their motherland. At the same time, we hope this pictorial will help promote understanding and friendship between Chinese Muslims and their friends elsewhere in the world.[100]

TRUTH WITHIN PURITY: EXPRESSIONS OF NA IDENTITY

The influence of recent shifts in government policy and socioeconomic conditions illustrates the importance of Islam in the ethnoreligious identity of the Hui in Na Homestead. To be separated from Islam would be to cut them off from their ancestry. When I asked young Hui why they believed in Islam, the vast majority responded: "Because we are Hui," or "Because we respect our parents and grandparents." To state-sponsored researchers, this indicated a confusion between customs and religion and a "subjective" belief in Islam.[101] I would argue, however, that it demonstrates the inextricable place of Islam in Na villagers' identity as Hui.

The interaction between changing government policies and Hui identity illustrates the dialectical relationship between ethnic identity and social context. The implementation of the responsibility system and more liberalized nationality policies was originally intended to stimulate economic development in backward minority areas. These policies allowed the Hui villagers more autonomy. In the context of this more liberalized setting, salient aspects of Hui ethnic identity emerged. These included not only a more active participation in the local market economy but also a return to a more conservative, revitalized Islam.

Islamic conservativism of Hui villagers is now publicized by the state in its efforts to improve socioeconomic relations with Third World Muslim nations. State-sponsored exposure to these foreign Muslims—in the interest of encouraging economic investment—has led Hui villagers to gain a more international perspective on their faith and has furthered Islamic revival. Liberalized economic and nationality polices have fostered a reexamination of the relation of Islam to Hui identity and economic action by local cadres. At the same time, this reevaluation has allowed the expression of an ethnoreligious identity rerooted in an Islamic heritage and adapted to the local context. The Hui are actively taking advantage of these favorable policies. In the process, their identity and the policies themselves are reformulated and reevaluated.

Islam is an integral part of the identity of Na villagers—not easily distinguished from their ethnic identity. While Stalinist policy may seek assimilation through economic development and modernization, attempting to strip away Shelley's "loathsome mask" to get to the "pure" individual underneath, among the Hui just the opposite has been found to be true. As Hui continue to prosper and develop, they have become even more interested in their ethnoreligious roots. This does not represent an idealized nativism. Rising Hui interest in their Islamic and Central Asian heritage has led, dialectically, to a new revitalized identity. Instrumentalist approaches, such as Leo Despres's definition of ethnicity as a "mask of confrontation"[102] are helpful for understanding opposition and symbolic representation, but in this case the masks are not easily removed or affixed. Interestingly enough, while seeking to employ a Stalinist policy of ethnicity that in theory should lead to the assimilation of minorities, the state, by registering the Hui as a nationality whose basic religion is Islam, has to some degree institutionalized and objectified this ethnoreligious identity. This local village now sees itself as part of a national imagined community that the state has helped to define. Policies that make a radical distinction between ethnicity and religion will serve only to alienate northwestern Hui from participation in the broader society.

While the renewed meaningfulness of Islam to the Hui might represent for some a fundamentalist revival of fanatical proportions, I argue that the unique ethnoreligious identity of these Hui communities reflects a return to ethnic roots—a rerooting, rather than a fanatic revival of Islam. The moral authority and purity (*qing*) of their identity as Hui is intimately tied to the truth (*zhen*) and authenticity of their religious heritage. Hui are motivated to take advantage of liberalized government economic and nationality policies in order to further express their understanding of *qing zhen* and its implication for their lives.

Outer portico of Niu Jie Mosque in Beijing (AD 916–1125). Note stand for preaching at center and curtain at right behind which women pray. Inscription over entry reads: "The Ancient Religion of the Pure and True (*Qing Zhen*)." Photo: Gladney.

FOUR

Ethnic Identity in Oxen Street: The Urban Experience

It seems that Max Weber was right to see a specific link between trade and certain sects . . . and that economic history is in this sense indebted to the history of heresies.
— *Louis Dumont,* Homo Hierarchicus

The Hui are China's most urbanized minority nationality. They constitute the vast majority of minorities in every Chinese city, with the exception of cities in the border regions of Tibet, Xinjiang, and Inner Mongolia. The ethnic identity of these urban Hui and the expression of that identity, however, is different from the northwestern Hui Muslim communities and the dispersed southeastern Hui lineages in many aspects. The issues and concerns facing these Hui as they seek to continue to adapt to changing urban life are well illustrated by the following conversation with a Hui cook at a small *qing zhen* restaurant in one northern city:

Near the railroad station there are often many small privately run (*geti*) food stalls where one can find a wide assortment of local specialties. On one stall, a large blue banner was hung with flowery white Arabic writing across the center, bordered by the Chinese for "Qing Zhen Restaurant, Hui Snacks" (*qing zhen fandian, Huimin xiaochi*). A smaller sign below proclaimed that this restaurant specialized in Hezhou beef hand-pulled noodles (*Hezhou niu lamian*). In the glass cabinet where the chile, garlic, and other spices were kept was a small mirror with the insignia of a yellow teapot and the characters for *qing zhen* clearly printed on its lid.[1] A young man was busily kneading the dough while keeping rhythm with the pop music on the large portable stereo cassette player. He wore the white Hui hat often seen on the street through-out northwest China but rarely found outside of mosques or restaurants in central and southern urban centers.

I approached the young cook and gave him the traditional Hui greeting, *A-salam ^calaykum*. He replied, *Alaykum a-salam* and offered me a stool. I explained that I was traveling through on my way to Beijing where I went to school. He immediately asked if I needed a place to stay. "There aren't any *qing zhen* hotels in the area." He suggested, "You'll have to go to the mosque and ask the ahong if anyone can take you in." He said most of the Hui in the city were concentrated near the mosque, which lay in the western side of the urban center, outside the old city walls. I explained that I would need to stay in the hotel in town for foreigners. He refused to believe that I was not Chinese and suggested several times that I must be from Xinjiang. Despite his looking at my student card, I still had difficulty convincing him.

From his accent I could tell he was not from Hezhou (presently Linxia, Gansu). He said he had relatives there and they taught him how to make the noodles in the Hezhou spicy style. "Besides," he added, "everyone knows Hezhou hand-pulled noodles are the best Hui noodles. I made a lot more money after I put up the Hezhou noodle sign. Even the Han like to eat the beef noodles, but they don't like the mountain taste (*shanwei*) of lamb."[2] It turned out that he did not own the restaurant, but was working under an assumed registration. *Getihu* registration is hard to come by and the application process is often time-consuming. He said he was working under his friend's name until he could get enough money to start his own restaurant.

After my third visit to the restaurant, Ma Xinhua explained he could not get a permit without his residence committee chairman's assistance. Unfortunately, they did not get along and he had to work under his friend's registration. As an unemployed youth (*daiye qingnian*, literally, "waiting-for-employment youth"), he had little choice but to try and open a restaurant or engage in some other small trade like fixing bicycles or selling clothing bought from Shanghai. He could not test high enough to get into high school, even though as a minority he received special consideration on the entrance exams. He opened the restaurant because his father and grandfather had all run noodle stands before 1949. During the 1950s collectivization campaigns, his father's small cafe was combined with the other small Hui restaurants into a large state-run Hui restaurant, and he went to work in a food-processing factory. His mother and sisters often come to help him in the noodle stand. "Its good he started this restaurant," his mother said, "maybe he will meet a nice Hui girl to marry." She was very much against his marrying a Han, but it was difficult to meet single Hui girls of the right age and background in the factories and institutes where most Hui work in the city.

On my fourth visit to the restaurant, the youth admitted, after making sure no one else was listening, that the owner who had put up the money to open the restaurant was a Han. This is a practice known among Hui as "wearing a hat" (*ding maor*). The owner knew that he could make money on a Hui restaurant. "Hui can't eat in a Han restaurant, but anyone can eat in a Hui restaurant, and many Han like the spicy noodles," Ma noted. He quickly explained that, although the restaurant was owned and registered to a Han, Hui handled all the food. "Not like the large state-run (*guojia bande*) Hui restaurant downtown," he complained, "where most of the waiters are Han and even some of the cooks. Many Hui won't eat there because it's not pure and true enough (*bugou qing zhen*)." The Hui concentrated around the mosque were all "united" (*tuanjie*), he said, and very few of them ate in the state-run restaurant. They preferred to eat at home or patronize a few well-known Hui restaurants. "But a lot of the young people and workers are more casual (*suibian*)," he added, "and, although they don't eat pork at home, they sometimes go to Han restaurants. You'll never see this outside the city in the Hui villages."

MAKING HUI IN THE CITY: THE URBAN PROBLEM

Maintaining the *qing zhen* lifestyle, getting an education, arranging a job, finding a mate, and achieving upward mobility are issues continually faced by the urban Hui, who are spread thinly throughout China in every city. With the liberalization of nationality and economic policies, many traditional Hui strategies have emerged to deal with these issues. Unlike his northwestern co-religionists in Na village, Ma Xinhua, the cook in the small cafe described above, is not concerned about Islamic doctrinal issues. He had never heard of the various Hui Sufi orders, and he went to mosque only twice a year during the Corban and Ramadan holidays. Young Ma told me that he thought the main difference between the "Old Teachings" (*lao jiao*) and the "New Teachings" (*xin jiao*) was that the former did not eat crab or rabbit.

Unlike the Hui along China's southeast coast, he knew little about his foreign Muslim ancestry. Like 75 percent of the other urban Hui I surveyed, he said he was Hui because his parents were, and different from Han in that he abstained from pork. Many of his concerns revolve around the problems facing other urban youth: employment, marriage, education, and other more mundane concerns. Because he is a member of the state-recognized Hui nationality, however, these issues and his strategies for resolving them take on a different meaning for him in the city.

Although the Hui inhabit every major metropolitan center and are considered China's main urban ethnic group, they have received little attention in the growing anthropological literature on China's cities. The comprehensive Whyte and Parish study of urban life in contemporary China makes only passing mention of Muslims. Unfortunately, the study also drastically underestimates the population of the Hui in Beijing, stating there are only 16,000 Hui Muslims in the city,[3] whereas the 1982 census numbered 184,693 Hui, with 46 mosques and hundreds of *qing zhen* restaurants. Morton Fried's ethnography of a Chinese city in Anhui neglected the important Hui community and mosque complex in the city, their role in the local market, and the government's treatment of them (partly because he was not allowed in the mosque).[4] Ma Xinhua lives in a city where the Hui are concentrated in one area; the issues of Hui identity are even more pronounced in cities where the Hui are widely dispersed. In this chapter I discuss these different conditions of Hui urban life and introduce the cultural, social, and political aspects of Hui urban identity with particular reference to the Niujie (Oxen Street) community in Beijing.

OXEN STREET, AN URBAN HUI ENCLAVE

Based on the 1982 census, the Hui people represent almost two-thirds (57 percent) of the minority residents of Beijing. All 55 of China's minority nationalities can be found in Beijing, constituting 3.5 percent of the 9,230,687 population; the Hui minority are 2 percent of the total population. In other Chinese cities, the Hui occupy an even higher percentage of the ethnic minorities: In Tianjin, the Hui constitute 87 percent of the minority residents, 142,847 out of a total of 163,637; and in Shanghai, the Hui represent 89 percent of the minority residents, 44,123 out of 49,552.

The Hui are spread throughout Beijing, especially concentrated in several neighborhoods, including Oxen Street, Ma Dian, Haidian, Chongwai, Chaowai, Chaonei, and Sanlihe. While there have not been any published data on the exact distribution of the Hui in Beijing based on the 1982 census, a good indication of Hui concentration is the location of mosques and *qing zhen* restaurants (see Map 3). While there are relatively few privately run restaurants in Beijing, the state restaurants have been established in areas of higher Hui concentration. The restaurants indicated on the map do not include smaller *qing zhen* cafes or *getihu*-run food stands. They represent only those published on city maps. Most of the more than 40 mosques existing in Beijing before 1949 have been reopened or rebuilt (Table 8).[5] The presence of a mosque generally indicates at least 100 Hui families (500 individuals), with more famous mosques, like the Niujie Mosque, serving hundreds of households.

The Oxen Street area of the Xuanwu city district in the southeast corner of the city has the highest concentration of Hui. Oxen Street is known for the largest and oldest mosque in Beijing, the Niujie Libaisi, (also known as the Wanyu Lou), founded in the Liao Dynasty (A.D. 916–1125).[6] One legend has it that the mosque was established by the Liao Emperor Jinzong in his 14th year, while another tradition suggests that the Northern Song Emperor Taizong in his 2nd year was the one responsible. Nasur al-Din, the son of a prominent Arab scholar, Guam al-Din, was supposedly the founding imam of the mosque. The street, Niu Jie, derives its name either as a homophonic representation of the fact that the street was near the Liu River, where willow (*liu*) trees and pomegranate (*shi liu*) trees grew, or, perhaps due to the fact that there was a concentration of beef butchers in that district during the Qing dynasty.[7] Stories dating from the Yuan dynasty relate that there were 2,953 households concentrated along Oxen Street where Han rarely dared to walk alone.[8] The street now has 2 small *qing zhen* restaurants, 8 *qing zhen* noodle and pastry shops, and several Hui *getihu* selling pastries and fruit. There are 51 *qing zhen* restaurants in the Xuanwu district, with 51 *qing zhen* meat shops and many *qing zhen* foodstuff stores selling pastries, noodles, and sundries. The ethnic flavor of the community is also enhanced by a Hui middle school at the northern end, a Hui elementary school just across from the west of the mosque, an imposing Hui hospital (*Huimin yiyuan*) at the south end of the street, and the Chinese Islamic Association just southeast of the mosque, built in the 1950s with large green domes, parapets, and other Arab architectual styles.

The population of the Oxen Street district is 55,722, with minorities accounting for 24.7 percent (13,755), of which 96.6 percent are Hui (13,307). The Hui are even more concentrated along Oxen Street itself. Out of a population of 2,446, 1,763, or 70.2 percent, are Hui. Of the 649 households along the street, 475, or 69.3 percent, are Hui. There are also 2 Mongolian and 2 Manchu households on Oxen Street. In neighborhoods on either side of the street the ratio of Han and Hui drops to about 50 percent, and continues to decline as one moves further away.

Tang Fang is a typical Niujie neighborhood. Located on Beiruilu, just west of Oxen Street, it is more than 50 percent Hui, with a few Manchu households. Table 9 indicates the multi-ethnic structure of the community.

Ma Dian is another typical Hui neighborhood, located in north central Beijing and representative of several Hui communities, like Haidian, Dong Bali, An He Qiao, and Qing He, which were originally outside of Beijing. As the city expanded, Han moved in, and the formerly all-Hui villages gradually became multi-ethnic neighborhoods of Beijing.[9] Ma Dian ("Horse Pasture" or "Caravansary") derives its name from the large sheep and horse market that formerly existed in the village, which lay at the terminus of a northern caravan route.[10] Concentrated around a central mosque, the former village was a coherent community of sheep and horse traders. On the central street of the village there were once as many as thirteen 13 shops with one shop selling as many as 30,000 head during the Daoguang period (1821–1850). At that time, the district sold more than 130,000 head a year. During the late Republican period, the caravan trade was superseded by locomotive transport, and heavier taxation led to decreased income and diversification of enterprise. By the 1930s, sheep trade fluctuated from 30,000 to 50,000 head per year.[11] Although the 1982 composition of the 923 households (3,278 people) was only 28.6 percent Hui, recent studies indicate that the community continues to maintain a strong solidarity. Table 10 gives the multi-ethnic structure of Ma Dian.

MAP 3 Hui Mosques and Restaurants in Beijing

Qinghe

Haidian

Heplingli

Deshengmen — Andingmen

Xizhimen
Dongzhimen

Di Anmen

Fuchengmen Xisi
Chaoyangmen

Imperial
Palace

Xidan

Dongdan Jianguomen
Chonwenmen

Xuanwumen
Huashi
Guangqumen

Niujie (Oxen Street)

Yongdingmen

▲ Mosques

△ Former Mosques

● Restaurants

TABLE 8 Beijing Mosques: Names, Location, and Founding

Name	Location	Founding
Libai Si	Niujie (Oxen Street)+	916–1125
Qingzhen Nusi	Niujie Shouliu Hutong*	1926
Qing Zhen Si	Dongsi (East Mosque)	1271–1368
Pushou Si	Funei Jinshi Fangjie	1271–1368
Faming Si	Andingmennei Ertiao Hutong	1271–1368
Qing Zhen Si	Andingmen Guan	–
Yongshou Si	Jiaozi Hutong	1662–1722
Qing Zhen Si	Qianmenwai Guanzhou Hutong	1368–1644
Qing Zhen Si	Tianqiao Fuchangjie	1926
Qing Zhen Si	Huashi (Flower Street)	1368–
Qing Zhen Si	Chongwenmenwai Tangzi Hutong	1821–1850
Qingzhen Nusi	Chongwenmenwai Liujia Hutong*	–
Qing Zhen Si	Tangdao Hutong	1883
Qing Zhen Si	Suzhou Hutong	1796–1820
Qing Zhen Si	Lumicang	1644
Qing Zhen Si	Douyacai Hutong	1796–1820
Qing Zhen Si	Wangfujing	1875–1908
Qing Zhen Si	Chaoyangmenwai Nanzhongjie	1662–1722
Qing Zhen Si	Chaoyangmenwai Xiapo	1662–1722
Qingzhen Nusi	Chaoyangmenwai Xianpu si*	–
Qing Zhen Si	Chaoyangmenwai Balizhuang	1736–1795
Qing Zhen Si	Zhongjian Zixiang	1862–1874
Qing Zhen Si	Dongzhimennei Nanxiaojie	1821–1850
Qing Zhen Si	Gulou hou	1911
Qing Zhen Si	Shishahai	1644
Qing Zhen Si	Nanfan Xihongmen	1368
Qing Zhen Si	Dongzhimenwai Erlizhuang	1271–1368
Qing Zhen Si	Anyongwai Daguan	1796–1820
Qing Zhen Si	Deshengmenwai Daguan	1662–1722
Qing Zhen Si	Deshengmenwai Ma Dian	1662–1722
Qingzhen Nusi	Deshengmenwai Xicun*	–
Qing Zhen Si	Xizhimenwai Nanguan	1736–1795
Qing Zhen Si	Xizhimennei Gouyan	1821–1850
Qing Zhen Si	Xisi Fenzi Hutong	1821–1850
Qing Zhen Si	Xi Dan	1875–1908
Qing Zhen Si	Xuanwumennei Shoupa Hutong	1821–1850
Qing Zhen Si	Xuanwumennei Niurouwan	1875–1908
Puning Si	Hepingmennei Huihuiying	1765

TABLE 8 Continued

Name	Location	Founding
Qing Zhen Si	Fuwai Sanlihe +	1794
Qing Zhen Si	Haidian	1662–1722
Qing Zhen Si	Xijiao Siwangfu	1662–1722
Qing Zhen Si	Xijiao Landingchang	1662–1722
Qing Zhen Si	Xijiao Anheqiao	1662–1722
Qing Zhen Si	Xijiao Shucun	1662–1722
Qing Zhen Si	Beijiao Qing He	1662–1722

+ Indicates attached woman's mosque; *Indicates woman's mosque

Sources: Wang Shoujie, "Beiping shi Huimin Gaikuang"; Sydney Gamble, Peking: A Social Survey, p. 511; Yang Yongchang, Mantan qingzhensi; personal interviews.

TABLE 9 Ethnic Composition of Tangfang Neighborhood, Niujie District, Beijing

Ethnic Group	Population	Percent	Male	Percent	Female	Percent
Han	1,272	40.94	601	39.23	671	42.6
Hui	1,814	58.38	918	59.92	896	56.89
Manchu	21	0.68	13	0.85	8	0.51
Total	3,107	100.00	1,532	49.31	1,575	50.69

Source: 1982 Census, unpublished report.

TABLE 10 Ethnic Composition of Ma Dian Neighborhood, Beijing

Ethnic Group	Population	Percent	Male	Percent	Female	Percent
Han	2,270	69.25	1,108	68.23	1,162	70.25
Hui	939	28.65	476	29.31	463	27.99
Manchu	65	1.98	39	2.40	26	1.57
Mongol	4	0.12	1	0.06	3	0.18
Total	3,278	100.00	1,624	49.54	1,654	50.45

Source: 1982 Census, unpublished report.

China Islamic Association Headquarters, Beijing, founded in 1957. Photo: Gladney

RECURRING TEXTS IN OXEN STREET

What does it mean to be a Hui in the city, and what influence does that
have on one's life, social interaction, and the effect of local government
policies? While it is difficult to generalize regarding the various important rituals and culturally shared ideas of identity in the city, there are
certain recurring texts that one finds often of interest to urban Hui,
including legends of origin, aspects of *qing zhen* lifestyle, religious holidays, traditional specializations and handicrafts, martial-arts practices,
and the organization of social space. These concerns represent shared
aspects of Hui identity that continually distinguish them from other
ethnic groups in the multi-ethnic urban setting, and regularly reaffirm
to themselves their unique ancestry. These cultural symbols serve as
important markers of Hui identity and influence inter-ethnic relations.
Their recent resurgence under liberalized policies reveals much about
changing Hui identity, its continued meaningfulness, and varied interpretations of the *qing zhen*.

THE LEGENDS OF FOREIGN ORIGIN. There are various legends of Hui origin and the arrival of Islam in China told by Hui from Beijing to Guangzhou. The most popular account is that the Tang Emperor Taizong was disturbed by the appearance in a dream of a turbaned man chasing a phantom. His interpreter told him: "The turbaned man is a Hui hui of the West. In Arabia is a Muslim king of great virtue. A great sage is born, with favorable omens."[12] The Emperor was so astounded by his dream and its import that he dispatched an ambassador to the Arab lands who returned with 3 Muslim teachers. Impressed with the scientific knowledge and civility of these teachers, the Emperor invited other Muslims to settle, build mosques, and propagate their faith. This legend is still repeated among the Hui who share the common belief that Islam entered China during the Tang at the Emperor's invitation.[13]

The veracity of this legend and other Chinese Muslim accounts of the early origin of Islam in China are discounted by Leslie[14] and other historians. They reason that the majority of the tales result from eighteenth- and nineteenth-century Hui attempts at legitimation through reference to imperial approval and ancient origin. "Nevertheless," Drake concludes, "the insistence upon the arrival of Mohammedanism as early as the T'ang dynasty; the suggestion of Mohammedan troops settling in northwest China; and the account of the early beginnings of Mohammedanism in Canton all reflect, however dimly, the actual facts."[15] For this study of ethnoreligious identity, the legends are important in that they continue to represent agreed-upon notions of Hui heritage.

There are also local stories told about the origin of the Hui in Beijing. The following account describes the origin of the Beijing Oxen Street Muslims and is engraved on a tablet in the Niujie Mosque, which was also supposedly founded by an Arab:

In A.D. 996 a *shai hai* [*shaykh*, elder] named Ge Wa Mo Ding came from the Western Regions (*xiyu*). This man often had strange dreams and gave birth to three sons. The eldest, Sai De Lu Ding, could tell the good or evil surrounding different graves. He left home with no reason for some unknown place and never returned. The second, Na Su Lu Ding, could read other people's minds. The youngest, Che Ah Dou Ding, could speak the language of birds. The two younger sons lived in seclusion and refused several official posts

Ramadam celebration at Niu Jie Mosque, June 1985. Photo: Gladney

Call to prayer from Chinese pavilion-style minaret, Niu Jie Mosque, taken in September 1937 by the protestant missionary Carter Holton. Photo: Holton. Courtesy of Harvard-Yenching Library.

offered to them. They became the imams of the mosque and settled permanently in the East. They prophesied that Beijing would become a center of prosperity where emperors would reign over great causes. As a reward for their loyalty to the Emperor, they were allowed to build mosques in the east of the city [the Dongsi Mosque] and in the south [the Niujie Mosque] and were given tombs inside the compound of the Niujie Mosque.[16]

In the southeastern corner of the Niujie Mosque are 2 small tombs belonging to 2 *shaykhs* who came from the West and were buried in the mosque. Inscriptions over the grave record that the west grave belongs to Ah Ha Mai De (Ahmed Bitan), an Afghan scholar who died in A.D. 1280; the east grave belongs to Ah Li (Ali Amad al-Din), a Bukharan, buried in A.D. 1283.[17] While these graves are not patronized like those of Muslim saints in the northwest,[18] they do represent the foreign origins of Chinese Islam to the Oxen Street Hui. I never saw anyone praying in front of the graves, nor was there incense lit for them, but, on several occasions after prayer, an elderly Hui would take me back to the graves and repeat the legend about these two saints and the arrival of Islam in Beijing.[19] An erudite Hui physician in Shanghai explained:

> I know I am a Chinese citizen and my home is China. However, I also know that, before migrating here from Henan, my earliest ancestors came from the West and were Muslim. This knowledge was handed down to me from my parents and, although I do not practice Islam, I will continue to pass it on to my children.

This Hui doctor went on to explain that she maintains the pork tabu, not out of religious persuasion, but out of "habit" and the belief that it is better for her health to abstain from pork.

ON EATING RIGHT: PORK ABSTENTION AND URBAN HUI IDENTITY. It is not surprising that, in the above conversation with the Hui physician, questions of ancestry immediately turned to pork abstention and maintaining a *qing zhen* lifestyle. Among the vast majority of urban Hui and Han I surveyed, the primary distinction noted between the two peoples was pork avoidance. This issue, while of real concern to Hui in the northwest, is not as paramount as it is in the city. In the northwest, Muslims are numerous. The Han are familiar with Hui customs and generally are sensitive to actions that might provoke the Hui.

Hui workers, Tian Shan Hui foodstuffs factory in Shanghai, producing *qing zhen* baked goods and candy. Photo: Gladney

Pork is the principal meat of China. Drawing found on side of market in Yangzhou. Ideograph is the Chinese term for "meat" (*rou*). Photo: Gladney

In most villages that are either Han or Hui, the issue is almost nonexistent. In Ningxia's Luo village, where there is almost an even mixture of Hui and Han, Hui homes tend to be adjacent to other Hui homes. Han are careful to keep their pigs in the yards, and, while mistakes do happen, people are aware of the issue and try to be sensitive.

The road that cuts through Na Homestead (see Chapter 3) is a major link between the Yongning county seat and several Han villages to the west. In the past, spirited confrontations arose when Han attempted to walk their pigs through the village on the way to market. When the village still had a wall, Hui said they would often close the gates on market days to prevent Han from bringing their pigs through. A compromise was reached where Han were allowed to take pigs on the road if they were tied up, and preferably covered, inside a cart. After being informed of this arrangement, I was surprised one day by a group of Han walking through with their pig freely driven on ahead of them—not even a leash to restrict its foraging. The Na villager I was with merely shrugged his shoulders and said, "There's nothing you can do" (*mei you banfa*).

In the northwest, more conservative Hui do not even mention the word for "pig" and have created various euphemisms like "black bug" or "black bastard" (*hei jinr*, from the Arabic) to avoid mentioning it. Some Hui with the surname Zhu, homophonous with the word for "pig," have changed their surnames, generally to Hei. The current chairman of the Ningxia Regional Government, Hei Boli, told me that his Hui ancestors changed their surname from Zhu to Hei. Hui born under the pig sign of the Chinese zodiac, when asked, will often reply that they are born under the "black" (*hei*) year. The pork tabu is accepted in the northwest where Hui are numerous. It is generally observed and rarely needs mentioning.

At the other end of the spectrum, southeastern Hui lineages who do not practice Islamic dietary restrictions are not very concerned about the pork question. It becomes an issue for them only when outside conservative Hui or foreign Muslims visit their village. Suggestions have been made that they cease raising pigs, but they have been doing so for centuries and there is no easy substitute. In the southern cities where Hui are few, there is generally less concern over *qing zhen* violations. Hui identity depends on lineage and ancestry, not on cultural maintenance. At one of the two Hui restaurants in Xiamen that open onto the street like most small southern cafes, I paused to look at the menu. A Han came up beside me and set down his bundle before walking in and ordering a bowl of noodles. It was only when I decided to go in and had to step over his bundle that I realized he had left a pole with large freshly butchered cuts of pork tied to either end. This would have incited a riot in the northwest and at least an altercation in most northern cities. My local Hui friend simply shrugged his shoulders and said there was no way to avoid it.

This is not the case in northern cities with larger Hui communities. Pork is neither so scrupulously avoided that it is rarely mentioned, nor so prevalent that people inevitably accept it. For these Hui, pork avoidance is described more as a matter of cleanliness than religiosity, like "germ" evasion in the West. The Qing dynasty Confucian Muslim scholar Liu Zhi (c. 1664–1730) once sought to describe (and legitimate) this avoidance in terms of proper Confucian condemnation of the pig itself:

> The pig's nature is greedy, essentially turbid, confused, and eats garbage; the meat has no nutrition and is unhealthy, uncouth. Accustomed to filth, it looks awkward and steals. Therefore we must prohibit pork.[20]

Hui continually justify pork avoidance in terms of the unhealthful qualities of the pig. Household products having to do with cleanliness, such as toothpaste, soap, shampoo and incense (see below), are all available from Muslim merchants certified as pure, with a *qing zhen* label.

Incidents involving pork are common in urban neighborhoods where the Hui live packed closely together. In Shanghai, where the Hui are thinly dispersed, Yang Guifu (pseudonym) complained that there was no way to avoid pork. His family of three generations lived in two and a half small rooms that were part of a 3-story complex built around a narrow courtyard. "The Han have nowhere to wash and cook their meat but in the courtyard or on the balconies. We put up with it, but we really wish we could move to where there are more Hui."

Han often cannot understand why the Hui are so upset about pork. For them, it is meat, the basic protein everyone craves. A foodstuffs store in Yangzhou that sold grains, sundries, and meat advertised the latter by painting a large red pig on the side of the store wall. Inside the outline of the pig was the Chinese ideograph for meat (*rou*), graphically depicting that pork, as far as Han are concerned, is merely meat—everything else is a qualified kind of meat, "beef meat" (*niu rou*) or "lamb meat" (*yang rou*). One Han said to me, "The Hui avoidance of pork doesn't make sense. They are like vegetarian Buddhist monks, but do not obtain any merit for giving up the meat." This misunderstanding is the subject of many ethnic tales and jibes told about why the Hui do not eat pork. I never heard these stories in the northwest, but encountered them frequently in cities when I mentioned I was studying the Hui. The following conversation reflects a typical encounter:

A Han saleswoman and man at the Huaqiao Hotel asked why I studied Hui, because "the Hui aren't very interesting" (*Huizu meiyou shenma yisi*). If I was interested in religions I should study Buddhism, since it was one of the "Three Great Religions" (*san da jiao*), whereas "the Hui religion is a small religion" (*Huijiao zhi shi yige xiaojiao*). Since this city was a place with few Hui and prominent Buddhist sites that attracted hundreds of Japanese tourists—the saleswoman spoke excellent Japanese—it was not surprising that they wondered why I came to Yangzhou nainly to study the Hui, despite the two interesting mosques in town and the ancient Islamic cemetery mentioned in the tourist brochures they sold at the counter. Though the ancient port of Yangzhou was a center in the Tang and Song dynasties for both Buddhism and Islam, few tourists, notably the Japanese, visit the Islamic monuments in the city. The salesman said Hui weren't interesting because they were mainly "backward" (*luohou*). When I asked why, they suggested because Hui history was too short and they had not had time to develop, but, when I countered that American society was advanced despite its short history of only 200 years, and that Islam had a history of over 1,300 years, they agreed that wasn't a very good reason. The man laughed and said that their opinion was probably influenced by "Great Han Chauvinism" (*Da Han zhuyi*).

They then said that "Hui aren't any different than Han" (*Huizu gen Hanzu meiyou shenma qubie*), but, when I asked if they had any special customs, the woman said, "They eat a lot of meat, much more than us, they'll eat any meat" (*Tamen chide hen duo rou, bi women chide duo, shenma rou dou chi*). "But I thought Hui didn't eat pork," I said; she went on that it was true for the older Hui but that the younger and middle-aged ate pork with gusto. Furthermore, they were much better off than Han because they "not only can eat pork, but the government gives them coupons and a special store to buy beef and lamb that we Han can't shop in." I then joked that they should try to find a Hui "spouse" (*duixiang*), but instead of laughing they said that a lot of Han now considered marrying a Hui a good thing, because they took those benefits into account.

Then I asked why it was that older Hui didn't eat pork. The woman answered that she thought one reason was that they thought pork (she said "meat" *rou*, but meant pork) was too dirty for some reason. She then said that she had heard a "legend" (*diangu*) about Hui not eating pork but couldn't remember, promising to go home and ask her family. The next morning she told me that the *diangu* had something to do with "Yuda" (Judas) the "traitor" (*pantu*) who betrayed Jesus, but was one of his 12 followers. Hui thought that in some ways the pig resembled this person and, because he was such a bad person, they refused to eat pork. When I asked why it was that Christians still ate pork, she said she wasn't sure and that it wasn't clear to her, but that was the legend she had heard.

I had not encountered this legend before, and it is one of the few that does not revolve around the idea that the Hui abstain from pork out of filial respect for their ancestor who at some time intermarried with a pig, as discussed in a later chapter.[21] A Chengdu truck driver recited the following slur regarding Hui ancestry:

Monkey for a brother	*hou didi*
Dog for a grandmother	*gou nainai*
A pig for his	*zhu shi ta*
ancestral tablet	*zuxian pai.*

While the PRC government has gone to great lengths to correct these traditional ethnic biases, long-held stereotypes still find their way into print. In a brief *Youth News* 31 December 1982 article, the Shanghai editor responded to a question regarding the difference between Hinduism and Islam. Hinduism, he wrote, is more glorious (*guangrong*) than Islam. "In Islam, one hand holds the sword while the other holds the Quran." He later noted that the Muslims revere the pig, and that is why they do not eat pork. That afternoon, several calls were made to the mosque and the City Commission for Nationality Affairs. Many Hui went to the office of the publisher to complain, and letters poured in. In the next issue, the weekly *Youth News* published a formal apology, and, on 13 January, went to press a day early to reveal on the front page that the 29-year-old editor had been fired (a rarity in China) and the 17-year-old writer severely reprimanded. The article, it stated, "hurt

Muslim religious feelings, was not beneficial to nationality unity (*minzu tuanjie*), and had a very bad influence."[22] A cadre from the City CNA explained to me that, while the writers were too young to understand (*qingnian bu dong shi*), this is still unacceptable in China today. This incident was familiar to many of the Beijing Muslims when they marched in the street against Salman Rushdie and was mentioned in their letter delivered to the government. In recent years, the State Commission for Nationality Affairs has attempted to incorporate more ethnic awareness into its elementary curriculum and, in 1985, published "nationality general knowledge" (*minzu changshi*) materials for middle-school students which stressed mutual respect and understanding for cultural differences.

THE RESTAURANT AS HUI PUBLIC SPHERE. The salience of the pork tabu for Hui in large and small cities throughout China has contributed to the importance of the restaurant as a center for cultural dissemination. While the mosque is central in the northwest, and perhaps the ancestral hall in the southeast, I propose that the importance of the pork tabu, the dispersion of the Hui in most cities, and the generally low attendance at mosque prayers contribute to making the Hui restaurant serve as a cultural center. The Niujie Mosque has from 50-100 Muslims at prayer there 5 times a day, with up to 600 in attendance on Friday, the main day of prayer (*zhu mari*). On holidays, over 1,000 cram into the main hall and fill the outlying courtyards. While, on these days, all generations are well represented, most of the 10 to 15 young people that attend prayer during the mid-week are Islamic students from the Chinese Islamic Society around the corner from the mosque. There is simply no time during the week for Hui workers in the city to leave their factories or institutes to go to mosque. In retirement years, Hui men and women find more time, and they make up the majority of worshipers (the women pray behind a curtain in the back of the Niujie Mosque). This lax attendance is acknowledged by all, and no one is troubled by it. Most Hui are satisfied to have one and a half to two days off every year to attend Corban and Ramadan festivities at the mosque. As a result, when Hui need a public place to discuss issues and meet associates, they usually end up at the restaurant.

Young people like to go to the large state-run restaurants in the evenings because they can have a *qing zhen* meal and also buy wine, beer, and cigarettes. Bai Ling (assumed name), a young Hui woman smartly dressed in jeans and a red T-shirt, told me that her parents would never let her meet boys at home. "Here my parents are glad to know that I am not in a Han restaurant, and boys like to eat here because they can't smoke and drink at home." One of the youths sitting with her admitted that he occasionally ate pork outside, but he never did at home. He liked to come here to eat because they had excellent lamb dumplings (*yangrou shuijiao*).

The Donglaishun ("Flows to the East") Restaurant on Wangfujing Street is the largest and most famous Hui restaurant in Beijing. Established in 1903 by 3 brothers (Ding Deshan, Defu, and Degui) as a porridge stall at the northern entrance to the Dong An bazaar, it began selling its famous lamb hot pot (*shuan yangrou*, literally "instant-boiled mutton") and obtained its current name in 1906. The 3-story building dates from 1930s, and the restaurant was collectivized in the 1950s.[23] The bottom floor is always packed with people eating lamb *jiaoze*, the majority of whom have to stand up to eat during meal hours in the crowded space. The 2nd floor serves the famous hot pot and, on the 3rd floor, people can order their well-known Beijing duck along with other stir-fried specialties. One of the cooks explained that many Han like to come here and eat Beijing duck because only vegetable oil is used, not lard as in some restaurants, and the duck tastes lighter and crisper. He also emphasized that even the most conservative Hui who will not eat in some of the other state-run Hui restaurants in town will come here because they know all of the cooks are Hui.[24] They have several smaller banquet rooms that have become popular with foreign tourist groups. Thus, they are always busy.[25]

In addition to the lively crowds inside the Donglaishun, there is always a large collection of Hui and Uigur congregating outside the restaurant. This phenomenon can be observed at all of the main Hui restaurants in every major city, especially on Fuzhou Road in Shanghai, Heping Road in Tianjin, and on Zhongshan (Sun Yat-sen) Road in Guangzhou. While there are many business transactions taking place, people with sundry goods to sell and money to trade, it primarily serves

Tombstone of Ibn Abd' Allah, found in Quanzhou in 1965, probably dating from the tenth to
eleventh centuries. Arabic inscription: "To
Allah belongs the order before and after. The
tomb of Ibn Abd' Allah ... Muhammad b.
Hasan ..." (Chen Dasheng, *Islamic Inscriptions
in Quanzhou,* p. 47). Chinese inscription:
"Grave of the Barbarian Guest." The Chinese
characters for "Barbarian" and "Grave" are written incorrectly, suggesting that they may have
been written by a first- or second-generation
Muslim immigrant. The stone is presently on
display at the Quanzhou Maritime Museum,
Fujian. Photo: Gladney.

Hui Muslims on the state-sponsored Hajj in 1980. After completing the pilgrimage
to Mecca, they are preparing to spend the night on Arafat Mountain. From *The Religious Life of Chinese Muslims,* p. 94, courtesy of the China Islamic Society.

as a social space where Hui can gather and exchange information. A 1988 study of nationalities in Beijing city reported that, on just the major streets of the city alone, there were 129 *qing zhen* restaurants, including 3 Xinjiang style restaurants. In addition, the study reported that there were 14 Korean restaurants, 4 Mongolian restaurants, and at least 3 Manchu.[26] In the city, the *qing zhen* restaurant has replaced the mosque as the locus for Hui cultural activity. Like the coffeehouses and public meeting places Jürgen Habermas writes were so important for developing civil society in the West, the *qing zhen* restaurant has become the center of the public sphere for Hui in the city.[27]

ETHNIC FESTIVALS AND RECURRING RITUALS. Two days a year in most large cities throughout China, Hui do not have to go to work or school, or, in some cases, are allowed to go home at noon. The government permits celebration of their "traditional nationality holidays" (*chuantong minzu jiere*). In the city, most youth know of Ramadan not as a month-long fast but as a Hui holiday that takes place one day a year. While for many the Corban (*Guerbang jie*) and Ramadan (*Kaizhai jie*) holidays represent time to go to the park or take in a movie, the Hui in Oxen Street go to the mosque, make *youxiang* (a flat, fried traditional Hui pastry), and, especially on the Ramadan holiday, visit the graves of their ancestors. While most conservative Hui in the northwest do not celebrate the Han holidays of *Zhongqiu*, *Qingming*, or even *Chun Jie* (Spring Festival), the Hui in most of China's cities gladly participate. The Hui *qing zhen* mooncakes (*yuebing*), eaten during the Mooncake Festival (*Zhongqiu*), are famous in Beijing. They are made with sesame and vegetable oil, not lard, so they are popularly regarded as light and savory. Hui also produce and sell *qing zhen zongzi*, *qing zhen yuanxiao*, *qing zhen la ba* porridge and other *qing zhen* desserts all consumed on Han Chinese festival days, though many of these foods are tied to Han religious practice.[28]

From early in the morning on the Ramadan holiday, Oxen Street is jammed with people. The Chinese Islamic Society announces the time for breaking the fast, and all mosques in the city generally follow. While there had been some differences in the past over when to break the fast between the Dongsi Mosque, mainly Yihewani, and the Niujie Mosque, primarily Gedimu, they now celebrate on the same day. This is not true in the northwest, where Islamic orders proliferate. During the Ramadan Festival I attended in Linxia in June 1985, the 3 main orders broke their fasts on 3 different days: the Qadariyya and other Sufi orders were on the 1st day, the Gedimu on the 2nd, and the Yihewani on the 3rd. Debates over the days to break fast, those who prayed in the mosque before breaking the fast (*houkai*) and those who prayed afterward (*qian-kai*), were the sparks that ignited violent sectarian clashes in Gansu, Qinghai, and Ningxia throughout the nineteenth and early twentieth centuries.[29] While there is one Jahriyya mosque on Mishi (rice-market) Street in Niujie, few of the local Hui are aware of or concerned about these differences. The festivals are a time of family celebration and "hot and noisy" (*renao*) activity.

On the Ramadan holiday, the gates of the mosque are opened, and people are allowed to crowd into the courtyard. Normally children do not play in the mosque and one can enter only through a side entrance. But, on this day, the children crowd around the sides of the courtyards and climb up on the surrounding shoe racks to watch their brothers, fathers, and grandfathers pray. The women pray in the reception room behind the minaret east of the courtyard, since the mosque is too crowded for them to use the usual curtained-off area. On the 1984 holiday, I estimated the Niujie Mosque had over 2,000 worshipers. At the 1983 Corban Festival I attended in the Dongsi Mosque, there were close to 1,000. There were many foreign Muslims from the diplomatic community as well as a large section of Uigurs.

The Niujie Mosque tends to be attended by local Hui, with many prominent imams, like Imam Hajji Abd Rahim Ma Songting, the eminent Hui scholar, reformer, and honorary president of the China Islamic Association, who was seated in the front of the mosque in 1984. Imam Al-Hajji Shi Kunbing gave a lengthy sermon on the Ramadan holiday, exhorting the worshipers to follow the example of the Prophet, who was loyal to his people and his faith. He admonished them, as Muslims in China, to work for their country's modernization and to remember they were Chinese citizens first. After the prayer, the Hui return to their homes for a feast or go to the Hui graveyard (*shangfen*) outside the city where they recite the Quran (*nianjing*) and clean the graves, in a manner similar to Han grave sweeping on Qingming.

Except for the ahong, their students, and a few elderly Hui, who often fast for all or part of the month, the majority of the younger Hui in Oxen Street do not fast during Ramadan. However, there are exceptions. Among some more conservative Hui urban communities, there are often many activities assisting those who fast, lasting the whole month. In Jiaxing city, Zhejiang province, there are 371 Hui households (1,180 people) in a city of 300,000. Hui factory workers number 680. Fewer than 100 are engaged in small businesses spread out among 130 work units. Before 1949, 90 percent of the Hui in the city were concentrated around the Ming-dynasty mosque on Danianxiang. Now, only 600 Hui live near the mosque, but they are a tight-knit community with 1 residence committee of 12 small teams, 4 of which are exclusively Hui. Over 100 people, one-sixth of the community, fast during the Ramadan month. Every night when the sun goes down, they gather in the mosque to pray and break fast. Their sustenance is provided by an elaborately organized system in which families take turns supplying the food and sundries for that night. The following is a record the mosque kept of the items donated for those fasting during the 1983 Ramadan:

92	*Youxiang bing* (large variety in pans)
2,010	Sesame seed cakes
1,050	Other sweet cakes
600	Lamb *baozi*
300	*Zongzi* (pyramid-shaped dumplings of glutinous rice wrapped in bamboo leaves)
30	kgm. of peaches
3	Whole cooked lambs
3	kgm. high-quality tea leaves
50	Face towels

In 1983, they also contributed over 800 yuan to the mosque and sent 100 yuan to Hui in Hainan Island to assist in rebuilding their mosque.

While many urban Hui do not know the Islamic history surrounding the festivals—one Beijing Hui told me that Corban was to honor Allah's sparing the life of Ishmael—their regular observance reinforces the Islamic aspect of their ethnic heritage. Urban Hui have also maintained traditional Hui earthen funerals in which the body is buried in a white cloth without a coffin or without the elaborate ceremonies of the Han. I was told that only one unlucky Oxen Street man was cremated during the Cultural Revolution when Hui were encouraged to reject their "feudal" funeral customs. Until the white-cloth ration coupons were abolished recently, the Hui received special increased allocations for funerals.

Like their modern Han friends, many Hui youth are opting for simple wedding ceremonies through state registration without any ritual and going on "traveling weddings" (*luxing hunying*) where the money normally spent on the ceremony is used for a honeymoon. Yet Hui wedding celebrations, when they do take place in the city, are often more conservative than Han weddings—without wine or cigarettes (see below). These recurring rituals, while not as elaborate as those among conservative Hui in the northwest, continue to serve as salient texts that give meaning to Hui ethnoreligious identity.

HUI SPECIALIZATION AND HANDICRAFTS. Hui are known in every small town in China for certain ethnic specializations: butchering beef and lamb, tanning leather, cobbling shoes, running small restaurants, processing wool, and carving stones and jewelry. In Oxen Street, there are several households that are famous for their long tradition of jade work. "Knowing-jade Hui" (*shiyu Huihui*) have been skilled at carving jade and especially "antiquing" jade (*zuo jiu*), a labor-intensive process of creating the right color and texture on the stone so that it appears ancient. Hui have also been known for their ivory carving and gold and silver work. The process was so involved and reaped such high rewards that they had the saying, "Do not sell for three years, Sell and eat for three years" (*San nian bu kai zhang, kai zhang chi san nian*). The sale of one piece of jade or carved ivory could earn so much that there was also the popular saying: "In the morning have nothing to eat, in the evening put your money in a car" (*Zao chen mei fan chi, wan shang you che zhuang*). Before 1949, outside Beijing's Front Gate (Qianmen), almost all the shops on Jadeware Street (Yuqi jie) were run by Hui. In addition to their skills with jewelry and jadeware (*zhubao yuqi*), Hui were known as excellent middlemen, particularly between foreigners and Han. With their exposure to Arabic and Persian in the mosque, they were reported to be adept at learning foreign languages.

The Jade Carver. Bai Shouyong is an elderly Hui jade craftsman. He is the 3rd generation of jade carvers, and his son is attempting to learn his special skills. Since the 1979 3rd Central Committee Plenum, the revival of traditional nationality handicafts has been encouraged. Bai and several of the old jade workers in Oxen Street set up a small cooperative to train young people to work jade in the traditional Hui style. They hoped to train mainly Hui, but several Han have also studied. In 1980, they would take a 100-yuan piece of jade, rework it, and sell it for 130 yuan. While few local Chinese can purchase the expensive stones, foreign tourists have shown considerable interest. One Burmese businessman has made several large orders, and it is thought that he resells the jade outside the country. While the artisans clearly sell their pieces in China as "antiqued" jade, the work is of such high quality that they are afraid they might be easily sold as real antiques elsewhere. In 1986, I spoke with one of the young workers at the tourist shop in the Summer Palace where they sell their wares. While there are plenty of foreign buyers, he lamented, even the master's son cannot exactly reproduce his special technique. He is afraid this skill might soon be lost.

"Now to return to the topic of the jewel and jadeware trade," one Hui author complained before 1949, "it was once regarded as the most profitable business, and the smartest children left school after two or three years to learn the trade."[30] Like many Republican-period Hui reformers, he blamed the inadequate education of the Hui for many of their economic and political woes. The jade trade declined in the Republican period with the shift of the capital to Nanjing (Nanking) and, especially in the north, was disrupted by the socioeconomic turmoil of the warlord years and the Sino-Japanese War. Before it could be substantially revived, the 1950s collectivization campaigns transformed the enterprise into a state-run operation, where antiquing was discouraged. Only recently has there been an attempt to recover this and other local handicraft traditions.

The Lantern Maker. He Keming is a 93-year-old Hui artisan in Shanghai. Since he was 12, he has been making paper and silk lanterns that are displayed during the Lantern Festival. His work is so well known that the *China Daily* referred to him as the "Lantern King" of Shanghai.[31]

He has developed a special technique of making small "gold-like coins" (*jinyin xiangqian*) to look like scales or feathers, and these make lantern figures, animals and birds, appear life-like. He is joined by his son, grandson, and 12 other members of the family in making lanterns. In 1984, from Lantern Day, 16 February, through 1 March, more than 180 of their works were on display at the Shanghai Youth Palace. He Keming displayed a golden dragon over 2 meters high with more than 2,000 golden scales.

His bright eyes glistening behind a shock of white bushy eyebrows and a full beard, Master He explained to me that his religion has helped him dedicate himself to his craft. Every morning at 3:00 a.m. he rises from his bed to recite the *Fatier* prayer, a text dedicated to one's ancestors. "My religion is for the service of people and to respect my ancestors; it is not for myself." During the Cultural Revolution, he was severely criticized for his "feudalistic" art, and, at one point, was encouraged to jump from an 8-story building. He turned to his accusers and claimed he wanted to live and "make revolution" (*gao geming*). "If they made me jump they would be opposing the revolution (*fan geming*)," he said with a wink, "so they let me live." During times when his art could not support him, he sold pastries on the street and ran a teahouse. In 1956, he was invited to join the Shanghai Arts and Crafts Institute; "Allah protected me" (*Zhenzhu baoyou*), he said. The main distinction of his work is a result of the influence of his faith. He says Islam prevents him from making the popular lantern figures of human personages, which would be idolatry. "But," he admits, "I have no problem making dragons!"

The Martial-Arts Specialists. "I travel all over the country because of *wushu* (Chinese traditional martial arts) competitions," Bai Minxiong (pseudonym) complained, "and its very difficult for me to maintain my *qing zhen* lifestyle." The Hui *wushu* boxing style is well known among martial artists, and few practice so hard as young Bai. Unlike many of his secularized Hui friends, Bai really struggles over the problems of maintaining his faith and *qing zhen* lifestyle while on the national-sports-competition circuit. He is often encouraged by his teammates to give up his "backward" ethnic customs. In some ways, his early training reflects the traditional way Hui learned martial arts. His father was a well-known ahong and martial-arts expert who taught his students *wushu* in the mosque compound. "You never know when you might be called on to defend your religion," Bai remembers his father telling him. A recent pamphlet, "Wushu Among Chinese Moslems," refers to this tradition of self-defense:

> In the centuries old feudal society, the Huis were cruelly exploited and ruthlessly suppressed whenever they showed the least resistance or discontent. In the Qing Dynasty (1644–1911), for instance, the rulers decreed that three or more Huis walking together with weapons on them would be severely punished, and, if they committed crimes, they would have the characters *hui zei* (meaning "Hui rebel") tattooed on their faces. This was meant to be a humiliation to them and at the same time served as a warning to the others. But it failed to intimidate the Hui people; they fought back and waged prolonged struggles in the course of which many heroes emerged from among them. . . . To foster perseverance and courage among the Hui people, their chiefs called upon them to go in for *wushu* as a "holy practice" in the struggle for survival and self-improvement.[32]

The Hui look up to famous *wushu* artists that took part in "righteous uprisings" (*qiyi*) against oppressive regimes. Under the banner of Zhu Yuanzhang, who established the Ming dynasty in a peasant revolt, were well-known Hui generals, including Chang Yuchun, Hu Dahai, Mu Ying, Lan Yu, Feng Sheng, and Deng Dexing.[33] Chang Yuchun is said to be the father of the famous "Kaiping spear method" (*Kaiping qiangfa*). In the Ming dynasty, 3 schools of spear play developed, the Yang, Ma, and Sha methods. These are typical Hui surnames, and Ma Fengtu, a famous Hui martial artist, argues that these were Muslim methods. The "18 fist-fighting exercise of the Hui" is a popular boxing method developed in the Ming. Wu Zhong, a Qing-dynasty Hui, developed the famous "8-diagram boxing" (*bajiquan*). When I visited the Hebei Hui autonomous county of Mengcun in 1985, known as the home of Hui *wushu*, I was given a demonstration of his method, together with the "6-combination" (*liu he*) spear play carried on by his descendants, 2 of whom participated in the national *wushu* competition that year.[34]

Much of Hui martial technique revolves around spear play. Wang

Xinwu, president of the Ningxia *Wushu* Committee and vice-president of the China *Wushu* Committee, argues that this may derive from the influence of Persian sword play.[35] Born in a Hui *wushu* center in Shandong, Master Wang won the 1975 National Tai Ji Quan championship and is one of 3 masters responsible for formulating the "combined 48 Peking style" of Tai Ji Quan [also known as Tai Ch'i].[36]

Famous twentieth-century Hui *wushu* artists include Ma Fengtu, Ma Qunxi, Ma Xianda, Ma Zhengbang, Zhang Wenguang, and Wang Ziping. Wang Ziping was born in 1881 in Mengcun, Cangxian county, Hebei province.[37] At 80, he accompanied Premier Zhou Enlai on his visit to Burma and demonstrated Chinese martial arts. During the Republican period, he became known for challenging several foreign boxers who claimed they could easily beat Chinese martial artists. *Wulin zhi*, a recent Chinese movie, portrayed his patriotic triumph in defeating a muscular Russian boxer employed by the Japanese to demonstrate the inferiority of the Chinese "sick man of East Asia" (*dongfang bingfu*). I saw the movie with a Hui friend in Yinchuan. He became quite upset that Wang Ziping's Hui identity was not disclosed; at one point, the film even portrayed his wife, in real life a devout Muslim, asking the Buddha to protect his life.

Wang Ziping's daughter, Wang Jurong, herself an accomplished martial artist in Shanghai, told me that his dedicated *qing zhen* life as a Muslim and his rigorous *wushu* exercise led to his long and healthy life. He developed a special set of exercises in 20 forms that would lead to health and longevity. "Wang Ziping himself also did [the exercise] regularly in his old age. The fact that he lived to 93 shows that this set of exercises is well worth the name of 'longevity.'"[38]

Zhao Changjun is the 27-year-old student of Ma Zhengbang, the famous Hui *wushu* master from Xi'an. He began studying *wushu* in the mosque when he was 6. During the Cultural Revolution, he continued his studies at home. He has won the National *Wushu* Championship 5 times (1980, 1981, 1982, 1983, and 1985) and has performed in over 20 countries. "I am a Hui, and I'm glad to be competing in Yinchuan, the capital of the Hui autonomous region," he told me at the 1985 National Competition, which he won. When I asked him why he worked so hard, he quietly told me: "As a Hui, I not only have to compete on behalf of my country, but I also fight for my people. I am Chinese first, but I am also Hui."

THE SOCIAL ORGANIZATION OF TIGHT URBAN SPACE. In most respects, urban Hui homes are very similar to those of their Han neighbↄrs. There is not much noticeable difference between Hui and Han homes, unlike the situation in the northwest. Islamic paraphernalia in most urban Hui homes is generally limited to posting an Islamic calendar that gives the Muslim and Roman dates in Arabic and Chinese, published by the Chinese Islamic Society. Occasionally one comes across an Arabic sign with the *Shahadah* or a Chinese sign indicating that this is a Muslim household (*Musilin zhi jia*) mounted over the door or on the wall. I rarely saw them anywhere else, but, in Tianjin's Hongqiao district, along Ma (horse) Road, where the Hui are most concentrated, many Hui homes mount a small green sign over the outside entrance with the Arabic *Shahadah*. A local told me that they want Han to be able to see clearly which homes are Hui to prevent them from inadvertently bringing pork in through the gateway.

Before the Cultural Revolution, many Hui homes in Oxen Street were distinguished by 3 incense pots with Quranic inscriptions (*luping sanshe*) placed on a low table next to a family Quran.[39] This stood in the usual place of ancestral tablets in traditional Han homes. Hajji Muhammad Ali Ma Yue, the former principal of the Niujie Hui Middle School and present Niujie Mosque administrator, explained that Hui use incense in a way much different from the Han. Its purpose is to provide a fragrance that cleans the body and lungs (*muyu xunxiang*). "Besides, incense is not Buddhist in origin—it originally came from the West (*an xi xiang*)," Hajji Ma noted; "Hui incense is longer and thinner than the kind Buddhists use and is produced in Dachang Hui autonomous county." That is why Hui like to make the distinction that they "stick incense" (*dian xiang*), not "burn incense" (*shao xiang*) as the Han do.[40]

He went on to describe how the incense was used to indicate purity. On the Ramadan holiday, Muslims bring incense into the mosque to indicate their lives have been purified through fasting. Young Hui brides burn incense at weddings to symbolize a pure and chaste life. As the incense fills one's lungs, Imam Ma maintains, it reminds us that

Islamic purity is internal. "Hui Muslims are just like our Niujie Mosque. On the outside it looks altogether Chinese in style. But on the inside it is Muslim, pure and true (*qing zhen*)."

THE SOCIOECONOMIC CONTEXT OF OXEN STREET HUI IDENTITY

From outward appearance it is practically impossible to tell who are Moslems in Peking. They differ from their neighbors principally in their social intercourse. The fact that they do not eat pork cuts them off from a good many social contacts, particularly since eating is connected with so much of the Chinese life. There are some Mohammedans in government employ, some have money shops and large stores, some run dairies, but by far the majority are dealers in mutton, or camel, or donkey and cart drivers, the caravan trade to the city being almost entirely in their hands.[41]

The cultural texts of Hui identity outlined in 1921 by Sydney Gamble above influence social interaction. Niujie Hui may not look different from their Han neighbors, but they regard themselves as different, and are perceived as outsiders by the Han insiders. This perception influences Hui identity and ethnic relations. Social changes over the last 40 years have had a pronounced effect on the expression of that identity in the multi-ethnic arena.

Radical and rapid socioeconomic change has taken place among the Hui in Oxen Street in the 40 years since the founding of the People's Republic. But for the many *qing zhen* restaurants and the imposing mosque, one would not know that it is an urban minority neighborhood that once resembled many ethnic ghettos found in most large cities. One 1930s observer wrote:

Some may ask whether in the world of business one might have a peaceful and prosperous life without education. Never! In Oxen Street there are countless beggars, peddlers, and men drawing a 2-wheeled cart, and many unemployed walking in the street with nothing to do—all of these prove my point to be true.[42]

This might well have described many Beijing neighborhoods in the 1930s. Yet it is interesting that the writer singles out Oxen Street as the worst example of what happens when one refuses to get an education. The author argues that everyone knows the Hui are less educated than the Han, and look what that did for Oxen Street.

Since 1949, the significant changes in Hui occupation can be broken down into 4 periods, all related to shifts in government policies: from 1949 to the Great Leap Forward (1949–1958), from the Great Leap Forward to the Cultural Revolution (1949–1966), from the Cultural Revolution to the 3rd Central Committee Plenum (1966–1978), and from 1979 until now. From 1949 to 1958, the city government assisted the local Hui in their drive for rapid economic development and recovery from the Civil War. The government recognized the relative poverty and lower education levels of the Hui compared to the Han and attempted to solve the unemployment problem in Oxen Street through collectivization and retraining of those young enough to study. In 1953, 54 percent of the Hui in Oxen Street were illiterate in Chinese; 40 percent could recognize basic characters, like "10 jin of lamb"; and 5.6 percent were middle-school level. Through establishing evening literacy courses, forming Hui schools that gave preference to local Hui in admittance, and training minority cadres, the state attempted to alleviate this situation. State-run *qing zhen* food stores and restaurants were established during this period to help rationalize the local economy. Hui holidays were permitted, and the mosque was restored. Through the active lobbying of the local *jiedao* committee, the government agreed not to allow any buildings to be constructed higher than the mosque within 250 meters. "Not like the Dongsi Mosque," one cadre complained, "where people look down on you from the apartment next door while you are praying." One Chinese Islamic Society representative said, "The older people in Oxen Street thank Allah and the Party for these changes in their lives."

The period from 1958 to 1966 saw several reforms that had restricting effects on Hui ethnoreligious expression. The Religious System Reform Campaigns closed many of the mosques in the city. The Socialist Reconstruction of Industry collectivized Hui private businesses and restaurants into larger state-run units. Interestingly enough, at the very time the state was establishing nationalities institutes and minority autonomous regions and counties, it also promoted policies that were later seen as detrimental to the Hui. This may be related to the strong emphasis upon separating religious from ethnic expressions of identity. The state was also concerned during the Great Leap Forward period and the subsequent famine to strengthen its control over minorities, particularly in the border areas, and to encourage national over local ethnic loyalties.

The Cultural Revolution period saw the continuance and radicalization of many of these assimilative policies. All mosques were closed and former Hui businessmen were criticized as capitalists. Chairman Mao's wife, Jiang Qing, is often quoted as saying: "If you follow socialism, why worry about ethnicity (*minzu*)?" All the signs for *qing zhen* foodstuff stores and restaurants were taken down. The "Hui Elementary School," originally Beijing's famous Northwest Middle School located across from the Oxen Street Mosque, changed its name in 1966 to "Oxen Street Number 2 Elementary School." While the Dongsi Mosque stayed open on Fridays, mainly for foreigners, the Oxen Street Mosque was closed and did not reopen until 1980. People were afraid to come to the mosque and risk being branded with the "4 hats and 8 characters" indicating feudalist superstition and anti-revolutionary reactionism. "The Red Guards loved to criticize me," Imam Shi Kunbing, the head imam of the Niujie Mosque, recalled, "and they liked to use the mosque as a place to make big-character posters (*dazi bao*)." Hui carried out their traditional funerals quietly, ate at home or at restaurants they knew were still *qing zhen* without the sign, and, when asked where they lived, often gave only their local street or a false address so people would not know they were from the Oxen Street district.[43]

From 1979 to the present may be seen as the 4th period created by shifts in government policy. After the fall of the Gang of Four in 1976 and the 3rd Central Committee Plenum in 1978, recognition was given to the importance of nationality identity. The director of the Oxen Street *jiedao* committee, Imam Al-Hajji Salah An Shiwei, said the new agenda includes the following: correcting the errors of the Cultural Revolution, restoring work units with nationality characteristics (nursery, elementary, middle, and religious schools, hospitals, restaurants, and stores), carrying out the new policy of strengthening minority education, training minority cadres, solving the "living problems" (*shenghuo wenti*) the Hui experience in maintaining the *qing zhen* lifestyle, allowing traditional Hui handicrafts and private businesses to reemerge, and repairing mosques and religious structures. Initially the Oxen Street Mosque was given 400,000 yuan for reopening and reconstruction, with further major repairs planned.

THE BUSINESS HUI: URBAN ENTREPRENEURIAL TRADITIONS. The Hui have long been known for their penchant for small enterprise. "8 legs on the ground, 2 knives" (*ba gen shang, liang ba dao*) was the characterization of the Oxen Street Hui: They operated food stands on small tables that sold either meat (beef and lamb) or pastries. Another version states: "Hui hui have two knives: one to cut the meat, the other to slice the pastry" (*Huihui liang ba dao, yi ba mai niurou, yi ba mai qie gao*). The Hui in Niujie, however, are no longer engaged in small private enterprises. As in most cities, the majority of the Hui are workers in factories. This has been the norm since the instigation of the 1950s Socialist Transformation of Industry Campaigns, when small businesses were combined into larger collectives. The radical shifts in Niujie occupation over the last 30 years are reflected in Table 11. These changes in occupation have led to major alterations in income and lifestyle. While Hui have traditionally been known as small merchants and tradesmen, their largest population is involved in agriculture. Table 4 demonstrated that, while the largest number of Hui are engaged in agriculture and husbandry (60.75 percent), they are more engaged in production and transport (22.25 percent) than any other nationality. This supports the traditional proclivity of Hui for trade, transport, and small enterprise. Table 12 reveals the occupational structure of some minorities in Beijing, with the Hui again much more represented in commerce, service, and factory production and transport than others. It is also interesting to note the high percentage of skilled Korean technicians (48.44 percent), due to their high level of education.[44]

While change in income and ownership of household luxury items is difficult to measure because of inflationary fluctuations and the cheaper availability of some new technologies, Table 13 helps provide some information about recent changes in Hui households. Formal employment, especially in the state sector, has dramatically increased in Oxen Street. In 1953, it was found that there were 3,000 unemployed Hui in Oxen Street, representing about 70 percent of the population.[45] Of the 1,305 Hui surveyed in 1983, 49.4 percent were employed, and 10.9 percent were retired (Table 11). Another 1983 survey revealed that, out of 1,701 Hui in one Oxen Street neighborhood, 888 were employed in the following professions: 724 (80.5 percent) factory and service work-

TABLE 11 Hui Occupational Change in a Niujie Neighborhood, Beijing by Percentage of those Employed, 1953–1983

	Total Employed	Factory Workers	Service Workers	Profes-sionals	Cadres	Skilled Workers	Farmers	Clergy	Busi-ness	Other
1953	33.1	19.5	0	1.1	0	5.3	2.9	11.7	39.6	19.9
1964	35.4	54.9	13.1	5.7	3.3	9.5	5.8	7.1	0	0.6
1983	49.4	55.2	15.9	5.1	5.1	1.7	0	0	0	17.0

Source: Beijing Niujie Administrative Committee interview.

Note: This study was conducted by the Oxen Street Subdistrict Administrative Office (Niujie Jiedao Shiwu Chu) on the Hui in one neighborhood of 6 streets, at 3 different periods. In 1953, there were 410 households studied (N = 1,580 Hui); 1964 also 410 households (N = 2,306); and 1983 there were 355 households studied (N = 1,305).

TABLE 12 Occupational Structure of Minorities in Beijing City, 1982 (%)

Occupation	Beijing City						Whole Country	
	Whole City	Minor-ities	Hui	Mongols	Korean	Manchu	Han	Minorities
Skilled Technical Staff	13.62	14.23	12.40	27.61	48.44	18.75	5.15	3.99
Administration	4.04	3.51	3.26	6.52	7.93	3.37	1.59	1.14
Office & related workers	4.30	4.40	4.17	7.26	7.37	4.26	1.32	1.02
Commercial workers	2.81	5.40	6.36	4.52	2.05	4.23	1.85	1.15
Service workers	7.23	9.29	10.14	7.91	5.46	8.32	2.27	1.29
Farming, forestry, fishing & animal husbandry	24.81	15.63	12.70	5.17	0.51	21.86	71.18	83.82
Factory, production & transport	41.75	47.25	50.67	40.44	27.53	43.98	10.56	7.54
Others	0.33	0.30	0.30	0.56	0.30	0.24	0.08	0.05

Source: 1982 census, adapted from Zhang Tianlu, Beijing Shaoshu minzu renkou, p. 25.

ers; 92 (10.2 percent) cadres and police; and 73 (8.1 percent) skilled technicians. The Beijing city CNA reported in 1984 that 60,000 of the Hui, one-third of the city's population, were workers in factories, with 2,000 Hui working in qing zhen restaurants, of whom 200 were cooks. There were just over 100 qing zhen restaurants in the city and about 250 small food stands (xiao chidian) (see Map 3). They noted that only about 3 to 5 out of

TABLE 13 Income and Household Commodities Change in Niujie,
Beijing, 1953–1983

	(a)*Household Monthly Income (yuan)*	*Individual Monthly Income (yuan)*	*Bicycles*	*Radios*	*Sewing Machines*	*Watches*	*Television Sets*
1953	36.12	6.12	5	2	1	0	0
1964	94.30	16.71	19	81	32	217	0
1983	125.30	34.08	519	256	187	831	349

Source: Beijing Oxen Street Administrative Committee interview.

Note: (a) Total of Hui households surveyed varied by year: 410 Households in 1953; 410 in 1964; 355 in 1983. In 1983, new commodities reported included: 76 washing machines, 243 electric fans, 9 refrigerators, 9 recorders.

10 workers in *qing zhen* restaurants were Hui and about half the workers in *qing zhen* food stores (*fanshipin*). This breakdown matches my own informal survey. The vast majority of Hui in Oxen Street are engaged in factory work or in service professions (*fuwuyuan*), such as clerks in department stores or waiters in restaurants. While statistics from the 1982 census are helpful, they are still inadequate for giving an accurate picture of Hui occupations because many of the categories, like "commerce," were too general, and the survey had no way of measuring private or sideline enterprises, many of which are under-reported. I could not obtain more reliable information on youth unemployment and the number of private enterprises (*getihu*) run by Hui, but I was often told by Hui residents and local officials that both were significantly higher than for the Han.

While there has been some reemergence of Hui private and collective enterprise, Beijing is particularly slow in granting *getihu* permits. The city CNA gave the following reasons for the relatively small number of private enterprises in Beijing as opposed to other cities:

(1) Desire for a stable guaranteed income which *getihu* businesses cannot provide.
(2) Discouragement of young people to engage in riskier private enterprises while awaiting state employment, in favor of encouraging retirees to become *getihu* who are less at risk.

(3) Difficulty in finding a place to set up shop, since most houses do not front onto the street and there is little open space.

(4) Continuing influence of Cultural Revolution ideas so that people are afraid of being labeled "capitalist tails" if they start their own businesses.

(5) Less need for *geti* activity in large cities than in the countryside, since there are larger stores that are well supplied.

(6) Tighter rules within Beijing for health control.

(7) More conservative nature of Beijing as a "model" city and national capital that needs to present a more orderly, clean appearance to the many visitors.

(8) Unwillingness of Hui to allow their children to be clerks or workers in small private enterprises, in favor of having them become workers with a secure income.

Ma Xinhua, like many of the Beijing youth I spoke to, would like to carry on his parents' or grandparents' entrepreneurial traditions of making a certain kind of food or maintaining a special handicraft. Parents complain that, while the collectivization of small industry has in general helped the economy, it has adversely affected one important nationality characteristic (*minzu tedian*) of the Hui: the skill for small business. The youth would also like more secure jobs in the state sector, but those are even harder to come by without the right connections and education. Many complain that Beijing is too conservative and that Hui young people should be given more opportunity to engage in activities that reflect their minority heritage.

While most elderly Hui in Oxen Street are glad their children have more secure jobs and a better chance to receive an education than they had when they were young, they would like to see more opportunity for engaging in small business and participating in the free-market economy. Some have traveled in rural areas and noted that many Hui are actively engaged in the thriving private market.[46] "We wish we could set up more Hui restaurants," one local Hui lamented; "the state-run restaurants are too few and too crowded. Besides, many devout Muslims (*qianchengde Mumin*) will eat only at small private *qing zhen* restaurants where they can be sure the food is really *qing zhen*. A small Hui food stand on this street could make a lot of money, and we Hui know how to do business." The traditional capacity for entrepreneurial activity among the Hui is an ethnic characteristic also often noted by their detractors.

In 1921, G. F. Andrew reported the following stereotypes Han repeated to him: "A Tibetan can eat (take in) a Mongol, a Chinaman can eat a Tibetan, but a Hwei-Hwei can eat the lot." And, "A Chinaman awake is not the equal of a sleeping Hwei-hwei."[47] When I asked a taxi driver to take me to the famous Hui market area in Xi'an he related a common slur that I heard again on several occasions: "Be careful of the 'larcenous' Hui (*zei Huihui*). Out of 10 Hui there are 9 thieves" (*Shige Hui hui jiuge zei*). While the Hui reject this kind of stigma, they also admit that Hui often make good business people and wish there were more opportunities in the city for Hui to engage in trade.[48]

THE GIRL NEXT DOOR: FINDING A MATE IN A HAN CITY. "I just don't know what to do," Yang Dexin (assumed name), my older Hui friend, told me; "both of my daughters should be married, but my wife and parents just won't allow them to marry a Han. Many of our friends' children have intermarried and we have seen how inconvenient it is. They never meet any Hui boys at work, and our neighborhood does not have any likely prospects. And young people today refuse to let us make the arrangements. They turn down everyone we suggest. I guess I'll go talk to the ahong and see if he knows of anyone." Yang Dexin had not been to a mosque in years. He was a member of the Communist Party and a cadre in a prominent institute. Yet he was still adamantly opposed to allowing his daughters to marry outside the Hui. Nevertheless, intermarriages often take place in urban areas, and studies indicate there has been some increase. Most recent intermarriages revealed in the 1982 census, however, suggest that the Hui in Beijing are continuing to follow the traditional pattern of bringing in Han brides rather than marrying their women out. This tradition continues despite official policy that encourages intermarriage. The following is drawn from a 1978 policy statement, based on an historical survey of ethnic intermarriage over the centuries in China:

> This serves as historical evidence of the fact that "interracial marriage" adds to unity among nationalities. . . . The "gang of four" totally negated "interracial marriage". . . . In fact, "interracial marriage" expands and strengthens economic and cultural exchanges among fraternal nationalities in our country. It is conducive to social development and pushes history forward.[49]

This is a sensitive issue among the Hui in Oxen Street. While local cadres did not discourage me from asking any economic or political questions in the course of my research, they warned that the Hui on Oxen Street would be upset if I asked about intermarriage. Conservative Hui are embarrassed if anyone in their family has intermarried, and will often deny it. As a result, I rarely asked this question in my Oxen Street interviews and had to rely on outside studies for data. The *jie dao* committee reported that, in the Oxen Street district, there were 37 mixed Hui/Han households, only 2 of which were Han men with Hui wives. There were no households on Oxen Street with 2 generations of intermarriages

Studies based on the 1982 census reports have revealed much regarding increasing intermarriage trends in two Beijing Hui neighborhoods. The demographer Zhang Tianlu reports that, whereas a survey of 350 households in the Niujie area found only 2 Hui-Han intermarriages in 1953, and another survey in 1964 turned up none, the 1982 census revealed 38 Hui-Han intermarriages out of 491 households.[50] In the multi-ethnic northern Beijing neighborhood of Ma Dian (described above), 11.2 percent of the 939 Hui have intermarried with either Han or Manchu, 7.8 percent of the 2,270 Han have intermarried with Hui or Manchu, and 80 percent of the 65 Manchu nationality members have intermarried with Han or Hui. Table 14 gives the multi-ethnic structure of the intermarriages. It is noteworthy that, as the concentration of Hui goes up, intermarriage decreases. In the Tang Fang neighborhood of Oxen Street (described above), there are a third more intermarriages among the Han than among the Hui. Of the 1,814 Hui, 10.2 percent have intermarried; among the 1,272 Han, 15.3 percent have intermarried; and among the 21 Manchu, 83.3 percent have intermarried.[51] In addition to the increased possibility of finding a Hui spouse in the Oxen Street area where Hui are more concentrated, this lower percentage of intermarriage may also have something to do with a more conservative Hui population. Clearly, when possible, the Hui tend to marry their own.

But when they do intermarry, it is important to know who marries out. Traditionally, the Hui have taken in Han girls and rarely married their women out. The continuation of this practice in the city is sub-

TABLE 14 Ethnic Composition of Households in Ma Dian

Household Type	Households With Han		Households With Hui		Households With Manchu	
	Households	*Individuals*	*Households*	*Individuals*	*Households*	*Individuals*
All Han	608	2,196	–	–	–	–
All Hui	–	–	250	845	–	–
All Manchu	–	–	–	–	6	21
Hui-Han Marriages	30	30	30	72	–	–
Manchu-Han Marriages	22	40	–	–	22	42
Hui-Manchu Marriages	–	–	2	5	2	2
Totals	660	2,266	282	922	30	65

Source: Adapted from Chen Changping, "Minzu renkou," pp. 48, 51.

TABLE 15 Composition of Ethnic Intermarriages in Tang Fang
          Niujie District

Household Type	Households	Individuals	Hui	Han	Manchu
Hui-Han Marriages					
Male Han–Female Hui	35	132	94	38	–
Male Hui–Female Han	17	76	52	24	–
Manchu-Han Marriages					
Male Manchu–Female Han	7	27	–	11	16
Male Han–Female Manchu	3	7	–	4	3
Totals	62	242	146	77	19

Source: Adapted from Chen Changping, pp. 72–74.

stantiated by the 1982 data in Table 15. There is a similar structure of intermarriage in Ma Dian, where slightly more of the intermarriages had Hui women marrying out, 7 out of 34 (20 percent), as opposed to Tang Fang where 11 percent of the intermarriages involve Hui women marrying out (24 out of 208). The interesting feature in comparing Manchu/Han and Hui/Han marriages in Ma Dian is that, among both

TABLE 16 Age Structure of Hui-Han Intermarriages in Tang Fang and Ma Dian Neighborhoods, Beijing

	Under 30		*31 to 40*		*Over 41*	
	N	*%*	*N*	*%*	*N*	*%*
Tang Fang	29	55.7	19	36.5	4	7.6
Ma Dian	17	56.7	10	33.3	3	10.0

Source: Adapted from Chen Changping, pp. 57, 74.

groups, 13.6 percent and 20 percent of the women marrying out were Hui and Manchu, respectively, whereas 86 percent and 80 percent of the women marrying in were Han. In Tang Fang, 67.3 percent of the Hui men and 70 percent of the Manchu men intermarried with Han women. Both Hui and Manchu seem to be reluctant to give their women away.

The age structure of intermarriage reveals that, in Ma Dian and Tang Fang, there is a much higher proportion of Hui/Han intermarriages among those under 30 years old (56.7 percent and 55 percent respectively) than those over 40 years old (10 percent and 7 percent respectively; see Table 16). Interestingly enough, this is the opposite among Manchu/Han intermarriages in Tang Fang, which decrease from 70 percent among those over 40, to 10 percent among those under 30. However, the data here may be too insufficient (only 10 Manchu/Han households in Tang Fang) to suggest any conclusions.

The question of intermarriage is a personal one that involves much decision making and debate. A Hui/Han intermarriage ceremony that I attended in 1984 in the Tianqiao district, a concentrated Hui area in south Beijing with 80–90 Hui households, was one of the few cases where a Hui woman married a Han man. However, in this case she did not marry out. After much discussion, the groom decided to move in, a traditional uxorilocal practice in Chinese society known as "seeking a son-in-law" (*zhao nuxu*). It is unfortunate that the census data discussed above do not indicate whether any of the intermarriages were uxorilocal. We might find that quite a common practice when the bride is a Hui. In this case, the couple had known each other since high school,

6 years ago, but did not become interested in each other until later. They became reacquainted through a mutual friend and decided to get married one year earlier. At first, the parents on both sides disapproved. Neither family had experienced any intermarriages, and the Hui were especially antagonistic to the idea. The Han side happened to live in the Oxen Street district and, since they were familiar with many Hui, they were the first to agree. After the groom promised that his family would clean all the pots when the bride ate with them and respect the Hui customs wherever possible, the bride's side reluctantly agreed. "Besides," her mother said, "the two are in their mid-twenties, both high school graduates, and there are no other prospects in sight."

It was only later, when they began to discuss lifestyle problems, that the groom accepted his father-in-law's invitation to move in. The bride's family would build the couple a separate room in the small family courtyard. Though the groom agreed to move in, atypically they were not planning to give their future child the bride's surname, the usual Chinese uxorilocal custom. "It was merely more convenient to live here than with my family," the groom cheerfully admitted.[52]

Most urban Hui intermarriages are simple and do not involve the mosque. This one was unique in that the girl came from a fairly religious family and she "believed in Islam in her heart" and encouraged her spouse to do the same. They went to the mosque together and spoke with the ahong. "Before I had no religion," the groom said, "I didn't believe in anything. But, after talking with the ahong, I became interested in the Hui religion and decided to believe." Imam Shi Kunbing of the Niujie Mosque relates the 4 conditions of his marrying a Han and Hui: They must (1) believe in only one God, Allah; (2) follow Muhammad's teachings; (3) agree to the rules of Islam regarding marriage, that is, no divorce or adultery; and (4) learn that the basis of this is all in the Quran.

On the day of the wedding, 5 ahong, 2 from the Niujie Mosque and 3 from the local Tianqiao Mosque, gathered in the home of the bride. After going to the groom's house for a short *qing zhen* meal and an exchange of gifts, the new couple returned to the bride's home accompanied by his family, their gifts, and the popping of firecrackers as they entered the alleyway. While the groom wore a Western-style suit, the bride was dressed in a traditional red velvet *qipao*. On the gateway to their yard they posted a large red sign with gold Arabic lettering of the *Qing Zhen Yan* instead of the traditional Chinese ideographs for "double happiness" (*shuangxi*). Over the door to the couple's new room they posted a new green placard with the Arabic *Shahadah* lettered in white. It was the first time the two families had met each other. After exchanging greetings in the courtyard, the couple went inside to meet with the ahong who were drinking tea and eating snacks.

When they entered the room, the 5 ahong were led in prayer individually by the senior Oxen Street Mosque ahong. The bride's father and bride's mother's brother (*jiujiu*) joined them in the room and donned white Hui hats. Portions of the Quran were recited by all the ahong simultaneously, and, when they finished, the senior ahong addressed the couple (*yizabu*). He asked if the woman was willing (*yuanyi*) to marry and if the man would accept (*jieshou*) her, and whether both parents agreed (*tongyi*). When they assented, he lectured them on the importance of Islam in their lives, belief in God, and preserving the Hui *qing zhen* lifestyle. "If your job makes it difficult for you to live the Hui life, then change your work. Its easy to change your job, but not your life." They then signed their names on a special certificate (*ijab*) that the ahong also signed, and the bride gave him some candy, her first act in her new but traditional role as wife and hostess. The two Yihewani ahong departed and the Gedimu ahong remained for the subsequent feast (*nanzhi ganjing*). No wine or cigarettes were served at the wedding. Later on that evening, the groom had a party with his friends where both items were in abundance.

The relatively low percentage of intermarriages that I found in Niujie and Ma Dian is far surpassed by the many Hui-Han intermarriages in southern urban areas. Among 20 Hui households I interviewed in Shanghai, there was not one without a member of the extended family married to a Han. There were Hui-Han intermarriages among all the married children in 7 of the households. One Hui student from a southern city told me that, though his parents were both traditional Hui, his wife was Han, his three sisters were married to Han, and all his cousins on both sides were married to Han. He began to eat pork at the age of 17 during a long hospital stay while away at school.[53] Now he eats pork all the time. His son, of course, is also registered as a Hui. He told me that his son was "100 percent Hui." When I asked him what he meant, he said, "My son's blood is Hui." While Pillsbury has noted that this is a common response among Hui in Taiwan, I rarely encountered it in the PRC, and then only in southern areas.[54] Hui indicated that the children of Han-Hui marriages were "just as Hui" as other Hui children.

EDUCATING FATIMA: RELIGIOUS ISSUES AND URBAN MOBILITY. The Third Tide of Islam in China during the late nineteenth century saw Beijing's establishment as the "cultural center of Chinese Islam." While Hui in the northwest saw religious conservativism and revival as the answer to their social and cultural problems, the Hui in Beijing and other major cities decided that education was the solution:

> [The decline of the Hui in Beijing] is associated with the following 4 things: (1) the degeneration of Islam among all religions, (2) the degeneration of China among the nations, (3) the degeneration of Beijing among the capitals, (4) the degeneration of Niujie where the Hui people are crowded together. In fact, it isn't the degeneration of the people but the backwardness of their education. . . . The relationship between education and living standard is one of cause and effect. Obviously, without education there would not be people of talent; without talented personnel there would be no better means of livelihood.[55]

The question of what kind of education was debated throughout the Republican period, with various private Hui schools attempting different combinations of secular and religious education. In the early days of the People's Republic, these private schools became secularized and nationalized. Religious education was now the responsibility of the mosque and home, whereas secular education was the responsibility of the state. Shortly after the establishment of the PRC, the Beijing city government combined the Hui middle schools of Cheng Da Normal School, Northwest Middle School, and Yanshan Middle School into the Hui Institute (Huimin Xueyuan). In 1963, the Hui Institute was changed to the Hui Middle School. In 1979, it was reopened under that name after being divided up during the Cultural Revolution as the Capital Middle School and the Number 135 Middle School.

In 1949, there were 19 Hui primary schools created out of former private "Muslim" (Mu zi) schools. By 1953, there were 28 Hui elementary schools, all of them renamed during the Cultural Revolution. Children were required to attend the schools in the neighborhoods where they lived. This is still mainly the case for Hui primary schools; there are now 13 Hui primary schools and 6 Hui nursery schools in Beijing, all in Hui concentrated neighborhoods. Primary education, now universally required throughout Beijing, is the area of real gain. In 1949, there were only about 2,700 Hui in primary school in Beijing. Now there are no Hui primary-school-age children not in school.

The curriculum in all these state-run institutions is set by the Ministry of Education and is exactly the same as for other schools, with the main differences that no pork is served at the schools and no tuition charged to Hui students. In 1985, the state CNA published a "nationality general knowledge" (*minzu changshi*) curriculum for the Hui middle schools. The state's goal of strengthening education among minorities reflects the call in the 1930s: "This research explains that, whenever nationality education work is seized upon (*zhua haole*), then nationality relations and nationality unity will be greatly strengthened."[56]

Despite much emphasis on minority education since the "golden period" of the 1950s, the Hui still lag behind the Han, especially in post-primary education.[57] Out of 364 Han who graduated from Beijing's Number 1 Middle School in 1982, there were 47 (12 percent) who went on to either college or higher technical schools. Out of the 7 Hui who graduated, not one went on.[58] Table 17 gives differences in Hui and Han high-school entrance from 1979 to 1981 in the Oxen Street district.

From 1979 to 1981, there was a slight decline among both Han and Hui in high-school entrance. Although the Hui constitute about one-fourth of the Oxen Street population, they represent only 5 to 14 percent of those entering high school. Less than 6 percent of the Oxen Street area Hui had attended middle school prior to 1955. A 1983 education survey of the Xuanwu district (where Oxen Street is located) found that, out of every 1,000 Hui, 5.1 percent are college graduates, 22.7 percent high-school graduates, 30.7 percent middle-school gradu-

TABLE 17 Ethnic Composition of Entering High School Students from Niujie, 1979–1981

	1979		1980		1981		Total	
	Han	Hui	Han	Hui	Han	Hui	Han	Hui
Students	54	3	37	2	35	2	123	10
Percentage of Ethnic Group	0.13	0.03	0.09	0.20	0.80	0.04	0.29	0.07
Percentage of Class	94.70	5.30	95.00	5.00	86.00	14.00	92.00	8.00

Source: Adapted from Beijing City Sociology Committee, p. 21.

TABLE 18 Ethnic Composition of Entering High School Students in Beijing, 1979-81

	1979	1980	1981	Total
Total	11,442	10,401	10,226	32,069
Han	11,263	10,190	10,021	31,474
Minorities	179	211	205	595
Percent Minorities	1.56	2.02	2.0	1.96

Source: Adapted from Beijing City Sociology Committee, p. 21.

ates, and 41.8 percent primary-school graduates. The same survey among Han in the Xuanwu district revealed that 23.34 percent are college graduates, 21.54 percent high-school graduates, 25 percent middle-school graduates, and 17.58 primary-school graduates. More than 4 times as many Han graduate from college as Hui in this area, and there are almost 2.5 times as many Hui with only an elementary school education as there are Han. Table 18 shows that about 2 percent of those entering high school from 1979 to 1981 were minorities in Beijing.

In 1982, 1.2 percent of the Han students who took the high-school exam were admitted, whereas only 0.67 percent of the minority examinees were admitted.[59] Table 19 reveals the dramatic increase in educational levels in Niujie since the 1950s, and, though the earlier statistics were not as reliable as the 1982 census, important shifts in education are discernable.

TABLE 19 Niujie Educational Levels, 1953–1982

| Year | Out of every 1,000 persons with some education | | | | Semi-Literate & Illiterate Above 12 Years Old |
	College	High School	Middle School	Elementary	
1953	8.3	23.3	30.1	323.1	40.1
1964	21.7	47.4	147.8	298.8	33.1
1982	28.0	226.0	346.2	197.9	12.0

Source: Zhang Tianlu, *Beijing shaoshu minzu renkou*, p. 27.

While it is generally true that the Hui educational level is lower than that of the Han majority among whom they live, at the national level Hui educational level has apparently fared rather well. Table 20 indicates that the Hui have kept pace with the national average and are substantially better educated than the other Muslim minorities.[60] The main advantage the Hui have is language. Other Muslim minorities have to contend with learning the Han language as a second language to enter middle school and university. The Hui speak the Han dialects wherever they live.

Some Hui parents in the Oxen Street district have told me that, while they are glad for the Hui schools and the priority Hui are now receiving in education, they feel their children would be more motivated to study if there were more ethnic content. Many of them remember that Hui schools in the early 1950s often invited famous Hui scholars such as Bai Shouyi and Ma Songting to give lectures on Hui history and on historic Chinese Muslim personages. The Hui middle school also offered Arabic as a second language, so children did not have to go to the mosque to learn it. Beijing Hui parents are not tempted to withdraw their children from school and send them to the mosque for religious education like many northwestern Hui. Instead, they argue that there is more of a need to integrate secular and religious education in order to motivate their children. They also point out that the Islamic schools, even with the course for training imams at the Chinese Islamic Association in the Oxen Street district, cannot supply enough imams for as many mosques as need them. One of the reasons is that many young men upon graduation use their Arabic or Persian to become inter-

TABLE 20 Educational Level of Muslim Minorities in China, 1982 (%)

Education Level	Hui	Uigur	Kazak	Dong-xiang	Kirghiz	Salar	Tadjik	Uzbek	Bao-an	Tatar	All Ethnic Groups	All China
University Graduate	0.5	0.2	0.4	0	0.3	0.2	0.2	0.2	0.2	38	0.2	0.5
Undergraduate	2.5	0.1	0.1	0	0.1	0.2	0.1	0.9	0.1	11	0.1	0.2
Senior Middle School	7.0	5.0	5.0	1	5.0	1.0	4.0	11.0	2.0	14	5.0	7.5
Junior Middle School	19.0	12.0	17.0	3	11.0	5.0	11.0	22.0	6.0	24	15.0	20.0
Primary School	30.0	37.0	49.0	8	40.0	18.0	38.0	40.0	12.0	40	37.0	39.9
*Illiterate	41.0	45.0	29.0	87	41.0	74.0	49.0	20.0	78.0	–	45.0	31.9

Source: Adopted from Population Census Office 1987, pp. xvi, 29.

Notes: *Population aged 6 and above who cannot read Chinese or can read very little.
All figures are estimates based on the Population Census Office diagram, p. 29, and p. 84

preters or translators overseas where they can travel and earn more money, instead of becoming imams. The distinction between ethnicity and Islam in the city is still too strong for most Hui parents, and they think it might help the country if the two were brought closer together.

GOVERNMENT POLICY AND URBAN STRATEGIES

The state's favorable policy toward its urban minorities is having a significant impact on their ethnoreligious identity. The Hui, as a minority nationality, receive many small "special considerations" that may be insignificant when taken alone but together are beginning to have an influence on their status and living conditions.

LIFESTYLE BENEFITS. Most work units with many Hui workers give a lifestyle bonus (*shenghuo butie*) of 4 to 6 yuan to help offset the cost of buying beef, lamb, or chicken, which are more expensive meats. While this is not a lot of money for the individual, a frugal family with several working members might save a fair amount over time. Urban Hui receive special oil and meat coupons that allow them to purchase beef, lamb, and vegetable oil in larger quantities at a reduced price. In Niujie, Hui could buy twice as much vegetable oil as Han and with their coupons they could buy twice as much beef or lamb from the state stores. Beef and lamb are becoming more popular among the Han with the result that the free-market price is considerably higher than for pork. The state ration system allows Hui to have better access to the limited supplies of beef and lamb at an affordable price.

Han co-workers of one young Hui factory worker I knew were constantly joking that, even though he ate pork, he continued to receive his 5 yuan a month and extra ration coupons. They thought he had the best of both worlds: He could buy oil and beef at a cheaper rate, and was not afraid to eat pork. No one was angry with him because, they said, "It is the government's money" (*guojia de qian*) and people should seek to receive all to which they are entitled.

PRIVILEGES IN EDUCATION AND BIRTH PLANNING. Like other minorities, the Hui in Niujie receive special consideration on their exams for entrance to middle school, high school, and college. In general, they receive 2 "levels" of 10 points each for college entrance preference. For example, if the threshold for college entrance on the state exams is 300 points, a Hui who scores 280 points will be accepted. This may make a difference. I knew a Hui who scored 281 on the exam and was admitted to Beijing Normal University (Beijing Shifan Daxue). His Han neighbor complained bitterly of this to me, since he scored 295 and was not admitted to the college of his choice, but had to go to a "television university" (*dianshi daxue*) where most courses are taught on video cassette. Athletes who place among the top 6 (*qian liu ming*) in provincial competitions are also given 2 stage preferences. Hence, it is conceivable that a Hui athlete could score 260 on the exam and still be admitted to college with a total score of 300, as the result of 4 stage preferences. Preference for high school and college minority education is just beginning to show long-term effects, and 1990 records should reveal a significant improvement over the 1979-to-1981 figures cited above.

Urban Hui are allowed to marry 2 years earlier than Han, but they are not allowed to have 2 children with urban residency. Only Hui with rural residency or those who recently moved to the city are allowed to have 2 children. This is leading to a growing number of hypergamous marriages between Hui women from the countryside and urban Hui who are interested in having at least 2 children (see Chapter 5). Most urban Hui, like the Han, do not want more than 2 children, especially if at least 1 is male.[61] Minority members also tend to receive other special considerations when there are opportunities for promotion, wage increase, or assignment for housing. It is a slight edge, but an edge nevertheless.

LOCAL RESPONSE TO FAVORABLE POLICIES. This edge is having an influence. In the Oxen Street district, out of 34 district representatives to the city government, 12 are Hui (35.3 percent), more than their one-fourth population ratio. Two Hui from this district are national Chinese People's Political Consultative Conference (CPPCC) representatives, 5 are city representatives, and 16 represent the district. For the first time, many young urban Hui are seeing participation in the local political organizations as an upward-mobility strategy.

TABLE 21 Ethnicity Selection among Offspring from
Intermarried Households in Ma Dian, 1982

Household Type	Total Households	Total Children	Select Hui	Select Han	Select Manchu
Hui-Han Marriage	30	33	33	0	—
Manchu-Hui Marriage	2	3	3	—	0
Manchu-Han Marriage	22	35	—	16	19

Source: Adapted from Chen Changping, p. 58.

The rise in the status of local Hui and possibilities for income and
lifestyle improvements through favorable policies have also led to a significant shift in Han-Hui relations. Once reluctant to marry Hui as culturally different, sometimes regarded as inferior to Han, many local
Han are now more open to interethnic marriage. The children of these
intermarriages are now invariably given minority status. Table 21
demonstrates that, in 1982, all the offspring of Hui intermarriages,
whether with Han or Manchu, were registered as Hui, whereas only 19
of the 35 children of Manchu/Han intermarriages chose Manchu status.

The fact that offspring of Manchu-Han marriages are less inclined to
be registered as minorities than the offspring of Hui intermarriages indicates the importance of preserving and passing on ethnic identity
among the Hui. This may be related to the special privileges accorded
the Hui due to their dietary restrictions, which are not applicable to
Manchu (see below). Out of 48 Hui-Han intermarriages in Tang Fang,
Oxen Street district, only 8 offspring chose to be Han. The government
requires parents to decide the registration of their children until the age
of 18 when they are allowed to choose for themselves. I have not yet
met anyone who chose Han registration in recent years.

In his fascinating comparison between three multi-ethnic communities based on the 1982 census, Zhang Tianlu found some interesting data
regarding interethnic marriage.[62] In the Niujie district, out of 38 Hui-
Han intermarried households with 45 offspring, 33 children, or 75.5 percent, were registered as Hui. By contrast, out of 6 Han-Manchu intermarriages, only 4 of the 8 children chose Manchu ethnicity (50 per-

cent). In Beimujialing Hui autonomous village on the outskirts of Beijing, there were 16 Hui-Han intermarriages. Of 19 children, 17 chose to be registered as Hui (89.47 percent). In the one Han-Manchu household, the 2 children were registered as Han. Most striking, however, was his discovery that in the Tanying Manchu and Mongol joint autonomous village, also in the rural suburbs of Beijing, there was a high number of intermarriages between Manchu and Han (146 out of 175 intermarriages in the village), 20 Mongol-Han intermarriages, 7 Mongol-Manchu intermarriages, 1 Hui-Han intermarriage, and 1 Hui-Mongol intermarriage. Of all children born to mixed couples, 76.8 percent registered as minorities; 73 percent of the Manchu-Han offspring chose Manchu nationality; 94 percent of the Mongol-Han offspring chose Mongol nationality; and 100 percent of the Hui-Han and Hui-Mongol offspring chose to be registered as Hui. Interestingly, children born to the Mongol-Manchu households registered only slightly more often as Mongol (60 percent) than as Manchu (40 percent). This indicates that there is not much of a difference in preference for nationality selection between urban and rural areas. When they have a choice, most people want to be a minority nationality in the People's Republic.

HUI POPULATION INCREASE. Hui preference for choosing minority status for their offspring of intermarriages is also found among other minorities. This trend, added to the higher birth rate among minority nationalities due to relaxed birth-planning policies, has led to a notable increase in the minority population. In 1981, the total fertility rate of minority populations, 5.05, was almost twice that of the rural Han, 2.76.[63] The total population growth for China since 1982 was 12.5 percent, but for the minorities it was 35.5 percent.[64] Figure 3 indicates that minorities have increased slightly in their percentage of the total population since 1978, from 5.8 percent to 6.7 percent.[65]

While population figures derived from the 1982 national census are fairly reliable, comparisons that rely on earlier census data, particularly with regard to minority areas, are highly suspect.[66] Table 22 indicates the growth of Muslim minorities in contrast to the total population growth. Hui and Boaon increases of 2.4 and 4.4 percent respectively are significantly higher than for Han (1.4 percent) and close to other minorities

FIGURE 3 Minorities as Percent of National Total

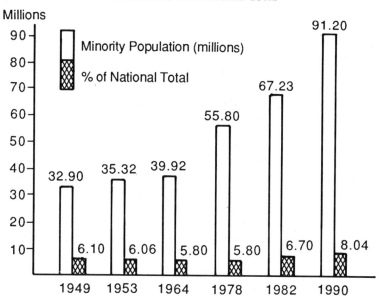

Source: Zhang Tianlu, "Population Growth among China's Minorities," p. 45.

(4.4 percent). This may indicate under-reporting in the past, or the coming forward of many who were previously registered as Han.[67] This is particularly true of the children of mixed marriages. Previously registered as Han, many of these offspring have come forward as minorities now that they are certain that the favorable policies toward minorities will be enforced. This trend has continued since 1982, with preliminary 1990 census results indicating that the minorities increased 35.5 percent, whereas the Han only increased 10 percent. The Tujia increased a whopping 101 percent over their 1982 population (from 2,834,732 to 5,704,223); the Manchu more than doubled their population, increasing 128 percent (from 4,204,160 to 9,821, 180); the Russian (Eluosi) nationality increased 360 percent (from 2,935 to 13,504); and the most dramatic was the 7-fold increase of Yunnan's Gelao minority, growing 714 percent, from 69,102 in 1982, to 437,997 in 1990.[68]

INCREASING EXCHANGE WITH FOREIGN MUSLIMS. The increased promotion of exchange with foreign Muslim countries is exposing more urban Hui to international aspects of their religious heritage. Among urban Hui,

TABLE 22 Population Growth of Muslim Minorities, 1953–1982

Ethnic Group	Population				Approximate annual average grown (%)		
	Midyear 1953	Midyear 1964	Midyear 1982	Midyear 1990	1982–1990	1953–1964	1953–1982
Hui	3,119,000	4,473,147	7,219,392	8,602,978	2.4	2.1	2.4
Uigur	3,640,125	3,996,311	5,957,112	7,214,431	2.6	0.8	1.7
Kazak	509,000	491,637	907,582	1,111,718	2.8	-0.3	2.0
Dongxiang	156,000	147,443	279,397	373,872	4.2	-0.5	2.0
Kirghiz	70,900	70,151	113,999	141,549	3.0	-0.1	1.6
Salar	30,600	34,664	69,102	87,697	3.4	1.1	2.8
Tadjik	14,400	16,236	26,503	33,538	3.3	1.1	2.1
Uzbek	13,600	7,717	12,453	14,502	2.1	-5.2	-0.3
Baoan	4,900	5,125	9,027	12,212	4.4	0.4	2.1
Tatar	6,900	2,294	4,127	4,873	2.3	-10.0	-1.8
All Minorities	35,320,360	39,923,736	67,233,254	91,200,314	4.4	1.1	2.2
Han	547,283,057	651,296,368	936,703,824	1,042,462,187	1.4	1.6	1.9

Source: Banister, *China's Changing Population,* pp. 322–323; *Renmin ribao,* 14 november 1990, p. 3.

Islamic knowledge tends to be higher than in rural areas, perhaps because of increased educational levels and more media exposure. The majority knew of Khomeini and the location of Mecca. Unlike the vast majority of Hui in rural areas, many urban Hui interviewed knew of and often read the magazine published by the China Islamic Association, *Zhongguo Musilin* (China's Muslims). Few were aware of and interested in the sectarian disputes in the Iran/Iraq conflict, but most knew of Shi[c]ism.

Foreign Muslims are often in the news in Beijing, and are to be found worshiping regularly in many mosques, especially at Dongsi. At the 1983 Corban service I attended, there were more than 200 foreign Muslims in attendance at the Dongsi Mosque.[69] Statements have been made in foreign-language newspapers about Chinese Muslims' support for the "Afghan, Arab, and Palestinian Muslim struggles."[70] At the 1986 Corban festival, there were 300 Chinese and foreign Muslims invited to a special reception at the International Club in Beijing, including heads of diplomatic missions from "34 Arab Islamic countries."[71] Ground has been broken for construction of a new 9-story "Muslim Building" for foreigners behind the Beijing Hotel on Wangfujing Street in which the entire ground floor will be a *qing zhen* restaurant.[72]

Donations are now being actively solicited from foreign Muslims by the Chinese Islamic Association. The "Muslim Foundation for Reconstructing Niujie Street" was recently established in 1984 to help turn the Niujie district into a Hui ethnic tourist area.[73] The *China Daily* article reported that, in 1983 alone, the Niujie Mosque received 56 delegations of more than 1,300 persons from Islamic countries. "We can't rely only on state funds," Zhang Shunzhi, vice-director of the Xuanwu district stated. "To speed reconstruction, we welcome donations as well as foreign investment. The foundation will link all those Muslims who want to help us." The funds, they said, will be used to make Niujie a cultural "show-window" for tourists to view China's Hui nationality.

As the Hui of Beijing have been more exposed to the "Islamic world" than other Muslims, this increased exchange cannot help but have an influence in the years to come. Several secularized urban Hui youth admitted to Beijing's Number 1 Foreign Languages Institute to learn Arabic and serve in the foreign service have come to local ahong to receive instruction on how to pray. They are afraid they might embarrass their foreign Muslim hosts if they do not learn the proper ritual behavior.

THE CULTURE OF PURITY: HUI IDENTITY IN THE CITY

This chapter has examined some of the interests and issues confronting the Hui in Oxen Street, an urban Hui community in Beijing. For them, ethnoreligious identity does not lie in the correct interpretations and applications of Islamic doctrines. Nor does it mean a strict accounting of genealogical descent from foreign Muslim ancestors. It lies somewhere in between. Constantly negotiated, variously expressed, Hui identity in the city is often difficult to describe. It has much to do with practical concerns such as maintaining the *qing zhen* lifestyle, finding a spouse, testing into the right school, and obtaining advantageous employment. Yet all these decisions are made from the perspective of a tradition that is inescapable. It must be reckoned with, even among those urban Hui who attempt to discount, hide, or reject it. For those who accept, reinterpret, and sometimes manipulate it, ethnoreligious identity is often authenticated and judged by one's *qing zhen* lifestyle.

Cultural traditions that are maintained or rejected represent one's ancestral heritage. The truth and relevance of urban Hui ancestry is expressed in terms of a pure (*qing zhen*) life.

The reemergence of many of these cultural traditions that mark urban Hui identity is related to the post-1979 liberalized nationality and economic policies. Hui ethnicity in Niujie was suppressed and altered during unfavorable periods when the state restricted ethnic expression. The main change in the expression of urban Hui identity can be traced to the 1958 labor and religious reforms. Hui businesses were closed and small merchants became workers in large state enterprises. At the same time, the state closed private religious schools and carried out sweeping educational reforms that brought all Hui children into public schools. The campaigns of the Cultural Revolution were but the continuation of the late 1950s policies that discouraged expressions of Hui ethnoreligious identity. When I asked urban Hui about the "10 lost years" of the Cultural Revolution and its effect on their ethnicity, several replied that it was really 20 years, from 1958 to 1978. Throughout this period, the Hui downplayed their identity out of fear of being regarded as feudalistic and receiving one of the 5 black labels.

Hui in the city are no longer reluctant to admit their ethnic heritage. The promulgation of recent policies and socioeconomic change has radically altered the ethnoreligious setting for Hui. Not only are the Hui prospering economically, but they are growing in population. As a direct result of this policy, Han are becoming more interested in marrying minorities, and the offspring of mixed marriages are increasingly choosing minority ethnicity. That one has the legal right formally to choose one's nationality at 18 demonstrates the state's strong hand in shaping ethnic identity in China. Many Hui are grateful for these recent improvements in policy. One Hui intellectual compared Deng Xiaoping's reforms with Abraham Lincoln's: "Our Deng, like your Lincoln, liberated all the blacks." The resurgence of Hui identity and its relevance in the social setting demonstrates that ethnic identity is quickly being disassociated from feudalism and backwardness in China.

It is a popular belief, particularly among those influenced by assimilationist ideas, that Hui in the urban areas of China have been thoroughly Sinicized. Measured against Middle Eastern Muslims, or even northwestern China conservative Muslim communities, the Hui hardly appear different from the Han. Because the Hui in urban areas are more secularized, rarely wear Muslim dress, and sometimes even (among the young) eat pork, they have generally been ignored and absented from the social landscape. Indeed, many accounts of China's cities have almost thoroughly ignored ethnicity, as if China's urban context, like China itself, was mono-cultural. This study has shown otherwise. Not only do Hui maintain a vibrant sense of their identity and community, but they play an important role, and have for centuries, in China's urban affairs. Hui traditions have influenced much of China's urban life, as anyone who stops for a skewer of roast mutton on almost any street corner or a "Mongolian hot pot" in many Hui restaurants will discover. These ethnic foods have become so popular that even Han restaurants have tried to imitate them; but locals know the Hui cooks still do it better.

Once the ethnopolitics of China's inner city—choosing an ethnic spouse, registering one's child as a minority, maneuvering for advantage in school, work and the marketplace, and celebrating regular ethnic festivals—are brought to light, we may discover a whole new, multicultural China. It seems extraordinary that this has so rarely been emphasized before. Perhaps it is because Westerners have been so caught up with the Chinese in general as the "Other," they fail to notice the "Others" within Chinese society, or chose to look for them only in the frontier borderlands where the "colorful" minorities are supposed to live (and where some Han believe they belong). This homogenization of Chinese society cries out for further deconstruction. It may reveal a whole new side to the generic Chinese world generally described in the ethnographic and travel literature. Certainly the Hui seem to maintain their own world within Chinese society, though most have overlooked it.

Changying Hui villagers during last stage of funeral prayer before the deceased (in *the tabuti*, wooden container at center) is carried to the graveyard where the body is buried, wrapped in white cloth, without the coffin, in accordance with Islamic regulation. Photo: Gladney

The Other Great Wall: Ethnic Endogamy and Exclusivity in a Hui Autonomous Village

It is thus the same with women as with the currency the name of which they often bear, and which, according to the admirable native saying, "depicts the action of the needle for sewing roofs, which, weaving in and out, leads backwards and forwards the same liana, holding the straw together."
— Claude Lévi-Strauss, The Elementary Structures of Kinship

Out of ten Hui families, nine are related

—*Hui proverb*

"Only 11 stops on bus number 342 from Red Temple (Hongmiao) station, Changying Hui village is not far from Beijing," a local Hui friend told me. "Just get off at the first *qing zhen* restaurant. If you see the small mosque at Xiao Guanzhuang, you've gone too far." Such are the ethnic signposts marking the way to Changying Hui autonomous village, as described by a Hui Niujie resident. He often visits his wife's relatives who live in this village, one of many satellite suburban villages on the outskirts of Beijing.

Changying is located 20 km. east of Beijing on the main road to Tongxian, Dachang Hui autonomous county, and Tianjin. I was never prepared for the long lines and crowded buses that turned the short distance into a 2-hour ordeal. Changying villagers are undaunted by this journey, however, regularly making the arduous trek into the city to peddle wares, buy sundries, and even report to work in one of the many small factories that ring Beijing's perimeter. At Guanzhuang, the closest bus stop to Changying, hundreds of bicycles parked tightly together—

deposited after a 2 km. ride from the village—indicate the close connections that Changying villagers maintain with Beijing, and with the world outside their concentrated Hui village. These connections are critical to local Hui identity.

It is this chapter's thesis that the social world of Changying Hui villagers is vitally influenced by their ethnoreligious identity. I argue that interaction with the outside world for the Hui in Changying is more restricted than for neighboring Han villages and, at the same time, more wide-ranging. This is illustrated by the intensive and extensive marriage networks maintained by Hui villagers. William Skinner has persuasively argued that the world of the Chinese peasant—once thought to be bounded by the local village—is at least as large as the standard marketing area, and tied vertically into a nested hierarchy of intermediate and central marketing centers.[1] William Lavely, in an extensive survey of a rural "marriage market" in Sichuan, has further proposed that marriage networks indicate interaction with a social world even larger than the standard marketing center.[2]

Hui ethnic identity has direct bearing on the boundaries of their social-spatial world. I suggest in this chapter that the marriage network maintained by the Hui in Changying suggests a social world much smaller than that of the Han, discretely bound by the confines of the village and production team. Yet it also may be more far-reaching. When Hui marry outside the team or village, their networks extend to distant Hui areas that are far beyond the areas where Han villagers would normally consider finding a spouse or sending a daughter. Hui develop networks with these distant Hui villages in order to maintain their ethnic identity.

In response to the problem of maintaining their ethnic identity while ensconced in Han-dominated areas, the Hui practice strict ethnic endogamy. For these Hui, ancestral heritage and ethnic identity are expressed through endogamy. While cultural traditions such as the pork tabu are important for urban Hui identity, the equal importance of the idea of endogamy for the ethnoreligious identity of the Hui was expressed well in the following statement made by a Beijing Hui intellectual: "There is a 'Great Wall' separating us Hui from the Han: We do not eat pork and we do not give them our women."

Ethnic identity is often preserved and expressed through mate selection. Charles Keyes suggests that the nature of ethnic identity is shaped by the structural oppositions of interacting ethnic groups, often expressed in marriage exchange.[3] This is clearly the case for the Hui in Changying. Their marriage practices are influenced by and reveal much about Changying villagers' ethnoreligious identity. The persistence and high rate of endogamous marriages within the Hui village are principal strategies for Hui in isolated northern villages for maintaining their community. Fluctuations in government policies have also influenced Changying marriage practices and ethnic identity. By considering the importance of marriage as practice, not as ritual, in the Hui villagers in Changying, we gain insight into the relevance of their Hui identity in the context of a northern suburban village.

ETHNOHISTORICAL ORIGINS OF A HUI AUTONOMOUS VILLAGE

Changying Huimin *xiang* is a former brigade (*dadui*) of Shuangqiao commune, located in the Chaoyang district (*shiqu*) of Beijing municipality. Beijing municipality administratively comprises 18 districts and counties, of which Chaoyang is the easternmost district. Chaoyang district has a population of over 1.5 million; Shuangqiao commune comprises 20,000 residents. In 1984, Changying brigade had 8,350 residents (2,200 households), comprising 11 production teams (*shengchandui*).

Teams numbered 1 through 8 are clustered tightly together and are 95 percent Hui, consisting of 5,020 residents. This represents the greatest concentration of Hui in one village throughout the Beijing suburban area, and one of the largest Hui villages in the North China Plain. There are also 3 almost completely Han production teams (Shilibaocun, Wuliqiaocun, and Gongzhufencun) under the administration of Changying brigade, but separated from the 8 Hui teams by 1 to 2 km. of fields and canals (see Map 4). In 1984, 85 percent of the households in Changying brigade were Hui and 15 percent Han. Five percent of the households within the 8 Hui teams are Han, but these Han no longer eat pork or raise pigs, in deference to their numerous Hui neighbors.

The Han who live within the 8 mainly Hui teams of Changying village are the only Han the Hui will entertain with their own eating utensils. Han who visit from outside the Hui teams are provided with a

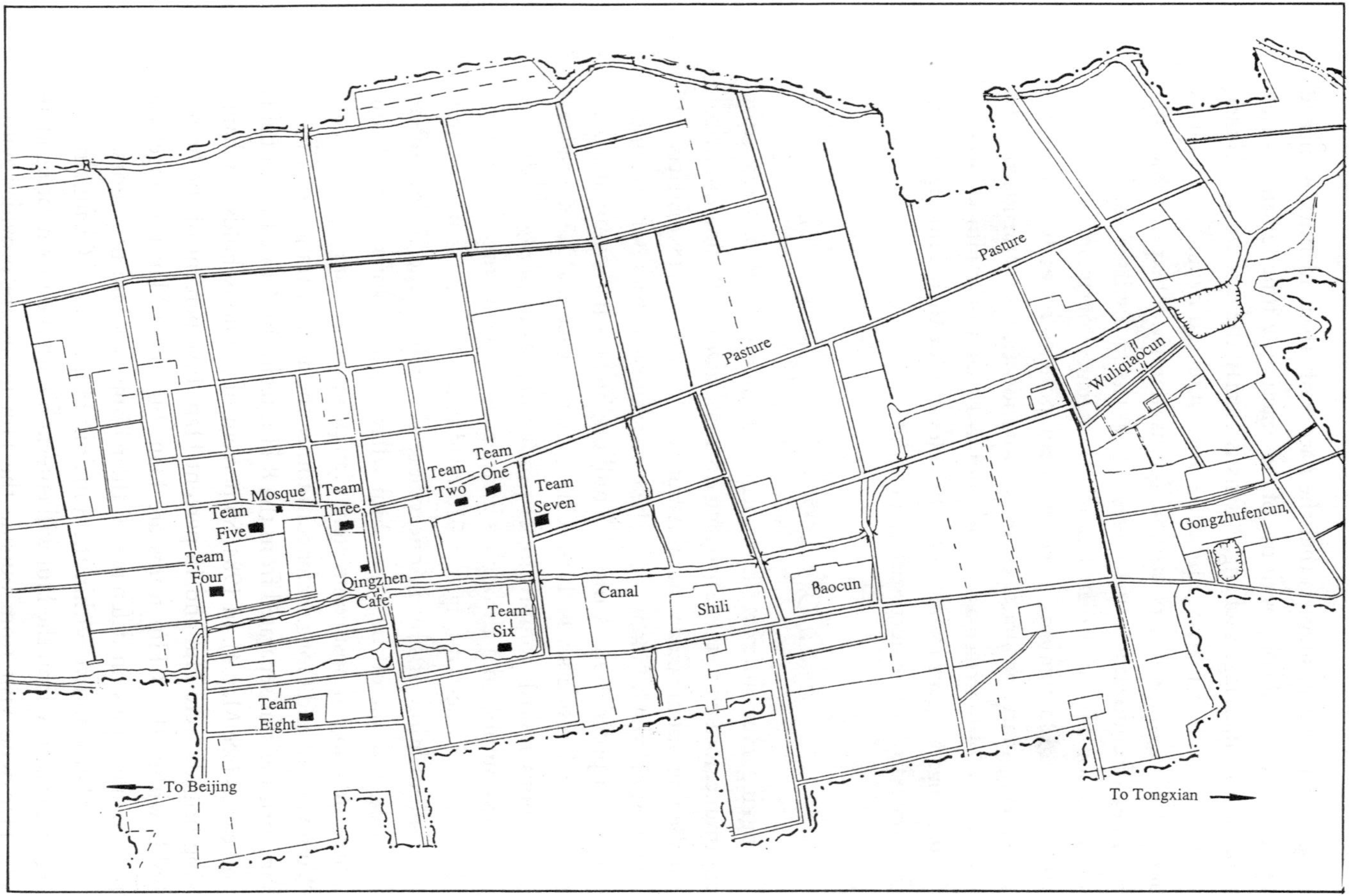

Map 4 Changying Hui Village

special set of bowls, cups, and chopsticks that the Hui never use. This tradition has been maintained since before 1949, as revealed in the following village description drawn from the autobiography of Zi Qi, a successful Hui businessman and reformer, born in Changying:

> Forty *li* east of Beijing, 10 *li* outside of Tongxian's West Gate, there is a hamlet called "Changying" 3 *li* long, intersected by 3 streets and 2 canals; the village residents number more than 600 households and are all Muslims (Mumin); there are also not more than 50 or 60 Buddhist families (*fojiaoren*), and, although they live in their midst, as they receive Islam's nurturing (*huijiao de xuntao*), they are completely polite in their diet (*yiqie yinshi limao*), all of them having been assimilated to the Hui (*huihuale*).[4]

The sense of coherence within these 8 Hui teams is such that the villagers exclusively refer to them when they mention Changying village. The 3 Han teams are always called by their proper village names. The grouping of these 11 production teams under the single administration of the Changying brigade, changed to Changying Hui autonomous village (Huimin *xiang*) in 1986, is thus an artificial one—a fact substantiated by the marriage-survey data. Hence, in this chapter, Changying village refers to the 8 Hui teams, and Changying brigade refers to the administrative unit that includes all 11 Hui and Han teams.

ETHNIC COHERENCE AND CHANGYING IDENTITY

Changying village has a long history of Hui ethnic independence and resilience. It has been known as a concentrated Hui village in northern Hebei since before incorporation into Beijing municipality after the 1949 Revolution. Even Hui villagers in Na Homestead in Ningxia told me they had heard of Changying. In 1956, Changying was recognized as a *minzu xiang* (nationality village), but, during the Cultural Revolution, this label smacked too much of local ethnic chauvinism, and was changed to Changying brigade. As a result of liberalized government policies and intensive lobbying by Changying brigade leaders, it was recognized as a Hui autonomous village (*Huimin zizhi xiang*) in 1986.

Village Hui ethnohistories that I collected were unclear as to ancestral origins prior to 4 or 5 generations back. Most Hui said they migrated to the Changying area from Shandong, but beyond that they knew only that their ancestors were Muslims who came from the West (*xiyuren*). As with many northerners, genealogical records are scarce and the few geneaologies in the village were destroyed during the Cultural Revolution. For these Hui, their ancestral home is Shandong. Beyond that, there was not much interest in or knowledge of their earliest ancestors, except for the fact that they were Hui Muslims. This contrasts to southeastern Hui lineages for whom descent from foreign Muslim ancestors is the most salient aspect of their identity.

Local gazetteers record that Changying (长营) originally meant "often thankful" or "many thanks." The first character for Changying was changed from "many" (常) to "long" (长) only recently—a 1931 inscription on a mosque stele preserves the original *chang* (often, many) character, homophonous with the present *chang* (long) character in Changying. *Ying* (营) also has the double meaning of "barracks" and "thanks."[5] Local Hui historians suggest that Hui militia were given this land at the beginning of the Ming dynasty as an expression of gratitude for their assistance in driving out a Mongolian army encamped there. Thus, Changying means either "many thanks" to the Hui who helped drive out the Mongols, or the "many barracks" of the Hui militia eventually established there.

This reflects the popular belief among the Hui that they played an important role in overthrowing the Mongols and establishing the Ming Chinese dynasty. While one would generally think that the Hui would take greater pride in their co-Central Asianists, there was a strong Chinese reaction following the overthrow of the Yuan against all Central Asians, many of whom were Muslim administrators appointed by the Mongols.[6] Perhaps for purposes of legitimation, Hui today often speak of how Muslims supported the Ming at the beginning of the dynasty, and at least one Hui scholar claims that the Ming Taizu Emperor, Zhu Yuanzhang, was himself a Muslim.[7]

A local story recorded by Zi Qi, the famous Changying resident, and retold to me indicates the tradition of Hui independence maintained by the village.[8] During the time of the Qing dynasty Tongzhi Emperor (1862–1874), as the Northwest Hui Rebellion raged in Shaanxi, Hui in Changying also expressed their dissatisfaction with the government's treatment of the Muslim minorities through social unrest and criminal acts. Local gazetteers record an incident in which Changying Hui villagers absconded with over 30,000 *liang* of the Emperor's silver as it passed through the village on the way to the capital. Imperial troops were soon dispatched to deal with the Hui bandits (*Huifei*), executing several score local Hui; but many of those responsible escaped. This incident contributes to the local belief that the Hui in Changying are fiercely independent and liable to acts of violence and larceny if provoked.

The Hui in Changying during the late Qing dynasty had many reasons for engaging in illegal ventures. Zi Qi described the abject poverty in the area due to the limited village farmland in Hui possession.[9] Hui admit that, over the years, their original land was let out and then sold off to Han who were more adept at agriculture. The Hui preferred to engage in trade and transport with Beijing. By 1949, over 40 percent of the land was in the hands of 5 Han households. After land reform, the government distributed a fairly equal proportion of the land to both Hui and Han. There are now over 8,600 *mu* of land in Changying (1.02 *mu* per person), with 6,000 *mu* devoted to rice and 1,260 *mu* planted with vegetable cash crops.

CHANGYING TRADITIONS OF RURAL ENTREPRENEURSHIP

With the recent economic reforms, Hui have once again begun to leave the land in favor of engaging in private business and small-scale industry. Very few Han are involved in sideline enterprises, but active Hui participation has significantly increased their income. This is similar to Na Homestead, where the Han basically left small trade to the so-called "crafty Hui," who they say are better at it. In 1980, average per capita annual income among the Hui was 145 yuan per year. By 1984, average income had risen to over 400 yuan, with many workers in small-scale factories earning over 1,000 yuan a year. This results from a substantial increase in participation among the Hui in small-scale industries and sideline enterprises. Many of these Hui have returned to the small enterprises their families had engaged in before 1949. Even the mosque is taking advantage of liberal economic reforms. It opened a mill for husking rice and making noodles in 1981, and with its 7 machines averages a monthly profit of 1,000 yuan. Much of its income has been devoted to helping the village through spending 10,000 yuan on a new bridge, asphalt road, and street lamps.[10]

Out of 3,000 laborers in Changying, 1,000 work in small factories, including a cotton-spinning factory (300), a car-repair factory (200), an air-conditioner factory (100), and a clothing factory (100). There are also 30 households involved in a fledgling dairy industry, which has purchased over 150 milk cows in the last 5 years. This is a new enterprise for the Hui in Changying. Prior to 1949, no one in the village had raised any livestock except sheep and horses. The milk is sold to a nearby Chaoyang district processing plant. Demand for the milk has grown with the recent substantial increase in Beijing residents' consumption of dairy products. Twenty households raise chickens as a sideline, and there are 10 *getihu* (individual economic households) engaged in various small enterprises. Nine households sell *shaobing* (pastries) and 1 household opened a small 7-table *qing zhen* restaurant in the village, the Deshun Guan ("The Obedient to Morality Cafe"). The father had run a cafe in the village until 1956 when he became a factory worker. Ever since the first week the son opened the cafe in July 1984, they have averaged a 25-percent profit margin. A new *geti* restaurant was established around the corner in 1986.

Except for the larger restaurants, most of these private *geti* small enterprises are unregistered, due to their temporary sideline nature, as well as the desire of the entrepreneurs to avoid taxation. While government statistics estimate that only 0.6 percent of economic enterprise is private in China, and thus not very significant, at the local level I found it to be otherwise. These small-scale entrepreneurs are changing the socioeconomic horizons of every village I entered. State statistics can never reveal the impact these businesses are having on the villagers, since their income and registration are in general far under-reported.

RELIGIOUS TRADITIONS AND CHANGYING IDENTITY. Like many other rural Hui, Changying residents say that they enjoy engaging in small business as an expression of their ethnoreligious heritage. They also feel responsible to give back part of their income to the mosque in appreciation of Allah's assistance. Mosque participation and influence in the village are important aspects of Changying life, but not as vibrant as I found in more conservative northwestern Hui villages. Average Friday attendance is about half that found in Na Homestead (7.9 percent in Changying versus 13 percent in Na Homestead).

Changying is quite unique in that one-third of those at prayer are generally women, who gather in their own small room southeast of the main prayer hall and connected with it by an intercom system. Although in North China public participation of women in prayer is generally rare and women mosques (*nu si*) are few, women's participation in Changying religious life is strong. Half the 650 individuals (12.9 percent of the village) who fasted during the month of Ramadan in 1984 were women. I found even more participation in Yunnan, where there were many women imams and separate women's mosques, which may reflect the influence of Southeast Asia, where women's participation and ordination is more common.

In the more conservative Muslim areas of the northwest, women are more restricted from public participation in ritual and leadership. It was explained to me by many northwest Hui that the reason their women are not allowed a larger role in public ritual and leadership is that Hui women's blood is not considered pure. As one Na Homestead villager explained: "Our women carry Han blood in them; since so many of our ancestors have intermarried with the Han and brought in Han women, we do not allow women to take part in funerals or other public rituals."

On the rare occasions when Hui men do bring in Han women as spouses in the northwest, there seems to be less concern with their religious conversion than with their willingness to "lead a Hui life" and bring their children up in the ways of *qing zhen*. In order to do this, women are traditionally often ritually cleansed prior to marriage, through the drinking of soda water (said to clean the large intestine) or the consuming of teas that had burned Quranic texts dissolved in them. While I never witnessed this, and was told it happened less in recent years in the northwest, it was a tradition often discussed, which reveals Hui concerns with ritual and moral purity, particularly where women are concerned. The following account by the missionaries Mildred Cable and Francesca French, who traveled throughout the northwest and spent most of their time staying and talking with women, also reflects this concern:

> It is not unusual for a Tungan [Hui] to marry a Chinese woman from a Con-
> fucian home, and the strain thus introduced has greatly affected the race, but
> before a girl enters the Moslem household she must submit to the most elab-
> orate purifications in order to cleanse her from any defilement contracted
> when she was a "pig-eating *kaper*" (infidel). Only after fastings and drastic
> cleansing may she enter the "clean" household of the husband. The tragedies
> of the Tungan women and their many humiliations and sufferings have made
> of them a disciplined and controlled class.[11]

In Changying, unpurified blood was not as great an issue, and the
women said the men also had Han blood. There was, of course, concern
with pork pollution, but, since few intermarriages took place, it was
not an ongoing concern. Barbara Pillsbury has argued that this notion
of "blood ethnicity" for the Hui in Taiwan is a strong factor in their
identity.[12] As I have not found the Hui consistent in their responses, it
is difficult for me to draw any conclusions. It may very well be that,
where emphasis on blood ethnicity is strong, Hui women's participation in religious activity outside the home is more strictly curtailed.[13]

The seventeenth-century mosque is staffed by 2 local ahong, and
from 5 to 10 students. One ahong had studied in Beijing's Niujie and
Dongsi Mosques before 1949 and the other had studied in mosques in
Ma Dian and Tianjin. Three out of a group of 10 *halifat* were recently
selected to continue their studies at the Beijing Dongsi Mosque. Except
for the ahong, villagers know nothing about the various Hui Islamic
orders—so critical to northwestern Hui identity. Some know that they
are Gedimu and that other ahong in Beijing are trained differently from
theirs. Since distinctions in Islamic orders are of no concern to the villagers, they maintain frequent contacts with both Yihewani and Gedimu
ahong and *halifat* from Beijing.

Before 1949, there were 5 mosques in Changying, including 2
women's mosques. Four small mosques were converted to nursery
schools in 1958 during the Religious System Reform Campaign, leaving
the one remaining large mosque (see Map 4). The present mosque
became a factory in 1966 at the start of the Cultural Revolution and
reopened as a mosque in 1982. During that entire period, the ahong continued to meet secretly with many of the local Hui and chanted the
scriptures (*nianjing*) whenever it was requested of them. While most

chanting takes place in Hui homes today, caution required them at that time to meet privately at the graveyard. During the "Smash-4-Olds" Campaign, each production team was required to run a pig farm.

The ahong recognizes that, except for holidays, few young people come to the mosque. There are about 100 elderly worshipers at daily prayer, with up to 400 on Fridays, and most of the villagers in attendance at 3 festival services held on Corban, Ramadan, and the Prophet's Birthday. Foreign Muslims residing in Beijing often come and celebrate with the villagers. This does not mean that the young people do not believe in Islam or fail to respect the traditions of their ancestors, he assured me, but that they are just too busy. Some of them smoke and drink outside their homes, but none are known to have violated the locally accepted norms of *qing zhen*. While all the Hui in the village continue to maintain traditional Hui Islamic funeral customs—very elaborate in Changying—fewer than half since 1979 have invited the ahong to read at their weddings. Intermarriage with Han, as we shall see, is still extremely rare.

LOCAL POLICIES AND ETHNIC RESURGENCE. Changying was reconstituted as a Hui autonomous village in 1986. Village leaders expect many benefits to accrue from this new status, including increased control over local planning and development policies, further jurisdiction over tax revenue disbursement, more representation by Hui in township and district policy meetings, and greater flexibility in meeting local needs. In early 1986, the municipal government and State Commission for Nationality Affairs financed the building of a large *qing zhen* restaurant equipped to entertain and eventually house foreign Muslim guests. Changying is only 12 km. from the Beijing Sanlitun diplomatic district and is often visited by foreign Muslim delegations interested in the mosque and rural Muslim life. The mosque regularly accepts requests to slaughter sheep and cattle ritually for foreign Muslims. This contact is encouraged by the district and municipal leadership and will continue to have a growing influence on the Changying Hui villagers.

Minority policies promulgated since 1979 in Changying have also had an important influence on the Hui. Nationality policies have allowed each couple to have 2 children under the minority-family-planning policy. Benefits for nationalities also include the providing of

Hui agriculturalist with beard trimmed in the Jahriyya Sufi style, Wuzhong, Ningxia. Photo: Gladney

Xining Hui Muslim women with traditional head covering (*gai tou*). Note black head covering for younger woman behind the foreground figure. Veils come in green, black, and white, depending on age and marital status. They generally cover the hair and neck, leaving the face exposed. Photo: Gladney

extra ration coupons for Changying factory workers. Now that Changying has become an autonomous village, they have more control over village administrative decisions and dispersal of local tax revenues. They are still under the administration of the Shuangqiao township, Chaoyang district government, but they have more flexibility in planning and application of policies than other, non-autonomous villages.

The greatest emphasis has been placed upon raising the educational level of Hui villagers. In 1958, over 90 percent of the Hui were found to be illiterate. By contrast, almost all the children above age 10 in the neighboring Han teams could read. The commune had to send in outside accountants to handle the brigade paperwork for the Hui. By 1980, there were 8 Hui college students from the village, 650 high-school students, 3,000 middle-school students, and 3,000 primary-school students. The municipality and district government donated 300,000 yuan to build a nationality primary school (*minzu xiaoxue*) in Changying, with the plan of making it into a cultural center for all Beijing suburban villages to emulate. The faculty are paid a higher wage than in other primary schools, and there is twice the budget for the children's meals and snacks. Out of 647 students, 85 percent are Hui, a proportion higher than any other nationality school in Beijing. The faculty are 30 percent Hui. Of the first class, 95 percent entered middle school, and 50 percent of those tested into high school.

There are still problems to overcome, however. The Hui principal said that Hui parents do not value education as much as the Han do. They would rather have their children help out with the family sideline enterprise. The brigade government has developed special training programs to help families realize the importance of a public education. One of the issues the local officials have yet to address, however, is the nature of education for these Hui. The imam mentioned that, while desire for "Han" learning was low, many of the younger Hui were quite motivated to study Islamic history and Quranic languages. There were four *manla* studying in the mosque and hoping to test into the Beijing *madrassah* at the Niujie Mosque the following year. After 2 years' studying with the mosque imams, and 2 years in Beijing, they would hope to be ordained and sent out to other villages to teach. The Party secretary countered that this was not regarded as education by the state and therefore could not be encouraged in state schools. It was part of religion, according to him.

One of the most difficult questions I had to ask in China concerned education. The way to pose the question in Chinese is, literally: "What is your cultural level?" (*nide wenhua chengdu duoshao*). "Culture" here refers only to learning in state-sponsored schools and literacy in Chinese characters. I still remember asking this question of an elderly Hui *hajji* in Hezhou, who answered that he "had no culture." This Islamic scholar had spent 12 years living in the Middle East, was fluent in Persian, Arabic, and a master of the Islamic natural sciences. Efforts to integrate "nationality general history" (*minzu changshi*) into the state-school curriculum do not even begin to address this issue of pervasive Han chauvinism. It may be a strong factor that keeps Hui children from wanting to go to mainly Han schools.

The positive effects of some minority policies have been significant enough that the Han villagers in Changying brigade were very interested in remaining part of the village administration once it became a Hui autonomous village. By remaining in the village, the Han teams become a minority within a minority and receive several benefits, including increased representation in the local government and inclusion in development and educational programs. This was also the case in Na Homestead, where the 3 Han teams voluntarily rejoined the village administration once the commune system was dismantled. During the Cultural Revolution, the Han teams were administratively separated from the all-Hui Na Homestead, but specially requested readmittance to the village in 1982. If minority nationality benefits are such that even the neighboring Han production teams wish to be closely aligned with a minority administrative unit, then it is evident that these favorable policies are making an important contribution to the villagers' lives.

ETHNORELIGIOUS MARRIAGE TRADITIONS IN CHANGYING

During interviews with Hui married women in Changying, I became accustomed to the response that their natal home was within Changying village, and that they were generally born in the team in which they were still residing or in one of the 7 others nearby. This was consistent with what I found in other Hui villages such as Na Homestead: The wives and daughters-in-laws generally married in patrilocally from another household within the team, or from a Hui household in a village nearby; daughters married out to a household in a Hui village that was very near their original home.

Every so often, however, I would be surprised to find that a daughter-in-law had come to Changying from a distant Hui village in Shandong, or a daughter had married out to a Hui family as far away as Ningxia. When I told Niujie Hui residents that I was interviewing Hui in Changying, I found several with relatives there. Finding a Hui spouse is not a major issue in the northwest where Hui are numerous. Religious issues, such as which Islamic order one's mate must belong to, often supersede ethnic concerns. Intermarriage with Han is almost inconceivable for these Hui. In urban areas, on the other hand, intermarriage with Han is resisted in some Hui communities like Niujie but is an accepted eventuality in Shanghai and Guangdong. Along the southeast coast, Hui lineages are concerned more with maintaining lineage continuity than with finding a Hui spouse or preserving ritual *qing zhen* purity.

Unlike the Hui in the northwest or in southeastern lineages, for Hui living in pockets of isolated Hui communities in Han majority areas (*zaju huimin diqu*), finding an appropriate Hui spouse can be a difficult task. It is a pressing issue for Hui who wish to preserve their ancestral traditions and maintain their Hui community. Intermarriage with Han is almost non-existent in these areas, but locating a Hui spouse may be challenging—especially if one does not want to marry the boy next door. The patterns Hui have established and the networks they have developed to solve this problem tell us much about Hui identity. Like the weaving of the vine that holds the straw roofs together in Lévi-Strauss's analogy, the movement of Changying women has much to do with the continuing ethnoreligious coherence of this Hui community.

HUI MARRIAGE PRACTICE IN CHANGYING. I conducted a marriage survey of Hui women in Changying village in the summer of 1984. That was an appropriate time because most Hui marriages, like those of their Han neighbors, take place during the Spring Festival, so that the majority of marriages through 1984 could be included. With the help of the Changying village leadership, a total survey of all living Hui women related to the most senior male in the family was conducted. Both women in Changying and those who had left the village as a result of out-marriage or migration were included. Unmarried women were also included in order to provide a base for follow-up study. I tried to survey all of the Hui families in the village with as many members present as possible, since the study relied not on household registers but on their memories of living women relatives (women tend to disappear from family oral histories).

Perhaps as a result of the patrilineal and patrilocal Chinese tradition that the Hui maintain, I found that many women were forgotten over the years. In several of my earlier interviews, when I asked how many children were in the household, the parents would respond by naming only the sons. Married daughters would often be omitted and sometimes totally lost track of if they had married out more than 10 years earlier. This revealed much about Hui social hierarchy within the family and across gender lines.

There are 799 families in the marriage survey drawn from the 8 Hui teams of Changying village. This represents all the known Hui women from 3 generations related to these 8 teams, the Hui village of Changying brigade. Data from 200 families have been analyzed, amounting to 1,131 women, among whom 796 were ever married.[14]

Village leaders told me that *tongyangxi* or minor marriage,[15] in which an adopted daughter is raised and later married to a son, was never practiced among the Hui in Changying, so all marriages are adult marriages. No data were collected on divorced, widowed, or remarried women, who do not exceed 5 percent of all women in the village. The survey was focused on the movement of women, so such changes in marital status are not significant for the study. Uxorilocal marriage was very rare. Couples that marry within the team live so close to both husband's and wife's original homes that it is more convenient to reside virilocally; uxorilocality is generally avoided within the team.

NO HUI FOR HAN: INTERMARRIAGE IN CHANGYING. There were only 2 Han women who married into Changying out of the 546 women surveyed, both of them married Hui men within the last 8 years. Chen Guizhen,

a Han from the Chaoyangmenwai Nanxiaojie district in Beijing, wed-
ded the youngest of Wang Yuming's 2 sons in 1981. After she moved
into her husband's household in Team 8, she continued to commute to
a factory in the Chaoyangmenwai district near her natal home. The
other Han woman is a factory worker who married a Hui soldier from
Changying while he was stationed in her home in Wenzhou, Zhejiang.
They now live there together.

Intermarriage between Hui women and Han men from outside Changying is virtually unknown. The ahong and village elders could not ever
remember having heard of such a case. There are a few cases of Hui
women marrying Han men from within the 8 teams, but even these unions were opposed by most villagers. In 1956, for example, a Han man
from within the 8 Hui teams married a local Hui woman. Even though
this man had previously accepted Hui dietary restrictions and religious
practices, most of the Changying villagers were still adamantly opposed
to the marriage. After a prolonged dispute involving the entire village,
the wedding was allowed to take place on the condition that the husband convert. He did, and is now registered as a Hui.

Officially, Han conversion to Islam at the time of intermarriage with
a Hui should not involve a change in ethnic registration. However, all
Han I knew of who had intermarried with Hui before the 1982 census
were registered as Hui. Since the census, these spouses are no longer
allowed to change their ethnicity, whether they convert or not. They
should be known as Muslim Han (*xinyang yisilanjiao de Hanzu* or
Hanzu Musilin). I often asked throughout China whether a Han who
believes in Islam could become a Hui. Hui workers and farmers always
agreed this was possible. Only cadres and intellectuals were inclined to
deny the possibility. Conversely, when I asked if Hui could lose their
ethnicity through atheism or violation of *qing zhen*, not one Hui said
that it would be possible. Such a person would merely be known as a
"bad Hui," never a Han. This reveals that Hui rarely make the distinction between ethnicity and religion, and, according to most Hui, ethnic
change is unidirectional: Han can become Hui, but Hui cannot become
Han.

ETHNIC ENDOGAMY IN CHANGYING VILLAGE. During my first visit to the mosque, the ahong told me that, before 1949, he had performed most of the weddings and thus knew where most of the women came from and went to. Even though many young people no longer have a traditional Hui wedding with the ahong present, he is still cognizant of current events. Many parents consult with the ahong when they have questions about the suitability of a marriage. When a local match cannot be found, ahong can also ask other ahong from distant mosques if there are any appropriate unmarried youth. Thus, the ahong are a good place to begin one's study of marriage exchange in any Hui village.

The ahong said that, before 1949, over 60 percent of the women married within Changying village, 10 percent of the remainder married within the commune, and about 10 percent married to or from Beijing city. Now, however, with recent enforced policies restricting urban migration, there are few Hui marriages between Changying and Beijing. Instead, there has been an increase in marriage with the rural Hui from neighboring Dachang Hui autonomous county. From before 1949 until now, mosque records indicate that the vast majority of Hui women marry within Changying village. This was substantiated by my survey (see Table 23). The data are arranged in a hierarchy of place and distance so that we can see if women are moving from within the team and the brigade (essentially all-Hui), the commune, the district, or farther out.

The most striking feature this table displays is the high incidence of marriage within the brigade and teams. Over 33 percent of the daughters who married out of their present family into a neighboring family stayed within the same team; 17.9 percent of wives married into their current family from another family within the same team. Adding brigade and team marriages together, we find they account for over 79.2 percent of out-marrying daughters, and 52.3 percent of in-marrying wives. This is almost twice the percentage in similar surveys conducted among Han villagers.[16]

As this survey relies on the memories of the families interviewed, early out-marriages might tend to be under-reported. Assuming that there should be a fairly even flow of women who marry within the teams, the record appears somewhat unbalanced. Hence, a breakdown

TABLE 23 Migration in Marriage to and from Changying Village, 1922–1984 by Provenance or Destination

Destination or Provenance	Out-Marrying (Daughters)		In-Marrying (Wives)	
	N	%	N	%
Within Team	84	33.6	98	17.9
Within Brigade	89	35.6	188	34.4
Neighboring Brigade	25	1.0	55	10.0
Neighboring Commune	4	1.6	11	2.0
Neighboring District or County Within 40 kilometers	11	4.4	55	10.0
Distant County Beyond 40 kilometers	1	0.4	93	17.0
City	36	14.4	46	8.4
Total	250	91.0	546	99.9

Source: Family Survey.

Note: Figures for marriage in and out of the team are unequal because not all the women in the survey household have been tabulated and need to be checked against household registers, unavailable at the time of the research. The survey was also only conducted on the Hui families in Teams 1 through 8, so instances of inter-marriage with the 3 Han villages within the brigade are not recorded. Hence, women from the 8 Hui teams who came from or went to the 3 Han teams in marriage would be recorded, but no women from the 3 Han teams would be included if they were exchanged with the Hui teams. This would also account for imbalance in the figures at the brigade level.

of marriages within the most recent 10 years is presented in Table 24.

The data from the most recent 10 years, which we would expect to be more accurate, indicate an even higher incidence of marriage within the team and brigade. The in- and out-marriage numbers are more balanced at the brigade level in the 1974–1984 period, with a total of 140 wives and 130 daughters marrying within Changying. Most of the increase in intra-team marriage is at the expense of marriages into the city. Table 24 shows a 5-percent reduction in out-marriages to the city over Table 23 and a 3-percent reduction in in-marriages.

In their study of marriage within Chen village, a southern Han village, Chan et al. found that endogamous marriage within the lineage was so tabu that its recent initiation by poorer villagers who could not

TABLE 24 Migration in Marriage to and from Changying Village, 1974–1984 by Provenance or Destination

Destination or Provenance	Out-Marrying (Daughters)		In-Marrying (Wives)	
	N	%	N	%
Within Team	60	35.9	39	16.7
Within Brigade	70	41.9	101	43.3
Neighboring Brigade	15	8.9	26	11.1
Neighboring Commune	3	1.7	3	1.2
Neighboring District or County Within 40 kilometers	4	2.3	19	8.1
Distant County Beyond 40 kilometers	0	0.0	32	13.7
City	15	8.9	13	5.5
Total	167	99.5	233	99.6

Source: Family Survey.

find outside spouses constituted a veritable "marriage revolution."[17] Lineage endogamy was encouraged by local government policies in order to break down local lineage power. This was gradually adopted by the poorer villagers as a preferred marriage strategy, accounting for 70-80 percent of the total marriages. Villagers found many advantages to marrying someone next door:

> A married daughter who lived just down the lane provided parents with one more household to turn to in addition to their married son's. Occasionally she would kill one of her chickens and invite them over to eat; and if her mother were ill, a married daughter would hurry over to help out. To be sure, parents still depended financially on their sons in old age, and they still felt that married sons stayed in the family and that married daughters were lost to someone else's.[18]

The convenience of keeping Hui daughters nearby has been known to Changying villagers for a long time. While this may be a recent trend among the Han in Chen village, the Hui in Changying have preferred not to marry their daughters out since before 1949, as Table 23 indicates. Poverty has kept Chen villagers from being able to bring in wives. Ethnicity keeps Changying villagers from wanting to bring in outside Han women, or marry their daughters out to non-Hui villages. Economic considerations are also an important factor in Changying, contributing to their preference for endogamy. Government policies have restricted marriage of Changying women into the city, and have led to their own rapid economic development as an autonomous village. Changying daughters may well have few preferable hypergamous destinations outside the village.

Endogamy is one of the most important ways Hui in this community express their descent from foreign Muslim ancestry. They keep their community pure by not marrying their daughters to non-Hui and not bringing in Han women. The above tables also demonstrate that, for the Hui, there are important levels of endogamy. Since we know that virtually all out-marrying daughters are going to Hui homes, and in-marrying wives are coming from Hui families, it becomes important to ask how far out these networks extend, and how ingrown they have become. Ethnic identity leads the Hui to bring in wives from much farther away than the Han. It also leads them to consider marrying women from an even closer radius. In order to preserve the purity of their descent, Hui in Changying do something that Han would never do: They engage in surname endogamy. By this practice, thought immoral and even unhealthful by most Han, Hui seek to perpetuate their community. It is the closest level in a hierarchy of intimate endogamous relations.

MARRIAGE BONDS IN A CLOSE-KNIT COMMUNITY. For the Hui in Changying, the obvious preference is to find a mate within one's team. Barring that, one should try at least to find someone from the other neighboring 7 teams within the village. Of course, most younger Hui say they would much prefer to marry into the city, but strict control over migration to the capital from the countryside makes that almost impossible. With the improvement in the living conditions and education in the suburban villages, there has been a trickle of urban women out to Changying.

But, for most Changying Hui women, their world is fairly bounded by the village and team.

Each of the 8 Hui teams comprises primarily families with one surname. From Team 1 to 8, they are: Zhang, Hai, Yin, An, Ma, Zhang, Xia, and Bai and Wang (both the last in Team 8). These surname groups may be better understood as clans instead of lineages, since the Hui do not recognize that all of those with the same surname are descended from the same ancestor. The Hui maintain the belief that their surnames were translated into Chinese from the names of their foreign Muslim ancestors during the Yuan and Ming dynasties. This, they explain, is the reason they feel free to engage in endogamous marriages with other Hui of the same surname—a practice eschewed by the Han as unfilial.[19]

Out of the 200 families recorded in my survey, there are 34 with surname endogamous marriages (see Table 25). Seventeen of those marriages took place in the last 10 years. One family, surnamed Zhang, has had 2 surname endogamous marriages in 2 generations. The surname Zhang is the most numerous in Changying, representing the majority in both Teams 1 and 6. These are frequently encountered surnames among Hui villagers in North China. This survey of Changying Hui surnames presented in Table 25 is the first systematic analysis of Hui surnames based on one extended community. Comparisons of other communities in other regions of China are needed before we can draw any generalizations as to the frequency and distribution of these Muslim surnames.[20]

This high rate of same surname endogamy is extraordinary in the Chinese context, where it is regarded as immoral at best and genetically unhealthful at worst. The principal of the Hui elementary school suggested that one of the reasons Hui do not do well in school is that they have a high rate of mental birth defects. Hui preference for close marriage with their relatives, he argued, has led to a high incidence of mental illness among their offspring (*jinhunbing*). More than 20 out of every class of 600 Hui students have severe learning disabilities to the extent that they cannot continue school beyond the 1st grade—a condition he attributes to too close intermarriage. This reflects a common view

TABLE 25 Changying Hui Surnames and Surname Endogamy

Surname	N	%	Surname Endogamous Marriages		Within Last 10 Years	
			N	%	N	%[a]
Zhang	234	20.70	20	58.8	10	58.8
Ma	114	10.00	6	17.6	2	11.8
An	99	8.70	1	2.9	1	5.9
Yang	78	6.90	2	5.9	1	5.9
Wang	59	5.20	3	8.8	2	11.8
Bai	48	4.20	–	–	–	–
Hai	43	3.80	–	–	–	–
Guan	38	3.30	–	–	–	–
Li	36	3.10	–	–	–	–
Hou	29	2.50	1	2.8	1	5.9
Wu	27	2.40	–	–	–	–
Jin	22	1.90	1	2.8	–	–
Qin	22	1.90	–	–	–	–
He	22	1.90	–	–	–	–
Du	18	1.60	–	–	–	–
Liu	18	1.60	–	–	–	
Xue	18	1.60	–	–	–	–
Kang	16	1.40	–	–	–	–
Mu	14	1.20	–	–	–	–
Xia	14	1.20	–	–	–	–
Yi	13	1.20	–	–	–	–
Ding	12	1.10	–	–	–	–
Gao	11	1.00	–	–	–	–
Chen	10	0.88	–	–	–	–
Wan	10	0.88	–	–	–	–
Xiao	10	0.88	–	–	–	–
Hu		0.79	–	–	–	–
Hao	8	0.70	–	–	–	–
Mao	7	0.62	–	–	–	–
Han	6	0.53	–	–	–	–

TABLE 25 (Continued)

Surname	N	%	Surname Endogamous Marriages		Within Last 10 Years	
			N	%	N	%[a]
Liang	4	0.35	—	—	—	—
Hui	3	0.26	—	—	—	—
Cao	2	0.12	—	—	—	—
Dai	2	0.12	—	—	—	—
Feng	2	0.12	—	—	—	—
Lu	2	0.12	—	—	—	—
Lou	2	0.12	—	—	—	—
Xu	2	0.12	—	—	—	—
Zhong	2	0.12	—	—	—	—
Zhao	2	0.12	—	—	—	—
Bi	1	0.08	—	—	—	—
Fan	1	0.08	—	—	—	—
Hong	1	0.08	—	—	—	—
Ping	1	0.08	—	—	—	—
Su	1	0.08	—	—	—	—
Wei	1	0.08	—	—	—	—
Total	1,094		34	100.0	17	50.0

Notes: [a]Percent in last two columns is of total surname endogamous marriages

among nationality cadres working among the Hui: Much of their economic and educational problems stem from their close intermarriage. As a result, the 5-generations law is strongly promoted among the Hui: no intermarriage with anyone that is a close relative within 5 generations. This criticism of Hui endogamy was also found as one of the main points on a "large-character poster" (*dazibao*) targeting the Hui during the Cultural Revolution:

> Posters were seen in Peking in autumn 1966 calling for the abolition of Muslim customs. One poster proposed that the authorities should:

Close all mosques.
Disperse [religious] associations.
Abolish Koran study.
Abolish marriage within the faith.
Abolish circumcision.

Another poster listed a 10-point program for the eradication of Islam. Included were:

Immediate abolition of all Islamic organizations in China.
Moslem priests must work in labor camps.
Moslem burial practice must be replaced by cremation.
Abolish observance of all Moslem feasts and holidays.[21]

This represents a traditional Han criticism of the Hui, reflecting Han values of filial piety and scientism, which repeat themselves in various "scientific" policies aimed at reforming the Hui. Interestingly, the effort to prevent close in-marriage and endogamy within the Hui ethnic group goes against the 1957 marriage law, which discouraged intermarriage between ethnic groups. In most Hui villages I visited, if a Hui couple or their parents really wanted them to get married and they were too closely related according to the 5-generations law, they generally found a way to get around it. This is an excellent example of the adaptation of central policy to local-level and individual ethnic situations that are perceived as uniquely problematic for certain ethnic groups under special circumstances.

FAR AWAY HUI: REMOTE PROVENANCES AND DESTINATIONS OF CHANGYING WOMEN. Most Changying women stay within their team or the brigade when they get married. But, when they do move outside the village in marriage, they tend to go to or come from Hui villages quite distant from Changying. There is a rather large gap between the number of women marrying within the brigade and team, and those marrying outside the district (see Table 23). Very few marriages occur outside Shuangqiao commune but within Chaoyang district. Even though there are many Hui satellite villages within the suburban Chaoyang district, few Hui wives come from them and few Hui daughters marry out to these Hui villages. Between 1922 and 1984, only 2 percent of wives married into Changying from within the district, while 27 percent of wives married in from neighboring or distant rural areas within or beyond 40 km. Most of these distant places were areas with concentrated Hui villages.

According to Table 23, 47.4 percent of the wives marrying into Changying came from outside the brigade. The majority of these women came from known Hui areas. It would be very interesting to know the ethnic compositions of the communities these women married in from. Unfortunately, 1982 census data at the village and county level for minority population have not yet been made public. In order to find out if the women came from Hui areas, I interviewed Hui leaders and scholars familiar with the distribution of Hui villages in the North China Plain. I found that Hui tended to marry their daughters out to distant areas that were not major Hui centers. Hui daughters-in-law who married in, however, tended to come from villages nearby that were almost all-Hui. Changying Hui apparently prefer to bring in wives and daughters-in-law from concentrated Hui areas. Fifteen percent of the wives who married in came from villages that were over 70 percent Hui. Once they have decided to marry a daughter out, however, it seems that there is less concern that they are destined for a Hui area. Only 6 percent of the daughters who married-out went to villages with over 70 percent Hui. Of the out-marrying daughters, 67.5 percent went to villages where there were fewer than 30 percent Hui. I have already noted that the vast majority of Hui women will be marrying Hui no matter where they go, even to a village that is mostly Han. I have so far found only 2 cases of marriage with Han women, and informants could never remember any cases of Changying Hui women marrying Han outside the 8 Hui teams in the village. These Han living among the Hui in Changying village, as I have described, had already accepted the Hui way of life.

It is noteworthy that often the women move in only one direction. The largest group of wives marrying into Changying from Hui areas (32.6 percent) come from Dachang Hui autonomous county, less than 40 km. away. However, there are as yet no cases of Changying daughters marrying out to Dachang. The imbalance of women exchanged between villages in Dachang and Changying may be explained by the continuing practice of marriage hypergamy in contemporary China. Lavely suggests:

As economic inequality has been reduced within local units, disparities between higher level units have become more pronounced. The result has been an increasing tendency for marriage out of poor areas and into wealthier areas, a kind of geographical hypergamy.[22]

Madsen, Chan, and Unger[23] have discussed how men from poorer Han villages often have difficulty finding wives. The local girls marry up and out. Dachang Hui women may wish to marry into Changying because it is a suburban village near Beijing city. In China, prosperity and opportunities to work in suburban factories often come with proximity to urban centers. When local Changying daughters marry outside of Changying—and they seldom do—they prefer to go to Beijing. With the recent enforcement of restrictions on migration to the city, however, out-marrying Changying daughters must find other destinations. Of the few that do marry out of Changying, the majority, the survey reveals, choose to marry far beyond the district to distant Hui areas that are probably economically much better off than Changying. If they marry within the area at all, they are likely to stay within the bounds of the commune, and marry into all-Hui villages like Yangzha. In that case, ethnic choice is intimately tied to state policy.

PRESERVING PURITY THROUGH ETHNIC ENDOGAMY: ETHNORELIGIOUS STRATEGIES AND GOVERNMENT POLICY IN CHANGYING

This chapter has focused on one rural Hui community on the outskirts of Beijing and its efforts to preserve the purity of its ethnoreligious identity through mate selection. For these Hui, *qing zhen* is expressed in maintaining the purity and cohesiveness of their community through marriage endogamy. Ethnic endogamy expresses their belief in uninterrupted descent from Muslim ancestors. Its maintenance insures the continuance of that heritage for future Hui generations. In order to preserve *qing zhen*, these Hui spread throughout isolated Han majority areas have developed extensive marriage networks that connect them with Hui communities throughout northern, if not all, China. While there are many other concerns confronting them, the issue of community maintenance through the exchange of Hui women reveals much about their ethnic identity and the social context of Hui life in Changying.

Many questions remain about the resilience of Hui identity. The Hui have survived as a people throughout a 1,200-year history in China while other groups, like the Chinese Jews and the Khitans, disappeared or assimilated. It may very well be that the strong conservativism in Hui marriage practices that this study has disclosed provides an initial insight into the preservation of Hui identity. The refusal by Hui to marry their women out and their willingness to bring Han women in, who then raise Hui children, is certainly a most effective strategy for preserving ethnic coherence. Hui in the city, we have found, are also more conservative than their Han and Manchu neighbors when it comes to allowing their children to intermarry (see Chapter 4). When they do intermarry, the offspring are almost always regarded as Hui. Intermarriage is starting to increase in many urban areas where Hui are more dispersed, however, and it may signal more rapid loss of their coherence as an ethnic community in those areas. Coupled with the pork tabu, endogamy becomes a powerful force for preserving ethnic exclusivity.

It has often been assumed that ethnic groups, including the Hui, maintained community identity through endogamy. This study has suggested that this is the case for the Hui in Changying. The "other Great Wall" exists in China between Hui and Han in the rural areas at the great divide of marriage practice. The study also takes us a step farther in discovering the important impact of shifts in government policies on marriage networks, and thus on the social world of Hui villagers and their national identity. Liberalized economic and nationality policies have allowed more freedom in the movement of women throughout the country, and, together with the restrictions imposed on urban migration, have led to the strengthening and expansion of networks linking distant Hui communities. Restricted urban migration has also contributed to increased endogamy within Changying, where recent village prosperity discourages women from finding acceptable affinal alliances outside the village. Cut off from mates in the city, they must go farther away to marry hypergamously. Moreover, the recent favorable policies in Changying that have led to religious and economic resurgence have also made it a desirable destination for outside rural Hui women.

Marriage will become even more of an issue, since the community is faced with increasing industrialization and urbanization as Beijing gradually expands to the east and south (it is bordered by mountains to the west and north). Changying is also within 30 km. of the airport, where development has been rapid in the last few years. The Lido Holiday Inn, Jianguo, and Great Wall Sheraton hotels are all within 20 km. of Changying, but as yet culturally remote from the villagers, who have never visited these Western hotels and know little about them.

Within several years, Changying will most likely be in the same position as Ma Dian is today. Once a former all-Hui suburban village, Ma Dian is now only 28 percent Hui and has a growing rate of intermarriage with Han (see Chapter 4). Changying Hui villagers have friends and relatives in Ma Dian whom they consider to be losing some of their ethnic distinctiveness. "The Hui in Beijing are not *qing zhen* enough," I was told by one Changying dairyman; "we like to go there for business but we would never want to live in the city. Its just not convenient enough for Hui there." Convenience, he later explained, refers to the comparative ease with which Changying Hui find a Hui spouse for their children, have more than one child, and obtain a *qing zhen* meal— all very difficult prospects for Hui in the city.

This study has also told us something about the social world of Hui villagers. In some ways it is much smaller than that of their Han neighbors, in that Hui rarely marry beyond the confines of their village, and even prefer to find a mate from within their own production teams. Unlike the Han, Hui do not hesitate to engage in same surname endogamy. Only enforced government policy stands in the way of even more frequent endogamous marriage within Changying. In poor Han villages, the government has sought to encourage village and lineage endogamy to keep women from marrying up and out.[24] In Changying, however, the local government has tried to discourage endogamy. Local cadres believe that Hui preference for endogamy has led to birth defects among the children of these close marriages; this reflects Han ideas of propriety.

At the same time, this study has revealed something about the networks connecting Hui communities. The Hui in Changying exchange women in marriage with other Hui villages hundreds of kilometers away. This marriage network is maintained by contacts through the ahong and business associates. It needs to be further studied. The networks that connect disparate Hui communities are tenuous but important. They have assisted the Hui in preserving and expressing an ethnic identity that extends well beyond their local identity.

Government efforts to develop Changying's dairy industry, encourage interaction with visiting foreign Muslims, and improve their educational level have given the Hui confidence in the stability of nationality policies and a willingness to express more openly their Hui identity. Liberalized nationality policies have allowed the Hui to expand their business and marriage contacts. Policies restricting hypergamous marriage with mates in the city have led to increased endogamy and the need to find mates from farther away. Privileges accorded Changying villagers as members of an autonomous village have spurred their local economy and led to an improvement in their position compared to other more distant rural Hui villages. Hui from these distant areas are becoming more interested in improving their liaisons with Changying villagers through intermarriage and business relations.

With the rise in their income, the Hui are talking about sending the ahong and local religious leaders on the Hajj, building a better women's mosque, and expanding their reputation as a *Huimin xiang*. In turn, the government is interested in further improving conditions in Changying village as an example of its favorable policy toward rural Muslims and perhaps further attracting foreign Muslim investment.

The Hui in Changying feel that these better times are a result of Allah's blessing for their maintaining a *qing zhen* village. They are proud of their ethnoreligious heritage and are determined to maintain the purity of their identity. The exchange of Hui women in marriage is one of the main strategies for preserving that identity in isolated Hui villages. The phrase "Out of 10 Hui families, 9 are related" is often used by Han to express their disapproval of Hui close intermarriage and the so-called "unfilial" practice of surname endogamy. Yet, for the Hui, this phrase expresses the unity of their identity and strength of their community. Hui are not only one family because of descent from a common ancestry, they also maintain that bond through extensive marital networks. Ethnic endogamy embodies their ideas of uninterrupted descent from a Muslim ancestry and the preservation of the purity of that ancestry through establishing affinal relations with all other Hui throughout China, as "one family under Heaven."

Ding Hui Lineage hall, Chendai, Fujian. Note the sign just left of the entrance that mentions the display of the Hui Historical Museum and Archive inside the hall. Photo: Gladney

SIX

Ethnic Invention and State Intervention in a Southeastern Lineage

At the end of five days' journey, you arrive at the noble and handsome city of Zaitun [Quanzhou], which has a port on the sea-coast celebrated for the resort of shipping, loaded with merchandise, that is afterwards distributed through every part of the province. . . . It is indeed impossible to convey an idea of the concourse of merchants and the accumulation of goods, in this which is held to be one of the largest and most commodious ports in the world.

—*Marco Polo*[1]

In February 1940, representatives from the China Muslim National Salvation Society in Beijing came to Quanzhou, Fujian, to interview Ding lineage members who reside in Chendai town, Jinjiang county. In response to a question on his ethnic background, Mr. Ding Deqian answered: "We are Muslims [Huijiao *ren*], our ancestors were Muslims."[2] It was not until 1979, however, that these Muslims became *minzu*, an accepted nationality. After attempting to convince the state for years that they belonged to the Hui nationality, they were eventually accepted. The story of the late recognition of the members of the Ding lineage in Chendai town as members of the Hui nationality by the State Commission for Nationality Affairs reveals much about the dialogue of ethnogenesis and state policy in China.

Outside Quanzhou, there are 13 villages with the single surname of Ding, numbering over 16,000 and known as *wan ren Ding* (the 10,000-person Ding). When I spoke with members of the Ding lineage in 1984, they also strongly affirmed their identity as Hui people (Hui-

min), 20th generation descendants of Arab and Persian ancestors. They
pointed to an abundance of preserved family genealogies, gravestones,
stele inscriptions, and dynastic records as undeniable proof of this ancestry. For these Hui, their claim to nationality status is based on the veracity (*zhen*) of their ancestral heritage, rather than the purity (*qing*) of
their Islamic belief.

If the evidence is so overwhelming that the Ding lineage are descendants of Arab and Persian ancestors, why did it take so long for them
to be recognized officially as members of the Hui minority? The answer
lies in the nature of their lifestyle and the current policy of national
identification in the People's Republic of China. Ding identity is radically different from the Hui identity of Na villagers described in Chapter 3, representing the other extreme of ethnoreligious expression
among the Hui in China.

NO PIGS FOR THESE ANCESTORS:
THE MEMORY OF MUSLIM ANCESTRY IN CHENDAI

Along China's southern coast are several lineages of Hui for whom
Islamic purity is not nearly as critical as the truth of foreign ancestry to
their ethnic identity and understanding of *qing zhen*. Most of the lineages that were not recognized, and several that have yet to be officially
accepted as Hui, are located along the southeast coast and include Hui
surnamed Ding, Guo, Jin, Bai, Ma, Huang, and Pu (see Map 5). In Quanzhou, Fujian, a typical response to a question about Hui ancestry was:

> Of course I know my family are descended from foreign Muslims. My ances-
> tor was an Arab, and our name was changed to Jin in the Ming dynasty. We
> have our family genealogy to prove it. . . . We are Hui because we are
> descended from these foreign ancestors.[3]

This interview was conducted in a Hui household that ignores Islamic dietary restrictions and practices Chinese folk religious traditions in ancestral worship. While cognizant of their Islamic heritage, these Hui have
not practiced Islam nor attended the mosque for generations. Because
they do not follow Islamic practices, until recently the Chinese State
Commission for Nationality Affairs did not recognize many of these

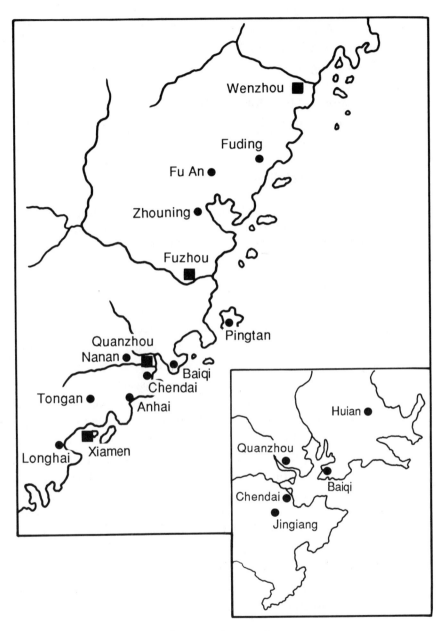

MAP 5 Hui Lineage Locations on the Southeast Coast

individuals in Quanzhou as members of the Hui nationality.

It is not surprising that, under a Chinese policy resembling the cult-unit model described above, the Chendai Hui, who lack most of the outward cultural traits that should distinguish them as Hui, would have difficulty in being officially recognized. Chendai Hui in almost every respect are culturally similar to their Han nationality neighbors: They speak the Southern Min (Hokkien) dialect, light incense to ancestors in their lineage temple, do not believe in Islam, and, remarkably, publicly disregard all Islamic dietary restrictions. The last item is most critical for understanding why it has taken so long for the Ding in Chendai to attain recognition as Hui. As Pillsbury's research among Hui in Taiwan revealed:

> First, among [Han] Chinese—who not only eat pork (usually taking considerable pleasure in doing so) but who also eat and use it ritually—not eating pork has become a token, and indeed *the* main token, of the Chinese Muslims' dissociative ethnic identity.[4]

This feature of Hui dietary restrictions, rather unique in Chinese society, has led to a continuing series of articles by Hui authors explaining and defending why the Hui do not eat pork.[5] Yet there are Hui who do not follow Islamic dietary restrictions, the Fujian Hui for example. Many urban Hui youths in Shanghai and Beijing say they respect their family's traditions while at home but are more casual (*suibian*) when outside, often eating in Han restaurants. There are also many instances in China of Hui who do not believe in Islam, but continue to emphasize their Hui ethnicity. However, since the Chendai Hui do not fit many of the cultural criteria of what Hui are like, their official recognition has been late in coming. Under the current ethnic-identification policy in China, which, as I have argued above, relies on a Stalinist cultural-trait approach, these Hui did not fit the cultural criteria. Hence, they were not recognized by the state until 1979 when changes took place, not in cultural criteria, but in sociopolitical conditions.

The purpose of this chapter is not only to introduce the ethnographic data on a controversial southeastern Hui lineage but also to analyze why existing ethnic-identification policy in China has difficulty justifying their inclusion as part of the Hui nationality. Since they have been recognized as members of the Hui minority, the influence of local government policies has led to further changes in their ethnic identity. I also provide an example of how modern Western ethnicity theory has difficulty identifying similar "Taiwanese Hui" in Taiwan, who have almost lost their ethnic identity under unfavorable government policies and state that they are "not Hui."[6] By contrasting these divergent approaches to the ethnic identification of the Hui minority in Fujian and Taiwan, I propose to show that a dialectical approach more fully accounts for the nature of their ethnic identity through the interaction of government policy and their specific social context.

THE CULTURAL BASIS FOR CHENDAI HUI IDENTITY

The essence of ethnic identity is the idea of descent—the idea, factual or fictive, of belonging to a group of people descended from ancestors different from the others with whom a group interacts. Discovering how these ancestral connections are transmitted and then appropriated in a socially relevant way is one of the primary tasks in the study of ethnic identity. Records, legends, stories, symbols, and rituals become the most critical texts by which people transmit their sense of "otherness." In the case of the Hui in Chendai, they are in the unique position of possessing numerous historical artifacts that authenticate their descent from "foreign" ancestors; their *otherness* has been etched in stone.

Investigations in Quanzhou over the last few decades have unearthed "more than 200 pieces of structural stone components of Islamic gravestones, grave cover stones, mosques, and Muslim residences."[7] While many of these stone inscriptions are unintelligible to present Hui descendants of the Ding lineage in Chendai, the symbolic fact that their ancestors' graves bear Arabic inscriptions has great importance for their identification with these *fan ke* (barbarian guests) or *semu ren* (colored-eye persons)—the official Chinese terms for foreign Muslim residents of Quanzhou before the Ming dynasty when the term *Huihui* became widely used. Present Ding residents can point to the graveyards of their ancestors as important texts of their present Hui identity.

HISTORICAL MONUMENTS TO HUI ISLAMIC HERITAGE. In a highly symbolic move, in August 1980, the Ding lineage relocated its earliest ancestors' graves to the historic Lingshan Holy Islamic Tombs outside Quanzhou. These historic tombs are among those monuments preserved by the Chinese government's Historic Artifacts Bureau, and generally belong to foreign Muslim or famous Hui personages buried in Chinese soil. These include the various tombs and monuments erected to the supposed Muslims who served as officials, militia, and merchants from the Southern Song through Qing dynasties (eleventh through nineteenth centuries) and are buried in special graveyards in southern China, predominantly in Quanzhou, Guangzhou, and Yangzhou. Historic tombs also contain the graves of Hui who played a major role in China's development and interaction with the West. These individuals included Zheng He, Hai Rui, Sai Dianchi (Sayyid 'Ajall), Li Zhi, and, more recently, the Panthay Rebellion leader, Du Wenxiu.[8]

Historical arguments regarding the Muslim ancestry of certain figures like Hai Rui, Li Zicheng, or Li Zhi have little bearing on this study.[9] More important is the recognition the Chinese government accords the significant role these purported Muslims played in China's development. Acknowledgment of the contribution they made to Chinese history greatly influences modern Hui self-understanding. Many Hui look to these historic figures as foreign Muslim ancestors who legitimate their descent from a high religious and cultural tradition. This knowledge also figures prominently in present-day Hui interaction with government policy and leads to a growing awareness of their place internationally.

The historic tombs of Arab and Persian ancestors of the Hui in Quanzhou are also important in the interaction between Islamic identity and government policy.[10] In 1961, the Fujian provincial government declared the Lingshan Muslim Tombs and the Ashab Mosque in Quanzhou (founded in A.D. 1009–1010) to be historic monuments.[11] Since 1979, the state, provincial, and city governments have provided substantial funds to restore these structures, to the extent that now the tombs have been refurbished and rededicated with a large tract of land and a sign at the entrance proclaiming: "Lingshan Holy Islamic Tombs." All tourist maps for Quanzhou city highlight these two Islamic sites as important attractions.

The Lingshan Tombs are primarily those of two Muslim saints, who,

Ashab Mosque, Quanzhou city (c. 1009), also known as the Qing Jing Si (Pure and Clean Mosque). Note Persian architectural style in the portico and Arabic inscription along the length of wall above the window, which opened onto the main prayer hall. Photo: Gladney

Holy Islamic Tombs, Lingshan cemetery, Quanzhou city, containing the two saints, Imam Sayid and Imam Waggas, said to have arrived in China from Medina in the early seventh century. Photo: Gladney

according to legend, were said to have been sent to China by the Prophet Muhammad and buried in their present location during the Tang dynasty (seventh to tenth centuries). According to He Qiaoyuan's 1629 *Minshu*, the two Muslim saints buried in Quanzhou are Imam Sayid and Imam Waggas from Medina. These were 2 of 4 foreign Muslims said to have visited southern China during the Wu De period of the Tang Emperor Gao Zu (A.D. 618–626).[12] Substantial research has been carried out on the more than 300 Islamic carvings and artifacts left by the Muslim communities concentrated in Quanzhou when it was a key international harbor on the southeast coast, from the Tang to the Yuan dynasties (seventh to fourteenth centuries).[13] The government's efforts to refurbish historic Islamic monuments in China have attracted increasing foreign Muslim attention and investment.

The Ding graveyard is presently located on the southeast hillside of Lingshan Hill outside the Renfengmen Gate of Quanzhou. It was moved to this location and refurbished by provincial authorities and members of the Ding lineage in August 1980. The style of the two tombs is similar to those found in other Muslim graves in Quanzhou, with what has been called a pagoda-shaped tomb cover[14] resting on a rectangular stone base of 5 tiers. Each tier is intricately carved with Islamic designs of clouds, lotus petals, a full moon, and Quranic inscriptions.[15] Behind the tombs is a tablet in Chinese and Arabic indicating that this is the first ancestor of the Ding lineage in Chenjiang (now Chendai) and the ancestor of the 4th generation of the Ding lineage from Jinjiang county.[16] On the back of the tablet is this Chinese inscription:

> I bought this famous hill Luyuan and it was my intention to have my parents buried here, my brothers all agreed with me without objection. Litchis are planted to give shade just as our ancestors shall protect us forever. Mind you, my descendants, safegaurd this important place. Written by Uncle Chengzhai in the 8th month of the 2nd year of Xuantong (A.D. 1910).[17]

This verse is significant, for it clearly sets forth the "rights and obligations" of Ding descendants to maintain the traditions of their ancestors. In return for preserving their identity, they will be "protected forever." The survival of the Ding lineage as a people supports the veracity of this promise. "Ethnicity in its deepest psychological level is a sense of survival. If one's group survives, one is assured of survival, even if not in a personal sense."[18] If nothing else, the Ding are tenacious survivors.

In addition to stone inscriptions on tombstones attesting to the Ding lineage's descent from foreign Muslim ancestry, there are numerous imperial edicts, originally inscribed in public places, depicting the important historical position of their Muslim forbears.[19] While these do not specifically name Ding members as descendants, and are written in a classical style (*wenyan*) unintelligible to modern Chinese speakers, they do serve as important symbols signifying the glory of Hui past. Ding residents of Chendai town pointed out several of these important edicts inscribed in the ancient Quanzhou Qingjing Mosque. One such inscription on a pedestal built against the east wall under the second arch in the passage from the entrance dates from A.D. 1407 and reads:

> The Emperor of the Great Ming instructs Miri Haji: I think he who is sincere and honest will revere God and serve the Emperor; he will also guide the good people, thus giving invisible support to the royal system. Therefore God will bless him, and he shall enjoy infinite bliss. You, Miri Haji, have long since followed the teachings of Muhammad; you are pious and honest, and are guiding the good people; you also revere God and serve the Emperor with loyalty. Such good deeds deserve praise and approval. Thereby I am giving you this imperial edict to protect your abode. No official, military, or civilian personnel should despise, insult, or bully them; whoever disobeys my order by doing so should bear the blame. This edict is hereby issued on the 11th day of the 5th month of the 5th year of Yongle.[20]

The original scroll from which this edict was copied was discovered in the home of Lan Xiaoyang, the hereditary imam of the Puhading Mausoleum in Yangzhou, and is now kept in the Beijing Minorities Cultural Palace.[21] The edict, originally composed in Chinese, Persian, and Mongolian, was posted in mosques all over China by Hui in order to protect themselves against discrimination at that time and to document imperial endorsement for future generations. It is an important legitimation text for the Ding lineage and other Hui attesting that theirs is a religious and cultural heritage valued by the Chinese host rulers since imperial times. This text legitimates the dignity of their ancestry in the face of ethnic discrimination. It also documents the Ding lineage's early incorporation into the Chinese state system. The text thus becomes meaningful to Hui at any time when their cultural traditions are brought into question.

RITUAL REMEMBRANCE OF DING IDENTITY. Probably more significant for the Hui descendants of the Ding lineage than stone inscriptions, which rarely impinge upon their daily lives, are the prescriptions for properly remembering their ancestors recorded in their genealogy.[22] These prescriptions are adhered to 4 times a year when the Ding lineage celebrates the traditional Chinese agricultural holidays and remembers its ancestors. Like their Han Chinese neighbors, Ding members go to their ancestral lineage temple, burn incense, perform *baizu* rituals, and make offerings. Unlike their Han neighbors, however, they strictly prohibit the use of pork or pork by-products in the offerings. When asked why, they say, "It is because we are descended from Hui ancestors, and they have instructed us in our genealogy not to offer them pork." This is spelled out in the *siyue* (offering arrangements) section of their genealogy in the following prescriptions:

> On the dates of the ancestor's birth and death, the offerings for the worship are the same. But on the death date, a whole ox should be added in the worship. The ox used should be of the size of the ox which was offered in the worship of the feudal princes. Since our ancestors have served as high officials of the state since long ago, the offerings have been used until now, in order to spread out the honors of our ancestors. . . . Our ancestors' instructions must not be disobeyed.[23]

In addition to beef, several vegetables and seafood, including razor clams, are prescribed. Tea is also placed on the ancestral altar, to assist the departed in "cleaning his mouth" of any pork residue before encountering his ancestors. Most significantly, instead of the traditional paper money burned by Han villagers as an offering to the ancestors for their afterlife, these Hui have burned red paper with Islamic inscriptions. I could not find out where this tradition originated, but local Hui said that, when there was an ahong available in the mosque, they would ask him to write Quranic scriptures on the paper. They said that it would help "purify" the deceased upon his meeting with Allah in the afterworld.[24] (With the Han, the burning of the object is for the use of the ancestor in the afterworld.) This parallels the placing of Quranic-text-inscribed bricks and other objects with the deceased in the graves that I have witnessed in the northwest. For most Hui, and Muslims throughout Central Asia who do not have access to the Quranic text in Arabic, the text itself takes on talismanic quality and is used in burial, healing, and adornment to gain protection and power.

Other distinctions that Ding members maintain include the making of a certain Hui food, a large deep-fried pastry, known as *youxiang*, on holidays. On the 1st day of the 6th month according to the agricultural calendar, this *youxiang* cake is prepared and the day is referred to as *baibing jie*, "cake-offering day."[25] Eating this food on holidays distinguishes Hui throughout China. That these rituals have been continued through the centuries attests to the Ding lineage's strong desire to "not disobey" the demands of its ancestors.

The regularity of these rituals at the lineage temple also helps reinforce the ethnic identity, the "otherness," of the Ding lineage.[26] While modern Ding members might not be able to read their genealogies in classical Chinese, or explain why they cannot eat or use pork on ritual holidays, nevertheless they are regularly reminded that their ancestors were different, and that this difference is maintained by ritual remembrance of them. Pu Zhenzong, in 1940, told his interviewers that, even though he is no longer Muslim, he is descended from Muslims, and that "the Pu family has had a secret custom—never offer pork in ancestor worship."[27]

Ding members have maintained this tabu against pork during ancestral rituals for centuries. They have an explanation for this in the form of this often-told legend, related to me as follows:

> Our ancestors were very sincere Muslims. At the time of our 11th-generation ancestor, Ding Qirui, who served during the Ming dynasty as a government secretary in the Ministry of Justice, he was accused with a trumped-up charge of attempting to usurp the throne of the Emperor. Because of this, the Emperor attempted to exterminate the Ding family. The main mark of the Ding family was their being Muslims. In order to save their lives, the Ding family could not "practice Islam (religion) for 100 generations" (*baidai zhanyang*). Thus, at that time, we began to become assimilated to the Han (*tonghua*).

This is the same story, almost word for word, told to the investigation team that interviewed the Chendai Hui, Ding Deqian, in February 1940.[28] It has become an accepted text to explain the reason for the Ding Hui leaving Islam and eating pork. In the 1940 interview as well as in mine, the Ding members explained that the saying "Practice Islam for a hundred generations" is taken from an inscription on a wooden tablet on the front of their lineage temple, parallel to another inscription on the temple itself: "Pacify ourselves for future success" (*Suiwo sicheng*).[29] In both interviews, the Ding speakers pointed out that their ancestral temple was structured in the shape of the Chinese character for *Hui*, one small square within a larger one, signifying they are of the Hui people. Most Han ancestral halls have covered corridors connecting the hallways on the perimeter with the main hall in the center of the courtyard. The absence of these connecting corridors is the one feature that differentiates their hall from Han lineage halls.

That so much emphasis is placed upon the legend illustrates the ritual significance attached by the community to violating the dietary tabu. In addition to Hui Islamic concerns, Fujianese traditions of totemic prestation and ritual offerings may play a role. In a fascinating article, Stuart Thompson has recently argued that the early use of the pig as the central part of food prestation may indicate the primary role of pork in the elementary structures of Taiwanese ritual.[30] I was surprised on several occasions when Fujianese locals mentioned the common belief that the reason Hui did not eat pork was that their earliest ancestor mated with a pig. One Hui from the Baiqi Guo lineage village told me another story—that the Hui may have also descended from a donkey, since Hui proscribed horse flesh in diet and ritual, and since early Hui "temples" often had an image of a donkey copulating with a man hidden in the wall behind the altar. This fantastic tale is highly suspect, since the Hui who related it was a member of a branch of the Guo lineage which had converted to Christianity in the 1920s, long after they had assimilated Fujianese folkways; he may have had reason to want to criticize Hui Muslim practices. Nevertheless, it illustrates the common pervasive belief in the close relationship between food tabu and ancestry in the Fujian cultural region. In an interview with Chinese anthropologists from Xiamen University, I was shown photographs of a genealogical pictorial portfolio belonging to the She minority, native to the Wu Mountains, which illustrated their own belief that they are descended from the union of a dog and human. Many of their ritual garments contain totemic representations of the dog. It is not surprising that many such ethnic stories and generally derisive references to Hui ancestry should originate in this area.

The forced-assimilation legend is extremely important for providing textual support through which modern Ding members interpret their behavior. More than the genealogy and stone inscriptions, the legend not only ties them to their ancestors but explains the difference between them and their Han neighbors, as well as why they differ from other Hui who maintain Islamic customs. The legend summarizes a common experience of suffering and persecution that Hui throughout China say took place during the Ming dynasty when, by imperial decree, they were no longer allowed to speak Arabic or Persian, wear foreign dress, or live in completely separate Muslim communities. It was at that time, they say, that Hui lost their former high status under the fallen "foreign" Mongolian dynasty and were forced to be Sinicized in a Chinese dynasty that prohibited foreign names, clothes, and languages.[31]

THE ETHNOGENESIS OF HUI IDENTITY. This common experience of suffering and forced assimilation may have been what galvanized the Hui ethnic consciousness into a single minority where there were once Arab, Persian, Turkish or Mongolian Muslim communities living in China. More than anything else, this may have forged a "pan-Hui" identity where there was none before.[32] Members of the Pu lineage in Quanzhou discuss how, as a consequence of their persecution as Hui, they changed their name from the foreign sounding *Pu* to the more Chinese *Wu* character. On their tombstones they often wrote "Wu's tomb" on the front side, but secretly inscribed "Pu's tomb" on the back.[33] This is in response to the widescale persecution of the descendants of Pu Shougeng, the influential Hui customs master in Quanzhou, at the end of the Yuan dynasty.[34]

The legend of Ding persecution for practicing Islamic Hui customs, coupled with the texts and stone inscriptions that document their history, provide a powerful identity which present-day Ding lineage members draw upon in the midst of social change. What is important is not the historical veracity of these texts, but how they become meaningful to the Ding today. In other words, the ability to claim membership in a distinct ethnic group by tracing one's lineage to a common ancestor is not significant if it does not serve as the basis for social action. If the texts discussed above were not salient for current Ding members' social life, they would not occupy a place of importance in their claim to ethnic identity. In China, however, the social and cultural significance of these texts may not lead to state recognition, as in the case of the Ding until 1979. These texts gain even more significance when they may serve to legitimate cultural claims to ethnicity. Under a Stalinist nationality policy in China that stresses historical cultural traits for ethnic identification, it is not surprising that these texts, which evidently have always been available to the Ding, have once again become crucial to their recognition by the state and the rediscovery of their ethnic roots. The re-emergence of this relevance is related to changes in the social context as a result of recent government policies. The validity (*zhen*) of one's ethnic ancestry has now become an important issue in this altered sociopolitical setting.

Socioeconomic Factors in Chendai Hui Identity

The Ding have lived in Chendai since the Wanli period of the Ming dynasty (1573–1620), where they supposedly fled from Quanzhou to avoid persecution. Since that time, they have been known for their specialized aquacultural economy. Chendai town is on the Fujian coast and well suited to cultivating razor clams for which the Ding lineage are famous. Before 1949, they were not engaged only in this industry but also produced opium and had many small factories that made woven bags and sundry goods. These goods were exported extensively and led to the migration of many Ding Hui to Southeast Asia and Hong Kong in their business endeavors. After 1955, when private industries were collectivized in China, these small factories were either curtailed or transferred to the larger commune, in which the Ding lineage occupied 7 brigades.

Since 1979 and the implementation of the economic reform policies in the countryside, the Ding members have once again become engaged in private small factories producing leather shoes and plastic goods, like the brightly colored plastic sandals, rugs, and other sundries found in most Chinese department stores.[35] Of the 3,350 households in the 7 villages (former brigades) in Chendai (in which 92 percent are Hui) over 60 run small factories. (In larger factories there are over 100 workers; in smaller ones only 10 or more.) Workers can work as long as they wish, usually 8 to 10 hours a day, 7 days a week. As a result, they have begun to do extremely well; several Ding families have registered as *wanyuan hu* (10,000-yuan families), with one family presently banking at least 100,000 yuan ($33,000 US). Average annual income in Chendai in 1983 was 611 yuan per person; in Jinjiang county it was only 402 yuan in 1982.[36] By 1984, Chendai income reached 837 yuan per person for the town, while the Hui averaged 1,100 yuan. Their income increased 33 percent in 1985 (see Table 26).

As income from small enterprise has risen, the structure of the labor force has changed dramatically. Involvement of laborers in industry has grown to almost 3 times the 1978 number (see Table 27). Finally, income from sideline enterprises in agriculture and small industry has also grown at an incredibly rapid rate (see Table 28). Although the Hui constitute only one-seventh of the town's population, they account for over one-third of the income (township records). In 1984, Chendai was the first town in Fujian province to become a *yiyuan zhen* (100,000,000-yuan town). Over half the Hui in the town have their own 2-story homes paid for with cash from their savings. Color television sets are owned by almost every household, and there are over 550 motorcycles in the 7 all-Hui villages. This growth has signaled new prosperity for the Ding as they seek to take further advantage of favorable government policies.

ETHNIC ASPECTS OF DING PROSPERITY. Ding Hui do not attribute their prosperity to industriousness alone. Since they were recognized as part of the Hui nationality in 1979, they became eligible for assistance as members of an underprivileged minority. They have received several government subsidies that have spurred their economy. From 1980 until 1984, the government has given over 200,000 yuan to the 7 Hui teams. With the funds they built a running-water system, ponds for rais-

TABLE 26 Chendai Factory and Industry Income, 1979–1985 (yuan)

1979 — 1,440,000	1983 — 8,780,000
1980 — 3,220,000	1984 — 29,040,000
1981 — 5,630,000	1985 — 35,000,000
1982 — 6,150,000	

Source: Township records.

TABLE 27 Chendai Town Changes in Labor Force, 1978–1985 (%)

	Agriculture	Industry
1978	69.9	30.1
1984	19.9	80.1
1985	14.0	86.9

Source: Township records.

TABLE 28 Chendai Town Changes in Income from Agricultural and Industrial Sideline Enterprises, 1979–1984 (1,000 yuan)

1979	1980	1981	1982	1983	1984
334	492	746	1,177	1,388	1,777

Source: Township records.

ing fish, and the means to expand their razor-clam industry. The Ministry of Education has given 40,000 yuan to build a middle school and 33,000 yuan for a primary school. They also receive benefits as a minority nationality in preference for high-school and college entrance. Under special birth-planning policies for minorities, they are allowed to have 1 more child than the Han. Hui representation in the local government is also higher than their proportion in the population. Two of the 10 Party Committee representatives (*changwei*) are surnamed Ding, as well as the town's Party secretary.

Over 50 percent of the Ding lineage members have overseas relatives—

mainly in the Philippines, Indonesia, and Singapore—a higher proportion than among their Han neighbors. They have reestablished communication with these relatives and have been assisted by frequent remittances. This outside income is an important factor in the rapid economic development of the 7 Ding villages. All 7 Hui villages have elementary schools, thanks to donations from overseas relatives, averaging 20,000 yuan each. Neighboring Han villages have 1 elementary school for every 3 or 4 villages. The Ding say that their close and frequent contact with overseas relatives is a result of their strong feelings of ethnic identity, which they say surpass those of neighboring Han lineages with respect to their relatives overseas.

These government subsidies and special benefits are important factors in the Ding Hui claim to ethnic minority status. The manipulation of ethnic identity for special favored treatment has been well documented by anthropologists and is an important factor in explaining why the Ding lineage's ethnic identity has become even more relevant. Changes in socioeconomic conditions and the local political economy are conducive to rapid ethnic change. Even before such policies were promulgated, however, Ding Hui occupied a distinct ecological and commercial niche that they had maintained for generations. It is significant that part of the *jipin* (requirements of remembrance) stipulated in their genealogy was the offering of razor clams to their ancestors.[37] This indicates that almost an ethnic specialization of labor was maintained in southern Fujian where Hui were known to be involved in selected aquacultural industries. The Guo in Xiamen city were known before Liberation to be excellent repairmen and builders of motorboats. Virtually all mechanical repair shops were staffed by these Hui.

Hui were known throughout Chinese history as specialized tradesmen in such areas as transport, wool trade, jewelry, and small food stands. Specializations ranged widely in scale and varied regionally according to the socioeconomic position of the Hui in urban or rural settings. These ethnic specializations were virtually lost after the 1955 collectivization reforms but have rapidly resurged since the 1978 Economic Liberalization Policy. Not only in Quanzhou, but throughout China, Hui have prospered at an incredible rate through strong participation in small private businesses and industry—in many places far surpassing their Han neighbors.[38] Local Hui say that they are gifted as small businessmen, and new economic policies have allowed them to express that aspect of their ethnic identity.

ETHNIC PRESERVATION AND MARRIAGE ENDOGAMY. Ding members, through the centuries, also maintained control over out-marriage. A cursory reading of the Ding genealogy reveals a high number of marriages with the mainly Muslim surnames of Guo, Bai, Yang, Jin, Ma, Huang, and even Ding. While surname endogamy is not preferred among the Ding lineage, they have a significantly higher number of in-marriages with other same surname lineage members than the Han in Jinjiang county. About 10 percent of the Ding lineage are married to same surname spouses. I do not have information for the pre-1949 endogamous practice among the Hui, and, while James Watson (personal communication) reports that surname endogamy rose sharply in the Pearl River Delta in the 1950s and 1960s, the local Han and Hui agree that Hui endogamy is still much higher than Han. Marriage is prohibited, however, between those related more closely than 5 generations. With the recent increase in Ding prosperity, there has been a growth in surname endogamy among young people unwilling to marry poorer people outside the lineage. I interviewed one Ding family from Huatingkou village whose 30-year-old son was married to a 26-year-old woman also surnamed Ding.

When the Ding do marry out, spouses are often found among the 4 other Hui surname groups in Quanzhou. The head of one Hui household in Quanzhou surnamed Jin said his family traditionally were allowed to marry only those with the surnames Guo, Ding, Bai, Ma, and Jin—mainly Hui surnames in Quanzhou.[39] Even though this household does not practice Islam, they claim descent from Arab ancestors and referred to their preserved genealogy, which demonstrated that descent. The front gateway to their home had an Arabic and Chinese *duilian*, which stated they were a Muslim household (*Musilin zhi jia*). At the same time, in their courtyard a small incense shrine to a local deity was mounted on a large ornamental rock. Such are the seeming contradictions in Hui life in Quanzhou.[40]

The "Taiwanese Muslims" are those Hui descendants described by the Taiwan China Muslim Association as "20,000 Taiwan-born descendants of Chinese Muslims who came to this island 300 years ago with the hero Koxinga [Zheng Chenggong]."[41] They are concentrated in several coastal towns and share a limited number of surnames, including Guo, Chen, Hong, Fu, Mu, and Pu. Their most prominent lineage is the Guo lineage in Lugang, of which one section is named for and inhabited mainly by this lineage, the Guo Zhu Li (Guo Family Section).[42] There is good evidence to suggest that these Guo are descended from the same ancestors as the Guo lineage in Fujian, Huian county, Baiqi township. Both Guo lineages claim descent from the Tang dynasty General Guo Ziyi,[43] although the accuracy of this claim has been questioned.[44]

There is evidence that an ancient mosque formerly stood in Lugang, and the China Muslim Association once sent mainlander Hui from Taibei to Lugang to instruct the Taiwanese Muslims in Islam and help bring them back into the faith. In a similar move, from 1983 to 1985, the China Islamic Society in the People's Republic of China brought 4 ahong from the Ningxia Hui Autonomous Region to teach in the 4 remaining mosques in Fujian in order to help instruct the newly recognized Hui in the Islamic faith. Both attempts, in Taiwan and Fujian, were ineffectual, however, and the last ahong in Fujian returned to Ningxia during the 1986 Spring Festival. The reason why there is a need for such instruction on both sides of the Taiwan Strait is the same: Both communities practice Chinese folk religion, and in most other respects are culturally indistinguishable from the Han communities in which they live.

The Guo lineage on the mainland, however, was recognized by the Chinese Nationalities Commission as being Hui in the early 1950s. After some political lobbying, they were able to convince the state of their claims to minority status, a process that took the Ding another 20 years. The Guo in Taiwan, however, no longer claim that they are Hui, nor do they seem to have any interest in doing so. While the Guo in

Fujian recognize themselves as Hui, their relations in Taiwan "except for those about fifty or older—say they are not."[45]

> Except for the elderly who still remember having once "done Hui"—having once lived the Hui "way of life"—virtually all Taiwanese of Muslim descent agree they are no longer Muslims.[46]

Like the Chendai Ding lineage, these so-called Taiwanese Muslims claim descent from Arab and Persian ancestors, and it is because of this recognition that they do not include pork in the food offerings to their ancestors, lest they "ruin their mouths." "As their descendants, the Kuos [Guo] must be filial and take pains not to offend them."[47] This recognition of descent from Muslim ancestors is critical for understanding why Hui on one side of the strait claim to be Hui, and why those on the other side feel they are no longer able to be considered so. Perhaps it is premature to predict that "it may well be that visitors to Lukang, Taiwan, a mere decade from now might likewise find no more Hui."[48]

This prediction, while giving insight into the changing identity of Hui in interaction with the Han majority and Taiwan government policy, does not adequately take into account the enduring presence of what it means, or meant, for these Taiwanese Muslims to be different from their Han neighbors. Confusion also arises when the analytical distinction between being Hui and practicing Islam is not made. The Taiwanese Muslims are certainly not practicing Muslims, but that does not mean that Hui identity may no longer be relevant to them. The maintenance of the pork tabu in ancestor worship indicates that, at the ritual level, there is still some significance attached to Hui identity among the Taiwanese Muslims. In the present social context, their ethnic identity may continue to recede in significance and total assimilation may very well take place. But it is also possible that Hui identity may become more relevant to them if Taiwan's policies toward ethnic minorities ever undergo reform similar to those on the mainland. This is all the more plausible, given the increasing discussions of reunification of Taiwan with the mainland. In that case, the Lugang Guo would certainly be recognized as members of the Hui nationality and eligible for the attendant privileges. Hui ethnic identity, though presently almost totally lost, would once again be sociopolitically salient.

It is not surprising that the Lugang Guo have adopted many of the customs of their Taiwanese neighbors, given that their social context has for centuries been unfavorable to the expression of ethnic identity. They have been dispersed among a Han majority for 300 years. In the nineteenth century, they experienced 50 years of a policy of assimilation under the Japanese administration, who discouraged "foreign religions." They have been subjected to the Nationalist policy that identifies Hui primarily in terms of their religious belief (see below). And, they have been geographically and linguistically isolated from other, mainland Hui who arrived with the Nationalists. What is significant is that these individuals maintain any recognition at all of their separateness from their Han neighbors and that this is still important in their lives in terms of ritual and social interaction. What is at issue here is not whether they are descended from Hui ancestors, which is clearly the case. Rather, we need to examine how relevant that ancestry is for their daily lives, and how that idea has changed in its expression over time, as I have argued for the Chendai Hui above.

An important factor is the role of the elderly in maintaining and transmitting the sense of Hui identity to future generations. While younger Guo in Lugang have evidently rejected Hui identity, this identity is apparently acknowledged by their parents and grandparents. In a fascinating story, Robert Weller (personal communication) recounted how, after working with his research assistant in Taiwan for over a year, he discovered for the first time that she was descended from Hui ancestors when he attended *baizu* rituals in their home. The parents would offer only beef to their ancestors, not pork, in deference to their Hui ancestry. This ancestry also came as a surprise to the research assistant. Previously, she had no idea why her parents had refused to offer pork to their ancestors, who continue to receive recognition as Muslims through regular rituals. These rituals perpetuate an idea of separateness which may lead to a reemergence of ethnic identity, should the social context and government policy change. I have noticed that ethnic identity among China's Hui often does not become especially salient until retirement years. While Hui identity may not presently be meaningful to this youth, this does not guarantee that it will remain meaningless as she grows older.

A certain Guo lineage of 383 members who migrated from Baiqi, Huian county to a village outside Xiamen, have also lost all major outward cultural traces of their ethnic ancestry. Despite their practice of Chinese folk religion, they maintain they are different from their Han neighbors, even though they feel that the label *Hui* might no longer be appropriate for them. I submit that it may be possible that, while the younger Guo in Taiwan no longer feel they should be called Hui, they may be reluctant to see themselves as being like their non-Hui neighbors in every respect. This sense of otherness is often the basis for ethnic identity. "It is this sense of belonging to a particular people in contrast to some other people or peoples that constitutes the essence of ethnic identity."[49] While it may no longer be meaningful for young Guo in Taiwan to identify with mainland Hui, they probably still retain some kind of psychological sense of belonging to their own people. Hui identity is often compared to American Jewish identity,[50] and this same sense of belonging is portrayed well by Theodor Reik, a psychoanalyst who explained his feelings about Jewish identity in the following:

> By this admittedly very personal concept of one's people as an extension of one's family I am attempting to explain to myself emotional facts that, often elusive in character, are hard to comprehend. A man can prefer to be together with others and even avoid his own people; he can feel estranged from them— but he can never be a stranger to them. The very intimacy of the experience, which is nothing but common memories that have become unconscious, excludes the possibility of cutting a tie that was formed, not alone by the same blood, but by the same rhythms of living. It is neither congeniality nor consanguinity that speaks here, but the common destiny of our ancestors, of ourselves, and of our children, which forms a bond stronger than relations of any other kind.[51]

ISLAMIC BELIEF AND HUI IDENTITY. At issue here is not the Lugang Guo lineage's identity as Hui, but their inability to admit Islamic belief, which disqualifies them as Hui under Nationalist policy. As discussed in Chapter 2, this policy regards the Hui as a religious group, not an ethnic group. Until 1939, the Hui were regarded as Huimin (Hui people) under Sun Yat-sen's policy of the 5 peoples of China—the Han, Mongolian, Tibetan, Manchurian, and Hui (meaning all the Muslim peoples of China). The policy changed when Chiang Kai-shek presided over the 1st National Congress of the Chinese Hui People's National Salvation Association in Chongqing and declared that all non-Han groups within

China are sub-varieties of an ancient Chinese race. Under this policy the Hui were not considered a separate *minzu* (people, nationality), but a religious group with special characteristics, and are to be referred to as Huijiaoren or Huijiaotu. For Lugang Guo, who are certainly no longer Muslim in religious belief and ritual, it becomes irrelevant and perhaps impossible to call themselves Hui under current Nationalist policy.

As a result of the Nationalist policy, which maintains all Chinese peoples are descended from one race, ethnic differences in Taiwan tend to split along Mainlander/Taiwanese and class lines.[52] Only the aborigines (*gaoshan zu*) receive a nationality status, similar to that on the mainland. The Hui are not regarded as an ethnic group, because there is no such category under the current policy. The Hui associate with the broader Taiwanese society of which they are a part.

The Nationalist policy toward the Hui has been called the *da Hanzu zhuyi* (Great Han Chauvinism) policy and strongly criticized by Hui and government leaders on the China mainland:

> Politically, the Nationalist reactionaries basically do not recognize Huihui are a people, they only recognize they are a "religious organization (*zongjiao tuanti*)," they call Hui people "Hui religious disciples (Huijiaotu)" or "internal nationalities with exceptional lifestyle customs (*neidi shenghuo xiquan teshu zhi guomin*)." The great Hui laboring people are the same as the Han and each minority people, you cannot basically even talk of them having political power [under the Nationalists].[53]

The Communist Party leaders of the People's Republic of China have recognized that the Hui are a distinct *minzu* (nationality, people) since before the 1949 Revolution. This distinction was brought home to Chairman Mao Zedong and other early Party leaders on the Long March. That historical experience and rationale have influenced considerably the PRC's policies toward the Hui and other minorities. In an interview with a Taiwanese Manchu, who are also not recognized as a nationality under the Nationalists, Pamela Crossley reported the following complaint: "Why can't we have a policy of 'nationalities unity' (*minzu tuanjie*), like they do on the mainland?"[54] The divergence between the PRC and Taiwan policies regarding religion and nationality has also affected Hui identity and its expression in both societies. It is particularly relevant to understanding the recent ethnic transformation of the Hui in Chendai, discussed below.

PUBLIC POLICY AND ETHNIC REVITALIZATION IN CHENDAI

PRC policy that accords special privileges to these recently recognized Hui along the southeast coast and encourages their interaction with foreign Muslim governments has had a significant impact on their ethnic identity. Fujian provincial and local municipal publications proudly proclaim Quanzhou as the site of the 3rd most important Islamic holy grave and the 5th most important mosque in the world.[55] Religious and government representatives from over 30 Muslim nations were escorted to Muslim sites in Quanzhou as part of a state-sponsored delegation in spring 1986. Foreign Muslim guests are frequently hosted by the local Quanzhou City Islamic Association.

As a result of this contact, construction of the Xiamen International Airport was partially subsidized by the Kuwaiti government. The Kuwaitis were also assisting in the building of a large hydroelectric dam project along the Min River outside Fuzhou. A Jordanian businessman visiting in spring 1986 offered to donate $1.5 million US to rebuild the Qingjing Mosque.[56] The many Islamic relics in Quanzhou are evidence of a long history of friendly exchanges between China and the Muslim world.[57] As a result of China's growing trade with Third World Muslim nations, it is only natural that these historical treasures should be displayed and made available to foreign Muslim visitors. It is also not surprising that the descendants of these early foreign Muslim residents in Quanzhou—the Ding, Guo, Huang, Jin, and other Hui lineages—are interested in further interaction with foreign Muslim relations.

The historic Hui tombs take on added international significance in the present government's improving relations with foreign Muslim governments. These tombs have become objects of ethnic tourism and pilgrimage for foreign Muslims, as well as urban and northwest Hui in China who wish to explore their Islamic "roots." Hui Party cadres often make a point of visiting historic Muslim tombs, such as the large monument and public park outside Kunming, Yunnan, dedicated to the father of Zheng He, the fifteenth-century Ming explorer and Muslim eunuch. Hui visitors to these historic Muslim tombs reaffirm their international Islamic heritage.[58] As Eaton has found for pastoral nomads in Pakistan,[59] tombs often serve to link local systems of culture into a larger cultural framework. In this case, historic shrines as objects of veneration and tourism remind local Hui of their international and religious roots.[60] Before Zheng He departed on his early fifteenth-century voyage to Hormuz Island in Persia, he inscribed the following request for protection, thus demonstrating the significance the tombs represented at that time for China's Muslims:

> The imperial envoy, general and eunuch Zheng He went to Hormuz and other countries in the Western Seas on an official mission. He offered incense here on [30 May 1417]. May the saints bless him. This was recorded and erected by the Zhenfu Pu Heri.[61]

International Islamic attention cannot but influence the self-perception of the Ding lineage as Hui descendants. It has also led to a kind of ethnic revitalization and rediscovery of their Muslim heritage. In 1984, the possibility was raised of constructing a mosque in Chendai so that the Hui there could begin to learn more about Islam. The Quanzhou Mosque is too far from Chendai (15 km.) to be of practical use for them, and it is now without a resident ahong. In November 1984, a grass-roots organization of Ding Hui leaders was recognized by the government as the Jinjiang County Chendai Town Commission for Hui Affairs. This is quite significant in that formal voluntary associations outside initial government sponsorship are generally considered illegal in China, and, in this case, the state recognized the organization well after it was founded.

One of the Commission's first acts was to establish a small museum in the ancestral hall displaying articles substantiating their foreign Muslim ancestry. The ancestral hall possesses the ritual objects and ancestral tablets on the domestic altar typical of other Hokkien temples.[62] Locals affirmed that rituals of the domestic cult, lighting incense daily, and providing special offerings on festivals and feast days, resembled the practices of other Fujianese families. The main difference here is that there was no pork admitted into the ancestral hall. Ding members told me that they often rinse their mouths with tea before making offerings to their ancestors, as a way of cleansing residue that might be offensive to them. In addition, they often offer tea at funerals so that the deceased can have a clean mouth when s/he meets Muslim ancestors in the afterworld.

Perhaps of more importance, this ancestral hall received special township-level support and approval. Ancestral halls are now allowed in China, but generally not patronized by the state. The township provided some funding for the ancestral hall, reasoning that it also contained a historical museum of the history of the Hui, and, thus, foreign relations in China. I have never seen another ancestral hall with a museum inside; it was the best hall I visited in Fujian.

The Commission has also asked to be recognized as an autonomous minority county, but this has not been worked out because of redistricting difficulties. The Commission even suggested that, in 1987, they would have a Ramadan celebration, and, in 1988, they wanted to encourage many of the Ding to fast. This possible revitalization of a new Islamic identity for the Hui in Chendai is important to watch as it becomes increasingly relevant for them in their altered social context.

Prosperity has come to the Ding lineage as a result of government minority assistance and of increased contacts with overseas relatives. Economic prosperity has been accompanied by ethnic and even religious revival. The growing Muslim identity of the Fujian Hui in interaction with changing sociopolitical conditions and government policy reveals a dialectical process that is the basis for ethnic change. These lineages have always maintained a Hui identity, which, in conjunction with recent events, is only now beginning to take on a decidedly Islamic commitment.

The benefits attached to recognition of the Ding as members of the Hui nationality have led other southeastern lineages with traditional Hui surnames to apply for minority nationality status. As a result, the population of the Hui in Fujian is growing at a rapid rate. Ding lineage members have been located on Pingtan Island (over 5,000 Hui were recognized in 1982) and several other areas in smaller numbers (see Table 29).

BECOMING ETHNIC IN CHINA

In addition to the Ding lineage, there are also other communities who have been recognized recently or are seeking recognition. The majority of the Guo lineage was recognized as Hui in the 1950s, with its largest concentration in 9 villages of Huian county, giving them the name "Jiuxiang Guo" (9-township Guo). They number upwards of 16,000. Descen-

TABLE 29 Fujian Ding Lineage Distribution by County, 1986

Chendai	16,000	Huian	100
Pingyang	2,000	Pingtan	4,800
Fu An	1,000	Ningzhou	300
Fuding	3,500	Tongan	200
Fuzhou	300	Jinjiang An Haizhen	400
Nanan	300	Jinjiang Dongshizhen	150
		Total	29,050

Source: Chart displayed in Central Ancestral Hall.

dants of the Ding, Guo, and other Hui lineages have been recognized in Fuding (1982, 3,000 Hui); Moziping outside Xiamen city (383 Hui named Guo from Huian, Baiqi); Wenzhou city, Zhejiang province; and several villages in Guangdong province.[63] These Hui all lay claim to nationality status based on historical and genealogical evidence of their descent from Arab or Persian ancestors. The recognition of these Hui has led to a dramatic increase in the population of national minorities in Fujian province, from 13,000 in the 1953 census to 31,060 in the 1982 census and to over 60,000 in 1985 (estimate of the Quanzhou Historical Research Society).[64]

The process of application for recognition as members of the Hui nationality is often long and tedious. Recognition among southeastern lineages rests primarily on establishing genealogical proof through research into *jiapu* (genealogical) records, since there are few cultural markers indicating Hui identity for these lineages. Official government recognition rests on the historical truth (*zhen*) of claims to Muslim ancestry. However, in some cases where the genealogical records are lacking, cultural traits of the Hui become more important for establishing identity. This has led to the resurgence of some Hui practices among these unrecognized lineages. Purity of practice has begun to resurface as a means to reinforce claims to the truth of descent. The two poles of *qing zhen* are being pulled together as a result of these local policies.

The Dong Jie Guo (East Street Guo) include 919 households of 4,871 people surnamed Guo, who are concentrated in several blocks of Quanzhou city and have not yet been recognized as Hui. Since 1983, they have made application to be recognized to the State Commission for Nationality Affairs. There has been no decision, however, because of the lack of evidence supporting the East Street Guo's claim to Muslim ancestry. They lost their genealogy during the Cultural Revolution, and other historical sources fail adequately to document their claim to gradual remigration from Baiqi into Quanzhou during the Qing dynasty. Many of their members have also migrated to other areas, making historical demonstration of their origins even more difficult to establish (see Table 30).

The Guo application materials discuss the remnants of evidence pointing to their ancestry in the various preserved Guo genealogies, discovered by researchers of the Quanzhou Historical Society. During interviews, various members of the East Street Guo repeatedly mentioned several Hui cultural practices that they have preserved and are now continuing to practice. These include the refusal to eat pork on ancestral holidays, the intermarriage with other Hui surnames, and the funeral custom of *kaijing*, where the procession to the graveyard is led by an elder with an open Quran. Once again, although they do not read the Quran, it possesses special ritual importance in Baiqi. Like other Hui, they traditionally placed their Qurans, which had been passed down through the generations, on top of the highest rafter of their homes. While most Qurans were burned with their geneaologies as feudal superstitions during the Cultural Revolution, one family had hidden theirs and allowed me to photograph it. It was a hand-copied Quran, dating from the seventeenth century.

Interestingly, the Guo also contend that they have a strong ethnic solidarity. They say that they have maintained a "united nationality" (*minzu tuanjie*) characteristic, revealed in the phrase: "East Street Guo hit people without saying a word" (*Dongjie guo, da ren bu yong shuo*). They gave evidence of intermarriage with the other Hui surname communities in Quanzhou and expressed dismay that the state was dragging its feet on recognizing them.

The East Street Guo took their case to a local institute specializing in the study of the early history of Quanzhou. The institute's scholars are assisting them to collect historical documents and oral accounts that demonstrate their connection to the recognized Hui lineage in Baiqi. In addition, the Guo have decided that it would help their case if they

TABLE 30 Dongjie (East Street) Guo under Application for
Recognition as Members of the Hui Nationality, 1986

Origin	Residents	Migrants	Total
Dongjie	450		450
Xingzhai	1,976		1,976
Yingtou	619	193	812
Tangxi	248		248
Daping	716	325	1,041
Hongdun	282		282
Houjinglong	42	20	62
Total	4,333	538	4,871

Source: Interview with East Street Guo Committee.

revived those cultural practices associated officially with being Hui. They are discussing giving up pork and encouraging their children to study Arabic. When I met with members of this group, they asked me to assist in their application process. They wanted to know what foreign Muslims do that makes them appear different from others around them, and which of their cultural traditions were Muslim. Unsuccessfully attempting to maintain "anthropological distance," I convinced them that I knew little about this; nevertheless it illustrates the important role that foreign scholarship and international connections play in local ethnic identity, particularly when state recognition is at stake.

In order to support their claim to nationality, East Street Guo have begun to revive many ethnic practices associated with the Hui minority. The dialectical interaction between cultural meanings and changing social contexts that has led to the reemergence, even re-invention, of a more relevant ethnic and Islamic identity for these Hui lineages along the southeast coast was also found to be relevant for the "reflowering" of Islam that Nagata studied in Malaysia:

> Ethnic identity then is a unique blend of affective, expressive and basic ties, sentiments and loyalties with (sometimes blatantly) instrumental, calculated, political interests, and the latter are explained and given meaning by the former. The two ends of the *Gemeinshaft-Gesellschaft* continuum here come full circle.[65]

Examination of this case of changing ethnic identity on the southeast coast has demonstrated the influence of government intervention and policy in shaping the resurgence of ethnic identity and practice. In this case, we have traced the rising ethnic consciousness of a people the state only recently recognized as a nationality. The Ding are now starting to adopt and revive many of the traditional markers of Hui ethnicity, spurred by state recognition as a nationality. An overemphasis on the cultural traits of the Hui, their religion, eating customs, business abilities, and other distinguishing features to the exclusion of the social manipulation of ethnicity can lead to confusion over what makes a Hui a Hui. A cultural-trait approach to ethnicity would exclude the Chendai Ding from official recognition as Hui, as it effectively did until 1979 in the PRC, and still does for Hui in Taiwan. Focusing on the social adaptation of the Hui to varying ecological environments under different government policies to the exclusion of the cultural continuities of Hui identity can lead to an assimilationist interpretation, as in the Taiwanese Muslims. Attention must be given to how cultural meanings are shaped under different social contexts and, especially in the Taiwan and Fujian cases, under different government policies.

Under China's socialist policy, which, especially since 1979, has distinguished clearly between the ethnic and religious expressions of a nationality's identity, Hui such as the Chendai Ding are given the option to express their ethnic identity without reference to Islamic belief and practice. We have even found that, in the case of Quanzhou, the Communist Party has gone so far as to send four imams from the northwest to Fujian in order to help preserve and revive that identity. Under Taiwan's Nationalist policy, which stresses the Islamic condition of Hui ethnicity, Guo lineage members in Lugang who no longer practice Islam have no grounds for being considered Hui. I submit that discussions of who the Hui are will be fruitful only if we examine how they have adapted under different socioeconomic circumstances and how their expression of ethnic identity and its relevance differs in those situations.

In some cases, Hui expressions of ethnicity will take on a decidedly religious emphasis, as with many northwest Hui communities. For these cases, as we have seen above, Islamic purity is the main emphasis in the expression of *qing zhen* and Hui identity. In the case of this south-eastern lineage, the interpretation of *qing zhen* dictates only the preservation of one's true ancestry and the ability to demonstrate the veracity of that claim. In still other cases, we shall see that a closer combination of purity and veracity, *qing* and *zhen*, will be stressed. More of a non-religious ethnic identity will be prominent, especially in situations where young Hui may attempt to make use of special leadership opportunities for minorities to rise in the ranks of the Communist Party and other organizations. While Islam is an important and undeniable aspect of Hui heritage, in some contexts it is not necessarily critical for modern expression of Hui identity.

The Hui discussed in this chapter are not concerned with the Islamic ritual purity of a *qing zhen* lifestyle. The core of their identity is stripped bare in their emphasis upon the truth (*zhen*) of their genealogy. Their purity as Hui resides in the truth of this ancestry, rooted in the idea of descent from foreign ancestors who came from the West. Over the entrance to the tomb of the second Islamic saint in Yangzhou was displayed a Chinese epigraph proclaiming the foreign origin of Islam: "The Dao Originates in Western Lands" (*Dao yuan xi tu*).

Unlike other ethnic groups who appeared and then disappeared through the centuries of China's development, such as the Xiongnu and the Jews, and even some who ruled dynasties, like the Khitan, Tangut, and Jurchen, the Hui survived. While the Hui along the southeastern coast have lost much of the cultural and religious distinctiveness normally associated with Hui identity, they have somehow managed to preserve the core of that identity. In the midst of a vast Han majority and beset by many centuries of assimilative policies, their identity has re-emerged as socially relevant in the context of a new state policy that favors minority identity.

The "Dao Tang" (Ritual Center) of a Sufi *shaykh* belonging to the qadariyya Order in Hezhou, Gansu, the "Chinese Mecca." Note pictures on wall of Sufi tombs throughout the Middle East where the *shaykh* lived for nine years. Quranic texts are in Arabic and Chinese. Pot on table holds a large incense stick, typical of Sufi mosques and tombs in northwestern China. Photo: Gladney

SEVEN

Conclusion:
National Identity in the Chinese Nation-State

There are always periods when the State as organism has problems with its own collective bodies, when these bodies, claiming certain privileges, are forced in spite of themselves to open onto something that exceeds them, a short revolutionary instant, an experimental surge. A confused situation: each time it occurs, it is necessary to analyze tendencies and poles, the nature of the movements. All of a sudden, it is as if the collective body of the notary publics were advancing like Arabs or Indians, then regrouping and reorganizing: a comic opera where you never know what is going to happen next (even the cry "The police are with us!" is sometimes heard).
         —Gilles Deleuze and Felix Guattari, A Thousand Plateaus:
         Capitalism and Schizophrenia

The Salman Rushdie protest in China in May 1989 brought Hui together from all corners of the country: There have been many Hui students at the Central Institute for Nationalities, where the protest began, from Ningxia, Quanzhou, and Changying, and many of the residents of Beijing's Oxen Street community joined in the procession. Representatives from each of the four communities I have described in the preceding chapters may actually have come together in the protest march through the streets of Beijing. There were certainly a wide mixture of Muslims represented: Hui, Uigur, Kazak, and Kirghiz, all crying out for justice, demanding respect for the government's policy of religious freedom and nationality rights. It is here that we are introduced to the growing "fourth tide" of Islam in China—a tide that mixes ethnic nationalism with international religious politics. In the face of this tide, the

Chinese government blinked. While they were right in the midst of planning a horrendous military crackdown on the pro-democracy student protests, the government surprisingly granted all of the demands of the Muslims, seeking to use the event as a propaganda point in the national media. As if to say, "Protest is allowed in China, look at the law-abiding Muslim nationalities," the state sought to deflect criticism from its planned suppression of the university students. The students had no legitimate voice by which to address the state. Their organizations were unrecognized and illegal. The Muslims, however, by virtue of their being recognized minority nationalities, had been given a voice, an identity, by the state, that they have turned effectively to their own advantage. After 30 years, they have proved themselves adept at ethnic nationalism and primordial politics in the People's Republic.

The Western press briefly noted the Salman Rushdie Incident, but did not go on to make the interesting connection between the Muslim protest and the Beijing student uprising, which was initially also led by a Muslim Uigur from Xinjiang, Wu'er Kaixi (Uerkesh Daolet). The lull following the Hu Yaobang memorial and May Fourth protests, which had ended with the Beijing students resolutely promising they would not disrupt the imminent visit by President Gorbachev, was broken by a few supposedly insignificant Muslims (much is made of their constituting less than 2 percent of China's population) demanding a bit more religious respect. In the students' call for "no more phoney dialogue," one finds a crucial subtext: the demand for real participation of all the peoples who form the People's Republic. No longer content with past tokenism, the students expressed their frustration on posters, in such slogans (often in English), as: "You can't cheat all of the people all of the time," and "Why can't Li Peng, the people's Prime Minister, come out to meet the people?"—a protest especially appropriate when the People's Liberation Army and People's Police were so devastatingly employed. Most survivors of the June Fourth massacre say that it did not surprise them that the state ordered a crackdown, but that the People's Army, the so-called liberators of the people (whom they had thought were with them), actually fired on the people. For one fleeting instant, the cry, "The police are with us!" (parodied in the Deleuze and Guattari quotation above) had been heard on Tiananmen Square.

THE PEOPLE OF THE PEOPLE'S REPUBLIC: FINALLY IN THE VANGUARD?

It is notable that perhaps the greatest pro-democracy demonstration to have ever taken place in China was led by a Uigur from Xinjiang: As a Muslim minority he had a legitimate voice officials may have been hesitant to silence. And, as Uigur money changers have often rationalized: If he were arrested, what could the police do, exile him to Xinjiang? The participation of the Muslims in the recent political unrest demonstrated the wide complexity and energy of the movement. The Uigur student leader was joined by a host of other minority nationalities students and teachers, far disproportionate to their population. At least 3 students from the Nationalities Institute were killed during the incident, including a Muslim Kazak and a Tujia minority.

It is not surprising that, though Wu'er Kaixi became the darling of the Western press, his Muslim and Uigur background was rarely discussed. In one personal interview, he said: "If I am to be the leader of a national movement inside and outside of China, people won't listen to me if they think I am a 'barbarian' minority." Nevertheless, he frequently admits that it is his ethnic background that most made him aware of the oppression of the government in minority areas and the economic backwardness of his own people. Born to Uigur parents who raised him in Beijing (they were translators of Mao's works into Uigur), he went to high school in Xinjiang and spent summers with Kazak hersdmen in the Tian Shan Mountains. Always an outspoken individual, he was dismissed from his high school for writing an editorial condemning a teacher who had struck a student in class, published in a newspaper he had helped start. This did not prevent him, however, from testing out of Xinjiang in the national college examination into the capital's Central Institute for Nationalities, whence he then tested into the Beijing Normal University, because, he said, he wanted to train to become a teacher in order to return to Xinjiang and help raise the educational level of his people. His fluid command of Beijing-accented Mandarin, combined with his fearless disregard for his own safety (he was the student leader in hospital garb who confronted the Prime Minister Li Peng, chastising him on national television for coming late to the meeting with the students), led him to be elected chairman of the Beijing Universities Students' Autonomous United Association, and after the crackdown, number 1 on the state's 21 most wanted list. Criticized for his flamboyant lifestyle while seeking to organize an exile Democracy Movement in the United States and France, he has shrugged it off: "As a Uigur I don't enjoy saving my money and not having fun like the Han. Maybe I'll go back to trading, or open a restaurant; that's what we Uigur do best."[1]

Not the only minority student leader on Tiananmen Square, Wu'er Kaixi was joined by many of his former classmates from the Central Institute for Nationalities. One minority student was arrested two months after the crackdown walking down the path to his village in southern Yunnan province. Local police had been on the lookout for him, and they were alerted by the new bicycle he was riding in the poor rural area. Wang Zhengcun was the Chairman of the Central Institute for Nationalities student pro-democracy organization, who also made the most wanted list with Wu'er Kaixi (2 minorities out of 21 on the list). When the first list was published with Wang's name on it, however, an interesting error was discovered. In the section after age, place of birth, and work unit, in the place that records nationality (where Wu'er Kaixi was listed as a Uigur), Wang Zhengcun was reported on national television as being a member of the "Ku Cong" nationality (*minzu*). The Ku Cong, however, are not an official nationality in China, and show up on none of the lists. When I asked about this, I was told that the Ku Cong, originally a forest-dwelling people in Yunnan, have been trying unsuccessfully since the 1950s to get recognized as a separate nationality. They were classified as "Yellow Lahu," a supposed branch of the Lahu, and have been in disagreement about it ever since. Wang Zhengcun, known to feel strongly about this, always wrote "Ku Cong" in the space for nationality on his residency and student registration cards, even though he knew it was not an accepted category. When the Public Security Bureau looked up his file, they reported that he was a Ku Cong *minzu*, as he had written. The second time the 21 most-wanted list appeared in the national press, however, his status was changed to Ku Cong *ren* (person, not nationality), and later he was simply listed as a member of the Lahu nationaliy (*minzu*).

One of the few women student leaders on the Square, and also a member of dubious nationality, was Liu Yan. At the time also a student at the Nationalities Institute, she came from a multi-ethnic household. Her father was a Han, but her mother was born to a Mongolian father and Russian mother (enabling Liu's mother to become a Russian translator). When Liu turned 18, she was allowed to decide her nationality, and chose to be Mongolian, because, she told me, "It seemed more exotic than Han or Russian." Hers is an excellent example of how nationality status in China may have little to do with one's true feelings of ethnicity.

Cai Jingqing is a Hui student now living in exile due to her participation in the Pro-Democracy Movement. A straight-A student at Beijing University before the crackdown made her flee the country, Cai grew up in a middle-class Hui family near Niujie. Although her father was a bus repairman, she and her three brothers grew up with a healthy respect for education, and all are now in the United States pursuing graduate careers. One brother studies advanced physics at Boston University, another is studying conducting with the Boston Philharmonic conductor, Seiji Ozawa, and she is a 4.0 student at Wellesley, as well as a star basketball player. In a *New York Times* interview with Fox Butterfield, she stated that she and her Chinese classmates had given up hope: "After all the events in Eastern Europe and the Soviet Union, they think China missed its chance to modernize and become democratic. They are all very depressed."[2] It is interesting that, like most of the Wu'er Kaixi articles, the interview with Ms. Cai failed to mention that she is a Hui, with a Muslim family background.

Yet the nationality factor was of major concern to students in the Salman Rushdie protest as well as the Tiananmen Movement. When a rumor circulated in Beijing that the state might employ minority soldiers who could not speak the Han language to suppress the students, Uigur and other minority students immediately went to all the train stations to serve, if necessary, as translators able to inform the soldiers of the true nature of their peaceful demonstration. Reflecting belief in such a rumor, and traditional Han ethnocentric biases against minorities, one Harvard graduate student, who was a frequent commentator on the Democracy Movement in the United States, on 5 June made the following statement in an ABC Nightline interview with Ted Koppel:

"According to a phone conversation I made with a student in China today, most of the troops that made most of the killings were not Han, not of Han nationality, but of those—national minorities. So it is apparently easier for a different nationality, people from a different nationality to kill people of a different nationality."[3] He argued that, since the 27th Army was based in Inner Mongolia, it was probably composed of Mongolians. After being telephoned by numerous incensed Mongolian and other Chinese students residing in the United States, who told him that there were no Mongolians in the 27th Army, and that it was the Han army that was used to suppress and execute many Mongolians suspected of being members of an underground counter-revolutionary movement during the Cultural Revolution,[4] the student retracted his statement on the 7 June Nightline program and apologized for relying on false rumors. Unlike the Soviet Union, China has few minorities serving in its military.

This is not the first time minorities have been at the forefront of social protest, as events in Mongolia, Ningxia, Xinjiang, and Tibet have demonstrated. On 10 December 1988, the People's Liberation Army opened fire on demonstators in Tibet, killing several. The Shadian Incident in Yunnan in 1975, discussed above, led to the massacre of over 1,600 Hui. This study has shown that, in many other respects, the minorities have led the Han in national reforms. In Ningxia, the building of Hui mosques opened the way for the reopening of Han temples. Hui entrepreneurism has pushed the limits of the free-market system. Minorities were the first openly and brazenly to reject the 1-child family policy, which most Han in rural areas are also now ignoring. Government cadres, we have seen, have been more reluctant to crack down on minority expressions of limited autonomy. In the process, the Han have also pushed for further reforms. The nationalities, as identified peoples, have a legitimate voice for such actions, given them by the state. They do not represent illegal voluntary associations, such as the student and worker unions in Beijing. The state cannot deny them the right to organize without changing the constitution. Wherever possible, minorities have effectively used the state-assigned labels for their own benefit— turning an originally assimilationist policy to their own advantage.

The labels, now owned by the peoples themselves, were institutionalized by the state. From the beginning, the Chinese state reserved the right to determine who were considered to be a people. In exchange for their support for the founding of the Chinese nation-state, they were offered participation and power sharing. While, for many peoples, this has remained merely a promise, nevertheless it is still held up as a legislated ideal. The PRC is not a new Chinese empire built on top of the old—the leadership no longer claims to rule under the divine Mandate of Heaven. As the People's Republic, the supposed representatives of the people, must maintain the myth, if not the reality, that they are responsive to the people's demands. It is not surprising, therefore, that many of the large-scale protests we have seen in the last 10 years in China have been led by peoples officially designated as members of, albeit generally absent from, the political process: Tibetans, Mongolians, Uigurs, and Hui Muslims. Now the Han, perhaps for the first time, have been subjected to the full brutality of the state, *their* People's Government, in which the Han have always thought to have been in the vanguard—a level of violent repression the minorities claim they have been experiencing from the very beginning. As Roderick MacFarquhar has suggested, the crushing of the Pro-Democracy Movement on June 4th may have led to the "Tibetanization of all China."[5]

THE SOCIAL LIFE OF LABELS

The state in China has assigned ethnic labels to the peoples identified by them—labels often arbitrary and defined primarily by the state. Nevertheless, over the last 40 years, it can be argued that these labels have taken on a life of their own. Like material commodities, which Arjun Appadurai convincingly argues gain enduring sociopolitical value beyond their original intent, these state designations have contributed to a growing awareness of nationalism.[6] Bernard Cohn's suggestion that these legal statuses led to the objectification and, in some cases, creation, of identities—perhaps previously present but loosely defined—is certainly relevant to the nationalities in China.[7] Perhaps related to the traditional role of the Confucian Chinese state to name the essence of things, these designations take on superordinate status in China. In his recent book, Lynn White has argued that, in China, labels, such as *right-*

est, worker, and *landlord,* have controlled access to employment, education, residence, and food rations—the substance of debate in every political conflict.[8] They have certainly meant a great deal in determining
one's access to state affirmative-action programs and political representation for minorities. It is not surprising that hundreds, perhaps thousands, of groups who perceive themselves to be ethnic, are seeking
nationality status from the Chinese state.

The Hui are perhaps the clearest case of a people who emerged in
their present "pan-Hui" identity through a long process of ethnogenesis
under the Chinese state. Hui in China, no matter where one travels,
now refer to themselves as Hui people (Hui *min*). Descended from Persian, Arab, Mongolian, and Turkish Muslims, the people now known as
the Hui emerged in a protracted process of ethnogenesis. Now these
diverse peoples, who thought of themselves primarily as Muslims until
the beginning of this century, see themselves as one nationality, united
by a common imagined ethnohistory. This bond includes not only the
traditionally accepted Hui Muslims who speak the mainly Han dialects,
but also the Tibetan, Mongolian, Thai, Hmong, Mien, and Hainanese
Muslims, who now all call themselves and are registered by the state as
Hui. The Hui may be one of the few peoples ever to become a nationality before they fully thought of themselves as an ethnic group, at least
in not such inclusive terms. That the Hui see themselves and their religion as "pure and true" adds an ironic twist to the state's power to label.
By accepting the term, *Pure and True Religion* for *Islam,* it tacitly legit-
imized a people generally thought to be less civilized than the majority.
This chauvinism found its most derogatory expression in the Ming dynasty by adding to the Chinese ideograph for Hui (回) the radical   for
"dog" or "beast" (犭回).[9] In this case the state's authority to label was
certainly intended to exclude and insult, rather than to enlist.

OBJECTIFIED ETHNONYMS IN THE NORTHWEST

While the Hui may be one of the more extreme examples of this invention and evolution of ethnicity, the reach of the state in the objectification of other nationalities in the northwest is also clearly seen. The
present-day Uigur are concentrated in the oasis cities of the Xinjiang

Uigur autonomous region and are known as the settled oasis-dwelling Muslim Turkic-speaking people of the Tarim Basin. The ethnonym *Uigur* was revived by the Soviets in the 1930s, however, as a term for those oasis peoples who had no name for themselves other than their locality, *Kashgar-lik, Turpan-lik, Aksu-lik,* as well as *Taranchi, Turki,* and *Sart.* The term was adopted by a Chinese Nationalist warlord in Xinjiang in 1934 upon the suggestion of his Soviet advisor. The ethnonym itself, however, had dropped out of usage after the fifteenth century when it referred to the settled oasis peoples of the Tarim Basin, who were Buddhist and expressly non-Muslim. Once these peoples began to convert to Islam, from the tenth to fifteenth centuries, they rejected the ethnonym *Uigur,* which to them meant heathen.[10] It was gladly revived by the 6 million oasis-dwelling Turkic Muslims in Xinjiang as their ethnonym, since this acceptance brought with it recognition by the state, as well as an autonomous region. This reconceptualization of their ethnohistory struck deep chords in their agreed upon sense of commonality as an autochthonous Central Asian people in opposition to the Han, descended from a historic Turkish empire, in a poetic recreation of historical imagination.[11] Other terms for the Muslim peoples of Xinjiang, such as *Uzbek, Kazak, Tatar, Kirghiz,* and *Tadjik,* were also taken over by the Chinese from the Soviets, and these ethnonyms are not without their problems.[12]

In this regard, the Yugur nationality, who are concentrated in their own autonomous county in Gansu's Hexi corridor, are also extremely problematic. It is this modern group that most preserves the linguistic, cultural, and religious ties with the Uigur empire's past. Known as the Yellow Uigur (Shari Yugur) who fled to Gansu after the Kirghiz invasion of A.D. 840, which had conquered the Uigur kingdom and dispersed the tribal confederation, the Yugur are the only remnants of the original Uigur kingdom to preserve much of their former Turkish language, written with Old Uigur script until the nineteenth century. Manichaean practices in their Lamaist-Buddhist religion are also still present,[13] and they now are divided into 3 groups speaking Turkish, Mongolian, and Chinese dialects—all recognized as belonging to one nationality, the Yugur.[14] One wonders why they did not inherit the label *Uigur* from the seventh–ninth century Buddhist kingdom, whence they fled, instead of the oasis-dwelling Muslims in Xinjiang.

Several other nationality identities in the northwest are of significant interest. I have already discussed the problematic identifications of the Dongxiang, Salar, and Baoan Muslims, who are found only in China. Each group speaks a combination of Turkic, Mongolian, and Han dialects, and, within each individual nationality, there are some that speak only one or the other language—they are not all tri- or bilingual. The Baoan derive from Mongolian-speaking Tibetan Lamaists, later identified as the Tu (or Monguours), who, upon conversion to Islam, formed a new collectivity eventually registered by the state as the Baoan.[15] The Dongxiang ("East Village") derived their name from a Hezhou suburb. That the state chooses to identify these Muslim peoples individually in the northwest, to accept their own formulations of identity and ethnonym, and then to legalize them, but at the same time refuses individual recognition to the Tibetan, Mongolian, Bai, and Hainan Muslims, lumping them all together as "Hui," certainly reflects pragmatic sociopolitical decisions. This process and the effect of the distinct identifications of these peoples in their separate ethnogeneses cries out for further study.

This objectification of ethnic identities based on state-assigned labels was emphasized to me recently by a Han scholar who went to Xinjiang in the early 1950s as a language student and teacher. After taking a one-month truck ride from Xi'an to Urumqi, she was assigned to a predominantly Uigur village that also had Kazak and Hui residents. At the time, she noticed that there was little division among them as Muslims. They worshiped in the same mosque and generally made little reference to their national identities. On a 1987 return trip, however, she found that they no longer prayed together and seemed to have a much stronger sense of their ethnic difference from each other.[16] This, of course, was the intention of Soviet Central Asian nationality policies: the creation of a plurality of Turkic ethnicities that would help prevent pan-Turkic unification.[17] This policy has led, however, to other results in China.

THE HARDENING OF ETHNONYMS IN THE SOUTHWEST

In Southwest China, a plethora of officially designated nationalities masks an even greater ethnic complexity. As anthropologists have begun to study the ethnohistories of these groups, they have found that many are umbrella associations, registered during the 1950s identification campaigns, which included many peoples who did not necessarily think of themselves in the same way the state did, but were happy to be registered as something other than Han. A striking example is provided by the Bai people of Yunnan, whom C. P. Fitzgerald identified as the Minjia.[18] In the famous study by Francis L. K. Hsu, *Under the Ancestor's Shadow*, these people were simply identified as Han.[19] For years, Sino-anthropologists have assigned this book to their students as an excellent ethnography of Chinese, that is, Han, traditional society. Detailed ethnographic research by a Japanese anthropologist, Hiroko Yokoyama, however, has uncovered their ethnic complexity and ethnogenesis as the Bai.[20] David Wu reports that these people have gone to great lengths to maintain their minority status and in no way wish to be mistaken for, or assimilated to, the Han.[21]

Lin Yueh-hwa's discussion of the Yi (formerly Lolo) people in Sichuan also typically depicts a uniform history of a people which "is an old one in China. . . . Ever since ancient time, the Yis have been a member of the family of Chinese nationalities."[22] This "colonization" of ethnic history by the regime in power masks a wide sociocultural variety among a people now labeled as the Yi. They comprise at least 3 separate ethnolinguistic groups who were, for the most part of their history, independent of Chinese rule. Stevan Harrell suggests that the rewriting of "the history of the history of the Yi" from their own, Chinese, and Western missionary accounts is required to find out who and why they have become what they are.[23]

The Qiang are a people whose identity has been conceived by an even greater stretch of the historical imagination. Distributed throughout Southwest and Central China, their name has been found by Chinese ethnohistorians to date from as early as the Shang dynasty. A fantastic leap is made to the modern century, however, in arguing that the peoples in Sichuan identified as such are direct descendants of these obscure nomadic peoples.[24] Through a sifting of historical, archaeological, and ethnographic materials, one Chinese researcher from Taiwan has demonstrated that the peoples found all over China during several periods and identified as Qiang in the historical records cannot possibly be related.[25] This represents just another instance of a Confucian preoccupation with the "rectification of names." The term *Qiang*, according to the linguist Robert Ramsey, probably only indicated "pastoralist" in the early Chinese texts, and this was used to apply to any shepherding people.[26] Nationality identification in some cases in China may be engaged in the somewhat Procrustean art of fitting modern peoples into the ethnonyms found in classic texts.

Incredible linguistic diversity and multiplicity found throughout the southwest makes it almost impossible to identify many of these groups on the basis of language alone, though this is what was mainly attempted by the 1950s ethnologists constrained to follow a Stalinist model. Dai Qingxia, a Chinese linguist, has recently shown that, within a single Jingbo (Kachin) family in Yunnan, there are generally 2, and perhaps 3, languages in use, depending on the generations present.[27] Ramsay elaborates on how these umbrella nationalities were created in China through language politics:

> At least two of these groups—Tsaiwa (or Atsi) and Lashi—are known to range over the Chinese side of the border. The languages that they speak natively are believed to be closer genetically to Burmese than to Jingpo. But since these tiny ethnic groups use Jingpo in their dealings with outsiders, the Chinese government classes them together and calls their languages "dialects" of Jingpo.[28]

In each of these cases the label the state has assigned, no matter how ill-suited, has led to the crystallization and expression of identities within the designated group along pan-ethnic lines.[29] While ethnogenesis and the rise of pan-ethnic identities have occurred throughout history, particularly with the incorporation of native peoples by nation-states, China represents an incubated process: What normally takes several generations for most ethnic groups has for many of the identified nationalities in the PRC occurred in the last 30 years.

The increasing appeal of minority identity has led to an explosion of nationalism in the southwest and throughout China. Zhang Tianlu, a Chinese demographer, mentioned to me that in Shizhu, a county in southwestern Sichuan, the 1982 census counted only 19 people who claimed to be members of the Tujia minority. In 1984, however, when the county applied to be an autonomous Tujia county, they reported that there were now more than 218,000 Tujia! These Tujia had formerly

Hui men at prayer near a local tomb at the Lingwu Muslim cemetery, Ningxia, the Gobi Desert. These graves were described by Pickens as "Beehive Tombs" and are found throughout the northwest. Photo: Gladney

Tomb complex of Naqshbandi Jahri Saint Ma Hualong in Zhang Jiachuan, Gansu, said to contain the head of the saint with his body buried at the small tomb in Jinji, Ningxia (c. 1930s). Regarding this tomb complex, the missionary Claude Pickens wrote: "To say in Kansu and Ningsia that one has visited this place means much in friendship among Moslems in the northwest and most parts of China." Photo: Pickens. Courtesy of Harvard-Yenching Library.

identified themselves as Han in 1982 and now were not afraid to come forward to claim their real national identity. It is clear from this case and many others that the distinction between Han majority and minority nationality is an ambiguous one that is in the midst of state-minority contestation. The 1990 census revealed that the Tujia had increased 101 percent, from 2.8 million in 1982 to 5.7 million, indicating an explosion of ethnicity in China among many peoples who have shifted their nationality category from Han to minority.

"SUB-ETHNIC" IDENTITIES AND THE QUESTION OF HAN ETHNICITY

Ethnic identities are not entirely absent outside of the officially recognized minority nationalities. Unrecognized peoples live very ethnic lives: Emily Honig in a series of fascinating articles has documented the plight of the Subei people in Shanghai, who, though not an official nationality, occupy several lower economic niches and have been stigmatized for such a long time that they have begun to think of themselves, and act, as an ethnic group.[30] While Western scholars have been aware of cultural diversity within the Chinese for some time, these difference have generally been explained as "regional," or "sub-ethnic." This is because the vast majority of China scholars have accepted that 94 percent of China belongs to one ethnicity—the Han. Ethnographies on people such as the Hakka are said to teach us generalities about the rest of Chinese society, precisely because the Hakka are Han.[31] Minority studies, no matter how close they are to the so-called "Han" in language, social structure, and culture, such as the Hui, are rarely included in studies of "Chinese" society, simply because they are not Han. Ethnic differences within Han society, while readily accepted as separate cuisines, cultures, and languages outside of China, within China are regarded as local dishes, customs, and dialects. The Cantonese, Sichuanese, and Hunanese are somehow not what they eat.

These extra-nationality associations cast doubt on the concept of the Han: The assumption that 94 percent of China constitutes one ethnic group is accepted by Chinese and most Western scholars. This should give us pause; perhaps we also have been taken in by the same political justification for Chinese nationalism as proposed by Sun Yat-sen. Fred Blake's important study, *Ethnic Groups and Social Change in a Chinese*

Market Town, has identified a plethora of ethnic groups defined by language, place, and occupation, including Hakka, Cantonese, and Hokkien, in the New Territories outside Hong Kong.[32] While these groups are not recognized as "minorities" in China, no one has objected to his depiction of them as vibrant ethnic groups. This is perhaps because of their living under Hong Kong's jurisdiction. What will happen to these so-called ethnic groups once Hong Kong reverts to China? Will Blake be criticized for confusing sub-regional identity with ethnicity? Clearly the issue of state hegemony and nationality identification requires further attention.

When the assumption of Han ethnicity is challenged, Sinologists often point to the Chinese language as the unifying factor: All Han speak Chinese, whereas the minorities do not (except, of course, for the Hui, She, Manchu, and the vast majority of bilingual minority youth). The major branches of Chinese, including Wu, Min, Kejia (Hakka), Yue (Cantonese), Huizhou, Xiang, Gan, as well as Northern, Northwest, Southern, and Southwest Mandarin, are all referred to as dialects. However, modern linguists generally distinguish a dialect from a language in terms of mutual intelligibility. Except for the Mandarin branches, the others listed are all mutually unintelligible, and several "dialects" within them, such as Southern and Northern Min (Quanzhou and Fuzhou dialects), represent entirely different and mutually exclusive speech communities. To resolve this dilemma, John De Francis suggests that, while linguistically these are actually separate languages, politically they have been unified under one nation-state, and therefore should be accepted as one language with many dialects.[33] This, of course, ignores the minority languages, which are also part of the Chinese state. It is perhaps in reaction to this that S. Robert Ramsay entitled his book, *The Languages of China*, emphasizing the plurality of Chinese languages and cultures. In a discussion of the rise of China as a nation-state and its effort to modernize and nationalize its population, Ramsay discusses the priority placed on language reform in unifying the country. The development of the "common language" (*putong hua*) based on Beijing Mandarin was indispensable to the development of China as a unified nation.[34] The denial of differences among the Chinese languages was thought to be critical to the legitimation and modernization of the nation, in much the same way that I discussed in Chapter 2 with regard to Sun Yat-sen's emphasis on the unification of the Chinese "sheet of loose sand" into one unified race.

Without the political necessity for a unified language system, China's linguistic diversity could be easily compared to other multi-lingual nations. In fact, Y. R. Chao, the respected Chinese linguist, suggested, "While there is relative uniformity of speech in the Mandarin-speaking regions, from Harbin to Kunming, from Chungking to Nanking, the dialects in the east and south vary from one another as much as French from Spanish or Dutch from German."[35] In his recent linguistic analysis of Chinese, Jerry Norman concurs with this comparison of Chinese with the Romance languages:

> In view of these parallels, it would not be surprising if we found about the same degree of diversity among the Chinese dailects as we do among the Romance languages, and in fact I believe this to be the case. To take an extreme example, there is probably as much difference between the dialects of Peking and Chaozhou as there is between Italian and French; the Hainan Min dialects are as different from the Xian dialect as Spanish is from Rumanian.[36]

The Romance example is intriguing, particularly as we anticipate the unification of the European community. Ramsay argues that Chinese is unlike Romance in that China is one nation, and that political unity drives the languages together rather than apart (though certainly Belgium would provide a counter-example).[37] If Europe unifies, will that then make all of the Romance languages dialects? This absurd suggestion points to the fact of the importance of the political context in distinguishing dialects from languages, sub-ethnicities from ethnicities and nationalities. In the modern world, it is often the nation-state that feels compelled to make, or attempts to make, this taxonomic division.

Chinese scholars will also often point to Chinese ideographs as binding all Han together, since they can all read them, no matter what their "regionalect" (to use De Francis's neologism). But the natural response is to ask about the Japanese, or Mateo Ricci, who perhaps knew as many or more ideographs as any Chinese scholar-official: Does that make them Chinese as well? A more serious reply is to compare Chinese characters to Latin in the Middle Ages: Most of the Europeans (except the Germans) used it as a *lingua franca*, at least in the written script, but it bound few of them together. Most linguists would agree that there is little that ties the spoken language to the written Chinese ideographs; meaning, as in any language or signifying system, is attached much more obliquely. In China, however, through imperial examinations and continual language reforms, the state has exerted a tremendous influence on shaping the Chinese language(s). As with language, so with nationality.

A similar structural argument is offered about the Chinese family. Since the vast majority of Chinese have similar household economic and kinship structures, this relates them all as one ethnicity, no matter what language they speak. But this structural argument has also been disputed by anthropologists along linguistic lines. There are many very culturally different peoples with the same kinship structures. Yet there is nothing culturally deterministic about kinship systems.

But there are problems with these linguistic parallels. Ethnicity is not determined by language, as there are many multi-lingual ethnic groups. As I have argued above, ethnicity is an intensely political phenomenon; an ongoing dialectical mixture of self-perception, other-designation, and state-definition. The state has had many reasons for defining most of China as one "nationality," speaking one "language." Understanding the substance of these social and political relations, rather than reducing them to pure linguistic, cultural, or ethnic essences, is what is needed in our understanding of the development of Chinese society, nationality, and the state.

The question then becomes: When did these peoples begin to think of themselves as ethnic? For most, the process certainly did not begin with the nationality-identification campaigns in the 1950s. The spread of the Chinese state always came into conflict with other cultures, whether dominated by peoples who identified with the descendants of the Wei River Valley or one of the 11 dynasties dominated by non-Chinese peoples. As I have argued, however, these cultural and even ethnic oppositions were fundamentally different in an empire seeking to establish rule over subject peoples than for a nation-state seeking legitimacy through a rhetoric of participation in governance. This enlistment required identification for purposes of representation and census-taking. This is the juncture where ethnicity began to become crucially salient and, for some, even invented. A parallel process has been documented in India, where Richard G. Fox has noted the production of "national cultures" and the "making of the Hindian." Fox reports:

> Hindu nationalists maintain that underneath the superficial diversity of India's sects and castes lies an essential unity, a "unity in diversity." Anyone who recognizes India as a geographical homeland and as a cultural heartland is a true Indian, that is, a Hindian. Hindus, Muslims, Sikhs, Untouchables, and Christian Indians, no matter their superficial sectarian identities, partake of this essential Hindian unity, if they would only put aside their squabbles and recognize it.[38]

While India has been portrayed as the most multi-cultural of nations, and often contrasted to the culturally monolithic China, we see here the same kind of ethnic nationalist argument employed by Sun Yat-sen with regard to the diversity within Chinese society. One must only wait to see if the "Hindian" will emerge from India much the same way as the "Han" in Chinese society—the recent upsurge in decided Hindu nationalism suggests otherwise.

In China, the process of ethnogenesis is not completed, since individuals in every new generation become incorporated into the state and begin to conceive of themselves in ethnic terms. This often happens at census registration, job application, or matriculation into state-run schools. I recently asked a Han colleague when it was that he first realized he was a Han. No mono-cultural individual, he grew up in the cosmopolitan Manchurian city of Harbin, long a center of Sino-Soviet trade and northeastern ethnic diversity, populated by Russians, Manchurians, Koreans, Mongols, Olonqen, Daur, Hezhe, and Hui. Yet this 32-year-old intellectual, now conducting post-doctoral research at Harvard, grew up in Harbin without ever realizing that he belonged to a distinct nationality. "The first time I knew I was a Han," he told me recently, "was when I was 17 years old and I registered for work. I filled out the form and the man there told me to write *Han* in the blank category for nationality (*minzu*). I didn't know what to write." It was when he applied for a job in the state-controlled sector that this Han fully realized his official nationality status. It had little meaning for him until that time. Another Han from Beijing told me that she first realized she was Han when she entered school at 7. She recalled her teacher saying that she must not make fun of her playmate because he did not

Owen Lattimore, while traveling in the Mediterranean, encounters Hui and Uigur Muslim pilgrims on their Hajj to Mecca, 1937. Original caption: "Mecca-bound Hami and Turfan pilgrims, Greece–Egypt, on boat." Photo: Lattimore. Courtesy of Peabody Museum, Harvard University, and reproduced with the permission of David Lattimore.

Gate formerly outside the Di An city in southern Ningxia with proclamation: "Do not divide Hui from Han." Pickens's note with the 1933 photo reads: "Do not divide Moslems and Christians." Photo: Pickens. Courtesy of Harvard-Yenching Library.

eat pork, since she was Han and he was Hui. "Some people like ice cream, some others don't," the girl's teacher told her; "it's because different people like different things. You should respect the Hui, just as he should respect you, a Han." Han ethnicity is the unmarked category in China that must be learned in state schools.

No Weberian "subjective belief" in common ancestry or political action will change one's ethnicity in China.[39] Unauthorized "associations" of unrecognized groups are still illegal—unlike Irish in Chicago or Jews in New York, who have political power despite their not being officially classified as underprivileged minorities in the United States. Only the officially designated underprivileged minorities and Native Americans find parallels with the minority nationalities of China and the Soviet Union. Unrecognized groups are not *ethne* for the Chinese state—no matter how much they themselves think they are. Under the all-seeing eye of Jeremy Bentham's authoritarian panoptican, as Foucault so vividly portrayed for the modern totalitarian regime, all behavior is monitored.[40] In the multi-ethnic world of China, the state's panoptic power is improved if those under observation and control are divided into certain cells or accepted categories of ethnicity and tradition. However, after delineating the cells, the state cannot guarantee that the created communities within do not take on lives of their own.

THE RISE OF "UNITED NATIONALITIES"

Despite the continued diversity that we have seen among these communities, a process of ethnogenesis has also brought them closer together, in dialectical interaction with state policy and local traditions. Through acceptance of the ethnic label assigned by the state, increased communication, education in special state minority schools, and the desire for more political power through larger numbers, ethnic groups are beginning to argue for the national unity of their people—a process of pan-ethnic nationalization noted by Benedict Anderson.[41] The Hui traditionally quoted a Chinese translation of a *hadith*, "All Hui under Heaven are one family." The *hadith* referred to all Muslims in the wider Islamic *Umma*, but it is now taken by the Hui as referring only to the unity of their own people. This saying occasionally arose when I asked

Hui informants what was unique about them as a people.

I once greatly embarrassed a famous Hui calligrapher, however, when I asked him to inscribe for me the phrase "All Hui under Heaven are one family." This phrase was criticized during a 1958 campaign against "local nationalism" (*difang minzu zhuyi*) which sought to discourage local ethnic identities in favor of broader national unity.[42] Out of fear of later being accused of local nationalism, my Hui artist friend suggested instead that he write the state's preferred slogan, "Nationalities Unite" (*Minzu tuanjie*). This slogan serves as an official contradiction of the Hui phrase, since it is intended to encourage all minorities to unite together with the Han majority for the good of the country. The slogan "Nationalities Unite" is still prominently displayed in every minority area. A magazine devoted to minority culture uses it as a title; until recently, it graced the main entrance of the Central Institute for Nationalities in Beijing; and a holiday, "United Nationalities Day," has recently been named to emphasize its importance.[43]

Hence, it came as quite a surprise to me when, during several interviews with Hui informants, the Hui used the same phrase "Nationalities Unite" to refer to their own solidarity when threatened by outsiders. To a question I often asked about what they saw as a characteristic of being Hui, several responded: "We Hui nationality are very united" (*Womende Hui minzu hen tuanjie de*). They thus reinterpreted the meaning of the phrase *Minzu tuanjie* as "Nationality Unity," instead of the plural "United Nationalities"—a translation entirely permitted by Chinese grammar (since there are no plurals in Chinese), but completely opposite to the state's original intent. Without changing the Chinese phrase, they have radically altered its meaning. This slogan, for many Hui, is now often taken to mean the solidarity of their own ethnic group vis-à-vis other nationalities and the dominant hegemony—a far cry from its official public meaning. The East Street Guo used the phrase to refer to their solidarity when fighting with the Han. The protesters in the Rushdie Incident frequently called for nationality unity, and often meant only among Muslims. In short, the Hui have perhaps unconsciously substituted the meaning of their traditional phrase "All Hui under Heaven are one family"—now out of favor with the state—for the state's own "Nationalities Unite," by changing the original intent of the phrase to fit their own preferred interpretation. These shifts and manipulations of meaning, tradition, and history demonstrate the dynamism of the internal and external dialogics in forging a new pan-Hui ethnic identity.

MANY ORGANS OF THE CHINESE BODY POLITIC. The myth of the unity of all the people of China as one socialist entity has not been entirely accepted by the peoples. The creation of a "body without organs," to use Deleuze and Guarttari's phrase, has yet to take place.[44] It is as if the separate body parts now wish to go their own ways. Claude Lefort argues that the idea of the "people as one" is fundamental to the totalitarian vision.[45] In China, the state has not yet been able to convince all the peoples that it is the same as the nation. The two need not be conflated. If the state is primarily Han, the nation most certainly is not. The inexorable unification of peoples, once thought inevitable in Marxist theory, can no longer be counted on, and this is one reason assimilation theory is so inappropriate for the post-modern era. As James Clifford notes:

> Throughout the world indigenous populations have had to reckon with the forces of "progress" and "national" unification. The results have been both destructive and inventive. Many traditions, languages, cosmologies, and values are lost, some literally murdered; but much has simultaneously been invented and revived in complex, oppositional contexts. If the victims of progress and empire are weak, they are seldom passive.[46]

The Soviet "melting pot," once thought the most assimilative due to the application of thoroughgoing Russification programs since the Stalinist era, has now erupted in a "cauldron" of ethnicities.[47] This is strongly related to local perceptions of national power and opposition.

The eruption of national feelings in the Soviet Union has as much to do with "taking the lid off" through the policy of openness (*glaznost*) as it has to do with the settling of national borders. The Sino-Soviet rapprochement and the ending of the war in Afghanistan, I would argue, has had more of an impact on local expression of ethnicity than any internal reforms. As one Kazak told me in Alma Ata in 1988: "The Russians have no right to repress us any longer. In the past, we were willing to go along with it for the sake of national security and the threat of being dominated by an outside power. Now there is no need for such centralized control." In his Birmingham speech on 12 May 1904, Joseph Chamberlain predicted: "The day of small nations has long passed away. The day of empires has come." Fortunately this has not been borne out. The rise of the nation-state has seen the return of a plethora of legally identified "small nations" that has assisted the renewed salience of local ethnic identities.

In China, for perhaps the first time in history, there is no longer any real perceived national security threat from her neighbors: the Soviets, Vietnamese, Indians, Japanese, Taiwanese, or even the British colonial authority in Hong Kong. All outside powers have fully accepted Chinese sovereignty. Even China's right to rule Tibet has not been called into question by the United Nations. The encirclement doctrine, upon which Nixon and Kissinger constructed the Sino-American normalization, is no longer relevant to current geopolitical relations. It ended with Gorbachev's visit to Beijing. It is no coincidence, then, that the students, and the broader citizenry, chose that moment to call for greater individual autonomy. The nationalities, having sought this for many decades, gladly joined in, and may have helped lead the way.

ETHNIC PLURALISM IN CHINESE SOCIETY

The conquest of the earth, which mostly means the taking of it away from those who have a different complexion or slightly flatter noses than ourselves, is not a pretty thing when you look into it too much. What redeems it is the idea only. An idea at the back of it; not a sentimental pretence, but an idea; and an unselfish belief in the idea—something you can set up, and bow down before, and offer a sacrifice to.

—*Joseph Conrad,* The Heart of Darkness

Traditional approaches to the study of ethnic minorities in China have stressed their assimilation into Chinese culture, their "Sinicization".[48] Certainly, a give and take will occur wherever two cultural traditions interact. However, in the case of the Han, this has become the accepted idea, in Conrad's sense, that is rarely seriously challenged: Ethnic change in China is assumed to be uni-directional, the inexorable grinding down of any foreign culture that comes into contact with the mono-lithic Chinese.[49] Even studies that admit a wide cultural diversity within Chinese society are pessimistic about the possibilities of main-taining, let alone reviving, those cultures different from the Han, or considering whether these "foreign" cultures might have exerted tremen-dous influence on what we now know as "the Chinese." In their exhaus-tive and textured study of eighteenth century China, which widely discusses the place of minorities in Qing Manchu society, Naquin and Rawski conclude: "Cultural change was overwhelmingly one way."[50] This supports the general assumption that the Manchu, like other "for-eign" dynasties before them, culturally fell before the Han juggernaut. However, in her new study of the Manchu at the end of the Qing dy-nasty, Pamela Crossley rejects this conclusion as being insensitive to the complexities of "Chinese" identity, as well as Manchu. "The 'siniciza-tion' of the Manchus has been accepted as fact," Crossley states, "with too little sustained examination either of the 'sinicization' concept itself or of the particulars of Manchu existence in the later Qing period."[51] While most anthropologists have long rejected assimilationist and "melting-pot" theories of ethnic change, Crossley perceptively notes that one of the reasons it may have held sway in China studies is due to a turn in intellectual history. In 1957, Mary Wright questioned Karl Wittfogel's thesis that the conquest dynasties had not in fact been assim-ilated by the Chinese, as generally assumed. In accepting Wright's thesis that the Manchus lost their statutory place in Chinese society after the Taiping War, and that there was a "restoration" of a Confucian state, most historians readily agreed that the Manchu had become thoroughly assimilated.[52] While most scholars now reject the "restoration" hypoth-esis, they continue to assume the Manchu lost their identity with their legal privileges. By contrast, Crossley argues that this may have all the more fostered Manchu identity, particularly in the garrison areas of the cities in which they lived:

> The crystallization of Manchu ethnic identity that began under the pressures of the Taiping War had, by the first decade of the twentieth century, gained expression in a new vocabulary of ethnicity—applied by the Manchus to them-selves as the Chinese applied similar terms to themselves—and in the demand that China's imminent political reorganization should make the Manchu

homeland in the Northeast an autonomous territory, free of rule by the Chinese government.[53]

While the demand for a Manchu homeland has yet to be met, some recent progress has been made. There were no autonomous Manchu nationality administrative units set up in the 1950s when most minorities received some county-level autonomous units, and there were none as of 1982 (perhaps because of lingering resentment toward the feudal Qing empire). Since that time, 3 autonomous counties have been established in the northeast. Village after village across northern China has publicly declared itself Manchu, and the Manchu, formerly reluctant to admit their ethnicity, due, they say, to fear of "Leftist Han chauvinist" persecution, are coming out in large numbers. Though the first Chinese census in 1953 recorded only 2.4 million Manchu, and that figure had only grown to 2.6 million in 1978, by the 1982 census it had doubled to 4.3 million.[54] Since 1982, the Manchu have more than doubled their population, from 4.3 million to 9.8 million (128 percent).[55] This is an extraordinary increase in 6 years, especially considering that the Manchu are one of the few minorities who are not permitted to have more than one child. Their population increase was certainly not due to fertility!

This kind of ethnic category-shifting, where formerly registered Han reveal that they were really ethnic all along, wreaks havoc on Sinicization theory and state demographers. An overemphasis on the supposed ability of the Chinese, namely Han, culture inexorably to assimilate others has diverted attention from issues of power, state domination, and the resilience of ethnic identity. It is certainly in the interests of the regime in power to promote the idea that there is something in Chinese society that inevitably assimilates everything in its path. This perspective was best articulated in psychosocial terms by Hsien Rin in his article on the Chinese "synthesizing mind." He argued:

> In sum, the Chinese look at people in their life circumstance as a whole, and the structure of their society tends to be homogeneous. In Chinese society there is little tendency to segregate the few minority groups, either economically or geographically.[56]

This statement is so revealing of the "great Han" perspective, and so contrary to the actual situation in China, that George DeVos and Lola Romanucci-Ross, the editors of the volume in which the article appeared, felt constrained to add:

> [Communities of Hakka or Muslims, however, have separately existed for many generations.—ed.].[57]

Through focusing on the Sinicization of minorities, generally referred to in Chinese as Hanification (*Han hua*), less attention has been paid to their integration by the Chinese state (*Zhongguo hua*).

This may be one reason why the Hui have generally been overlooked in studies of Chinese society. Even though they are the largest Muslim group and the second largest minority, and have played significant roles throughout Chinese history—virtually severing the empire in half during the mid-nineteenth century Hui Rebellions, and powerbrokering in the northwest between Japanese, Nationalist, and Communist armies during the warlord era of the first half of this century—little has been written on them in the past. It was generally assumed that, if the Hui were not already Hanified, completely "Chinese" Muslims, they inevitably would be:

> Most Chinese neither think nor know much about the Hui, but the aggressive Hanification of Hui territory in the 20th century indicates to me the Chinese imperative for domination of the frontier. "Sovereign rights," "national defense," "stable borders"—such concepts have begun to eliminate the old vague distinctions between the central kingdom and the various barbarians. The traditional ways of thinking must be replaced by a coherent national identity, one which must by sheer force of numbers be a *Han* identity.[58]

This conclusion must necessarily be reached if *Chinese* is equated with *Han*, which I have argued does not necessarily have to be the case, especially given the dubious nature of Han-ness. The problem is that, for Westerners, *Chinese* is an ethnic designation. Whereas, in China, *Chinese* (*Zhongguo ren*) refers to those who live in China, minority or otherwise. Whether they like it or not, those residing in China are Chinese (citizens, at least), though perhaps not of Han ethnicity.

At times in China's history, the state certainly has attempted to assimilate those it regarded as barbarians into some notion of civilized identity. In the modern era, however, the Chinese nation-state has been predicated on the idea, if not the myth, of pluralism. In the past, hegemonic empires, many established by foreigners, may have allowed pluralism, but from it they certainly did not derive their raison d'être. If the Chinese state pursues more multi-ethnic policies, as it has officially done since 1978, then there is further hope for the Hui and other ethnic minorities. Attention to the state's role in influencing Hui identity takes us beyond positions that saw the Hui as assimilated Chinese Muslims,[59] as if there was some pure unassimilated Muslim community, defined by a reified notion of Islam in the Middle East.[60] It also helps to understand how the Hui as a collection of Muslim peoples could manage to survive for 1,200 years and evolve into their current identity.

The Sinicization paradigm also ignores the tremendous contributions Muslims and other minorities have made to Chinese culture. In the past, many regions and cities were governed by famous Muslim officials, like Sayyid 'Ajall; state expeditions were led by Muslim explorers, like Zheng He; and contributions were made to Confucian scholarship by Muslim gentry schooled in the classics, like Liu Zhi and Ma Zhu. The Muslim astronomer Jimal al-Din introduced a Western calendar to China that was used for over 400 years. The architect Ikhtiyar designed Beihai Park and much of the capital city. The famous "Hui hui cannon" was, of course, built by Muslims (the military engineers Alaw al-Din and Ismail), and had a long-term impact on the development of Chinese weaponry (which, it must be noted, they are now exporting back to the Middle East).[61] Famous Yuan and Song dynasty poets were Muslims, including Gao Kegong (A.D. 1248-1310) and Zhao Zhan, a tradition that continues today, with several Hui Muslim authors enjoying a widespread audience throughout the country, such as Gao Shen (Ningxia), Bai Chongyi (Xinjiang), Ma Zhiyao (Ningxia), Ma Li (Jilin), and Zhang Chengzhi (Beijing).[62]

Despite assumptions of Sinicization, the pluralism of the Chinese state is fundamental to its founding ideas, and one of the main subjects of the 1980 reforms; it is also one of the main planks of the Pro-Democracy Movement in China. It comes as no surprise that the minorities in Beijing flooded the streets, and that there were sympathetic outbursts in the minority regions for these reforms. Liao Gailong, summarizing the 1980 reforms in a 1981 speech, noted that a necessary concomitant of Deng's position was the need for further pluralism and nationality autonomy:

> Comrade Deng Xiaoping's speech on August 18 points out the principle for revising the constitution: our constitution must be perfected, must be clear and accurate, and must genuinely ensure that the masses of people can enjoy adequate democratic rights and the right to manage the state and various enterprises and businesses, that various *nationalities can really practice regional autonomy*, that the people's congresses at various levels will be improved, and so on. The principle of disallowing the over centralization of power will also be reflected in the constitution. These were Comrade Deng Xiaoping's words. ... In particular, we must take effective measures to *conscientiously strengthen the national autonomous power* of the autonomous regions of various nationalities and strengthen national unity. Because of the prolonged sabotage by Lin Biao and the "Gang of Four," the contradictions among nationalities are rather intense at present. In particular, we must correctly implement our policy of national autonomy in Xizang [Tibet] and Xinjiang to resolve the national contradictions in these regions.[63]

Incorporation into the Chinese state may not always have involved assimilation, but it most certainly has required efforts at legitimation. Norma Diamond has shown how the Miao (Hmong) through history have constantly adapted and reformulated their expressions of ethnic identity to local constructions of Han power and state incorporation in Yunnan.[64] Monumental efforts in the Ming dynasty to reconceptualize Islam in terms of Confucian morality and discourse certainly represent the most valiant attempt at legitimation vis-à-vis the Chinese world order by Muslims. More fundamentally, Hui efforts to present themselves as orderly, in harmony with the state and their social surroundings, have always had accommodation as the goal—*not* Sinicization.

Internal Hui Islamic debates over orthopraxy and orthodoxy reflected this struggle to be true to Islamic visions of reality while not appearing disruptive to the Chinese state. Factional disputes were often taken to Chinese courts by Hui who accused other orders as being heterodox (*xie jiao*).[65] The so-called "New Teachings" were proscribed by the state for this reason. All these movements saw themselves as reformist: *more orthodox* in terms of Islam. "Heterodox" to the Chinese state meant disorderly, factional, and, therefore, a threat—it had nothing to do with Islam. No wonder Sufi reformers sought to present themselves as more "pure," more "orthodox," than their predecessors, and, when this was not accepted by the state, they went underground—just as Buddhist sectarian organizations became secret once they threatened local authority. It is also not surprising that the Naqshbandi conflict in China took as its most symbolic focal point of contention a seemingly innocuous point of ritual: the chanting of the *dhikr*; one group (Khufiyya) maintained that silent remembrance was orderly, not confused (*luan*), while the other (Jahriyya) claimed their practice of vocal remembrance as being more true, more fundamentalist, to the dictates of their order. Even so, the chanting of remembrance I have observed in China tends to be more restrained, more controlled, with less evidence of dancing, trance, or glossolalia than Sufi practice elsewhere in the Muslim world—evidence of a preoccupation with order in a Chinese state that feared anything it could not control.

There is nothing inherently secret or rebellious to Sufism. Some Sufis, not all, became violent against the state in China only when their survival was at stake. It is interesting that Islamic associations (what Lipman terms "solidarities") are translated as "factions" in China (*jiao pai*).[66] The creation of the Sufi *menhuan* in China, and its basis in lineage, may have had just as much to do with the need to form sociopolitical institutions vis-à-vis the Chinese state as with Chinese preoccupations with inheritance and hierarchical family organization. The *Xi Dao Tang*, a non-Sufi Chinese-oriented reform movement, was virtually annihilated by a Hui official in the Qing government who perceived it as a commercial and political threat. This had very little to do with religion or issues of cultural assimilation. It had much more to do with material aggrandizement and survival in the harsh environment of Northwest China.

THE WIDE EXPRESSION OF HUI IDENTITY. The diverse expression of the Muslim communities now recognized as Hui *minzu* may be seen as attempts to preserve ethnic integrity and identity in dialectical interaction with the state and other oppositional ethnicities in each local sociopolitical context. For Hui communities in Northwest China, Islam is taken by the Hui as the fundamental marker of their identity—to be

Hui is to be Muslim. Islam becomes the signifying practice of identity. The meaning of *qing zhen* for these Hui is expressed in Islamic ritual purity. Islamic movements have arisen in these communities as Hui reformers sought to resolve the tensions created by adapting the ideals of *qing zhen* to the Chinese social world. Government policy that permits freer expression of Hui ethnic identity has also allowed the resurgence of Islam. In response to the rerooting of Hui identity in Islam, local government cadres have reformulated central policies in recognition of the important place of Islam in northwestern Hui identity.

In southeastern Hui lineages, genealogical descent is the most important aspect of Hui identity—to be Hui is to be a member of a lineage that traces its descent to foreign Muslim ancestors. The concept of *qing zhen* for these Hui on the southeast coast is embodied in the veracity of their claims to foreign ancestry. Recent state recognition of these lineages as members of the Hui nationality has led to ethnic resurgence among previously unrecognized Hui lineages throughout the nation. In turn, contact with state-sponsored Hui and foreign Muslim delegations has led to a growing interest for many of these Hui in their ethnoreligious roots, and even in practicing Islam.

Hui urban communities tend to express their identity in terms of cultural traditions such as the pork tabu, entrepreneurship, and craft specializations. For these Hui, *qing zhen* means the cultural maintenance of those markers salient to their identity. To be Hui in these urban communities is to express the purity of one's ancestral heritage through living a Hui lifestyle. This leads to the growing influence of institutions such as the restaurant in preserving and expressing Hui identity in the city. Liberalized nationality and economic policies have contributed to the cultural and economic expansion of those specializations and small businesses that most reflect urban Hui descent from Hui ancestors.

In northern rural Hui communities that are isolated among Han majority areas, ethnic identity is often expressed and perpetuated through strategies of community maintenance. One of these strategies is ethnic endogamy. To be Hui in these communities is to be ensconced in a community that expresses its foreign Muslim ancestry through the maintenance of a tradition of endogamy; *qing zhen* is expressed in maintaining the purity and cohesiveness of their community through mar-

riage with other Hui. In order to preserve *qing zhen*, Hui marriage networks extend hundreds of kilometers beyond their immediate village.
The promotion of government policies on urban migration, nationality
marriage, surname endogamy, and birth planning have led to the expansion, and in some cases contraction, of Hui endogamous practices over
time. Depending on fluctuations in government policies, Hui have
often had to go far beyond their local area to find a Hui spouse. At other
times they have been less willing to marry outside the confines of their
village, lest they disrupt the cohesion of their community. Hui community interests concerning marriage and the changes in movement of Hui
women through marriage over time reveal the important influence of
government policy on Hui identity.

I have argued in the previous chapters that the Hui people, once
members primarily of religious communities, through interacting with
changing social contexts and state policy now very much see themselves
as a bona fide ethnic group. Their solidarity is clearly seen when conceptions of ethnic identity do not become preoccupied with the search for
a set of static or common cultural criteria. The diversity of ethnic
expressions found among the four communities discussed reveals that
Hui identity is dynamically involved with and adapted to distinct social
contexts. Everywhere, however, such identity has been particularly
influenced by state policies implemented at the local level. Hui ethnic
identity is no longer meaningful solely in terms of Islam, as Israeli
would have us believe.[67] Islam was once the defining characteristic of
Hui-ness in China. Now it is only one marker of that identity. In a letter from the Protestant missionary Martin Taylor to Claude Pickens,
dated 17 October 1936, he wrote in reference to a convert, Wang Hui-
zeng, that, though Wang "used to be a huei huei . . . now he was a Christian." This indicates that Wang, once he converted, was no longer
thought of as a Hui. I knew of two cases in Changying and Najiahu
where former Han villagers were now known as Hui. However, though
this was true in the past, recent Han converts to Islam in China, as I was
told by Yang Yongchang of the China Islamic Association, could no
longer be considered Hui. They should properly be referred to as "Han
Muslims." I was also freequently told by Hui informants that, though
a Han could conceivably convert to Islam and become a Hui, as had

happened in the past, a Hui could never become a Han, no matter what he or she did. The Hui in Quanzhou, who no longer believe in Islam and violate Islamic dietary restrictions, certainly attest to this new social reality. The Hui have moved from being a religious community to an ethnic nationality. While Islam is intimately related to Hui ancestry, as we have seen in Na Homestead, it may not always be as salient to Hui ethnic expression in every social context, as in Quanzhou. Yet Islam cannot be ignored or divorced from Hui identity either, as the state has attempted to do in the past. We must look at each Hui community, its interests, involvements, and dialogue with the state in specific contexts before coming to a more consistent understanding of Hui identity.

In each context, Hui will stress those markers of identity, those signifying practices, that most express to themselves, and to the salient others with whom they are in dialogue, their unique ethnicity. I was surprised to find that the Hui in Xinjiang tend to stress their origins inside the pass of China proper.[68] Not only do they not take on Central Asian Muslim characteristics in dress, language, and lifestyle, but Hui mosques noticeably symbolize their origins in Gansu, Ningxia, and Shaanxi. Rarely inscribed with Quranic verses outside the main prayer hall, like other Central Asian mosques, they instead are labeled in Chinese, and their names reflect their places of origin, similar to *tongxiang hui* (same-village societies) among the overseas Chinese communities. The title of one mosque, the Ning Gu Si, reveals in its first two characters that it is from *Ning*-xia, *Gu*-yuan county, where the people originating from that region worship. The largest Hui mosque in Urumqi is the Shaanxi Great Mosque, and it is ensconced in a neighborhood of Hui who migrated to Xinjiang from Shaanxi, beginning in the early part to this century.

In a recent fascinating paper, Boris Riftin, the Soviet folklorist and scholar of Dungan [Hui] literature in Soviet Central Asia, gives several textual examples of how the Dungans in Kirghizia emphasize their Chinese origins in their local folklore. By contrast, analysis of popular mythology among the Hui in China proper (Gansu, Ningxia, Shaanxi, and Henan), revealed a literature devoted to Quranic and Islamic figures and themes. Riftin concludes:

We can say then in general peculiarly Muslim features are characteristic for the folklore of the Huizu living in China and only a very small degree for the folklore of the Soviet Dungans. . . . The Huizu in China, living amidst the Chinese and not always in compact groups, can stress their ethnic identity practically only through Muslim practices and beliefs. But the Soviet Dungans, living in Kazakhstan and Kirghizia, surrounded by other Muslim peoples, differ from them not only by their language and by some elements of traditional life common with the Chinese (e.g., they have fans of the Chinese type), but also by stressing in their folk-lore peculiarly Far-Eastern, in the last analysis Chinese or common with the Chinese, plots (e.g., meeting the king of dragons) and images (dragons, all sorts of evil spirits: gui, yaoguai, jing, etc.).[69]

These Dungan were originally from Gansu, but their religious and ethnic practice, their symbolic representations of themselves in folklore, dress, and ritual, had altered in their new Central Asian context. The Hui, to preserve their ethnoreligious distinctiveness in Xinjiang, like their brethren in Soviet Central Asia, stress those elements of their identity that set them apart from the Uigur and other Muslim peoples of Xinjiang. Thus, in their clothing, architecture, language, and even folklore, we find that they emphasize continuities with their place of most recent origin, China inside the pass. This is not cultural assimilation. It represents shifts in cultural style, power oppositions, and dialogic interplay within a new sociopolitical environment.

THE EXTENSIVE UNITY OF HUI IDENTITY. While I have found remarkable diversity among the Hui, it has also been established that they regard themselves as "one family under Heaven," and one "united nationality." The idea that all Hui are one people becomes particularly meaningful when called into question by radical shifts in socioeconomic contexts. It became especially relevant to many Hui when they migrated from different backgrounds to Taiwan with the Nationalists in the late-1940s. Pillsbury reports that this idea of a common familial affinity sustained and united this diverse community:

It is significant that the complex of sentiments underlying this expression was able to function as a common denominator of so large a population of such heterogeneous background. In terms of geographical origins, these Muslims came from all four corners of China — Manchuria and Yunnan, Sinkiang and

Fukien—thousands of miles, and not long ago, many months' journey apart. They came from diverse linguistic groups, many speaking dialects (such as Cantonese and Mandarin) or even languages (Chinese and Uighur) which are mutually non-intelligible. They came from tiny villages and cities as large as six million. They represented occupational backgrounds as diverse as rice farmer, merchant, camel driver, pastoral herder, school teacher, provincial governor and military general.[70]

Various religious and socioeconomic networks that link disparate Hui communities together have been mentioned in this study. These networks deserve further research. They support and reinforce Hui shared ideas of a common ancestry. Religious networks include links between Sufi leaders and the appointed members of their orders, extending hierarchically from the *murshid* through his personally chosen *reyisi* and ahong to the individual follower (*mulide*). Non-Sufi religious networks are often established by influential ahong who attract students from all over China, as we have seen for Linxia, Gansu, and Weishan, Yunnan. Itinerant Hui book salesmen who travel throughout China peddling the Quran and popular religious works reveal the importance of these religious and trade networks. As purveyors of information about distant Hui communities, these peripatetic Hui are another example of the tenuous ties between Hui communities. Social networks developed through the exchange of women in marriage also link isolated Hui communities. We have seen that one village, Changying, has built contacts through establishing and maintaining affinal ties with distant Hui villages located hundreds of kilometers away, contacts often initiated and maintained by the itinerant ahong.

Socioeconomic networks linking Hui communities were strongest before 1949 in the wool and leather long-distance trade, which the Hui dominated along the Yellow River throughout the north, and along the Burma Road in the southwest. Smaller-scale trade networks have re-emerged in recent years with policies allowing freer participation in the market economy. Hui tradesmen from the northwest are found throughout China, selling carpets and sundry factory goods in Lhasa, buying tea in Yunnan, ordering textiles in Shanghai, and trading money in Beijing. In each place they travel, mosques and newly established private *qing zhen* restaurants are the nodes in the extended network that sustains them.

State incorporation has contributed much to this process of ethnogenesis. The construction of roads, improved telecommunications, and establishment of national representative organizations have brought the formerly isolated Hui communities together as never before. State-sponsored associations whose purpose was to carry out state policies and improve nationality conditions, such as the Nationality Affairs Commission, the Nationalities Institutes, and the Chinese Islamic Association, are also playing important roles in the establishment of Hui networks and the strengthening of a transnational pan-Hui identity. While the Nationalities Institutes were set up to educate the minorities in Han culture, incorporating the future nationality leaders into the Han vision of the state, they have often led to the building of national associations among minorities who have come from around the country to study. Rather than assimilate into the Han, the students tend to keep to their own minority groups. Throughout China, Hui can subscribe to the periodicals *China's Muslims (Zhongguo Musilin)* and *Muslim World (Musilin shijie)*, receiving them in one's town or village through an incredibly efficient postal system. These state-sponsored organizations endorse the unity of Hui identity, and facilitate the building of relationships among Hui throughout China. The China Islamic Association has reported that, from 1980–1987, it had organized 25 delegations of 73 members to Islamic countries, hosted 36 groups from more than 20 countries and regions, sponsored over 2,000 pilgrims on the 1986 Hajj, trained over 129 *manla* Islamic students from 6 nationalities at the Chinese Islamic Theological College (*jingxue yuan*) in Beijing from over 27 provinces and regions, sent 10 students to study at the Al-Azhar in Egypt in 1982, with a second group in 1986, 3 of whom went to Libya, and began sending students to Pakistan from Xinjiang and Gansu.[71] These state-sponsored national organizations have promoted international exchange with the Muslim world, and assisted inter-referentiality among the disparate Hui communities, which Michael Fischer suggests ethnicity may be fundamentally about.[72] These state-sponsored enterprises have contributed to the objectification and crystallization of a national ethnic group from what were once isolated "patchwork" communities and more fluid identities. Few villagers need be isolated any more.

International business networks with foreign Muslims are starting to reemerge with the establishment of state-sponsored "Hui Muslim Construction Collectives" that gain contracts in Third-World Muslim countries. Recent trade agreements between Xinjiang and bordering Soviet Central Asian republics will cause import-export volume to grow 75.6 percent in 1987.[73] While local trade is dominated mainly by Turkic-speaking Muslims, Hui in Xinjiang say they hope to participate as much as possible, and have already reestablished contacts with their Dungan relatives in the Soviet Central Asian Republics of Kazakhstan and Kirghizia. International ties are beginning to be reestablished with the Islamic world as more Hui are undertaking the Hajj and state-sponsored foreign Muslim delegations visit rural Hui areas. The advent of Islamic tourism in China has literally redrawn the map for foreign Muslims and exposed local Hui to international Islam as never before.

Before 1949, several of these networks were nonexistent, and many of them were disrupted in the early 1950s. Their reemergence and the effect they are having on Hui identity are a result of liberalized economic and nationality policies. Many of them came together in the Salman Rushdie protest, which began at the Central Institute for Nationalities, and received encouragement and approval from the Chinese Islamic Association, the State Commission for Nationality Affairs, and even visiting foreign Muslim dignitaries, such as Iran's President Khameini. The incident illustrates the nationalism and transnationalism of China's fourth tide of Muslim identity. The creation of a pan-ethnic identity is intimately tied to these transnational organizations and movements, as they have furthered Hui ethnogenesis, the reconceptualization of local identities in terms of a broader imagined community.

THE DIALECTICS OF NATIONALITY POLICY AND HUI IDENTITY

Contrasting Nationalist and Communist policies toward the Hui are an important illustration of Hui interaction with different social contexts created by different policies. In Taiwan, Hui identity is regarded solely in terms of religion. Thus, for the Taiwanese Muslims who no longer practice Islam, Hui identity has no tangible relevance. Hui who came from the mainland have sought to adapt themselves to this policy, express their Islamic identity, and, at the same, time continue to emphasize the ethnic and blood differences that distinguish them from the Han.[74] In the PRC, the Hui are free to express their identity without reference to religion. At one time, ethnic expression was encouraged to the point of excluding religious expression, and Hui Islamic identity was suppressed. Now that freer religious expression has been allowed, Islamic resurgence has taken place in those areas where Islam is the most salient expression of Hui ethnoreligious identity. Even where Islam is no longer of central importance to local Hui identity, however, Islam has begun to take on new meaning, as we have seen among Hui lineages on the southeast coast. In both Taiwan and mainland China, the state has attempted to define Hui identity in terms of its own state ideology. In response, the Hui in both places have reformulated their own ethnic ideologies in dialogical fashion in order to preserve and express their identity.

In his illuminating discussion of Geertz's approach to ideology and utopia, Paul Ricoeur discusses the role of ideology as the integration or preservation of identity:

> Even if we separate off the other two layers of ideology—ideology as distortion and as the legitimation of a system of order or power—the integrative function of ideology, the function of preserving an identity, remains. It may be that our regressive analysis can go no further, because no group and no individual are possible without this integrative function.[75]

Ideology as power has been the focus of Michel Foucault's study of the "modes of objectification which transform human beings into subjects." One of these modes is the process in which the subject is "either divided against himself or divided from others."[76] The past divisive policies that were promulgated under a state ideology that pitted minority against majority, and Hui against Han, have been repudiated by the present state council. The reversal of these policies has led to a new dynamic process of ethnic expression and objectification. Hui identity is once again being transformed in the process. The state accepts the idea of Hui identity for its own purposes of integration and nation-building. The Hui adapt and manipulate this policy for purposes of self-preservation. Through the dialogical interaction of the two, Hui identity is formed and altered.

The state reconstructs mosques and historic Islamic sites as places for tourism and religious pilgrimage for the Hui and foreign Muslims. As a result, local Hui identity often becomes expanded in its perspective. Hui villagers, many for the first time, experience participation in the national and international Islamic world. Expanded awareness of the importance of Islam to Hui identity leads local government officials to revise policies that had previously encouraged a stricter distinction between ethnicity and religion. Many of these policies were originally intended to encourage economic development and the Four Modernizations. In the process, they have allowed freer religious expression of Hui identity. With this resurgence of ethnoreligious identity, socioeconomic development has also improved.

This dialectic is illustrated well by shifts in policies toward Hui entrepreneurism. Once criticized as "capitalist tails" who thrived on business ventures, the Hui were constantly accused as maintaining feudalist, anti-socialist, and exploitative practices. At the 1987 Congress of the Chinese People's Political Consultative Conference, a delegate called for the minorities to have a "freer hand in their own affairs."[77] While the stated purpose of increased minority autonomy is to help stimulate the local economy, it has also led, in a dialectical fashion, to the further resurgence of ethnic identities. In a recent interview, Fei Xiaotong suggested that socioeconomic development of minority areas would be enhanced if the minorities themselves played a greater role. Minority participation in economic development should be encouraged, rather than continuing the former policies of providing government assistance to minority areas and promoting minority customs, such as traditional songs and dances. Professor Fei specifically suggested that Hui entrepreneurial talents should be given more freedom in order to assist the expansion of local market economies:

> In July and August last year, I visited Linxia Hui Autonomous Prefecture, Gansu Province, during which I was deeply impressed by the fact that the Hui people there are very smart traders. They have been blessed with this talent from their ancestors, who nurtured trading skills during centuries-long commercial dealings between farmers and herdsmen. This tradition has been developed mainly due to their geographical locations, which are inserted between the Qinghai-Tibet Plateau inhabited by nomadic groups and the

country's farming areas. . . . I think that the Hui people might play a significant role in the development of these two regions.[78]

This recognition of the unique contribution Hui entrepreneurial abilities might make to economic development is a significant shift from past criticisms of these characteristics as capitalistic and feudal. A new Islamic college recently set up in Xi'an advertized courses in small business and "Muslim entrepreneurism" as well as improved opportunities for foreign travel that training in Arabic and Persian would provide. That the market is, and always has been, an important focal point for the expression of Hui identity may have less to do with any inherent cultural characteristics than it has to do with issues of power and state control. Ann Anagnost has recently argued that it is in the free market that the state exercises the least control, and this is why it has always posed a threat to the state, providing a space for alternative constructions of power, ritual fairs, and ethnic identity.[79] For the Hui, the market provides a public sphere for autonomous expression within the hegemony of the Chinese state.

Now that the state once again has promoted policies favorable to the Hui and other minorities, there has been a resurgence in those aspects of ethnic identity most relevant in each social context. In China, people now want to be ethnic, or at least members of a minority nationality. Children of mixed marriages choose to be registered as a minority. Han young people in Beijing are willing, and perhaps even prefer, to find minority spouses. While autonomous regions, counties, and villages were thought to possess little real autonomy, this study has shown that enough benefits are attached to them for people to want them. Not only in Chendai, Fujian, where the Ding have applied for recognition as an autonomous county, but throughout China autonomous administrative units have become important issues in contemporary ethnopolitics. In China, as well as the USSR, autonomy may not mean much, but it does give people a voice in the political process and a legal wedge by which to push for social change. This is the kind of voice the students were calling for in Tiananmen Square, and the Muslims expressed in the Rushdie protest.

ETHNICITY AND NATIONALISM IN THE PEOPLE'S REPUBLIC

Understanding of the Hui and other ethnicities in China in the past has been hampered by models and policies that could not account for the wide diversity and present unity of ethnic expression. Models that relied on a cultural-trait analysis, such as the Stalinist and cultural approaches, do not begin to account for the dynamic context and politicized nature of ethnicity in China. In the example of the Hui, these models foundered on the similarity between Hui and Han, and on the diversity found within the Hui. Although the Hui did not fit the Stalinist model, the government chose to recognize them on the basis of prerevolutionary ideas for the political goals of incorporation and state-building, in a careful rewriting of history. Utilitarian situational approaches had trouble with the continued meaningfulness and power of ethnic identity in the face of hegemonic oppression. Attention to power relations in the ongoing dialectic between the state and local ethnic groups, both externally and internally, is critical for our understanding of the current resurgence of ethnic identities, their significance, and salience in the modern world. Foucault reminds us that the state is compelled to address a plethora of nonnegotiables:

> The state is superstructural in relation to a whole series of power networks that invest the body, sexuality, the family, kinship, knowledge, technology and so forth. True, these networks stand in a conditioning-conditioned relationship to a kind of "meta-power" which is structured essentially round a certain number of great prohibition functions; but this meta-power, with its prohibitions, can only take hold and secure its footing where it is rooted in a whole series of multiple and indefinite power relations that supply the necessary basis for the great negative forms of power.[80]

Ethnicity is one meta-power that is constantly negotiated between state and self: The dialogue is ongoing and regularly redefined in changing social contexts. The role of the state must not be over-privileged. Even the most totalitarian of regimes has its limits. Ethnic identity has a power and resilience of its own that acts in dialectical fashion with the state apparatus. At the same time, ethnicity itself need not be over-essentialized. Peoples disappear, or merge into other groups through processes of ethnogenesis. The emphasis here is upon relations, not essences.

The state has the power to rewrite history, to colonize it, and attempt to control it through the editing of textbooks, the locking of libraries, and the censoring of the press. It cannot, however, control historical memory. Icons of ethnic history are not easily dislodged from the imaginations of minority peoples. The state can attempt to define art, by strictly monitoring what is displayed in museums and what is collected or burned. An official in the Ministry for Art and Culture of the Ningxia autonomous region told me the reason they did not collect the extraordinary Arabic-Chinese calligraphic representations that only the Hui produce was: "They are not art. They are religious items." And yet, in the free market and in the home, this genre is flourishing. Perhaps most dramatically in China, the state has exercised, in Foucault's words, "the hegemonic power over language." "Standard speech" (*putong hua*) has followed the ideograph as the most effective state-imposed means of national control throughout Chinese history. Yet declaring that Cantonese, Sichuanese, and Shanghainese are but dialects has not stopped anyone from continuing to speak them—and to think their own thoughts in them. Among the minorities, language reform has meant the creation of some, the rewriting of others, and the loss of many vernaculars. Yet, for those groups that take language as the main marker of their ethnicity, much has been preserved. They have just added another, which helps mainly in dechipering what's on the television set.

Hui identity is rooted in the idea, factual or fictitious, of descent from foreign Muslim ancestors. This idea links all Hui together—religious and non-religious, ahong and cadre, farmer and factory worker—under the shared belief that "All Hui under Heaven are one family." When this shared idea of descent interacts with changing social contexts, new expressions of identity emerge in dialectical relation to the old. This leads to the wide variety of Hui ethnoreligious expression in different social settings. As I have described in the preceding discussion of four Hui communities, expressions of Hui identity and understandings of *qing zhen* will be altered and adapted to each specific context. Cultural symbols of Hui identity, such as the pork tabu, Islamic ritual, genealogy, occupational specialization, and endogamy become salient for each Hui community in the social situation where they express their ancestral heritage. Which markers of identity become salient in each context often has much to do with state policy and power. These policies are often influenced by international alignments and shifts in relations.

Since the founding of the PRC, international and strategic considerations—particularly the desire for Third-World, often Muslim, investment—have encouraged favoritism toward minorities, so that goals of pluralism and assimilation have constantly shifted, depending on local and international politics. Chinese Marxists were surprised that these identified groups did not fade away with the land reforms, collectivization, and erosion of class-based loyalties. Ethnicity is a vertical phenomenon that often cuts across class and socioeconomic stratification. It has maintained its salience despite the land-reform campaigns and other efforts to reduce class differences in Chinese and Soviet societies, which, it was thought, would lead to the disappearance of social and ethnic difference. Charles Keyes, following Max Weber, has suggested the metaphor of a gyroscope for understanding ethnicity: Rooted in constructed notions of descent and ancestry, it is constantly changing and propelled by its very dynamism. This has certainly been true for the Hui across China, and their notions of self, history, and Islam (which they translated *qing zhen*). This notion was perfectly expressed by Ma Zhu, an early Qing-dynasty scholar, who in 1681 published a work on Islam, which he titled: *Qing zhen zhi nan* (The compass of *qing zhen*).[81]

In recent years, the Hui have been significant players in China's efforts to maintain close political-economic ties with largely Muslim, Middle Eastern nations (which involve trade, development contracts, silkworms, and the like). No wonder, then, that a small protest over a minor Chinese book much less known than Salman Rushdie's garnered such a quick, vigorous response on the part of PRC officials: They immediately confiscated and destroyed all copies of the book *Sexual Customs*, fired the Shanghai editors, and required official apologies from the authors. This is reminiscent of the strong and rapid response to the 1982 Shanghai *Youth News* article that also denigrated Islam (Chapter 4). In both cases the state acted swiftly to preserve the image of fairness toward Muslims.

In the 1989 Beijing crackdown, whole university departments were closed and teachers dismissed or arrested. While many nationality students took part in the protest, actions against the Nationality Institutes were much more restrained. The Sociology Department at Beijing University was closed. The Anthropology (Ethnology) Department at the Central Institute for Nationalities was left open. Both departments had many students in the Square. This illustrates the perceived importance that nationalities have in influencing China's domestic and international relations from the point of view of the state. They have a voice to challenge accepted notions of nationality, and legitimately struggle to redefine nationalism beyond the expression of power by those who regard themselves as representatives of all the people.

As we have discovered, China's nationality policy is a "derivative discourse," combining Western, Japanese, and Soviet notions of nationalism, awkwardly constructed on top of traditional ideas of identity. The contradictions and complementarities of these discourses, mainly inculcated in China at the beginning of this century, have combined with China's traditional notion of country and race as defining nationality to produce a multi-level debate on Chinese national identity that continues to rage across the country.

As an indication that not only the Hui (and some anthropologists) are intensely interested in the question of national identity in China, in 1988 a controversial film led to an intensive debate over this question throughout the country before being banned by the government in May 1989. It may have significantly influenced the political and theatrical events leading up to the June 1989 protest.[82] The 6-segment, 4-hour film series, *River Elegy (He shang)*, aired twice in China on national television. The film seriously called into question the generally accepted tokens of Chinese identity—the Great Wall, the dragon, the Qin Emperor who first unified China, and the technological inventions of compass, paper, and gunpowder—instead revealing an interest in the racial origins of Chinese society. After reviewing China's economic backwardness, and many defeats over the last hundred years at the hands of foreign nations (many of whom made use of technologies invented by Chinese), the film's narrator states:

History chose the Chinese, but the Chinese have failed to choose history. . . . To save our civilization, we must open our door and welcome *science* and *democracy*. . . . Why is it so difficult for social change to occur in China? Perhaps it is because we always worry: If we change our ways, will we still be Chinese? It never occurs to us that, as the countries of the West underwent their many social changes during the last 300 years, no one there worried if after these changes they would still be Italian or German. *Only in China do we worry about our identity so much.*[83]

In search of the origins of Chinese identity and nationhood, the film looks back to the Yellow River, as both the cradle of Chinese civilization, and its source of disappointment. The environmental origin of the Chinese "species" becomes a sociobiological, even racial, determinant:

Where are the roots of the Chinese found? Probably every yellow-skinned Chinese knows that the Chinese nation was nurtured by the Yellow River. Yellow water, yellow earth, and yellow people, a mystic, natural connection. It is almost as if we were trying to convince the world that the yellow skin of the yellow people was dyed yellow by the Yellow River.[84]

This discourse of nationalism can be seen to have roots in Sun Yat-sen's notion of a great Chinese race, later promoted by Chiang Kai-shek and the Nationalists, to the exclusion of all ethnic diversity in China. It continues to influence the debate on ethnic nationalism today in China, and what it means to be Chinese. Contradictions in the defining the "Others" within Chinese society have finally led to a sincere questioning of "Self."

The "fourth tide" of ethnic nationalism among Muslims is caught up in the national debate over national identity. The Muslims, and other minorities, have much at stake in this debate. If it should resolve itself in a traditional Chinese racist approach, as it did in the "Han chauvinist" periods of the Cultural Revolution and Anti-Rightest Campaigns, they have much to fear. If, however, their call for pluralism has been heard, we may see a new openness throughout Chinese society, a rediscovery and reflowering of many different ethnic roots, once subsumed for nationalistic goals as merely "regional" or "sub-ethnic." While this may be a threat to an insecure rulership, it may also be the only way to engender the support of all the people of the People's Repubic without resorting to force.

As the Hui and other ethnic groups interact with local contexts, both their ethnic identity and the government policies influencing them will change. This interaction has led to the Hui emerging as a people who are an important thread in the fabric of Chinese society. The Hui are no longer "strangers in a strange land" as the Protestant missionary G. Findley Andrew suggested in the 1920s.[85] With recent favorable nationality policies that have allowed freer expression of Hui identity, special nationality privileges, and further exposure to the Islamic world, we should expect newer Hui collectivities and interpretations of *qing zhen* to emerge, and certainly, a fourth tide in Chinese Islam.

Notes
Appendixes
References
Index

Notes

PREFACE

1. Nathan Glazer and Daniel P. Moynihan, *Beyond the Melting Pot;* Manning Nash, *The Cauldron of Ethnicity.*
2. Peter Stallybrass and Allon White, *The Poetics and Politics of Transgression,* p. 5. (emphasis in the original)
3. Partha Chatterjee, *Nationalist Thought and the Colonial World: A Derivative Discourse.*
4. Clifford Geertz, "Blurred Genres: The Refiguration of Social Thought," p. 19.
5. Benedict Anderson, *Imagined Communities: Reflections on the Origins and Spread of Nationalism.*

1. MUSLIM NATIONALISM IN CHINA

1. For more information on these protests, see the sketchy but fascinating news accounts and radio broadcasts reported in the Beijing China News Agency, "Publication Ban Sought"; Beijing New China News Agency, "Government Bans Book"; China Communication Service, "'Sex Habits Book' Causes Controversy in Beijing"; China Communication Service, Hong Kong, "Writer of 'Sex Habits' Has Been Suspended for Examination"; Gansu Provincial News Agency, "Lanzhou Muslims Riot Over Publishing of Book"; *Huaqiao ribao,* "San qian Musilin xuesheng Beijing youxing"; Qinghai Provincial News Agency, "Qinghai Muslims Demand Author's Punishment"; *Shijie ribao,* "Zhongguo xinwen chubanzhe chajin *Xing Fengsu* Yi Shu"; Tokyo Kyodo, "Muslim Students Demonstrate," and "Muslim Students Decry Sacrilege." I am grateful to the Wenner-Gren Foundation for Anthropological Research that provided conference travel funding to Beijing in early 1990, which allowed me to interview many of the participants in the Rushdie protest.
2. Orville Schell, *Discos and Democracy: China in the Throes of Reform,* pp. 73–84.
3. Ke Lei and Sang Ya, eds., *Xing fengsu,* pp. 45–46, 74–75, 105–113, 130–131.

4. Except, apparently, for the uprising in Urumqi, Xinjiang, where Uigur Muslims arrested during the protest in the public square had still not been released up to one year later. This may be due to the proximity of Xinjiang to Soviet Central Asia, where Muslim nationalist movements are more of a threat to Chinese interests. It has led to increased ethnic tension in Xinjiang, as apparently only Uigur protesters were arrested, while several Hui Muslims, who the Uigur claimed first brought the Chinese book *Sexual Customs* to the local Uigurs' attention, were not prosecuted. For Hui and Uigur relations in Xinjiang, and intra-Muslim conflict in China, see Dru Gladney, "Pivotal Pawns? Hui-Uigur Relations and Ethnoreligious Identity in Xinjiang," and Andrew D. W. Forbes, *Warlords and Muslims in Chinese Central Asia.*

5. Gansu Provincial News Agency, "Lanzhou Muslims Riot Over Publishing of Book," p. 59.

6. *The Economist,* "Beijing's Copycat Scandal"; *Los Angeles Times,* "Chinese Muslims Protest 'Sex Habits' Book"; *New York Times,* "Muslim Students March in Beijing: 2,500 Protest a Book that they say Blasphemes Islam."

7. For Joseph Fletcher's discussion of the "three tides" of Islam in China, see "The Sufi paths (*ṭuruq*) in China." A discussion of these three tides follows.

8. Rudolf Löwenthal, "The Mohammedan Press in China," pp. 242–246.

9. Barbara Pillsbury, "China's Muslims in 1989: Forty Years Under Communism," pp. 6–7.

10. Liu Zekuan, "Huijiaoren weishenma bu chi zhurou," p. 14. See also Ibrahim T. Y. Ma, "Weishenma bu chi zhu rou," and Ma Jian, "Huimin weishenma bu chi zhurou?"

11. A translation of the document is presented in Appendix A.

12. Anderson, pp. 46–49.

13. While much ink has been spilt on the Rushdie incident, and several have noted the transnational implications of the event (Gyatri Spivak, "Reading *The Satanic Verses*"; Charles Taylor, "The Rushdie Controversy"; Peter van der Veer, "Satanic or Angelic? The Politics of Religious and Literary Inspiration"), nowhere do we find, even in the recent wide-ranging compilation of the articles surrounding the event by Lisa Appignanesi and Sara Maitland, *The Rushdie File,* speculation regarding the possibility of the Rushdie scandal's being mimicked effectively elsewhere by Muslims with local complaints, as in China, though I suspect this will not be an isolated example.

14. See Arjun Appadurai, "Disjuncture and Difference in the Global Cultural Economy."

15. Mayfair Mei-Hui Yang, "The Gift Economy and State Power in China," p. 26.

16. Chatterjee.

17. Clifford Geertz, "The Integrative Revolution: Primordial Sentiments and Civil Politics in the New States."

18. Qinghai Provincial News Agency, "Qinghai Muslims Demand Author's Punishment," p. 53 (emphasis mine).

19. For excellent recent summaries of Soviet nationality policy and ethnology, see Julian Bromiley and Viktor Kozlov, "The Theory of Ethnos and Ethnic Processes in Soviet Social Sciences"; Regina E. Holloway, "The Study of Ethnicity: An Overview"; Rasma Karklins, *Ethnic Relations in the USSR: The Perspective From Below;* and Teodor Shanin "Ethnicity in the Soviet Union: Analytical Perceptions and Political Strategies." While the borrowed and limited Chinese term *minzu* conflates the categories of identity, Soviet ethnological vocabulary distinguished in Russian between *ethnos, nationalnost,* and *narodnost* (roughly equivalent to ethnicity, nationality, and peoplehood). For the changing usage in Chinese, see Wang Mingfu, "'Minzu' bian." Soviet ethnology in the 1960s began to move away from essentializing studies of "primitive minority customs" to more processual and historical studies of ethnogenesis and ethnic change, but this had little influence on Chinese ethnology due the breakdown in Sino-Soviet relations.

20. Quoted from a 19th-century Chinese Muslim tract, in Marshall Broomhall, *Islam in China,* pp. 304–305.

21. Clifford Geertz, *Islam Observed: Religious Development in Morocco and Indonesia,* p. 79.

22. Mildred Cable and Francesca French, *The Gobi Desert,* p. 72.

23. Donald D. Leslie, *The Survival of the Chinese Jews,* p. 102.

24. Ma Shouqian, "Yisilanjiao zai Zhongguo weishenmo you chengwei Huijiao huo Qingzhenjiao?" p. 156.

25. Yang Yongchang, *Mantan Qingzhensi.*

26. Ma Shouquian, "Yisilanjiao."

27. Henri M. G. d'Ollone, *Recherches sur les Musulmans Chinois.*

28. G. G. Warren, "D'Ollone's Investigations on Chinese Moslems," pp. 406–407.

29. *Ci Yuan,* III, 1817.

30. In Ma Shouqian "Yisilanjiao," p. 157.

31. See Dru C. Gladney and Ma Shouqian, "Interpretations of Islam in China: A Hui Scholar's Perspective."

32. Robert Henry Matthews, *Matthews's Chinese-English Dictionary.*

33. Ibid.

34. Vernon Fowler, "The Truth about Zhen," p. 41.

35. I am grateful to Prof. Farhat Ziadeh for his suggestion of *tahára* as the best Arabic approximation of the Chinese *qing zhen.*

36. Louis Dumont, *Homo Hierarchicus,* pp. 59–60.

37. Marvin Harris, *The Rise of Anthropological Theory,* pp. 366–370, and Roy A. Rappaport, *Pigs for the Ancestors,* p. 78.

38. Mary Douglas, *Purity and Danger: An Analysis of the Concepts of Pollution and Taboo,* pp. 122–128.

39. Arnold van Gennep, *Tabou et Totemism à Madagascar,* p. 314. See Michael
    Lambeck's discussion of van Gennep's approach to tabu and its usefulness for
    understanding embodiment in Africa, in "Taboo as Cultural Practice in
    Mayotte."
40. Ahmad Salah Jamjoom, "Notes on a Visit to Mainland China," p. 208.
41. Victor Turner, *The Forest of Symbols,* p. 50.
42. Stuart E. Thompson, "Death, Food, and Fertility," p. 73. In his perceptive treat-
    ment of the symbolic structural relations between the offerings and prestations
    of rice and pork in Taiwanese funerary rituals, Thompson argues that it is
    meat, and especially pork, that is by far the most important ritual element in
    offerings to the ancestors and gods: "The transformation from ghost to ancestor
    is both marked and accomplished by the switch in food prestations. There is a
    shift from *ts'ai-fan* to *sheng-li,* which is also a shift from rice to pork. Concom-
    itantly, those said to be chiefly responsible for providing the offerings switch
    from agnates to affines," p. 86.
43. Julia Kristeva, *Powers of Horror: An Essay on Abjection.*
44. Emile Durkheim, *The Elementary Forms of the Religious Life,* pp. 52–57. For a
    classic anthropological analysis of the ecological basis for the pork tabu, see
    Rappaport.
45. I use the term *ethnoreligious* to refer to this perspective of the Hui as it expresses
    both ethnic and religious commitments. This avoids the problem of attempting
    invidious distinctions between ethnicity and religious ideology, as has been
    often proposed in China's nationality policy (see Chapter 3).
46. Bernard S. Cohn, "The Census, Social Structure and Objectification in South
    Asia," p. 230.
47. Judith Banister, personal communication.
48. Sun Yat-sen, *The Three Principles of the People,* pp. 23–25, cited in H. Yuan Tien,
    China's Population Struggle, pp. 7–9.
49. For excellent introductions to the early history of Islam in China, see especially
    Donald Leslie *Islam in Traditional China;* Jonathan N. Lipman, "The Border
    World of Gansu, 1895–1935," pp. 288–299; Ma Qicheng, "A Brief Account of
    the Early Spread of Islam in China"; Imke Mees, *Die Hui–Eine moslemische
    Minderheit in China;* Nakada Yoshinobu, *Kaikai minzoku no shomondai;* P.
    Dabry de Thiersant, *Le Mahométisme en Chine et dans le Turkestan Oriental;* Bar-
    bara Pillsbury, "Muslim History in China: A 1300-year Chronology." Morris
    Rossabi, *China and Inner Asia from 1368 to the Present Day,* provides a seminal
    introduction to the complex history of Inner Asia. For Inner Asia in general,
    see Denis Sinor, *Inner Asia: A Syllabus.* For a helpful overview, and for pre-13th
    century, see his recent definitive edited volume, *The Cambridge History of Early
    Inner Asia.* For the incorporation of Inner Asia by China in the 18th and 19th
    centuries, see Joseph Fletcher's "Ch'ing Inner Asia c.1800." For an excellent

recent review of the early sources, see François Aubin, "Chinese Islam: In Pursuit of its Sources."

50. Ma Shouqian, "Yisilanjiao," p. 156.

51. Most of these terms derived from early Chinese descriptions of the Middle East, such as found in Du Huan's Tang-dynasty travelogue, *Jing xing ji* (Record of scriptural travels; see Gladney and Ma). That Arabia was known as early as the 7th century in China as the land of the "Celestial Square" certainly reflects early Chinese knowledge of the importance of the Kaba Stone to Arabs and Muslims. See J. V. G. Mills's marvelous translation of a Ming-dynasty Muslim's account of travels to the "Western Shores" in *Ma Huan, Ying-yai Sheng-lan: "The Overall Survey of the Western Shores" (1433)*. For a survey of early Chinese knowledge of and expeditions to the Middle East, see Leslie, *Islam in Traditional China*, pp. 20–27.

52. Early Muslim accounts, interpretations, and legends of their history in China, the late Ming and Qing classical Chinese Islamic texts have been collected in an extremely useful compendium, *Compilation of Hui and Islamic Chinese Classical Documents (Huizu he Zhongguo Yisilanjiao guji ziliao Huibian)*, of 9 volumes with over 65 individual books (*juan*), available from the publication office of the Ningxia Academy of Social Sciences, Yinchuan City, Ningxia Hui autonomous region. Useful compendia also include the *Hui History Collection 1949–79*, 712 pages, published in 1979, and the 2-volume, *Chinese Islamic Historical Research Materials 1911–49 (Zhongguo Yisilanjiao shi cankao ziliao)*, 1,824 pages, published in 1985. Both were published by the Ningxia Nationalities Publishing Society. In *Hui hui minzu bian Huaxia* (The spread of the Hui hui nationality in China), the Gansu Provincial Nationalities Affairs Commission has compiled interesting earlier accounts of the Hui in Ningxia, Gansu, Henan, Yunnan, Hebei, Shandong, Qinghai, Xinjiang, Guizhou, Liaoning, Guangxi, Hubei, Guangdong, and Lhasa.

53. Morris Rossabi, *Khubilai Khan*, p. 71. See also François Thierry, "Empire and Minority in China," p. 83. Ch'en Yüan, *Western and Central Asians in China*, p. 2, suggests that the Yuan classified the population according to conquest; thus the people in Yunnan and Sichuan, who were conquered last, were known as Han *ren*. "Southerners" referred to the people living in present-day Fujian, Zhejiang, Jiangxi, Guanzhou, Hunan, Guizhou, Guangxi, Jiangsu, Anhui, and Hubei. People who did not live under the rule of the Jin or Song were referred to as Han in his view. It is noteworthy that the classification of peoples by the Yuan may have been according to political, not cultural, criteria.

54. For a recent discussion of the earliest appearance of the term *Hui-hui* in a Southern Song dynasty (960–1127) text, see Tang Kaijian, "*Meng xi bi tan* zhong 'Hui hui'—ci zai shi," pp. 73–74, who concludes that the term probably referred to a variety of peoples, including the Uigur and other Central Asians, under the

Western Xia dynasty (1034–1224), and later was more narrowly defined under the Mongols to refer to Muslims. For further discussion of the origin of the term *Hui* to indicate Muslims in China, see Leslie, *Islam in Traditional China,* p. 196; Lipman, "The Border World of Gansu," pp. 288–295; and Barbara Pillsbury, "The Muslim Population of China: Clarifying the Question of Size and Ethnicity."

55. William Samolin, *East Turkistan to the Twelfth Century: A Brief Political Survey,* p. 73.

56. Barbara Pillsbury, "Blood Ethnicity: Maintenance of Muslim Identity in Taiwan," p. 45.

57. Bai Shouyi, *Huizu, Huijiao, Huimin Lunji.*

58. Walker Connor, *The National Question in Marxist-Leninist Theory and Strategy,* p. 53, quotes the following statement by Stalin in 1923 that revealed his early intention of passing on their nationality policy to China: "We must here, in Russia, in our federation, solve the national problem in a correct, *a model way,* in order to set an example to the East, which represents the heavy reserves of our revolution." (emphasis in original)

59. Barbara Pillsbury, "Cohesion and Cleavage in a Chinese Muslim Minority," p. 45.

60. Svetlana Rimsky-Korsakoff Dyer, *Soviet Dungan Kolkhozes in the Kirghis SSR and the Kazakh SSR.*

61. Moshe Yegar, "The Panthay (Chinese Muslims) of Burma and Yunnan."

62. Sinor, p. 47.

63. The situation is even further confused by references to minorities in China as *non-Chinese* (e.g., see Franz Michael's discussion of "Non-Chinese Nationalities and Religious Communities" in *Human Rights in China,* pp. 269ff). While *Chinese* is often used to indicate an ethnic group outside of China, within China it refers to all citizens of the People's Republic, with the Han as the majority nationality. Though Tibetans, Uigurs, and Mongols certainly do not see themselves as Chinese culturally, and may even object to being considered Chinese citizens as part of the Chinese nation-state, this is nevertheless as of now a *fait accompli.*

64. See Dru C. Gladney, "The Ethnogenesis of the Uigur."

65. Cohn.

66. Raphael Israeli, *Muslims in China,* p. 122.

67. Cited in Fletcher, "The Taylor-Pickens Letters on the Jahri Branch of the Naqshbandiyya in China," p. 6. For a description of the 1933 Samuel Zwemer trip across China with Claude Pickens, see Pickens, "Across China in Two Weeks." For discussions of Protestant missions to Muslims in China, see François Aubin, "*L'apostolat protestant en milieu musulman chinois*"; and Mees, pp. 44–55.

68. Lila Abu-Lughod, "Zones of Theory in the Anthropology of the Arab World," pp. 278–280. See also Arjun Appadurai's "Theory in Anthropology: Center and Periphery," for a discussion of the hierarchical notion of place in social science, that some places define the center of discourse by which social scientists pass judgment on the "authenticity" of other places, or peoples, on the periphery.

69. Dale F. Eickelman and James Piscatori, *Muslim Travellers: Pilgrimage, Migration and the Religious Imagination,* p. 12.

70. Wulsin, "Non-Chinese Inhabitants of the Province of Kansu, China." Some of the more than 2,000 photographs of Wulsin's expedition are reproduced in Mary Ellen Alonso, ed., *China's Inner Asian Frontier* with an excellent introduction to the complex cultural makeup of Chinese Inner Asia by Joseph Fletcher, "A Brief History of the Chinese Northwestern Frontier, China Proper's Northwest Frontier: Meetingplace of Four Cultures." Another recent pictorial of Muslims in China appeared in *Aramco World Magazine,* 1985. Tragically, in Chinese the magazine bore the title most eschewed by China's Muslims: *Hui jiao zai Zhong guo,* "Hui religion in China." The Chinese Islamic Association published pictorials of Muslims in China in 1957, 1965, and 1981, with the text in Chinese, Arabic, and English.

71. Interestingly enough, Israeli ends up with this assimilationist position as a consequence of his argument that, due to the failure of the 19th-century Hui rebellions to establish *Dar-al-Islam* in China, there was no alternative for the Hui but to follow the succession of "uneasy co-existence" to "rebellion," and, finally, to "Sinicization." (*Muslims in China,* p. 29). In the *Cambridge Encyclopedia of China,* Israeli concludes: "From then on, one could indeed speak of 'Chinese Muslims' and no longer about 'Muslims in China'" (pp. 330–332). For the role of politics in the assimilation of the Hui prior to 1949, see Mees.

72. Isaac Mason, "The Mohammedans of China: When, and How, They First Came."

73. Owen Lattimore, *Pivot of Asia: Sinkiang and the Inner Asian Frontiers of China and Russia,* p. 119n20.

74. John Steinhardt, "Minority groups in Xinjiang strengthen Middle East ties: Muslim Groups Defiant."

75. Judith Banister, *China's Changing Population,* p. 316. See also Thomas Heberer, *China and Its National Minorities,* who states that the Hui are "not different ethnically and linguistically from the Han," p. 73. Susan Naquin and Evelyn Rawski, *Chinese Society in the Eighteenth Century,* state that the Hakka and Hui were "both Han groups," p. 128.

76. John Lawton, "The People," p. 44.

77. Barbara Pillsbury, "The Muslim Population of China: Clarifying the Question of Size and Ethnicity," p. 51.

78. Fazlur Rahman, *Islam,* p. 172.

79. Ruth Mandel reports that the practice of *taqiya,* or dissimulation, is often seen among the Alevis Shiites as part of their "dissociative" and defensive response to centuries of persecution; see "The Making of Infidels and Other Ethnics," pp. 8–9.
80. Population Census Office, *The Population Atlas of China,* p. xvi.
81. See Fletcher, "Brief History of the Chinese Northwestern Frontier."
82. A. Doak Barnett, *China on the Eve of the Communist Takeover,* p. 182.
83. Barbara Pillsbury, "Muslim Population in China According to the 1982 Census."
84. Population Census Office, *The Population Atlas of China,* pp. 26–39.
85. Guo Wu Yuan, *Di san ci quan guo renkou pucha Shougong huizong Ziliao zongbian,* Vol. IV *Nationalities Population,* 1983.
86. Hajji Yusuf Chang, "The Hui (Muslim) Minority in China: An Historical Overview," p. 73.
87. For a discussion of the high degree of accuracy of the 1982 Chinese national census, see Banister, *China's Changing Population.* While there is under-reporting among Hui, and several groups have been admitted in recent years previously unrecognized as Hui (see Chapter 6), a figure of no more than 10 million Hui, and from 15–20 million Muslims seems the best estimate. I translate Chinese administrative terms in the following manner, arranged according to administrative size: *sheng* (province), *qu* (region), *shi* (city), *shiqu* (city district), *xian* (county), *zhen* (town), *xiang* (township) or *gongshe* (people's commune), *dadui* (brigade), *cun* (village), or *xiaodui* (team). Confusion arises in that the commune system was in the process of returning to a village system during my fieldwork, and government administrative units (e.g., *zhengshi cun* or *xingzhen cun* "official village") do not necessarily conform to natural traditional units (e.g., *ziran cun* "natural village").
88. Jonathan N. Lipman, "Hui-Hui: An Ethnohistory of the Chinese-Speaking Muslims," p. 112.
89. Ma Weiliang, "Yunna Daizu, Zangzu, Baizu, he xiao liangshan Yizu diqu de Huizu."
90. Boris Riftin, "Muslim Elements in the Folklore of the Chinese Huizu and the Soviet Dungans."
91. See Dyer, *Soviet Dungan Kolkhozes,* and Victor H. Mair, "Chinese Language Reform and Dungan Script in Soviet Central Asia."
92. Female imams are very unusual in North China and I encountered them only in Yunnan. They lead the women in prayer, never the men, and are responsible for mosque administrative duties. Among the Yihewani (see below) in Qinghai and Gansu, I encountered many girls enrolled in the local Islamic schools learning Arabic, though it was unclear whether they aspired to be formal imams.
93. Dru C. Gladney, "Ethno-religious Factionalism and the Panthay Muslim Rebellion in Yunnan, 1855–1873."

94. Hiroko Yokoyama, "Ethnic Identity among the Inhabitants of the Dali Basin in Southwestern China."

95. Xue Wenbo, "Lasa de Huizu," p. 148. See also Triloki Nath Sharma, "The Predicament of Lhasa Muslims in Tibet."

96. Tibet Academy of Social Sciences interview.

97. Keng-fong Pang, "Austronesian-speaking Hui of Hainan Island: A Southeast Asian Islamic Identity?"

98. *Zhongguo shaoshu minzu,* pp. 57–68, and Banister, *China's Changing Population,* pp. 322–333.

99. Joseph Fletcher, "The Sufi 'paths' (*ṭuruq*) in China." It is one of the greatest tragedies of recent Inner Asian scholarship that Joseph Fletcher died at 49 in 1984. Praised recently as one of the few "complete Asianists" (Rhoads Murphy, "Presidential Address: Toward the Complete Asianist"), he was one of the few scholars who possessed the myriad languages and determined dedication necessary to begin to fully address the intricate historical links between China and Inner Asia. Several of his works in progress are being edited by a committee of his colleagues and students. A summary of his published and unpublished works is provided in *Late Imperial China* 1985.6 2:110–113, and a recent conference on Islam in China was held in his memory at Harvard University, 14–16 April 1989, entitled: "The Legacy of Islam in China: An International Symposium in Memory of Joseph F. Fletcher." For his correspondence with Claude Pickens, a Protestant missionary in Northwest China who contributed much to Fletcher's understanding of Islam in this area, see Joseph Fletcher, "The Taylor-Pickens Letters."

100. Feng Zenglie, "'Gedimu' bayi."

101. Aside from perhaps a few remaining cultural influences deriving from the large communities of Persian Muslims in the earliest period of Islam in China, there is no institutionalized Shi'ism among the Hui, which contradicts Raphael Israeli's thesis (see Jonathan N. Lipman, "Shi'ism in Chinese Islam"; Xue Wenbo, "Shiya pai dui Zhongguo-Sunnai pai de ying xiang"). There is at least one Shi'i community among the Uigur in Khotan, and many of the Persian-speaking Tadjik are Shi'ite. Nevertheless, cultural and political contacts are strong between China and Iran.

102. Robert Ekvall, *Cultural Relations on the Kansu-Tibetan Border,* p. 19.

103. G. Findlay Andrew, *The Crescent in North-West China,* p. 10.

104. Martin King Whyte and William L. Parish, *Urban Life in Contemporary China,* pp. 27–29. R. Bush, *Religion in Communist China,* pp. 270ff, F. Joyaux, *Les Musulmans en Chinese Populaire,* Kao Hao-jan, *The Imam's Story;* M. R. Khan, *Islam in China,* J. Lindbeck, "Communism, Islam and Nationalism in China," and Yang I-Fan, *Islam in China,* give critical accounts of the effects of the Land Reform, Social Transformation, and other campaigns on rural and urban Hui communities prior to 1960 in the New China. For an unabashedly positive evaluation, see Ding Yimin, *Xin Zhongguo de Huihui minzu.*

105. Iwamura Shinobu, "The Structure of Moslem Society in Inner Mongolia."
106. James A. Millward, "The Chinese Border Wool Trade of 1880–1937," p. 45.
107. An excellent portrayal of the important role itinerant Hui merchants have played among Tibetan nomads is found in the opening scenes of the 1986 film *Horse Thief*, directed by Tian Zhuangzhuang and produced by the Xi'an Film Company. The mediating role of the Hui throughout China was explored in a panel at the 1988 Association of Asian Studies Annual Meetings, entitled: "Hui Between the Worlds: Chinese Muslims as Ethnoreligious Mediators."
108. Earlier Sufi communities and other Islamic orders existed in China and may have been involved in several minor disturbances within the foreign Muslim communities. See Chen Dasheng, "Quanzhou Yisilanjiaopai yu yuanmou yisiba dizhanluan xingzhi shishen," pp. 53–64, for an interesting inquiry into Islamic factional disputes that led to the 10-year Isbah disturbance in Quanzhou at the end of the Yuan dynasty (14th century). Jin Yijiu, "The System of *menhuan* in China," pp. 34–35, notes that the Yuan History (*Yuan shi*) records the presence of dervishes (*dieliweishi*) in some mosques, and that Ibn Battuta apparently encountered a Sufi mystic in China in the mid-14th century: "I was told . . . that a considerable personage was in that neighborhood, who was upwards of two hundred years old; that he never ate, drank, spoke, or took any delight whatever in the world, his powers were so great and so perfect; and that he lived in a cave without the city, in which also his devotions were carried on."
109. John Spencer Trimingham, *The Sufi Orders in Islam*, p. 10.
110. *Menhuan* is the Chinese technical term describing the socioeconomic and religious organization of Sufi brotherhoods linked to the "leading descent line" of the original Sufi founder, extending through his appointed descendants to the leader himself and from him to Muhammad. For a more detailed discussion, see Jin Yijiu, "The System of *menhuan* in China," and "Sufeipai yu Zhongguo menhuan," pp. 187–203; Jonathan N. Lipman, "Sufi Muslim Lineages and Elite Formation in Modern China: The *Menhuan* of the Northwest"; Ma Tong and Wang Qi, "Zhongguo Yisilanjiao de jiaopai he menhuan"; Nakada.
111. Joseph Fletcher, "The Sufi 'paths' (*ṭuruq*) in China."
112. See John O. Voll, *Islam: Continuity and Change in the Modern World*, pp. 33–86, and Rahman, pp. 237–260.
113. Early 20th-century Western travelers in northwest China were struck by the non-religious political nature of some of these *menhuan* which were instrumental in organizing many of the large and small Hui rebellions. Owen Lattimore, *Inner Asian Frontiers of China*, p. 185, observed: "Different religio-political families—in the name, characteristically, of different sects of Islam—began to struggle against each other both for hegemony as between Moslems and for control of external relations as between Moslems and Chinese." The sociopolitical role of these *menhuan* has been the main focus of Chinese histor-

ians, especially during the 1950s Land-Reform Campaign when large *menhuan* landholdings were expropriated as allegedly belonging to feudal landlords. The most controversial victim of this critique was Ma Zhenwu, the Naqshbandiyya Jahriyya Shagou branch leader in Ningxia, whose vast holdings were confiscated in 1958 (see the October 1958 document, "Chinese Moslems Expose the Crimes of Ma Chen-wu" in Donald MacInnis, *Religious Policy and Practice in Communist China,* pp. 167–175). Jin Yijiu, "The System of *menhuan* in China," p. 41, reflects this critical Chinese Communist historiography of the "feudal" nature of the *menhuan:* "To carry out cruel feudal exploitation of believers through all kinds of ways is the second characteristic of the Menhuan system. . . . Under the name of religion, [the *Jiaozhu,* leader] deceived believers, and oppressed and exploited them. The Jiaozhu outdid secular landlords in exploitation."

114. Charles L. Pickens, "The Four Men Huans."

115. See Ma Tong, *Zhongguo Yisilan jiaopai yu menhuan zhidu shilue;* Mian Weiling, *Ninqxia Yisilan jiaopai gaiyao,* pp. 45–117; Yang, Mohammed Usiar Huaizhong, "Sufism among the Muslims in Gansu, Ningxia, and Qinghai."

116. In 1934, W. A. Saunders went to Gansu to investigate some of the differences between Chinese Islamic Orders. When he asked a local postmaster specifically about the difference between the "Old and New Sects," the Chinese Muslim "laughed at the notion of anyone, even a Moslem, getting all the sects tabulated and pigeonholed." W. A. Saunders, "Hsuan Hua Kang," p. 69.

117. For accounts of the 19th-century Hui rebellions in the northwest, see Wendjang Chu, "Ch'ing Policy Towards the Muslims in the Northwest"; Gao Zhanfu, "Guanyu jiaopai zhizheng zai qingdai xibei Huimin qiyi zhong xiaoji zuoyong de tantao," pp. 245–261; Lipman, "Border World," pp. 134ff; Yang Mohammed Usiar Huaizhong, "Lun shiba shiji Zhehelinye Musilin di qiyi."

118. Stevan Harrell and Elizabeth Perry, "An Introduction," and Susan Naquin, *Millenarian Rebellion in China.*

119. See Israeli, *Muslims in China,* pp. 155–180.

120. Dru C. Gladney, "Muslim Tombs and Ethnic Folklore: Charters for Hui Identity," pp. 507–508.

121. In Ma Tong, *Zhongguo Yisilan jiaopai . . . ,* p. 330.

122. For a survey of literature on Sufism, see Idries Shah, *The Way of the Sufi;* John A. Sublian, *Sufism: Its Saints and Shrines;* and Trimingham, *The Sufi Orders in Islam.*

123. Yang Mohammed Usiar Huaizhong, "Sufism among the Muslims."

124. Andrew D. W. Forbes, "Survey Article: The Muslim National Minorities of China," p. 75, regards the popularity of tombs among the Hui as "probably due to isolation from the Islamic mainstream." On the other hand, Joseph Trippner, "Islamische Gruppe und Graberkult in Northwest China," argues that

these "grave-worshiping cults" give evidence of the pervasive influence of Shi^cism among the Hui. Alternatively, I suggest, "Muslim Tombs," pp. 501–517, that the tombs reveal a wide variety of Hui religious meaning, serving as important charters that link different Hui communities to their foreign Muslim heritage.

125. See Yang Mohammed Usiar Huaizhong, "Sufism."
126. Cited in Jin Yijiu, "The System of *Menhuan* in China," pp. 40, 42. For a philological comparison of mystical terms in Daoism and Sufism, see Toshihiko Izutsu, *Sufism and Daoism.*
127. Ma Tong *Zhongguo Yisilan, jiaopai yu menhuan zhidu shilue,* pp. 328–354. An interesting example is provided by the Jiucaiping *menhuan,* a branch of the Qadiriyya in Haiyuan county, southern Ningxia, who say their order is the "flagpole of Ali" and venerate Fatima as *hange laomu* (Arabic, "true" venerable mother), who resembles the Buddhist Guanyin (see Mian Weiling, *Ningxia Yisilan,* p. 102), or perhaps even more closely "Mazu" and the "Venerable Eternal Mother" (*wusheng laomu*), popular among Chinese heterodox sects, such as the White Lotus and the Religion of Unity (*Yi Guan Dao*) currently outlawed in Taiwan (Robert P. Weller, *Unities and Diversities in Chinese Religion,* p. 50).
128. Joseph Fletcher, "The Naqshbandiyya in Northwest China." This is a lengthy revision of an earlier unpublished manuscript, "Brief history of the Naqshbandiyya in China," currently being edited and revised by Jonathan Lipman for publication and upon which much of the following narrative is based.
129. See Trippner, pp. 142–171.
130. Annemarie Schimmel, *Mystical Dimensions of Islam,* p. 357.
131. "Sufism." For more of the Naqshbandiyya in Central and Inner Asia, see Ikbel Ali, *Islamic Sufism,* pp. 97–112; Schimmel, pp. 363–373; Shah, pp. 141–158; Subhan, pp. 286–309; and Trimingham, pp. 62–66.
132. Ma Tong, *Zhongguo Yisilan jiaopaiyu menhuan zhidu shilue,* pp. 223–247.
133. Fletcher, "Naqshibandiyya in Northwest China," goes on to speculate about the gift of a Sufi text that the Mawlana Makhdum passed on to Ma Laichi, known in Chinese as the *Ming sha le.* Arguing that *sha le* may be a Chinese transliteration for *sharh,* or "commentary," he suggests it may mean the "Commentary on Brightness" (the translation of the Chinese character *ming*). There is a work of that name by an Indian mystic, Nizam ad-Din Thanesari (d. 1627), which is a commentary of Fakhr ad-Din Ibrahim 'Iraqi (d. 1289), in turn an abridged version of the *Wisdom of the Prophets,* by the famous Spanish mystic Ibn al-'Arabi (d. 1240). If this was indeed the Indian commentary by Thanesari, it supports the possibility that Mawlana Mahkdum was an Indian, and may explain certain mystical elements in Khufiyya Sufism, as well as its less political attitude, which is characteristic of Indian Sufism. Another possibility Fletcher raises is that the *Ming sha le* may have been the "Ashi' 'at al-'Lama'at" (Beams of

light of the Lama'at) by the famous Turkish Naqshbandi mystic and poet, the Maulana ᶜAbdu'r-Rahman Jami (d. 1492).

134. Yang Mohammed Usiar Huaizhong, "Sufism." Fletcher, "Naqshbandiyya in Northwest China," dates his death in 1753.

135. Joseph Fletcher, "Brief History of the Naqshbandiyya in China," p. 38; Schimmel, pp. 172, 366.

136. See Joseph Ford, "Some Chinese Muslims of the 17th and 18th Centuries," pp. 153–155, and Joseph Fletcher, "Central Asian Sufism and Ma Ming-hsin's New Teaching."

137. For more on the distinctions between vocal and silent *dhikr* in Sufi remembrance, see Hamid Algar ("Silent and Vocal Dhikr in the Naqshbandiyya Order," pp. 44–45), which he argues were not exclusive, but practiced by Qadiriyya, Naqshbandiyya, and Kubrawiyya in Central Asia. Fletcher, "Naqshbandiyya in Northwest China," suggested that, by the time Ma Mingxin studied in Yemen, both forms were used and there was no real conflict in the Middle East between those advocating one or the other. It became a heated debate in China upon Ma Mingxin's return, however.

138. The two letters of the Taylor-Pickens correspondence referring to the transmission of Sufism in China are reprinted in Joseph Fletcher, "The Taylor-Pickens Letters on the Jahri Branch of the Naqshbandiyya in China," pp. 20–26, with explanatory notes by Jonathan Lipman. The Jahriyya saying was often repeated to me and recorded in Ma Tong, *Zhongguo Yisilan jiaopaiyu menhuan shilue*, p. 365.

139. Fletcher, "Naqshbandiyya in Northwest China."

140. See Ho-dong Kim, "The Muslim Rebellion of the Kashgar Emirate in Chinese Central Asia, 1864–1877."

141. Gladney, "Ethno-religious Factionalism."

142. For interesting similar connections between Buddhist sects, see Susan Naquin, "Connections between rebellions: sect family networks in Qing China."

143. Mian Weiling, *Ningxia Yisilan*, p. 68.

144. Donald MacInnis, *Religious Policy and Practice*, p. 172.

145. Ma Tong, *Zhongguo Yisilan*, p. 431; Mian Weiling, *Ningxia Yisilan*, p. 70. Given the rebellious history of the Naqshbandi Jahriyya in China (see Bai Shouyi, *Huimin qiyi*, and Yang Mohammed Usiar Huaizhong, "Sufism"), the Chinese government has made important efforts to incorporate present leadership wherever possible. The current *murshids* (Sufi leader, Chinese *jiaozhu, laorenjia, baba, taiye*, depending on the order, see Glossary) for the Shagou and Banqiao *menhuan* in Ningxia, while not Communist Party members, are regional vice-chairmen in the People's Political Consultative Conference (Zhengxie) and the People's Government (Renmin Zhengfu). In recent years, several of these Muslim leaders have accompanied state-sponsored delegations to foreign Muslim nations.

146. See Trimingham, pp. 55–58.
147. Ma Tong, *Zhongguo Yisilan*, pp. 451–455; Yang Mohammed Usiar Huaizhong, "Sufism."
148. Ernest Gellner, *Nations and Nationalism*, p. 103.
149. Jonathan Lipman, "Patchwork Society, Network Society: A Study of Sino-Muslim Communities."
150. Claude L. Pickens, "The Challenge of Chinese Moslems," p. 414.
151. The activity surrounding these tombs is similar to the festivals that take place at large shrine complexes, or *dargâhs*, in India, Pakistan, and Central Asia (see Richard Maxwell Eaton, *Sufis of Bijapur 1300–1700: Social Roles of Sufis in Medieval India*, p. xxiv, and David Gilmartin, "Shrines, Succession, and Sources of Moral Authority," pp. 221–240), which may give some credence to Fletcher's suggestion that at least the Khufiyyah may have been influenced by Indian mysticism.
152. Various reasons are given for the significance of these 6-pointed hats, including the symbolism of God's creating the earth in 6 days and resting on the 7th. Interestingly, the source for this tradition is not found in the Quran (Th. Emil Homerin, personal communication).
153. Trimingham, p. 11.
154. Claude Pickens, "The Challenge of Chinese Moslems."
155. Anonymous, "Japanese Infiltration Among Muslims in China," p. 127. This report and "Peoples and Politics of China's Northwest" have been published by Derk Bodde in three articles—"China's Muslim Minority," "Japan and the Muslims of China," and "Chinese Muslims in Occupied Areas."
156. Fletcher, "Naqshbandiyya in Northwest China."
157. Rudolf Löwenthal, *The Religious Periodical Press*, pp. 211–250.
158. "Japanese Infiltration," p. 27.
159. Ma Shouqian, "The Hui People's New Awakening at the End of the 19th Century and Beginning of the 20th Century."
160. See Louis Schram, "The Monguors of the Kansu-Tibetan Frontier."
161. Jonathan N. Lipman, "The Third Wave: Establishment and Transformation of the Muslim Brotherhood in Modern China," p. 21.
162. For a history of the Yihewani (Ikhwan) in China see, especially, ibid., pp. 14–21, as well as Chinese works by Ma Kexun ("Zhongguo Yisilanjiao Yihewani pai de changdaozhe: Ma Wanfu"), Ma Tong (*Zhongguo Yisilan yu menhuan zhida shilue*, pp. 127–154), Mian Weiling (*Ningxia Yisilan*, pp. 118–131), and Ye Zhengang ("Ningxia Yihewanyi zhuming jingxuejia Hu Gaoshan").
163. Richard Maxwell Eaton, "The Political and Religious Authority of the Shrine of Baba Farid," pp. 334–335.
164. Lipman, "Third Wave," p. 9.
165. See Ma Ximing, "Xi'an de jizuo Qingzhensi," and Wolfgang Franke's 1979 visit report, "A Note on the Ancient Chinese Mosques of Xian & Quanzhou."

166. This special art form, which combines floral Arabic calligraphic Quranic content with Chinese form, is unique to the Hui and begs further study. An initial paper has been presented on the subject (see Joseph Fletcher, Mary Ellen Alonso, and Wasma'a Chorbachi, "Arabic Calligraphy in Twentieth-Century China"), but much work needs to be done on this incredible combination of Eastern and Central Asian aesthetics.

167. See Dale F. Eickelman's discussion of the Salafiyya reform movement in Morocco (*Moroccan Islam: Tradition and Society in a Pilgrimage Center,* pp. 226–228). In China the order is also referred to by outsiders as the Santaijiao (3-bowing teaching) for their emphasis upon three prostrations during prayer instead of the 1 (Yihewani, also referred to as Yitaijiao) or 10 (Gedimu) prostrations of other orders. See also Da Yingyu, "Zhongguo Yisilanjiao Sailaifeiye pai shulue."

168. Andrew, p. 56.

169. Described in Lipman, "Border World," pp. 197–199.

170. For more on this fascinating movement, which Lipman says "seems to defy classification" (ibid., pp. 144–146), see Ma Tong, *Zhongguo Yisilan yu menhuan zhida shilue,* pp. 155–209, and Zi Heng's summary in "Zhongguo Yisilanjiao Xi Dao tang shilue" and the other informative articles in the newly published collection *Xi Dao tang shiliaoji* (Collected materials of the Xi Dao Tang).

171. Yang Mohammed Usiar Huaizhong, "Sufism."

172. Ma Tong, *Zhongguo Yisilan yu menhuan zhida shilue,* 477–482.

173. See also Trippner, pp. 154–155. Jin Yijiu, "The System of Menhuan in China," p. 39, suggests that, after many of the Gedimu converted to Sufism in the 18th and 19th centuries, in the 20th century the Sufis began to convert to the Yihewani (Ikhwan), citing a 1950 survey of Zhangjiachuan where it was reported that 53 out of 216 Jahriyya Sufi mosques had converted to the Ikwan.

174. Compare Johannes Fabian's discussion of African religious movements, in "Six Theses Regarding the Anthropology of African Religious Movements."

175. 17th- and 18th-Century Hui Muslim literature in China also reflects this debate; see Donald Leslie, *Islamic Literature in Chinese, Late Ming and Early Ch'ing: Books, Authors and Associates,* and H. D. Hayward, "Chinese-Moslem Literature: A Study in Mohammedan Education." For Hui literature during the Republican period, see Löwenthal. Isaac Mason, "Notes on Chinese Mohammedan Literature," lists 318 titles, and C. L. Ogilve and S. M. Zwemer, "A Classified Bibliography of Books on Islam in Chinese and Chinese-Arabic," list 95 publications. See also Ludmilla Panskaya's *Introduction to Palladii's Chinese Literature of the Muslims.*

176. See William R. Roff, "Islam Obscured? Some Reflections on Studies of Islam and Society in Asia," pp. 8–10.

177. Broomhall, de Thiersant, and Israeli, *Muslims in China,* share this view of Sinicized Islam. See Ch'en Yuan's influential but misleading thesis regarding the

transformation into Chinese of all Muslim and other foreign visitors who entered China—their becoming "Sinicized"—*Western and Central Asians in China Under the Mongols: Their Transformation into Chinese.* Ch'en writes: "As the dicussions in this book are limited to the Western Regions, the Mongol, Khitan, and Jurchen peoples are not touched. Because the civilization of these peoples was primitive in character, it is not surprising that they should become sinicized. As regards the people of Japan, Korea, Liu-ch'iu, and Annam, who have been using the written language and institutions of China for a long time, their sinicization is also not to be wondered at. But the Uighur, T'u-chüeh, Persians, Arabs, and Syrians all had languages and religions of their own. . . . Nevertheless, once their people came to China, they adopted Chinese customs. . . . These citations tend to show that the people of Hsi-yü [Western regions] were quite numerous in ancient times. But these people made no contribution to Chinese civilization; so nothing may be said about them" (pp. 3–4, 7).

178. See Clive S. Kessler, *Islam and Politics in a Malay State: Kelantan 1838–1969*, pp. 19–20, and Eickelman, *Moroccan Islam*, pp. 10–13.

179. E.g., Max Weber, *Ancient Judaism* and *The Protestant Ethic and the Spirit of Capitalism.*

180. Geertz, *Islam Observed*, p. 97, and Dale F. Eickelman, *The Middle East: An Anthropological Approach*, pp. 12–13.

181. In MacInnis, *Religious Policy*, pp. 169–170.

182. This interpretive scheme is influenced by H. Richard Niebuhr's analysis of Christian social ethics; see *Christ and Culture.*

183. Jürgen Habermas, *The Structural Transformation of the Public Sphere*, pp. 7–10.

184. James Piscatori, *International Relations of the Asian Muslim States*, pp. 17–27.

185. *China Daily*, "Xinjiang's pilgrimage to Mecca," p. 1.

186. For China's political and military relations with the Middle East, see Yitzhak Shichor's recent book, *East Wind over Arabia: Origins and Implications of the Sino-Saudi Missile Deal*, as well as his earlier work, *The Middle East in China's Foreign Policy, 1949–1977.*

2. ETHNOGRAPHIC RESEARCH AND THE CHINESE STATE

1. Fei Xiaotong, "Ethnic Identification in China," p. 60.

2. *Renmin ribao* "Guanyu 1990 nian ren kou pucha zhu yao shu ju de gongbao" (Announcement regarding the most important statistics of the 1990 population census) 14 November 1990, p. 3.

3. J. V. Stalin, *Works, 1907–1913*, XI, 349.

4. Ibid., p. 351.

5. Jin Binggao, "The Marxist Definition of Nationality: Its Origin and Influence," p. 67. The recent publication in *Minzu yanjiu* (Nationality research, 1988, no. 4) of several papers given at the 1986 national conference in Shanghai where Stalin's principles were discussed reveals that, though the principles are begin-

ning to be questioned for the first time, they are still held as most appropriate for China. The journal published a similar discussion of the term *minzu* in 1983 (no. 6).

6. State Commission for Nationality Affairs, ed., *Minzu lilun yu minzu zhengce*, p. 39.
7. Fei Xiaotong, "Ethnic Identification," p. 67.
8. Ibid., p. 77.
9. Stevan Harrell, "Ethnicity, Local Interests, and the State: Yi Communities in Southwest China."
10. Wang Mingke, "Zhongguo gindai Jiang, Yiang, Diqiang, zhi yanjin."
11. *Zhongguo shaoshu minzu.*
12. He Yan, "Mingdai Xiyu yu zhongyuan wangchao guanxi shulun," p. 5, a prominent young Hui scholar, has found evidence of Hui communities maintaining the use of Persian and Arabic well into the Ming dynasty and possibly the Qing.
13. See Paul Wexler, "Research Frontiers in Sinto-Islamic Linguistics."
14. Cable and French, p. 246.
15. Hill Gates, "Ethnicity and Social Class," p. 243.
16. Raoul Naroll, "On Ethnic Unit Classification," p. 286.
17. Frederik Barth, ed., *Ethnic Groups and Boundaries.*
18. Edmund R. Leach, *Political Systems of Highland Burma.*
19. Fredrik Barth, "Introduction," p. 12.
20. Fei Xiaotong, "Ethnic Identity," p. 77.
21. Connor, pp. 7–19.
22. Lewis Henry Morgan, *Ancient Society*, pp. 1–18.
23. Tong Enzheng, "Morgan's Model and the Study of Ancient Chinese Society," pp. 182, 194.
24. Ibid., p. 185.
25. Fei Xiaotong, "Zhonghua minzu de duoyuan jiti geju," pp. 4, 7, 8.
26. Ibid., pp. 11, 13.
27. Ibid., pp. 16, 18.
28. Nathan Glazer and Daniel P. Moynihan, *Beyond the Melting Pot*, p. 37.
29. Gates.
30. Immanuel Wallerstein, "Social Conflict in Post-Independence Black Africa: The Concepts of Race and Status Group Reconsidered."
31. Fredrik Barth, "Pathan Identity and its Maintenance"; Leo A. Despres, "Introduction"; Gunnar Haaland, "Economic Determinants in Ethnic Processes."
32. Abner Cohen, *Custom and Politics in Urban Africa: A Study of Hausa Migrants in Yoruba Towns;* Brian L. Foster, "Ethnicity and Commerce."
33. Abner Cohen, *Two Dimensional Man: An Essay on the Anthropology of Power and Symbolism in Complex Society.*
34. Rodolfo Stavenhagen, *Social Classes in Agrarian Societies;* Wallerstein.

35. See Abner Cohen's "Retribalization" in *Custom and Politics,* and S. R. Charsley, "The Formation of Ethnic Groups," p. 377. For Abner Cohen, *Two Dimensional Man,* p. 97, "ethnicity is fundamentally a political phenomenon." In the Ronald Cohen and John Middleton classic volume on ethnic incorporation processes among African tribal peoples (*From Tribe to Nation in Africa*, pp. 10–11), ethnicity is also most often conceived in terms of the political and sociohistorical contexts of incorporation and their effect on the ethnic groups, or tribes, involved. The "major criteria," they suggest, for studying ethnic incorporation are "of sociopolitical structure."
36. Pillsbury, "Cohesion and Cleavage," pp. 63ff, and "Blood Ethnicity," p. 3.
37. Pillsbury, "Cohesion and Cleavage," p. 222.
38. Ibid., p. 67.
39. Pillsbury, "Blood Ethnicity," pp. 18–22.
40. Pillsbury, "Cohesion and Cleavage," p. 148.
41. Edward Shils, "Primordial, Personal, Sacred and Civil Ties," p. 135.
42. Michael M. J. Fischer, "Ethnicity and the Post-Modern Arts of Memory," p. 195.
43. Peter Worsley, *The Three Worlds,* p. 246.
44. Jay O'Brien, "Toward a Reconstitution of Ethnicity: Capitalist Expansion and Cultural Dynamics in Sudan," p. 899.
45. Eric Wolf, *Europe and the People Without History,* p. 6.
46. Heberer, pp. 37–38. Based on published Chinese sources, Heberer also reports application for minority status by the following groups: the Pingwu-Tibetans, on the Sichuan-Gansu border; the Deng, a Tibetan group on the Chinese-Indian border and numbering about 20,000; the Laji, numbering 1,500, from the Maguan district in Yunnan; the Khmer, totaling about 2,100; the Mangren, with 500 persons; the Hu, living in Xishuangbana prefecture, with over 2,000; the Ku Cong in Yunnan, with a population of over 25,000; and the Sherpas in Tibet, who number about 400.
47. Charles F. Keyes, "Introduction" and "The Dialectics of Ethnic Change."
48. Michelle Z. Rosaldo, "Toward an Anthropology of Self and Feeling," p. 137. Mikhail Bakhtin's (*The Dialogic Imagination*) notion of dialogue may be useful in understanding how ethnic identity is formed out of a continuing dialogical relation between Self and Other, group and state (see Gladney, "Dialogic Ethnicity: The State and National Identity in China").
49. George E. Marcus and Michael M. J. Fischer, *Anthropology as Cultural Critique.*
50. Judith A. Nagata, "In Defense of Ethnic Boundaries: The Changing Myths and Charters of Malay Identity," p. 92; Gladney, "Muslim Tombs."
51. George Devereux, "Ethnic Identity: Its Logical Foundations & its Dysfunctions," p. 49.
52. Keyes, "Introduction," p. 208.
53. Keyes, "Dialectics," pp. 18, 25.

54. Michael Banton, "The Direction and Speed of Ethnic Change," p. 50.
55. For the relevance of dialogical theory to the ethnographic endeavor, see also James Clifford, *The Predicament of Culture: Twentieth-Century Ethnography, Literature, and Art,* pp. 39–44.
56. Manning Nash, *The Cauldron of Ethnicity in the Modern World.*
57. G. Carter Bentley, "Ethnicity and Practice." For a discussion of the influence of Soviet nationality policy on ethnic identities in Russia and the resurgence of ethnicity in the USSR, see John A. Armstrong, "The Ethnic Scene in the Soviet Union: The View of the Dictatorship"; Elizabeth E. Bacon, *Central Asians Under Russian Rule: A Study in Culture Change,* pp. 15–27; Julian S. Bromiley, *Soviet Ethnology and Anthropology Today,* pp. 55–80; M. M. Eminov, *The Development of Soviet Nationality Policy and Current Soviet Perspectives on Ethnicity,* pp. 55–80, 114–115; Richard Pipes, *The Formation of the Soviet Union,* pp. 1–49; Teodor Shanin, "Ethnicity In the Soviet Union," pp. 409–415; Bromiley and Kozlov, pp. 425–430. Rasma Karklins, pp. 77–100, represents one of the first attempts to present the Soviet nationality's own perspective "from below."
58. John Comaroff, "Of Totemism and Ethnicity: Consciousness, Practice and the Signs of Inequality," p. 303. (emphasis in the original)
59. For a review of the relations between ethnicity, class, and the nation-state, see Brackette Williams, "A Class Act: Anthropology and the Race to Nation Across Ethnic Terrain," pp. 415–444.
60. For an excellent discussion of the role of the state in influencing Islam in China and the construction of Muslim identities, see François Aubin, "Islam et Etat en Chine populaire," pp. 170–176.
61. E. K. Francis, *Interethnic Relations,* p. 114.
62. David Maybury-Lewis, "Living in Leviathan: Ethnic Groups and the State," p. 221.
63. Eugen Weber, *Peasants Into Frenchmen: The Modernization of Rural France, 1870–1914.*
64. Jean-Jacquest Rousseau, *The Social Contract,* p. 49.
65. Thomas Hobbes, *Leviathan,* p. 141.
66. Lloyd Fallers, *The Social Anthropology of the Nation-State,* p. 3.
67. Charles F. Keyes, "The Basis of Ethnic Group Relations in Modern Nation-States," p. 15.
68. Gellner, p. 55.
69. Ibid., p. 56.
70. Eric Hobsbawm, "Introduction: Inventing Traditions," p. 4.
71. See Leach.
72. E. E. Evans-Pritchard, *The Nuer.*
73. Rupert Emerson, *From Empire to Nation,* p. 95. See also Connor, p. 39.
74. See Yitzhak Brudny, "The Rise and Fall of the Political Contract: Russian Nationalism and the Soviet State"; John B. Dunlop, *The Faces of Contemporary*

Russian Nationalism; Alexander Yanov, *The Russian Challenge and the Year 2000.*

75. Edward Allworth, "Ambiguities in Russian Group Identity and Leadership of the RSFSR."
76. Thierry, p. 78.
77. Charles Mckhann, "Naxi-Han History and the Transformation of the 'Mee-biuq' (Sacrifice to Heaven) Ritual."
78. Shelley Rigger, "Voices of Manchu Idendity."
79. Sun Yat-sen, *The Three Principles of the People: San Min Chu I,* pp. 2, 5.
80. See Anonymous, "Peoples and Policies of China's Northwest," p. 49.
81. Chiang Kai-shek, *China's Destiny,* pp. 39–40.
82. Pillsbury, "Blood Ethnicity," p. 261.
83. China Encyclopaedia Committee. *Minzu,* p. 30.
84. Eric Hobsbawm, "Mass-Producing Traditions," p. 266.
85. Anderson, p. 87.
86. V. Y. Mudimbe, *The Invention of Africa,* p. 12.
87. This has led to an interesting line of argument. While many agree that Soviet nationality studies are important given the "fact" that almost half the Soviet Union is non-Russian, most argue that, by the same token, nationality studies in China are of less significance since the minorities make up only 6%. This argument relies on a fundamental acceptance of the notion of the Han nation-ality as one unified group. A recent attempt to describe China as a "cultural mosaic" composed of many sub-Han ethnicities is presented in Leo Moser's sur-vey, *The Chinese Mosaic: The Peoples and Provinces of China.*
88. Edgar Snow, *Red Star Over China;* Harrison E. Salisbury, *The Long March: The Untold Story.* In *Red Dust,* Nym Wales, wife of Edgar Snow, reproduced her fas-cinating Yenan interviews with several of the Long Marchers. Hsu Meng-ch'iu, official historian of the Long March, described how, after narrowly escaping slaughter at the hands of the "fierce Lolos" and "wild Tibetans" in Sichuan, the "Red Army marched on to north Shensi [Shaanxi], pursued by three cavalry elements—those of Ma Hung-k'uei, Ma Hung-p'ing, and Chiang Kai-shek. Because of the speed of the cavalry, many Red troops in the rear were cut off and captured" (Wales, p. 74). The first two were (Hui) Muslim warlords who controlled most of Ningxia and Gansu. Hsu also records several graphic accounts of "barbarians" sweeping down out of the mountains upon the hapless Long Marchers, screaming "Woo-woo-woo" in unintelligible dialects—reminis-cent of American western accounts of encounters with native Indians.
89. Mao Zedong, "Appeal of the Central Government to the Muslims."
90. See Forbes, "Survey Article," p. 77, and Lindbeck.
91. Snow, p. 320.
92. Forbes, *Warlords and Muslims,* p. 157.
93. Henry G. Schwarz, *Chinese Policies Towards Minorities,* pp. 13–17.
94. Connor, p. 89.

95. June Dreyer, *China's Forty Millions*, p. 17.

96. CASS News Research Institute, eds., *Zhongguo gongchandang xinwen gongzue wenjian huibian*, pp. 407–408.

97. Connor, p. 38.

98. Vivienne Shue, "The Fate of the Commune."

99. Mayfair Mei-Hui Yang, p. 26.

100. Gilles Deleuze and Felix Guattari, *A Thousand Plateaus: Capitalism and Schizophrenia*, pp. 149–160.

101. Claude Lefort, *The Political Forms of Modern Society: Bureaucracy, Democracy, and Totalitarianism*, pp. 279–280.

102. David Deal, "National Minority Policy in Southwest China, 1911–1965"; Dreyer, *China's Forty Millions;* David Wu, "National Minority Policy and Minority Cultures in Asia."

103. Ma Weiliang, "Minzu wenti yu jieji douzheng de guanzi," quoted from Joint Publications Research Service, 76883, pp. 71–73.

104. See Connor.

105. Hobsbawm, "Mass-Producing Traditions," pp. 13–14.

106. Heberer, pp. 21–22.

107. Clifford Geertz, personal communication.

108. Thomas Barfield, *The Perilous Frontier: Nomadic Empires and China*, pp. 44–59.

109. Edward Shils, *Center and Periphery: Essays in Macro-sociology.* While center-periphery theory has its limits of usefulness in social theory (see Appadurai, "Theory in Anthropology"), Vivienne Shue, *The Reach of the State*, pp. 31–72, finds Edward Shils's approach helpful for understanding traditional Chinese ideas of hierarchy and central authority.

110. Thierry, pp. 76, 94.

111. Pamela Kyle Crossley, "Thinking about Ethnicity in Early Modern China."

112. Anderson, pp. 41–49.

113. Michael Moerman, "Ethnic Identity in a Complex Civilization: Who are the Lue?" p. 1215.

114. Several of these photographs have been published in Isma⁽il R. Fârûqî and Lois Lamyâ'l, *The Cultural Atlas of Islam* and displayed with other Hui artifacts in the Lowie Museum of Anthropology at the University of California, Berkeley, as well as the Harvard-Yenching Library. I donated requested slides from the fall 1983 trip to the Nationalities Research Department of the Central Institute for Nationalities.

115. Clifford Geertz, *Works and Lives: The Anthropologist as Author,* p. 143n.

116. Bakhtin, p. 301.

117. See Anderson.

118. See Andrew; Broomhall; and Israeli, *Muslims in China.*

119. See Norman K. Denzin, "On the Ethics of Disguised Observation," and Kai T. Erikson, "A Comment on Disguised Observation in Sociology."

120. Marcus and Fischer, p. 165.

121. Edward Said, *Orientalism.*
122. James Clifford, "Introduction: Partial Truths," p. 12.
123. Philip Carl Salzman, "The Lone Stranger and the Solitary Quest."
124. Mary Louis Pratt, "Fieldwork in Common Places," p. 27.
125. Marcus and Fischer, p. 166.
126. Geertz, *Works and Lives,* pp. 23–24.
127. James A. Boon, *Other Tribes, Other Scribes,* p. 4. See also Kathleen Gough, "Anthropology: Child of Imperialism"; Murray L. Wax, "On Fieldworkers and Those Exposed to Fieldwork: Federal Regulations and Moral Issues."
128. The notion of extraterritoriality may not be entirely gone from modern China. Certainly the "Special Economic Zones," primarily in the coastal areas where these territories were first established, bears some relation to China's colonial past. Interestingly, the literary critic Rey Chow suggests that the important role of the Western media in China in broadcasting the 1989 Tiananmen protest was allowed only because of this tradition of extraterritoriality in China. Few totalitarian regimes would tolerate the live coverage by foreign media of their crackdown on their own civilians with the tacit acceptance of the Western press as not subject to China's own laws. Chow writes: "Nowadays, instead of guns, the most effective instruments that aid in the production of the 'Third World' are the technologies of the media. It is to these technologies—the bodies of the Western journalist and camera person, their voices, their images, their equipment, and the 'reality' that is broadcast in the U.S. and then 'faxed' back to China— that extraterritoriality is extended, and most of all by Chinese communities overseas who must, under the present circumstances, forget the history of extraterritoriality in Sino-Western relations." Rey Chow, "Violence in the Other Country: China as Crisis, Spectacle, and Woman."
129. George E. Marcus, "Afterword: Ethnographic Writing and Anthropological Careers."
130. R. David Arkush, *Fei Xiaotong and Sociology in Revolutionary China,* p. 268.
131. Ibid., p. 269, quoting Hu Sheng, *Zhexue yanjiu,* October 1958.
132. See Fei Xiaotong, "Ethnic Identification."
133. I was able often to use this argument to gain entré into Han communities for comparisons with the Hui. As a *minzu* (nationality), the Han also attend the nationalities institutes, usually in inverse proportion to their population: The Beijing Central Institute for Nationalities had 7% Han and 93% minorities. The study of Han as a nationality is beginning to gain popularity in China with a recent major conference and a publication series (see Xu Jieshan). Most of these studies seek to reveal the vast diversity of customs found among the Han, but have not yet raised the issue of the legitimacy of the ethnic category itself.
134. Geertz, *Islam Observed.*
135. Michel Foucault, "Truth and Power," p. 109.
136. This is similar to Weber's use of "ideal types" for the purposes of comparative

analysis. Weber never reified societies nor compared societies as wholes, but always contrasted cross-cultural institutions within them, such as law, marriage, religion, etc. Typology, for Weber, was a means of focusing on what is "typically important in the historical realization of religious ethics. This is important for the connection of religions with the great contrasts of economic mentalities" (see Max Weber, *The Sociology of Religion*, p. 37). For a discussion of Weber's use of type, and its later misuse by other sociologists, see Guenther Roth and Reinhard Bendix, *Scholarship and Partnership: Essays on Max Weber*, pp. 111ff.

3. ETHNORELIGIOUS RESURGENCE IN A NORTHWESTERN SUFI COMMUNITY

1. John F. Burns, "Chinese City is True to Moslem Self"; Jim Mann, "China's Uighurs—a Minority Seeks Equality"; Steinhardt.
2. Zhang Tongji, "Najiahucun de Huizu zhishi qingnian sixiang zhuangkuang," p. 12.
3. Wang Yiping, "Najiahucun de zongjiao zhuangkuang," p. 9.
4. Zhang Tongji, p. 11.
5. Ma Yin; Ya Hanzhang, *Minzu wenti yu zongjiao wenti.*
6. Najiahu, which I translate "Na Homestead," is a brigade (*dadui*) belonging to Yanghe commune (*gongshe*). Now that Yanghe has become a township (*xiang*), Na Homestead can be considered a large village, comprising 11 teams (*xiaodui*).
7. Marcel Mauss, *The Gift*, p. 10.
8. Wang Yiping, p. 7.
9. A 1964 report collected by the county "United Front Office" (Tongzhanbu) claimed that, in 1954, over 200 were worshiping at the mosque 5 times daily, 9.5% of the total Hui population, whereas present participation stands at only 80 worshipers, 4.7% (cited in ibid., p. 8, and Gong Weiduan, "Yongnin xian Na Jiahu cun shi diaocha," p. 37). The population of the village has almost doubled since that time (see Table 6).
10. Wang Yiping, p. 7, and Gong Weiduan, p. 38.
11. As elsewhere in Central Asia, in Hui villages any elder who possesses advanced Islamic knowledge (*Ahlin*) or who can read the Quran is generally recognized as an ahong (imam). Among the traditional non-*menhuan* Gedimu or Khufiyya, the "teaching" (*kaixue*) ahong is recognized as the preacher (*woerzu*) and responsible for delivering the main Friday sermon (*hutubai*). The mosque is generally administered by a committee (*siguan weiyuanhui*) that replaced the traditional "3-leader system" (*sandaozhi* or *zhangjiao zhidu*) in 1958, after the Democratic Reform Campaign (*minzhu gaige*)—among the Jahriyya, the term *zhangjiao* ahong, for the teaching ahong, is preserved. The assistant to the teaching ahong is now known as the *zhangxue* ahong; the mosque administrator in

charge of daily affairs is the *si shifu* or *si guan zhuren*. The teaching ahong among the Gedimu and Yihewani is often transferred (*sanxue*) to another mosque after an average of 3 years. An elder with minimal Islamic knowledge is known as a "second ahong" (*er* ahong) or even, "primary-school ahong" (*xiaoxue* ahong).

12. The largest mosque in Ningxia, located in Tongxin, dates from the late 16th century. It was spared destruction by Red Guards during the Cultural Revolution because it was the site where Chairman Mao Zedong declared the first Hui autonomous county on 20 December 1936. Weizhou was the site of the oldest and largest mosque in Ningxia, but it was destroyed in 1966. It was under reconstruction in 1985, but the former Islamic architecture is not being restored.

13. The only available figures on Ningxia for the average wage of workers in state-owned units was 936 yuan per year and in collective owned units 646 yuan per year in 1982 (State Statistical Bureau, *Statistical Yearbook of China–1983*, p. 488). This does not reflect typical rural income, which averaged about 400 yuan according to most areas I surveyed.

14. Population Census Office, p. 206.

15. Zhu Yuntao, "Najiahucun chanye jiegou de diaocha," p. 6.

16. The study revealed that individual giving among 6 households in a Gedimu village averaged 7.52%, among 6 households in a Jahriyya village 11.99%, and among 5 households in a Yihewani village 9.34%.

17. Out of a population of 1.3 million in 1981, the Hui are 35.2% (489,571), the Dongxiang 15.9% (223,240), the Baonan 0.53% (7,683), and the Salar 0 .27% (4,364).

18. For further information on the economic situation in Linxia, see Linxia Hui Autonomous Prefectural Basic Situation Committee, eds., *Linxia Huizu zizhizhou gaikuang*. Other helpful introductions to Hui autonomous counties that I have been able to collect include *Dachang Huizu zizhixian gaikuang, Minhe Huizu Tuzu zizhixian gaikuang, Mengcun Huizu zizhixian gaikuang, Menyuan Huizu zizhixian gaikuang, Hualong Huizu zizhixian gaikuang*, and *Changji Huizu zizhizhou gaikuang*. For the Hui in Gansu, see Ma Tong, *Gansu Huizu shi ganyao*.

19. 17 April 1987, p. 1. All names used in this study are real unless pseudonyms are indicated.

20. See Michael M. J. Fischer, *Iran: From Religious Dispute to Revolution*. A rather new development is the sending of Hui *manla* to mosques in Xinjiang where Arabic language study is much more advanced due to the influence of the Arabic script in Uigur and the proximity to Pakistan with its recently opened Karakoram highway. In September 1987, while visiting a mosque in Kashgar, I met a Hui *manla* from Hezhou who was studying there for 6 years for precisely those reasons. He mentioned his desire to travel to Mecca through Pakistan and how much more inexpensive and convenient the Hajj had become since the

opening of the road. He served at the only Hui mosque among the 160 Uigur mosques in the city.

21. Hui women's head coverings (*gaitou*) veil the hair, forehead, and neck, but leave the face exposed. In heavily populated Hui areas, particularly among communities influenced by the Yihewani, such as Linxia, Gansu, and Xining, Qinghai, almost all women over 12 years of age wear them. While it is not a consistent practice in every area, young unmarried women often wear green, married women tend to wear black, and older women white, generally after their husbands die or their grandchildren are born.

22. Zhang Tongji, p. 11.

23. Ibid., pp. 11–12.

24. For unbelief in Taiwan, see Stevan Harrell, "Belief and Unbelief in a Taiwan Village."

25. Wang Yiping, p. 7.

26. I heard of at least 3 other cases of elderly party members becoming ahong in Pingluo, north of Yinchuan.

27. Zhang Tongji and Zhang Yongqing, "A Study and Analysis of the 'Dual Functions' of Islam in Xiji, Ningxia." Cited in Donald E. MacInnis, *Religion in China Today*, p. 259.

28. The question of the unbelief of committed believers, and the seemingly unproblematic acceptance of that apparent contradiction among Taiwanese folk religionists is addressed in detail by David K. Jordan and Daniel L. Overmeyer, *The Flying Phoenix: Aspects of Chinese Sectarianism in Taiwan*, pp. 173–180, 270.

29. Wang Yiping, p. 9.

30. Ibid.

31. See Zhang Tongji, p. 11.

32. These studies were conducted over a 2-month period in December 1984 and January 1985 by a team of researchers from the Ningxia Academy of Social Sciences (NASS) as part of a national project, "Investigation on typical village socioeconomics" ("Nongcun shehui jingji dianxing diaocha"). Na Homestead was one of two villages in Ningxia region selected for study. Some of the results of the study have been published in Wang Yiping, Zhang Tongji, Zhu Yuntao, and Gong Weiduan.

33. Zhang Tongji, p. 11.

34. Wang Yiping, p. 8.

35. Zhang Tongji, p. 11.

36. Wang Yiping, p. 9.

37. Zhang Tongji and Zhang Yongqing, pp. 256–257.

38. *China Daily*, "Middle East trade links sought by Ningxia," 17 November 1984.

39. Wang Yiping, p. 8.

40. Ibid., p. 9.

41. The freedom-of-religion policy is stated in Article 35 of the "Draft of the

Revised Constitution of the PRC" and is summarized in an editorial in *Hongqi* (Red flag), No. 12, 16 June 1982.

42. *Huizu jianshi*, p. 29; Ya Hanzhang.

43. Bai Shouyi, "Huihui minzu de xingcheng," pp. 5–6; Ma Shouqian "Yisilanjiao."

44. Ma Ruling, "Zailun Yisilanjiao yu Huihui minzu xingcheng de guanxi," p. 32.

45. Barth, "Introduction."

46. See Fabian, "Six Theses."

47. See Geertz, *Islam Observed*, and "'Internal Conversion' in Contemporary Bali"; Weber, *The Protestant Ethic*. In response to the effort to distinguish clearly between Islam and Hui ethnic identity, northwest Hui authors have recently produced numerous articles arguing the inseparable interrelation of Islam with the historical formulation of Hui identity and customs. See Lin Song, "Shilun Yisilanjiao dui xingcheng woguo Huizu suo ji de jueding xing zuoyong"; Ma Guyuan, "Yisilanjiao yu Huizu fengsu"; Ma Sukun, "Huizu de xingcheng yu Yisilanjiao"; and Yu Zhengui "Ningxia Musilin de bianqian he zongjiao shenghuo."

48. This legend is also recorded in a Shaanxi Gazetteer (in Gong Weiduan, p. 34). For more information on Sayyid 'Ajall, the Bukharan Muslim governor of Yunnan, Sichuan, and Shaanxi during the Yuan dynasty and his son, Nasredin, see Jacqueline Armijo-Hussein, "The Sinicization and Confucianization in Chinese and Western Historiography of a Muslim from Bukhara Serving Under the Mongols in China"; Bai Shouyi, "Sai Dianchi Shan Sidinb zhuan"; Bai Shouyi and Yang Huaizhong, eds., *Huizu renwu zhi, Yuandai*, pp. 12–50. For Muslims in China under the Mongols, see Rossabi, *China and Inner Asia*, pp. 257–295. Note also in this legend the failure to mention the Han co-villagers in teams 1 and 11.

49. See Gong Weiduan, p. 34.

50. Discussed by A. Doak Barnett, *Communist China and Asia*, pp. 29–32.

51. See Ding Yibo, "'Zhengce ahong' qianjian," pp. 1–2.

52. Hui continue to say that pigs are the only animals that copulate with or devour their young; they believe that pork is the meat with the least protein and the most susceptible carrier of disease.

53. Xinzhaizi Mosque was torn down during the Cultural Revolution and rebuilt in 1983–1984 with 50,000 yuan donated by local Hui. It belongs to the traditional Gedimu Islamic faction, with 200 households in the village within the mosque's *jiaofang* (religious or teaching area). It is visible from the road. We often called it the "Mexican Mosque" because of its bright colors and tall twin minarets (*wangyue lou*, literally, "watching-the-moon tower"), which resemble the bell towers of Catholic cathedrals in Meso-America.

54. MacInnis, *Religious Policy*, pp. 169–170.

55. Shadian Hui History Editorial Committee, eds. *Shadian Huizu shiliao*, pp. 46–57.

56. For a 1951 report on Shadian and its history, see Jiang Yingliang, *"Diannan Shadian Huijiao nongcun diaocha,"* pp. 644–653.

57. See Gladney, "Ethno-religious Factionalism and the Panthay Muslim Rebellion."

58. *Shadian Huizu shiliao*, p. 52.

59. Ibid., pp. 194–200.

60. George DeVos, "Ethnic Pluralism."

61. Keyes, "The Dialectics of Ethnic Change."

62. Paul Ricoeur, "The Model of the Text."

63. See Pierre Bourdieu, *Outline of a Theory of Practice*, p. 16; Bentley, "Ethnicity and Practice."

64. Ekvall, p. 19, traveling outside Hezhou (Linxia), reports: " . . . so for that night we stopped in a little Moslem world. The children were called I-si-mer (Ismael) Fa-ti-mai (Fatima) Er-pu-tu (Abdul)."

65. Bourdieu, pp. 136, 137–138. (emphasis in original)

66. Yang Huaizhong interview. See also Muhammed Usiar Huaizhong Yang, "Lun shiba shiji" and "Lüe lun sufeipae zai Zhongguo neidi Yisilanjiao zhong de fazhan." Professor Yang, "Sufism among the Muslims in Gansu," gives the 1986 population estimates of Muslims in Ningxia as 374,112 Yihewani (30.4%), 364,112 Jahriyya (27.4%), 229,280 Khufiyya (17.2%), 228,556 Gedimu (17.2%), and 103,463 Qadariyya (7.8%).

67. Joseph Fletcher, "The Naqshbandiyya and the *Dhikr-i Arra*," pp. 115–116, also found this inconsistency among the early Central Asian Naqshbandiyya, as the following quotation from the famous 16th-century Naqshbandi Khoja Ah mad Kasani reveals:

> The lords of the Naqshbandiyya have preferred the silent (*khufi*) remembrance, but some of them, if necessary, also perform the vocal (*jahri*) remembrance, just as when Khoja Ah mad Yasawi was appointed to set out for Turkestan, he saw that the inhabitants of that place did not take to the silent remembrance; so he immediately took up the way of the vocal remembrance, and thus the *dhikr-i arra* was created.

68. Pillsbury, "Cohesion and Cleavage," p. 174.

69. The family of a well-known Hui elder in Yinchuan distributed over 3,000 yuan ($1,000 U.S.) at his funeral in 1985.

70. *Ningxia huabao.*

71. Cable and French, pp. 166, 168.

72. Ekvall, p. 23.

73. Owen Lattimore, *The Desert Road to Turkestan*, p. 17.

74. Francis L. K. Hsu, *Under the Ancestors' Shadow*, p. 196.

75. See Yokoyama, p. 2.

76. Weller, pp. 37–42.

77. Compare P. Steven Sangren, *History and Magical Power in a Chinese Community.*

78. Stevan Harrell, "When a Ghost Becomes a God."
79. Gladney, "Muslim Tombs," p. 507–510.
80. MacInnis, *Religious Policy*, p. 172.
81. See Norma Diamond, "Rural Collectivization and Decollectivization in China—A Review Article"; Nicholas R. Lardy, "Agricultural Reforms in China," pp. 99–102; and Shue "Fate of the Commune."
82. Zhu Yuntao, p. 4.
83. Ibid., pp. 1, 3.
84. Fan Changjiang, *Zhongguo de xibei jiao*, p. 312.
85. Ibid., p. 307.
86. The reporter Daniel Sutherland called Gansu "A Third World within China." For further economic information on Gansu, see the helpful report by the World Bank, *China: Growth and Development in Gansu Province.*
87. See Sha Ren, "Neimenggu Huhehaoteshi Huizu jinqin hun wenti."
88. Morris Rossabi, "The Tea and Horse Trade with Inner Asia during the Ming."
89. This reflects a common policy of incorporation through the giving of titles and limited government-sanctioned power. The Jahriyya Sufi *shaykh*, Ma Zhenwu, before his arrest in 1958, held the following positions: member of the Commission on Nationalities Affairs under the Committee on Political and Military Affairs of the Northwest; governor of the Guyuan Hui People's autonomous *zhou;* member of the National Committee of the Chinese People's Political Consultative Conference; and vice-chairman of the Chinese Islamic Association. MacInnis, p. 173.
90. Dreyer, *China's Forty Millions*, p. 263.
91. Developing the northwest Muslim areas and correcting past policy mistakes was stressed to S. Enders Wimbush during his interviews with nationality officials as early as 1981: "Acutely aware of the failures of Chinese nationality policy in the past several decades, specialists in Urumqi and Beijing are seeking solutions to the most pressing minority complaints among China's substantial Muslim population." Enders S. Wimbush, *Nationality Research in the People's Republic of China: A Trip Report.*
92. But see Husain Haqqani, "Repression and Revival—the Dichotomy of Islam in China."
93. Ma Tong, *Zhongguo Yisilan jiaopai*, p. 152.
94. "Middle East trade links sought by Ningxia," *China Daily*, 14 November 1984, p. 2.
95. "Overseas investors sought for Ningxia," *China Daily*, 20 June 1984, p. 2.
96. "An Islamic Investment Corporation," *Beijing Review* 17:25 (1986) and "Chinese Oil Workers in Iraq," *Beijing Review* 12:37 (1986).
97. See Fletcher, "Central Asian Sufism."
98. Andrew, pp. 45–46.
99. For the growing literature on the relevance of tourism to ethnic change, see

Kathleen Adams, "Come to Tana Toraja, 'Land of the Heavenly Kings': Travel Agents as Brokers in Ethnicity"; Eri Cohen, "The Impact of Tourism on the Hill Tribes of Northern Thailand"; Nelson Grayburn, "Tourism: The Sacred Journey"; D. M. Greenwood, "Tourism as an Agent of Change: A Spanish Basque Case"; and Valene Smith, ed., *Hosts and Guests: The Anthropology of Tourism.*

100. China Islamic Association, *The Religious Life of Chinese Muslims,* p. 7.

101. Wang Yiping, p. 8.

102. Leo A. Despres, "Ethnicity: What Data and Theory Portend for Plural Societies."

4. ETHNIC IDENTITY IN OXEN STREET

1. The ubiquitous "teapot" insignia found in Hui restaurants from Urumqi to Kunming generally inscribed with the characters for *qing zhen* reflects the former custom of leaving a pot of water outside the restaurant for ritual washing (Niujie Ahong interview). This assisted the maintenance of a *qing zhen* lifestyle and reinforced Hui ideas of cleanliness.

2. This is a typical shared perception of lamb meat in China. In a Foreign Languages Press publication describing the rinsed mutton (*shuanyang rou*) specialty of Beijing's famous Donglaishun Hui restaurant, there are several statements guaranteeing the meat used is of superior quality and lacks the bad taste often associated with lamb: "The meat is extraordinarily tender, tasty and not at all rank. . . . The meat is white and tender and does not have the rank smell of meat from older sheep." (Liu Junwen, *Beijing: China's Ancient and Modern Capital,* p. 240) Ch'en Yuan, *Western and Central Asians in China,* p. 288, records that the early Ming historian Wang Fuzhi (1619–1692) noted in his history of the western regions that the "barbarian poets" of the Yuan dynasty, Guan Yuanshi and Sa Tianxi, had attempted to improve upon the "decadent tendencies" of Song poetry, "but the smell of sheep penetrated their work."

3. Whyte and Parish, pp. 296, 306.

4. Morton Fried, *Fabric of Chinese Society.*

5. See Wang Shoujie, "Beiping shi Huimin gaikuang."

6. See Yi Gong, "Beijing Niujie Libaisi liangwen ahlabowen de guke."

7. See Lin Song, "Everyday Life of Chinese Muslims in Beijing," pp. 196–200; Wang Shoujie, *Niujie Huimin Shenghuo tan.*"

8. Jiang Weitang, "'Gang zhi' suojide qingchu Beijing Niujie Huimin qu."

9. See Wang Shoujie, "Beiping shi Huimin gaikuang," p. 3.

10. Cai Wenpo, "Ma Dian zhi Huimin xianzhuang."

11. Wang Shoujie, "Beiping shi Huimin gaikuang," p. 8.

12. In Leslie, *Islam in Traditional China,* p. 74.

13. This legend is found in the 17th- or 18th-century anonymous *Huihui yuanlai* (The origin of the Hui) and reproduced in several Western accounts (Broomhall, pp. 61–83; G. Devéria, "Orienede l'Islamisms en Chine (deux légendes

musulmanes chinoises, pèlerinages de Ma Fou-tch'ou" pp. 312–329; Isaac Mason, "The Mohammedans of China," pp. 46–53; Edward Harper Parker, *Studies in Chinese Religion,* pp. 245–251.) See also Tazaka, pp. 193–198. A Soviet Hui Dungan version is also discussed in Svetlana Rimsky-Korsakoff Dyer, "T'ang T'ai-tsung's Dream: A Soviet Dungan Version of a Legend on the Origin of the Chinese Muslims."

14. Leslie, *Islam in Traditional China,* pp. 60–78.

15. F. S. Drake, "Mohammadanism in the T'ang Dynasty," p. 23.

16. A version of this story is given in Wang Shoujie, "Niu jie Huimin Shenghuo tan," p. 2; the historical background is in Yang Yongchang, pp. 60–62.

17. Yang Yongchang, p. 60.

18. Gladney, "Muslim Tombs," pp. 513–517.

19. Note that the second son, Na Su La Ding, bears resemblance to the famous Yuan dynasty official Nasredin (also, Na Su Lu Ding), the supposed ancestor of the Hui in Na village, Ningxia (see Chapter 3) and of the Ding in Chendai, Fujian (see Chapter 6).

20. Cited in Lin Song, "Everyday Life of Chinese Muslims in Beijing," pp. 210–211. This Confucian repugnance for the unhealthful aspects of pork and pigs was shared by villagers in Taiwan, who, according to Stuart Thompson, "Death, Food, and Fertility," p. 100, characterized pigs as "depraved, gluttonous, dirty, and licentious creatures, representative of unbridled sexuality and uncontrolled fertility, all in marked contrast to pure, moral, agnatic fertility." Hui often give these characteristics as their basis for pork avoidance.

21. Pillsbury ("Cohesion and Cleavage," p. 273) records a Hui-origin myth that they refer to in response to derogatory Han tales about Hui ancestry. Hui say that they are descended from the filial son of Adam who did not eat pork. The unfilial son ate pork, and he is the earliest ancestor of the Han.

22. For similar denigrating ethnic stereotypes directed toward the Hui in Taiwan, and ensuing eruptions of conflict, see Barbara Pillsbury, "No Pigs for the Ancestors: Pigs, Mothers and Filial Piety Among the 'Taiwanese Muslims,'" pp. 11–14; Israeli, "Muslims in China: Islam's Incompatibility with the Chinese Order."

23. See Ding Futing, et al., "Beijing Donglaishun yangrouguan fajia shi."

24. Over 174 *qing zhen* recipes of the famous Hui chef, Ma Shikui, are presented in a *qing zhen* cookbook (Ma Shulin, ed., *Zhongguo qingzhen caipu*).

25. See Chen Jo-hsi's (*The Execution of Mayor Yin and Other Stories from the Great Proletarian Cultural Revolution,* pp. 151–168) delightful description of Keng Erh's back-door maneuvers to be assured a taste of hot pot during the Cultural Revolution. The restaurant he regularly sought entré to undoubtedly was the Donglaishun.

26. Sha Zhiyuan, et al., *Beijing de Shaoshuminzu,* pp. 302–307. The 150 nationality restaurants are listed by name and address for the main streets of Beijing only.

There are undoubtedly many more on smaller streets and privately owned that are not on the list. A Uigur who was selling digital watches outside the Yanqun Lou (Spring Swallow) Hui restaurant in Tianjin suggested that the Hui like to do business at home while the Uigur prefer to travel long distances. They go to Tianjin and Shanghai for clothes and textiles, Hangzhou and Suzhou for silk, and Guangzhou and Hainan for electronic goods and motorcycles brought in from Hong Kong. In every place, and especially Beijing, due to the large foreign population, they trade local currency (*renminbi*) for foreign-exchange certificates (*waihuijuan*). He said the Uigurs look more like foreigners and were less suspect. They take their goods back to Xinjiang and sell or trade them for a profit. He is generally away from home 6 months out of the year. (See Gladney, "Ethnogenesis of the Uigur.")

27. Habermas, pp. 7–9.
28. Lin Song, "Everyday Life," p. 231, reports that, while Hui eat lamb dumplings (*jiaozi*) all year long, many conservative Beijing Hui do not prepare the dumplings at New Years and Spring Festivals to distinguish themselves from the Han who celebrate by eating dumplings at that time.
29. See Fletcher, "The Naqshbandiyya in Northwest China."
30. Wang Shoujie, "Niu jie Huimin Shenghuo tan," p. 10.
31. Luo Jianguo, "Lantern 'king' brightens exhibit."
32. Ma Xianda, "Chinese Moslems and Wushu," pp. 3–4.
33. Not only do the Hui believe there were many Hui generals who helped overthrow the Yuan, in a fascinating example of ethnohistory, one Hui historian has argued that he is a direct descendant of the Ming Taizu Emperor, Zhu Yuanzhang, who was married to a Muslim and he himself may have been a Muslim. (Hajji Yusuf Chang, "The Ming Empire: Patron of Islam in China and Southwest and West Asia, pp. 1–4 and "Chinese Islam and the Hui Minority: Past, Present and Future").
34. See *Mengcun Huizu zizhixian gaikuang.*
35. Wang Xinwu, "Huizu wushu chutan," p. 38.
36. Chang Jingcun, "Huizu quanshi yishi—ji Wang Xinwu," p. 4. Wang Xinwu is pictured demonstrating his Tai Ji Quan [also known as Tai Ch'i] style in *Inside Kungfu*, September 1985, p. 11, and discussed in the report on an Australian team's participation in the 1985 China National *wushu* Championship that took place in Yinchuan, Ningxia, which I attended.
37. Wang Peiqin and Bi Jing, "Wang Ziping: A Great Patriotic Fighter," pp. 8–13.
38. China Sports, ed., *Wushu Among Chinese Moslems*, p. 115.
39. An antique collection and description is pictured in *Zhongguo Musilin* 1:49 (1984). Several exquisite antique porcelain vases and incense holders with Islamic insignia are on display in the reception room of the Oxen Street Mosque.
40. This distinction between "sticking" and "burning" incense was emphatically made by the caretaker to Botham during his fascinating visit to a saint's tomb

in the Dongxiang area, Gansu. See Mark E. Botham, "A Saint's Tomb in China."
41. Sydney Gamble, *Peking: A Social Survey*, p. 373.
42. Wang Shoujie, "Niu jie Huimin Shenghuo tan," p. 23.
43. Wang Shoujie (ibid., p. 18) reported this same practice during the later Republican period when Hui were reluctant to admit they were from such a poverty-stricken area: "At best they would name the Chu Zhang Lane or the Fa Yuan Temple."
44. See Lee Chae-Jin, *China's Korean Minority*, pp. 51–74.
45. Wang Shoujie, "Niu jie Huimin Shenghuo tan," p. 9.
46. While earlier studies of "ethnic enclave enterprises" generally denigrated their contributions to ethnic solidarity and economic development (e.g., Edna Bonacich, "A Theory of Middlemen Minorities"; Michael Piore, "The Role of Immigration in Industrial Growth: A Case Study of the Origins and Character of Puerto Rican Migration to Boston"), recent studies suggest that ethnic-based businesses often exploit non-economic resources and are well-adapted to small and mid-level modern urban enterprises (Illsoo Kim, *The New Urban Immigrants: Korean Immigrants in New York*; Roger Waldinger, "Ethnic Enterprise and Industrial Change: A Case Study of the New York Garment Industry"; Bernard Wong, "The Role of Ethnicity in Enclave Enterprises: A Study of the Chinese Garment Factories in New York City").
47. Andrew, p. 63.
48. Hill Gates (personal communication) suggests that, as an urban minority found in every large market center, the Hui are one of the most likely groups to engage in the "petty capitalist mode of production."
49. "Kwangming Daily on History of Interracial Marriages," *FBIS* 190 (29 September 1978), p. E6. Quoted in Banister, *China's Changing Population*, p. 319.
50. Zhang Tianlu, "Beijing shaoshu minzu renkou zhuangkuang fenxi," p. 30.
51. The following figures are from Chen Changping's 1983 MA Thesis, "Minzu renkou biandong yu yizu tonghun yanjiu." I am grateful for his allowing me access to the study. For the common Muslim practice throughout the Middle East of marrying only non-Mulsims in, and the preference for father's brother's daughter marriages (*bint ᶜamm*), see Eickelman, *The Middle East*, p. 128.
52. While Sydney Gamble (*How Chinese Families Live in Peiping*, pp. 198–242) gave extensive descriptions of several traditional weddings in Beijing, he did not cite any cases of uxorilocal or minor marriage. More study needs to be done on this before we can tell if this case of uxorilocal marriage is typical in northern cities. Whyte and Parish (pp. 144–45) found that, though urbanites expressed an openness to living "wherever there is room," and even some new preferences for uxorilocal marriage, their data revealed that only 3% of couples lived with the wife's parents, with the vast majority establishing their own separate neo-local residence according to work and school assignments, generally related to the husband's work unit. Male-oriented arrangements, they concluded, continue to be the norm.

53. In order to insure that Hui in Beijing can stay in the hospital without fear of violating *qing zhen,* the city built a Hui hospital in the Niujie district. While this hospital practices only Western and Chinese traditional medicines, Hui doctors interviewed in Beijing, Xi'an, and Shanghai have said that there are certain Hui treatments for illnesses that differ from the Han, and claim that Islamic practices had an early influence on Chinese traditional medicine. These have never been catalogued systematically.

54. Pillsbury, "Blood Ethnicity." The emphasis that Pillsbury found among Hui upon their blood being different from Han may be related to the Nationalist policy that asserts that Hui and Han are all of one race and blood (see Chapter 6). Hui in Taiwan, in reaction to this policy, may attempt even more to emphasize their ethnic differences from Han in terms of blood.

55. Wang Shoujie, "Niu jie Huimin Shenghuo tan," pp. 18–19.

56. Beijing City Sociology Committee, et al., eds., "Beijing she sanzaju shaoshu minzu jiaoyu wenti diaocha baogao," p. 19.

57. Ibid.

58. Ibid., p. 20.

59. Ibid., p. 21.

60. According to the 1982 census, the overall educational level of minorities is quite low. The illiteracy rate of the total minority population aged 12 years and above is 45.54%, with the illiteracy rate of the Dongxiang Muslim minority the highest, at 86.84%. There are no university students among the Dongxiang, the Blang, the Lahu, or the Hani (Akha). The Tatar people are the most educated among the minorities, with an illiteracy rate of 8.89%, due to the fact that they, along with the Uzbeks, live almost exclusively in urban areas and are the descendants of well-educated Central Asian Muslims (Population Census Office, p. xvii). For further discussion of minority education in China, see Heberer, pp. 48–51, and Lee Chae-jin's excellent study.

61. Whyte and Parish, pp. 161–162.

62. Zhang Tianlu, "Beijing shaoshu minzu renkou," p. 32.

63. Ansley J. Coale, "Rapid Population Change in China, 1952–1982," p. 63; H. T. Li, T. Song, and C. Li, "Current Fertility State of Women of Han and Minority Nationalities in Rural Areas."

64. "Ethnics post a faster population increase," *China Daily,* 14 November 1990, p. 1.

65. Susan Greenhalgh, "Shifts in China's Population Policy, 1984–86: Views from the Central, Provincial, and Local Levels," discusses the effect of recent shifts in Chinese population policy on fertility and population growth, noting that minority population should continue to grow faster than the Han under the new policy. Beijing Hui with an urban registration are allowed to have only 1 child, however. Their population increase will largely result from in-marrying peasant women with rural registrations (who are allowed to have 2 children, see Chapter 5) and intermarriage.

66. See John S. Aird, "Population Studies and Population Policy in China"; Judith

Banister, "An Analysis of Recent Data on the Population of China"; C. Li, "The Quality Control of the 1982 Population Census in China," pp. 325–344.

67. Banister, *China's Changing Population*, p. 321.

68. "Results of China's Census: Minority Nationalities" in Summary of World Broadcasts, Part 3: The Far East, Second series, No. 7174 (4 November 1982), p. 1. Quoted in Banister, *China's Changing Population*, p. 321.

69. "Chinese Muslims celebrate," *China Daily*, 21 September 1983.

70. "Moslems celebrate festival in Beijing," *China Daily*, 19 September 1983.

71. "Muslims join in festival," *China Daily*, 18 August 1986, p. 3.

72. "Muslim restaurant," *China Daily*, 17 April 1987.

73. "Muslims kick off donation campaign," *China Daily*, 7 November 1984.

5. THE OTHER GREAT WALL

1. William G. Skinner, "Marketing and Social Structure in Rural China," p. 32; and Skinner, "Chinese Peasants and the Closed Community: An Open and Shut Case."

2. William R. Lavely, "A Rural Chinese Marriage Market."

3. Keyes, "Introduction," p. 5.

4. Zi Qi, *Zi Qi zishu*, p. 3. Note that in the quotation, the Han are referred to as "Fojiao *ren*" ("Buddhists"), while the Hui as "Huijiao *ren*" (Muslims).

5. *Ci Yuan* III, 1958–1959.

6. See Armijo-Hussein.

7. Hajji Yusuf Chang, "The Ming Empire," pp. 1–5.

8. Zi Qi, pp. 5–10.

9. Ibid.

10. Lu Yun, "Rural Muslims."

11. Cable and French, p. 167.

12. Pillsbury, "Blood Ethnicity."

13. See Barbara Pillsbury, "Being Female in a Muslim Minority in China."

14. More extensive data and analysis are presented in Dru Gladney, "Muslim Marriage Endogamy in China: A Strategy for Preserving Muslim Minority Identity?"

15. See Arthur Wolf and Chieh-shan Huang, *Marriage and Adoption in China, 1845–1945*.

16. Lavely, p. 8, reports less than 26% of marriages within the commune. William L. Parish and Martin K. Whyte (*Village and Family in Contemporary China*, p. 169) found as many as 45% of their informants married within the village.

17. Anita Chan, Richard Madsen, and Jonathan Unger, *Chen Village: A Recent History of a Peasant Community in the People's Republic of China*, pp. 186–191.

18. Ibid., pp. 190–191.

19. Ibid., p. 186. Hugh D. R. Baker (*Sheng Shui: A Chinese Lineage Village*, pp.

174–175) also found strict observance of surname exogamy required the building of extensive inter-village marriage networks in Sheung Shui.

20. In the northwest, Ma is the most prominent surname, with other Hui surnames not found on this list, including: Fen, Ga, Gai, Ha, Hei, Huang, Jing, Na, Nie, Niu, La, Peng, Sa, Sai, She, Shen, Shi, Sun, Ye, Yü, Zheng, and Zhou. Leslie (*Islamic Literature,* pp. 64–65, 189–192) gives the most comprehensive list of Hui Muslim surnames based on the occurrence of the names of Hui authors in the Ming and Qing dynasties. His helpful chart includes lists of Hui surnames also noted by Iwamura Shinbou, *Chūgoku Kaikyō shakai no kozo* II, 15, and Jin Jitang, "Huijiao minzu shuo," pp. 6–7. The frequency of certain Hui surnames, like Ma and Hui, in some areas has led to many puns and sayings, the most often heard of which is: "Out of 10 Hui there are 9 named Ma; if they're not named Ma, then Ha, if not Ha, then La" (see also Andrew, *The Crescent in Northwest China,* p. 25).

21. MacInnis, *Relgious Policy,* p. 292, emphasis mine.

22. Lavely, p. 7.

23. Richard Madsen, *Morality and Power in a Chinese Village,* p. 36, and Anita Chan et al., p. 187.

24. Anita Chan et al., p. 186.

6. *Ethnic Invention and State Intervention in a Southeastern Lineage*

1. Marco Polo, *The Travels of Marco Polo,* pp. 317–318.

2. Zhang Yuzhi and Jin Debao, "Dao Chendaixiang qu–baogao," p. 1.

3. Personal interview. See Huang Tianzhu and Liao Yuanquan, "Mantan Quanzhou diqu Ahlabo Musilin de houyi ji qi yiji," for the changing of the surnames of several Hui lineages in Quanzhou during the Ming dynasty. Bai Shouyi and Ma Shouqian, "Jizhong Huihui jiapu zhong suofanying de lishi wenti," discuss the background for this discriminatory policy.

4. Pillsbury, "Blood Ethnicity," p. 5. (emphasis in original)

5. See Ma Ibrahim T. Y., Ma Jian, and Liu Zekuan.

6. Pillsbury, "Cohesion and Cleavage," p. 145.

7. Huang and Liao, p. 201. Artifacts discovered thus far have been laboriously catalogued, photographed, and translated into Chinese, Arabic, and English by the Fujian Foreign Maritime Museum (Chen Dasheng, ed., *Islamic Inscriptions in Quanzhou*). The representations, calligraphy, and photography are all excellent in this significant volume, which is largely a reproduction and expansion of Wu Wenliang's *Quanzhou zongjiao shike.* While the translation from Chinese to English is quite good, it is hoped that future editions might consider translating the Arabic on the stone inscriptions directly into English, rather than having the English translations based on the Chinese translations of the Arabic.

8. See Gladney, "Ethno-religious Factionalism," and "Islam Preserved."

9. For the debate in China on these individuals, see Bai Shouyi, "Sai Dianchi"; Bai and Yang; Chen Sadong, "Li Zhi de jiashi, guju ji qi qi mubei"; Pei Zhi, "Hai Rui shi fo Huizu." Also see Tazaka Kōdō, "Ri Jisei wa kaikyōto ka?" cited in Lipman's "Border World," p. 293, asserting that Li Zicheng was raised in a Muslim household. Chan Hok-Lam, *Li Chih, 1527–1602, in Contemporary Chinese Historiography,* pp. 8–9, discounts the idea that Li Zhi's ancestors changed their surname from Li to Lin in the 14th century in rejecting an Islamic heritage.

10. Yitzhak Shichor's analysis, in "The Role of Islam in China's Middle-Eastern Policy," of the interplay between Middle Eastern foreign relations and China's treatment of its Muslim minorities does not reflect the importance of the minorities themselves in interacting with policy; yet it remains the best treatment of the subject. See also John O. Voll, "Muslim Minority Alternatives: Implications of Muslim Experiences in China and the Soviet Union," which distinguishes important differences between Muslim identity in China and Russia, resulting from divergent ethnic policies.

11. For important discussions of the dating and name of the Persian-style Ashab mosque in Quanzhou, see Chen Dasheng, *Islamic Inscriptions,* pp. 8–10; Wu Wenliang, "Zailun Quanzhou Qingjingsi de shijian shiqi he jianzhu xingshi," pp. 83–101; and Zhuang Weiji, "Quanzhou Qingjingsi de lishi wenti." See also Wolfgang Franke's 1979 report, "A Note on the Ancient Chinese Mosques at Xian and Quanzhou."

12. Wahb Abu Kabcha is said to be buried in Guangzhou's famous "Bell Tomb." The fourth saint is buried in Yangzhou (see Liu Binru and Chen Dazue, "Yangzhou 'Huihui tang' he yuanda Alabowen de mubei"). The early Tang date of this visit by foreign Muslims is hotly debated by Chinese Muslims and scholars—see Chen Dasheng, "Quanzhou Yisilanjiaopai," pp. 167–176, and *Islamic Inscriptions,* pp. 95–101; and Yang Hongxun, "A Preliminary Discussion on the Building Year of Quanzhou Holy Tomb and the Authenticity of its Legend," pp. 16–38.

13. Hugh Roberts Clark's 1981 dissertation, "Consolidation on the South China Frontier: The Development of Ch'uan-chou 699–1126," provides a wealth of information regarding the early rise of Quanzhou as a key maritime harbor, with particular attention paid to the role of local elites in its development. For his discussion of the early Muslim community in Quanzhou and their role in its economic development, see pp. 60–65, 216–217. For the influence of Islam on Quanzhou's history and customs, see Huang Tianzhu and Wu Youxiong, "Yisilen wenhua dui Quanzhou de yinxiang."

14. Chen Dasheng, *Islamic Inscriptions,* p. 56.

15. For translation and description, see ibid., pp. 107–108.

16. See Quanzhou Foreign Maritime Museum, ed., *Symposium on Quanzhou Islam,* pp. 207–213.

17. Chen Dasheng, *Islamic Inscriptions,* p. 108.

18. DeVos, p. 17.

19. In a recent paper, "The Role of the Mosque in the Reacceptance of Islam by Muslim Descendants in Quanzhou during the Ming Dynasty," Chen Dasheng traces the important role that mosques played in reviving the Muslim communities along the southeast coast. Like the Ashab Mosque, they were generally rebuilt as the first acts of reformers who sought to re-Islamicize the assimilated former Muslim communities.

20. Chen Dasheng, *Islamic Inscriptions*, p. 11.

21. Ibid., pp. 11–12.

22. The importance of this genealogy is not its authenticity, but its acceptance by the current members of the Ding clan in validating their descent from foreign Muslim ancestors. It is also the basis for their continuing ancestral rituals. For an excellent analysis of the genealogy, see "Chendai Dingxing yanjiu," by the Investigation Section of Quanzhou Foreign Maritime Museum.

23. Ibid., pp. 42–43.

24. A recent documentary entitled *Islam in Quanzhou (Yisilanjiao zai Quanzhou)*, produced by the Quanzhou Tourism Bureau, filmed the yearly *baizu* rituals at the Ding ancestral graves in the Lingshan Islamic graveyard, including the burning of incense and paper with Quranic texts, offering of fruit and food, and the prayers of an ahong sent from Ningxia.

25. Huang Qiuren, "*Mantan Quanzhou Huizu fengsu.*"

26. DeVos, p. 26.

27. Zhang and Jin, p. 2.

28. Ibid.

29. Ding share the belief that they are descended from Nasredin, the son of Sai Dianchi Sayyid 'Ajall, the famous Governor of Yunnan, Sichuan, and Shaanxi during the Yuan. They say that the 3rd characters of both texts cited above, when put in alignment, are the characters *zhan si*, the Chinese personal name of Nasredin (Ding Zhansi), indicating a hidden reflection of their foreign ancestry in the inscriptions over the entrance to their ancestral hall. Note that both the Na (Chapter 3) and Ding lineages claim descent from the same foreign Muslim ancestor.

30. Stuart Thompson, "Death, Food, and Fertility," p. 78. In an interesting parallel to the Hui, Thompson notes that Taiwan villagers also maintain a tabu on pork consumption which takes place from the time of death to the funeral banquet by the surviving agnatic descendants of the deceased and their wives. Eating pork at this time would be regarded as unfilial, "It would be like eating the dead person's flesh," p. 96. This connection between pork flesh and the flesh of the deceased may indicate why it is widely held among Han that the Hui do not eat pork because they were at some point descended from the offspring of the union of their primordial ancestor with a pig. Hui, of course, regard this as insulting and strongly reject this Han notion of filiality.

31. See Wing-tsit Chan, "The new awakening of Islam," p. 209.
32. See Bai Shouyi, "Huihui minzu de xingcheng."
33. Zhang and Jin, p. 2.
34. Leslie, *Islam in Traditional China*, pp. 65–66. Chen Ziqiang, "Pu Shougeng shiliao kaoban."
35. The Party secretary of Chendai town said they made enormous profits from a recent exhibition and sale of their leather shoes in Beijing. The exhibition opened on 20 August 1986 in Beijing and the entire stock was sold out within 3 days, although they had reserved the hall for 10. They made a profit of over 10,000 yuan each day. Ding relatives from overseas bring shoes with them on their visits to the villages. "When we get a new shoe," he explained, "we tear it apart and copy it as fast as we can. People like our new foreign styles."
36. Population Census Office, p. 175.
37. "Ding Clan Genealogy," p. 30.
38. I have discussed this phenomenon in a preliminary paper suggesting that Weber's hypothesis regarding China and minority entrepreneurship may be relevant for understanding economic activity in contemporary China, particularly among the Hui. See Dru C. Gladney, "The 'Weber Thesis' and Economic Action in Post-Mao China."
39. Ding relatives from the Philippines visited Chendai recently, revealing that they were members of a "Five Surname Association" (Wuxing Hui) of Hui in Southeast Asia, including Guo, Ding, Bai, Jin, and Ma.
40. I have refrained from referring to Hui such as the Ding, Jin, and Guo as the "Quanzhou Hui" in general, as some publications do, since there are other later Hui immigrants from Shandong, Anhui, and Henan living in Quanzhou, Fuzhou, and Xiamen who are more culturally Muslim in their lifestyles (see Terada Takanobu, "Mingdai Quanzhou Huizu zakao").
41. Chinese Muslim Association, *Islam in Taiwan*, p. 4.
42. See Ts'ai Mao-t'ang, "Hui-jiao zai Lugang."
43. Pillsbury, "Blood Ethnicity," p. 31.
44. See the Investigation Section of Quanzhou Foreign Maritime Museum, "Baiqi Guoxing bu shi Guo Ziyi de houyi er shi Huizu ren," pp. 213–216, where it is demonstrated that the Guo genealogies do not support the claim to descent from Guo Ziyi. Elderly Guo in Baiqi, Fujian, however, still speak of being descended from Guo Ziyi, and their ancestral home, they claim, is Fenyang, Shanxi, where Guo Ziyi originated. During ancestral holidays before Liberation, Guo ancestral halls displayed small lanterns adorned with the characters for Fenyang, referring back to their ancestral home. Even recent funerals of elder Guo have had the characters for Fenyang printed on a red cloth that is buried on top of the coffin.
45. Pillsbury, "Cohesion and Cleavage," p. 145.
46. Pillsbury, "Blood Ethnicity," p. 34.
47. Ibid., p. 33.

48. Pillsbury, "Cohesion and Cleavage," p. 240.

49. Charles Keyes, "Dialectics of Ethnic Change," p. 4.

50. Pillsbury, "Blood Ethnicity," pp. 5–6.

51. Quoted in G. Carter Bentley, "Theoretical Perspectives on Ethnicity and Nationality," Part 1, p. 52.

52. See Gates.

53. Unpublished document entitled "Huizu," in a 1974 series, Zhongguo xiaoshu minzu jiankuang (The basic situation of China's minority nationalities).

54. Pamela Crossley, *Orphan Warriors*, p. 218.

55. See the pamphlet compiled by the Committee for Protecting Islamic Historical Relics in Quanzhou and the Research Centre for the Historical Relics of Chinese Culture. Yang Hongxun, pp. 1–15.

56. A resolution on the use of the funding has not yet been reached however, as local authorities are afraid of causing damage to the remains of the Ashab Mosque during restoration. The Jordani, however, is not willing to construct a new mosque with his funds. The influx of this large contribution has caused considerable dissension within the Hui community.

57. Min Tong, "Youha wanglai de jian zheng," pp. 131–135.

58. See Jamjoon for an interesting account of a Saudi delegation's visit to Islamic sites in China.

59. Eaton, "Political and Religious Authority," p. 355.

60. See Gladney, "Muslim Tombs," pp. 497–507.

61. In Chen Dasheng, *Islamic Inscriptions*, p. 96. Compare Eaton's ("Political and Religious Authority," p. 341) Punjab case of the power of Bâbâ Furîd to protect a certain ᶜAbd Allâh Rumî from highway robbers as he traveled southwest from Ajudhan to Multan in the early 16th century. Mills provides a discussion of Zheng He's voyages and a translation of Ma Huan's 15th-century Chinese account, including a visit to Mecca, the city of the "Heavenly square" (*tian fang*), and the miraculous "bright light" that he reported rose from the prophet's tomb in Medina (pp. 1–34, 173–179). The influence of this account among China's early Muslims may account for the belief that the Holy Islamic Tombs in Quanzhou also emitted a bright light at night, thus the name of their location became *Ling shan* ("spiritual or brilliant mountain"; see He Qiaoyuan, *Minshu*, p. 21.

62. Weller, pp. 26–27.

63. See Huang and Liao.

64. Early estimates ranged widely from 1,000 in 1910 (Broomhall, p. 215) to 850,000 in 1911 (*Qing Minzhengbu*, cited in Lipman, "Border World," p. 303) to 471,750 in 1935 (*China Yearbook, 1935–1936*).

65. Nagata, "In Defense of Ethnic Boundaries," p. 112.

7. NATIONAL IDENTITY IN THE CHINESE NATION-STATE

1. Wu'er Kaixi, personal interview, December 1989.
2. *New York Times*, "Voice from Tiananmen Now Heard at Wellesley," 22 February 1990, p. A18.
3. "Strife Continues in China," ABC News Nightline, Show No. 2096, Ted Koppel interview, 5 June 1989.
4. For more information on the *neiren dang* (internal party) suppression during the Cultural Revolution in Inner Mongolia, the widespread arrests and tortures of Mongolians, see William R. Jankowiak, "The Last Hurrah? Political Protest in Inner Mongolia."
5. Roderick MacFarquhar, "The End of the Chinese Revolution."
6. Arjun Appadurai, "Introduction: Commodities and the Politics of Value."
7. Cohn.
8. Lynn T. White, III, *Policies of Chaos: The Organizational Causes of Violence in China's Cultural Revolution.*
9. In Jonathan Lipman, "Border World," p. 293, citing Tazaka Kōdō, *Chūgoku ni okeru kaikyō no denrai to sno guzū.*
10. See Gladney, "The Ethnogenesis of the Uigur"; Juten Oda, "Uighuristan," p. 22; Justin Jon Rudelson, "Uighur Ethnic Identity Change in the Oases of Chinese Turkestan."
11. Hayden White, *Metahistory: The Historical Imagination in Nineteenth Century Europe*, p. 81.
12. For a discussion of the problematic nature of these Central Asian identifications in the Soviet Union, see Enders S. Wimbush, "The Politics of Identity Change in Soviet Central Asia."
13. These Manichaean artistic representations are wondrously depicted in the caves of Bezeklik, near Turfan; see Albert von LeCoq, *Buried Treasures of Chinese Turkestan.*
14. See Henry G. Schwarz, *The Minorities of Northern China: A Survey*, pp. 57–74; Saguchi Tōru, "Historical Development of the Sarïgh Uyghurs." *Zhongguo shaoshu minzu*, p. 289.
15. Schram, pp. 63–65.
16. Gladney, "Pivotal Pawns?"
17. Hélène Carrère d' Encausse, "The Stirring of National Feeling," p. 274. See also Wimbush, "The Politics of Identity," pp. 69–78.
18. C. P. Fitzgerald, *The Tower of Five Glories: A Study of the Min Chia of Ta Li, Yunnan.*
19. Hsu.
20. Yokoyama.
21. David Wu, "Chinese Minority Policy and the Meaning of Minority Culture: The Example of the Bai in Yunnan, China."

22. Lin Yueh-hwa, "Yizu of Liang Shan, Past and Present," p. 90.

23. Stevan Harrell, "Ethnicity, Local Interests, and the State." See also David Bradley, "The Yi Nationality of Southwestern China: A Linguistic Overview."

24. *Zhongguo shaoshu minzu*, p. 289.

25. Wang Mingke. See also Sun Hongkai, "A Preliminary Investigation into the Relationship Between Qiong Long and the Languages of the Qiang Branch of Tibeto-Burman."

26. S. Robert Ramsay, *The Languages of China*, p. 273.

27. Dai Qingxia, "On the Languages of the Jingpo Nationality."

28. Ramsay, p. 271.

29. In a similar fashion, in Taiwan, the Aborigines are a group of 10 separate ethnolinguistic groups that have only recently begun to accept and manipulate their status as the Gaoshan minority for certain benefits under the Nationalist Government in a pan-Aboriginal movement. They have accepted the label of the state, are using it for their own purposes and are beginning to organize as a pan-ethnic collectivity. See Hsieh Shih-Chung, "Ethnic Contacts, Stygmatized Identity, and Pan-Aboriginalism: A Study on Ethnic Change of Taiwan Aborigines."

30. Emily Honig, "The Politics of Prejudice: Subei People in Republican-Era Shanghai"; and "Pride and Prejudice: Subei People in Contemporary Shanghai."

31. See Myron Cohen, *House Divided, House United: The Chinese Family in Taiwan*. The statement about the Hakka being Han was made to me personally by Professor Cohen and is widely accepted. It is interesting, however, that the Hakka, like the Cantonese, call themselves "Tang people" (Tang *ren*). When asked if they would like to be considered a minority nationality, most Hakka (and Cantonese) say no, and willingly accept Han nationality status, perhaps as a way of avoiding further stigmatization.

32. Fred C. Blake, *Ethnic Groups and Social Change in a Chinese Market Town*.

33. John De Francis, *The Chinese Language*, pp. 54–57.

34. Ramsay, pp. 4–16.

35. Yuen Ren Chao, *Aspects of Chinese Sociolinguistics*, p. 87.

36. Jerry Norman, *Chinese*, p. 187.

37. Ramsay, pp. 17–18.

38. Richard G. Fox, "Hindu Nationalism in the Making, or the Rise of the Hindian," p. 68.

39. Max Weber, *Economy and Society*, II, 389.

40. In this powerful metaphor depicting the modern hegemonic state as a "panoptican," Foucault (*Discipline and Punish: The Birth of the Prision*, pp. 195–230) describes the central control tower of a circular prison in which all prisoners can be seen by the watcher, but he himself cannot be seen, which leads, as Bentham pointed out, to total submission: "To be incessantly under the eyes of the inspector is to lose in effect the power to do evil and almost the thought of want-

ing to do it" (in Fallers). I am grateful to Ann S. Anagnost ("The Mimesis of Power") for first indicating the relevance of this metaphor to the modern Chinese state.

41. Anderson, pp. 41–49.

42. June Dreyer, "The Islamic Community of China," p. 34.

43. *Renmin ribao* (overseas edition), "Yixie renda daibiao lianhe jianyi jueding yige 'minzu tuanjie' re," p. 4.

44. Deleuze and Guattari, p. 149.

45. Lefort, p. 279.

46. Clifford, *The Predicament of Culture*, p. 16.

47. The phrase is from Manning Nash, *The Cauldron of Ethnicity*, which seems a better metaphor than "melting pot" for our day.

48. Dreyer, *China's Forty Millions*, pp. 264–265; Heberer.

49. See Ch'en Yuan's discussion of 168 individuals in the Yuan dynasty who became "Sinicized" by virtue of their mastering Chinese and passing the imperial examinations.

50. Naquin and Rawski, p. 129.

51. Crossley, *Orphan Warriors*, p. 223.

52. See Mary Clabaugh Wright, *The Last Stand of Chinese Conservativism*, pp. 51–56; and Karl A. Wittfogel and Feng Chia-sheng, *History of Chinese Society: Liao;* cited in Crossley, *Orphan Warriors*, pp. 224–225.

53. Crossley, *Orphan Warriors*, p. 228.

54. Banister, *China's Changing Population*, p. 322.

55. Heberer, p. 11.

56. *China Daily,* 14 November 1990, p. 1.

57. George DeVos and Lola Romanucci-Ross, *Ethnic Identity*, pp. 141–142.

58. Lipman, "Border World," pp. 284–285. (emphasis in the original)

59. Broomhall; Israeli, *Muslims in China.*

60. This rather "Orientalist" interpretation by Westerners who often rely on preconceived Middle East-centered notions of Islam is prevalent among many early chroniclers of the history of Islam in China. In his article "Muhammadanism (in China)," p. 590, Martin Hartmann wrote: "Islam, which with its rigid doctrine of uniformity does not on principle express itself in creeds, and tends to repel by the defiant and arrogant tone of its adherents, and which, above all, contrasts with Buddhism in its being essentially a political religion, could not strike root in China save under the protection of the strong [Mongol] hand." For the historiography of Muslims in China from Chinese and Western perspectives, see Armijo-Hussein. For the study of Muslim societies as the indigenized Islamic communities wherever they are to be found, see the volume edited by William Roff, ed., *Islam and the Political Economy of Meaning.*

61. See Lin Song, "Everyday Life," pp. 197–198; Bai Shouyi and Yang Huaizhong, *Huizu renwu zhi, Yuan dai;* Bai Shouyi and Yang Huaizhong, *Huizu renwu zhi, Ming dai.*
62. See Schwarz, *Minorities of Northern China,* p. 203.
63. Liao Gailong, "The '1980 Reform' Program in China 1986," pp. 88–89, emphasis mine.
64. Norma Diamond, "The Miao and Poison: Interactions on China's Southwest Frontier," pp. 1–25.
65. Yang Mohammad Usiar Huaizhong, "The Eighteenth Century Gansu Relief Fraud Scandal."
66. Lipman, "Sufi Muslim Lineages and Elite Formation in Modern China"; Ma Tong, *Zhongguo Yisilan jiaopai.*
67. Cited in Fletcher, "The Taylor-Pickens Letters on the Jahri Branch of the Naqshbandiyya in China," p. 14.
68. Xinjiang Academy of Social Sciences, "Xinjiang Huizu de laiyuan," p. 85.
69. Riftin, p. 519.
70. Pillsbury, "Cohesion and Cleavage," p. 4.
71. Reported in MacInnis, *Religion in China Today,* pp. 241–242.
72. Fischer, "Ethnicity and the Post-Modern Arts of Memory," p. 223.
73. "Xinjiang–Soviet trade rises," *China Daily,* 4 April 1987, p. 2.
74. Pillsbury, "Blood Ethnicity."
75. Paul Ricoeur, *Lectures on Ideology and Utopia,* p. 258.
76. Michel Foucault, "The Subject and Power," p. 208.
77. "Freer reign urged for minorities," *China Daily,* 4 April 1987, p. 1.
78. Fei Xiaotong, quoted in "Minorities hold key to own prosperity," *China Daily,* 28 April 1987, p. 4.
79. Anagnost.
80. Foucault, "Truth and Power," p. 122.
81. Ma Zhu, *Qing Zhen zhi Nan.* 8 juan. 1681. For a description, see Leslie, *Islamic Literature in Chinese,* p. 35.
82. See Gladney, "Bodily Positions and Social Dispositions: Sexuality, Nationality and Tiananmen."
83. Su Shaokang, *He Shang,* Segment 2. (emphasis added)
84. Ibid., Segment 1.
85. Andrew, p. 12.

Appendix A Hui Islamic Orders in China

Name	Other Names	Place of Origin	Leaders[a]	Initial Period	Original Location	Adherents[b]	Present Distribution
				Non-Sufi Orders			
Gedimu[c]	Laojiao[d] Lao Ga "Old Teaching"	Arabia Persia Central Asia	Merchants Officials Soldiers	7th century to 14th century migrations	Southeast Coast (Guangzhou[Canton] Quanzhou, Hangzhou, Yangzhou) Silk Road (Kashgar, Turfan, Lanzhou, Linxia, Wuzhong, Yinchuan, Xian)	4,000,000	Xinjiang; Gansu; Qinghai;Ningxia; Yunnan; Shaanxi; Henan; Hebei; Shandong; Heilongjiang
Yihewani[e]	Ikhwan Xinxinjiao "New New Teaching" Aihelisunnai Zuningjiao, Sadid	Arabia	Ma Wanfu (Ma Guoyuan)	1889	Gansu (Hezhou) Linxia	1,500,000	All China, esp. urban areas
Sui pai	Yitaijiao	Gansu, Guanghe	Ga Suge (Ga Su Hajji)	1937	Gansu, Linxia	1,000,000	Gansu; Ningxia; Qinghai; and all China
Bai pai	Salafiyya Sailaifeiye Santaijiao	Gansu, Guanghe Huangzhaojia, Baizhuang	Ga Baizhuang (Ma Debao)	1937	Gansu, Linxia	50,000	Gansu; Qinghai; Ningxia; Xinjiang; Shaanxi, Xian

APPENDIX A *Continued*

Name	Other Names	Place of Origin	Leaders[a]	Initial Period	Original Location	Adherents[b]	Present Distribution
Xi Dao Tang[f]	Hanxue pai Xinxinjiao "New New Teaching"	Gansu, Taozhou Old City	Ma Qixi (Ma Mingren)	1901	Gansu, Lintao	10,000	Gansu, Lintao: Qinghai; Ma Ying; Xinjiang
				Sufi Menhuan			
Qadariyya[g]	Gadelinye Ka-di-lin-ye Xinjiao "New Teaching"	Central Asia	Khoja Abd Alla	1674	Gansu, Linxia Qinghai, Yingzhong	100,000	Gansu; Qinghai; Ningxia; Xinjiang; Shaanxi; Sichuan
Da Gongbei	Great Gongbei Qi Men	Central Asia	Qi Jingyi [Yang Shijun]	1690	Gansu, Linxia West Gate	80,000	Gansu, Linxia; Shaanxi, Xixiang; Sichuan, Langzhong; Qinghai; Ningxia; Xinjiang
Houzihe		Shaanxi, Xian, Guande Men	Master Yang [An Yilun]	1750s	Qinghai	5,000	Qinghai, Houzihe
Xiangyuantang		Xinjiang	Hai Kuo [Sha family]	1766	Xinjiang	2,500	Gansu, Lanzhou, Dongxiang, Linxia; Ningxia, Yinchuan
Ah Men		Arabia	Muhammad Nuvideeni	1861	Gansu	500	Gansu, Lanzhou, Panjiaba, Gaolan

APPENDIX A *Continued*

Name	Other Names	Place of Origin	Leaders[a]	Initial Period	Original Location	Adherents[b]	Present Distribution
Jiucaiping		Qinghai, Houzihe	An Hongxiong [Ma Jinsong]	1895	Ningxia, Xiji	5,000	Ningxia, Xiji Jiucaiping, Haiyuan, Guyuan
Qi Men	Ji Men	Xinjiang	[Ma Demin]	1905	Gansu; Qinghai	1,000	Ningxia, Guyuan Liangjiabao and Tanshan
Khufiyya[h]	Hufuye Khanyya Xinjiao "New Teaching"	Central Asia	Khoja Afaq	1671	Xinjiang; Qinghai; Gansu	491,500	Sinjiang; Gansu; Qinghai; Ningxia; Shaanxi; Sichuan; Yunnan
Bijiazhang		Central Asia	Ma Zongsheng [Ma Guozhen]	1675	Gansu, Linxia	20,000	Gansu, Linxia Batang, Yangwashan, Hezheng Dagutai, Yadang, Heitupo; Xinjiang; Qinghai; Ningxia
Xiao Liu Men		Gansu, Linxia	Liu Mou [Ma Rong]	1740s	Gansu, Lanzhou Xiao Xihu	2,000	Gansu, Linxia, Lanzhou
Mufuti		Central Asia	Ma Shouzhen [Ma Xiao]	1683	Gansu, Linxia, Tangle	100,000	Gansu, Linxia, Tangle, Zhaizigou, Qiaorou, Hezheng Jiniwan, Dongxiang; Qingnai, Nanchuan; Xinuang

APPENDIX A *Continued*

Name	Other Names	Place of Origin	Leaders[a]	Initial Period	Original Location	Adherents[b]	Present Distribution
Lin Tao		Gansu, Tangle	Ma Yuhuan [Hajji Ma Dawu]	1796	Gansu, Linxia	5,000	Gansu, Linxia Bafang, Wataotou, Tangle, Liuchuan
Huasi	Flowery Mosque	Arabia	Ma Laichi [Ah Gugu]	1741	Gansu, Linxia	150,000	Gansu, Linxia Xixiang, Nanxiang, Guanghe Sanjiaji, Hezheng Shijiaji, Yadang, Daxiao Nancha; Qinghai, Xunhua, Xining; Ningxia, Yinchuan; Xinjiang, Urumqi
Hongni Xionghu Men		Gansu, Dongxiang, Guanghe	Ma Zedi [Ma Guotai]	1751	Gansu, Dongxiang	50,000	Gansu, Dongxiang Hongnixiang, Hezheng
Taizisi Hu Men		Gansu, Dongxiang	Gederu [Ma Guozhong]	1860	Gansu, Linxia Guanghe	60,000	Gansu, Linxia Guanghe Nangou, Tangle
Qinghai Xian Men		Central Asia	Xian Meizhen [Xian Yufeng]	1700s	Qinghai, Bazhangou	2,000	Qinghai, Bazhangou
Ningxia Xian Men		Qinghai	Xian Linyuan [Xian Chunyi]	1931	Ningxia, Xiji Qiancha	3,000	Ninxia, Xiji; Guyuan; Gansu, Lanzhou

Name	Other Names	Place of Origin	Leaders[a]	Initial Period	Original Location	Adherents[b]	Present Distribution
Liu Men		Qinghai	Liu Ye	1795	Gansu, Lanzhou	500	Gansu, Lanzhou
Beizhuang	Baizhuang	Xinjiang, Shanian	Ma Baozhen [Ma Shaozong]	1816	Gansu, Linxia Dongxiang	80,000	Gansu, Dongxiang Qungai, Beizhuang, Sucheng, Leshan, Guanghe Zongjia, Zhenghe Hezheng Hongya, Daxiao Nancha; Qinghai, Xining; Xinjiang, Urumqi
Ding Men		Xinjiang Ye Erqiang	Dingxiang [Ga Ahong]	1800s	Gansu, Linxia Hualinshan	500	Gansu, Linxia, Lanzhou
Jiangoujing		Qinghia, Datong	Huazhe Dongjini Xini [Ma Ahong]	1850s	Gansu, Lanzhou Xujiawan	1,500	Gansu, Lanzhou, Jingtai
Hong Men		Gansu, Jingtai Jiantou Jing	Er Zezi (Hong Hairui) (Zhou Taoren) (Ding Wanming)	1874	Ningxia, Guyuan	4,000	Ningxia, Guyuan, Tongxin
Wenquan Tang		Arabia	Ma Wenquan [Ma Xing]	1851	Gansu, Lanzhou Gengjiazhuang	500	Gansu, Lanzhou, Linxia; Qinghai; Xunhua

APPENDIX A *Continued*

Name	Other Names	Place of Origin	Leaders[a]	Initial Period	Original Location	Adherents[b]	Present Distribution
Yantou		Gansu, Linxia	Hajji Han (Han Zhenzhe)	1900s	Gansu, Linxia Dahejia Meipo	5,000	Gansu, Linxia Dahejia Liuji, Batang, Lanzhou
Gao Zhaojia		Gansu, Linxia [Reng Yixi]	Ma Yiheiya	1911	Gansu, Linxia, Liuji Gaozhaojia	1,000	Gansu, Linxia, Liuji
Tonggui		Gansu, Lanzhou	Ma Guanglin [Qiao Dianma Ahong]	1900s	Ningxia, Tonggui	1,000	Ningxia, Tonggui; Yongning, Pingluo; Gansu, Pingliang
Salajiao		Qinghai, Xunhua	Suwa Lemanzi [Ma Heizile]	1959	Qinghai, Xunhua	500	Qinghai, Xunhua; Gansu, Linxia
Ling Ming Tang		Xinjiang	Ma Lingyi [Shaan Zijiu]	1879	Gansu, Lanzhou	3,000	Gansu, Lanzhou, Tangle, Guanghe; Qinghai; Xinjiang
Ming Yue Tang		Gansu, Lanzhou	[Ma Reniu]	1940s	Ningxia, Guyuan, Sanying	500	Ningxia, Guyuan
Fa Men		Arabia	(Fa Zhen)	1920s	Gansu, Linxia	1,500	Gansu, Linxia
Jahriyya[i]	Zheherenye Xuanhuagang Xinjiao "New Teaching"	Yemen	Ma Mingxin 'Abdal-Kaliq b. az-Zayn al-Mizjaji	1744	Gansu, Linxia; Qinghai, Xunhua	750,000	Gansu; Qinghai; Ningxia; Xinjiang; Shaanxi; Sichuan; all China

Appendix A Continued

Name	Other Names	Place of Origin	Leaders[a]	Initial Period	Original Location	Adherents[b]	Present Distribution
Banqiao	Jinji pai Maqiao pai	Gansu, Pingliang	Ma Datian [Ma Tengai]	1813	Ningxia, Wuzhong	60,000	Ningxia, Wuzhong, Lingwu, Tongxin, Qingtongxia; Gansu, Linxia, Lanzhou; Xinjiang, Urumqi, Yanqi; Yunnan, Shadian; Beijing; Tiantin
Nanchuan		Ningxia, Banqiao	Ma Jinxi [Ma Tengni]	1890	Gansu, Zhangjiachuan, Nanchuan	30,000	Gansu, Zhangjiachuan, Linxia
Shagou	Honglefu pai	Gansu Ningxia	Ma Yuanzhang (Ma Zhenwu) [Ma Liesun]	1875	Ningxia, Honglefu, Xiji	600,000	Ningxia, Xiji, Guyuan, Haiyuan; Gansu, Pingliang; Xinjiang; Yunnan; Jilin; Hebei; Shandong
Beishan	North Mountain	Ningxia, Shagou	Ma Yuanlie [Ma Dianwu]	1920	Gansu, Zhangjiachuan, Beishan	50,000	Gansu, Zhangjiachuan, Weicheng, Guanghe
Xin Dianzi		Ningxia, Xiji	Ma Jiwu	1920	Ningxia Xiji Xindianzi	10,000	Ningxia, Xiji; Gansu

Appendix A *Continued*

Name	Other Names	Place of Origin	Leaders[a]	Initial Period	Original Location	Adherents[b]	Present Distribution
Kubrawiyya[j]	Khubulinye Dawantou Zhang men	Arabia	Mohidin (Muhuyindeni) [Zhang Hairu]	1370[k] or 1660s	Gansu, Dongxiang Dawantou	20,000	Gansu, Dongxiang Dawantou, Tangwang, Heishishan, Chenjiaketuo, Shawa, Shuangshu, Ahlimadu, Tangle Shanwan, Caonan, Yangjiazhuang, Fengtai, Taogonggou, Lanninan

Sources: Primarily Ma Tong, *Zhongguo Islanjiaopai yu menhuan*, *Zhongguo Yisianjiaopai menhuan suyuan*. Also Fletcher, "The Naqshbandiyya in Northwest China"; Jin Yijiu, "Sufeipai yu Zhongguo menhuan"; Lipman, "The Border World of Gansu"; Ma Tong and Wang Qi, "Zhongguo Yisilanjiao de jiaopai he menhuan"; Mian Weiling, *Ningxia Yisilan jiaopai le gaiyao*; Trippner, "Islamische Gruppe and Braberkult in Nordwest China"; Yang Mohammed Usiar Huaizhong, "Sufism among the Muslims in Gansu, Ningxia, and Qinghai."

Notes: [a]Present leaders, where known, are placed in brackets. Former prominent leaders are placed in parentheses.

[b]Population figures are estimates based on Ma Tong, *Zhongguo Yisilan jiaopai menhuan zhidu shilue*, and personal interviews conducted with religious and government leaders between 1983 and 1986.

[c]Sunni, Hanafi, Mosque-centered communities, traditionalist, no hereditary leadership.

[d]Note that Trippner's schema (p. 17) places the Gedimu within the Wahhabi, continues to use the confusing Laojiao ("Old Teaching"), Xinjiao ("New Teaching"), and Xinxinjiao ("New New Teaching"), and tends to arrange groups according to geographic, rather than historical or religious, affiliation.

[e]Sunni, Hanafi, Reformist Wahhabi Islamic brotherhood (Ikhwan), Mosque-centered, no hereditary leadership.

[f]Reformist, Mosque-centered, no inherited leadership, emphasizes Chinese scholarship.

[g]Earliest Sufi *menhuan*, Qadiri *tariqa*, dispersed, often centered on tombs, inherited leadership.

[h]Naqshbani *tariqa*, now decentralized into smaller Mosque-centered *menhuan*.

[i]Naqshbandi *tariqa*, connected through *menhuan*, hereditary leadership.

[j]Kubrawiyya *tariqa*, concentrated in small Mosque-centered communities, hereditary leadership.

[k]For difference in dates, compare Yang Mohammad Usiur Huaizhong forthcoming and Ma Tong, pp. 451-455.

A Select Glossary of Hui Chinese Islamic Terms

The Hui in China primarily speak the languages and dialectics spoken by the people among whom they live. Lacking a distinct language of their own, they have nevertheless infused these mainly Chinese (Han) languages with Islamic terminology derived from several sources, including Arabic, Persian, Turkish, and other Central Asian languages. Known as "Hui speech" (*Huihui hua*), the phrases and vocabulary items do not comprise a language of their own but serve as linguistic markers of ethnic and religious identity.

There are no non-Chinese verbs in Hui speech, and many of the terms they use represent a unique mix of Chinese and foreign languages, permeated by translations and transliterations of Islamic lexical items. For example, "Arabia" is rendered Ah la bo 阿拉伯, but "Arabic" is expressed as Ah wen 阿文, literally, the "literature of Arabia," with Arabia represented by only the first syllable. Other terms are direct transliterations of Persian or Arabic terms, such as ahong 阿訇 for "teacher," drawing upon the Persian *akhund*, rather than the Arabic *imam*. Many terms are purely Chinese translations of the Islamic meaning, such as Qing Zhen 清真 for Islam, referring to the pure and true religion. Other words can be expressed in either Arabic, Persian, or Chinese, such as the Arabic An la 安拉, the Persian Hu da 胡达, or the Chinese Zhen Zhu 真主 (True Lord), all of which refer to Allah. Folk, Buddhist, and Daoist traditions have also exerted an influence on Hui terminology, such as the use of the Buddhist term *wuchang* 无常 (impermanence) for death by Hui throughout China, or the Daoist-influenced terms *Dao tang* 道堂 for the main prayer hall used by the leader of a Sufi order in the northwest, and *Dao zu* 道祖 to refer to the Sufi master or saint who is the originator of the order. Other terms serve as transliterations of the foreign words, but at the same time employ Chinese ideographs with their own meaning, e.g., one Hui term for "Hell" is *Duozuihai*

多罪海, a transliteration of the Persian *Duozakh*, with the added Chinese meaning of "the sea of many transgressions."

I have noticed that the use of these terms generally marks outsider/insider status, as Hui will often use the Arabic- or Persian-derived terms among themselves, saving the Chinese terms for when they speak with non-Muslim Han. It also seemed to me that, in the Hui villages or neighborhoods, daily speech was influenced more by Persian, whereas theological terminology used in the mosque by the ahong and *manla* was dominated more by Arabic-derived terms. There is also significant variation regionally, with the more technical Arabic and Persian terms much more prevalent in the northwest than in the southeast or urban areas (a Hui in Shanghai will be just as confused when asked directions to the *maisijide* 麦斯吉德 [mosque] by a northwestern Hui as his Han conterpart).

This glossary was complied primarily from my field notes, with considerable assistance derived from comparison with other lists, especially that of Professor Yu Zhengui and Ahong Su Dunli.[1] Andrew Mason's 1919 list was one of the first Western attempts to translate these terms, and Barbara Pillsubury's excellent glossary based on her fieldwork in Taiwan was the most recent addition, both of which provided very helpful comparisons.[2] I did not include terms from these lists that I did not hear in use or were unrecognized by my informants, so this represents an "up-dated" glossary. Unfortunately, it is still terribly limited due to the wide geographic and dialectical variation found among the Hui. More rigorous linguistic and speech performance analysis is necessary before we can begin to note the distribution and influence of earlier Islamic languages on the development of Hui speech in China. Origins of the Chinese terms, where known, are indicated by the letters in parentheses following the terms (A = Arabic, P = Persian, T = Turkish, C = Chinese, A/C = combination of Arabic and Chinese).

I offer this glossary as a tool for those interested in carrying out further research on Islam in China or tracking down the Chinese ideographs for many of the terms used in this book. A working knowledge of many of these terms is required for any cursory reading of the enormous body of Hui Islamic literature, sociological, or religious studies of Islam in China, the Chinese Quran, or even the local newspapers and gazetteers in Muslim areas of China. The incorporation of foreign terms into Chinese is a haphazard affair, since there exists no systematic method to romanize these terms in Chinese, as *romaji*, *katagana*, or *hinagana* are employed by the Japanese. Chinese generally translate the meaning of a term, or approximate the sound of the foreign lexical item,

[1] Yu Zhengui and Su Dunli, *Ningxia Yisilanjiao changyong ciyu huibian.*
[2] Andrew Mason, *List of Chinese Moslem Terms*; Barbara Pilsbury, "Cohesion and Cleavage," p. 275–283.

with considerable distortion, and sometimes combine both methods in one term (such as the term *Sufei pai* 苏非派 for Sufism, which joins the tranliterated characters for *Sufi* with the Chinese term *pai*, 派 for school or faction). Unless one's ear is attuned to the unique phraseology and lexical peculiarity of Hui expressions in China, it is easy to miss the distinctiveness of Hui national cultural and social interaction. I suspect that it is the total lack of awareness of this unusual vocabulary of the Hui in China that has led China scholars to assume that Hui differ little from the Han. They speak only Chinese, the argument goes, so they must be Chinese, or "Chinese Muslims." Yet this assimilationist perspective ignores the tremendously complex and subtle distinctiveness of the Hui linguistic codes and ethnoreligious vocabulary. Expert code switching that Hui frequently engage in when among the Han, using Han Chinese terms for Islamic terms, like *libaisi* 礼拜寺 (prayer temple) for *qingzhen si* 清真寺 or *maisijide* 麦斯吉德 (mosque), helps to mask and thus, perhaps preserve, the elusiveness of this identity. The use of Arabic or Persian numbers between Hui merchants in the marketplace also helps them gain a linguistic edge over the Han they are bartering with, and may even contribute to their reputation as being crafty or larcenous. I hope this introduction to Hui speech will help to contest this image, as well as to assist others in recognizing and becoming familiar with these subtle ethnolinguistic differences a great deal more quickly than I did.

Ahdan (A) 阿丹 — Adam

ahbudeke (P) 阿布得可 — small ritual washing (*jiemei*)

ahheileti (A) 阿黑勒提 — afterlife

Ahla (A) 阿拉 — Allah

Ahlabo (C) 阿拉伯 — Arabia

Ahlahu (A) 阿拉乎 — Allah

Ahli (A) 阿利, 阿里 — Ali (Muhammad's son-in-law)

Ahlin (A) 阿林 — "one with knowledge," those with advanced Islamic knowledge

Ahmu (A) 阿木 — common Muslims without much Islamic knowledge

ahong (P) 阿訇, 阿衡, 阿洪 — "teacher," imam or anyone with advanced religious knowledge and able to read the Quran in Arabic

Ahshula (A) 阿舒拉 — tenth day of first month on Islamic calender, eating of bean porridge in mosque to commemorate the ascension of Adan (Adam), Nuha (Noah), Yibolaxi (Abraham) and Musa (Moses); and commemorates

	the assassination of Housainiyuce (Hossein)
Ahwen (A/C) 阿文	Arabic
Ahye 阿叶	Quranic scriptures
Ahyete (Ahye) (A) 阿叶特	The belief that the Quran is one of the great miracles (*qiji*) of the world
aibi (A) 埃毕	unforeseen future
Anla (A) 安拉	Allah
Anlahu (A) 安拉乎	Allah
Anlahu ahkebai (A) 安拉乎额克白	"God is Most Great"
Anlahuteahlia (A) 安拉乎特阿两	"Great God!"
Anseliamu ahlaikong (A) 安色俩目阿来空	"Peace be to you"
Anseliamu, erlaikumu 安色俩目, 尔莱库目	"Peace be with you"
aulade (A) 奥拉德	personal prayer before and after each prostration
Baba (C) 巴巴	Sufi *menhuan* term for son of the saint
Balehudaya (P) 巴勒胡达亚	Great God!
baierxi (A) 白尔西	the awakening at resurrection
bailia (A/P) 白俩	disasters created by Allah to test the faithful and punish the wicked
baileketi (A) 白勒克提	to live under another's good fortune (*zhan guang*), lucky
Balatiye (A) 白拉提夜	"Day of pardoning (*shemian*)," 14th night of 8th Islamic month when Allah considers the fate of each person; Muslims gather in mosque for all-night prayer and *taobai*
ban ahong (C) 搬阿訇	Gedimu and Yihewani process of selecting ahong by mutual agreement among believers
Banbudade (P) 拜布打得	first time of prayer between one hour before sunrise and sunrise
Banda (P) 邦答	first time to prayer between one hour before sunrise and sunrise
bande (P) 板得	servants of God
Bangke (P) 邦克	the call to prayer
bangkelou (P/C) 邦克楼	minaret

Banqiaopai (C) 板桥派   Banqiao sub-order of Jahriyya Sufi *menhuan*

Baoan (C) 保安   Baoan (Bonan) nationality

Beijing (C) 北京   Beijing, Peking

bideerti (A) 比得尔提   actions not consonant with the Quran

biemale (P) 别马勒   to be sick

Bisimingle (A) 必思命了   Bismillah

Bixishite (P) 比喜世忒   Paradise

Bosiwen (P/C) 波斯文   Persian

Buli (C) 哺乳   third time of prayer, between four hours after noon and sunrise

canwujimi (C) 参悟机密   contemplate the depths of Allah

changdao (C) 常道   Sharia, Sufi term for first stage of initation, meditation, or enlightenment

Changying (C) 常营   Changying village, Beijing

chaduah (A/C) 茶都阿   tea that ahong has read or blown prayers over, taken in aiding illness

Chantou Hui (C) 缠头回   "Turbanned Hui," generally referring to Uigurs and other Muslims who wear turbans

Chaojin (C) 朝觐   Hajj, the pilgrimage to Mecca

Chenli (C) 晨礼   first time of prayer between one hour before sunrise and sunrise

chuanfan (C) 传饭   practice of inviting ahong to homes for regular meals

chuanyi (C) 穿衣   Ordination of ahong (lit., "donning clothes")

chuiduah (A/C) 吹都阿   blowing or reading of prayer by ahong over salt, sugar, or tea to aid in illness

chusannietie (C) 出散乜贴   to give alms

cilian (C) 慈悯   beneficial rain given by Allah

dadian (C) 大殿   main prayer hall of the mosque

dajiawangren (C) 搭救亡人   *nietie* given by relatives in remembrance of the deceased

dajin (C) 大净   complete ritual washing, shower (*linyu*)

dale (C) 大了   Sufi *menhuan* and Gedimu practice of reading the entire Quran and

	singing many praises in one sitting; some orders read only important sections
Dangranbai (C) 当然拜	the prayer on Quran and Ramadan that all Muslims make, the "of course prayer"
dannian (C) 单念	reading of Quran by one appointed person while others listen, system used mainly by Yihewani
danyijiaofangzhi (C) 单一教坊制	Yihewani and Gedimu "mosque neighborhood" or "parish," one mosque for a village; Khufiyya and Qadariyya in many areas also follow this system, i.e., not related to a *menhuan*
Daocheng (C) 道乘	Ṭarīqa, the middle stage of Sufi initation, meditaton, or enlightenment
Daohao (C) 道号	Sufi *menhuan* special name for the saint, often in Arabic
Daomen (C) 道门	Islam, "the school or order of the Way (Dao)"
daopu (C) 道谱	Jahriyya practice of writing genealogy of the saints (*silsila*) on graveclothes of deceased which become a "ticket to heaven" (*tiantang piao*) or "touch of the saint"
daotang (C) 道堂	Sufi *menhuan* term for the saint's residence, also becomes a Sufi teaching and ritual center
daotong (C) 道统	Sufi *menhuan* term for system of transmitting the *silsila*
Daozu (C) 道祖	Sufi term for originator, master, or earliest saint of the order
Daozu taiye (C) 道祖太爷	Sufi *menhuan* term for the earliest saint who founded the order
dashiman (P) 答失蛮	scholar, ahong
dasuan (C) 打算	reckoning for one's good and evil actions
daxian (C) 大限	time and age of deceased at death
daxuanlici (C) 大宣礼词	call to prayer in a loud voice
desitale (P) 得斯塔勒	turban used in prayer (*chantou bu*)

diaoguan (C) 吊罐 — shower pot used in *dajin*

dieleweishi (T) 迭勒威士 — dervish, "poor student," Qadariyya Sufi *menhuan* term for mendicant Sufi

dieli weishi (T) 迭力威士 — dervish, mendicant Sufi

diewu (P) 迭屋 — devil

Digele (P) 底格勒 — third time of prayer, between four hours after noon and sunrise

diyan (C) 谛言 — Confession of faith ("attending to the word")

Donggan (T) 东干 — Dungan (Tungan), term for Hui used in Xinjiang and Soviet Central Asia

dongnaifusi (A/C) 动乃夫斯 — lose one's temper

dongshihui (C) 董事会 — traditional committee responsible for administrating mosque assets

Dongxiang (C) 东乡 — Dongxiang nationality

duah (A) 都阿 — prayer

dunya (*jinshi*) (A) 顿亚 — the present life

Duositani (P) 多斯塔尼 — brother Muslims, friends

Duositi (P) 多斯弟 — brother Muslim, friend

Duozaihai (P/C) 哆灾海 — Hell ("Sea of many calamities")

Duozehe (P) 朵则核 — hades, hell

Duozuihai (P/C) 多罪海 — Hell ("Sea of many transgressions")

Dusanbai (P) 堵闪白 — Monday

dushiman (P) 杜失蛮 — enemy; members of opposing religions

ecili (A) 厄司力 — ritual washing of the deceased

er ahong (C) 二阿訇 — ahong with minimal Islamic knowledge, also known as "primary-school ahong" (*xiaoxue ahong*)

erbude (A) 尔布得 — God's servants

Erde (A) 尔德 — the first prayer after Qurban and Ramadan

erde (A) 尔德 — feast-day or holiday (Arabic, '*Id*)

Erdide (A) 尔梯德 (Katibin) — Spirit responsible for recording the good and evil deeds of all humankind (Katibun)

erlin (A) 尔林 — those with advanced Islamic knowledge

erlesuotikahai (A/P) 尔勒所提卡亥 — place of judgment

ermaili 尔麦力 — banquet for iman given by followers on special occasions, or festival in honor of saint

ermamai (A) 尔马麦 — turban used in prayer (*chuantou bu*)

Ersa (A) 尔撒 — Jesus

Ersajiaoren (A/C) 尔撒教人 — Christian

Ershayi (A) 尔沙义 — fifth time of prayer, after dark

Ershiwu sheng (C) 二十五圣 — The 25 famous saints, from Adam to Muhammad

Ershi zhiren (C) 二氏之人 — Jews and Christians

Ersule (A) 尔素勒 — third time of prayer, between four hours after noon and sunrise

erzhangjiao (C) 二掌教 — Ming and Qing dynasty term for *xuanliyuan*, one who calls faithful to prayer

erzabu (*erduobu*) (A) 尔杂布 — Suffering or punishment for wrongdoing

Erzilaylie (A) 尔孜拉衣勒 — Spirit with power over life and death of all things, including its own (Azrail)

Fadimajire (C) 法蒂玛忌日 — Fatima's remembrance day. On night of 4th day of 9th Islamic month women gather in the mosque to hear the ahong talk about Fatima's moral example, give *nietie*, and later invite ahong to homes for meals

Faerxi (P) 法而西, 法日善 — Persia (Fars)

fali (A) 法力 — practice of opening *Quran* at random and looking for one's fortune when confronted with disasters

faliduo (A) 法力朵 — requirement of all Muslims to pray five times a day and once a week on Friday

fanke (C) 番客 — barbarian guest, foreigner

Fatima (A) 法提玛 — Fatima (Muhammad's daughter)

fayi (A) 法义 — benefit

Fazhili (A) 法只力 — first time of prayer between one hour before sunrise and sunrise

Feidiye (A) 费递也 — prayer on behalf of deceased by relatives seeking atonement

Feimusilin (A/C) 非穆斯林 — Non-Muslim

Fuchao (C) 付朝	Hajj at four times of year other than Ramadan
fugongbai (C) 附功拜	voluntary prayer beyond the other five, often in the middle of the night by pious Muslims
fugongzhai (C) 付功斋	voluntary fast outside of the month of Ramadan
fuqing (C) 浮情	principles of this world
fusheng (C) 复生	resurrection
Gadelinye (A/C) 嘎德林耶	Qadariyya Sufi *menhuan*
gadui (A) 尕兑	qadi, Islamic judge, role played by ahong in China when there are Islamic disputes
Gaideerye (A) 盖得尔节	Qadr, 27th night of Ramadan
gaitou (C) 盖头	headcovering worn by women that leaves the face exposed but covers hair and neck
gaiwancha (C) 盖碗茶	traditional Hui tea with dried raisins, dates, apples, and "brick tea" in a cup with a lid, lit., "lid bowl tea"
gaomani (A) 高马尼	"people," term ahong uses to refer to his followers
gaomu (A) 高目	"people," term ahong uses to refer to his followers
ganhalamu (A/C) 干哈拉目	to do illegal or uncanonical actions
Gebulai (A) 格卜来	Kibla
gedele (A) 格得勒	Fate, the plan Allah has for all persons, expressed in Chinese by *qianding, dingran, dingduo, fapai*
Gedimu (A/C) 苏非派	"Ancient, old," traditional Chinese Islam
gei kouhuan (C) 给口唤	Sufi *menhuan* practice of oral transmission of succession upon death of saint
geiyamaiti (A) 给亚麦提	resurrection day
Geiyasi (A) 给亚斯	new theology developed from Quranic doctrine
gemisu (A) 格密素	Tunic or shirt worn by deceased
gongbei (A/C) 拱北	tomb of the saint, "rounded dome"
gongyang (C) 供养	room and board expenses provided by Muslims to *mala*
guanming (C) 官名	official Han name used in registration

Guannei (C) 关内	all of China inside the Jiayuguan Pass
guazhang (C) 挂帐	erecting a tent or curtain for the ordination service
Guerbangjie (A/C) 古尔邦节	Corban, 'Id al-Adha, feast of the sacrifice
gugu (C) 姑姑	Jahriyya *menhuan* term for elder
Gulanjing (A) 古兰经	*Quran*
gunahe (P) 固纳核	sin, transgressions
guohaile (A/C) 过海勒	Sufi *menhuan* practic of giving banquets and *nietie* to saint and poor Muslims
Guojiaminzu shiwu weiyuanhui (C) 国家民族事务委员会	State Commission for Nationality Affairs (SCNA)
gutubu (A) 古土布	"main one," Jahriyya Sufi *menhuan* term used by *reyisi* for saint
habibu (A)	close friend
Hadisi (A) 哈底斯	Hadith sayings of the Prophet
haerlai (A) 哈尔来	halal, lawful
hagegeti (A) 哈给格提	truly!
haidingye (A) 海顶耶	special alms or gift given to imam, especially to the Jahriyya Sufi saints from their followers
haji (A) 哈吉	*hajji*, one who has completed the Hajj, the pilgrimage to Mecca
halamu (A) 哈拉木	haram, unlawful
hali (A) 哈力	fate, honor, position
haliali (A) 哈俩力	"legal, canonical," also wife
halifa (A) 哈里发	"successor," student in preparation to become an ahong; Khufiyya *menhuan* term for main successor of saint
Hanafei (A) 哈纳肥	Hanafi school of Islamic law
Hanbaili (A) 罕白黑	Hanboli school of Islamic law
hange (A) 罕格	"true!"
Hange Laomu (A/C) 罕格老母	"True Mother," ref. to Fatima generally
hangesiti (A/P) 罕格斯提	"truly"
Hangeteahlia (A) 罕格特阿两	"True God!"
Han kitabu (C/A/T) 汉凯它布	"Chinese book," *Quran* or theological works translated into Chinese
Hanming (C) 汉名	Han name

hanyi qingzhensi (A/C) 罕乙清真寺 — central mosque where all Muslims of an order gather on special ritual occasions

Hanxuepai (C) 汉学派 — *Xidaotang*, lit., "Han studies order"

Hanzhiguo (C) 汉志国 — Hedjaz, Hijaz

Hanzu (C) 汉族 — Han nationality

Hasakezu (C) 哈萨克族 — Kazak nationality

hasu (A) 哈苏 — respected Muslim

hatige (A) 哈提格 — pest

hawande (P) 哈完得 — term ahong uses for his followers

henzeile (A) 狠贼勒 — "pig," stupid person

hetenai (A) 核特乃 — circumcision, performed with son is 12-years-old, "To follow the requirements of the Sunna"

houkai (C) 后开 — "to break the Ramadan fast after prayer"

Houking (A) 候孔 — Islamic law

huaer (C) 花儿 — "huar," Northwestern antiphonal singing often practical by Hui

huansuoliatie (A) 唤索两提 — person in rural mosques who strikes a wooden clapper (*bangzi*) to call the faithful from the fields to prayer, often stands on roof of mosque building if no minaret

Huayuan (C) 花圆 — Paradise ("flower garden")

huazhe (P) 华者 — sir, mister

Huda (P) 胡达 — Term for Allah used by some Hui

Hudateahlia (P) 胡达特阿两 — Most exalted God!

Hudaya (P) 胡达亚 — My God!

Hufeiye (A/C) 虎非耶 — Khufiyya Sufi *menhuan*

Hufuye (A/C) 虎夫耶 — Khufiyya Sufi *menhuan*

Huihui (C) 回回 — Hui nationality

Huihui hua (C) 回回话 — "Hui speech" that incorporates Islamic Arabic and Persian terms

Huijiao (C) 回教 — Early term for Islam

Huijiaotu (C) 回教徒 — Early term for Muslim

Huili (C) 会礼 — the first prayer after Qurban and Ramadan

Huizu (C) 回族 — Hui nationality

hulier (A) 户力尔 — divorce, wife leaving husband

hunaile (P) 户乃勒	skill, ability
Hunli (C) 昏礼	fourth time of prayer, before the night sets in after sunset
huonian (C) 伙念	reading of Quran unanimously, "group reading"
Huoyu (C) 火狱	Hades, Hell
hushinude (P) 胡失怒得	satisfied, happy
hutubai (A) 呼图白	the sermon on Friday
jianxiebai (C) 间歇拜	prayer after breaking the fast where one rests and prays at the same time
jiaocheng (C) 教乘	Sharia, Sufi term for first stage of meditation or enlightenment
jiaofang (C) 教坊	Yihewani and Gedium "mosque neighborhood" or "parish," one mosque for a village; Khufiyya and Qadariyya in many areas also follow this system, i.e., not related to a *menhuan*
Jiaomen (C) 教门	Islam, religion, "the school or order of faith"
jiaopai (C) 教派	order, faction, solidarity
jiaoxia (C) 教下	Sufi *menhuan* saint's term for his followers
jiaozhu (C) 教主	Leading imam or ahong of mosque; Sufi term for head *shaykh* or saint of the order
jihade (C) 吉哈德	Jihad, "Holy war"
jikeer (A) 即克尔	*dhikr*, words of remembrance;
jikele (A) 即克勒	Jahriyya Sufi *menhuan* include all terms for Allah and Shahadah; Khufiyya *menhuan* include only *Ablabu* and first half of Shahadah
jingming (A/C) 经名	Quranic name
jingtang jiaoyu (C) 经堂教育	educational system in the mosque
jingtangyu (C) 经堂语	"Hui speech" that incorporates Islamic Arabic and Persian terms
jingwen daxue (C) 经文大学	*madrassah* for adults in mosque
jingwen xiaoxue (C) 经文小学	*madrassah* for children in mosque
jizhuci (C) 记主词	Sufi *menhuan* term for remembering the names of Allah
juli (C) 聚礼	main prayer of week on Friday

junbai (A) 佳白	white overcoat, often worn by Yihewani ahong
kabin (P) 卡宾	bridewealth
Kafeile (A) 卡费勒	infidels, other than Jews or Christians, "Kafir"
kaixue ahong (C) 开学阿訇	main ahong invited to teach in Gedimu and Yihewani mosques
kaizhai (C) 开斋	to break ("open") the fast
Kaizhaijie (C) 开斋节	'Id al-Fatr, feast-day at end of Ramadan
kanfaleti (A) 坎法勒提	penalties for transgressions, fines
kan kouhuan (C) 看口唤	wait for the opportune moment "see if Allah provides"
kaomizi (P) 考来子	eight
kebule (A) 刻布勒	haughty person
Keerkezizu (C) 柯尔克孜族	Kirghiz nationality
Keerbai (A) 克尔白, 克而拜, 克而卜	Ka'ba, the holy black stone at the center of Mecca
kefan (A) 克凡	graveclothes, men's have 3 parts, women's have 5 parts; must be of common rough white cloth, not silk or fine fabric
Kehefu (A) 克核夫	18th chapter of the *Quran*, often read on Friday
kelamaiti (A) 克拉长提	miracle performed by saint
Kelangjing 可兰经	*Quran*
Kelimai shehadi (A) 克立麦·舍哈特	*Shahadah* in Arabic
kouhuan (C) 口唤	oral transmission of succession or other important responsibilities, "permission"
kouhuanle (C) 口唤了	death
Kounei (C) 口内	All of China inside the Jiayuguan Pass
Kubulinye (A/C) 库布林耶	Kubrawiyya Sufi order
Kuburenye (A/C) 库布忍耶	Kubrawiyya Sufi order
Kufutan (P) 虎夫坦	fifth time of prayer, after dark
kufuye (A) 库夫勒	to deny Allah or one's faith
Layilahe (A) 嗜一嗜合	Beginning of *Shahadah*
laojiao (C) 老教	"old teachings" earlier reference to Gedimu, Khufiyya, and Jahriyya

laorenjia (C) 老人家 — Sufi *menhuan* term for the saint; also general term of respect for imam

legeibu 勒给布 (*qilaman*) 其拉漫 — spirit responsible for recording the good and evil deeds of all humankind (Kiramun)

lehamamin (A) 勒哈玛民 — one who is merciful and philanthropic

lehemu (A) 勒黑木 — those who will obtain Allah's mercy

Leyuan (C) 乐圆 — Paradise ("garden of happiness")

Lianchao (C) 联朝 — Hajj at any time other than Ramadan

liaojing (C) 了经 — Sufi *menhuan* and Gedimu practice of reading all the important sections of the *Quran* in one sitting

Liaoye (C) 了夜 — "Day of pardoning (*shemian*)," 14th night of 8th Islamic month when Allah considers the fate of each person; Muslims gather in mosque for all-night prayer and *taobai*

libai (C) 礼拜 — prayers facing Mecca, including: five times a day, once on Friday, twice a year on Islamic holidays, and supplemental prayers

libaisi (C) 礼拜寺 — mosque, "prayer temple"

licigei (A) 力兹给 — life, subsistence

lieshang (C) 列圣 — holy saint enlightened by Allah, without miraculous powers and not mentioned in the *Quran*

lingnian (C) 领念 — reading of *Quran* antiphonally after the prompting of a leader

lisanlai (A) 力撒来 — the mission given by Allah to the prophets

lishu jiaofangzhi (C) 隶属教坊制 — Sufi *menhuan* mosques related through system of appointment of mosque leaders by the saint

Liu Zhi (C) 刘智 (刘介廉) — Liu Zhi, Qing dynasty Confucian Muslim scholar

luha (A) 鲁哈 — soul (*linghun*), departs the body at death, spirit

Luoze (P) 罗则 — The Ramadan Fast (also Fenzhai, Bizhai, Bazhai)

lunnian (C) 轮念 — reading of *Quran* passages in consecutive succession

mahabubu (A) 麦哈补布	close friend
Ma Hualong (C) 马化龙	Ma Hualong
Maianseliamu (A) 麦安色俩目	"And peace be with you"
Maielibu (A) 麦恶力布	fourth time of prayer, before the night sets in after sunset
maihaile (A) 麦海勒	bridewealth
Maijia (A) 麦加	Mecca
maikeluhai (A) 麦克鲁亥	actions that are impolite and to be avoided, but not sinful; ghost; pest
mailaike (A) 麦来克	angel
mailekulimaoti 麦赖库力毛提	spirit with power over life and death of all things, including its own
mailiouyi (A) 麦力欧义	troublesome ghost, pest
mainale (A) 麦那勒	minaret
maisijide (A) 麦斯吉德	masjid, mosque
maisilai (A) 麦斯莱	Islamic questions and principles
malzazi (A) 麦扎孜	false or fake
maiti (A) 买提	corpse
Ma Laichi (C) 马来尺	Ma Laichi
maliayike (A) 麦俩义克	myraid heavenly hosts
Malike (A) 马立克	spirit responsible for Hell
Ma Mingxin (C) 马明心	Ma Mingxin
Manke (A) 满克	Mecca
manla (A) 满拉	"one with knowledge," students in preparation to become ahong
maogeifu (A) 毛给夫	place of judgment
maolia (A) 毛俩	director, leader, Jahriyya Sufi *menhuan* term for saint
maoti (A) 毛提	respectful term for death, returing to Allah (*guizhen*), lit., "impermanence"
Ma Wanfu (C) 马万福	Ma Wanfu
menhuan (C) 门宦	"saintly descent group or school," sociopolitical institution based upon the family of the saint and his followers, or his appointees
meishui (C) 没水	ritually unwashed (lit., "without water")
Menkele 门克勒	spirit responsible for examining the deceased in the grave before resurrection (Munkar)

miaizenai (A) 米艾则乃	minaret
mihaladi (A) 米哈拉比	place where prayer leader stands, mihrab
Mikayile 米卡衣勒	spirit responsible for the subsistence of the elements and all things ("Michael the Archangel")
minbaile (A) 闵拜勒	minbar, place where *hutubai* is preached
minzu (C) 民族	nationality, ethnic group
minzu xiaoxue (C) 民族小学	nationalities primary school
Minzu Xueyuan (C) 民族学院	Institute for Nationalities (college)
Molike (A) 模力克	Maliki school of Islamic law
minzu zhongxue (C) 民族中学	nationalities middle school
Modina (A) 默德那, 默底纳	Medina
Mori (C) 末日	last day of the world
moguo (C) 抹锅	to give *nietie* (lit., "pass through the frying pan")
Moshishengren (C) 末世圣人	Muhammad, ("Prophet of the last age")
muanjin (A) 穆安津	one who calls the faithful to prayer from the *xuanlita*
mubaha (A) 木巴哈	permissable actions
mucitehabu (A) 木司特罕布	voluntary prayer
muerjizi (A) 穆尔吉孜	miracles that only the Prophet can do
muhailisu (A) 穆亥力素	honest and good Muslim
Muhamode (A) 穆罕默德	Muhammad
muleshide (A) 穆勒师德	*murshid*, advisor; main term for saint used by Khufiyya and Qadariyya Sufi *menhuan*, also used by Jahriyya Sufi *menhuan*
mulide (A) 穆力德	"disciple," Sufi *menhuan* term for students of the saint
Mumin (A/C) 穆民	Muslim
munafele (A) 穆纳费格	nominal believer, two-faced
Musa (A) 母撒	Moses
mushenlike (A) 木什力克	polytheists
Musilin (A) 穆斯林, 穆思林	Muslim, one in submission to Allah
muzi xiaoxue (C) 穆孜小学	muslim primary school
Najiahu (C) 纳家户	Najiahu, Na Homestead, Ningxia region
naifei yicibati (A) 乃非·伊司巴提	division of the *Shahadah* into

	negative half "nothing but Allah" (*wanwufeizhu*) and postive "there is only Allah" (*weiyou zhenzhu*)
Naikele 乃克勒	spirit responsible for examining the deceased in the grave before resurrection (Nakir)
naimazi (P) 乃麻孜	prayer, term often used in Ningxia
Nainai (C) 奶奶	Jahriyya Sufi *menhuan* term for mother of the saint
Naisala (A) 奈撒拉	Christian
Nakeshiban (T) 那革石板	Naqshbandiyya (Sufi order)
Nale (A) 那勒	Hades, Hell
nang (T) 馕	nan, baked flat bread
Nasulading (A/C) 纳苏拉丁	Nascredin, son of Sayyid Edjell
nayibo haji (A) 纳义卜·哈吉	one who goes on the Hajj on behalf of another
Neidi (C) 内地	China proper, exclusive of the northwest and Xinjiang
nian (C) 念	recitation of the *qingzhen yan*
nianpinganjing (C) 念平安经	invitation to ahong to read and pray in one's home
Nianye (C) 念夜	"Day of pardoning (*shemian*)," 14th night of 8th Islamic month when Allah considers the fate of each person; Muslims gather in mosque for all-night prayer and *taobai*
niermaiti (A) 尼尔买提	food that Allah provides
nietie (C) 乜贴	alms, donation
nikaha (A) 尼卡哈	wedding vows presided over by ahong
ningyetie (A) 宁叶贴	alms, donation
nianzhiganjing (C) 念知感经	invitation to ahong to read and participate in banquet thanking Allah for special favor
Niujie (C) 牛丁	Niujie, "Oxen Street," Beijing neighborhood
Nushengji (C) 女圣忌	Fatima's remembrance day, on night of 4th day of 9th Islamic month women gather in the mosque to hear the ahong talk about Fatima's moral example, give

	nietie, and later invite ahong to homes for meals
oucili (A) 欧司力	complete ritual washing, shower (*linyu*)
oushele (A) 欧什勒	ten-percent tithe
paili (P) 拍尼	spirits (*jingling*) created out of fire by Allah
panmizi (P) 盼米子	five
Panthay	Burmese term for Hui in Yunnan
Panzhisanbai (P) 盼只闪白	Thursday
pilahan (C) 披拉汗	Jahriyya practice of writing genealogy of the saints (*silsila*) on graveclothes of deceased which become a "ticket to heaven" (*tiantang piao*) or "touch of the saint"
pilahan (P) 披拉汗	1. clothing; 2. Jahriyya Sufi *menhuan* term for saint's *daopu*
po (C) 破	one-half
posai (P) 婆塞	kiss
qiankai (C) 前开	"to break the Ramadan fast before prayer"
qianliang (C) 钱粮	assets of mosque reserved for mosque restoration
Qianli Hui hui shiyi jia 千里回回是一家	"All Hui within a thousand miles are one family"
qijingming (C) 起经名	to be given a Quranic name
qirenyigou duah (A/C) 七人一狗都阿	practice of asking ahong to write the names of the seven saints and one dog on a paper which, when hung on one's wall, will lead to good fortune, based on the legend in 18th chapter of *Quran*
qingkaizhai (C) 请开斋	host those fasting in one's home during Ramadan
qingliananzhe (C) 清廉者	successful, skillful Muslim
qingzhen (C) 清真	Islamic "purity and truth"
qingzhen Daoshi (C) 清真道士	Islamic Daoist master
qingzhen canguan (C) 清真餐馆	*qingzhen* (halal) restaurant

qingzhen heshang (C) 清真和尚	Islamic (Buddhist) monk
Qingzhenjiao (C) 清真教	Islam
qingzhensi (C) 清真寺	mosque, "pure and true temple"
Qingzhenyan (C) 清真言	*Shahadah*, the confession in Chinese that there is no God but Allah, and Muhammad is his Prophet
Qingzhen zhi nan (C) 清真之南	*The Compass of Islam*, book by Ma Zhu
qishubai (C) 奇数拜	three prostrations of prayer after the last time of prayer
qisongqian (C) 超送钱	*nietie* given by relatives in remebrance of the deceased at the funeral
Quanzhou (C) 泉州	Quanzhou
reyisi (A) 热依斯	Jahriyya Sufi *menhuan* term for main leaders appointed by saint in different district, often relatives of the saint
ruzhai (C) 入斋	to begin (enter) the fast
saibaibu (A) 塞白布	"opportunity," sudden illness
Saierdi Wageshi (A) 赛尔弟斡歌土	Sayyid Waqqas (reputed cousin of Muhammad, who arrived in China A.D. 676)
Sailafeiye (A/C) 赛来费耶	Salafiyya Islamic order
saiyide (A) 赛以德	sayyid
Salazu (C) 撒拉族	Salar nationality
Sanbai (P) 闪白	Saturday
Sandajiao (C) 三大教	"the three great faiths," Confucianism, Buddhism, Daoism
sandaozhi (C) 三道制	traditional mosque administrative committee in Yuan, Ming, and Qing comprised of imam, *hetuibu*, and *muanjin*
sankaizhai (C) 散开斋	to give alms during Ramadan to those fasting
Santaijiao (C)	Salafiyya, lit., "Three prostrations teaching"
sanxue (C) 散学	resgination or transfer of ahong from mosque
sanzhangjiao (C) 三掌教	traditional mosque administrative

	committee in Yuan, Ming, and Qing comprised of imam, *hetuibu*, and *muanjin*
sanzi (C) 闪子	traditional crisp shoe-string pastry
saogande (P) 扫干得	an emotional vow
Sashen (P) 撒申	second time of prayer, between one and three hours after noon
Seliamaiti (A) 色俩买提	"Peace be to you"
Semuren (C) 色目人	foreigner, generally Central Asian
Sewabu (A) 色瓦布	expression of thanks, "May Allah reward you"
sexiangshi (C) 色相世	world or reality, objective existence
Shafeier (A) 沙肥尔	Sha'fi school of Islamic law
Shagoupai (C) 沙沟派	Shagou sub-order of Jahriyya Sufi *menhuan*
Shamu (P) 沙目	fourth time of prayer, before the night sets in after sunset
shaihai (A) 筛海	"elder," especially used by Qadariyya *menhuan* for the saint, *shaykh*, *sheikh*
shaitani (A) 筛塔尼	cunning devil, Satan (*sandan*)
Shangli (C) 晌礼	seocnd time of prayer, between one and three hours after noon
Shate (C) 沙特	Saudi Arabia
shefaerti (A) 舍法尔提	advocacy of Muhammad before Allah on behalf of faithful Muslims on the day of reckoning
shelierti (A) 舍里尔提	Islamic instructions; the first stage of Sufi discipline (*daocheng*)
shemizi (P) 舍米子	six
shenchao (C) 身朝	to go on the Hajj personally
shenggao (C) 升高	to go to Heaven
shenghua (C) 生化	creation
Shengji (C) 圣纪	Prophet's Day, twelfth day of third Islamic month
shengming (C) 圣名	Sufi *menhuan* term for saints of previous generations
shengren (C) 圣人	"holy person," often used to refer to the Prophet, who according to legend is the last of 124,000 holy persons of four different grades
shengren de pinji (C) 圣人的品级	grades of the holy persons:

1. *shengren*; 2. *yinsheng*; 3. *dasheng*;
4. *zhisheng*

shengwu (C) 圣物   Sufi *menhuan* articles used by the saint

shengxing (C) 圣行   *sunna*, "way of the Prophet" or "holy way"

shengxingbai (C) 圣行拜   the prayer that individuals add on their own before and after five times of prayer that will protect them from hell because of "righteous action" (*shengxing*)

Shenshen (C) 婶婶   Jahriyya *menhuan* term for the daughter-in-law of the saint

shesan (C) 舍散   give alms

shexide (A) 舍西德   religious martyr (*sheshen zhe*)

Shi jia Hui hui jiu jia qin 十家回回九家亲   "Out of ten Hui families, nine are related"

shibude (C) 使不得   what one shouldn't do

Shidaitianxian (C) 十大天仙   Ten great angels

shide (C) 使得   permissable actions

Shige Hui hui jiuge Ma 十个回回九个马   "Out of ten Hui, nine are surnamed Ma"

shi ren (C) 认识   confession of God

Shiye (P) 什叶   Shi'i Islamic sect

shixizhi (C) 世袭制   Sufi *menhuan* term for system of succession

shizhe (C) 使者   prophets enlightened by Allah, also *Tianshi* and *Yincha*, with Muhammad as the last of 25 mentioned in the Quran

Shizijiao (C) 十字教   Christianity ("religion of the cross")

shoujie (C) 受戒   ritual purity maintained by those on the Hajj (lit., "initiation")

shumi (A) 舒密   unfortunate, unlucky

sidatianxian (C) 四大天仙   Ningxia Hui belief in four angels as the most powerful

sifei (C) 寺费   mosque income depending on donations

siquan weiyuanhui (C) 寺管委员会   mosque administrative committee, replaced traditional committee in 1958 during Democratic reforms (*minzhugaige*) *sishifu* (C) 寺师付 — main administrator of daily mosque affairs and upkeep

song ahong (C) 送阿訇 — ceremony of escorting ahong to new mosque

song qingzhen yan ru jiao (C) 涌清真言入教 — conversion to Islam

suan zhu (C) 算珠 — counting beads, prayer beads

Subuha (A) 素布哈 — first time of prayer between one hour before sunrise and sunrise

sudegefetule (A) 索得格费吐勒 — alms given during Ramadan

Sufei (T) 苏飞, 苏非, 苏费 — Sufi

Sufeipai (C) 苏非派 — Sufism

sufenye (A) 麦粉耶 — close friend

suidaike (A) 虽代盖 — alms

suifati (A) 碎法提 — immoral

Suilatui (A) 碎拉推 — the bridge leading to Paradise over Hades

Sulatai Sulaqiao (A) 遂拉台 (A) 苏喇桥 — bridge over Hell

sule (A) 苏勒 — sura, chapter of the *Quran*

Sunaiti (A) 逊奈提 — *Sunna*, the way, the path, the example of the Prophet's life

suodege (A) 索得格 — required alms

suoliate (A) 索俩特 — time of prayer

sutan (A) 苏坦 — sultan

tabuti (A) 塔布提 — wooden bed or platform used to carry deceased to graveyard, kept in mosque

taiye (C) 太爷 — Sufi *menhuan* term for deceased saint

Tajikezu (C) 塔吉克族 — Tadjik nationality

tangduah (A/C) 糖都阿 — sugar that ahong has read or blown prayers over, taken in aiding illness

tangping (C) 汤瓶 — water pot used in *xiaojin*

tanlaxi Bingliaxi (A) 坦拉西·丙两西 — a pledge made to God

taobai (A) 讨白 — confession (*qianhui*); among Sufis, confession to the saint, repentance

taoheide (A) 讨黑德 — monotheism, "there is only Allah"

Taolate (A) 讨拉特 — Old Testament (*jiuyue*) of the Bible

Tataerzu (C) 塔塔尔族 — Tartar nationality

tegedile (A) 特格底勒 — fate

tehazhude (A) 特罕朱德 — voluntary prayer beyond the other

	five, often in the middle of the night by pious Muslims
tekanbule (A) 特坎布勒	conceited person
Telasayang (P) 特拉撒扬	Christian
telaweha (A) 特拉威哈	prayer after breaking the fast where one rests and prays at the same time
tenasuibu (P) 别乃碎布	unlucky
tetuanwoer (A) 特团渥尔	voluntary prayer beyond the other five, often in the middle of the night by pious Muslims
teyanmen (A) 特严门	ritual washing with clean and when no water is available
tianminzhai (C) 天命斋	fast the whole month of Ramadan
Tianxia Hui hui shiyi jia 天下回回是一家	"All Hui under Heaven are one family"
Tianxia qingzhensi Hui hui jian 天下清真寺回回见	"In all mosques under Heaven Hui meet"
tianxian (C) 天仙	"heavenly spirits, angels" angelic beings in Islam
Tiaojinjiao (C) 挑筋教	Judaism, lit., "Plucking sinews religion"
Tianfang (C) 天房, 天方	Mecca (lit., "heavenly square"), Ka'ba
tianmingbai (C) 天命拜	requirement of all Muslims to pray five times a day and once a week on Friday
Tiantang (C) 天堂	Paradise, Heaven
Tuerji (T) 土尔基	Turkey
tujin (C) 土净	ritual washing with clean sand when no water is available
Tujueyu (T/C) 土决语	Turkish
tuoliage (A) 脱俩个	divorce, husband leaving wife
tuoligeti (A) 脱力格提	the correct way; in Sufism, the second stage of discipline, involving deep levels of *nian* (recitation), *li* (prayer), and *zhai* (fast) and breathing techniques
wang yue lou 望月楼	minaret ("moon-watching tower")
wanmizi (P) 弯米子	nine
Wansheng zhi lingshen (C) 万圣之领袖	Muhammad ("leading spirit of a thousand saints")

wazhibu (A) 瓦志布   the prayer on Qurban and Ramadan that all Muslims make

weipaizhi (C) 委派制   Jahriyya Sufi *menhuan* succession by selection of saint

weitele (A)   three prostrations of prayer after the last time of prayer

Weiwuerzu (C) 维吾尔族   Uighur nationality

woerzu (A) 沃尔祖   preacher, one responsible for delivering the *Hutubai*

wofati (A) 沃法提   death of a renowned person

wogefu (A) 沃格夫   waqf, properties and assests of mosque

wohayi (A) 沃哈义   enlightenment of the prophet, also *tianqi* and *moshi*

woli (A) 沃力   "friend of Allah," *menhuan* term for saint, *wali*

wubali (A) 乌巴力   pitiful

wuchang (C) 无常   respectful term for death, returning to Allah (*quizhen*), lit., "impermanence"

wuduyi (A) 乌杜义   small ritual washing (*jiemei*)

Wuge da Ma 五个大马
Wuge xiao Ma 五个小马   five great "horses" and five small "horses"; refers to the ten Hui warlords who dominated the northwest in the Republican period

wugong (C) 五功   five tenets (literally "works" or "deeds") of Islam

wushibai (*Wufanbai*) (C) 五时拜 (五番拜)   five times of prayer

wusu (P) 屋苏   anxiety, fear

Wuzibeikezu (C) 乌孜别克族   Uzbek nationality

xianjibuhao (C) 显迹不好   "unlucky portent"

xianzhi (C) 先知   prophet of less stature than *shizhe*, but often interchanged

Xiaojiao (C) 小教   "The little faith," Islam

xiaojin (C) 小净   small ritual washing (*jiemei*)

Xiaoli (C) 宵礼   fifth time of prayer, after dark

xiaomaer (A) 稍麻尔   small mosque

xiaoming (C) 校名   Han name used in school

xiaoye (C) 消夜	Sufi *menhuan* and Gedimu practice of inviting ahong to home party for the deceased on night of death
xiaoxuanlici (C) 小宣礼词	call to prayer in a quiet voice, also arrangement of worshipers in proper order for prayer
Xibei (C) 西北	northwest, mainly Ningxia, Qinghai, Gansu, and Shaanxi
Xidaotang (C) 西道堂	Xi Dao Tang, lit., "Western School or Mosque"
xinchao (C) 心朝	to go on the Hajj in one's heart when prevented from actual participation by phsysical or financial limitations
xinjiao (C) 新教	"new teachings" earlier reference to Khufiyya, Jahriyya, and Yihewani
xinjiao (C) 行教	propagate religion, proselytize
xinmizi (P) 新米子	seven
xinnaiti (A) 逊奈提	the prayer that individuals add on their own before and after five times of prayer that will protect them from hell because of "righteous action" (*shengxing*)
xinren zhu (C) 信认主	confession of God
xinshiti (A) 欣买提	will, ambition
xinxingjiao (C) 新行教	"new way teachings"
xinxinjiao (C) 新新教	"new new teachings" earlier reference to Yihewani and Xidaotang
xiyuren (C) 西域人	"person from the West," foreign ancestors
xualita (C) 宣礼塔	minaret, lit., "tower for disseminating doctine"
xuanliyuan (C) 宣礼员	one who calls the faithful to prayer from the *xuanlita*
xuanpinzhi (C) 选聘制	Yihewani and Gedium system of succession through agreement among the mosque members
xueke (C) 学课	salary of ahong, usually given at end of year
xueliang (C) 学粮	salary of ahong paid in grain

Yalanbi (A) 亚兰毕   "My savior!"
yanduah (A/C) 盐都阿   salt that ahong has read or blown
                                            prayers over, taken in aiding
                                            illness
yao kouhuan (C) 要口唤   requesting intervention of ahong in
                                            dispute
yaomudini (A) 夭目底尼   the last day of reckoning
Yaomugei yamaiti (A) 夭目给亚麦堤   Resurrection Day
Yaomuhesanbu (A) 夭目黑撒布   Day of Judgment
Yaotoujiao (C) 摇头教   "Shaking head religion" former Han
                                            term for Sufism
yashantou (C) 压山头   Sufi *menhuan* practice in southern
                                            Ningxia of placing cloth or paper
                                            inscribed with Quranic texts by
                                            the saint underneath a stone on
                                            the top of a mountain and allow-
                                            ing the elements to dissipate it
Ye (C) 爷   Ningxia Sufi *menhuan* term for the
                                            Sufi saint (*jiaozhu*)
Yehude (A) 叶呼得   Jew, thrifty person
Yekesanbai (P) 叶克闪白   Sunday
yemizi (P) 叶米子   ten
yemizi (P) 叶米子   one
Yesu hui (C) 耶稣会   Christianity
Yibolaxin (A) 易卜腊觋   Abraham
  Yibucixin (A) 易卜剌觋   Abraham
  Yinbolaxi (A) 伊伯拉觋   Abraham
Yibulisi (P) 以不理思   Satan
Yihewani (A/C) 依黑瓦尼   Yihewani, Ikwan, the Muslim
                                            Brotherhood in China
yihimaer (A) 以吉马尔   agreement, consensus
Yiliaxi (A) 义两西   "My god!"
yimani (A) 伊玛尼   faith, with particular reference to the
                                            belief in Allah, the angels, the
                                            Quran, the Prophet, the afterlife,
                                            and the Plan of Allah
yinbulisi 伊不里斯   Hebrew for "tricky devil"
yincigatui (A) 饭剌嘎推   Yihewani formal prayer on behalf of
                                            deceased seeking their atonement
Yindusitang (T) 饭都斯唐   Hindustan
ying (C) 营   barracks, often a Hui or Manchu
                                            village that was a former garrison

Yinzhili (A) 尹知力 — New Testament (*xinyue*) of the Bible

Yisila (A) 以思啦 — Israel

Yisilafeile 伊斯拉飞勒 — Spirit responsible for the last trump when all things perish, and the next trump when all will rise from the dead (Asrafil)

Yisilanjiao (A/C) 伊斯兰教 — Islam

Yisiliamu (A) 伊斯俩目 — Islam

Yisimuzati (A) 伊斯目杂提 — The earliest name of Allah

yixinshunshou (C) 一心顺受 — submission

yizabu (A) 义扎布 — vows of agreement in response to ahong's questioning of bride and groom

yizazi (A) 义扎孜 — "transmission" of authority to succeeding saint in Sufi orders

Yizede, teahlia (A/P) 依则得, 特阿两 — "Most holy and exalted Allah"

youshui (C) 有水 — state of having ritually washed (lit., "with water")

Youtaijiao (C) 犹太教 — Judaism

youxiang (C) 油香 — "fragrant oil cake," traditional Hui pastry

yuanjing (C) 园经 — Sufi *menhuan* and Gedimu practice of reading the entire *Quran* singing many praises in one sitting; some orders read only important sections

zakate (A) 扎卡特 — *zakat*, alms; tythe of 2.5% for commodities and cash, 5–10% for agricultural produce, and particular percentages for livestock

Zamier Qingzhensi (A/C) 扎米尔清真寺 — A famous mosque

zaohua (C) 造化 — creation, fortunate

zaonie (C) 造孽 — to do something one should not do

Zebule (A) 则布勒 — Psalms of the Od Testament

zei Huihui (C) 贼回回 — larcenous Hui

Zhaijie (C) 斋戒 — The Ramadan Fast (also *Fenzhai, Bizhai, Bazhai*)

Zhangjiachuan (C) 张家川 — Zhangjiachuan, Gansu province

zhangjiao ahong (C) 掌教阿訇 — main ahong in charge of the

mosque; Jahriyya Sufi *menhuan* term for main ahong

zhangjiaozhidu (C) 掌教制度   traditional administration of mosque by an imam, *hetuibu* (preacher), *muanjin* (*xuanliyuan*), and *muza-weier* (master of the mosque). After 1958, replaced by administrative committee

zhangxue ahong (C) 掌学阿訇   assistant to *kaixue* ahong

Zhannai (A) 展乃   Paradise, Heaven

zhanxian (C) 沾仙   Jahriyya practice of writing genealogy of the saints (*Silsila*) on graveclothes of deceased which become a "ticket to heaven" (*tiantang piao*) or "touch of the saint"

Zhebolayile 哲伯拉依勒 (Jiabolie 加伯列) (A)   spirit responsible for the period between the New and Old Testaments (the *jiabolie*); Angel of revelation, past and future (Gabriel)

zhehelinye (A/C) 哲赫林耶   Jahriyya Sufi *menhuan*

zhemuerti (A) 哲麻尔提   Yihewani and Gedimu "mosque neighborhood" or "parish," one mosque for a village; Khufiyya and Qadariyya in many areas also follow this system, i.e., not related to a *menhuan*

zhenazi (A/C) 折那孜   carry out or participate in a funeral

zhencheng (C) 真乘   *haqiqah*, last or highest stage of meditation, enlightenment, or initiation for Sufis

zhengchao (C) 正朝   Hajj during the 8th–20th days of the 12th month on the Islamic calendar

zhenni (A) 镇尼   spirits (*jingling*) created out of fire by Allah (Ginn, Genii)

Zhenzai (C) 真宰   Allah, "The first cause"

Zhenzhu (C) 真主   Allah, "True God"

zhicheng (C) 至乘   *haqiqah*, last or highest stage of meditation, enlightenment, or initiation for Sufis

Zhisheng (C) 至圣   most exalted holy one, the Prophet

Muhammad; Also the fourth
grade of holy ones which also
includes five grades: 1. *Daxian*;
2. *Zhizhe*; 3. *Lianshi*; 4. *Shanren*;
5. *Yangchang*

zhongdao (C) 中道   middle stage of initiation, meditation, or enlightenment for Sufis

Zhongguo Yisilanjiao Xiehui (C)   China Islamic Association
中国伊斯兰教协会

Zhuanxianzhi (C) 传贤制   Sufi *menhuan* term for the earliest
founders of the order; Jahriyya
include the first 3 generations,
Qadariyya include first 7
generations

Zhuhude (P) 朱呼得   Jew, thrifty person
Zhuhuderen (P/C) 朱呼德人   Jews
Zhuma (A) 主麻   main prayer of week on Friday, Friday
zhumanietie (C) 主麻乜贴   alms collected on Friday for
expenses of mosque staff

zhumingbai (C) 主命拜   requirement of all Muslims to pray
five times a day and once a week
on Friday

zizhiqu, zhou, xian, xiang (C) 自治区,   autonomous region, prefecture,
州, 县, 乡   county, village, township
zhuxue (C) 住学   reside in the mosque while studying
under the ahong

zuodeng zhi yan nian (C) 作澄之言念   confession of faith
Zuhehe (A) 祖核勒   second time of prayer, between one
and three hours after noon

zuojing (C) 坐静   meditation and all-day prayer in
mosque during last 10 days of
Ramadan

zuosunnaiti (A/C) 做逊奈提   circumcision, performed when son
zuosun (A/C) 作逊   is 12 years old, "to follow the
zuoheitina (A/C) 作黑提那   requirements of the Sunna"

References

Anonymous. "Japanese Infiltration Among Muslims in China." Unpublished report. Office of Strategic Services, Research and Analysis Branch, 1944.
——. "Peoples and Politics of China's Northwest." Unpublished report. Office of Strategic Services, Research and Analysis Branch, 1945.

Abu-Lughod, Lila. "Zones of Theory in the Anthropology of the Arab World," *Annual Review of Anthropology* 18: 267–306 (1989).

Adams, Kathleen. "Come to Tana Toraja, 'Land of the Heavenly Kings': Travel Agents as Brokers in Ethnicity," *Annals of Tourism Research* 11: 469–485 (1984).

Aird, John S. "Population Studies and Population Policy in China," *Population and Development Review* 8.2: 85–97 (1982).

Algar, Hamid. "Silent and Vocal Dhikr in the Naqshbandiyya Order," *Akten des VII. Kongresses fur Arabistik und Islamwissenschaft* 3.9 (1976).

Ali, Ikbal. *Islamic Sufism.* Delhi: Idarah-I Adabiyat-I Delli, 1933.

Allworth, Edward. "Ambiguities in Russian Group Identity and Leadership of the RSFSR." In *Ethnic Russia in the USSR: The Dilemma of Dominance.* Ed. Edward Allworth. New York: Pergamon Press, 1980.

Alonso, Mary Ellen, ed. *China's Inner Asian Frontier.* Cambridge: The Peabody Museum, Harvard University, 1979.

Anagnost, Ann S. "The Mimesis of Power." Paper presented at the Conference on "Anthropological Perspectives on Mainland China, Past and Present," Center for Chinese Studies, University of California, 22 November 1986.

Anderson, Benedict. *Imagined Communities: Reflections on the Origin and Spread of Nationalism.* London: Verson Press, 1983.

Andrew, G. Findlay. *The Crescent in North-West China.* London: The China Inland Mission, 1921.

Appadurai, Arjun. "Introduction: Commodities and the Politics of Value." In

The Social Life of Things: Commodities in Cultural Perspective. Ed. Arjun Appadurai. Cambridge: Cambridge University Press, 1986.

——. "Theory in Anthropology: Center and Periphery," *Comparative Studies in Society and History* 13: 745–761 (1986).

——. "Disjuncture and Difference in the Global Cultural Economy," *Public Culture* 2.2: 1–24 (1990).

Appignanesi, Lisa, and Sara Maitland, eds. *The Rushdie File*. New York: SUNY Press, 1990.

Aramco World Magazine. Muslims in China: A Special Issue. Washington, D.C.: The Aramco Corporation 36.4 (1985).

Arkush, R. David. *Fei Xiaotong and Sociology in Revolutionary China*. Cambridge: Council on East Asian Studies, Harvard University, 1981.

Armijo-Hussein, Jacqueline. "The Sinicization and Confucianization in Chinese and Western Historiography of a Muslim from Bukhara Serving Under the Mongols in China." In *The Legacy of Islam in China: An International Symposium in Memory of Joseph F. Fletcher*. Ed. Dru. C. Gladney. Conference Volume. Harvard University, 14–16 April 1989.

Armstrong, John A. "The Ethnic Scene in the Soviet Union: The View of the Dictatorship." In *Ethnic Minorities in the Soviet Union*. Ed. E. Goldhagen. New York: Praeger, 1968.

Asiaweek. "China: The Other 60 Million." 50.50: 35 (1979).

Aubin, François. "Islam et Etat en Chine populaire." In *L'Islam et l'Etat*. Ed. Olivier Carre. Paris: Presses Universitaires de France, 1982.

——. "*L'apostolat protestant en milieu musulman chinois*." In *Actes du IV Colloque International de Sinologie, Chantilly-1983*. Taipei: Variétés Sinologiques, 1983.

——. "Chinese Islam: In Pursuit of its Sources," *Central Asian Survey* 5.2: 73–80 (1986).

Bacon, Elizabeth E. *Central Asians Under Russian Rule: A Study in Cultural Change*. Ithaca and London: Cornell University Press, 1980. 1st ed. 1966.

Bai Shouyi 白寿彝, "Sai Dianchi Shan Siding zhuan" 赛典赤瞻思丁传 (Biography of Sai Dianchi Shans Al-din), *Qingzhen Yuebao* 31 (1947). Reprinted in *Zhongguo Yisilanjiaoshi cankao ziliao xuanbian, 1911–1949* 中国伊斯兰教史参考资料选编, 1911–1949 (China Islamic history reference material selections, 1911–1949). Ed. Li Xinghua 李兴华 and Feng Jinyuan 冯今源. Vol I. Yinchuan: Ningxia People's Publishing Society, 1985.

——. "Huihui minzu de xingcheng" 回回民族的形成 (The nature of the Hui nationality), *Guangming ribao*, 17 February 1951.

——. *Huimin qiyi* 回民起义 (Hui rebellions). 4 vols. Ed. Bai Shouyi. Shanghai, 1953.

——. *Huizu, Huijiao, Huimin lunji* 回族, 回教, 回民论集 (Collected Essays on the Hui nationality, Hui religion, and the Hui people). Kowloon: n.p., 1974.

Bai Shouyi and Ma Shouqian 马寿千. "Jizhong Huihui jiapu zhong suofan-ying de lishi wenti" 几和回回家谱中所反映的历史问题 (Several historical problems reflected in Huihui genealogies), *Beijing Normal University Journal* 2 (1958). Reprinted in *Huizu shilun ji* 1949–1979 回族史论集 (Hui history collection 1949–1979). Ed. Chinese Academy of Social Sciences Ethnology Department and Central Nationalities Institute Ethnology Department, Hui History Team. Yinchuan: Ningxia People's Publishing Society, 1984.

Bai Shouyi and Yang Huaizhong 杨怀中, eds. *Huizu renwu zhi, Yuan dai* 回族人物志, 元代 (Annals of Hui personages, Yuan dynasty). Yinchuan: Ningxia People's Publishing Company, 1985.

——. *Huizu renwu zhi, Ming dai* 回族人物志, 明代 (Annals of Hui personages, Ming dynasty). Yinchuan: Ningxia People's Publishing Company, 1988.

Baker, Hugh D. R. *Sheung Shui: A Chinese Lineage Village*. Palo Alto: Stanford University Press, 1968.

Bakhtin, M. Mikhail. *The Dialogic Imagination*. Ed. Michael Holquist. Tr. Caryl Emerson and Michael Holquist. Austin: University of Texas Press, 1981. Russian ed. 1975.

Banister, Judith. "An Analysis of Recent Data on the Population of China," *Population and Development Review* 10.2 :241–7 (1984).

——. *China's Changing Population*. Stanford: Stanford University Press, 1987.

Banton, Michael. "The Direction and Speed of Ethnic Change." In *Ethnic Change*. Ed. Charles Keyes. Seattle: University of Washington Press, 1981.

Bao Jianxing 保健行. "Zhehelinye jiaopai zai Guizhou sheng de chuanbo" 哲赫林那教派在贵州省的传播 (The spread of the Jahriyya order in Guizhou province). In *Zhongguo Yisilanjiao yanjiu wenji*. Ed. Chinese Islamic Research Committee. Yinchuan: Ningxia People's Publishing Society, 1988.

Barfield, Thomas. *The Perilous Frontier: Nomadic Empires and China*. Cambridge, MA: Basil Blackwell, 1989.

Barnett, A. Doak. *Communist China and Asia*. New York: Vintage Books, 1960.

——. *China on the Eve of the Communist Takeover*. New York: Praeger, 1963.

Barth, Fredrik. "Introduction". In *Ethnic Groups and Boundaries: The Social Organization of Cultural Difference*. Ed. Fredrik Barth. Boston: Little, Brown, 1969.

——. "Pathan Identity and its Maintenance." In *Ethnic Groups and Boundaries: The Social Organization of Cultural Difference*. Ed. Fredrik Barth. Boston: Little, Brown, 1969.

Battuta, Ibn. *Voyages d'Ibn Battuta*. 4 vols. Ed. and Tr. C. Défrémey and B. R. Sanguinetti. 2nd ed. Ed. Vincent Monteil. Paris: E. Leroux, 1979. 1st ed. 1853–1858.

Beijing China News Agency (Beijing Zhongguo Xinwen She) 北京中国新

闻社. "Publication Ban Sought." Reproduced and Translated in the Foreign Broadcast and Information Service *FBIS-CHI*-89-092, 15 May 1989, p. 52.

Beijing City Sociology Committee, et al., eds. "Beijing shi sanzaju shaoshu minzu jiaoyu wenti diaocha baogao" 北京市散杂居少数民族教育问题调查报告 (Research report on the problem of education among dispersed minorities in Beijing city), *Central Institute for Nationalities Journal* 1: 18–26 (1984).

Beijing New China News Agency (Beijing Xinhuashe) 北京新华社. "Government Bans Book." In *FBIS-CHI*-89-150, 15 May 1989, p. 53.

Beijing Review. "Chinese Oil Workers in Iraq," 12: 37 (1986).

——. "An Islamic Investment Corporation." 17: 25 (1986).

Bentley, G. Carter. "Theoretical Perspectives on Ethnicity and Nationality," Part 1, *Sage Race Relations Abstracts* 8.2: 1–53 (1983).

——. "Theoretical Perspectives on Ethnicity and Nationality," Part 2, Bibliography, *Sage Race Relations Abstracts* 8.3: 1–26 (1983).

——. "Ethnicity and Practice," *Comparative Study of Society and History* 1: 24–55 (1987).

Blake, Fred C. *Ethnic Groups and Social Change in a Chinese Market Town*. Honolulu: The University Press of Hawaii, 1981.

Bodde, Derk. "China's Muslim Minority," *Far Eastern Survey* 15.18: 281–284 (1946).

——. "Japan and the Muslims of China," *Far Eastern Survey* 15.20: 311–313 (1946).

——. "Chinese Muslims in Occupied Areas," *Far Eastern Survey* 15.21: 330–333 (1946).

Bonacich, Edna. "A Theory of Middlemen Minorities," *American Sociological Review* 37: 583–594 (1973).

Boon, James A. *Other Tribes, Other Scribes; Symbolic Anthropology in the Comparative Study of Cultures, Histories, Religions and Texts*. Cambridge: Cambridge University Press 1982.

Botham, Mark E. "A Saint's Tomb in China," *Moslem World* 14.2: 185–186 (1924).

Bourdieu, Pierre. *Outline of a Theory of Practice*. Cambridge: Cambridge University Press, 1977.

Bradley, David. "The Yi Nationality of Southwestern China: A Linguistic Overview." In *Minority Nationalities of China*. Ed. Charles Li and Dru C. Gladney. Amsterdam: Mouton Press, Forthcoming.

Bromiley, Julian S. *Soviet Ethnology and Anthropology Today*. Mouton: The Hague, 1974.

Bromiley, Julian S., and Viktor Kozlov. "The Theory of Ethnos and Ethnic Processes in Soviet Social Sciences," *Comparative Studies in Society and History* 3: 425–437 (1989).

Broomhall, Marshall. *Islam in China: A Neglected Problem*. New York: Paragon Book Co., 1910.

Brudny, Yitzhak. "The Rise and Fall of the Political Contract: Russian Nationalism and the Soviet State." PhD dissertation, Princeton University, Forthcoming.

Burns, John F. "Chinese City is True to Moslem Self," *Los Angeles Times*, 13 June 1984, p. Y4.

Bush, Richard. *Religion in Communist China*. Nashville: Abingdon, 1970.

CASS (Chinese Academy of Social Sciences) News Research Institute, eds. *Zhongguo gongchandang xinwen gongzuo wenjian huibian* 中国共产党新闻工作文件汇编 (Collected documents of China's Communist Party's news work). Vol. I. Beijing: New China Publication Society (1980).

Cable, Mildred with Francesca French. *The Gobi Desert*. 1987 Reprint. Boston: Beacon Press, 1942.

Cai Wenpo 蔡文波. "Ma Dian zhi Huimin xianzhuang" 马甸之回民现况 (Present situation of Ma Dian Hui People), *Yue Hua*, May 25 (1930).

Chan, Anita, Richard Madsen, and Jonathan Unger. *Chen Village: A Recent History of a Peasant Community in the People's Republic of China*. Berkeley, Los Angeles, and London: University of California Press, 1984.

Chan, Hok-Lam. *Li Chih, 1527–1602, in Contemporary Chinese Historiography*. New York: M. E. Sharpe, 1980.

Chan, Wing-tsit. "The New Awakening of Islam." In *Religious Trends in Modern China*. Ed. Wing-tsit Chan. New York: Columbia University Press, 1953.

Chang Hajji Yusuf. "The Hui (Muslim) Minority in China: An Historical Overview," *Journal. Institute for Muslim Minority Affairs* 8.1: 62–78 (1987).

———. "The Ming Empire: Patron of Islam in China and Southeast and West Asia," *Journal of the Malaysian Branch of the Royal Asiatic Society* 61.2: 1–44 (1988).

———. "Chinese Islam and the Hui Minority: Past, Present and Future." In *The Legacy of Islam in China: An International Symposium in Memory of Joseph F. Fletcher*. Ed. Dru C. Gladney. Conference Volume. Harvard University, 14–16 April 1989.

Chang Jingcun 常憬存. "Huizu quanshi yishi—ji Wang Xinwu" 回族拳师轶事 (The story of a Hui boxing master—Wang Xinwu), *Ningxia ribao*, 23 July 1983.

Changji Hui Antonomous Prefectural Situation Committee, eds. *Changji Huizu zizhizhou gaikuang* 昌吉回族自治州概况 (Changji Hui autonomous prefectural basic situation). Urumqi: Xinjiang Nationalities Publishing Society, 1985.

Chao, Yuen Ren. *Aspects of Chinese Sociolinguistics*. Stanford: Stanford University Press, 1976.

       References

Charsley, S. R. "The Formation of Ethnic Groups." In *Urban Ethnicity*. Ed. Abner Cohen. ASA Monograph No. 12. London: Tavistock, 1974.

Chatterjee, Partha. *Nationalist Thought and the Colonial World: A Derivative Discourse*. London: Zed Books, 1986.

Chen Changping 陈长平. "Minzu renkou biandong yu yizu tonghun yanjiu" 民族人口变动与异族同婚研究 (Research on changes in nationality population and inter-ethnic marriage). MA Thesis, Central Institute for Nationalities, Beijing, 1983.

Chen Dasheng 陈达生. "Quanzhou lingshan shenmu niandai chushen" 泉州灵山圣墓年代初探 (A tentative inquiry into the date of the Lingshan Holy Tomb at Quanzhou). In *Symposium on Quanzhou Islam*. Eds. Quanzhou Maritime Museum. Quanzhou: Fujian People's Publishing Society, 1983.

———. "Quanzhou Yisilanjiaopai yu yuanmou yisiba xizhanluan xingzhi shishen" 泉州伊斯兰教派与元末亦思巴奚战乱性质试探 (Tentative inquiry into the Islamic sects at Quanzhou and the 'Isbah' disturbance toward the end of the Yuan dynasty). In *Quanzhou Yisilanjiao yanjiu lunwen xuan* 泉州伊斯兰教研究论文选 (Symposium on Quanzhou Islam). Ed. Quanzhou Maritime Museum. Quanzhou: Fujian People's Publishing Society, 1983.

———. "The Role of the Mosque in the Reacceptance of Islam by Muslim Descendants in Quanzhou during the Ming Dynasty." In *The Legacy of Islam in China: An International Symposium in Memory of Joseph F. Fletcher*. Ed. Dru C. Gladney. Conference Volume. Harvard University, 14–16 April 1989.

———, ed. *Quanzhou Yisilanjiao shike (Islamic Inscriptions in Quanzhou.)* 泉州伊斯兰教石刻. Tr. Chen Enming. Yinchuan: Ningxia Peoples Publishing Society and Quanzhou: Fujian People's Publishing Society, 1984.

Chen Enming 陈恩明. "*Sunni pai yu Shiye pai de zhuyao qubie*" 逊尼派与十叶派的主要区别 (Main differences between Sunni and Shi'i orders). In *Zhongguo Yisilanjiao yanjiu wenji* 中国伊斯兰教研究文集 (Compendium of Chinese Islamic research). Ed. Chinese Islamic Research Committee. Yinchuan: Ningxia People's Publishing Society, 1988.

Chen Jo-hsi. *The Execution of Mayor Yin and Other Stories from the Great Proletarian Cultural Revolution*. Bloomington: Indiana University Press, 1978.

Chen Sidong 陈泗东. "Li Zhi de jiashi, guju ji qi qi mubei" 李贽的家世, 故居及其妻墓碑 (Li Zhi's family, ancient residences, and his wife's gravestone), *Wenwu* 1 (1975). Reprinted in *Huizu shi lun ji* 回族史论集 1949–1979 (Hui history collection 1949–1979). Ed. Chinese Academy of Social Sciences Ethnology Department and Central Nationalities Institute Ethnology Department, Hui History Team. Yinchuan: Ningxia People's Publishing Society, 1984.

Chen Ziqiang 陈自强. "Pu Shougeng shiliao kaoban" 蒲寿戌史料考辨 (Verifying historical material related to Pu Shougeng). In *Symposium on Quanzhou*

Islam. Ed. Quanzhou Maritime Museum. Quanzhou: Fujian People's Publishing Society, 1983.

Ch'en Yüan. *Western and Central Asians in China Under the Mongols: Their Transformation into Chinese*. Tr. and annotated by Ch'ien Hsing-hai and L. Carrington Goodrich. Monumenta Serica Monograph XV. Los Angeles: Monumenta Serica at the University of California, 1966.

Chiang Kai-shek. *China's Destiny*. New York: Roy Publishers, 1947. 1st ed. 1943.

China Communication Service (Zhongguo Tongxun She) 中国通讯社. "'Sex Habit Books' Causes Controversy in Beijing." In *FBIS-CHI*-89-092, 15 May 1989, p. 52.

China Communication Service, Hong Kong (Zhongguo Tongxun She Xiang Gang) 中国通讯社, 香港. "Writer of 'Sex Habits' Has Been Suspended for Examination." In *FBIS-CHI*-89-092, 15 May 1989, p. 53.

China Daily. "Moslems celebrate festival in Beijing," 19 September 1983, p. 3.

———. "Chinese Muslims celebrate," 21 September 1983, p. 1.

———. "Overseas investors sought for Ningxia," 20 June 1984, p. 2.

———. "Middle East trade links sought by Ningxia," 14 November 1984, p. 2.

———. "Xinjiang's pilgrimage to Mecca," 28 March 1984, p. 1.

———. "Muslims kick off donation campaign," 7 November 1984, p. 3.

———. "Muslims join in festival," 18 August 1986, p. 3.

———. "Freer reign urged for minorities," 4 April 1987, p. 1.

———. "Xinjiang—Soviet trade rises," 4 April 1987, p. 2.

———. "Keep rural girls in school," 17 April 1987, p. 1.

———. "Muslim restaurant," 17 April 1987, p. 3.

———. "Minorities hold key to own prosperity," 28 April 1987, p. 4.

China Encyclopaedia Committee. "Minzu" (Nationality). In *Zhongguo dabaike quanshu* (The complete encyclopaedia of China). *Minzu* Volume. Beijing: China Complete Encyclopaedia Publishing Society, 1986.

China Handbook, 1937–1945. New York: Macmillan, 1947.

China Sports, ed. *Wushu Among Chinese Moslems*. China Sports Series 2. Beijing: *China Sports Magazine*, 1984.

China Yearbook. Published annually by Routledge & Kegan Paul.

China Islamic Association (Zhonghuo Yisilanjiao Xiehui) 中国伊斯兰教协会. *The Religious Life of Chinese Muslims*. Beijing: Foreign Languages Press, 1981.

Chinese Muslim Association (Zhongguo Huijiao Xiehui) 中国回教协会. *Islam in Taiwan*. Taipei: Chinese Muslim Association, 1969.

Chow, Rey. "Violence in the Other Country: China as Crisis, Spectacle, and Woman." In *Third World Women and Feminist Perspectives*. Ed. Chandra Mohanty, et al. Bloomington: Indiana University Press, 1990.

Chu Wen-djang. "Ch'ing Policy Towards the Muslims in the Northwest." PhD dissertation, University of Washington, 1955.

Ci Yuan 词源 (Etymologies). 5th ed. 4 vols. Beijing: Shangwu Yinshuguan, 1982.

Clark, Hugh Roberts. "Consolidation on the South Frontier: The Development of Ch'uan-chou 699–1126." PhD dissertation, University of Pennsylvania, 1981.

Clifford, James. "Introduction: Partial Truths." In *Writing Culture: The Poetics and Politics of Ethnography*. Ed. James Clifford and George E. Marcus. Berkeley: University of California Press, 1986.

———. *The Predicament of Culture: Twentieth-Century Ethnography, Literature, and Art*. Cambridge: Harvard University Press, 1988.

Coale, Ansley J. "Rapid Population Change in China, 1952–1982." Committee on Population and Demography, Report No. 27. Washington, D.C.: National Academy Press, 1984.

Cohen, Abner. *Custom and Politics in Urban Africa: A Study of Hausa Migrants in Yoruba Towns*. London: Routledge & Kegan Paul, 1969.

———. *Two Dimensional Man: An Essay on the Anthropology of Power and Symbolism in Complex Society*. Berkeley: University of California Press, 1974.

Cohen, Eri. "The Impact of Tourism on the Hill Tribes of Northern Thailand," *Internales Asienforum* 10.1, 2: 5–38 (1979).

Cohen, Myron. *House Divided, House United: The Chinese Family in Taiwan*. New York: Columbia University Press, 1976.

Cohen, Ronald and John Middleton, eds. *From Tribe to Nation in Africa*. Scranton: Chandler Publishing Co., 1970.

Cohn, Bernard S. "The Census, Social Structure and Objectification in South Asia." In *An Anthropologist Among the Historians and Other Eassays*. Ed. Bernard S. Cohn. Delhi: Oxford University Press, 1987.

Comaroff, John. "Of Totemism and Ethnicity: Consciousness, Practice and the Signs of Inequality," *Ethnos* 52.3.4: 301–323.

Connor, Walker. *The National Question in Marxist-Leninst Theory and Strategy*. Princeton: Princeton University Press, 1984.

Conrad, Joseph. *The Heart of Darkness*. New York: Viking Press, 1975. 1st ed. 1902.

Crapanzano, Vincent. *The Hamadsha: A Study in Moroccan Ethnopsychiatry*. Berkeley: University of California Press, 1973.

Crossley, Pamela Kyle. *Orphan Warriors: Three Manchu Generations and the End of the Qing World*. Princeton: Princeton University Press, 1990.

———. "Thinking about Ethnicity in Early Modern China," *Late Imperial China* 11.1: 1–35 (1990).

Da Yingyu 达应庾. "Zhongguo Yisilanjiao Sailaifeiye pai shulue" 中国伊斯兰教赛来菲耶派述略 (A brief narration of China's Islamic Salafiyya order).

In *Zhongguo Yisilanjiao yanjiu wenji* (Compendium of Chinese Islamic research). Ed. Chinese Islamic Research Committee. Yinchuan: Ningxia People's Publishing Society, 1988.

Dachang Huizu Zizhixian Gaikuang, eds. *Dachang Huizu zizhixian gaikuang* 大厂回族自治县概况 (The situation of the Dachang Hui autonomous county). Shijiazhuang: Hebei People's Publishing Society (1985).

Dai Qingxia. "On the Languages of the Jingpo Nationality." In *Minority Nationalities of China*. Ed. Charles Li and Dru C. Gladney. Amsterdam: Mouton Press, Forthcoming.

Deal, David. "National Minority Policy in Southwest China, 1911–1965." PhD dissertation, University of Washington, 1971.

De Francis, John. *The Chinese Language: Fact and Fantasy*. Honolulu: University of Hawaii Press, 1984.

Deleuze, Gilles and Felix Guattari. *A Thousand Plateaus: Capitalism and Schizophrenia*. Minneapolis: University of Minnesota Press, 1987.

Denzin, Norman K. "On the Ethics of Disguised Observation," *Social Problems* 15: 502–504 (1968).

Despres, Leo A. "Introduction." In *Ethnicity and Resource Competition in Plural Societies*. Ed. Leo A. Despres. The Hague, Paris: Mouton Publishers, 1975.

———. "Ethnicity: What Data and Theory Portend for Plural Societies." In *The Prospects for Plural Societies*. Ed. David Maybury-Lewis. Washington, D.C.: The American Ethnological Society, 1984.

Devereux, George. "Ethnic Identity: Its Logical Foundations and its Dysfunctions." In *Ethnic Identity: Cultural Continuities and Change*. Ed. George De Vos and Lola Romanucci-Ross. Palo Alto: Mayfield Publishing, 1975.

Devéria, G. "Orienede l'Islamisme en Chine (deux légendes musulmanes chinoises, pèlerinages de Ma Foutch'ou)." In *Centenaire de l'Ecole des Languages Orientales*. Paris: n.p., 1895.

De Vos, George. "Ethnic Pluralism: Conflict and Accommodation." In *Ethnic Identity: Cultural Continuities and Change*. Ed. George De Vos and Lola Romanucci-Ross. Palo Alto: Mayfield Publishing, 1975.

De Vos, George and Lola Romanucci-Ross, eds. *Ethnic Identity: Cultural Continuities and Change*. Palo Alto: Mayfield Publishing, 1975.

Diamond, Norma. "Rural Collectivization and Decollectivization in China—A Review Article," *Journal of Asian Studies* 44.4: 785–792 (1985).

———. "The Miao and Poison: Interactions on China's Southwest Frontier," *Ethnology* 21.1: 1–25 (1988).

Diao, Richard K. "The National Minorities of China and Their Relations with the Chinese Communist Regime." In *Southeast Asian Tribes, Minorities, and Nations*. Ed. Peter Kunstadter. Princeton: Princeton University Press, 1967.

"Ding Clan Genealogy." 丁氏谱 In *Quanzhou wenxian congkan di san zhong* 泉州文献丛刊第三种 Quanzhou documents collection, No. 13. Quanzhou:

Quanzhou Historical Research Society, 1980.

Ding Futing 丁福亭, Ma Xiangzi 马祥字, Ding Yuzhang 丁裕长, Wang Liwen 汪季文. "Beijing Donglaishun yangrouguan fajia shi" 北京东来顺羊肉馆发家史 (The historical development of the Donglaishun Lamb restaurant), *Guangming ribao*, 20 March 1962. Reprinted in *Huizu shilun ji* 1949–1979 (Hui history collection 1949–1979). Ed. Chinese Academy of Social Sciences Ethnology Department and Central Nationalities Institute Ethnology Department, Hui History Team. Yinchuan: Ningxia People's Publishing Society, 1984.

Ding Yibo 丁一波. "'Zhengce ahong' qianjian" "政策阿訇"浅见 (Humble opinion about policy ahong), *Ningxia tongzhan lilun taolunhui lunwen* (Ningxia United Front theory discussion meetings thesis) 34 (1984).

Ding Yimin 丁毅民. "*Xin Zhongguo de Huihui minzu*" 新中国的回回民族 (New China's Hui nationality). Beijing: n.p., 1958.

Douglas, Mary. *Purity and Danger: An Analyis of the Concepts of Pollution and Taboo*. New York: Praeger, 1966.

Drake, F. S. "Mohammedanism in the T'ang Dynasty," *Monumenta Serica* 8: 1–40 (1943).

Dreyer, June. *China's Forty Millions: Minority Nationalities and National Integration in the People's Republic of China*. Cambridge: Harvard University Press, 1976.

——. "The Islamic Community of China," *Central Asian Survey* 1.2/3: 32–49 (1981).

Dumont, Louis. *Homo Hierarchicus*. Chicago: University of Chicago Press, 1980. First ed. 1966.

Dunlop, John B. *The Faces of Contemporary Russian Nationalism*. Princeton: Princeton University Press, 1983.

Dunn, Ross. E. *The Adventures of Ibn Battuta: A Muslim Traveler of the 14th Century*. Berkeley: University of California Press, 1986.

Durkheim, Emile. *The Elementary Forms of the Religious Life*. Tr. Joseph Ward Swain. New York: The Free Press, 1915.

Dyer, Svetlana Rimsky-Korsakoff. *Soviet Dungan Kolkhozes in the Kirghiz SSR and the Kazakh SSR*. Oriental Monograph Series No. 25. Canberra: Australian National University Press, 1979.

——. "T'ang T'ai-tsung's Dream: A Soviet Dungan Version of a Legend on the Origin of the Chinese Muslims," *Monumenta Serica* 35: 545–570 (1981–1983).

Eaton, Richard Maxwell. *Sufis of Bijapur 1300–1700: Social Roles of Sufis in Medieval India*. Princeton: Princeton University Press, 1978.

——. "The Political and Religious Authority of the Shrine of Baba Farid." In *Moral Conduct and Authority: The Place of* Adab *in South Asian Islam*. Ed. Barbara Daly Metcalf. Berkeley: University of California Press, 1984.

Economist, The. "Beijing's Copycat Scandal," 20 May 1989.

Eickelman, Dale F. *Moroccan Islam: Tradition and Society in a Pilgrimage Center.* Austin and London: University of Texas Press, 1976.

———. *The Middle East: An Anthropological Approach.* New Jersey: Prentice-Hall, Inc., 1981.

Eickelman, Dale F. and James Piscatori. "Social Theory in the Study of Muslim Societies." In *Muslim Travellers: Pilgrimage, Migration and the Religious Imagination.* Ed. Dale F. Eickelman and James Piscatori. London: Routledge, 1990.

Ekvall, Robert. *Cultural Relations on the Kansu-Tibetan Border.* Chicago: Chicago University Press, 1939.

Emerson, Rupert. *From Empire to Nation.* Boston: Beacon Press, 1960.

Eminov, M. M. *The Development of Soviet Nationality Policy and Current Soviet Perspectives on Ethnicity.* Bloomington: Indiana University Press, 1976.

Encausse, Hélène Carrère d'. "The Stirring of National Feeling." In *Central Asia: 120 Years of Russian Rule.* Ed. Edward Allworth. Durham and London: Duke University Press, 1987.

Epstein, A. L. *Politics in an Urban African Community.* Manchester: Manchester University Press, 1958.

Evans-Pitchard, E. E. *The Nuer.* Clarendon: Oxford University Press, 1940.

Erikson, Kai T. "A Comment on Disguised Observation in Sociology," *Social Problems* 12: 366–373 (1967).

Fabian, Johannes. "Six Theses Regarding the Anthropology of African Religious Movements," *Religion* 11: 109–126 (1982).

———. *Time and the Other: How Anthropology Makes its Object.* New York: Columbia University Press, 1983.

Fallers, Lloyd. *The Social Anthropology of the Nation-State.* Chicago: Aldine, 1974.

Fan Changjiang 范长江. *Zhongguo de xibei jiao* 中国的西北角 (China's northwest corner). Tianjin: Public Publishing House. Ed. Chinese Academy of Social Sciences. Beijing: New China Publishing Society, 1980. 1st ed. 1936.

Fan Wenlan 潘文兰. *Han minzu xingcheng wenti taolunji* 汉民族形成问题讨论集 (Collection of discussions of the formation of the Han nationality). Peking: Sanlian, 1957.

Fârûqî, Isma⁹îl R. al and Lois Lamyâ'l. *The Cultural Atlas of Islam.* New York: Macmillan, 1986.

Fei Xiaotong 费孝通. "Ethnic Identification in China." In *Toward a People's Anthropology.* Ed. Fei Xiaotong. Beijing: New World Press, 1981.

———. "Zhonghua minzu de duoyuan yiti geju" 中华民族的多元一体格局 (Plurality and unity in the Configuration of the Chinese nationality), *Beijing daxue xuebao* 4: 1–19 (1989).

Feng Zenglie 冯增烈. "'Gedimu' bayi" "格迪目" 八议 ("Gedimu" eight opinion). In *Xibei Yisilanjiao yanjiu* (Northwest Islam research). Ed. Gansu

Provincial Ethnology Department. Lanzhou: Gansu Nationality Publishing Society, 1985.

Firth, Raymond. *We, the Tikopia*. London: Allen and Unwin, 1936.

Fischer, Michael M. J. *Iran: From Religious Dispute to Revolution*. Cambridge: Harvard University Press, 1980.

——. "Ethnicity and the Post-Modern Arts of Memory." In *Writing Culture: The Poetics and Politics of Ethnography*. Ed. James Clifford and George E. Marcus. Berkeley: University of California Press, 1986.

Fitzgerald, C. P. *The Tower of Five Glories: A Study of the Min Chia of Ta Li, Yunnan*. Westport: Hyperion Press, 1973. 1st ed. 1941.

Fletcher, Joseph F. "The Naqshbandiyya in Northwest China." Unpublished manuscript, Harvard University, n.d.

——. "Central Asian Sufism and Ma Ming-hsin's New Teaching," *Proceedings of the Fourth East Asian Altaistic Conference*. Ed. Ch'en Chieh-hsien. Taibei: National Taiwan University, 1975.

——. "The Naqshbandiyya and the *Dhikr-i Arra*," *Journal of Turkish Studies* 1: 113–119 (1977).

——. "Brief History of the Naqshbandiyya in China." Unpublished manuscript, Harvard University, 1978.

——. "Ch'ing Inner Asia c. 1800." In *The Cambridge History of China*. Vol. X, Part 1, *Late Ch'ing 1800–1911*. Ed. John King Fairbank. Cambridge: Cambridge University Press, 1978.

——. "A Brief History of the Chinese Northwestern Frontier, China Proper's Northwest Frontier: Meetingplace of Four Cultures." In *China's Inner Asian Frontier*. Ed. Mary Ellen Alonso. Cambridge, Peabody Museum, 1979.

——. "The Sufi 'paths' (*turuq*) in China." Unpublished manuscript, Harvard University. French version published as "Les 'voies' (*turuq*) a soufites en Chines." In *Les orders mystiques dans l'Islam, cheminements et situation actuelle*. Ed. Alexandre Popovic. Paris, 1988.

——. "The Taylor-Pickens Letters on the Jahri Branch of the Naqshbandiyya in China." Ed. Jonathan N. Lipman. *Central and Inner Asian Studies* 3: 1–35 (1989).

Fletcher, Joseph, Mary Ellen Alonso, and Wasma'a K. Chorbachi. "Arabic Calligraphy in Twentieth-Century China." In *The Legacy of Islam in China: An International Symposium in Memory of Joseph F. Fletcher*. Ed. Dru C. Gladney. Conference Volume. Harvard University, 14–16 April 1989.

Forbes, Andrew D. W. "Survey Article: The Muslim National Minorities of China," *Religion* 6.2: 67–87 (1976).

——. *Warlords and Muslims in Chinese Central Asia*. Cambridge: Cambridge University Press, 1986.

——. "The 'Cîn-Hô' (Yunnanese Chinese) Caravan Trade with North Thailand During the Late Nineteenth and Early Twentieth Centuries." Paper presented to the Regional Workshop on Minorities in Buddhist Politics, Chulalongkorn University, Bangkok, Thailand, 24–28 June 1987.

Ford, Joseph. "Some Chinese Muslims of the 17th and 18th Centuries," *Asian Affairs* (New Series) 5.2: 144–156 (1974).

Foster, Brian L. "Ethnicity and Commerce," *American Ethnologist* 1: 437–448 (1974).

Foucault, Michel. "Truth and Power." In *Power/Knowledge*. Ed. Colin Gordon. New York: Pantheon Books, 1972.

———. *Discipline and Punish: The Birth of the Prision*. New York: Vintage Books, 1975.

———. "The Subject and Power." In *Michel Foucault: Beyond Structuralism and Hermeneutics*. Ed. Hubert L. Dreyfus and Paul Rabinow. 2nd ed. Chicago: University of Chicago Press, 1983.

Fowler, Vernon. "The Truth About Zhen," *Asian Review* 1.1: 26–42 (1987).

Fox, Richard G. "Hindu Nationalism in the Making, or the Rise of the Hindian." In *Nationalist Ideologies and the Production of National Cultures*. Ed. Richard G. Fox. Washington: American Ethnological Society, 1990.

Francis, E. K. *Interethnic Relations*. New York: Elsevier, 1978.

Franke, Wolfgang. "A Note on the Ancient Chinese Mosques at Xian and Quanzhou." In *Ma Da Zhongwenxi 1980 nianchi 1981 niandu biye jinian kan* 马大中文系一九八〇年齿一九八一年度比业纪念刊 (Malaysia University Chinese Department 1980–1981 graduate memorial publication). Kuala Lumpur: University of Malaysia, 1981.

Fried, Morton. *Fabric of Chinese Society*. New York: Octagon, 1969. 1st ed. 1953.

Furnivall, J. S. *Netherlands India*. Cambridge: Cambridge University Press, 1939.

Gamble, Sydney. *Peking: A Social Survey*. New York: George H. Doran Company, 1921.

———. *How Chinese Families Live in Peiping*. New York and London: Funk & Wagnalls, 1933.

———. *North China Villages: Social, Political, and Economic Activities Before 1933*. Berkeley and Los Angeles: University of California Press, 1963.

Gansu Provincial Nationalities Affairs Commission, Gansu Provincial Nationalities Research Institute, eds. *Hui hui minzu bian Huaxia* 回回民族遍华夏 (The spread of the Hui hui nationality in China). Gansu: n.p., n.d.

Gansu Provincial News Agency (Gansu Sheng Xinwenshe) 甘肃省新闻社. "Lanzhou Muslims Riot Over Publishing of Book." In *FBIS-CNI-89-092*, 15 May 1989, p. 59.

Gao Mingkai 高名凯 and Liu Zhengtan 刘正埮. *Xiandai Hanyu wailaici yanjiu* 现代汉语外来词研究 (Research on foreign terms in modern Chinese).

Beijing: Wenzi Gaige Chubanshe, 1987.

Gao Zhanfu 高占福. "Guanyu jiaopai zhizheng zai qingdai xibei Huimin qiyi zhong xiaoji zuoyong de tantao" 关于教派之争在清代西北回民起义中消极作用的探讨 (Discussion regarding the inactive role of factional struggles in the Qing dynasty northwest Hui rebellions). In *Xibei Yisilanjiao yanjiu* 西北伊斯兰教研究 (Northwest Islam research). Ed. Gansu Provincial Ethnology Department. Lanzhou: Gansu Nationality Publishing Society, 1985.

——. "Yisilanjiao hunying zhidu yu Huizu hunying xisu de yanjiu" 伊斯兰教婚姻制度与回族婚姻习俗的研究 (Research on the Islamic marriage system and Hui marriage customs). In *Zhongguo Yisilanjiao yanjiu wenji* 中国伊斯兰教研究文集 (Compendium of Chinese Islamic research). Ed. Chinese Islamic Research Committee. Yinchuan: Ningxia People's Publishing Society, 1988.

Gates, Hill. "Ethnicity and Social Class." In *The Anthropology of Taiwanese Society*. Ed. Emily Ahern and Hill Gates. Stanford: Stanford University Press, 1981.

Geertz, Clifford. "The Integrative Revolution: Primordial Sentiments and Civil Politics in the New States." In *Old Societies and New States*. Ed. Clifford Geertz. New York: Free Press, 1963.

——. *Islam Observed: Religious Development in Morocco and Indonesia*. Chicago and London: University of Chicago Press, 1968.

——. "Internal Conversion' in Contemporary Bali." In *The Interpretation of Cultures*. Ed. Clifford Geertz. New York: Basic Books, 1973.

——. "Blurred Genres: The Refiguration of Social Thought." In *Local Knowledge*. Ed. Clifford Geertz. Ithaca: Cornell University Press, 1983.

——. *Works and Lives: The Anthropologist as Author*. Stanford: Stanford University Press, 1988.

Gellner, Ernest. *Nations and Nationalism*. Ithaca: Cornell University Press, 1983.

Gennep, Arnold, van. *Tabou et Totemism à Madagascar: Etude descriptive et théorique*. Paris: E. Leroux, 1904.

Gilmartin, David. "Shrines, Succession, and Sources of Moral Authority." In *Moral Conduct and Authority: The Place of Adab in South Asian Islam*. Ed. Barbara Daly Metcalf. Berkeley: University of California Press, 1984.

Gladney, Dru C. "The 'Weber Thesis' and Economic Action in Post-Mao China." Unpublished manuscript, 1982.

——. "Muslim Tombs and Ethnic Folklore: Charters for Hui Identity," *The Journal of Asian Studies* 46.3: 495–532 (1987).

——. "Muslim Marriage Endogamy in China: A Strategy for Preserving Muslim Minority Identity?" Paper presented at The Middle Eastern Studies Association Annual Meetings, Los Angeles, 3–5 November 1988.

——. "Dialogic Ethnicity: The State and National Identity in China." Paper presented at the Seminar on National Identity in Post-Colonial Third World

States, the Institute for Advanced Study, Princeton, 13 December 1989.

——. "Bodily Positions and Social Dispositions: Sexuality, Nationality and Tiananmen." Paper presented at the American Ethnological Society Annual Meetings, Atlanta, March 1990.

——. "The Peoples of the People's Republic: Finally in the Vanguard?" *The Fletcher Forum of World Affairs* 12.1: 62–76 (1990).

——. "The Ethnogenesis of the Uigur," *Central Asian Studies* 9.1: 1–28 (1990).

——. "Islam Preserved: Ethnic Identity and Adaptation in a Southeastern Hui Lineage." In *Minority Nationalities of China*. Ed. Charles Li and Dru C. Gladney. Amsterdam: Mouton Press, Forthcoming.

——. "Ethno-religous Factionalism and the Panthay Muslim Rebellion in Yunnan 1855–1873," under revision.

——. "Pivotal Pawns? Hui-Uigur Relations and Ethnoreligious Identity in Xinjiang." In *Hui Muslims in Chinese Society*. Ed. Dru C. Gladney. Forthcoming.

Gladney, Dru C. and Ma Shouqian. "Interpretations of Islam in China: A Hui Scholar's Perspective," *Journal, Institute for Muslim Minority Affairs*, 10.2: 475–486 (1989).

Glazer, Nathan and Daniel P. Moynihan. *Beyond the Melting Pot*. Cambridge: MIT Press, 1974.

Gong Weiduan 宫为端. "Yongning xian Na Jiahu cun shi diaocha" 永宁县纳家户村史调查 (Yong Ning county Na Homestead history investigation) *Ningxia shizhi yanjiu* 宁夏史之研究 1: 34–40 (1987).

Gough, Kathleen. "Anthropology: Child of Imperialism," *Monthly Review* 19.11: 12–27 (1967).

Grayburn, Nelson. "Tourism: The Sacred Journey." In *Hosts and Guests*. Ed. V. Smith. Philadelphia: University of Pennsylvania Press, 1977.

Greenhalgh, Susan. "Shifts in China's Population Policy, 1984–86: Views from the Central, Provincial, and Local Levels," *Population and Development Review*, 1987.

Greenwood, D.M. "Tourism as an Agent of Change: A Spanish Basque Case," *Ethnology* 11: 80–91 (1972).

Guo Wuyuan Renkou Pucha Bangongshi 国务院人口普查办公室 (State Population Census Office). *Di san ci quan guo renkou pucha shougong huizong ziliao zongbian* 第三次全国人口普查手工汇总资料汇编 (The third national census hand-counted collected population statistics). Vol. IV. *Ge minzu renkou* 各民族人口 (Various nationalities population). Beijing: State Population Census Office, 1983.

Haaland, Gunnar. "Economic Determinants in Ethnic Processes." In *Ethnic Groups and Boundaries: The Social Organization of Cultural Difference*. Ed. Fredrik Barth. Boston: Little, Brown, 1969.

Habermas, Jürgen. *The Structural Transformation of the Public Sphere*. Tr. Thomas Burger and Frederick Lawrence. Cambridge: MIT Press, 1989. 1st ed. 1962.

Handler, Richard. "On Sociocultural Discontinuity: Nationalism and Cultural Objectification in Quebec," *Current Anthropology* 25.1: 55–71 (1984).

——. "On Dialogue and Destructive Analysis: Problems in Narrating Nationalism and Ethnicity," *Journal of Anthropological Research* 41.2: 171–182 (1985).

Haqqani, Husain. "Repression and Revival—the Dichotomy of Islam in China," *Far Eastern Economic Review* 15: 54–55 (December 1983).

Harrell, Stevan. "Belief and Unbelief in a Taiwan Village." PhD dissertation, Stanford University, 1974.

——. "When A Ghost Becomes a God." In *Studies in Chinese Society*. Ed. Arthur P. Wolf. Palo Alto: Stanford University Press, 1974.

——. "Ethnicity, Local Interests, and the State: Yi Communities in Southwest China," *Comparative Studies in Society and History* 32: 515–548 (1990).

Harrell, Stevan and Elizabeth Perry. "An Introduction." In "Symposium: Syncretic Sects in Chinese Society." Ed. Stevan Harrell and Elizabeth Perry. *Modern China* 8.3: 283–305 (1982).

Harris, Marvin. *The Rise of Anthropological Theory*. New York: Crowell, 1968.

Hartmann, Martin. "Muhammadanism (in China)." In *Encyclopeadia of Religion and Ethics*. Ed. James Hastings. VIII, 888–895. New York: Charles Scribners, 1951.

Hayward, H. D. "Chinese-Moslem Literature: A Study in Mohammedan Education," *Muslim World* 23: 356–377 (1933).

He Qiaoyuan 何乔远. *Minshu* 闽书 (History of Minjiang, Fujian), 1629.

He Yan 和羑. "Mingdai Xiyu yu Zhongyuan wangchao guanxi shulun" 明代西域与中原王朝关系术论 (Brief discussion of Ming dynasty relations between Western countries and the central plains), *Zhongyang minyuan xuebao* 中央民院学报 5: 3 (2 July 1985).

Heberer, Thomas. *China and Its National Minorities: Autonomy or Assimilation?* Armonk: M. E. Sharpe, 1989.

Hechter, Michael. *Internal Colonialism: The Celtic Fringe in British National Development,* 1536–1966. London: Routledge and Kegan Paul, 1975.

——. "Ethnicity and Industrialization: The Proliferation of the Cultural Division of Labor," *Ethnicity* 3.3: 214–224 (1976).

Hobbes, Thomas. *Leviathan*. New York: Fontana Publishers, 1962. 1st ed. 1651.

Hobsbawm Eric. "Introduction: Inventing Traditions." In *The Invention of Tradition*. Ed. Eric Hobsbawm and Terence Ranger. Cambridge: Cambridge University Press, 1983.

——. "Mass-Producing Traditions: Europe, 1870–1914." In *The Invention of Tradition*. Ed. Eric Hobsbawm and Terence Ranger. Cambridge: Cambridge University Press, 1983.

Holloman, Regina, and Serghei A. Arutiunov, eds. "The Study of Ethnicity: An Overview." In *Perspectives on Ethnicity*. The Hague: Mouton, 1978.

Honig, Emily. "The Politics of Prejudice: Subei People in Republican-Era Shanghai," *Modern China* 15.3: 243–274 (1989).

———. "Pride and Prejudice: Subei People in Contemporary Shanghai." In *Unofficial China: Popular Culture and Thought in the People's Republic*. Ed. Perry Link, Richard Madson, and Paul G. Pickowicz. Boulder: Westview Press, 1989.

Hsieh Shih-Chung. "Ethnic Contacts, Stygmatized Identity, and Pan-Aboriginalism: A Study on Ethnic Change of Taiwan Aborigines." Paper presented at a conference "Taiwan Studies: An International Symposium," University of Chicago. 7 July 1986.

Hsien Rin. "The Synthesizing Mind in Chinese Etho-Cultural Adjustment." In *Ethnic Identity*. Ed. George De Vos and Lola Romanucci-Ross. Chicago: University of Chicago Press, 1982. 1st ed. 1975.

Hsu, Francis L. K. *Under the Ancestors' Shadow*. Palo Alto: Stanford University Press, 1968. 1st ed. 1948.

Hu Sheng. *Zhexue yanjiu*, October 1958.

Hua Nianci 花念慈 and Zhang Sui 张绥. "Jianshu Yisilanjiao zai Shanghai de fazhan" 简述伊斯兰教在上海的发展 (A brief narration of the development of Islam in Shanghai). In *Zhongguo Yisilanjiao yanjiu wenji* (Compendium of Chinese Islamic research). Ed. Chinese Islamic Research Committee. Yinchuan: Ningxia People's Publishing Society, 1988.

Hualong Hui Autonomous County Basic Situation Committee, eds. *Hualong Huizu zizhixian gaikuang* 华隆回族自治县概况 (Hualong Hui autonomous county basic situation). Xining: Qinghai Nationalities Publishing Society, 1984.

Huang Qiuren 黄秋润. "Mantan Quanzhou Huizu fengsu" 浅谈泉州回族风俗 (A simple talk on Islamic custom at Quanzhou). In *Symposium on Quanzhou Islam*. Ed. Quanzhou Foreign Maritime Museum. Quanzhou: Fujian People's Publishing Society, 1983.

Huang Tianzhu 黄天柱 and Wu Youxiong 吴幼雄. "Yisilan wenhua dui Quanzhou de yinxiang" 伊斯兰文化对泉州的影响 (The influence of Islamic culture on Quanzhou), *Ningxia shehui kexue* 5: 64–68 (1986).

Huang Tianzhu 黄天柱 and Liao Yuanquan 廖渊泉. "Mantan Quanzhou diqu Ahlabo Musilin de houyi ji qi yiji" 漫谈泉州地区阿拉伯穆斯林的后裔及其遗迹 (An Informal talk on the Moslem descendants of the Quanzhou area and their heritage). In *Symposium on Quanzhou Islam*. Ed. Quanzhou Foreign Maritime Museum. Quanzhou: Fujian People's Publishing Society, 1983.

Huaqiao ribao (Overseas Chinese daily) 华乔日报. "San qian Musilin xuesheng Beijing youxing: ti yaoqiu yancheng *Xing fengsu* zuozhe" 三千穆斯林学生

北京游行: 提要求严惩性风俗作者 (Three thousand Beijing Muslim students protest: Request severe punishment of the author of *Sexual Customs*). 13 May 1989.

Huizu Jianshi Editorial Committee, eds. *Huizu jianshi* 回族简史 (Brief history of the Hui). Yinchuan: Ningxia People's Publishing Society, 1978.

Huxley, Julian, and A. C. Haddon. *We Europeans: A Survey of "Racial" Problems.* New York: Harper, 1936.

Investigation Section of Quanzhou Foreign Maritime Museum, eds. "Baiqi Guo xing bu shi Guo Ziyi de houyi er shi Huizu ren" 白奇郭姓不是郭子仪的后裔而是回族人 (The 'Guo' Clan of Bai Qi are descendants of Moslems rather than those of Guo Ziyi). In *Symposium of Quanzhou Islam.* Ed. Quanzhou Foreign Maritime Museum. Quanzhou: Fujian People's Publishing House, 1983.

———. "Chendai Dingxing yanjiu" 陈埭丁姓研究 (A study of the 'Ding' clan). In *Symposium on Quanzhou Islam.* pp. 202–212. Ed. Quanzhou Foreign Maritime Museum. Quanzhou: Fujian People's Publishing Society, 1983.

Israeli, Raphael. *Muslims in China.* London and Atlantic Highlands: Curzon & Humanities Press, 1978.

———. "Muslim Plight Under Chinese Rule." In *Islam in Asia Minor.* Ed. Raphael Israeli. London and Atlantic Highlands: Curzon & Humanities Press, 1982.

———. "Islam." In *Cambridge Encyclopedia of China.* Ed. Brian Hook. Cambridge: Cambridge University Press, 1982.

———. "Muslims in China: Islam's Incompatibility with the Chinese Order." In *Islam in Asia*, Vol. II. Ed. Raphael Israeli and Anthony H. Johns. Boulder, Westview Press, 1984.

———. "Is there Shi'a in Chinese Islam?" *Journal, Institute for Muslim Minority Affairs* 9.1: 49–66 (1988).

Iwamura Shinobu 岩材忍. "The Structure of Moslem Society in Inner Mongolia," *Far Eastern Quarterly* 8.1: 34–44 (1948).

———. *Chūgoku Kaikyō shakai no kozo* 中國回教社會の構造. 2 vols. Tokyo: Nippon Hyōronsha 1950.

Izutsu, Toshihiko. *Sufism and Daoism.* Berkeley and Los Angeles: University of California Press, 1983.

Jamjoom, Ahmad Salah. "Notes of a Visit to Mainland China," *Journal, Institute of Muslim Minority Affairs* 6.1: 208–218 (1985).

Jankowiak, William R. "The Last Hurrah? Political Protest in Inner Mongolia," *The Australian Journal of Chinese Affairs* 21 (1989).

Jiang Weitang 姜纬堂. "'Gang zhi' suojide qingchu Beijing Niujie Huimin qu" 冈志所记的清初北京牛街回民区 (What "Gangzhi" remembers clearly of the Beijing Niujie Hui area at the beginning of the Qing), *Minzu yanjiu* 4: 39–44 (1984).

Jiang Yingliang 江应梁. "*Diannan Shadian Huijiao nongcun diaocha*" 滇南沙甸回教农村调查 (Southern Yunnan Shadian Hui village investigation). Reprinted in *Huizu shi lun ji* 1949–1979 回族史论集 (Hui history collection 1949–1979). Ed. Chinese Academy of Social Sciences Ethnology Department and Central Nationalities Institute Ethnology Department, Hui History Team. Yinchuan: Ningxia People's Publishing Society, 1984. 1st ed. 1951.

Jin Binggao. "The Marxist Definition of Nationality: Its Origin and Influence," *Central Nationalities Institute Journal* 3: 64–67 (1984).

Jin Jitang 金记唐. "Huijiao minzu shuo" 回教民族说 (Speaking of the Hui religion). In *Huizu, Huijiao, Huimin Lunji* (Collected essays on the Hui nationality, Hui religion, and the Hui people). Ed. Bai Shouyi. Kowloon: n.p., 1974. 1st ed. 1936.

Jin Yijiu 金宜久. "The System of *menhuan* in China: An influence of Sufism on Chinese Muslims," *Ming Studies* 19: 34–45 (1984).

——. "Sufeipai yu Zhongguo menhuan" 苏非派与中国门宦 (Sufism and China's menhuan). In *Xibei Yisilanjiao yanjiu* 西北伊斯兰教研究 (Northwest Islam research). Ed. Gansu Provincial Ethnology Department. Lanzhou: Gansu Nationality Publishing Society, 1985.

Jordan, David K. and Daniel L. Overmeyer. *The Flying Phoenix: Aspects of Chinese Sectarianism in Taiwan*. Princeton: Princeton University Press, 1986.

Joyaux, F. "Les Musulmans en Chinese Populaire," *Notes et Etudes Documentaires* 2915, 1962.

Kao Hao-jan. *The Imam's Story*. Hong Kong: Dragonfly Books, 1960.

Karklins, Rasma. *Ethnic Relations in the USSR: The Perspective From Below*. Boston: Allen and Unwin, 1986.

Ke Lei 柯勒 and Sang Ya 桑娅, eds. *Xing fengsu* 性风俗 (Sexual customs). Shanghai: Shanghai Cultural Publishing Society, 1989.

Kessler, Clive S. *Islam and Politics in a Malay State: Kelantan* 1838–1969. Ithaca: Cornell University Press, 1978.

Keyes, Charles F. "Introduction." In *Ethnic Adaptation and Identity: The Karen on the Thai Frontier with Burma*. Ed. Charles Keyes. Philadelphia: ISHI, 1979.

——. "The Dialectics of Ethnic Change." In *Ethnic Change*. Ed. Charles F. Keyes. Seattle: University of Washington Press, 1981.

——. "The Basis of Ethnic Group Relations in Modern Nation-States." In *Ethnic Processes in the USA and the USSR: Material of the Soviet American Symposium*. Ed. V. I. Kozlov. Moscow: INION, The Academy of Sciences, 1984.

Khan, M. R. *Islam in China*. New Delhi: n.p., n.d.

Kim Ho-dong. "The Muslim Rebellion of the Kashgar Emirate in Chinese Central Asia, 1864–1877." PhD Dissertation, Harvard University, 1986.

Kim, Illsoo. *The New Urban Immigrants: Korean Immigrants in New York.* Princeton: Princeton University Press, 1981.

Kristeva, Julia. *Powers of Horror: An Essay on Abjection.* Tr. Leon S. Romleiz. New York: Columbia University Press, 1980.

Lambeck, Michael. "Taboo as Cultural Practice in Mayotte." Paper presented at the American Ethnological Society Annual Meetings, Atlanta, 26–29 April 1990.

Lardy, Nicholas R. "Agricultural Reforms in China," *Journal of International Affairs* 32.2: 91–104 (1986).

Lattimore, Owen. *The Desert Road to Turkestan.* Boston: Little, Brown, 1929.

———. *Pivot of Asia: Sinkiang and the Inner Asian Frontiers of China and Russia.* Boston: Little, Brown, 1950.

———. *Inner Asian Frontiers of China.* New York: American Geographical Society, 1951.

Lavely, William R. "A Rural Chinese Marriage Market." Paper presented at the Morrison Seminar in Demography, Stanford University, 7 February 1983.

Lawton, John. "The People." In *Muslims in China: A Special Issue, Aramco World Magazine* 36.4. Washington, D.C.: The Aramco Corporation, 1985.

Leach, Edmund R. *Political Systems of Highland Burma.* Cambridge: Harvard University Press, 1954.

Le Coq, Albert von. *Buried Treasures of Chinese Turkestan.* Oxford: Oxford University Press, 1985. 1st ed. 1928.

Lee Chae-Jin. *China's Korean Minority: The Politics of Ethnic Education.* Boulder: Westview Press, 1986.

Lefort, Claude. *The Political Forms of Modern Society: Bureaucracy, Democracy, and Totalitarianism.* Ed. Roger B. Thompson. Cambridge, MA: Polity Press, 1986.

Leslie, Donald Daniel. *The Survival of the Chinese Jews: The Jewish Community of Kaifeng.* Leiden: E. J. Brill, 1972.

———. *Islamic Literature in Chinese, Late Ming and Early Ch'ing: Books, Authors and Associates.* Canberra: Canberra College of Advanced Education, 1981.

———. *Islam in Traditional China: A Short History to 1800.* Camberra: CCAE, 1986.

Lévi-Strauss, Claude. *The Elementary Structures of Kinship.* Boston: Beacon Press, 1969.

Li, C. "The Quality Control of the 1982 Population Census in China." Paper presented at the meeting of the International Statistical Institute, Madrid, 1983.

Li, H. T., T. Song, and C. Li. "Current Fertility State of Women of Han and

Minority Nationalities in Rural Areas," *Population and Economics*, 1983.

Liao Gailong. "The '1980 Reform' Program in China (Part IV)." Speech made in 1981. In *Policy Conflicts in Post-Mao China*. Ed. John P. Burns and Stanley Rosen. Armonk: M. E. Sharpe, 1986.

Lin Song 林松. "Shilun Yisilanjiao dui xingcheng woguo Huizu suo ji de jueding xing zuoyong" 识论伊斯兰教对形成我国回族所记的觉定形作用 (Thesis regarding the role of Islam in the form of China's Hui people's decision making), *Shehui kexue zhanxian* 3 (1983).

———. "Everyday Life of Chinese Muslims in Beijing." In *Urbanism in Islam*. Proceedings of the International Conference on Urbanism in Islam. Vol. IV. Tokyo: The Middle Eastern Culture Center, 22–28 October 1989.

Lin Yueh-hwa. "Yizu of Liang Shan, Past and Present." In *The Prospects for Plural Societies*. Ed. David Maybury-Lewis. Washington, D.C.: The American Ethnological Society, 1984.

Lindbeck, J. "Communism, Islam and Nationalism in China," *Review of Politics* 12: 473–488 (1950).

Linxia Hui Autonomous Prefectural Basic Situation Committee, eds. *Linxia Huizu zizhizhou gaikuang* (Linxia Hui autonomous prefectural basic situation). Lanzhou: Gansu Nationalities Publishing Society, 1986.

Lipman, Jonathan N. "The Border World of Gansu, 1895–1935." PhD dissertation, Stanford University, 1981.

———. "Patchwork Society, Network Society: A Study of Sino-Muslim Communities." In *Islam in Asia*. Ed. Raphael Israeli and Anthony H. Johns. Vol. II. Boulder: Westview Press, 1984.

———. "The Third Wave: Establishment and Transformation of the Muslim Brotherhood in Modern China." Paper presented at the China Colloquium of the Henry S. Jackson School of International Studies, University of Washington, 20 February 1986.

———. "Hui-Hui: An Ethnohistory of the Chinese-Speaking Muslims," *Journal of South Asian and Middle Eastern Studies* 11.1, 2: 112–130 (1987).

———. "Sufi Muslim Lineages and Elite Formation in Modern China: The *Menhuan* of the Northwest." In *The Legacy of Islam in China: An International Symposium in Memory of Joseph F. Fletcher*. Ed. Dru C. Gladney. Conference Volume. Harvard University, 14–16 April 1989.

———. "Shi'ism in Chinese Islam." In *Encyclopaedia Iranica*, Forthcoming.

Liu Binru 刘彬如 and Chen Dazuo 陈达祚. "Yangzhou 'Huihui tang' he yuandai Alabowen de mubei" 扬州"回回堂"和元代阿拉伯文的墓碑 (Yangzhou "Huihui temple" and the Yuan dynasty Arabic gravestones). Reprinted in *Huizu shi lun ji* 1949–1979 回族史论文集 (Hui history collection 1949–1979). Ed. Chinese Academy of Social Sciences Ethnology Department and Central Nationalities Institute Ethnology Department, Hui History Team. Yinchuan: Ningxia People's Publishing Society, 1984. 1st ed. 1962.

Liu Junwen. *Beijing: China's Ancient and Modern Capital*. Beijing: Foreign Languages Press, 1982.

Liu Zekuan 刘泽宽 "Huijiaoren weishenma bu chi zhu rou" 回教人为什么不吃猪肉 (Why Muslims do not eat pork), *Nanhua wenyi* 1: 14 (1932).

Los Angeles Times. "Chinese Muslims Protest 'Sex Habits' Book," 13 May 1989.

Löwenthal, Rudolf. "The Mohammedan Press in China." In *The Religious Periodical Press in China*. Peking: Synodal Committee on China, 1940.

Lu Yun. "Rural Muslims: Prayer and Progress, the Changying Mosque, Beijing," *Beijing Review*, 18 August 1986, p. 19–20. Reprinted in D. MacInnis, *Religion in China Today*. Maryknoll: Orbis Books, 1989.

Luo Jianguo. "Lantern 'king' brightens exhibit," *China Daily*, 5 February 1984, p. 27.

Ma Guyuan 马古原. "Yisilanjiao yu Huizu fengsu" 伊斯兰教与回族风俗 (Islam and Hui customs), *Qinghai minzu xueyuan xuebao* 2 (1983).

Ma Ibrahim T. Y. (Ma T'ien-ying 马天英). "Weishenma bu chi zhu rou" 为什么不吃猪肉 (Why abstain from pork). Taipei: Chinese Muslim Association, n.d..

Ma Jian 马建. "Huimin weishenma bu chi zhurou?" 回民为什么不吃猪肉 (Why do Hui people not eat pork?), *People's Daily*, 17 February 1951.

Ma Kexun 马克勋. "Zhongguo Yisilanjiao Yihewanyi pai di changdaozhe: Ma Wanfu" 中国伊斯兰教伊赫瓦尼派的倡导者—马万福 (The leader of China's Ikwan: Ma Wanfu). In *Yisilanjiao zai Zhongguo* (Islam in China). Ed. Gansu Provincial Ethnology Department. Yinchuan: Ningxia People's Publishing Society, 1982.

Ma Qicheng 马启成. "A Brief Account of the Early Spread of Islam in China," *Social Sciences in China* 4: 97–113 (1983).

Ma Ruling 马汝邻. "Zailun Yisilanjiao yu Huihui minzu xingcheng de guanxi" 再论伊斯兰教与回族形成的关系 (Discuss again the relationship between Islam and the Hui nationality's form), *Ningxia University Journal* 20: 32–37 (1984).

Ma Shouqian 马寿千. "Yisilanjiao zai Zhongguo weishenme you chengwei Huijiao huo Qingzhenjiao?" 伊斯兰教在中国为什么又称为回教或清真教 (Why is Islam in China called Huijiao or Qingzhenjiao?), *Guangming ribao*, 9 October 1979. Reprinted in *Huizu shilun ji* 1949–1979 (Hui history collection 1949–1979). Ed. Chinese Academy of Social Sciences Ethnology Department and Central Nationalities Institute Ethnology Department, Hui History Team. Yinchuan: Ningxia People's Publishing Society, 1984.

——. "The Hui People's New Awakening at the End of the 19th Century and Beginning of the 20th Century." In *The Legacy of Islam in China: An International Symposium in Memory of Joseph F. Fletcher*. Ed. Dru C. Gladney.

Conference Volume. Harvard University, 14–16 April 1989.

Ma Shulin 马书林, ed. *Zhongguo qingzhen caipu* 中国清真菜谱 (China's *qing-zhen* cookbook). Dictated by Chef Ma Shikui. Beijing: People's Publishing Society, 1982.

Ma Sukun 马苏昆. "Huizu de xingcheng yu Yisilanjiao" 回族的形成与伊斯兰教 (Hui nature and Islam), *Xinjiang ribao*, 5 March 1983, p. 3.

Ma Tong 马通. *Zhongguo Yisilan jiaopai yu menhuan zhidu shilue* 中国伊斯兰教派与门宦制度史略 (A history of Muslim factions and the *menhuan* system in China). Yinchuan: Ningxia People's Publishing Society, 1983. 1st ed. 1927

——. *Zhongguo Yisilan jiaopai menhuan suyuan* 中国伊斯兰教派门宦溯源 (Tracing the source of China's Islamic Orders and *menhuan*). Yinchuan: Ningxia People's Publishing Society, 1986.

——. "China's Islamic Saintly Lineages and the Muslims of the Northwest." In *The Legacy of Islam in China: An International Symposium in Memory of Joseph F. Fletcher*. Ed. Dru C. Gladney. Conference Volume. Harvard University, 14–16 April 1989.

——. *Gansu Huizu shi gangyao* 甘肃回族史纲要 (*An outline of Gansu Hui history*). Lanzhou: Gansu Provincial Commission for Nationality Affairs, Gansu Provincial Nationalities Research Department, n.d.

Ma Tong and Wang Qi 王琦. "Zhongguo Yisilanjiao de jiaopai he *menhuan*" 中国伊斯兰教的教派和门宦 (The religions factions and *menhuan* of China's Islam). In *Xibei Yisilanjiao yanjiu* (Northwest Islam research). Ed. Gansu Provincial Ethnology Department. Lanzhou: Gansu Nationality Publishing Society, 1985.

Ma Weiliang 马为良. "Minzu wenti yu jieji douzheng de guanxi" 民族问题与阶级斗争的关系 (The relationship between the nationality problem and class struggle), *Minzu yanjiu* 3: 1–6, 11 (1980). Translated in U.S. Joint Publications Research Service 76883, pp. 65–77.

——. "Yunnan Daizu, Zangzu, Baizu, he xiao liangshan Yizu diqu de Huizu" 云南傣族、藏族、白族和小梁山彝族地区的回族 (Yunnan Dai, Tibetan, Bai, and Little Liangshan mountain Yi minority area Hui peoples), *Ningxia shehui kexue* 1 (1986).

Ma Ximing 马希明. "Xi'an de jizuo Qingzhensi" 西安的几座清真寺 (Xi'an's several mosques). In *Zhongguo Yisilanjiao yanjiu wenji* (Compendium of Chinese Islamic Research). Ed. Chinese Islamic Research Committee. Yinchuan: Ningxia People's Publishing Society, 1988.

Ma Xianda. "Chinese Moslems and Wushu." In *Wushu Among Chinese Moslems*. Ed. China Sports. China Sports Series 2. Beijing: *China Sports Magazine*, 1984.

Ma Xueliang 马学良 and Dai Qingxia 戴清夏. "Minzu he yuyan" 民族和语言 (Nationality and language), *Minzu yanjiu* 1: 6–14 (1983).

Ma Yin 马寅, ed. *Zhongguo xiaoshu minzu changshi* 中国少数民族常识 (General knowledge of China's minority nationalities). Beijing: China Youth Press, 1984.

———. ed. *China's Minority Nationalities.* Beijing: People's Publishing Society, 1989.

Ma Zhu 马注. *Qing Zhen zhi Nan* 清真指南 (The compass of Islam). 8 juan. 1681.

Ma Zikuo 马兹廓. "Linxia Gongbei Siyuan" 中国伊斯兰教参考资料选编 (Tracing the source of Linxia *gongbei*). In *Zhongguo Yisilanjiao cankao ziliao xuanbian, 1911–1949 (China Islamic history reference material selections, 1911–1949).* Ed. Li Xinhua and Feng Jinyuan. Vol. I. Yinchuan: Ningxia People's Publishing Society, 1985.

MacFarquhar, Roderick. "The End of the Chinese Revolution," *The New York Review of Books* 36.12: 8–10 (1989).

MacInnis, Donald E. *Religious Policy and Practice in Communist China.* New York: Macmillan, 1972.

———. *Religion in China Today: Policy and Practice.* Maryknoll: Orbis Books, 1989.

Madsen, Richard. *Morality and Power in a Chinese Village.* Berkeley, Los Angeles, and London: University of California Press, 1984.

Mair, Victor H. "Chinese Language Reform and Dungan Script in Soviet Central Asia." In *The Legacy of Islam in China: An International Symposium in Memory of Joseph F. Fletcher.* Ed. Dru C. Gladney. Conference Volume. Harvard University, 14–16 April 1989.

Mandel, Ruth. "The Making of Infidels and Other Ethnics." Paper presented at the American Anthropological Association Annual Meetings, Chicago, 18–22 November 1987.

Mann, Jim. "China's Uighurs—a Minority Seeks Equality," *Los Angeles Times, Sunday,* 13 July 1985.

Mao Zedong. "Appeal of the Central Government to the Muslims," *Tou-cheng,* 12 July 1936, pp. 1–3.

Marcus, George E. "Afterword: Ethnographic Writing and Anthropological Careers." In *Anthropology as Cultural Critique.* Chicago: University of Chicago Press, 1986.

Marcus, George E., and Michael M. J. Fischer. *Anthropology as Cultural Critique.* Chicago: University of Chicago Press, 1986.

Mason, Isaac. *List of Chinese-Moslem Terms.* Shanghai: China Continuation Committee on Work for Moslems, 1919.

———. "Notes on Chinese Mohammedan Literature," *Journal of the North China Branch of the Royal Asiatic Society* 56: 172–215 (1925).

———. "The Mohammedans of China: When, and How, They First Came," *Journal of the North China Branch of the Royal Asiatic Society* 60: 1–54 (1929).

Matthews, Robert Henry. *Matthews' Chinese-English Dictionary*. Cambridge: Harvard University Press, 1943.

Mauss, Marcel. *The Gift: Forms and Functions of Exchange in Archaic Societies*. New York: Norton, 1962.

Maybury-Lewis, David. "Living in Leviathan: Ethnic Groups and the State." In *The Prospects for Plural Societies*. Ed. David Maybury-Lewis. Washington, D.C.: The American Ethnological Society, 1984.

Mckhann, Charles. "Naxi-Han History and the Transformation of the 'Meebiuq' (Sacrifice to Heaven) Ritual." Paper presented to the American Anthropological Association Annual Meetings, November 1988.

Mees, Imke. *Die Hui—Eine moslemische Minderheit in China: Assimilationsprozesse und politische Rolle vor 1949*. Munich: Minerva-Publikation, 1984.

Mengcun Huizu Zizhixian Gaikuang 孟村回族自治县概况, eds. *Mengcun Huizu zizhixian gaikuang* 孟村回族自治县概况 (The situation of the Mengcun Hui autonomous county). Shijiazhuang: Hebei People's Publishing Society, 1983.

Menyuan Huizi Zizhixian gaikuang, eds. 门源回族自治县概况 *Menyuan Huizu zizhixian gaikuang* 门源回族自治县概况 (Menyuan Hui autonomous county basic situation). Xining: Qinghai Nationalities Publishing Society, 1985.

Mian Weiling 勉维霖. *Ningxia Yisilan jiaopai gaiyao* 宁夏伊斯兰教派概要 (An outline of the Islamic factions of Ningxia). Yinchuan: Ningxia People's Publishing Society, 1981.

———. "Ningxia Huizu Yisilanjiao de jiaopai fenhua qiantan" 宁夏回族伊斯兰教的教派分化浅谈 (Brief discussion of the distribution of Ningxia Hui Islamic factions). In *Xibei Yisilanjiao yanjiu* (Northwest Islam research). Ed. Gansu Provincial Ethnology Department. Lanzhou: Gansu Nationality Publishing Society, 1985.

Michael, Franz. "Non-Chinese Nationalities and Religious Communities." In *Human Rights in the People's Republic of China*. Ed. Yuan Liwu. Boulder: Westview Press, 1988.

Mills, J. V. G. *Ma Huan, Ying-yai Sheng-lan: "The Overall Survey of the Western Shores" (1433)*. Cambridge: Cambridge University Press, 1970.

Millward, James A. "The Chinese Borker Wool Trade of 1880–1937." In *The Legacy of Islam in China: An International Symposium in Memory of Joseph F. Fletcher*. Ed. Dru C. Gladney. Conference Volume. Harvard University, 14–16 April 1989.

Min Tong 闵桐. "Youhao wanglai de jian zheng." 友好往来的见证 (Testimony to friendly discourse). In *Symposium on Quanzhou Islam*. Ed. Quanzhou Foreign Maritime Museum. Quanzhou: Fujian People's Publishing Society, 1983.

Minhe Hui and Tu Autonomous County Basic Situation Committee 民和回族土族自治县概况, eds. *Minhe Huzu Tuzu zizhixian gaikuang* 民和回族土族自治县概况 (Minhe Hui and Tu autonomous county basic situation). Xining: Qinghai Nationalities Publishing Society, 1986.

Minzu tuanjie 民族团结 (United nationalities magazine). "Twenty nine provinces, cities, and autonomous regions' minority nationality population" 2: 38–39, 3: 46–47 (1984).

Minzu Wenti Research Society, eds. 民族问题研究会 *Huihui minzu wenti* 回回民族问题 (The question of the Hui nationality). Beijing: Nationalities Publishing Society, 1982.

Moerman, Michael. "Ethnic Identity in a Complex Civilization: Who are the Lue?" *American Anthropologist* 67.5: 1215–1230 (1965).

——. "Being Lue: Uses and Abuses of Ethnic Identification." In *Essays on the Problem of the Tribe*. Ed. June Helm. Seattle: University of Washington, 1968.

Morgan, Lewis Henry. *Ancient Society*. Tucson: University of Arizona Press, 1985. 1st ed. 1878.

Moseley, George. *The Party and the National Question in China*. Cambridge: MIT Press, 1966.

Moser, Leo J. *The Chinese Mosaic: The Peoples and Provinces of China*. Boulder and London: Westview Press, 1985.

Mudimbe, V. Y. *The Invention of Africa: Gnosis, Philosophy, and Order of Knowledge*. Bloomington: Indiana University Press, 1988.

Murphy, Rhoads. "Presidential Address: Toward the Complete Asianist," *Journal of Asian Studies* 47.4: 747–755 (1988).

Nagata, Judith A. "In Defense of Ethnic Boundaries: The Changing Myths and Charters of Malay Identity." In *Ethnic Change*. Ed. Charles Keyes. Seattle: University of Washington Press, 1981.

——. *The Reflowering of Malaysian Islam: Modern Religious Radicals and Their Roots*. Vancouver: University of British Columbia Press, 1984.

Nakada Yoshinobu 中田吉信. *Kaikai minzoku no shomondai* 回回民族の諸問題 (Studies on the Hui people). Tokyo: Ajia keizai kenkyūjō, 1971.

Naquin, Susan. *Millenarian Rebellion in China: The Eight Trigrams Uprising of 1813*. New Haven: Yale University Press, 1976.

——. "Connections between Rebellions: Sect Family Networks in Qing China," *Modern China* 8: 337–360 (1981).

Naquin, Susan and Evelyn S. Rawski. *Chinese Society in the Eighteenth Century*. New Haven: Yale University Press, 1987.

Naroll, Raoul. "On Ethnic Unit Classification," *Current Anthropology* 5: 283–291, 306–312 (1964).

——. "Who the Lue Are." In *Essays on the Problem of the Tribe*. Ed. June

Helm. Seattle: University of Washington Press, 1968.

Nash, Manning. *The Cauldron of Ethnicity in the Modern World*. Berkeley: University of California Press, 1989.

New York Times. "Muslim Students March in Beijing: 2,500 Protest a Book that they say Blasphemes Islam," 13 May 1989, p. A3.

———. "Voice from Tiananmen Now Heard at Wellesley," 22 February 1990, p. A18.

Niebuhr, H. Richard. *Christ and Culture*. New York: Harper and Row, 1951.

Ningxia ribao (Ningxia daily). "Tongxin xian zhongshi zai xiaoshu minzu zhong fazhan dangyuan" 同心县重视在少数民族中发展党员 (Tongxin county emphasizes the development of Parly members within minority nationalities), 8 November 1984.

———. "Women ye shi xibei ren" 我们也是西北人 (We are also northwesterners), 22 November 1984.

Ningxia huabao (Ningxia pictorial) 2 (1983). Yinchuan: Ningxia People's Publishing Society, 1984.

Norman, Jerry. *Chinese*. Cambridge: Cambridge University Press, 1988.

O'Brien, Jay. "Toward a Reconstitution of Ethnicity: Capitalist Expansion and Cultural Dynamics in Sudan," *American Anthropologist* 88.4: 898–907 (1986).

Oda, Juten. "Uighuristan," *Acta Asiatica* 34: 22–45 (1978).

Office of Strategic Services, Research and Analysis Branch. "Japanese Infiltration Among Muslims in China." Unpublished report, 1944.

———. "Peoples and Politics of China's Northwest." Unpublished report, 1945.

Ogilve, C. L. and S. M. Zwemer. "A Classified Bibliography of Books on Islam in Chinese and Chinese-Arabic," *Chinese Recorder*, October 1917.

Ollone, Henri M. G. d'. *Recherches sur les Musulmans Chinois*. Paris: E. Leroux, 1911.

Pang, Keng-fong. "Austronesian-speaking Hui of Hainan Island: A Southeast Asian Islamic Identity?" In *The Legacy of Islam in China: An International Symposium in Memory of Joseph F. Fletcher*. Ed. Dru C. Gladney. Conference Volume. Harvard University, 14–16 April 1989.

Panskaya, Ludmilla. *Introduction to Palladii's Chinese Literature of the Muslims*. Oriental Monograph Series 20. Canberra: Australian National University Press, 1977.

Parish, William L. and Martin K. Whyte. *Village and Family in Contemporary China*. Chicago: University of Chicago Press, 1978.

Parker, Edward Harper. *Studies in Chinese Religion*. London: n.p., 1910.

Pei Zhi 佩之. "Hai Rui shi fo Huizu" 海瑞是否回族 (Was Hai Rui a Hui nationality?), *Guangming Daily*, 26 November 1959. Reprinted in *Huizu shi lun ji* 1949–1979 (Hui history collection 1949–1979). Ed. Chinese Academy of

Social Sciences Ethnology Department and Central Nationalities Institute Ethnology Department, Hui History Team. Yinchuan: Ningxia People's Publishing Society, 1984.

Pickens, Claude L. "Across China in Two Weeks," *The Chinese Recorder* 64: 625–628 (1933).

——. "The Challenge of Chinese Moslems," *The Chinese Recorder* 68: 414–417 (1937).

——. "The Four Men Huans," *Friends of Moslems* 16.1 (1942).

Pillsbury, Barbara L. K. "Cohesion and Cleavage in a Chinese Muslim Minority." PhD Dissertation, Columbia University, New York, 1973.

——. "No Pigs for the Ancestors: Pigs, Mothers and Filial Piety Among the 'Taiwanese Muslims.'" Paper presented at the Symposium on Chinese Folk Religions, University of California, Riverside, 24 April 1974.

——. "Blood Ethnicity: Maintenance of Muslim Identity in Taiwan." Paper read at the Conference on Anthropology in Taiwan. Portsmouth, New Hampshire, 19–24 August 1976.

——. "Being Female in a Muslim Minority in China." In *Women in the Muslim World*. Ed. Lois Beck and Nikki Keddie. Cambridge: Harvard University Press, 1978.

——. "Muslim History in China: A 1300-Year Chronology," *Journal, Institute for Muslim Minority Affairs* 3.2: 10–29 (1981).

——. "The Muslim Population of China: Clarifying the Question of Size and Ethnicity," *Journal, Institute for Muslim Minority Affairs* 3.2: 35–58 (1981).

——. "Muslim Population in China According to the 1982 Census," *Journal, Institute for Muslim Minority Affairs* 5.1: 231–3 (1984).

——. "China's Muslims in 1989: Forly Years Under Communism." Paper presented at a Conference on Muslim Minority/Majority Relations, City College of the City University of New York, New York, 24–26 October 1989.

Piore, Michael. "The Role of Immigration in Industrial Growth: A Case Study of the Origins and Character of Puerto Rican Migration to Boston." Working Paper No. 112, Department of Economics, MIT, 1973.

Pipes, Richard. *The Formation of the Soviet Union*. New York: Atheneum, 1980.

Piscatori, James. *International Relations of the Asian Muslim States*. Asian Agenda Report 2. New York: The Asia Society, 1986.

Polo, Marco. *The Travels of Marco Polo*. Ed. W. Marsden. New York: Dorset Press, 1987. 1st ed. 1908.

Population Census Office of the State Council of the People's Republic of China and the Institute of Geography of the Chinese Academy of Sciences. *The Population Atlas of China*. Oxford: Oxford University Press, 1987.

Pratt, Mary Louis. "Fieldwork in Common Places." In *Writing Culture: The Poetics and Politics of Ethnography*. Ed. James Clifford and George E. Marcus. Berkeley: University of California Press, 1986.

Qinghai Provincial News Agency (Qinghai Xinwenshe) 青海新闻社. "Qinghai Muslims Demand Author's Punishment." 15 May. In *FBIS-CHI*-89-093, 16 May 1989, p. 52.

Quanzhou Foreign Maritime Museum, ed. *Symposium on Quanzhou Islam*. Quanzhou: Fujian People's Publishing Society, 1983.

Rahman, Fazlur. *Islam*. New York: Doubleday Anchor Books, 1968.

Ramsay, S. Robert. *The Languages of China*. Princeton: Princeton University Press.

Rappaport, Roy A. *Pigs for the Ancestors*. New Haven: Yale University Press, 1984. 1st ed. 1968.

Renmin ribao. "Yixie renda daibiao lianhe jianyi jueding yige 'minzu tuanjie' ri" (Some People's Government delegates joined together to support the establishment of a "United Nationalities" holiday). Overseas edition. 28 March 1990, p. 4.

Ricoeur, Paul. "The Model of the Text: Meaningful Action Considered as a Text." In *Paul Ricoeur: Hermeneutics and the Human Sciences*. Ed. and Tr. John B. Thompson. Cambridge: Cambridge University Press, 1981.

———. *Lectures on Ideology and Utopia*. Ed. George Taylor. New York: Columbia University Press. 1986.

Riftin, Boris. "Muslim Elements in the Folklore of the Chinese Huizu and the Soviet Dungans." In *The Legacy of Islam in China: An International Symposium in Memory of Joseph F. Fletcher*. Ed. Dru C. Gladney. Conference Volume. Harvard University, 14–16 April 1989.

Rigger, Shelley. "Voices of Manchu Identity, 1635–1935." Unpublished paper, Harvard University, 26 May 1989.

Roff, William R. "The Meccan Pilgrimage: Its Meaning for Southeast Asian Islam." In *Islam in Asia*. Vol. II. Ed. Raphael Israeli and Anthony H. Johns. Boulder: Westview Press, 1984.

———. "Islam Obscured? Some Reflections on Studies of Islam and Society in Asia," *L'Islam en Indonesie* 1.29: 7–34 (1985).

———, ed. *Islam and the Political Economy of Meaning*. New York: Social Science Research Council, 1987.

Rosaldo, Michelle Z. "Toward an Anthropology of Self and Feeling." In *Culture Theory: Essays on Mind, Self, and Emotion*. Ed. Richard A. Shweder and Robert A. LeVine. Cambridge: Cambridge University Press, 1984.

Rossabi, Morris. "The Tea and Horse Trade with Inner Asia during the Ming," *Journal of Asian History* (Weisbaden) 4.2: 135–168 (1970).

———. *China and Inner Asia from 1368 to the Present Day*. London: Thames and Hudson, 1981.

———. *Khubilai Khan: His Life and Times*. Berkeley: University of California Press, 1988.

Roth, Guenther and Reinhard Bendix. *Scholarship and Partnership: Essays on Max Weber*. Berkeley: University of California Press, 1971.

Rousseau, Jean-Jacques. *The Social Contract*. Tr. Maurice Cranston. London: Penguin, 1968. 1st ed. 1762.

Rudelson, Justin Jon. "Uighur Ethnic Identity Change in the Oases of Chinese Turkestan." Unpublished paper, Harvard University, 1988.

Rushdie, Salman. *The Satanic Verses*. London: Viking, 1988.

Saguchi Tōru. "Historical Development of the Sarïgh Uyghurs," *Memoirs of the Research Department of the Tōyō Bunko* 44: 1–26 (1986).

Said, Edward. *Orientalism*. New York: Random House, 1978.

Salisbury, Harrison E. *The Long March: The Untold Story*. New York: Harper & Row, 1985.

Salzman, Philip Carl. "The Lone Stranger and the Solitary Quest," *Anthropology Newsletter*, 16 May 1989.

Samolin, William. *East Turkistan to the Twelfth Century: A Brief Political Survey*. The Hague: Mouton, 1964.

Sangren, P. Steven. *History and Magical Power in a Chinese Community*. Palo Alto: Stanford University Press, 1987.

Saunders, W. A. "Hsuan Hua Kang," *Friends of Moslems* 8.4: 69–71 (1934).

Schell, Orville. *Discos and Democracy: China in the Throes of Reform*. New York: Anchor Books, 1989.

Schimmel, Annemarie. *Mystical Dimensions of the Islam*. Chapel Hill: University of North Carolina Press, 1975.

Schram, Louis. "The Monguors of the Kansu-Tibetan Frontier," *Transactions of the American Philosophical Society* 51.3: 1–65 (1961).

Schwarz, Henry G. *Chinese Policies Towards Minorities: An Essay and Documents*. Occasional Paper No. 2. Bellingham: Western Washington State College, Program in East Asian Studies, 1971.

———. *The Minorities of Northern China: A Survey*. Bellingham: Western Washington University Press, 1984.

Sha Ren 沙任. "Neimenggu Huhehaoteshi Huizu jinqin hun wenti" 内蒙古呼和浩特市回族近亲婚问题 (The problem of close-relative marriage among the Hui people in Huhehot city, Inner Mongolia), *Minzu xue yu xian dai hua* 民族学与现代化 No. 4 (1986).

Sha Zhiyuan 沙之沅, Fu Li 富丽, Yu Liming 徐理明, Bai Jingyuan 白静源, eds. *Beijing de Shaoshuminzu* 北京的少数民族 (Minority nationalities of Beijing). Beijing: Beijing Yanshan Chubanshe, 1988.

Shadian Hui History Editorial Committee, eds. *Shadian Huizu shiliao* 沙甸回族史料 (Shadian Hui history). Yunnan: n.p., 1989.

Shah, Idries. *The Way of the Sufi*. New York: E. P. Dutton, 1969.

Shanin, Teodor. "Ethnicity in the Soviet Union: Analytical Perceptions and

Political Strategies," *Comparative Studies in Society and History* 3: 409–423 (1989).

Sharma, Triloki Nath. "The Predicament of Lhasa Muslims in Tibet," *Journal, Institue for Muslim Minority Affairs* 10.1: 21–27 (1989).

Shichor, Yitzhak. *The Middle East in China's Foreign Policy, 1949–1977.* Cambridge: Cambridge University Press, 1979.

———. "The Role of Islam in China's Middle-Eastern Policy." In *Islam in Asia.* Vol. II. Ed. Raphael Israeli and Anthony H. Johns. Boulder: Westview Press, 1984.

———. *East Wind over Arabia: Origins and Implications of the Sino-Saudi Missile Deal.* Berkeley: Institute of East Asian Studies and the Center for Chinese Studies, University of California 1989.

Shijie ribao "Zhongguo Xinwen Chubanzhe chajin *Xing Fengsu* yi shu: Zeling Shanghai Wenhua Chubanshe tingye zhengdun" 中国新闻出版署查禁〈性风俗〉一书,责令上海文化出版社停业整顿 (China News Publication Agency bans the book *Sexual Customs*: Instructs the Shanghai Cultural Publication Society to close down and reorganize). 15 May 1989.

Shils, Edward. "Primordial, Personal, Sacred and Civil Ties," *British Journal of Sociology* 8: 130–145 (1967).

———, ed. *Center and Periphery: Essays in Macro-sociology.* Chicago: University of Chicago Press, 1975.

Shue, Vivienne. "The Fate of the Commune," *Modern China* 10.3: 250–283 (1984).

———. *The Reach of the State: Sketches of the Chinese Body Politic.* Stanford: Stanford University Press, 1988.

Sinor, Denis. *Inner Asia: A Syllabus.* Bloomington: Indiana University, 1969.

———, ed. *The Cambridge History of Inner Asia.* Cambridge: Cambridge University Press, 1990.

Skinner, G. William. "Marketing and Social Structure in Rural China," Part II. *Journal of Asian Studies* 24.3 (1965).

———. "Chinese Peasants and the Closed Community: An Open and Shut Case," *Comparative Studies in Society and History* 13.3 (1971).

Smith, Valene, ed. *Hosts and Guests: The Anthropology of Tourism.* Philadelphia: University of Pennsylvania Press, 1977.

Snow, Edgar. *Red Star Over China.* New York: Grove Press, 1938.

Spivak, Gyatri Chakravorty. "Reading *The Satanic Verses*," *Public Culture* 2.1: 79–99 (1989).

Stalin, J. V. *Works.* 1907–1913. Volume XI. Moscow: Foreign Languages Publishing House, 1953.

Stallybrass, Peter, and Allon White. *The Poetics and Politics of Transgression.* London: Methuen, 1986.

State Commission for Nationality Affairs, ed. *Minzu lilun yu minzu zhengce* 民族

理论与民族政策 (Nationality theory and nationality policy). Beijing: State Commission for Nationality Affairs Education Department, 1983.

State Statistical Bureau. *Statistical Yearbook of China—1983*. English ed. Hong Kong: Economic Information & Agency, 1983.

Stavenhagen, Rodolfo. *Social Classes in Agrarian Societies*. New York: Anchor Press, 1975.

Steinhardt, John. "Minority groups in Xinjiang strengthen Middle East ties: Muslim Groups Defiant," *South China Morning Post*, 11 March 1987, p. 9.

Su Shaokang, 苏晓康, Director. *He Shang* 河殇 (River elegy). 6-part film. Beijing, 1989.

Subhan, John A. *Sufism: Its Saints and Shrines*. Lucknow: Lucknow Publishing House, 1960.

Sun Hongkai, "A Preliminary Investigation into the Relationship Between Qiong Long and the Languages of the Qiang Branch of Tibeto-Burman." In *Minority Nationalities of China*. Ed. Charles Li and Dru C. Gladney. Amsterdam: Mouton Press, Forthcoming.

Sun Yat-sen. *The Three Principles of the People: San Min Chu I*. Tr. Frank W. Price. Taipei: China Publishing Company, 1924.

Tang Kaijian 汤开健. "*Meng xi bi tan* zhong 'Hui hui'—ci zai shi" 〈梦溪笔谈〉中"回回"一词再释 (Another examination of the term *Hui hui* in the *Meng xi bi tan*), *Minzu yanjiu* 1: 69–74 (1984).

Taylor, Charles. "The Rushdie Controversy," *Public Culture* 2.1: 118–22 (1989).

Tazaka Kōdō 田坂興道. "Ri Jisei wa kaikyōto ka?" 李自成は回教徒か? (Was Li Zicheng a Muslim?), *Tōho gakuhō* 12.2: 91–110 (1941).

———. *Chūgoku ni okeru Kaikyō no denrai to sno guzū* 中國における回教の伝來とそる弘通 (The transmission and diffusion of Islam in China). Tokyo: Tōyō Bunko, 1964.

Terada Takanobu 寺田高信. "Mingdai Quanzhou Huizu zakao" 明代泉州回族杂考 (General study of Ming dynasty Quanzhou Hui), *Minzu fancong* 2: 38–45 (1986).

Thierry, François. "Empire and Minority in China." In *Minority Peoples in the Age of Nation-States*. Ed. Gérard Chaliand. London: Pluto Press, 1989.

Thiersant, P. Dabry de. *Le Mahométisme en Chine et dans le Turkestan Oriental*. 2 vols. Paris: E. Leroux, 1978.

Thompson, Stuart E. "Death, Food, and Fertility." In *Death Ritual in Late Imperial and Modern China*. Eds. James L. Watson and Evelyn S. Rawski. Berkeley: University of California Press, 1988.

Tien, H. Yuan. *China's Population Struggle: Demographic Decisions of the People's Republic, 1949–1969*. Columbus: Ohio State University Press, 1973.

Ting, Daoud. "Islamic Culture in China." In *Islam—The Straight Path*. Ed.

K. W. Morgan. New York: Ronald Press, 1958.

Tokyo Kyodo. "Muslim Students Demonstrate." In *FBIS-CHI*-89-091, 12 May 1989, p. 23.

———. "Muslim Students Decry Sacrilege." In *FBIS-CHI*-89-092, 15 May, 1989, p. 52.

Tong Enzheng. "Morgan's Model and the Study of Ancient Chinese Society," *Social Sciences in China*, Summer, 1989, pp. 182–205.

Trimingham, John Spencer. *The Sufi Orders in Islam*. Oxford: Clarendon Press, 1971.

Trippner, Joseph. "Islamische Gruppe und Graberkult in Nordwest China" (Muslim groups and grave-cults in northwest China)," *Die Welt des Islams* 7: 142–171 (1961).

Ts'ai Mao-t'ang 蔡茅堂. "Hui-jiao zai Lugang" 回教在鹿港 (Islam in Lukang), *China Times*, Taipei, 10, 11 August, 17 November 1973.

Turner, Victor. *The Forest of Symbols*. Ithaca: Cornell University Press, 1967.

Veer, Peter van der. "Satanic or Angelic? The Politics of Religious and Literary Inspiration," *Public Culture* 2.1: 100–105 (1989).

Voll, John O. *Islam: Continuity and Change in the Modern World*. Boulder: Westview Press, 1982.

———. "Muslim Minority Alternatives: Implications of Muslim Experiences in China and the Soviet Union," *Journal, Institute for Muslim Minority Affairs* 6.2: 332–353 (1985).

Waldinger, Roger. "Ethnic Enterprise and Industrial Change: A Case Study of the New York Garment Industry." PhD dissertation, Harvard University, 1983.

Wales, Nym. *Red Dust: Autobiographies of Chinese Communists as told to Nym Wales*. Stanford: Stanford University Press, 1952.

Wallerstein, Immanuel. "Social Conflict in Post-Independence Black Africa: The Concepts of Race and Status Group Reconsidered." In *Racial Tensions and National Integration*. Ed. Ernest O. Campbell. Nashville: Vanderbilt University Press, 1972.

Wang Mingfu 王明甫. "'Minzu' bian" 民族变 (Changes in "nationality"), *Minzu yanjiu* 6: 1–23 (1983).

———. "Minzu yanjiu shuyu zhi tan" 民族研究术语摅谈 (Taking up the technical terms of nationality research), *Minzu yanjiu* 4: 43–54 (1988).

Wang Mingke 王明珂. "Zhongguo gudai Jiang, Qiang, Diqiang zhi yanjiu" 中国古代姜、羌、氏羌之研究 (Reseach on China's ancient Jiang, Qiang, and Diqiang peoples). MA thesis, Taiwan National Normal University, Taibei, 1983.

Wang Peiqin and Bi Jing. "Wang Ziping: A Great Patriotic Fighter." In *Wushu Among Chinese Moslems*. China Sports Series 2. Beijing: *China Sports Magazine*, 1984.

Wang Shoujie 王寿杰. "Niu jie Huimin Shenghuo tan" 牛街回民生活谈 (Discussion of the lifestyle of the Oxen Street Hui), *Yue hua*, 25 May, 5 July 1930.

———. "Beiping shi Huimin gaikuang" 北京市回民概况 (A survey of the Hui people of Beiping), *Li gong* 李工, 1 May 1937.

Wang Xinwu 王新武. "Huizu *wushu* chutan" 回族武术初谈 (An introductory discussion of Hui *wushu*), *Wulin* 武林 10: 38–39 (1983).

Wang Yiping 王一平. "Najiahucun de zongjiao zhuangkuang" 纳家村的宗教状况 (The religious situation in Najiahu village), *Ningxia shehui kexue* 9: 7–9 (1985).

Warren, G. G. "D'Ollone's Investigations on Chinese Moslems," *New China Review* 2: 267–289, 389–414 (1920).

Wax, Murray L. "On Fieldworkers and Those Exposed to Fieldwork: Federal Regulations and Moral Issues." In *Contemporary Field Research*. Ed. Robert M. Emerson. Boston: Little, Brown, 1983.

Weber, Eugen. *Peasants Into Frenchmen: The Modernization of Rural France, 1870–1914*. Stanford: Stanford University Press, 1976.

Weber, Max. *Ancient Judaism*. Ed. and tr. Hans H. Gerth and Don Martindale. Glencoe: Free Press, 1952.

———. *The Protestant Ethic and the Spirit of Capitalism*. Tr. Talcot Parsons. New York: Charles Scribner, 1958.

———. *The Sociology of Religion*. Tr. Ephraim Fischoff. Boston: Beacon Press, 1963. 1st ed. 1922.

———. *Economy and Society*. 2 Vols. Berkeley: University of California Press, 1978.

Weller, Robert P. *Unities and Diversitiies in Chinese Religion*. Seattle: University of Washington Press, 1987.

Wexler, Paul. "Research Frontiers in Sino-Islamic Linguistics," *Journal of Chinese Linguistics* 4.1: 47–82 (1976).

White, Hayden. *Metahistory: The Historical Imagination in Nineteenth Century Europe*. Baltimore and London: Johns Hopkins University Press, 1987. 1st ed. 1973.

White, Lynn T., III, *Policies of Chaos: The Organizational Causes of Violence in China's Cultural Revolution*. Princeton: Princeton University Press, 1989.

Whyte, Martin King, and William L. Parish. *Urban Life in Contemporary China*. Chicago: University of Chicago Press, 1984.

Williams, Brackette. "A Class Act: Anthropology and the Race to Nation Across Ethnic Terrain," *Annual Review of Anthropology* 18: 401–444 (1989).

Wimbush, Enders S. *Nationality Research in the People's Republic of China: A Trip*

Report. Santa Monica: Rand Corporation, 1981.

——. "The Politics of Identity Change in Soviet Central Asia," *Central Asian Survey* 3.3: 69–78 (1985).

Wittfogel, Karl A., and Feng Chia-sheng. *History of Chinese Society: Liao.* Philadelphia: American Philosophical Association, 1949.

Wolf, Arthur, and Chieh-shen Huang. *Marriage and Adoption in China, 1845–1945.* Stanford: Stanford University Press, 1980.

Wolf, Eric. *Europe and the People Without History.* Berkeley: University of California Press, 1982.

Wong, Bernard. "The Role of Ethnicity in Enclave Enterprises: A Study of the Chinese Garment Factories in New York City," *Human Organization* 4.2: 120–130 (1987).

World Bank. *China: Growth and Development in Gansu Province.* Washington, D.C.: The World Bank, 1988.

Worsley, Peter. *The Three Worlds.* Chicago: University of Chicago Press, 1984.

Wright, Mary Clabaugh. *The Last Stand of Chinese Conservativism.* Stanford: Stanford University Press, 1957.

Wu, David. "National Minority Policy and Minority Cultures in Asia," *Southeast Asian Journal of Social Science* 16.2 (1988).

——. "Chinese Minority Policy and the Meaning of Minority Culture: The Example of the Bai in Yunnan, China," *Human Organization*, Forthcoming.

Wu Wenliang 吴文良. *Quanzhou zongjiao shike* 泉州宗教石刻 (Religious inscriptions in Quanzhou). Peking: n.p., 1957.

——. "Zailun Quanzhou Qingjingsi de shijian shiqi he jianzhu xingshi" 再论泉州清静寺时期和建筑形式 (More on the formative period of the Qingjing Mosque and its architectural style). In *Symposium on Quanzhou Islam.* Ed. Quanzhou Foreign Maritime Museum. Quanzhou: Fujian People's Publishing Society, 1983.

Wulsin, Frederick R. "Non-Chinese Inhabitants of the Province of Kansu, China," *American Journal of Physical Anthropology* 8.3: 293–320 (1925).

Xinjiang Academy of Social Sciences. "Xinjiang Huizu de laiyuan" 新疆回族的来源 (The origins of the Hui of Xinjiang). In *Huihui minzu bian huaxia* 回回民族变华夏 (The spread of the Huihui nationality in China). Lanzhou: Gansu Provincial Nationalities Affairs Commission, Gansu Provincial Nationalities Research Institute, 1986.

Xu Jieshun 徐杰舜. *Han minzu lishi he wenhua xintan* 汉民族历史和文化新探 (New explorations in the Han nationality's history and culture). Guangxi: People's Publishing Society, 1985.

Xue Wenbo 薛文波. "Lasa de Huizu" 拉萨的回族 (The Hui of Lhasa). In *Hui hui minzu bian Huaxia* 回回民族变华夏 (The spread of the Hui hui nationality in China). Lanzhou: Gansu Provincial Nationalities Affairs Commission, Gansu Provincial Nationalities Research Institute, 1986.

——. "Shiye pai dui Zhongguo Sunnai pai de yingxiang" 什叶派对中国逊尼派的影响 (The influence of Shi'ism on Sunnism in China). In *Qingdai Zhongguo Yisilan jiao lunji* 清代中国伊斯兰教论集 (Essays on Islam in China during the Qing period). Ed. Ningxia Philosophy and Social Science Institute. Yinchuan: Ningxia People's Publishing Society, 1981.

Ya Hanzhang 牙含章. *Minzu wenti yu zongjiao wenti* 民族问题与宗教问题 (The nationality problem and the religion problem). Chengdu: Sichuan Nationalities Publishing Company, 1984.

——, ed. 民族形成问题研究 (Research on the question of ethnic formation). Chengchi: Sichuan Nationalities Publishing House, 1980.

Yang Hongxun. "A Preliminary Discussion on the Building Year of Quanzhou Holy Tomb and the Authenticity of its Legend." In *The Islamic Historic Relics in Quanzhou*. Ed. Committee for Protecting Islamic Historical Relics in Quanzhou and the Research Centre for the Historical Relics of Chinese Culture. Quanzhou: Fujian People's Publishing House, 1985.

Yang I-Fan. *Islam in China*. Hong Kong: Union Press, 1969. 1st ed. 1958.

Yang, Mayfair Mei-Hui. "The Gift Economy and State Power in China," *Comparative Studies in Society and History* 31.1: 25–54 (1989).

Yang Mohammed Usiar Huaizhong 杨穆罕默德 · 优什尔 · 怀中. "Lun shiba shiji Zhehlinye Musilin di qiyi" 论十八世纪哲赫林耶穆斯林起义 (On the 18th-century Jahriyya Muslim uprisings). In *Qingdai Zhongguo Yisilanjiao lunji* 清代中国伊斯兰教论集 (Essays on Islam in China during the Qing period). Ed. Ningxia Philosophy and Social Science Institute. Yinchuan: Ningxia People's Publishing Society, 1981.

——. "Lüe lun sufeipai zai Zhongguo neidi Yisilanjiao zhong de fazhan" 略论苏非派在中国内地伊斯兰教中的发展 (Discussion of the development of Sufism in internal China's Islam). In *Zhongguo Yisilanjiao yanjiu wenji* 中国伊斯兰教研究文集 (Compendium of Chinese Islamic research). Ed. Chinese Islamic Research Committee. Yinchuan: Ningxia People's Publishing Society, 1988.

——. "The Eighteenth Century Gansu Relief Fraud Scandal." In *The Legacy of Islam in China: An International Symposium in Memory of Joseph F. Fletcher*. Ed. Dru C. Gladney. Conference Volume. Harvard University, 14–16 April 1989.

——. "Sufism among the Muslims in Gansu, Ningxia, and Qinghai." In *Minority Nationalities of China: Language and Culture*. Ed. Charles Li and Dru C. Gladney. Amsterdam: Mouton Press, Forthcoming.

Yang Yongchang 杨永昌. *Mantan qingzhensi* 漫谈清真寺 (Brief discussion of mosques). Yinchuan: Ningxia People's Publishing Society, 1981.

Yanov, Alexander. *The Russian Challenge and the Year 2000*. Tr. Iden J. Rosenthal. Oxford: Basil Blackwell, 1987.

Ye Zhenggang 冶正纲. "Ningxia Yihewanyi zhuming jingxuejia Hu Song-shan" 宁夏伊赫瓦尼著名经学家虎嵩山 (The renowned scriptural scholar of the Ningxia Ikwan, Hu Gaoshan). In *Qing dai Zhongguo Yisilan jiao Lunji* 清代中国伊斯兰教论集 (Essays on Islam in China During the Qing Period). Ed. Ningxia Philosophy and Social Science Institute. Yinchuan: Ningxia People's Publishing Society, 1981.

Yegar, Moshe. "The Panthay (Chinese Muslims) of Burma and Yunna," *Journal of South-East Asian History* 7.1: 73–85 (1966).

Yi Gong 懿恭. "Beijing Niujie Libaisi liangwen Ahlabowen de guke" 北京牛街礼拜寺两方阿拉伯文的石刻 (Two Arabic inscriptions in Beijing's Oxen Street mosque), *Wen wu* No. 10 (1961). Reprinted in *Huizu shi lun ji* 1949–1979 (Hui history collection 1949–1979). Ed. Chinese Academy of Social Sciences Ethnology Department and Central Nationalities Institute Ethnology Department, Hui History Team. Yinchuan: Ningxia People's Publishing Society, 1984.

Yokoyama, Hiroko. "Ethnic Identity among the Inhabitants of the Dali Basin in Southwestern China." Paper presented on the 87th Annual Meeting of the American Anthropological Association, Phoenix, 16–20 November 1988.

Yu Zhengui 余振贵. "Ningxia Musilin de bianqian he zongjiao shenghuo" 宁夏穆斯林的变迁和宗教生活 (Ningxia Muslim's change and religious life). In *Xibei Yisilanjiao yanjiu* (Northwest Islam research). Ed. Gansu Provincial Ethnology Department. Lanzhou: Gansu Nationality Publishing Society, 1985.

Yu Zhenggui and Su Dunli 苏敦理. *Ningxia Yisilanjiao changyong ciyu huibian* 宁夏伊斯兰教常用词语汇编 (Collection of frequently used Ningxia Islamic terms). Unpublished paper. Yinchuan: Ningxia Academy of Social Sciences, Nationality Religion Office, 1981.

Zhang Tianlu 张天路. "Population Growth Among China's Minorities," *China Reconstructs* 32.11: 45–46 (1983).

——. "Beijing shaoshu minzu renkou zhuangkuang fenxi" 北京少数民族人口状况分析 (Analysis of the Beijing minority nationality population situation), *Zhongguo shaoshu minzu renkou* 中国少数民族人口 2.6: 22–23 (1986).

Zhang Tongji 张同济. "Najiahucun de Huizu zhishi qingnian sixiang zhuang-kuang" 纳家户村回族知识青年思想状况 (Najiahu village Hui intellectual youth situation), *Ningxia shehui kexue* 9: 10–12 (1985).

Zhang Tongji and Zhang Yongqing 张永青. "A Study and Analysis of the 'Dual Functions' of Islam in Xiji District (Ningxia Province) and Their Relation to Building a Spiritual Civilization," *Ningxia Social Sciences* 2 (1986).

Tr. and Reprinted in D. MacInnis, *Religion in China Today*. Maryknoll: Orbis Books, 1989.

Zhang Yuzhi 张玉志 and Jin Debao 金德宝. "Dao Chendaixiang qu—baogao" 到陈埭去报告 (Trip to Chendai village—report). Unpublished report. Quanzhou: n.p., 1940.

Zhongguo Musilin 中国穆斯林 (Chinese Muslim), 1957–1961, 1981-present.

Zhongguo Shaoshu Minzu 中国穆斯林, ed. *Zhongguo shaoshu minzu* 中国少数民族 (China's minority nationalities). Beijing: People's Publishing Society, 1981.

Zhongguo Encyclopedia Committee. "Minzu" (Nationality). In *Zhongguo dabaike quanshu* 中国大百科全书 (The complete encyclopeadia of China). *Minzu* Volume. Beijing: China Complete Encyclopeadia Publishing Society, 1986.

Zhu Yuntao 朱云涛. "Najiahucun chanye jiegou de diaocha" 纳家村产业结构的调查 (Najiahu village industrial production structure research), *Ningxia shehui kexue* 9: 1–6 (1985).

Zhuang Weiji 庄为玑. "Quanzhou Qingjingsi de lishi wenti" 泉州清静寺的历史问题 (Historical problems of Qingjing Mosque at Quanzhou). In *Symposium on Quanzhou Islam*. Ed. Quanzhou Foreign Maritime Museum. Quanzhou: Fujian People's Publishing Society, 1983.

Zi Heng 子亨. "Zhongguo Yisilanjiao Xi Dao tang shilue" 中国伊斯兰教西道堂史略 (Brief History of China's Islamic School of the Western Dao). In *Xi Dao tang shiliaoji* 西道堂史料辑 (Collected materials of the history of school of the Western Dao). Ed. Qinghai Institute for Nationalities Nationalities Research Department and the Northwest Institute for Nationalities Nationalities Northwest Research Department. Yining: n.p., 1987.

Zi Qi 子岐. *Zi Qi zishu liushi nian da shiji* 子岐自述六十年大事记 (An autobiography of the great 60 year's events by Zi Qi). Beijing: n.p., 1934.

Index

Harvard East Asian Monographs

49. Endymion Wilkinson, *The History of Imperial China: A Research Guide*

50. Britten Dean, *China and Great Britain: The Diplomacy of Commercial Relations, 1860–1864*

51. Ellsworth C. Carlson, *The Foochow Missionaries, 1847–1880*

52. Yeh-chien Wang, *An Estimate of the Land-Tax Collection in China, 1753 and 1908*

53. Richard M. Pfeffer, *Understanding Business Contracts in China, 1949–1963*

54. Han-sheng Chuan and Richard Kraus, *Mid-Ch'ing Rice Markets and Trade, An Essay in Price History*

55. Ranbir Vohra, *Lao She and the Chinese Revolution*

56. Liang-lin Hsiao, *China's Foreign Trade Statistics, 1864–1949*

57. Lee-hsia Hsu Ting, *Government Control of the Press in Modern China, 1900–1949*

58. Edward W. Wagner, *The Literati Purges: Political Conflict in Early Yi Korea*

59. Joungwon A. Kim, *Divided Korea: The Politics of Development, 1945–1972*

60. Noriko Kamachi, John K. Fairbank, and Chūzō Ichiko, *Japanese Studies of Modern China Since 1953: A Bibliographical Guide to Historical and Social-Science Research on the Nineteenth and Twentieth Centuries, Supplementary Volume for 1953–1969*

61. Donald A. Gibbs and Yun-chen Li, *A Bibliography of Studies and Translations of Modern Chinese Literature, 1918–1942*

62. Robert H. Silin, *Leadership and Values: The Organization of Large-Scale Taiwanese Enterprises*

63. David Pong, *A Critical Guide to the Kwangtung Provincial Archives Deposited at the Public Record Office of London*

64. Fred W. Drake, *China Charts the World: Hsu Chi-yü and His Geography of 1848*

65. William A. Brown and Urgunge Onon, translators and annotators, *History of the Mongolian People's Republic*

66. Edward L. Farmer, *Early Ming Government: The Evolution of Dual Capitals*

67. Ralph C. Croizier, *Koxinga and Chinese Nationalism: History, Myth, and the Hero*

68. William J. Tyler, tr., *The Psychological World of Natsume Sōseki*, by Doi Takeo

69. Eric Widmer, *The Russian Ecclesiastical Mission in Peking during the Eighteenth Century*

70. Charlton M. Lewis, *Prologue to the Chinese Revolution: The Transformation of Ideas and Institutions in Hunan Province, 1891–1907*

71. Preston Torbert, *The Ch'ing Imperial Household Department: A Study of its Organization and Principal Functions, 1662–1796*

72. Paul A. Cohen and John E. Schrecker, eds., *Reform in Nineteenth-Century China*

73. Jon Sigurdson, *Rural Industrialism in China*

74. Kang Chao, *The Development of Cotton Textile Production in China*

75. Valentin Rabe, *The Home Base of American China Missions, 1880–1920*

76. Sarasin Viraphol, *Tribute and Profit: Sino-Siamese Trade, 1652–1853*

96. Richard Wich, *Sino-Soviet Crisis Politics: A Study of Political Change and Communication*

97. Lillian M. Li, *China's Silk Trade: Traditional Industry in the Modern World, 1842–1937*

98. R. David Arkush, *Fei Xiaotong and Sociology in Revolutionary China*

99. Kenneth Alan Grossberg, *Japan's Renaissance: The Politics of the Muromachi Bakufu*

100. James Reeve Pusey, *China and Charles Darwin*

101. Hoyt Cleveland Tillman, *Utilitarian Confucianism: Ch'en Liang's Challenge to Chu Hsi*

102. Thomas A. Stanley, *Ōsugi Sakae, Anarchist in Taishō Japan: The Creativity of the Ego*

103. Jonathan K. Ocko, *Bureaucratic Reform in Provincial China: Ting Jih-ch'ang in Restoration Kiangsu, 1867–1870*

104. James Reed, *The Missionary Mind and American East Asia Policy, 1911–1915*

105. Neil L. Waters, *Japan's Local Pragmatists: The Transition from Bakumatsu to Meiji in the Kawasaki Region*

108. William D. Wray, *Mitsubishi and the N.Y.K., 1870–1914: Business Strategy in the Japanese Shipping Industry*

109. Ralph William Huenemann, *The Dragon and the Iron Horse: The Economics of Railroads in China, 1876–1937*

110. Benjamin A. Elman, *From Philosophy to Philology: Intellectual and Social Aspects of Change in Late Imperial China*

111. Jane Kate Leonard, *Wei Yuan and China's Rediscovery of the Maritime World*

112. Luke S. K. Kwong, *A Mosaic of the Hundred Days: Personalities, Politics, and Ideas of 1898*

113. John E. Wills, Jr., *Embassies and Illusions: Dutch and Portuguese Envoys to K'ang-hsi, 1666–1687*

114. Joshua A. Fogel, *Politics and Sinology: The Case of Naitō Konan (1866–1934)*

115. Jeffrey C. Kinkley, ed., *After Mao: Chinese Literature and Society, 1978–1981*

116. C. Andrew Gerstle, *Circles of Fantasy: Convention in the Plays of Chikamatsu*

117. Andrew Gordon, *The Evolution of Labor Relations in Japan: Heavy Industry, 1853–1955*

118. Daniel K. Gardner, *Chu Hsi and the Ta Hsueh: Neo-Confucian Reflection on the Confucian Canon*

119. Christine Guth Kanda, *Shinzō: Hachiman Imagery and its Development*

120. Robert Borgen, *Sugawara no Michizane and the Early Heian Court*

121. Chang-tai Hung, *Going to the People: Chinese Intellectual and Folk Literature, 1918–1937*

122. Michael A. Cusumano, *The Japanese Automobile Industry: Technology and Management at Nissan and Toyota*

124. Steven D. Carter, *The Road to Komatsubara: A Classical Reading of the Renga Hyakuin*

125. Katherine F. Bruner, John K. Fairbank, and Richard T. Smith, *Entering China's Service: Robert Hart's Journals, 1854–1863*

126. Bob Tadashi Wakabayashi, *Anti-Foreignism and Western Learning in Early-Modern Japan: The* New Theses *of 1825*

127. Atsuko Hirai, *Individualism and Socialism: The Life and Thought of Kawai Eijirō (1891–1944)*

128. Ellen Widmer, *The Margins of Utopia:* Shui-hu hou-chuan *and the Literature of Ming Loyalism*

129. R. Kent Guy, *The Emperor's Four Treasuries: Scholars and the State in the Late Ch'ien-lung Era*

130. Peter C. Perdue, *Exhausting the Earth: State and Peasant in Hunan, 1500–1850*

131. Susan Chan Egan, *A Latterday Confucian: Reminiscences of William Hung (1893–1980)*

132. James T. C. Liu, *China Turning Inward: Intellectual-Political Changes in the Early Twelfth Century*

133. Paul A. Cohen, *Between Tradition and Modernity: Wang T'ao and Reform in Late Ch'ing China*

134. Kate Wildman Nakai, *Shogunal Politics: Arai Hakuseki and the Premises of Tokugawa Rule*

135. Parks M. Coble, *Facing Japan: Chinese Politics and Japanese Imperialism, 1931–1937*

136. Jon L. Saari, *Legacies of Childhood: Growing Up Chinese in a Time of Crisis, 1890–1920*

137. Susan Downing Videen, *Tales of Heichū*

138. Heinz Morioka and Miyoko Sasaki, *Rakugo: The Popular Narrative Art of Japan*

139. Joshua A. Fogel, *Nakae Ushikichi in China: The Mourning of Spirit*

140. Alexander Barton Woodside, *Vietnam and the Chinese Model: A Comparative Study of Vietnamese and Chinese Government in the First Half of the Nineteenth Century*

141. George Elison, *Deus Destroyed: The Image of Christianity in Early Modern Japan*

142. William D. Wray, ed., *Managing Industrial Enterprise: Cases from Japan's Prewar Experience*

143. T'ung-tsu Ch'ü, *Local Government in China under the Ch'ing*

144. Marie Anchordoguy, *Computers, Inc.: Japan's Challenge to IBM*

145. Barbara Molony, *Technology and Investment: The Prewar Japanese Chemical Industry*

146. Mary Elizabeth Berry, *Hideyoshi*

147. Laura E. Hein, *Fueling Growth: The Energy Revolution and Economic Policy in Postwar Japan*

148. Wen-hsin Yeh, *The Alienated Academy: Culture and Politics in Republican China, 1919–1937*

149. Dru C. Gladney, *Muslim Chinese: Ethnic Nationalism in the People's Republic*

150. Merle Goldman and Paul A. Cohen, eds., *Ideas Across Cultures: Essays on Chinese Thought in Honor of Benjamin I. Schwartz*